Intellectuals at a Crossroads

SUNY series, INTERRUPTIONS:
Border Testimony(ies) and Critical Discourse/s

Henry A. Giroux, editor

[redacted]

Intellectuals at a Crossroads

The Changing Politics of China's Knowledge Workers

Zhidong Hao

State University of New York Press

Published by
State University of New York Press, Albany

Printed in the United States of America

For information, address State University of New York Press,

90 State Street, Suite 700, Albany, NY 12207

Production by Michael Haggett

Marketing by Michael Campochiaro

Library of Congress Cataloging-in-Publication Data

Hao, Zhidong, 1952–
Intellectuals at a crossroads : the changing politics of China's knowledge workers / Zhidong Hao.
p. cm. — SUNY series, interruptions—border testimony(ies) and critical discourse/s)
Includes bibliographical references and index.
ISBN 0–7914–5579–3 (alk. paper) — ISBN 0–7914–5580–7 (pbk : alk. paper)
1. Professional employees—China—Political activity. 2. Intellectuals—China—Political activity. 3. Knowledge workers—China—Political activity. 4. China—Intellectual life—1949– 5. China—Politics and government—1949– I. Title. II. Series.
HD8038.C55H36 2003
320.951'088—dc21 2002044772

10 9 8 7 6 5 4 3 2 1

To the Four Most Important Women in My Life

My Mother (1909–1974)
A loving and sweet peasant woman who lived in hardship all her life and whom I can only join in my dreams.

Jiachun
My much loved wife, who endured all of those sleepless nights while I worked on the book.

Kate (Huikun)
My daughter, whom I did not have much time to take out for fun.

Eva Richter
The devoted friend whose support has made possible my life in the United States.

Contents

List of Tables and Figures

List of Abbreviations

ACFTUs	All China Federation of Trade Unions
APD	Association for the Promotion of Democracy
BRC	bureaucratic ruling class
CAS	Chinese Academy of Science
CASS	Chinese Academy of Social Sciences
CCD	culture of critical discourse
CCP	Chinese Communist Party
CPPCC	Chinese People's Political Consultative Conference
DL	Democratic League
DPGs	democratic parties and groups
GMD	Guomindang (or KMT, the Nationalist Party)
MC	moneyed class
NATO	North Atlantic Treaty Organization
NGO	non-governmental organization
NPC	National People's Congress
NSF	National Science Foundation
ODM	Overseas Democracy Movement
PAN	National Action Party (Mexico)
PLA	People's Liberation Army
PRI	Institutional Revolutionary Party (Mexico)
PMC	professional-managerial class
PRC	People's Republic of China
SOEs	state-owned enterprises
TVEs	township and village enterprises
VOA	Voice of America
WC	working class
WTO	World Trade Organization

Foreword

I became acquainted with Zhidong Hao in the early 1990s when he sent me his Ph.D. thesis to read. Although I am an historian and he a sociologist, we were both working on a similar topic at that time: the role of the intellectuals in post-Mao China. Like my own work, most scholarly treatment of China's intellectuals has been done by historians. Therefore, Hao, as a sociologist, brings a new approach to the topic and asks different questions, which he answers in a different analytical framework. He uses an extensive questionnaire of a representative sample of intellectuals, whom he interviewed on long extended trips to China. In addition, he brings a comparative perspective that adds a new dimension to the discourse on the changing role of China's intellectuals in present-day China.

Another important difference between Hao's and my own work and that of most of my colleagues is that whereas our interest in the relationship between China's intellectuals and the state arose from a scholarly curiosity about the change in the traditional role of the intellectuals as leaders of their society in Confucian China to their denigration under the rule of Mao Zedong (1949–76), Hao's interest was sparked by his own experiences in China and by the fortuitous circumstances that brought him to the United States.

Hao was born in 1952, three years after China's Communist revolution in a poor mountainous village in China's Shanxi Province. He attended the only middle school with a little over 1,000 students in a county populated by 260,000 people, almost all of whom were peasants. In 1966, when he was fourteen years old and in his second year of middle school, Mao launched the Cultural Revolution, in which Mao called on students "to rebel against authority" and to show concern with state affairs in his effort to purge those in the Party and in the establishment whom Mao believed were not obeying his orders and conspiring against him. Like other students at the time, Hao joined in the rebellion against those in authority in the belief that their overthrow would bring about a freer, fairer society. But as Mao found in 1968 that he could no longer control the students he had mobilized against his supposed "enemies," he then sent them away to work in factories and in the countryside. Thus in 1970, Hao was employed as a cement worker in a power construction company. After two years of backbreaking work, in 1972 he was selected by his work unit as a worker-peasant-soldier-student and was sent to Nankai University in Tianjin to study English. After graduation in 1975, he taught middle school, but since the Cultural Revolution was still raging, the education system was chaotic and the students not interested in learning.

When the Cultural Revolution ended in the fall of 1976 and Mao's successor Deng Xiaoping subsequently came to power with a program of reform that opened China to the outside world, Hao was employed in 1980 by the foreign languages department at Hebei Teachers University to teach English. In 1984, he went to East China Normal University in Shanghai for an M.A. degree in English and returned to Hebei in 1986.

In the post-Mao period, Hao still retained the concern with "state affairs," which he had developed in the Cultural Revolution. In addition to having become disillusioned by the difference between the idealistic promises of Mao and his supporters and the chaos and repression their policies had created, Hao read the many books, written by intellectuals in the aftermath of the Cultural Revolution, about their persecution and that of their families and colleagues. Nevertheless, he asked how was it possible for these intellectuals who had participated so enthusiastically in the Communist revolution and in its government to be destroyed by the system they had helped to establish. Moreover, with great expectations of a more democratic society after Mao's death in 1976, Hao became more and more disappointed by the fact that movements against critical intellectuals still continued into the reform period of Deng Xiaoping.

Thus, with help from some American friends, he made his way in 1988 to the United States and to the City University of New York. Initially, he decided to pursue a Ph.D. degree in English. But since that discipline was not directly related to his concern over the fate of China's intellectuals, a year later he transferred to the sociology department in order to better understand why such a tragic fate had befallen China's intellectuals and to find out what was happening to them in the post-Mao era. Fortunately, the well-known sociologist Stanley Aronowitz was in the Sociology Program and although he was not a China expert, he was interested in intellectuals and had done extensive research on the topic. Under his direction, Hao received his Ph.D. in sociology in 1995.

In addition to his work on Chinese intellectuals, Hao has written articles on a variety of other topics—nationalism, gender, modernization, Chinese political culture, and prostitution in China. In 2002–2003, he did research in Taiwan as a Fulbright Scholar on the roles of intellectuals in the unification and independence movements. He expects to continue researching and publishing in this area.

As a child growing up in his poor village in China, all that Hao dreamed about was being able to wear leather shoes and own a wristwatch. Today, because of profound changes in China and in his own life, Hao has not only acquired these consumer items, but in addition to coming to the United States, earning a Ph.D., and teaching in a university, as this book demonstrates, he has written a significant work about the trials, tribulations, and extraordinary transformation of China's intellectuals now underway in present-day China.

Merle Goldman
Boston University

自动对号的观众

Figure Can't Help But See (Part of) Oneself in the Picture (*Zidong dui hao de guanzhong*)
Source: Ding Cong, 1999 (Vol. 1), p. 82.

Preface

This project has a long history. It began in 1990 when I was a graduate student at the City University of New York, and it subsequently became the subject of my Ph.D. dissertation. After I received my degree in 1995, I decided to conduct further research with an eye to expanding the dissertation to a book. I went back to China in 1996 to interview still other intellectuals. In 1997 I toured the United States to interview exiled dissidents. From 1993 to 2001, I interviewed a total of 123 intellectuals, some individually and others in groups. Among those interviewed, both here and in China, were writers, professors in various disciplines, researchers in the social and natural sciences, journalists, artists, engineers, lawyers, doctors, graduate and undergraduate students from a variety of disciplines, political dissidents, and administrators who also viewed themselves as intellectuals.

Wherever possible, I have tried to give the reader a real sense for each person we meet, some of whom we will follow throughout the book. For their own protection, I have given most of the interviewees fictitious names. But if their points of view have already been published, I use their real names. These include Wang Yuanhua, Xiao Gongqin, Xu Jilin, Wang Xiaoming, Deng Weizhi, Huang Ping, Zheng Yefu, Yan Jiaqi, Hu Ping, Zheng Yi, Su Shaozhi, Su Xiaokang, Chen Kuide, Liu Bingyan, Wang Ruowang, and Ni Yuxian.

What does this book do and what is its thesis? Empirically, we will try to make sense of the range of Chinese intellectuals and their activities in the 1990s. China's intellectuals are not a large and undifferentiated entity. Rather, they are a fragmented yet overlapping constellation of types, each defined by its intellectual orientation and social function.

We will focus on three out of four types, whom we see as building blocks rather than as straitjackets. As the preceding cartoon implies, the reader or viewer may find something of him- or herself in one or another description.

Theoretically, the book attempts to reconceptualize intellectuals and their political and social roles as critical, organic, and professional. It also explores the possibility of intellectuals forming a class and the roles they can play in that capacity. While choosing to play these roles, intellectuals face various ethical dilemmas. Though they may not resolve them, the ways in which they manage these conflicts determine the extent to which they can influence social change.[1]

The basic layout of the book is as follows: Chapter 1 develops the framework of a political sociology of intellectuals. It identifies four types of intellectuals and four political roles: revolutionary intellectuals in power, and organic, critical, and unattached (bourgeoisified and professionalized) intellectuals. These roles are based on various powerfully held ideological foundations. While fulfilling these roles, intellectuals may be caught between an ethic of responsibility and an ethic of ultimate ends, between 'morality' and 'power,' or *Dao* and *shi,* and between vocation and profession. Dual and split personalities are in fact the perennial lot of intellectuals.

Chapter 2 examines the historical change in the politics of intellectuals from the Mao era (1949–76) to the first period of Deng (1977–89). It is a transition from a high degree of uniformity to the beginning of fragmentation. In the Mao era, most intellectuals conformed to the Party line. This conformity was the result of two factors: the intellectuals' own willingness to learn to work for the new regime, and the coercion of various movements, including the Thought Reform of the early 1950s, the Hundred Flowers movement in 1957, and the Cultural Revolution from 1966 to 1976. There were, to be sure, intellectuals who were critical of the Party in the Mao era, but their number was small and the consequences they suffered were a severe deterrent.

The Deng era took two opposing tracks. The first period saw intellectuals both within and without the system challenging the Maoist Party line, with the support of the more enlightened Party leadership. Once he was firmly in power, however, Deng launched campaigns against "bourgeois liberalization" and "spiritual pollution." With the help of orthodox organic intellectuals, he cracked down on the liberal intellectuals within the Party. Not surprisingly, his politics antagonized many intellectuals, who then became even more critical. Meanwhile, Deng's economic reform continued and it bourgeoisified and professionalized a large number of others. Thus began the fragmentation of China's intellectuals.

Chapter 3 examines the critical intellectuals. It opens with an analysis of the social environment in the 1990s and beyond: the crackdown of the 1989 democracy movement, the rapidly changing political economy, and the widening public space available for critical intellectuals. It then discusses the critical debates among liberals, neoconservatives, various nationalists and the New and Old Left on subjects ranging from the humanist spirit to nationalism and modernity. This chapter also explores the politics of the liberal democratic intellectuals in the democracy movement inside and outside China. The critical intellectuals especially display some diverse and interesting political orientations.

Chapter 4 focuses on the bourgeoisified and professionalized intellectuals. Since 1989, some intellectuals have become private entrepreneurs, while others have become their managers or technical experts. With the change in these intellectuals' positions has come a change in their intellectual culture. There has been a shift from politics with a strong infusion of morality to unabashed moneymaking.

Meanwhile, a majority of intellectuals have begun to be professionalized. But because this change is only just beginning, and the Party is not willing to relinquish its control, these intellectuals have little professional autonomy. They are generally attached neither to the Party nor to the private entrepreneurs. As a result, they may experience hardships, leading to psychological imbalance, in various aspects of their lives: sub-par income and housing, limited funding for research, problems with research equipment, and delays in, or outright lack of, promotion. They will almost certainly focus on further professionalization, and this indicates an intellectual model that is different from the traditional one.

Chapter 5 explores the status of organic intellectuals. We first explain what constitutes a class, and why most of China's classes are still in formation: the cadre class of the Party and the state, the private entrepreneurs, the professional-managerial middle class, the working class, and the peasants. We then discuss the intellectuals organic to these classes. Since many of these classes are still in the process of developing their organic intellectuals, we focus on those of the Party and the state. Our survey includes Party theorists and journalists, young economists, the new scholar-officials, members of the small democratic parties, and researchers in the academies of social sciences and in other research organizations. Because of their varied and often contradictory class locations, organic intellectuals suffer most acutely from dual and split personalities.

Chapter 6 discusses the possibility of intellectuals forming a new class, with arguments for and against the proposition. We then identify the bases of an intellectual class: cultural capital as their economic base, the culture of critical discourse as their ideological base, the "calling" and the humanist spirit as their political base, and intellectual communities and parties as their organizational base. Our conclusion: Intellectuals do have the potential to become a class, but it will be a flawed class in need of transformation and transcendence.

Chapter 7 summarizes the changing politics of knowledge workers in China and discusses their future. With the crises of Chinese modernity in ecology, in the social and political arenas, and in education, intellectuals as a class will find their efforts well spent in looking for an alternative to the current political and economic system, in social movements, and in education. At the same time, however, intellectuals face the task of transforming themselves, that is, of transcending their own flaws brought about by their culture of critical discourse.

The appendix is a study note on the concept of the intellectual. We review the transition of Chinese intellectuals from literati to modern intellectuals, and we compare it with the development of the intellectual in the West. We also review the various definitions of an intellectual: *educational* and *professional, cultural* and *social,* as well as *critical.* Most usefully for our readers we explain how we have used each term in the book.

Finally, a few words on methodology should help the reader better approach the book.[2] Roughly speaking, sociologists use three different approaches in their research, with three different methods and three different ways of thinking about the world: the positivist, the interpretive, and the critical. *The positivist researcher* uses the survey method and believes that social behavior can be understood by finding the relations among variables. For example, we can find out whether humanistic intellectuals are more critical than technical intellectuals by looking at the jobs they do, the books they read, the kind of people they associate with, and so forth. That is, however, not what we did. We conducted a limited survey of a purposive sample of 101 technical intellectuals in two universities and one factory primarily to gather some demographic data. I report only the findings about their living conditions in the middle of the 1990s. No correlations are calculated. Statistics from the census and my tabulations of journal articles are also limited to the purpose of demographics. They are very useful, but they are not the statistical analyses generally found in the sociological literature.

The interpretive researcher engages in field research, or participant observation, or ethnography. The philosophy here is that social behavior is more complicated than can be understood by a mere survey. We need to analyze what people say, do, and actually think. We need to analyze metaphors, symbols, and the many other ways in which people express themselves. We need to interpret the subjective meanings. To do this—to describe the norms, values, and beliefs of a culture or society based on direct observation and analysis, we need to live among them, observe them, and interview them. That is largely what I did (although I stayed in hotels or with my own family). In the summer of 1994, I observed labs and research institutes, attended classes, and visited faculty dorms. I also attended their parties, lunches, and dinners. Altogether, as I have said, I joined the lives of 123 intellectuals over roughly an eight-year period. The reader will see that I have incorporated many of their direct opinions and testimony into the study of these intellectuals. Their own words and emotions and their own actions help us better understand who they are and what they do.

The critical researcher uses the historical-comparative method. The philosophical underpinning here is that social behavior is governed by larger forces such as political and economic structures and processes. It emphasizes the interdependence of events and factors, the mutual interaction and reciprocal effects that occur over a period of time. In addition to this historical study, the researcher compares societies and events in order to better understand the world of those he or she studies. That is what I have done in this project. We ask the following questions: How did the literati transform into today's intellectuals? What are the events or factors that influence intellectuals' changing politics? What is the impact of the June 4 massacre? What is the effect of the market economy? What is the relationship between the intellectuals and the Party? Is it or is it not true that intellectuals need the Party as much as the Party needs intellectuals? In other words, is the relationship, or co-optation, mutual and reciprocal? How do China's intellectuals compare with intellectuals in the West? Intellectuals and the sociology of intellectuals, after all, are an international phenomenon. There are differences, but the similarities may be greater.

Max Weber's ideal type is chiefly a method of historical-comparative research, which we have also used in our analysis. Ideal types are instruments against which we can measure reality. Reality is always messy and fluid, but instruments of measurement can be constant. For example, people's height varies: the ruler shows us how they differ. The three different research methods just discussed are further examples of ideal types. Using those "rulers," the reader can measure to what extent this writer has been positivist, interpretive, and critical in his research. In our analysis of intellectuals, we constructed four ideal types: revolutionary intellectuals in power, unattached intellectuals, organic intellectuals, and critical intellectuals. In reality, one would be hard-pressed to distinguish clearly who is organic and who is critical. But our "measurement" allows us to say to what extent one is organic and another is critical, and when one seems to turn from one into the other. For in fact intellectuals do change from one position to the other. Each ideal type provides a basis for comparison and understanding. The reader will find how relevant and sensitive our measurements are to the empirical world of intellectuals.

I hope this explanation of methods will help our readers understand how I developed the book and how they can make the most of it. Enjoy the experience!

Acknowledgments

First, I want to thank the interviewees who opened their minds to me and helped me understand their worlds so that the reader could understand them as well. As I told them, I was there to *xun shi fang xue,* that is, "to learn from them and from their scholarship." Without their opening up to me about their own lives, and sharing their insights, there would not be a book like this.

Nor would this book be possible without the work and cooperation of my colleagues and friends in China. My own research was grafted onto a joint project by the City University of New York and by two universities and one research institute in China. I benefited a great deal from this joint research project. Sun Zhongxin, then a graduate student in sociology, assisted me in many of my interviews, as did Wang Yanxiu and Chen Zhiqing, two of my former students in China. My heartfelt thanks go to all of them.

Of course, no such book is possible without the support of the many scholars in the field. Throughout its history, many have read at least part of this work, and have discussed with me some of the issues involved. They include Stanley Aronowitz, Paul Montagna, Lily M. Hoffman, Peter Kwong, Merle Goldman, Xu Jilin, David Chu, Timothy Cheek, John Israel, Richard Madsen, Steven Brink, Alvin So, Roz Bologh, Leslie Howard, Eva Richter, David Robinson, Bob Alford, and Huang Ping. To be more specific, Professors Aronowitz, Montagana, Hoffman, and Kwong helped me greatly with my Ph.D. dissertation, on which this book is based. Without their encouragement as I broadened into comparative sociological studies, and without their initial critiques on my work, this book would never have been born.

I especially want to thank David Chu, who read the first drafts of the book and made meticulous comments. He encouraged me to rethink and reorganize the entire project following the formidable tradition of China studies, and he has saved me, I am sure, from a good deal of embarrassment. I am also deeply indebted to Professors Cheek, Israel, and Madsen, reviewers from the State University of New York Press. Their painstaking reading accompanied by extensive and valuable comments helped me vastly enhance the manuscript. Special thanks go to Prof. Merle Goldman, who kindly read several versions of the manuscript and made valuable suggestions for revisions. She graciously agreed to write the foreword for this book despite her busy schedule. Professor Goldman's example of scholarship and kindness has been an inspiration to me ever since I came to know her in the early 1990s.

Without the advice, suggestions, and critiques of these and other scholars, the book would not be at its current level of scholarship. I am grateful to all those who helped along the way, but any errors of fact or interpretation must be entirely my own responsibility. If the book can inspire further discussion on China's intellectuals and stimulate other scholars to construct more elaborate models of analysis, perhaps any errors may be forgiven.

Ding Cong, one of the most well-known and well-respected cartoonists in China, has allowed me to use his cartoons to illustrate some of the ideas in the book. I believe that both my readers and I deeply appreciate his kindness and generosity.

I am forever indebted to Judith C. Protas, whose editorial comments and weighing of every word greatly helped me to clarify my ideas and communicate them to the reader. Her dedication to the project and her help with whatever I sent her have remained a great inspiration to me. If there is still any language error in the text, it is my doing in (re)revision. I greatly appreciate the assistance of Whittier College librarians, especially Julie Ellis, Ann Topjon, and Mary Ellen Vick. Thanks also go to my daughter, Kate Hao, and several Whittier students, especially Elise Chatlaine, Georgi Gospodinov, and (Michael) Long Truong who have assisted me with my research and who have typed up corrections or otherwise put the book together. Lo-Ling Chang from Taiwan assisted me in putting together the indexes. And I would like to thank Howard Myerson for helping me come up with the title of the book.

A number of institutions provided generous financial support to our joint project as well as to my own research, without which the book would not exist. They are the United Board for Christian Higher Education in Asia, the Graduate School and University Center of the City University of New York, Whittier College Research grants, and the Whittier College Dean of Faculty's Office. The Department of Sociology, Anthropology, and Social Work at Whittier also provided unlimited support in every possible way. I want to thank all of them for their unstinting help.

Last but by no means least, I would like to express my gratitude to Priscilla C. Ross, the Director of SUNY Press, to Michael Haggett, Production Editor, to Marilyn Silverman, Copy Editor, and to everybody else whose names I do not know or may have missed, but who have been involved in producing this book, for making sure that the book appears in front of the reader in the most professional manner.

Chapter One

Introduction: Toward a Political Sociology of China's Intellectuals

> If the way the world works can be explained, it is not an eternal way;
> if the concept one uses can be explained, it is not an eternal concept.
> *(Dao ke dao, fei heng dao; ming ke ming, fei heng ming.)*
> —Lao Zi, *Dao De Jing*[1]

Tackling a "political sociology of China's intellectuals" seems to be an impossible task. First of all, from "literati" to "intellectuals," China's educated elite has a history of over 2,500 years, whereas sociology, developed in the West, has a history of only about 150 years. The sociology of intellectuals is an even younger field. As a social group, the European "intelligentsia" (the closest resemblance to China's intellectuals) did not emerge until the 1860s in Poland and Russia (Gella 1976), and the educated elite in France and in the United States did not identify themselves as "intellectuals" until the end of the nineteenth century. Thus, the sociological study of the group as a stratum is relatively new.

Second, the most accomplished scholars in the sociology of intellectuals, such as Weber, Gramsci, Mannheim, Shils, Parsons, Lipset, and Gouldner are Western. To be sure, they have all incorporated Chinese intellectuals into their historical-comparative research and have provided us with numerous insights, which will greatly inform our discussions in the book. Their focus, however, is largely on the Western and cross-cultural development of intellectuals.

Third, the most recent scholarship on Chinese intellectuals, both Western and Chinese, treats intellectuals mainly from a historical or a literary point of view, although many studies do use a sociological perspective. As a matter of fact, the best-known scholars in the field, including Merle Goldman (Harvard University), Timothy Cheek (Colorado College), Yu Ying-shih (Princeton University), Yan Buke (Beijing University), and Xu Jilin (Shanghai Normal University), are all historians. Among other scholars who have done substantive work are Perry Link in language and literature (Princeton University), Tu Wei-ming in Chinese philosophy (Harvard University), Jin Yaoji (or Ambrose Y. C. King) in sociology (The Chinese University of Hong Kong), and Andrew Nathan in political science (Columbia University).

Thus, a politico-sociological study of Chinese intellectuals poses a major challenge. Not only do we need to bridge the gaps between the ancient and the contemporary, China and the West, but we also need to integrate history, the humanities, sociology, and political science. It is not an easy task, but since scholars such as these have already laid the foundations, we can at least help construct the building.

In this chapter, we will lay out some of the major issues concerning a political sociology of China's intellectuals. We will focus on a historical-comparative study of intellectuals' political roles: revolutionary, organic, critical, unattached, and professional. We will examine their ideological dispositions and ethical dilemmas underlying their political roles. We analyze the dilemmas they face between an ethic of responsibility and an ethic of ultimate ends, between *Dao* (morality and values) and s*hi* (power), and between vocation and profession. These dilemmas lead to intellectuals' dual or split personalities. We will finally evolve a typology of China's intellectuals and their politics. Using various historical and theoretical perspectives to achieve a synthesized politico-sociological approach, this chapter serves as a foundation for our later exploration of various groups of contemporary intellectuals. (For an examination of the historical development of the intellectual in China as well as in the West, and the various definitions of intellectuals, see the appendix.)

Four Types of Intellectuals and Four Political Roles

Politics deals with power distribution, and sociology deals with individuals in group interaction. A political sociology of Chinese intellectuals may be said to deal with how intellectuals in China handle their power relations with the state: in other words, the political roles of intellectuals in relation to the state.

One way of thinking about the political roles of today's intellectuals is outlined in Lipset and Basu's aptly titled essay, "The Roles of the Intellectual and Political Roles" (1976). They compare and contrast intellectuals across nations and discern four orders of understood political roles. These include the *gatekeeper,* or the innovative spokesperson for contending tendencies; the *moralist,* or the conscience of society; the *preserver,* helping to frame the legitimization of old or new authority; and the *functionary* who maintains the social order as bureaucrats, judges, educators, and various other experts and professionals. The *gatekeeper* and the *moralist* seem to follow the critical tradition of intellectuals, while the *preserver* and the *functionary* seem to be what we may call 'organic intellectuals.'

But what does "organic" mean, if we know what it means to be critical? In his analysis of intellectuals, Gramsci (1971:13) emphasizes their *political attitudes or affiliation.* On the one hand, he does agree that intellectual activity must be "distinguished in terms of its intrinsic characteristics," with, at the highest level, the "creators of various sciences, philosophy, art, etc.," and at the lowest level "administrators," and "divulgers" of accumulated intellectual wealth. This reminds us of Lipset's creators, disseminators, and appliers (cited in Nettl 1969:97; see also the appendix). Gouldner's humanistic and technical distinction, that is, between intellectuals and intelligentsia, may also be seen as based on the intrinsic characteristics of intellectual activity: intellectuals being mainly critical and emancipatory, intelligentsia being technical and practical (1979:48). Gouldner's *intellectuals* would probably include Lipset and Basu's first and second layers, creators and distributors, but would exclude most scientists and engineers, whereas *intelligentsia* would include most scientists, engineers, physicians, and some lawyers, or in a word, those we tend to call "professionals." Gramsci would probably agree with both Lipset and Gouldner on the differences among roles, albeit with some reservations.

Gramsci (1971:12), however, also believes that this intrinsic aspect is not the most important factor in reaching "a concrete approximation of reality."[2] A more fruitful way to approximate the reality of intellectuals should view them in the "ensemble of the system of relations in which these activities (and therefore the intellectual groups who personify them) have their place within the general complex of social relations" (Gramsci 1971:8). This is where we see the difference between organic intellectuals and traditional intellectuals.

The closest definition Gramsci (1971:6) gives for *organic* intellectuals is that they "are for the most part 'specializations' of partial aspects of the primitive activity of the new social type which the new class has brought into prominence." In other words, it is these intellectuals who elaborate the various causes of the new class, the bourgeoisie. These include most of the functionaries that Lipset and Basu discuss. To be more specific, they accomplish this task on two superstructural levels. First, in civil society, they perform the function of ideological hegemony; and second, in political society, they perform the function of direct domination, or judicial government.

Therefore, "[t]he intellectuals are the dominant group's 'deputies' exercising the subaltern functions of social hegemony and political government" (Gramsci 1971:12). They are the advocates, organizers, and administrators of a mostly dominant group. However, they can also be organic to the working class. When Karl Mannheim (1936:158) speaks of intellectuals furnishing the theorists for the bourgeoisie, the conservatives, and the proletariat, he is, in fact, also talking about organic intellectuals. So is A. Joseph Schumpeter (1976:154), who says that intellectuals "staff political bureaus, write party pamphlets and speeches, act as secretaries and advisers, make the individual politician's newspaper reputation, which, though it is not everything, few men can afford to neglect."

In contrast, *traditional* intellectuals are the intellectuals of the rural type, "linked to the social mass of country people and the town (particularly small-town) petite bourgeoisie, not as yet elaborated and set in motion by the capitalist system" (Gramsci 1971:14–5). These resemble the unattached intellectuals Mannheim discusses (1936:155).

What is the value of Gramsci's characterization of intellectuals? The answer is that it highlights *the political relations between intellectuals and other social groups,* rather than their technical or cultural functions in society. Several issues, however, still need to be addressed. What other political roles do intellectuals perform? Do these social and political relations change? For example, how organic are organic intellectuals to, say, the industrialized bourgeoisie, or in the case of China, to the Chinese Communist Party (CCP)? Does the organicity change over time? What about the critical intellectuals who do not seem to be organic to either the capitalists or the working class, nor even linked to the rural masses? What about Mannheim's unattached intellectuals?

Mannheim (1936:155–6) believes that education levels the status and wealth differences among intellectuals. This does not mean, however, that individual intellectuals will not maintain their class and status ties or social interests. But it does mean that a "homogeneous medium" of multiple components has been created against which conflicting parties can "measure their strength." "With the increase in the number and variety of the classes and strata from which the individual groups of intellectuals are recruited, there comes greater multiformity and contrast in the tendencies operating on the intellectual level which ties them to one another" (p. 157).

It is only in this sense that intellectuals are "to a large degree unattached to any social class" (p.156). In this sense, they transcend their own social classes.

The contemporary meaning of this unattachedness may be embodied in professionalism. Both Brint (1994) and Flacks (1991:12) note that since the 1960s, there has been a tendency for the knowledge class in the United States to move from their concern with ordinary people's everyday experience, public welfare, and social movements to a concern with expert knowledge, instrumental effectiveness, and expert recognition. There is a parallel development in China in the 1990s. Although there are different meanings of unattachedness at different times, as we will see in our historical exploration of unattached intellectuals, it suffices to say now that these intellectuals strive to be objective, independent of politics, and unattached to any class.

However, intellectuals are not always happy with the unattached status. They take one of two courses of action to get out of the predicament, the dilemma of this middle-of-the-road position. One is to become affiliated "with one or the other of the various antagonistic classes" (Mannheim 1936:158). In Flacks's (1991:3) words, they "might try to link to social forces seeking to replace or overthrow established power centers." They thus become the organizers and participants of social movements, such as the Communists, working-class advocates, nationalists, feminists, and environmentalists (pp. 4–5, 13). Along with those who find a connection with the established power elites in the form of think tanks or managers (Dupuy 1991:80–1; Flacks 1991:3), they become what Gramsci would call "organic intellectuals."

It must be noted, though, that the rulers and their organic intellectuals need each other. For example, at the time of the founding of the People's Republic of China (1949), the CCP needed to enlist talented intellectuals in the minor parties to help reconstruct the country both politically and economically. Hence the name United Front. On the other hand, the minor parties needed the CCP to give them a chance to participate in that reconstruction, which they had sought desperately but hopelessly in the Republican era (Mazur 1997:52, 62–5, 70). The same can be said of the relationship between Deng Xiaoping and the intellectual reformers in the late 1970s (Kraus 1986:199). The intellectuals' identification with a social class or group, subordinate or dominant, does not, however, "free them from the disgust of the original members of that class" (Mannheim 1936:158). This is one of the emotional trials that triggered the dual and/or split personality, which we will discuss later in this chapter.

The other way out, according to Mannheim (1936:160–1), is to develop their own consciousness (not class consciousness, at least not in Mannheim's time) of their own social positions, and to strive to fulfill their mission as "watchmen in what otherwise would be a pitch-black night." They may be critical of the power elites and sympathetic to the "antagonistic class," but as in the case of some members of the New Left in Britain and in the United States, their space of discourse is in the universities and in the mass media. They can, however, easily switch to social movements as their discourse space (see Flacks 1991:8–12). These intellectuals, along with those engaged in social movements, are following the critical tradition.

Our analysis of Mannheim, Gramsci, and certain contemporary theorists yields at least three kinds of intellectuals according to their political roles: unattached, organic, and critical. In fact, some intellectuals have become so critical that they turn revolutionary. Indeed, Coser (1965:136) identifies at least four kinds of intellectuals. *Revolutionary* intellectuals like the Jacobins and the Bolsheviks hold power. Others advise those in power or serve them in bureaucratic functions, like the *Ideologues* under Napoleon, the Polish revisionists under Gomulka, the Fabians, and the members of Roosevelt's "brain trust." They connect with the established power elites, and we call them *organic* intellectuals. Still others criticize the powers that be, such as the "Old Testament prophets," who "may castigate political men for the errors of their ways." As also with the Dreyfusards and the Abolitionists, the critics may attempt "to shame men committed to an ethos of compromise by holding up absolute standards of moral righteousness." We call these people *critical* intellectuals. A fourth kind of intellectual may uphold "art for art's sake" and "have no relationship whatever with things political, for whom the world of politics is like a nightmare."[3] We call them *unattached* intellectuals.

Parallel developments of the four kinds of intellectuals have also occurred in China. Goldman and Cheek (1987) identify three kinds of Chinese intellectuals or three (political) roles intellectuals play. They include the ideological speakers for the state, academic and professional elites, and critical intellectuals (see also Cheek 1992:135). They correspond to Coser's last three kinds of intellectuals and three political roles. In the following discussion, we will expand these roles to include those of the revolutionary intellectuals in power, and we will also examine the various kinds of intellectuals in each category. Let us now trace the history of those developments in the context of this larger sociological scholarship, again comparing and contrasting China and the West.

Revolutionary Intellectuals in Power

In China, the 1911 Revolution seemed to have put many intellectuals in power, as we can see from the composition of the first Republican cabinet (see table 1 in the appendix). However, history did not really give this group a chance to rule. Chiang Kai-shek established a government that was populated with intellectuals,[4] but it was bogged down in constant civil wars as well as in the war against the Japanese invasion. History did give China's Communist intellectuals a chance, though. How did they do, then? To allow us to see the picture more clearly, we will compare the Jacobins in the French Revolution, the Bolsheviks in the Russian Revolution, and the Communists in the Chinese Revolution.

The Jacobins were members of one of the political clubs that were responsible for spreading the idea of *Liberty, Equality,* and *Fraternity,* the watchwords of the day. Coser (1965:146–7) observes that Jacobin intellectuals (lawyers, scientists, journalists, ex-priests, and former playwrights) were prominent as deputies to the National Convention. They were major agitators and leaders of mass organizations, including the Paris Commune. The very top leadership group of the government, the twelve men of the Committee of Public Safety, were all intellectuals: seven lawyers, one with a law degree; two army officers and engineers; one actor and playwright; and one Protestant minister. One can certainly say the same about the fathers of the Russian Revolution: Plechanov,

Lenin, and Trotsky, and about the top leadership group of the CCP. The Politburo members of the CCP, who made the revolution, such as Mao Zedong (1893–1976), Liu Shaoqi (1889–1969), Zhu De (1886–1976), Zhou Enlai (1898–1976), and Lin Biao (1907–71), were all intellectuals. Invariably, these revolutionary intellectuals were alienated, marginalized, and concerned about social inequalities at the time of the revolutions (see Coser 1965; Skocpol 1994; Yu Ying-shih 1993).

What did the Jacobins do, then? They wanted to "transform radically the very fabric of French society and to transform it in the image of reason and virtue, as interpreted by the philosophers, especially Rousseau" (Coser 1965:150). This was exactly the orientation of the Chinese Communist intellectuals after "liberation" as well as that of the Bolsheviks. They wanted to destroy the old world and create a new one. The Jacobins, the Bolsheviks, and China's Communists took many other similar steps. They all had created rituals and ceremonies to replace past memories. In France, festivals were created to honor "the Supreme Being, nature, the human race, the French People, liberty and equality, hatred of tyrants and traitors, friendship, temperance, mother-love, filial piety, and so forth" (p. 150). In China, festivals were created to honor the revolutionary past, such as the birthday of the Party, the May 4 Movement, Labor Day, Women's Day, and Army Day. And the same happened after the Russian Revolution (Kenez 1985:138). Street names and personal names changed in France as well as in China. Infants in France were given names such as Constitution, Marat, Montagne, or the names of other revolutionary intellectuals, rather than Christian names. In China there were suddenly a lot of personal names such as Liberation *(jiefang),* National Construction *(jianguo),* and National Day Celebration *(guoqing).* In France, people were supposed to wear simple long trousers rather than the knee breeches of the aristocracy. In China, people were supposed to wear Sun Yat-sen jackets, rather than the traditional style jackets and long gowns the gentry had worn.[5]

However, changing names, creating new festivals, and wearing different styles of dress were not enough. The Jacobins, the Bolsheviks, and the Chinese Communists all believed in a dictatorship for the same reason: for a harmonious society to exist, the government had to eliminate conspirators, factionalists, and all enemies of reason. The Jacobins sincerely believed that for the Republic of Virtue to prevail, the guillotine had to continue functioning (Coser 1965:151), thus the Reign of Terror. The same was true with the Bolshevists, who "saw the surrounding world as an amorphous mass of enemies and the party as shock troops of historical necessity" (p. 162). In many waves of terror (to use Solzhenitsyn's image), the ranks of the "enemies of the people" expanded from the kulaks (the rich peasants), the priests, the Nepmen (private businesspeople), and other "bourgeois specialists" at the end of the 1920s and the start of the 1930s to members of the Communist elite in the Great Purges of 1937–38 (Fitzpatrick 1999:190–217). Hundreds of professors were murdered (Krause 1991:20). And of the members of the Politburo between 1917 and 1923, "three died natural deaths, one committed suicide, five were executed by Stalin, and one, Trotsky, was murdered upon Stalin's orders" (Coser 1965:167).

That is what the CCP believed and did as well. It launched one movement after another after "liberation" simply because, as Mao said, "the class enemies still exist and they don't want to give up." The strategy then was to keep looking for enemies, or in Mao's words, to keep up "the continual revolution." The Party found enemies in the landlords and in the rich peasants in the Land Reform movement in the early 1950s. It found enemies in capitalists and bourgeois intellectuals in the Three-Anti and Five-Anti movements as well as in the Anti-Rightist movement of the 1950s. And finally in the 1960s, it found enemies in its own ranks, the heads of the Party committees at various levels. All during the Cultural Revolution, they found contemporary sinners, while still continuing their search among the previous social groups. The Chinese guillotines kept working alongside thought reform.

It is fair to say, though, that the Communists sincerely meant to construct a more equal and harmonious society, and they found that the guillotine and thought reform were the only way to do it. Still, we find it hard to understand the terror introduced by the Jacobins, the Bolsheviks, and the Chinese Communists. In France the Committee of Public Safety, which reigned by terror, was headed by Robespierre. Neither he nor Mao was a bloodthirsty man. The contemporaries of the former testified that he was a great man, a truly sweet person (Coser 1965:152). Mao, too, captured the affection of many Chinese.[6] Both intellectuals hoped for an equal and virtuous society. Why then did they create such terror among their people? We will discuss some of the reasons in the section on the ideological foundations of intellectuals.

Since the economic reform started in the 1980s, the Chinese revolutionary intellectuals' monopoly of economic power has been weakened, but they still hold political power, albeit through a new generation. Six of the seven Politburo standing committee members are engineers. They are Jiang Zemin, Li Peng, Zhu Rongji, Li Ruihuan, Hu Jintao, and Wei Jianxing. The seventh, Li Lanqing, has an M.B.A. The educated class has provided 93% of the provincial level cadres, 90% of the cadres of the Ting and Ju (the next lower-level departments), and 80% of the county level cadres (Wang Xiaohui 1997; see also Li Cheng 2000). They control the means of production, monopolize the use of violence and the production of ideology, and discipline other intellectuals, much as Lenin intended his Vanguard party to do (Aronowitz 1990:21; Gouldner 1979:79). The Chinese still maintain the revolutionary intellectuals' ideological dispositions, bureaucratic thinking, and monopoly of power, although to a much lesser degree than their predecessors because of economic reforms.

In the remainder of the book, we will refer to the revolutionary intellectuals in China as the *bureaucratic ruling class* (BRC) to differentiate them from the previous generation of revolutionary cadres. In the study of political elites in China, a distinction is made between technocrats and career bureaucrats (Goldstein 1994). While the former may be more concerned about analyzing and solving problems by using scientific methods, the latter are more interested in maintaining power and privilege. The current bureaucrats, however, are leaning toward the latter. They do have a more flexible and less dogmatic ideological disposition, as we have just mentioned, and are more likely to function as modern rational and impersonal bureaucrats, as defined by Weber (1946). But while they may be more flexible on economic issues, they appear to be very stubborn on political ones.[7] There will not be a separate chapter for them as there will be for the other major groups of intellectuals. But when we talk about "organic to," "unattached to," or "critical of," the BRC is almost always the object of the preposition.

Scholars in China studies have done many wonderful in-depth studies of various revolutionary intellectuals in power, such as Mao Zedong, Liu Shaoqi, Zhou Enlai, Tao Zhu (1908–69), Deng Tuo (1912–66), Wu Han (1909–69), Zhang Chunqiao (1917–91), and Yao Wenyuan (1931–),[8] and many of their findings will help us illuminate our discussions in this chapter. They provide further answers to the questions we have raised in this section about the behavior of intellectuals in power.

Organic Intellectuals

Rarely in power themselves, intellectuals have tried to exert their influence as advisers to those in power. This is what Shils (1969:31) means by "the intellectuals' authoritative exercise of power over concrete actions." Examples abound in China, India, and Europe. However, there is a difference between the Chinese literati and their Western contemporaries. Marx ([1888] 1978:145) wrote when he criticized Western intellectuals, "The [Western] philosophers have only *interpreted* the world, in various ways; the point, however, is to *change* it." In contrast, trying to change the world is what many Chinese intellectuals have been trying to do ever since Confucius, politically and/or culturally.

Nonetheless, Western intellectuals do have a tradition of political engagement, though to a lesser degree than China's intellectuals. Organic intellectuals have functioned as personal agents, counselors, tutors, or friends of the sovereign, as illustrated by Plato, Aristotle, Alcuin, Hobbes, Milton, Lord Keynes, and so forth. In fact, Geoffrey Chaucer (ca.1340–1400) held a number of official positions, including comptroller of the customs at the port of London and diplomat to the Continent. John Milton (1608–74) served as foreign secretary of the government of the Commonwealth, and Dante Alighieri (1265–1321), the Italian poet, served as one of the six magistrates of Florence, though only for two months.

The Western intellectuals' organic roles were strengthened in the past century since the emergence of the intellectual stratum after Marx's time; so were the organic intellectuals' roles in the former Soviet Union and Eastern Europe. In the 1930s in the United States, "[l]arge segments of the intellectual and educated communities flocked to support . . . the Communist and Socialist parties" (Lipset and Basu 1976:132). Roosevelt incorporated experts into his administration, as have other presidents, governors, and mayors. Coser (1965) describes four cases of such intellectuals. They are the Fabians in England, the "brain trust" in the United States, the *Ideologues* in France under Napoleon, and the revisionists in Poland under Gomulka. I will now summarize these cases as well as the case of the Soviet organic intellectuals, and we will then see to what extent they resemble those in China.

The Fabians were a group of intellectuals who were concerned with social problems such as poverty amid the industrial prosperity of England in the 1880s. But rather than starting a mass social movement or violent revolution, they wanted to influence change by inoculating the people in power with socialist ideas. At a time when the ruling circles were aware of the need for reform, and were receptive to reform ideas, the Fabians were able to get the attention of the rulers and to underwrite reform measures in government and education. To help with the government reform, they befriended those in power and advised them in private, including such leading politicians as Lord Asquith, Balfour, Churchill, and Lloyd George. They sat on innumerable committees, drafted programs and proposals, gave thousands of lectures, published books and reports, and wrote pamphlets and leaflets. They "transformed the intellectual climate of British political life. They founded [the journal] *The New Statesmen* and the London School of Economics; they were the intellectual godfathers of the modern Labor Party" (Coser 1965:179). The Fabians were enormously successful.

Roosevelt's "brain trust" refers to the large group of economists, agricultural experts, monetary experts, social workers, sociologists, and political scientists who came to the New Deal administration after the Great Depression. Although they "never created a coherent program or a common platform similar to that of the Fabians," they nonetheless influenced various agencies by shaping programs and influencing legislation and executive action (Coser 1965:184). To the brain trusters of the thirties, we may also add the Rand Corporation of the sixties, the American Enterprise Institute of the eighties, and numerous other professionals who have served or are serving the establishment (see Israel 1986:ix).

The term *Ideologues* was used derisively by Napoleon to refer to the Ideologists who, as heirs of the eighteenth-century Enlightenment, advocated, among other things, education as a means to teach rational and scientific principles so that a just and reasonable social order could be erected. In his ascendance to power, Napoleon courted these intellectuals for their influence on public opinion. He even joined one of their organizations, the Institut National, and "behaved like an *ideologue* on horseback. . . . [H]e appeared to the intellectuals as an incarnation of all the virtues they sought in enlightened men of power . . . their future philosopher-king" (Coser 1965:193–4). He wooed and won the most important men of letters, scientists, poets, philosophers, and so forth. After Napoleon's coup on November 9, 1799, the latter believed that their moment had come. But they soon found that Napoleon, his power consolidated, no longer needed them. He dissolved the section of the Institute devoted to moral and political sciences, and replaced the Enlightenment educational system with an authoritarian one. It was suddenly clear that "he profoundly disliked these 'men with a system'" who were not flexible to his needs. The honeymoon between intellect and power was now over (pp. 194–6). The intellectuals had hoped that Napoleon would provide them with more opportunities to implement their Enlightenment ideals than they had had from the Jacobins. They were quickly disillusioned.

The revisionists were a group of Polish intellectuals who, in 1955, began to question the Party's dogmatic interpretation of Marxism-Leninism and its monopoly in various intellectual fields. The sociologist Jozef Chalasinski was the first to urge that the Communists should not uncritically accept every assertion of Marxism. But Chalasinski and his fellow intellectuals remained within the Communist Party. They sincerely hoped that under their respectful pressure the Party would change. Outside, however, the criticism of the political tyranny over science, art, and literature, of the economic plans, and of the condition of the working class intensified. Attacks appeared in all of the leading cultural periodicals and student papers. Further disturbances, chiefly riots in a factory in June 1956, and an alliance between intellectuals and workers helped bring Gomulka into power. Gomulka proceeded to denounce the errors and crimes of the previous Stalinist regime and moved to democratize political institutions and to extend workers' control over their industrial life. Many intellectuals served in the councils of government, and helped him uncover the crimes and errors of the past.

However, history repeated itself. Like Napoleon, Gomulka found that he no longer needed the intellectuals once he had rooted out the die-hard Stalinists and consolidated his power. He had far more need of the old Party functionaries and the support of the Soviet Union. The intellectuals' attack on the system became an obstacle to his rule. So Gomulka banned their journals, expelled their editors from the Party, and arrested and sentenced to prison students who protested (Coser 1965:197–203).

So there they are, the Fabians, the "brain trust," the *Ideologues,* and the revisionists. They either helped the leaders into power, as did the *Ideologues* and revisionists, or helped them in their reform movements, as did the Fabians and the American "brain trust." While the latter two succeeded to a great extent in implementing their ideas, the former two succeeded only in helping the men in their ascendance to, and consolidation of, power. Both Napoleon and Gomulka found that the intellectuals' ideas hindered their authoritarian rule. And the intellectuals found themselves betrayed by those they had hoped would be their "philosopher-kings." All of these intellectuals opted to advise the rulers rather than to start a mass movement or a violent revolution, as the revolutionary intellectuals would have.

The development of the modern Russian organic intellectuals seems even more like that of China's. The first generation of Russia's men of letters tended to be employed "in chancelleries as secretaries and copyists, or were attached to newly established state institutions of learning (the Academy of Sciences and the University of Moscow) as official scribes and translators, or if more successful, to the [Czarist] court [in the eighteenth century] as its official bards and entertainers" (Nahirny 1983:36). During the Russian Revolution, the intelligentsia also served the Soviet regime as bureaucrats, propagandists, theorists, political educators, revolutionary writers, film and poster artists, and so forth. (Fitzpatrick 1970; Kenez 1985).[9] In this way, intelligentsia were brought under state control, and law, medicine, journalism, and engineering were made to serve the Party's cause and became what the Ehrenreichs (1979) would call the 'professional-managerial class' (PMC), in effect a part of the bureaucracy (Ehrenreich 1990:181; Jones and Krause 1991; Krause 1991; Ross 1988:110–1). By the 1970s and 1980s psychiatrists and other doctors were actually being used to persecute dissidents (Jones and Krause 1991:243). As Lenin claimed, and as Mao in 1942 agreed, the intelligentsia were indispensable for the working-class movement, although they were stupid, democratic, backward, and pitifully unreliable (see Nahirny 1983:14) And said Stalin in 1931, "no ruling class has managed without its own intelligentsia" (cited in Bell 1973:103).[10]

But the organic intellectuals also conflicted with the radical revolutionaries. For example, prominent Bolsheviks spoke up in defense of free expression at the same time the Leninists were suppressing the non-Bolshevik press. Some of the people's commissars even resigned in protest. Gorky had to use his position to protect and support intellectuals who were in trouble with the regime (Kenez 1985:39–40, 102). Lunacharsky (1875–1933), who was head of the commissariat from 1917 to 1929, was in charge of education and the arts. In his view, the Soviet Union had to implement a European and American cultural style: progressive and liberal education with equal access to educational opportunities, and freedom and creativity in both science and the arts. His policies were defeated, and he found himself plagued by other differences. Lunacharsky finally left the department. But while he still retained some official titles, he suffered a great many political humiliations in his last years (Fitzpatrick 1970:xv–xvi, 157, 309–10). He was luckier than some, however. Many intellectuals were unable to escape the firing squads and concentration camps of Stalin and his successors (see Fitzpatrick 1999:190–227; Gella 1976:16). Ilya Ehrenberg was another example of both "advise and dissent" (de Mauny 1984; Goldberg 1984).

What happened to the *Ideologues,* revisionists, and the Soviet intelligentsia also happened to the literati under the emperors and empresses and to the Chinese intellectuals under Mao and Deng, although there were some similar success stories of intellectuals influencing the powers, resembling those of the Fabians and "the brain trust." Rather than starting their own dynasties or mass movements, these intellectuals opted to advise the kings and emperors and the Party boss, and served them in various capacities. Intellectuals were supposed to follow the calling to *li de, li gong,* and *li yan,* that is, to "achieve great virtues, perform meritorious services," and "create great literary works." This underscores the fact that intellectuals were part of every ruling class in China's history, from feudal kings and emperors down to Communist and Guomindang regimes. That is what they were taught to do. The calling thus produced the *organic intellectuals*. We call them 'organic intellectuals' because they served an authority, whether the court or the Party, but in many ways they resembled the Jacobins in the sense that they did have some power, though not the ultimate power of the emperor. Their bureaucratic positions entrusted them with the power to administer local and departmental affairs, although it was the emperor or the Party Central Committee who had the final say.

In a book entitled *Rusheng yu Guo Yun* (Confucians and the fate of the nation), Liu Xiuming (1997) describes how literati strove to serve the various dynastic courts. Some examples are very illuminating. First and foremost, there is Confucius (551–479 B.C.E.). He was the founder and teacher of an entire system of ethical precepts for the proper management of society. It was Confucius who taught the emperors how to govern and the literati how to help him. Furthermore, he served as a senior official in the Kingdom of Lu (1100?–256 B.C.E.). To protect the kingdom's interests, he led the efforts to defeat a rebellious army, helped the king to deflect insults, and even executed a lower official, Shao Zheng Mao, who was critical of the nobles.[11] After he resigned from office, he wandered around the kingdoms offering his services whenever they were wanted or hoping to be hired again as an official

(Liu Xiuming 1997:25–30). He was the original organic intellectual. Other well-known scholar-officials described by Liu Xiuming include

Han Yu (768–824), poet and essayist
Du Fu (712–770), poet
Fan Zhongyan (989–1052), writer
Wang Anshi (1021–1086), writer and theorist
Zhu Xi (1130–1200), philosopher
Wen Tianxiang (1236–1283), poet and essayist
Wang Shouren (Yangming) (1472–1528), philosopher
Li Zhi (1527–1602), philosopher
Dong Qichang (1555–1637), painter, calligrapher, and connoisseur
Xu Guangqi (1562–1633), scientist

Many of the literati experienced frustrations and betrayals while serving the court, if they did not end up losing their lives in the process. Li Si (?-208 B.C.E.), the prime minister of Qin (221–206 B.C.E.), taught Qin Shi Huang, the first emperor, how to eliminate his enemies and at the same time how to gather talented people to his court. Though he was himself a Confucian, Li also advised the emperor to burn all of the Confucian books and to put to death those Confucians who did not obey the court, which the emperor obediently did. Li himself, however, was executed by the emperor's successor after failing in the court's power struggle (Liu Xiuming 1997:68–77). The emperor of the next dynasty, Han (206 B.C.E.–220 C.E.), benefited greatly from another great Confucian, Dong Zhongshu (179–104 B.C.E.). Dong later advised one of the most successful emperors of the dynasty, Wu Di, to follow only Confucius and no one else. He also served in the court, although he was never given very important positions. And he almost lost his life for his belief that an accident, like a fire, may indicate a need to behead the corrupt officials in court (p. 106). He spent most of his time writing scholarly works that elaborated on the Confucian teachings (pp. 98–108). Wang Anshi (or Wang An-shih) became prime minister of the court. But like many scholar-officials, he met resistance to his reform efforts and finally resigned from office (pp. 440–1).[12] The philosopher Li Zhi was an official for twenty years, but he did not like his job. He was more interested in critiquing a contemporary strand of Confucianism that emphasized Heaven's Way at the expense of human desires. He committed suicide in prison as a protest against persecution by the court because of his philosophy (Li Chunqing 1995:209–12; Liu Xiuming 1997:516–34).

There were successful scholar-officials. The Tang (618–907) dynasty's Yao Chong (642–721) and Song Jing (661–737) are prime examples. They not only helped Emperor Tang Xuanzong (685–762) in his power struggles and proposed reform measures, but also remonstrated with him when necessary (pp. 306–33). Literati like them were few, though.

Intellectuals were thus the "executive officers" of kings and emperors in various dynasties, their "deputies" as Gramsci would call them. They were supposed to, as Zhuge Liang (181–234) says, bend one's back to the task until one's dying day *(jugong jincui, si er hou yi)*. And they were supposed to, as Fan Zhongyan (989–1052) says, be the first to worry about the troubles of the world and the last to enjoy its pleasures *(xian tianxia zhi you er you, hou tianxia zhi le er le)*. Both refer to devotion to the emperor, or to a mission, usually given by one's masters or required by the literati tradition (see also Bol 1992). To become a scholar-official was the best way to save the world, because one would then, as Weber (1946:114–5) commented on politics as a vocation, hold the wheel of history. They were, however, constantly caught in power struggles and very few were able to influence politics the way Yao Chong and Song Jing did.

These were the earliest literati bureaucrats, or the bureaucratized intellectuals. Whenever a new dynasty was established, the new emperor would always surround himself with scholar-officials as advisers and administrators. For, as the saying goes, one can win a new dynasty on horseback but cannot govern from it (see also Tu Wei-ming 1993b:17–8; Jin Yaoji 1980:71).[13] Jin Guantao and Liu Qingfeng (1989:173–5) rightly pointed out that one reason why Chinese civilization survived is that every time an old dynasty was destroyed and a new one established, Confucian scholars helped reconstruct the society socially, politically, and economically. The same process has been repeated hundreds of times over the last several thousand years. Indeed, the traditional Chinese polity *(zheng tong)* could not have survived without the support of the Confucian ideology embodied and developed by the literati (Tang Bo 1988:67–9, 72–4).

What about modern organic intellectuals? Since they have followed the same tradition as the literati, we are bound to see many of them in government. For example, almost all the twelve members of the first Republican cabinet were from the educated elite (see table 8.1 in the appendix). Some intellectuals have certainly been in leadership positions, like the revolutionary intellectuals in power. But others, like the *Ideologues* and revisionists, have been in supporting roles and have kept meeting frustrations.

Table 1.1 gives us an idea of the occupational distribution of students returning from America in 1917, 1925, and 1937, indicating especially the percentage of those intellectuals engaged in government service. Of all the students back from America, the tendency was for about a third to be hired by the government. One would assume that returned students from Europe and Japan would also join the government in large numbers. We mentioned earlier in a footnote that in the Guomindang (GMD) government, about 90 percent were intellectuals, according to Jiang Tingfu (or T. F. Tsiang 1980). It is probably fair to say that most would have to be bureaucratic functionaries. Statistics also indicate that in 1945, out of the CCP Politburo's 42 members, 27 were known to have enjoyed a higher education (2 did not, and the educational status of the remaining 13 was unknown) (North 1965:380–1).

As a Party largely of intellectuals, the CCP managed to attract to its services many intellectuals, whom they then transformed for the Party's purposes. "In the manner of past Chinese governments, the Communist

Table 1.1 Occupational Distribution of American-Trained Students

Year[1]	1917	1925	1937
Education	39.19%	38.36%	28.13%
Government service	35.59%	15.41%	29.34%
Business [2]	11.66%	22.09%	13.45%
Foreign employ	1.90%	3.94%	4.60%
Professionals	8.27%	3.25%	2.60%
Social and Religious Work	3.39%	1.37%	1.30%
Others [3]	—	15.58%	20.58%
Unknown	—	13.36%	14.33%
Total	100.00%	100.00%	100.00%
Total number of persons	472	584	1152

Source: Reconstructed from Y. C. Wang. 1966. *Chinese Intellectuals and the West 1872–1949*, p. 514.

Notes:

1. Years were chosen in an attempt to give equal intervals.
2. Business includes banking, commerce, and industry.
3. Others include homemakers and the deceased.

leadership has sought to utilize the skills of the intellectuals and to indoctrinate them with an all-embracing ideology—the ideology being Marxism-Leninism rather than the traditional Confucianism" (Goldman 1967:1). In 1939, Mao wrote that recruiting intellectuals into the revolutionary ranks was one of the important conditions for the success of the Communist cause (1966:583).[14] Indeed, many intellectuals rushed to Yan'an, the mecca of the Chinese revolution. Or if they did not go to Yan'an, they supported the CCP from the GMD area.[15] We will now focus only on the organic intellectuals of the Party before "liberation," that is, the organic intellectuals dedicated to a social movement.[16] This will lay a foundation for chapters 2 and 5, our study of the organic intellectuals after "liberation."

The first sizable group of organic intellectuals in the Party was the League of Left-Wing Writers, established in March 1930. It was supported by Lu Xun (1881–1936), one of the most prominent writers and critics of the time, but it was first governed by Qu Qiubai (1899–1935) and later by Zhou Yang (1908–89), both of whom were Communist intellectuals (Goldman 1967:9–10). Its aim was to attack the Nationalist government and the rightist writers, and of course to spread Soviet literature and leftist programs (Holm 1991:30–3; Hsu 1983:569). It met dissent from some of Lu Xun's close confidants, though, such as Feng Xuefeng and Hu Feng, who tended to adhere to a less doctrinaire attitude toward others and in literary matters (Goldman 1967:11–17). Nonetheless, a great number of literary works that depicted the life of the ordinary people appeared. Included in them are Mao Dun's *Zi Ye* (The midnight), Lao She's *Luotuo Xiangzi* (The story of Xiangzi), and Nie Er's song *Yiyong Jun Jinxing Qu* (The song of the indignant and brave army) (Zheng Xian 1996:110), which is now the national anthem of the People's Republic of China.

Soon after, intellectuals in Yan'an went through the first round of thought reform in the Rectification Campaign of 1942. The campaign began with Mao's famous talk on art and literature. He urged writers to produce literature that would serve the Party and the working class. He called on the intellectuals to reform their bourgeois thinking and to become cogs and screws of the revolutionary machine (Holm 1991; Mao 1966; Vol. 3; see also Gao Xinmin and Zhang Shujun 2000). Most intellectuals willingly reformed themselves, like Ai Qing and He Qifang, both writers, and many began to write revolutionary literature. Holm's (1991) study of the Lu Xun Academy of Art (or Luyi) in

Yan'an describes how the Communists used various folk dance and drama genres such as stilt-walking, *yangge* dance, and *yangge* plays in promoting their ideologies: themes of rebellion, satires of established authorities, class hatred, and so forth. Some of the most famous works produced during the wartimes include *Brother and Sister Clear Wasteland (xiong mei kai huang)* and *White-Haired Girl (bai mao nu)*. Zhao Shuli's *Rhymes of Li Youcai* may be representative of the literature at the time. Here is a section of it:

> Join the Peasants' Union; it will make us stronger.
> Anybody cheats us, we can fetch him a good crack.
> Old Yen can't now press us any longer.
> All the stolen land back, all the squeezed cash back;
> Reduce all the rents to the last squeezed penny;
> Out with officials who want to get us on the run.
> We're going to be tough with them, we aren't having any.
> Join the Peasants' Union if you want to see it done.
> (quoted in Chesneaux 1973:138)

These works were quite effective in generating enthusiasm among the peasants and soldiers in their struggle against internal and external enemies (Holm 1991:275–6, 321–3).

While many followed the Party's directives in reforming art and literature, writers like Ding Ling and Xiao Jun, however, were reluctant to acknowledge any "problems." Wang Shiwei, the severest critic of the Yan'an government, refused to budge. In the spirit of Lu Xun, he criticized the inequality in Yan'an and the hypocrisy of the Party (see Dai Qing 1994; Holm 1991; Gao Xinmin and Zhang Shujun 2000:344–65). He became "the symbol of resistance" to Mao's definition of intellectuals' roles (Apter and Cheek 1994:xx), and he is a good example of organic intellectuals who also perform critical roles. Rather than blindly subordinating themselves to the Party, Wang is actually saying that they should criticize it. (He paid a price with his life.) This is an aspect of the intellectual we will further explore in this chapter. Figure 1.1 may help us understand the complexity of intellectuals' roles.

The Rectification Campaign went on to sweep the GMD area as well. Here the Communist intellectuals Ai Siqi, Chen Boda, and Zhou Yang led the charge. Again, there was resistance from more liberal intellectuals of the Left like Feng Xuefeng. The Party, however, continued its

Figure 1.1 The Size Doesn't Fit *(Chima bu heshi)*

fight to indoctrinate leftist writers and to influence the form and content of their work. It was helped by the more revolutionary organic intellectuals such as Ai, Chen, and Zhou as well as Kang Sheng, Hu Qiaomu, He Qifang, Guo Moruo, and Mao Dun (Apter and Saich 1994; Fogel 1987a:75; Goldman 1967:34–66; Wylie 1980). These were all writers, essayists, and/or scholars in China at the time, some more accomplished than others.

Mao faced four major struggles during the Yan'an period (1935–45). They were military against Zhang Guotao, territorial or administrative against Liu Zhidan, ideological against Wang Ming, and intellectual against Wang Shiwei (Apter and Saich 1994; Gao Xinmin and Zhang Shujun 2000). Mao would not have succeeded in any of these, especially the last two, without the support of the more organic intellectuals. Chen

Boda's and Ai Siqi's theoretical work on the Sinification of Marxism, for example, was especially helpful to Mao in his difficulties with Wang Ming (see Fogel 1987a, 1987b; Holm 1991:52–3; Wylie 1980), and Ai, Kang, Hu, Chen, and so forth all helped Mao in his struggle with the Wang Shiweis in the Party.

The Rectification Campaign was only the first of the CCP's serious efforts at reforming the intellectuals and making them more organic. As the CCP consolidated its national power, it continued to coerce more intellectuals into its fold, even while it continued to meet resistance from some. We would see more thought reform after "liberation," which we will discuss in chapter 2. For the moment we need only say that a group of organic intellectuals had already been developed before "liberation" and would continue to grow after it. Sometimes they resemble the Fabians and Roosevelt's "brain trust," but most often they resemble Napoleon's *Ideologues* and Gomulka's revisionists. Like all such groups, they had their graces and disgraces. While there may be such a group in every regime in every society, the literati tradition makes it more conspicuous and permanent in China. They continued to be one of the most important intellectual groups in both the Mao and Deng eras.

The GMD had its own share of organic intellectuals. Weng Wenhao (or Weng Wen-hao, 1889–1971); Jiang Tingfu (or T. F. Tsiang, 1895–1965); Fu Sinian (or Fu Ssu-nien, 1896–1950); and Luo Jialun (or Lo Chia-lun, 1897–1969), to name just a few, all held important positions in the GMD government in the 1930s and/or 1940s (see also Y. C. Wang 1966:414; Q. Edward Wang 2001). Hu Shih (1891–1962) was a prime example. He was a champion of the New Culture movement (1917–23),[17] and a critical intellectual in that regard. But he was also an ardent supporter of Chiang Kai-shek's chief policies in the 1930s and 1940s, including the suppression of internal dissension, and concessions to Japan in the Sino-Japanese dispute (Y. C. Wang 1966:409–15). He stressed that every government had a right to suppress subversive activities and praised Chiang for his extraordinary courage and ability. He thought that the assassination of Wen Yiduo (1899–1946) and Li Gongpu (1902–46) in 1946, two of the many intellectuals who protested the GMD policies, was only a "small incident in the midst of general progress toward democracy" (cited in Y. C. Wang 1965:415).[18] He suggested and then endorsed the demilitarization of Charhar and Hebei (Hopeh), that is, the withdrawal of Chinese troops from the two provincial regions, following an agreement drawn up between Chiang and the

Japanese government. He served as ambassador to the United States from 1938 to 1942, and as president of National Peking University in 1946, and became head of the Academia Sinica in 1958 until his death in 1962. Li Qingxi (2000) has also examined the various political roles Hu played in the Republican era and points out that he was far from "liberal," independent, and critical, contrary to what many Mainland Chinese intellectuals now tend to believe.

We have described the development of organic intellectuals in both China and the West, traditional and modern. We have focused on organic intellectuals' loyalty and service to those in power. However, as we have seen and will see more in our discussion, they can also be critical of the authorities they serve, which indicates a dual personality. We will further explore this aspect of the intellectual after discussing the critical, unattached, and professional intellectuals.

Critical Intellectuals

In the critical tradition in both China and the West, intellectuals want to be the "watchmen in what otherwise would be a pitch-black night" (Mannheim 1936:160–1) and to "shame men committed to an ethos of compromise" (Coser 1965:136). Ever since Confucius, in addition to governing the country as organic intellectuals to those in power, the Chinese intellectuals have been expected to function as the conscience of society and to shoulder the responsibility of uncompromising social criticism. In this section, we will look at some specific examples of intellectuals throughout history, so that we have a better idea of the tradition the contemporary critical intellectuals have inherited. We will start with those in the West.

Coser (1965:207–26) describes two examples of critical intellectuals, or "critics of power" in the West: the Abolitionists in America and the Dreyfusards in France. The Abolitionist movement was started in the 1830s by intellectuals who thought that American society was corrupt to the core if it allowed slavery to persist. The ownership of human beings contradicted the new country's professed values. The Abolitionists thus appealed to the conscience of society by serving as the conscience of society. It was an unpopular cause and they were less likely to gain political positions in the government, but that was not their concern. By 1838, the movement gathered more than 100,000 members in 1,300 abolitionist societies. In one year between 1837 and 1838, 412,000 petitions were sent to Congress, and in the following year

2,000,000 signatures for abolition were gathered. The movement had thirty to forty newspapers and held numerous "antislavery meetings, antislavery celebrations, antislavery bazaars, antislavery *soirees,* and antislavery festivals" (p. 213).

They finally succeeded, though it was a bloody success. But the interesting point is that they did not start the movement as politicians. Coser points out that the Abolitionists hardly thought about the issue in institutional terms. They did not know how to free the slaves, and once they were freed, what would happen to them. What they started was a moral movement, which eventually turned into a political one and led to the abolition of slavery. Coser says that had it been entangled in political details and compromises to begin with, one wonders whether the movement would have succeeded so thoroughly (1965:214–5). In the conclusion of the chapter, we will come back to similar dilemmas intellectuals face.

Much like the Abolitionists, the Dreyfusards too started their movement to defend a set of principles rather than to win political power. Alfred Dreyfus, an officer of the French General Staff, was wrongly convicted of espionage and sentenced to life in prison. The army knew it had made an error but did not want to correct it for fear it would hurt the cause of the military. Justice seemed at stake, according to Émile Zola, the famous French writer, and his comrades in arms, that is, other men of letters. "When force and fraud had become the instruments of government, he argued, the political order had lost its moral justification; it had become the duty of the citizen to oppose it" (Coser 1965:222). The Dreyfusards were defending an abstract idea of justice and did not much care about anything else. When Zola was accused of disturbing peace and was defending himself in front of a judge, he said, "I don't know the law and don't want to know it" (p. 223).

Indeed they were criticized by other men of letters for meddling in fields not their own. A famous literary critic, Ferdinand Brunetière, charged that Zola was "meddling in a problem of military justice" and it was "no less impertinent and preposterous than the intervention of a captain of gendarmerie in a question of syntax or prosody." It was absurd for the Dreyfusards, those writers, scientists, professors, and philologists, to coin the word *intellectual* to elevate themselves to the status of supermen, he said (Coser 1965:222). But that is exactly what an intellectual is all about. He was not going to restrict himself to performing his professional tasks. He was also going to concern himself with abstract justice, a universal idea, and to place it above the claims of the state and of social order. As true inheritors of the Enlightenment, the intellectuals believed that "their mission was to criticize the ruling powers when they interfered with reason and justice" (p. 223).

Like the Abolitionists, the Dreyfusards were not popular, either. While the Abolitionists were attacked or even murdered by anti-Abolitionist mobs, the Dreyfusards "were abused in public, attacked by mobs, cashiered from their positions in the diplomatic corps, or suspended from their university positions by a vindictive government . . . [some] had to part company with friends and loved ones because of the Affair" (Coser 1965:224). But eventually, both the Abolitionists and the Dreyfusards succeeded. Critical intellectuals played a key role in social transformation. Most importantly, in both France and America, they brought the moral questions of justice into the public arena and challenged people's consciences in the face of injustice. They accepted the fact that such challenges might jeopardize their political standing and uproot the nation's social order.

To Coser's examples, we may again add a number of Russian types: the intelligentsia, or *intelligenty,* who in the latter half of the nineteenth century would blend poetry and politics, and the populists, who merged with the peasant masses and the workers and organized a revolutionary vanguard that would lead the struggle for power. Some of these eventually became social democrats, such as Plechanov and Lenin (Nahirny 1983:89, 122, 131, 135–7). In the Soviet era, while intelligentsia were largely co-opted by the regime, there was no lack of dissidents, which explains the "psychiatric" prisons operated by the KGB, where dissenters were given punitive forms of therapy (Krause 1991:15), and the Gulags, the forced-labor camps for political prisoners. Yevgeny Ivanovich Zamyatin, the Soviet writer, rushed home to join the October Revolution but only to find himself unable to cope with the regime because he was too independent and critical. He finally had to go into exile. Another such example is Solzhenitsyn (see Le Guin [1973] 1977). Andrei Sakharov, of course, is a typical example of the great Russian dissidents. Championing intellectual freedom, he became the conscience of the Soviet intellectuals (see Bell 1973:97, 407). The USSR Nuclear Society, an informal research and lobbying group founded in 1989, was a watchdog organization, the sort of organization that critical intellectuals set up in the Soviet era (Krause 1991:249).

The Russian example greatly inspired both the Chinese revolutionaries and the dissidents. We will discuss this in the next section. But first of all, let us have a historical perspective of the traditional and modern intellectuals who were also concerned more with justice than with becoming officials, or organic to the powers, although the literati also needed to make a living, and the major way to do that was to become an official. They could not "live for" politics until they became modern intellectuals.[19] At any rate, there had always been literati who were critical of the status quo but who had sought to change the system from the *outside,* not from the *inside* as organic intellectuals did. But because they too might claim to follow the principle of *xiu qi zhi ping* (cultivating oneself, getting one's own house in order, governing one's own country, and bringing peace to the world), they became organic intellectuals once their group achieved power, again partly because there were few other ways to make a living. Indeed, the Communist intellectuals even became the ruling class. This was the first time that intellectuals came to real power. Our focus, however, will be on three groups of critical intellectuals: first, the *revolutionaries before they were in power;* second, those intellectuals who were critical of the powers from the outside, or *independent social and political critics;* and third, those who were critical of the tradition, not directly critical of the state power, whom we may call *cultural critics.*

Included among the *revolutionaries before they were in power* were the literati who participated in overthrowing one dynasty and establishing another. The Confucians participated in the earliest peasant uprisings. For example, Kong Fu, the eighth-generation grandson of Confucius, participated in Chen Sheng and Wu Guang's uprising against the Qin dynasty, not unrelated to the Qin emperor's burning of Confucian books and his execution of Confucians.[20] Kong died a martyr in the uprising (Liu Xiuming 1997:78). The rebellious peasants always needed the literati for advice and to help them write public notices as well. Another example is Pi Rixiu (ca. 833–83), a famous poet and thinker, who joined the Huang Chao Uprising against the Tang dynasty (618–907) (Liu Xiuming 1997:404–16). Other literati joined the Lulin Chimei Uprising in the late Western Han (206 B.C.E.–25 C.E.), and the peasant uprisings in the late Sui (581–618). The Taiping Uprising was even led by a member of the literati, Hong Xiuquan (1814–64).

But most likely, if the peasant uprising succeeded, many of these critical activists would become organic intellectuals. Some even became famous ministers of the new dynasties. Wei Zheng (580–643) of the early Tang, for example, was a *Daoist* monk when he was young. Later he joined a peasant uprising and ended up serving Taizong of the Tang dynasty as Jianyi Dafu, the adviser to the emperor whose major role was to criticize him and make suggestions. This was an institutional mechanism started in Western Han (225–06 B.C.E.) and ending in Ming (1368–1644). Wei became one of the most famous scholar-officials in China's history.

The literati joined the peasant uprisings because they believed that the dynasties were simply corrupt and needed a better emperor. As Chesneaux (1973:21) points out, the peasant revolts were more likely caused directly by the "abuses of the traditional regimes: excessive taxation, the exactions of officials, the brutality of a landlord, the neglect which led to disasters, and so on." But they "appealed to the Confucian principles of justice *(i),* the Way *(tao),* and the Will of Heaven *(t'ien).*" That gave the literati a good reason to participate in the peasant uprisings.

Like Hong Xiuquan of the Taiping Uprising, the revolutionaries such as Sun Yat-sen, Mao, and their colleagues started their own revolutions and became rulers themselves, based on the same principles of justice and moral imperatives. Sun Yat-sen, a medical professional educated in Hawaii and Hong Kong, turned political and revolutionary and adopted views even more radical than Kang Youwei and Liang Qichao, the constitutional reformists of the late Qing dynasty. Sun advocated what is known as *san min zhuyi,* the 'Three People's Principles': nationalism, democracy, and socialism. This meant a combination of a nationalist revolution to overthrow the Manchu dynasty, which had brought disasters and humiliations to the country; a democratic revolution to establish a republic to guarantee the proper function of government; and a social revolution to equalize land rights and prevent the ills of capitalism. Together with Huang Xing, a returned student from Japan, and Song Jiaoren, a traditional intellectual, Sun organized first the Revive China Society, and later his own party, the Chinese United League. Their goal was to implement the three principles, and they succeeded to some extent.

The legacy of the Chinese Communist Revolution began with the end of the May 4 Movement (1915–21), when Chen Duxiu (or Ch'en Tu-hsiu, 1880–1942), a professor of literature at Beijing University, and Li Dazhao (or Li Ta-chao, 1889–1927), the chief librarian of the university and a professor of economics and history, started the CCP in 1921. It was going to be a proletarian revolution and the Party was going to organize workers. Chen Duxiu, Zhang Guotao, and other Communist intellectuals spoke at meetings of workers' unions. The Communist intellectuals such as Deng Zhongxia, Zhang Guotao, Li Lisan, Liu Shaoqi, Shi Yang, and Guo Liang, played a major role in the labor organizations' strikes and protests in the 1920s (Chesneaux 1968; Kwan 1997; Perry 1993).[21] But the CCP later realized "the immense revolutionary potentialities of the peasantry" (Chesneaux 1973:157).

Indeed, look at the achievements of the peasant associations in Hunan in 1927 (Mao 1966:22–42), and in Guangdong from 1927 to 1928 (Marks 1984:253–62), and you will see the power of peasant movements, many of which were led by intellectuals. Chief among the achievements were taking over the village and county governments, and reducing the land rents (in Hunan) or even redistributing the land (in Guangdong). Seeing the enormous power of the peasantry, the CCP decided, as Lin Biao said, to "rely on the peasants, build rural base areas and use the countryside to encircle and finally capture the cities" (quoted in Chesneaux 1973:157). The Communist Revolution is, in a sense, a peasant movement, but led by revolutionary intellectuals. It was the revolutionary intellectuals who finally overthrew the Nationalist government and established the Communist regime, although in the name of the workers and peasants. We might call those who participated in the peasant uprisings and revolutions "radical critical intellectuals."

The second group, *independent social and political critics,* is typically not connected with peasant uprisings or revolutions although they may very well be on their way to becoming organic or revolutionary intellectuals. This group is becoming more typical of contemporary intellectuals, but the tradition really started a couple of thousand years ago. They are more like the Abolitionists and Dreyfusards.

In the Chinese tradition, Goldman (1981:3) points out, "Inherent in Confucianism was the obligation for any degree holder to speak out when the government deviated from Confucian ideals." These rights, however, were not legally guaranteed, but merely justified ideologically. From this belief in speaking out came the *qing yi,* 'pure opinion,' movements that have run throughout China's intellectual history (pp. 1–17), as well as "the tradition of the principled literati" that has survived up to this day (Goldman 1994:5–7). One well-known example is the case of the Danggu, or "party cases," in 166–169, at the end of the Eastern Han dynasty (25–220). Over three thousand leading scholars and university students launched a critical movement against the current politics, government policies, and the conduct of members of the imperial household as well as the eunuchs and the emperor. The movement was completely suppressed, with two to three hundred scholars and sometimes their whole families sentenced to death, exile, or imprisonment (Lin Yutang 1939:50). This was the first large intellectual protest movement in China and the start of the critical tradition that has descended to the present generation.

Another noteworthy intellectual critical movement originated in the academies. This was the Donglin Academy movement led by Gu Xiancheng, a deposed scholar-official who founded the academy in 1604 and who has left the motto for intellectuals: Family Affairs, National Affairs, and World Affairs, Everything Is of My Concern. Gu and his students began to criticize corrupt officials in their regular gatherings with scholars from other places. In effect, they reneged on their promise, made at the time of the academy's founding, not to get involved in politics. They spoke out against exploitation by government officials. They demanded open criticism and reform. The ruling clique, which was headed by a eunuch named Wei Zhongxian, eventually, between 1625 and 1626, cracked down on the Donglin intellectuals and in fact on academies all over the country, with some scholars executed and jailed and the academies destroyed. An early Qing scholar, Chen Ding, wrote 24 books about 120 of the Donglin rebels, to commemorate their intellectual tradition and courage (see also Goldman 1981:5; Chen-main Wang 1999:26–9). Deng Tuo, the revolutionary intellectual from the Beijing Communist Party Committee wrote the following to commemorate the critical tradition of the Donglin intellectuals (quoted by Liu Xiuming 1997:552): "Do not say that the scholars were just talking empty talk, Blood spilled where their heads rolled."[22]

The movement of independent social and political criticism continued in the May 4 era with intellectuals like Hu Shih, Chen Duxiu, and Li Dazhao (i.e., before they became organic or revolutionary), as well as Lu Xun. These voices made themselves heard through such independent periodicals as *Weekly Critic (Meizhou Pinglun)* and *New Youth (Xin Qingnian)*. As Chow Tse-tsung (1960:58–9) summarizes, the basic principles underlying the tenets of these intellectual leaders were Mr. Democracy and Mr. Science, the two main slogans of the day. Politically, they opposed political privileges for the few and advocated democracy and liberalism; socially, they opposed traditional thought and customs and advocated individualism, new family patterns, and equality between men and women. Ideologically, however, they cannot be easily categorized in this period before they became organic. Lu Xun, in fact, had always been independent. For example, he sympathized with the poor and the underprivileged but was not a Communist.[23] And his pen "was not for sale," comments Grieder (1981: 336). Even Li Dazhao, one of the intellectuals who introduced Marxism to the Chinese, maintained that Marxism should not be "accepted as a whole and applied uncritically to modern society" (cited in Chow Tse-tsung 1960:298).

In the Republican era under Chiang Kai-shek, there were numerous examples of independent intellectuals. Among them were many professors from the National Southwest Associated University, or Xinan Lianda, a wartime university in the 1940s composed of three institutions of higher learning: Beijing, Qinghua, and Nankai universities. These intellectuals include Wen Yiduo (poet), Pan Guandan and Fei Xiaotong (both sociologists), Zhang Xiruo (political scientist), and Wu Han (historian) (Israel 1998; Mazur 1996). Fei Xiaotong, a sociologist born in 1910 and trained in England, was one of them. In the 1940s, he criticized GMD politics, its corruption and power struggle, and analyzed the problems with Chinese society. He advocated democracy, law, and freedom of expression (Arkush 1986:111, 136; see also Israel 1998). He became a member of the Democratic League in 1946, a third party after the GMD and the CCP, and actively participated in rallies, speeches, and critical journalism.

The quintessential "third-party" political mind, however, may be said to belong to Zhang Junmai (or Chang Chun-mai, or Carsun Chang, 1886–1969). Zhang, in fact, is one of the interesting cases of a critical intellectual who tried to become organic and even ultimately a power holder. He was very critical of both the CCP and the GMD, being strongly opposed to a one-party dictatorship. In 1932 he founded his own party, the National Socialist Party of China, and made an attempt to ally with Yan Xishan, the ruler of Shanxi, and Li Zongren, the ruler of Guangxi. He wanted his party to be involved in the development of these provinces. None of his efforts, however, was successful, and he remained as he began, an independent social and political critic (Jeans 1997).[24]

But Chu Anping (1908–66?),[25] the editor of *The Observer,* is probably the most telling example of these independent intellectuals. In his letter to Hu Shih, one of the most prominent scholars of the time, inviting him to write for the journal, Chu criticized those who wanted to *li gong,* to "join the government." He believed that the best thing an intellectual should do is to be an independent observer and critic outside the powerhouse. Since the founding of the journal in 1946 in Shanghai, Chu had written many articles criticizing both the GMD and the CCP, especially for their respective control of public opinion in the areas under their rule (Xie Yong 1999a:250–4). A year after, the journal was banned by the GMD government. But its mission representing independent intellectuals remained: "freedom, democracy, progress, and reason" (see also Dai Qing 1990:176). In chapters 2 and 3, we will meet more critical intellectuals in the Mao and Deng eras who followed the Donglin or the Republican intellectuals; for example, the Rightists in 1957 and the intellectuals of the democratic movement in the past decade. It is obvious that the critical intellectuals have survived the past two thousand years along with their organic counterparts.

Discussion of these groups of critical intellectuals speaks mainly to their relations with the powers, namely, the state. The revolutionary intellectuals wanted to take over the government. The other critical intellectuals mainly wanted to change it, as did the Abolitionists, the Dreyfusards, and the Danggu and the Donglin literati, not necessarily to ascend to power themselves.

The third group of intellectuals, the *cultural critics,* may be less concerned with how the government functions but are critical of cultural traditions and revolutionary in their work. They sometimes overlap with the social and political critics, though. Hu, Chen, Li, and Lu, for example, were both political and cultural critics in the New Culture Movement in the May 4 period. Cultural criticism, by definition, may be only indirectly related to the powers. In fact, Chen Duxiu at first restricted the meaning of culture to only science, religion, morality, literature, music, the arts, and the like, not political, economic, and social actions (Chow Tse-tsung 1960:195). Like the *social and political critics,* however, these new intellectuals "called for a critical re-evaluation of China's cultural heritage in the light of modern Western standards" (Hsu 1983:493) because they believed that it was those Confucian standards that made China lag far behind the Western countries. That means China had to introduce science and democracy. While this movement eventually led some, like the Communist intellectuals, to start a political revolution, it inspired others to reform literature. For example, the modern intellectuals started a new literature based on the vernacular language rather than the classical, with Hu Shih and Chen Duxiu as their leaders. Still others started a movement of Chinese folk literature (Hung 1985).

The latter movement was led by such men as Liu Fu (Bannong, 1891–1934), Zhou Zuoren (1885–1967), and Gu Jiegang (1893–1934). The folklorists were to collect folk-songs, proverbs, dialect literature, legends, and children's literature, and to publish them in newspapers and journals. The significance of the movement lies first in the new intellectuals' criticism of the Confucian focus on morality in literature as opposed to the folk literature's focus on freedom, spontaneity, and sensitivity (Hung 1985:169). It lies also in the rethinking of intellectuals' roles: rather than serving only the aristocratic few, intellectuals should serve the majority of the people (Hung 1985:177–80). Those are some examples of critical intellectuals who found fault with traditional literary views and practice, found virtues in a folk literature that was looked down upon by the aristocratic intellectuals, and started to write in a new language.

Thus far we have seen at least three groups of critical intellectuals: the *revolutionaries,* or the rebels in both the peasant uprisings and intellectual revolutions; the *political and social critics* outside the power structure; and the *cultural critics,* that is, mainly the innovative men of letters. There tends to be an overlap among the three. The Communist revolutionary intellectuals later became organic intellectuals and some even entered the ruling class. We have considered them critical before they became organic. Like the Dreyfusards and Abolitionists, many critical intellectuals started their crusades driven by a moral imperative and sense of social justice. But the consequences of criticism these intellectuals suffered far surpassed any that the Dreyfusards and Abolitionists suffered. This has been true not only with the critical literati, such as the Danggu and Donglin literati, but also with today's intellectuals. It is important to remember that the three different kinds of critical intellectuals may overlap, and critical intellectuals can become organic intellectuals or even part of the ruling class. The organic intellectuals or members of the ruling class can also return to their critical roles, as Wang Shiwei did in the Yan'an era. We will further discuss this fluidity and complexity of both the critical intellectuals and their organic counterparts after we discuss the unattached and professional intellectuals. Figure 1.2 may illustrate how difficult it is to be critical.

Figure 1.2 "Media Supervision" and "Supervising the Media" *(Yulun jiandu yu jiandu yulun)*

Notes: "Media supervision" means the supervision of the government by the mass media, but "supervising the media" means the supervision of the mass media by the government.

Source: Ding Cong 1999 (Vol. 2), p. 46.

Unattached Intellectuals and Professionals

By *unattached* we mean unattached to politics. Our use of "unattached intellectuals" resembles Merton's (1968:266) use of the term. It refers to intellectuals (and this includes most academics) who play no part in formulating or implementing bureaucratic policies. As we mentioned earlier, Coser (1965:136) identifies a group of intellectuals who uphold "art for art's sake," and who view the world of politics as a nightmare.[26]

The "gentleman-litterateurs" of Russia in the eighteenth century may also be viewed as unattached intellectuals (see Nahirny 1983:42–9). These were a group of "superfluous people," who preferred dissipation to the disciplined life and who turned into intellectual dilettanti, shifting their interest to art, literature, and the theater. This aristocratic society and its salons thus created an autonomous cultural sphere, in which writers asserted an independent status, refusing to allow literature to become a state service, as organic intellectuals had previously in the czarist court. The same is true with the late nineteenth century Central European Jewish and gentry intellectuals who often led their lives "in search of truth" rather than in the service of employers (Eyal, Szelenyi, and Townsley 1998:71).

That closely resembles the *Daoist* tradition in China. Intellectuals who adhere to the *Daoist* tradition abhor becoming officials or even working for officials. Nor are they revolutionaries or reformers. They tend not to actively criticize the powers, either. They want to be free thinkers. They want to be free-floating and engage in their own studies of the world, unhampered by politics. Our definition here is close to that of Mannheim's, which refers to intellectuals who transcend their classes, as we mentioned earlier. These would be the traditional *Daoist yinshi,* whom we will discuss in the next section. Professionals, on the other hand, refer chiefly to modern intellectuals who are trained in the sciences and technical skills. With a few exceptions, they tend to keep their distance from politics, too. They are the modern "unattached intellectuals." We will now review the historical background of these two groups of intellectuals.

According to Yan Buke (1989:28), in the Warring States Period (475–211 B.C.E.), the time of Confucius, there emerged a group of free intellectuals *(wenxue youshi),* that is, "floating literary intellectuals," who devoted themselves to the "interpretation of concepts."[27] It was a time when independent groups of thinkers flourished and a "hundred schools contended." The kings would frequently consult with these *wenxue youshi* for help in ruling their states. This intellectual tendency fostered a group of intellectuals later on called *yinshi,* or "recluses." They were also called *yimin,* that is, "leisure folks," or "leisure intellectuals" (Ma and Chen 1992).

To the group of *yinshi,* we should add the Confucian gentry, most of whom were also averse to becoming officials. These included many scholars who performed extrabureaucratic services, and who enjoyed a leisurely but scholarly life outside the political structure. Many distanced themselves even further, becoming Buddhist monks and priests.[28]

What are some of the characteristics that made them such a special group? First, they tended to believe in *Daoism* (Taoism) or Buddhism, and to be concerned about individual freedom rather than becoming an official.[29] Zhuang Zi, one of the founders of *Daoism,* was a prominent example (Leng Chengjin 1997:4). He "did not wish to be 'harnessed' to an office but would rather exist 'like a [free] pig in a muddy ditch'" (Weber 1946:179). According to another story, the king of Chu sent two officials to invite Zhuang Zi to take the office of prime minister. Zhuang Zi was fishing at the time and paid little attention to them, simply telling them that he would rather live like a tortoise in a muddy ditch than be a dead one hanging in a grand hall (Zhang Hengshou 1984:98). A third story goes that he "was offered a high post by the king of Chu but replied by asking whether it was wise to be kept and fed like a pig and then be slaughtered and offered up on the sacrificial altar" (Lin Yutang 1939:118). He was determined not to become an official but to live his life as a philosopher and a writer. As Gramsci and Mannheim would put it, he refused to become an organic intellectual, preferring to remain unattached, culturally a free man.

Ji Kang (223–63) was another example. When one of his former friends, Shan Juyuan, invited him to come and serve Sima Zhao, a general, he wrote him a letter, listing nine what he called *huan,* that is, "worries," or reasons why he would not go. They include the loss of freedom to be alone playing *qin* (a musical instrument) and singing, for there would always be servants around. Scratching himself for lice would be difficult for he would have to wear formal clothes. Most importantly, he would not be tolerated for his criticism of Tang and Wu (two wise kings), Zhou (an accomplished politician), and Kong (Confucius).[30] And his temper could not allow him to refrain from expressing his views (Tang Yongde 1982:75–6). Those reasons characterize the ideal of a *yinshi,* whose freedom to do whatever he wanted to, from expressing political criticism to the pleasures of scratching for lice, might be lost once he became a scholar-official.

Second, the "leisure intellectuals" may have chosen not to become officials, but that does not mean they were not concerned about worldly affairs. As Ji Kang's letter shows, he was critical of kings and generals, and of Confucius and his disciples. But his desire to criticize would not be strong enough to make him join dissident forces to work out a new regime.

Third, how did they make a living? That brings us to another of their characteristics: believing that *Dao* was eternal while worldly fame and riches were transient as a fleeting cloud. *Yinshi,* uncharmed by worldly fame, tended to live simple but spiritually rich lives (see also Liu Xiuming 1997:196–204). They provided for themselves by farming, fishing, and hunting. Some would just build themselves huts in the mountains and read and write. They enjoyed as their companions simple woodcutters and herb-gatherers, as the following poem indicates:

> I asked the boy beneath the pines.
> He said, "The Master's gone alone
> Herb-picking somewhere on the mount.
> Cloud-hidden, whereabouts unknown."
> (quoted by Lin Yutang 1939:120)

On the other hand, their secluded lives gave them so much inspiration that some *yinshi* produced numerous landscape poems, describing mountains, rivers, and their personal emotions, of which our little quatrain is an example. These have been handed down from generation to generation. Some of the most famous landscape poets include Xie Lingyun (385–433), Tao Yuanming (365–427), Meng Haoran (689–740), and Chu Guangxi (707–60). Others lived by writing and teaching. One book of biographies entitled *Jin Shu: Yin Yi Zhuang* records a *yinshi* in the Jin dynasty (265–420), who had "three thousand students" (Ma and Chen 1992:161). Reading, playing music and chess, traveling, drinking, writing poetry and essays, teaching, visiting friends, and so forth, became a way of life for these *yinshi* (Ma and Chen 1992:126–7).

Fourth, it would be inaccurate to say that none of the *yinshi* wanted to become officials. Some y*inshi* agreed to advise kings and emperors, but their advice tended to follow their *Daoist* beliefs. For example, without becoming an official, Sima Chengzhen of the Tang dynasty advised Wu Zetian (624–705), the empress dowager, and Tang Zhong Zong, another emperor, to govern by doing nothing *(we wei er zhi).* He was dubbed the premier in the mountains *(shan zhong zaixiang)* (Ma and Chen 1992: 92). In fact, many of these men had been officials for sometime before they decided to become floating or recluse intellectuals. All four of these landscape poets were once officials. They escaped to nature only when they became tired of the chores and internal strife of officialdom. Xie Lingyun even neglected his duties and "lost" himself in the mountains while he was still an official (Wu Weihua 1982). Wang Wei (701–61), another famous landscape poet, lived a life of "half official and half recluse" (Ge Xiaoyin 1983).

Others, like Zhuge Liang, left the mountains to become officials (Ma and Chen 1992:63, 67). As the Confucian saying goes, *da ze jian ji tian xia, bu da ze du shan qi shen,* that is, "if they can become officials or otherwise perform meritorious services, they will help the world; but if they cannot do so, they will focus on perfecting themselves." Nonetheless, there is no doubt that *yinshi* became a way of life for some intellectuals, or at least for some time for some intellectuals.

We thus see in ancient times a group of intellectuals who escaped from officialdom to nature or otherwise refused to become officials. Although they might remain critical of the powers that be, that criticism was limited. However, these recluses could be prolific writers and brilliant thinkers. It is in all of these senses that we might call them "unattached intellectuals." The group enjoyed high prestige. In fact, their prestige was so high, and the need for their intellectual services so great, that frustrated Legalists like Shang Yang and Han Fei in the Warring States Period (475 -221 B.C.E.) and emperors like Zhu Yuanzhang of the Ming dynasty (1368–1644) had wanted those who refused to serve beheaded (Yan Buke 1989:29).

In modern times, this intellectual tradition of distancing themselves from officialdom has been taken over mainly by professionals. Let us now look in some detail at the transformation and transition of literati to modern intellectuals in this aspect (see more about the transition in the appendix). We will then have a better idea of the evolution of the professional stratum, and can better understand their contemporary development in chapter 4.

We have seen that the traditional literati were chiefly what are usually called "humanistic intellectuals," that is, those in the knowledge strata who lack technical training. As Weber (1946:427, 431, 432) points out, the special skills required for jurists, medical doctors, or technicians were not emphasized and tested as they were in the West. After the Warring States Period, mathematics lost its status in education, which used to consist of the six arts: ritual propriety, music, archery, horseback riding or charioteering, literature and/or calligraphy, and mathematics. Schools were not concerned with the natural sciences. What was valued were Confucian morals. Even the six arts were "'rituals' designed to discipline people's bodies and minds so that they can act suitably in all human situations" (Tu Wei-ming 1993b:6). Technological development would not bring the inventor much profit; neither would commerce (Y. C. Wang 1966:27–8, 35).

This, however, does not mean that humanistic intellectuals were not at all technical. Lin Tongqi (1980:46–7) observes that it has been overlooked by most historians that the Chinese "feudal *shi* was full of technical meanings." The six arts were actually perceived as six techniques. In addition, social activities such as divination, marriage, death, law and punishment, medicine, and architecture, were all performed by professionals in the field, who had the same social rank as *shi*. The word *shi* (scholar and/or official) actually also meant the same as another *shi,* meaning "things"; therefore, being a *shi* also refers to the ability to do things. Indeed, *fangshi* or *shushi* were those who were engaged in astronomy, mathematics, geography, medicine, agriculture, crafts, *yinyang* (application of the female and male cosmic principles in Chinese dualistic philosophy), and divination (Yan Buke 1996:12). There were even professional schools in the Tang dynasty (618–907) teaching calligraphy, mathematics, and law. There were Hua Tuo (?–208) and Li Shizhen (1518–93) in medicine, Zhang Heng (78–139) and Zu Chongzhi (429–500) in astronomy, Li Bin in irrigation works in the third century B.C.E., Shen Kuo (1031–95) in science, and Xu Guangqi (1562–1633) in agriculture (Yu Zuyao 1996:13, 24). Some of them might be unattached to officialdom, like *yinshi* in that sense, but others were traditional literati and had distinctive careers in politics.

Granted that the feudal *shi* was "full of technical meanings," professionals and scientists did exist to some extent, and sometimes they were one and the same; nonetheless this aspect of intellectualism had never been as developed as was the humanistic aspect. The literati were never tested for *shi* in order to hold office; instead, they were required to be deep in literature and Confucian classics. Even if a professional stratum had actually existed in such technical activities as medicine, they by and large did not have the same status as the literati. They were not considered as important enough for high office, though they were no less important in people's lives. This may have to do with the self-perfection ideal that said that one was "perfect" only when steeped in literature.[31] Therefore, it may be fair to say that technical intellectuals in the Western sense did not really exist in premodern times, although some unattached professionals did find a place in society.[32]

The technical intellectuals in the modern sense—technical and scientific—did not come into being until about a century and a half ago, mainly as organic intellectuals to the ruling class. The first sizable group of technical intelligentsia, the so-called *yangwu zhishi fenzi,* or "foreign matters" intelligentsia, emerged in the latter half of the nineteenth century as part of a Self-Strengthening movement (Li Changli 1989).[33] China was faced with Western "rational," imperial, and colonial attacks, and the traditional government was not able to preserve the Chinese culture. So, with the assistance of open-minded scholar-officials such as Weng Tonghe (1830–1904), Li Hongzhang (1823–1901), and Zhang Zhidong (1837–1909), new schools teaching "foreign matters," that is, Western languages, science, and technology, were established, and students were sent to Europe and America to learn Western civilization. Upon graduation, they were given jobs running factories, mines, textile mills, communications industries, the military, and foreign affairs. These were the organic intellectuals Gramsci is most concerned with, although in this case, the dominant group they were organic to was not the bourgeoisie but the feudal court.

Understandably, this newly born stratum of technical intelligentsia ran into trouble with the traditional literati. They brought home a different set of cultural capital, Western rather than Confucian. They argued that the West was more advanced than China in politics, industry, and the military. The traditional literati still believed that China was the center of the world; indeed, the very name of "China," Zhongguo, means center country, or middle kingdom. The technical intelligentsia insisted that to catch up with the West, China had to develop science and technology. The traditionalists thought that science and technology were but "the technology of carving a little wooden worm—an insignificant skill," or odd and wanton technique *(diao chong xiao ji,* or *qiji yin qiao),* compared with Confucianism with its thousands of years of tradition (Li Changli 1989:35).

The technical intelligentsia were employed to use their Western skills; they were not required to take the great imperial examinations testing their knowledge of the traditional Chinese literature. Without this background, they were often slandered by the traditional literati as "thugs in town," "small persons born in lower-class families," "foreign devils," "Chinese traitors," and "people who don't know how to read and write." (Of course, they meant in traditional Chinese.) Outnumbered by the traditional literati, the technical intellectuals more or less succumbed. Many of the schools teaching Western skills later became schools preparing students for the imperial examinations. Students trained overseas, like Ma Jianzhong (1840–1900), a political scientist from a French college, and Yan Fu (or Yen Fu, 1853–1921), a graduate from an English naval academy; either devoted themselves to preparing for the examinations or turned to translating Western literature (Yan) or writing grammar books (Ma) (Li Changli 1989:33–6). The Self-Strengthening Movement waned. The Western-trained intellectuals pursued their causes in other ways. They remained humanistic intellectuals but with the added values of Western education and ideology. Yan Fu, for example, introduced Western ideas to the Chinese by translating T. H. Huxley's *Evolution and Ethics,* J. S. Mill's *On Liberty* and *Logic,* Herbert Spencer's *Study of Sociology,* Edward Jenk's *History of Politics,* and so forth. (See also Grieder 1981:149–52.) These people were a blend of Western technical and Chinese humanistic intellectuals, a phenomenon in the transition from literati to modern intellectuals.

Around the time of the 1911 Revolution more and more people went abroad to study, and most of them studied science and technology. The statistics in table 1.2 show us the trend of the professionalization of intellectuals, as indicated by the percentages of students who studied business, science, and engineering in the United States over several decades, compared with students in other fields.

Table 1.2 Fields of Study of Chinese in the United States

Year	1914	1934–35	1951–52
Humanities	2.1%	13.4%	11.9%
Social Sciences	14.9%	25.5%	26.3%
Business, Science and Engineering	53.7%	61.1%	61.8%
Preparatory	29.5%	—	—
Total	100%	100%	100%
N = total no. of students known	747	931	2,773
Unknown	100	573	224

Source: Y. C. Wang. 1966. *Chinese Intellectuals and the West: 1872–1949,* pp. 510–1.

Notes:

1. The three dates separated by roughly equal intervals were chosen in an attempt to see a trend over the years.
2. *Humanities* include literature, history, philosophy, library science, journalism, and fine arts.
3. *Social sciences* include law, political science, economics, sociology, and education.
4. *Business, science, and engineering* include business, engineering, sciences, medicine, agriculture, and military sciences.

Over half of the students in America chose to study business, science, and technology. Although this is only about those students in the United States, we can already see the trend. The pattern of their employment after they returned from abroad also supports this trend. From table 1.1, we have already seen that although there was still about a third employed in the government, a sizable number were employed in various professional fields. Even in education and government services, one could find more professional experts. As a result of this trend, we would see more and more technical intellectuals in later years. One of the best-known examples is Zhan Tianyou (Jeme Tien Yau 1861–1919), a returned student, who was the first Chinese engineer to build a railway amid doubts from both the Qing government and Western powers. He also helped found the Chinese Society of Engineers in 1912 (Y. C. Wang 1966:465–70). With the rise in numbers, the status of the technical intellectuals was enhanced as well. Rather than viewed as inferior in training, these intellectuals had good jobs. They also developed a "highly inflated ego," believing that only they could save China (pp. 90–4).

Two more branches of this professionalization movement among intellectuals are also worth noticing: the emergence of a capitalist class and the rise of independent scholarship, both of which continued the tradition of unattached intellectuals, that is, unattached to officialdom.[34] Let us have a look at the first branch of the movement first.

To be sure, even in traditional China, there were literati who alternated between politics and businesses, or culture and commerce, such as one of Confucius' students, Zi Gong (Yu Zuyao 1996:16; see also He Qinglian 2001:131–42 for more examples in the Qing and Republican eras). Wang Daokun (1525–93), a prominent Huizhou scholar, even argued for a convergence of gentry and merchant (Brook 1998:215). He explained that commerce and scholarship would not contradict each other; in fact, the former often funded the latter. He also noted that many gentry families in the city alternated between the two vocations. But a sizable group of intellectuals did not become part of the capitalist class until the modern era when the old literati system was abolished. (One could even argue that a sizable capitalist class did not even come into being until the modern era, let alone intellectuals in the class.) T. V. Soong and H. H. Kung both received their education in the United States, from Vanderbilt and Yale universities, respectively, and became bankers and later ministers of finance. They helped finance Chiang Kai-shek's various endeavors (Y. C. Wang 1966:422–86). According to Y. C. Wang's account, 124 banks were established between 1928 and 1937 (p. 486). He Yimin (1992:112–16) gives us some idea of the development of a provincial capitalist class at the start of the twentieth century. According to his research in Sichuan Province, at least 24 intellectuals had opened coal mines or established factories that produced textiles, bricks, matches, and glass. Another 17 intellectuals participated in the management of the Chuan Han Railroad Company. Among the two groups, 23 members had a traditional educational degree, 13 received a modern education in Japan, and some had both. A capitalist class was indeed emerging, and a substantial part of it seemed to be composed of intellectuals.

Another branch of the professionalization movement occurred among humanistic intellectuals, who did not want to be either attached to political office or engaged in much political criticism. This is a parallel development of the professions in the humanities and social sciences. Indeed, according to Liu Mengxi (1996), a movement toward independent scholarship picked up momentum with the publications of Yan Fu's "On the Necessary Division of Scholarship and Politics" (1898), Liang Qichao's "On the Scholarship's Determining Things in the World" (1902), and Wang Guowei's *On the Dream of the Red Chamber* (1904). Rather than following the traditional route and becoming scholar-officials, the new intellectuals simply wanted to become scholars. The idea of "scholarship for scholarship's sake" was to become popular.

In Republican China, the years of revolution and counterrevolution had already seen some intellectuals who kept their distance from politics and produced excellent literary works (Yu Ying-shih 1997:203–12). These include Lin Yutang, Zhou Zuoren[35], Xu Zhimo, Liang Shiqiu, and Shen Congwen. These men did not like a literature that was nothing but revolution. Lin Yutang, for example, wrote novels and essays that attracted readers both in China and the West. This does not mean that they were not concerned about politics, but they were certainly not so concerned as to join the revolution. They were simply more neutral. Radical intellectuals criticized them. Liang was dubbed an "inferior running dog of the capitalists," and Lin's humorous writing was only to "make people laugh away the cruelty of a butcher [i.e., Chiang Kai-shek]" (Y. C. Wang 1966:406). In fact, Lu Xun ([1930] 1973b:46–8) charged that Liang was a "homeless," that is, *sang jia de,* and "tactless," that is, *fa,* "dog of capitalists." Although Lu claimed that Liang was indeed "a dog of capitalists," the words he used imply that Liang might not be that closely attached to the capitalist class as he was not closely attached to the CCP.[36] These criticisms, however, only prove that some intellectuals tried to keep a distance from politics. Their literary works were widely admired nonetheless.

Qian Zhongshu, a popular man of letters, is another example. During the existence of *The Observer,* arguably the most provocative political journal in the 1940s, he wrote four articles, all of which are about thoughts on literary and linguistic studies. Xie Yong (1999a:390–1) remarks that Qian was one of those rare scholars who could transcend the chaotic world of politics. Qian referred to himself as a "retired person." Apparently, it was his distance from politics that left him free to achieve the level of his scholarship. Modern history also has seen a group of such intellectuals. Chen Da, a sociologist, resigned an official post in the GMD government after only several months of service (Huang Weijing 1993:167). Chen Xingshen (or Shiing-shen Chern) wrote numerous mathematical papers but produced nothing in politics. Y. C. Wang (1966:393) notes that in Chen the trend toward specialization reached its peak.

To be sure, during the Qing dynasty (1616–1911), scholars had already begun to do some serious work in science rather than becoming scholar-officials or critics of government. It seemed that the literati were going to develop another intellectual orientation. Textual criticism, mathematics, archaeology, and geography made big strides (Y. C. Wang 1966:33–4; Liu Xiuming 1997:600–10). Or one can even trace this tradition of independent scholarly pursuit to early Confucians. For example, during the Warring States Period (475–221 B.C.E.), Confucians were not in the decision-making structures, and they exerted their influence over the cultural system through education (Tu Wei-ming 1993b:17). Even when the channel of upward social mobility opened to the literati, some chose to remain unattached, like the *Daoist yinshi.* One such example is Liu Yin (1249–93), who repeatedly defied summons of the Yuan (1206–1368) court to serve as a scholar-official and persisted in his self-development and scholarship, lonely and marginal to the center of power (Tu Wei-ming 1993b:57–92). But to become an official was still the calling of the day in much of premodern China. Besides, scholars' professional decisions were more or less influenced by politics: both the Qing and the Yuan dynasties were ruled by minorities, and each posed challenges of loyalty for politically oriented scholars. So other than *yinshi,* it was with the modern intellectuals that an independent and professional movement developed.

The move to professionalize intellectuals has continued. Jin Yaoji (1987:34, 63–6, 76, 80–3) identifies a new knowledge class composed of those engaged in creating and disseminating political, economic, and academic culture and knowledge. He is speaking chiefly of "professionalized" scholars, technical specialists and professionals such as political scientists, sociologists, psychologists, physicists, professors, journalists, lawyers, and doctors. Wen Chongyi (1989:94–6) of Taiwan identifies modern intellectuals as the professional and managerial class, as do the Ehrenreichs (Barbara and John Ehrenreich 1979). The professionals as such will be our modern "unattached" intellectuals. We will discuss their importance and their relationship to the powers in chapter 4.

The Ideological Foundations of Intellectuals' Political Roles

We have identified four political roles intellectuals play: revolutionary, organic, critical, and unattached/professional. We have also noted that these roles are not clear-cut; for example, being unattached or professional does not mean that the intellectual is not critical or revolutionary. Being organic does not mean that one is not critical. In addition, intellectuals tend to switch from one role to another: many, for example, turn from critical to organic or vice versa. Indeed, as Said (1994: vii) remarks, intellectuals are "figures whose public performances can neither be predicted nor compelled into some slogan, orthodox party line, or fixed dogma."[37] Nonetheless, we can still characterize their ideal typical roles, examine their changes, and try to understand why. In this section, we will discuss the ideological foundations underlying these political roles, which will help us understand intellectuals' "unpredictable" public performances. We will then explore the ethical dilemmas they face while playing these roles, and the resultant dual personality. We will thus add more complexity to the various dimensions of intellectuals' politics.

In addition to his discussion on the cultural dispositions of intellectuals (see the appendix for a cultural definition of the intellectuals), Shils (1969:40) has provided us with a comprehensive summary of what we may call their 'ideological dispositions.' These include the various principles guiding intellectuals' performance: "the rules of procedure, standards of judgment, criteria for the selection of subject-matters and problems, modes of presentation, canons for the assessment of excellence, models of previous achievement and prospective emulation." What specifically are these principles, the traditions guiding intellectuals' conduct?

The first and foremost of Shils's guiding traditions is the "awesome respect" and "serious striving for contact with the sacred." In China, however, the Confucian intellectual-civil servants produced a civil and aesthetic rather than a religious tradition (1969:41). This Sinicized tradition speaks to the intellectuals' desire to enter politics and to become organic intellectuals.

The "chief secondary tradition" of intellectuals is the distrust of authority and of tradition(!), including secular and ecclesiastical, familial, and communal. Their rebelliousness is nurtured by many subsidiary traditions such as scientism, romanticism, apocalypse, populism, and anti-intellectualism (Shils 1969:43).

Scientism, which was critical of the arbitrary and irrational, insists on testing everything before accepting or rejecting it. We mentioned earlier that science made big strides in the late Qing dynasty, and indeed, scholars in traditional China did not lack the scientific spirit in their work in the humanities, as Hu Shih would quickly point out (see Edward Wang 2001:61). But scientism as an ideology did not grip modern intellectuals until the May 4 period (1919–28), when *democracy* and *science* became the catchwords of the day. Hu Shih and Ding Wenjiang (or V. K. Ting, 1887–1936, the founder of Chinese geology) became the champions of scientific methods, and Chen Duxiu and Wu Zhihui (or Wu Chih-hui, 1865–1953) became the champions of a scientific worldview that unifies the natural and social worlds. Scientism in post-Mao China has been used by the government to legitimize its economic reforms, as when it declares that "practice is the criterion for testing truth" and that "science and technology are forces of production." It has also been used to legitimize technocracy, as when Deng's policies put scientific personnel in leadership positions. And it has been used as a source of liberal political values by politically oriented intellectuals (see Miller 1996:5–12, 61, 73–5, 183–283).

Romanticism, which seems to be contrary to scientism, values originality and spontaneity and disdains the bourgeois family, mercantile activity, the market, and civil society in general. Both of these traditions remind us of the unattached and professional stance of intellectuals. While the *Daoist* (Taoist) poets embody the romantic traditions characterized by originality and spontaneity, the fast-developing group of scientists and technicians certainly reflects the criticism of the arbitrary and irrational.

The *revolutionary and apocalyptic tradition* believes that "the evil world as we know it, so full of temptation and corruption, will come to an end one day and will be replaced by a purer and better world" (Shils 1969:45). The *populist tradition* believes "in the creativity and in the superior moral worth of the ordinary people, of the uneducated and unintellectual," as in Marxism (p. 46). The Communist movement in China is a good example of the revolutionary and populist tradition. Strongly resembling the revolutionary volunteerism of the Russian Populists, "go to the people," Li Dazhao was the earliest of Chinese revolutionaries to call on the young intellectuals to go to the villages, where the air is clear and life is humane, unlike the filth and evil of the city (see Meisner 1967:82–9). Indeed, the Communist movement prevailed by uniting the peasants and workers, that is, the "laboring classes," with intellectuals. The *anti-intellectual tradition of order* is the belief that "excessive intellectual analysis and discussion can disrupt the foundations of order" (Shils 1969:47). This is manifested in Plato's attitude toward poets and the ex-Confucian Li Si's burning of Confucian books in the Qin dynasty (221–206 B.C.E.). To that we must, of course, add Mao's persecution of intellectuals. This last tradition negates intellectuals themselves, ironically. But together with romanticism and revolutionism, it manifests a populist disposition. This is the distrust of authority and tradition that Shils refers to. The populist disposition helps us understand why some intellectuals are critics, and even revolutionaries.

This leads to what Gouldner (1979:32) calls an 'alienative disposition,' which is only natural since intellectuals are critical of the very powers to whom they are subordinate. They criticize society because they believe society can do better. This puts them "*in* the society without fully being *of* it" (Coser 1965:360). To Shils's list of intellectual ideologies, Gouldner also adds *autonomy,* or self-groundedness, which "refers to that which is capable of self-movement and self-direction, rather than to that which is externally driven" (p. 33). This is related to the culture of critical discourse (CCD), which advocates justifying one's arguments by the consent of the audience rather than by the authority of the speaker

(p. 28). This autonomous and alienative disposition explains why some intellectuals are critical of the powers that be and why organic intellectuals keep being frustrated by the powers they serve. It also explains why other intellectuals want to be unattached and professional, but may not be happy with their unattached status.

In addition, Gouldner (1979:83–5) identifies a serious flaw related to the culture of critical discourse. Intellectuals believe that they are the ones who know the rules. They monopolize the truth and make themselves its guardian, believing that their point of view is better than anyone else's. Mao, for example, believed that the revolution could succeed only when there was one unanimous thought leading it, that is, his thought.[38] The same is true with the Russian socialists, who thought that "[t]hey and they alone had access to 'true knowledge.' The task of the revolutionaries, therefore, was not to search for knowledge, for that was already achieved. Their duty was instead to bring the fruits of Marxist analysis to the proletariat." They were to lead the workers (Kenez 1985: 5–6). This leads to dogmatism, which will imply "a certain insensitivity to *persons,* to their feelings and reactions, and open the way to the disruption of human solidarity." Political brutality of the revolutionary intellectuals in power, then, "finds a grounding in the culture of critical discourse; the new rationality may paradoxically allow a new darkness at noon" (Gouldner 1979:84). The Bolsheviks, then, were so utterly convinced of the righteousness of their cause that they had no tolerance for opposing points of view (Kenez 1985:12). So were the Chinese Communists. Chapter 6 gives more examples in contemporary China.

These ideological dispositions may not, however, be the only variable that explains intellectuals' behavior. For example, to understand the political brutality of the revolutionary intellectuals in power, we also need to look into the political and bureaucratic positions they occupy, in addition to the flaws of the CCD they possess. Why is it that the revolutionary intellectuals like Mao and his colleagues wanted to persecute other intellectuals? Why did a party that advocated a "people's democracy" and a "united government" turn totalitarian, causing such human tragedies as the Anti-Rightist Movement (1957) and the Great Proletarian Cultural Revolution (1966–76) shortly after it assumed power?

In the French, Russian, and Chinese cases, the revolutionary intellectuals had monopolized not only speech but also political power in group relations. "Once they had achieved total power, once they had moved from the role of critic to that of dictator, the humanitarian, democratic, progressive man of the early Revolutionary Left became men who killed in a purely disinterested manner" (Coser 1965:152–3). Power indeed corrupts. To make matters worse, the nature of bureaucracy makes it difficult to redress things that go wrong. Marx notes that the bureaucrat believes that the world can be manipulated according to his ideas. Mannheim observes that the bureaucrat "does not understand that every rationalized order is only one of many in which socially conflicting irrational forces are reconciled" (cited in Coser 1965:153). This narrow-mindedness certainly is in line with the ideological dispositions of intellectuals, such as, paradoxically, the culture of critical discourse. The monopoly of power and the position of the bureaucracy certainly would not help to right wrongs.

The American founding fathers were all intellectuals: "sages, scientists, men of broad cultivation, many of them apt in classical learning. . . ." (Hofstadter 1963:145), and they were revolutionaries, too. Among other things, the difference between the two kinds of revolutions is the different system each has established. Intellectuals can be caught in the system they themselves have created, as were Liu Shaoqi, Tao Zhu, and so forth. Together with Deng Xiaoping, these three were viewed as the "biggest capitalist roaders" during the Cultural Revolution. Eventually they met their downfall, including death for Liu and Tao. Others can liberate themselves from the system they have created, at least to a much greater extent than did the Chinese revolutionary intellectuals. John Adams, Benjamin Franklin, Alexander Hamilton, Thomas Jefferson, James Madison, and so forth, managed to free themselves from what they had wrought.

Thus, the elitist and apocalyptic thinking of intellectuals coupled with a monopoly of power and a bureaucratic position will turn seemingly rational intellectuals into irrational bullies and dictators. The ideological, political, and bureaucratic processes designed to transform the world have transformed the intellectuals instead. "The machinery of power had acquired an impetus of its own, . . ." as Coser (1965:165) comments on the Bolshevik intellectuals' sweeping changes once in power. Mao had to launch one movement after another to purge real and imaginary enemies. The Jacobin and Bolshevik intellectuals had

> fallen victim to domination by the tools they had employed. He who desires to make the world over through the decisive action of a chosen elite, even though his intentions may be idealistic and democratic, is finally

caught in the inherent logic of his actions: Without participation of the governed in the political process, the tools of political action appropriate power . . . "mechanism becomes an end in itself." (p. 166)

Boggs (1993:44–5) also observes how Leninism turned "the masses it claimed to 'represent' into manipulated objects" and how "the methods and tools of politics took precedence over ultimate objectives." That is exactly what had happened in the Mao era.

Table 1.3 summarizes the ideological foundations underlying the various roles of the intellectual. We see that the revolutionary intellectuals share many ideological traits with the critical, while the organic intellectuals tend to lose many of those traits. The unattached tend to have traits that are less revolutionary but more autonomous and scientific. We will further explore these similarities and differences in chapter 6 on intellectuals as a class. If they seek to avoid the negative consequences accompanying the French and Chinese revolutions, intellectuals in power will have to take big steps to modify their ideological dispositions, change their bureaucratic thinking, and loosen their monopoly of power. That dilemma seems to be the lot of all revolutionary intellectuals.

These ways of thinking about the world, its social groups, and where their responsibilities lie provide the ideological base on which intellectuals perform their work, whether in science, technology, humanities,

Table 1.3 Intellectual Roles and Ideological Traits

Roles of Intellectuals	Major Ideological Traits
Revolutionary intellectuals in power	revolutionary and apocalyptic orientations, distrust of authority and tradition, culture of critical discourse, romanticism, populism, anti-intellectualism, ethic of responsibility
Organic	culture of critical discourse, scientism, ethic of responsibility
Critical	distrust of authority and tradition, striving for the sacred, culture of critical discourse, ethic of ultimate ends, autonomy
Unattached and Professional	striving for the contact with the sacred, scientism, autonomy, culture of critical discourse, ethic of ultimate ends, ethic of responsibility

Note: We will discuss intellectuals' ethics in the following section.

or the social sciences, but especially in their political roles. Although they are not the only variable in influencing intellectuals' behavior, these ideologies do help us understand why intellectuals engage in protest movements, including the Nationalist and Communist revolutions in China, and some of them become brutal when they monopolize the power. These ideologies also partly explain intellectuals' organic, critical, and unattached political roles. They help us understand intellectuals who switch roles from one to another.

Moreover, once intellectuals are in these roles and they are in contact with the powers, tensions and dilemmas will arise. These tensions will further complicate their political behavior. We will first discuss the tension between the ethic of responsibility and the ethic of ultimate ends, followed by more dilemmas in the subsequent section.

Ethical Dilemmas Facing Intellectuals

The dilemmas intellectuals face while playing their political roles include those between the ethic of responsibility and the ethic of ultimate ends, between *Dao* (morality and values) and *shi* (power), and between vocation and profession. These conflicts lead to intellectuals' dual and split personalities.

The Ethic of Responsibility and the Ethic of Ultimate Ends

The politicians who follow the ethic of responsibility are, as Weber (1946:121) would say, willing to use "morally dubious means or at least dangerous ones" to achieve an ethically good purpose. They are also willing to pay the price of possible evil ramifications caused by their use of ethically dangerous means. In the end, they do achieve what seems to be a lofty purpose, although they have left behind problems that are difficult to solve. Those are the *Communist intellectuals* who have made a revolution, used violent means, and achieved their purpose, and they are also organic intellectuals. On the other hand, while "[T]he politician [in our case, the organic intellectual] has to weigh consequences and adjust interests, the agitator [who follows an ethic of ultimate ends] stands for a set of ultimate and absolute values that cannot be compromised" (Coser 1965:208). The intellectuals who follow the ethic of ultimate ends will not use dubious means or compromise their integrity in any way. They know that it may take a long time to achieve their goals, but they will just keep burning "the flame of protesting against the injustice of the social order," as Weber (1946:121) says. These are the *critical intellectuals,* the agitators we just mentioned.

Let's first have a look at some specific examples of *organic intellectuals* who follow the ethic of responsibility. Their goal is to affect social change. (Again, we are talking about intellectuals pursuing politics mainly as a vocation, not as a way to make a better living.) In order to achieve their political goals, they must compromise their integrity by conforming to some of the norms and values of those in power if they want to stay in the powerhouse. These are the bureaucratized intellectuals, the deputies of the dominant class, from Confucius down to the organic intellectuals under the CCP and GMD regimes.

Zhao Bingwen (1159–1232), a Han literatus under the Jurchen rule of China, not only practiced a philosophy of the ethic of responsibility but also explained it. The Jurchen were a minority from northeast China. They established the Jin dynasty (1115–1234), which ruled a large part of China, the area north of the Huai River and the Qinling Mountains.[39] Southern China was ruled by the Southern Song (1127–1279), the remainder of the Song dynasty (960–1279). The Han literati in the northern part of China would then have to choose between loyalty to the Song dynasty and loyalty to the new ruler. This was the dilemma that literati had to face yet again during the later Yuan (1206–1368) and Qing (1616–1911) dynasties, both of which were ruled by minorities from the north. Zhao, however, coped with the conflict very well. He was a Hanlin academician and minister of rites. Despite all the dilemmas he faced, he was able to quell banditry and organize famine relief, and he was an adviser to the emperor (Bol 1995:120).

How did he do it? First of all, Zhao says, if you are born into a new order, you must accept its authority. You have no choice: history will not fault you for not being loyal to those in power before you were born. Second, rulers who "have in mind the interests of all under heaven" can be called "Han." Literati should have no shame serving them (Bol 1995:127). The question is *how* you serve them. Obviously, you have to cooperate with "evil men" if you "wish to ameliorate the problems" they have created (p. 127). That is moral. Literati should do the best as they can and "exercise their political responsibilities in the least harmful manner. . . ."(p. 126). But you are not supposed to pander to the interests of the powerful for your own purposes. That would be immoral. Third, a literatus can find his own identity if he follows the principles of *dao* and *wen. Dao* refers to the universal values of world harmony and integration, as well as personal moral conduct. *Wen* means to be well-versed in the classics, including history and philosophy. It means to be genuinely good at poetry, prose, and calligraphy, not simply memorizing and imitating other people's forms just to pass the examinations.[40]

Zhao believed that he was following both principles. By doing the right thing, he could use the dynasty's institutions to "further the common good" without letting himself become a mere servant or adjunct of a dynasty that would inevitably pass into history. Do the right thing, he urged, and don't blame your failure on the political environment (Bol 1995:140). (Zhao sounds like Weber. Or vice versa?)

As we just mentioned, Zhao was not the only one faced with the problem of political allegiance. Many literati actually served two dynasties, following an ethic of responsibility but rejecting conventional Confucian loyalty. Hong Chengchou (Hung Ch'eng-ch'ou 1593–1665) is a good example. One of the ablest of military commanders and scholar-officials, Hong had enjoyed 27 years of distinctive service to the Ming court before he was captured in a battle with the Manchu army, the offspring of the northern Jurchens. Two years after his capture, Hong joined his enemies. He helped them establish the Qing dynasty and then went on to help the Qing build a Chinese-style government in Beijing, defeating the Ming loyalists in the southeast and southwest and restoring political and economic order there (Mote 1999; Chen-main Wang 1999).

Hong himself never explained why he changed his political allegiance, but after analyzing his memorials to the court and his services to the Qing dynasty, Chen-main Wang (1999:250–2) concludes that Hong must have believed he was displaying a higher order of loyalty to China, its culture, and its people. Indeed, he suggested to Emperor Huang Taiji that he learn China's language and culture and follow the established Chinese political and economic systems. He also suggested that those Ming officials who were willing to serve should be used, and his conquered countrymen be pacified. The emperor acted upon his suggestions. Hong might have compromised his own integrity, but he was able to help protect the integrity of China's culture. Nevertheless, it is clear that he was troubled by his own politics. For example, in carrying out his mission to persuade Ming loyalists to surrender, he was often embarrassed when they denounced him for "serving two dynasties," or being an *er chen*. He was observed to be emotionally troubled on such occasions (Chen-main Wang 1999:155–6).

Zhan Tianyou was the first Chinese engineer to build a railway in China, as we mentioned earlier. It was built expressly, though, under the instruction of Yuan Shikai, the then governor-general of Zhili, so that the Empress Dowager's visit to the Western Tombs would be easier (MacKinnon 1980:64). It would, of course also make transportation in general easier. But if one follows the ethic of ultimate ends, one would probably not want to build the road in the first place just for the convenience of the Empress Dowager.

In the debate between "problems and isms" in the May 4 period, Li Dazhao, as Meisner (1967:110) points out, showed his commitment to the ethic of responsibility by sacrificing many of his beliefs and principles for the good of Bolshevism. On the other hand, Hu Shih, committed to the ethic of ultimate ends, preferred to engage in the pure study of problems, refusing to "soil his hands in the dirty and irrelevant business of politics." (See also Grieder 1981:331 and the next section.) Hu's friend, Ding Wenjiang, made a series of controversial political choices, including becoming a manager of a coal mine, serving under a warlord, and supporting an enlightened dictatorship. (Furth 1970; Grieder 1981: 346). Being a rationalist and pragmatist, Ding was practicing the ethic of responsibility. In general, when intellectuals came to Yan'an or otherwise chose to join the revolution, like Li Dazhao, they chose the ethic of responsibility. When Liu Shaoqi decided to comply with Mao during the Cultural Revolution, rather than leading an opposition force against him, he was practicing the ethic of responsibility: sacrificing himself and compromising his integrity so that the country would not be plunged into open civil war with further ruinous consequences (see Dittmer 1974:117; 1998:99). For much the same reasons, many intellectuals from the small democratic parties supported the CCP in its bloody crackdown of the 1989 democratic movement. They might not have agreed with the Party, but they had to pretend to if they were to remain in the power structure.

Organic intellectuals are good politicians in that sense and are able to participate in historical processes instead of looking on from the sidelines, as unattached or critical intellectuals must do. However, they have to struggle in order to deal with the evil consequences. They also have to suffer results of actions by the powers they support. For example, those who have supported either the violent revolution or the violent crackdown on the democratic movement will have to live with their "evil ramifications." Moreover, they are more likely to suffer the consequences of their compromise, such as the dual or split personality, which we will discuss in the next section.

It is not easy to follow an ethic throughout one's life. Hu Shih, for example, did soil his hands in dirty politics in spite of his resistance to politics. We mentioned earlier that Hu supported Chiang's policy of internal suppression and external concession (Y. C. Wang 1966:411–15). As we mentioned earlier, in 1946, he could see progress in democracy after Wen Yiduo and Li Gongpu were both assassinated. While advocating concessions to the Japanese, he could still see indications of a new strength and hope in his own people, reflected in their ability to suffer Japanese aggression in silence and dignity. In a rape charge against American marines in Beijing, he could see a cultural difference in that "The Americans did not attach as much importance to chastity as did the Chinese" (cited in Wang 1966: 415).[41] It is probably unfair to say that Hu was antidemocratic. He was a major voice in the May 4 Movement, the motto of which was Democracy and Science. It is also unfair to say that he was a traitor. We can probably say that in all of these efforts, he was, like Zhao Bingwen and Hong Chengchou, cooperating with evil to lessen evil. That seems to be true of both Nationalist and Communist intellectuals. It also seems to define an ethic of responsibility.

Let's now examine some critical intellectuals who follow an ethic of ultimate ends. Wen Yiduo, Li Gongpu, and other liberal intellectuals of Lianda we mentioned earlier were such intellectuals. Those of the democracy movement are another example. Democracy is the goal, and they will not settle for less. In addition, as Coser (1965:208) says about the Abolitionists, "Men who espouse such an ethic can never expect to reach office or even to become counselors to those in the seat of power, but they can mobilize opinion and prick the moral conscience of a nation—precisely what the Abolitionists accomplished." Coser suspects that if the agitators had made compromises, as politicians, or organic intellectuals, would do, the slavery issue would not have entered the realm of politics and finally been resolved (p. 215).

The *unattached* and *professional intellectuals* may also be said to follow the ethic of ultimate ends. Chen Yinke (or Chen Yinque, 1890–1969) was one of the few highly esteemed historians at the time of the founding of the PRC. He refused to become the head of one of the three Institutes of History at the Chinese Academy of Sciences unless he and his institute were allowed not to study Marxism and Leninism (Lu Jiandong 1995:102). He would not compromise his determination to keep a distance from politics. Had he accepted the invitation, thinking that by compromising on the issue of Marxism he would achieve the goal of advancing national scholarship, he would have become an organic intellectual, as many did at the time. He would have been following the ethic of responsibility. By refusing to become an official, he sacrificed an opportunity to serve the country at a higher level, although he pursued his scholarship to the best of his abilities. Following the ethic of ultimate ends, he would not compromise his academic integrity for the purpose of politics, as Fu Sinian did when, following the ethic of responsibility, he distorted history in one of his books to promote nationalism (Edward Wang 2001:173–5, 192).

It is important to note, Weber would tell us, that for a critical intellectual to follow an ethic of ultimate ends does not mean that he or she is not responsible. Neither does it mean that an organic intellectual who follows an ethic of responsibility is an unprincipled opportunist (1946:120). Our examples support Weber's views on this. It does say, though, that the former is concerned less with the immediate results than the latter is. Weber believes that the real world is governed by politicians who follow their own version of the ethic of responsibility: the end justifies the means. A politician needs to do whatever he needs to do to achieve his goals. Having said that, Weber also agrees that the two ethics "are not absolute contrasts but rather supplements, which only in unison constitute a genuine man—a man who can have the 'calling for politics'" (p. 127). In a sense, he is saying that an intellectual who "lives for politics" will need to be an organic intellectual or an intellectual in power, but he or she still needs to retain the critical ability. That seems to be an impossible task.

In fact, Zhao Bingwen was also asking the literati to do the same. Bol (1995:128) summarizes Zhao's idea well: "Devotion to the interests of the powerful is wrong, but a principled refusal to cooperate is also wrong. Literati cannot rely on the system to know how to act; yet they must act within the system. Chao [Zhao] leaves it up to literati as individuals to determine what is moral according to the situation." But neither Zhao nor Weber claimed that everybody could live up to Zhao's demand. The tension between the ethic of responsibility and the ethic of ultimate ends contributes to the unpredictability of intellectuals' political roles, their frustrations, and eventually their dual personality. Figure 1.3 helps us understand this ethical dilemma: sometimes you just

Figure 1.3 It Doesn't Matter Which Dynasties They Are From *(Bu lun chaodai)*

Notes: The original caption includes a dialogue between son, father, and mother.

Son: Papa, if Zhang Fei [from the Han dynasty] and Yue Fei [from the Song dynasty] had a fight, who would win?

Father: Of course Zhang Fei would win.

Mother: But they were not from the same dynasty. How could they even fight?

Father: Well, once you are engaged in a battle, you don't have time to think about dynasties.

Source: Ding Cong 1999 (Vol. 4), p. 60–61.

do what you have to do even if it does not make too much ethical sense. The way they manage the tension will determine the extent to which they influence social change. (They manage the tension, but do not resolve it; they cannot and should not resolve it. This should become clear in the next section.) The tension is further embodied in the following dilemmas intellectuals face.

Dao and S*hi,* and Vocation and Profession

Related to the two kinds of ethics are the conflicts between *Dao* (conscience, their own values and beliefs) and *shi* (power), and between vocation (*zhiye** as a calling) and profession (*zhiye* for a living).[42] These are more dilemmas that intellectuals have to face in deciding what roles to play and to what extent they can play those roles, which contribute to the dual or even split personality, the perennial lot of intellectuals.

Intellectuals often tend to be alienated and frustrated in their relationships with the powers. We have noticed earlier that among the organic intellectuals in the West, the Fabians seemed to be the most successful in having their voice heard by people in power. The *Ideologues* and the revisionists were less successful, and had only one way to handle their frustrations with, and betrayal by, the powers. The relationship ended in a divorce. The same happened with the Chinese literati and modern intellectuals. Success stories like Yao Chong and Song Jing, two prime ministers from the Tang dynasty, whom we mentioned earlier, are rare. Many organic intellectuals ended up frustrated and alienated, like Confucius himself, Dong Zhongshu and Wang Anshi of the literati, and Ding Ling and Xiao Jun of the modern intellectuals. They were lucky if they did not end up losing their lives, like Li Si of the Qin dynasty, Wang Shiwei of the Yan'an era, and Chen Bulei and Tian Jiaying under Chiang and Mao.

Yet intellectuals keep serving the people in power, and keep criticizing them, and keep on being frustrated. Why is that, then? Is there anything behind their political and critical orientations other than the ideological foundations we discussed earlier? We know that they are not happy with an unattached status and seek to connect with either the established powers or the latter's antagonistic forces (Flacks 1991; Mannheim 1936), that is, they enter politics. But why politics?

In his famous speech, "Politics as a Vocation," Weber succinctly points out the "inner enjoyments" politics can offer: "a feeling of power," to be able to "put one's hand on the wheel of history" (1946: 114–5). Another sociologist, Merton (1968:267), observes that for an intellectual to put his knowledge to work, he has to become part of a bureaucratic power structure. Merton does not elaborate on the possibility of social movements, but he notes that intellectuals "who have previously pledged their allegiance to political movements seeking to modify our economic and political structure have now in increasing numbers, it would seem, adopted the alternative of seeking to work these changes through constituted governmental authority."[43] They do this mainly by supplying the expert knowledge that decision makers need. One can be an unattached critical intellectual and serve as a gadfly, but he is effective only to a limited degree (Merton 1968:271–3). To be a professor is to stand on the sidelines looking on at the historical movements in progress (p. 266). There certainly would not be as much "inner enjoyment" as when one was holding the wheel of history.

Although Merton is talking about American intellectuals, the same is true of their Chinese counterparts. To cultivate oneself, put one's house in order, and govern one's country following the Confucian ethic has been the calling for intellectuals for over two thousand years, as we noted at the beginning of the chapter. The enjoyment to be found in *effectively* moving the wheel of history from within the government may have become part of the Chinese intellectuals' psyche. We are talking mainly about intellectuals who *live for* politics, to use Weber's term, that is, intellectuals who have chosen politics as their vocation, *zhiye**, rather than another *zhiye,* a profession. There are, of course, intellectuals who "live off" politics. Their participation in politics is mainly for wealth and fame *(fugui ronghua),* or for the glorification of their ancestors *(guang zong yao zu).* Politics for them is a profession. But we refer chiefly to those who enter politics as a vocation. Chen Bulei was a passionate intellectual who was very concerned about the future of China. When he decided to follow Chiang Kai-shek as a high-level party and government official, he thought Chiang was the one person who could save China, and he hoped to be able to help (Xu Jilin 1991:130–1). Tian Jiaying probably thought the same when he joined Mao. The same thought applies to numerous other intellectuals in the long history of China.

For Yan Buke (1989), the power that these intellectuals gravitate toward is *shi,* which inevitably comes into conflict with *Dao* (or *Tao*), which is one's conscience and morality in particular and culture in general. Correspondingly, Yu Ying-shih (1999:15–32), Y. C. Wang (1966: 8–10), and Link (1992:10–14) also discuss a degree of tension between the literati's political and moral functions. Yan comments that *shidafu,* or the "scholar-official," is a combination of culture and administration. The culture is the *Dao* while the administrative power is the *shi.* Or to use Wang's terms, the literati had the dual function of *morality* and *administration.* The scholar-official owed his allegiance to the emperor. But he also had a moral commitment to remonstrate with him if he found the emperor deviating from the Confucian administrative ethic (see also Bol 1992:5). This is what Tu Wei-ming (1993b:6, 19) calls the "inseparability of morality and politics" in the traditional Confucian belief.[44] But conflicts are bound to occur.

Cheek's (1997) monograph on Deng Tuo is by far the best account of this value conflict endured by Communist intellectuals. During the anti-Japanese war in the 1940s he served as editor of the Party's *Jin-Cha-Ji Daily* in the Jin-Cha-Ji Border Region. This was one of the CCP's bases in northern China, a large area composed of Shanxi, Chahar, and Hebei provinces. Deng believed in Mao's position on literature and art, which he agreed should serve the masses and should conform to the Party policy. At the same time, he was able to adhere to the principles of authenticity and historical accuracy in journalism. In spite of the rectification campaign in 1942, Deng and others in Jin-Cha-Ji were even able to establish an elitist poetry society, "The Yan-Zhao Poetry Society." Given the political squeeze of the time, one may safely assume that Deng's success was tied to the support he received from his area military commanders, who included Nie Rongzhen and Lu Zhengcao, both members of the poetry society.[45] Deng was very successful in working out a solution to the conflict between the role of the cog-and-screw of the revolutionary machine *(shi)* and the role of culture bearer *(Dao)*. In the end, however, when during the early years of the Cultural Revolution the institutional support disappeared, Deng was unable to manage the conflict.

In 1966, Deng committed suicide. The tension was resolved. That may be his way of maintaining his "integrity," or *qijie*. But is it possible to maintain one's *qijie* while seeking to serve within the bureaucratic apparatus, as Schwarcz (1986:250, 255–6) asks, without killing oneself? It seems that the conflict cannot and should not be resolved; it can and should only be managed.

A yet another but related conflict facing intellectuals is what Wu Mi calls a dilemma between one's profession *(zhiye)* and vocation *(zhiye*)*, which we mentioned briefly. Wu, a man of letters active in the first half of the twentieth century, explains the dilemma: intellectuals need a profession, something they can make a living with, but they also need a calling: the freedom to go wherever their intellect or feelings lead them, something they really like to do. The two seldom coincide (see Shen Weiwei 2001:571–2).[46] That freedom or calling is often constrained by the profession.

Wu uses a metaphor to explain the conflict between politics and culture, which we may apply to the conflict between profession and vocation: riding two horses at the same time, with a foot on each horse. When the horses run, the rider has difficulty controlling them, and he then runs the danger of being torn apart *(che lie),* one of the punishments used in ancient times:

> To be active in worldly affairs and achieve success [in politics] is one way of doing things. Or one may calmly retreat. When he sees how the grave difficulties [of politics] clash with his ideals, he puts all his heart into literature and art and thus enjoys himself. He may then achieve success in specific fields or write wonderful books. This is another way of doing things. But I am unfortunate in that I want to do both of them. (Wu Mi [1927] 1998:355; also cited in Luo Gang 1995:83–4)

Politics as profession and culture as vocation thus often conflict. Ding Wenjiang, for example, could not pass opportunities to serve in official positions for the political and economic modernization of the country, although he really enjoyed teaching and research (Furth 1970: 196).[47] Wu Han faced the same dilemma, although now politics seems to be his profession *(zhiye)* and his historical studies became his vocation *(zhiye**)*. He had wanted to remain in academia, but when he was called upon by the CCP to serve in the government as a deputy mayor of Beijing, he could not say no. Zhou Enlai "appealed to his loyalty to the nation and responsibility to the people and the revolution." To refuse to participate in the government would have meant negation of "the United Front coalition and the legitimacy of the new state in which he believed deeply" (Mazur 1996:424, 486; 1997:66–7). Wu tried to bridge the distance between *zhiye* and *zhiye**. Indeed, despite the heavy responsibilities in the city government between 1959 and 1965, he published on the average almost one major work a year. But vocation and profession wound up hurting each other, and finally the conflict hurt the man himself (see Fisher 1986; Mazur 1996, 1997).

This tension between profession and vocation afflicts not only organic and critical intellectuals, but unattached intellectuals as well. One may pursue "art for art's sake," or "scholarship for scholarship's sake," as Liang Qichao says (see Liu Mengxi 1996:64), but one may still maintain a passion for politics. One's *zhiye* does not provide enough room for one's *zhiye**. Politics, however, is always frustrating, as Liang himself experienced. Thus, the dual or split personality, which we will discuss in more detail in the next section, plagues not only the organic intellectuals but critical and unattached intellectuals as well. Though, since these two do not deal directly with politicians, the disruption is to a lesser degree. Examples also abound in traditional China. Ruan Ji (210–63) and Tao Yuanming (365–427) were still very much concerned with politics when they were away from the bureaucracy. This can be seen from many of their poems (Li Chunqing 1995:137–40). Indeed, some of these *yinshis'* political criticism was so sharp that they were executed by the powers at the time. Among the famous were Kong Rong (153–208), Ji Kang (223–62), and Yang Xiu (175–219) (Liu Xiuming 1997:204–26).

The Dual and Split Personalities: The Perennial Lot of Intellectuals

In the 1990s, although there were still many restrictions as to what scholars could investigate, one of the areas seemed to have opened up nicely: the study of certain intellectuals' "torn personalities." There are independent personalities, such as Gu Zhun's (1915–74) devotion to truth and justice, Chen Yinke's adherence to independence and freedom, and Chu Anping's upright spirit, Feng Youlan's mission of a cultured man (Ding Dong and Cai Zhongde 1999 [1992]:309–19; Xie Yong 1999a). But there are also dual personality *(shuangchong renge)* and split personality *(fenlie renge)* (Xu Jilin 1991, 1992). Xu observes that to survive in China's political power structure, intellectuals need to be flexible on the outside but straight on the inside *(wai yuan nei fang).* For example, when Huang Yanpei agreed to disband his organization, the Democratic League, in 1947 under pressure from the GMD, he was following the principle and exhibiting a dual personality: He yielded to the powers so that he could preserve and protect his people for future struggles. That is the idea of the ethic of responsibility. But not everybody could deal with the tension between the two ethics, or the tension between *Dao* and *shi*. Chen Bulei, who committed suicide in 1949 while serving Chiang Kai-shek as his chief secretary (Xu Jilin 1991: 40–58, 126–42), and Tian Jiaying, who also committed suicide while serving Mao as his secretary (Ye Yonglie 1999:419–22), are two prominent examples of the split personality. They were torn between their passion for politics and their inability to achieve the ideals they thought they could achieve. When the pressure grew too great, they could find no solution but to kill themselves.[48] These examples give us an idea of what the dual and the split personalities are all about.[49]

There are at least three basic reasons why intellectuals, whether organic, critical, or unattached and professional, especially the former two, may suffer from the frustrations and betrayals in their relationship with the powers, which lead to a dual or split personality. First, there are conflicts in values between the intellectuals and the powers they serve or criticize.[50] As our description of the *Ideologues* in France, the moderate Bolsheviks in the Soviet Union, and revisionists in Poland indicates, intellectuals often have a different agenda from the people in power. The *Ideologues* wanted an educational system that would teach the ideas of the Enlightenment, reason, and justice, but the dictator wanted to teach children authoritarianism. The revisionists valued freedom and equality, but Gomulka wanted bureaucratic control. In each case, there was a honeymoon period, but that was while Napoleon and Gomulka were ascending to power. They were not in power yet, and they needed the help of the intellectuals to get there. They endorsed the intellectuals' values and used them to articulate their goals and to attack their enemies. But once they were in power, other priorities took over. The intellectuals' values were put aside, causing alienation and frustration. The honeymoon was over.

Intellectuals face two choices: suffer dual or split personalities, or withdraw from politics to resolve the conflict. "My intention is to publish nothing which might displease the government; I am hence disposed to make any changes that might be required in that respect," said Daunou, once a proud enemy of Napoleon's imperial ambitions. Revisionists were also ousted from Gomulka's regime. Many intellectuals turned to academic, technical, and professional pursuits in both France and Poland, reacting similarly to similar historical circumstances (Coser 1965:196, 202). Guo Moruo, one of the most well-known men of letters, also said at the beginning of the Cultural Revolution that none of his works was of any value and should all be burned (Lu Jiandong 1995:465). Under the Mao regime, however, it was even impossible to withdraw from politics. But is it possible to avoid politics anywhere?

The Chinese intellectuals' value conflict demonstrated itself even before "liberation." For example, when they came to Yan'an to join the revolution, intellectuals faced what their French and Polish confreres had. Their values, they felt, coincided with the Party's values, including equality between the leaders and the led, and freedom to express their opinions. But as Wang Shiwei, Ding Ling, and Xiao Jun found out, they were not quite equal to Mao and they were not quite free. As more and more organic intellectuals would increasingly learn, they had far different values. Just as opium trade was important for the health of the Yan'an economy (see Apter and Saich 1994:223; Chen Yung-fa 1995), ideological hegemony was also a necessary evil for the sake of revolution (see Apter 1995). The Wang Shiweis had to accept it, just like Ding Ling, that is, developing a dual or split personality, or facing serious consequences, like Wang himself.

Other intellectuals in the CCP's history who were faced with this conflict also include Hu Feng, a writer, at the beginning of the People's Republic, some of the Rightists in the 1950s, and the so-called capitalist roaders, such as Teng Tuo's colleagues and friends Wu Han and Liao Mosha in the 1960s. In her aptly titled *China's Intellectuals: Advise and Dissent* (1981:18–60), Merle Goldman provides a detailed picture of organic intellectuals under the CCP who were also critical. Her examples include, among others, the Beijing Party Committee intellectuals Deng, Wu and Liao; in the propaganda department group Zhou Yang, Tian Han (1898–1968), Xia Yan (1900–95), and Mao Dun (1896–1981); and in the academic community the historians Jian Bozan (1898–1968), Wu Han, Zhou Gucheng (1898–1996), the philosopher Feng Youlan (1895–1990), and the economist Sun Yefang (1908–83).

Let us dwell on some more specific cases. Li Da (1890–1966), one of the founders of the CCP, who remained loyal to the revolution, was "a fellow traveler," committed to the advancement of orthodox Marxism despite the fact that he left the Party during the Republican era. He rejoined after "liberation" and continued his work in Marxist philosophy. But he was also an independent scholar. His loyalty to the Party did not prevent him from challenging Lin Biao's theory that Mao Zedong Thought was the pinnacle of Marxism (see Knight 1996; Song Jingming 1997). This remarkably independent criticism was something few dared undertake during the Cultural Revolution. He paid a price for his outspokenness, though, directly or indirectly: he died an enemy of the people when the hospital stopped his medication.[51] Many current dissident intellectuals such as Liu Binyan, a reporter, and Wang Ruowang, a writer, used to be organic to the Party but are now banished as enemies because they are critical of Party policies.

When Deng Xiaoping was on his way to power after the Cultural Revolution (1966–76), he needed the intellectuals' help in attacking the Gang of Four and repudiating Maoists.[52] But once he had consolidated his power, he shut down the *Democracy Wall* and other journals of dissent, and arrested their leaders, such as Wei Jingsheng and Liu Qing. His concerns over political control and social order took priority, not democracy and human rights. Some who were becoming organic intellectuals of Deng now became critical ones operating outside the power structure. Those who wanted to stay within the power structure had to conform to the Party line and be good organic intellectuals. A dual personality, if not a split personality, was inevitable.

Indeed, some literati risked their own lives and their families' lives when they spoke out against the emperor. Some even committed suicide in order to have a memorial presented to the throne (Y. C. Wang 1966: 10). An outstanding example is the well-known poet from the Warring States Period, Qu Yuan (340?-278? B.C.E.). Qu could not bear to see his ideals ignored and chose to commit suicide. Many intellectuals seem to have followed him down the long years of China's history.[53]

Let us come back to our example of Deng Tuo. During the revolutionary years, the cycle of promotion and demotion, of denunciation, of investigation, and of exoneration (Cheek 1997:106–7, 172–82) must have frustrated Deng Tuo. In the 1950s the Party's limitations on Deng's journalistic scope as editor in chief of the *People's Daily* would not help, nor would the limitations that Mao's 1942 "Yan'an Talks" continued to place on artistic personality and style (pp. 131–2, 147–9). Deng in the 1950s was no longer able to reconcile his role as the cog-and-screw of the revolution with his role as culture bearer, the accommodation we know he had managed in the 1940s (pp. 169–70, 193, 215–6). Now he wanted to resign from the chief editor's post, and he even thought about becoming a monk (pp. 180, 186). He felt that his inability to carry out his academic plans hung like "a millstone around [his] neck" (p. 197). One would assume that the "millstone" was political as well. Like other intellectuals, Deng was caught in a system he had helped to create, but that provided him with no safe exit, and in actual fact, no exit at all. He eventually followed in Qu Yuan's footsteps.[54]

The Chinese intellectuals under the GMD faced the same conflict between their moral and political functions. As we mentioned earlier, Fu Sinian, while serving in the government, remained critical of its officials. Hu Shih, an ardent supporter of Chiang Kai-shek, was also critical of Chiang's political rule, and he tried to balance his political aspiration and scholarly pursuit as Deng Tuo did (see Edward Wang 2001: 161, 179). Here is one of many examples. While in the United States in the 1950s, Hu Shih sponsored the magazine *Free China*. But the journal was banned because certain articles criticized GMD politics and even advocated establishing another party to compete with the GMD. One 1956 issue commemorating Chiang's birthday published articles advocating protection of freedom of speech, respect for the law and the constitution, and economic and defense reform. It was, in fact, a birthday gift of dissent. Hu Shih himself wrote an article entitled "Tell Two Stories of President Eisenhower to Commemorate President Chiang's Birthday," and suggested that Chiang do more by doing less. As a result of this open dissidence, not only was the magazine banned, but the copublisher Lei Zhen was court-martialed and imprisoned. Hu Shih questioned the trial procedures (the defense lawyer had had only a day and a half to consult related materials). He tried by every means to save Lei from imprisonment but failed, despite his longtime personal relationship with Chiang (Zhang Zhongdong 1989:363–87; see also Schwarcz 1986a:276–8).

Tao Baichuan, another well-known intellectual in Taiwan and a member of the State Supervisory Committee, argued that even if Lei Zhen violated the law by speaking his mind, he should be tried in a civil court instead of a military court. The trial itself was a violation of the law. But he too failed in his effort. Tao himself was well-known as an upright intellectual in the state government, not only for defending intellectuals but for impeaching corrupt officials. Chiang himself once said to him, "You are a well-established intellectual, but you are adamantly against the Party. I am very disappointed" (Li Hongxi 1989: 481–507, especially 500). Both Hu and Tao were critical but their influence was limited, as was the case with Communist organic intellectuals, which was against their ambitions.[55]

The second reason or conflict often leading to personality trauma is not unrelated to differing values. Politicians do not believe that the intellectuals' knowledge is necessarily better than theirs. In many cases, this may be true. In our discussion on the ideological foundations of intellectuals' political roles, we have discussed scientism and distrust of authority as part of their dispositions. Since it is the nature of the intellect to examine, ponder, and theorize before reaching a conclusion,[56] there is always a certain degree of what Merton (1968:264) would call "indeterminacy." The intellectual wants to spend more time to study, say, a social problem, before taking action. Politicians, however, "are often convinced that they have considerable knowledge.

"It is by no means evident to the policy-maker that the expert [i.e., the intellectual] has more competence in dealing with these problems than the policy-maker himself" (Merton 1968:265). The politician just knows he doesn't. The fact is, the politician probably does have more firsthand knowledge of social problems than intellectuals do. As Mao

(1966:773) says, "Many so-called knowledge elements [the literal translation of the word *intellectuals*] are in fact, comparatively speaking, most lacking in knowledge." To Mao, however, there are only two kinds of knowledge, of material production and of class struggle. He is right when he claims that intellectuals are lacking in these sorts of knowledge. Intellectuals are also lacking in the ins and outs of power struggles. So the politician, with more firsthand knowledge and the power to act fast, will make the decision, and the intellectual, with a different set of knowledge, will just have to follow. "He is on call, but is seldom regarded as indispensable" (Merton 1968:265). That creates conflict between master and man, resulting for the intellectual in frustration and the dual and split personalities.

The third reason for the intellectuals' angst is structural. Structurally, the politicians are the decision makers. When they consult with the organic intellectuals, they already have a general agenda. The policy is already set. All they need are specifics to implement the policy, or advice on the best way to carry it out. Organic intellectuals can provide alternative ways to implement the policy, but the policy has to be implemented. The intellectual has become a technician rather than a thinker, since he or she cannot question the policy itself. Or they can only do the kind of research corporate and political establishments have decided for them to do. And their advice can always be ignored (Aronowitz 1988:286–7, 326). Zhou Enlai, the premier under Mao, probably is the best example to illustrate this point (though he may not be the best example of an organic intellectual, for he was also in power). He seemed to be an ardent advocate for incorporating intellectuals into the socialist construction, as can be seen from his two talks on intellectuals in 1956 and 1962 (Liu Hongxia and Liu Guitian 1987:93–8). He seemed to have tried to protect intellectuals during both the Anti-Rightist Movement and the Cultural Revolution. However, policy was determined by Mao, and intellectuals were still persecuted. All Zhou could do was a degree of damage control. So structurally, organic intellectuals and the power holders are in two different positions. The former do not make major decisions, which defeats their ambitions.

These conflicts over values, knowledge, and authority in decision making lead to frustrations, which then result in dual and split personalities. Cheek's (1986, 1997) study of Deng Tuo shows us how the latter tried to balance between his conscience of an intellectual, his mission as a cultured man, and his loyalty to the Party's course. His eventual inability to manage the conflict must have contributed greatly to his decision to commit suicide. Caught in the clash between *Dao* and *shi* and unable to manage the conflict were also Tian Jiaying, Lao She, Jian Bozan, and many other organic intellectuals during the Cultural Revolution, who found their only escape in suicide.[57]

In sum, organic intellectuals do have a role to play in the power structure, but they are only assisting, and can be readily disposed of. To hold their positions, they have to abdicate their privilege of exploring policy options (Merton 1968:271). In other words, they have to sacrifice their values. Even if they are willing to do all this, their knowledge may still not be trusted or used. They may learn to adapt to the bureaucratic requirements by accommodating their interests, attitudes, and objectives to the bureaucracy, that is, surrender to the *shi.* They will be transformed into technicians to serve whomever is in power (pp. 268–9), which may contradict their intellectual orientations, that is, the *Dao,* or their "moral and cultural functions." All of these dilemmas lead to the trauma we have noted: the dual or even split personality.

The alternative, as we have said, is to withdraw from the bureaucracy and to become a critical intellectual. That is what many Chinese organic intellectuals did. In 1942, Ai Qing, the poet and an organic intellectual, was a critic of Wang Shiwei, the dissident, but in 1957, he became a critic of the cultural bureaucracy (see Wen Jize [1942] 1994, Teiwes 1979). Many intellectuals changed their allegiance after the June 4 massacre of 1989. Those may include Liu Binyan (journalist and former high-level cadre), Fang Lizhi (professor and former university president), Wang Ruowang (writer and former high-level cadre), Wang Ruoshui (editor and former high-level cadre), and Wang Meng (writer and former minister of culture). But now, unable to effectively influence politics, they may also suffer from a dual or split personality, or at least an alienated personality. They may face a conflict of profession and vocation.

They may not be happy with a totally unattached status, either, as the examples of Ruan Ji, Ji Kang, and Tao Yuanming show us. So intellectuals have constantly been torn between their need and desire for active political involvement, their instinct to be independent and autonomous, and their dependence on, and subordination to, the ruling bodies. The intellectual is forever alienated and will suffer the perennial personality problems.

This, however, is not necessarily undesirable. In a sense, intellectuals are always at a crossroads, and as they try to adjust, we see their politics constantly changing. In the process, they find what roles they can play and to what extent. That is the nature of the politics of intellectuals. And we can find some comfort in the success of some of them some of the times, like Deng Tuo in *Jin-Cha-Ji.*

The Chinese Intellectual: A Typology

We have distinguished four kinds of roles of intellectuals. There are the revolutionary intellectuals, subsequently the powers that be. And there are the rest: the intellectuals and professionals classified as organic, critical, or unattached, according to their political stance toward the powers that be. These attitudes can also be determined by their affiliation with other social groups or classes. We have also distinguished between humanistic and technical intellectuals according to their technical functions, a useful but less important distinction in a political sociology of intellectuals. Because they work in such disparate fields, humanistic intellectuals tend to be more critical of the status quo, and technical intellectuals less so. This, however, does not hold a 100 percent. A technical intellectual such as a scientist or engineer can be both very critical of the ruling class and politically active; a humanistic intellectual such as a journalist or professor can be very technical in orientation and not at all critical or political. Thus whether they are humanistic or technical, organic intellectuals can believe in the course of a certain class, for example, the moneyed class or the working class, and can serve as their political and economic advisers, executive officers, managers, and organizers. This includes lower-level bureaucrats if we define higher-level bureaucrats as part of a *bureaucratic ruling class,* which they and other organic intellectuals primarily serve. In China's case, the BRC is the revolutionary intellectuals in power, who may have been either humanistic or technical intellectuals.

In other words, within each stratum of intellectuals, technical or humanistic, there might be a strain of the "organic intellectual." We should, in fact, be able to "measure the 'organic quality' of the various intellectual strata and their degree of connection with a fundamental social group. . . ." (Gramsci 1971:12). The social groups Gramsci refers to include, for example, the new bourgeoisie: *the moneyed class* (MC) and *the working class* (WC). A technical intellectual's interests can include not only technical puzzles but also advocacy of a certain class, say the MC, and criticism of another, say the BRC. In this case, we may have a hybrid type: the "organic technical intellectual." By the same token, we may also have a humanistic intellectual whose interests include not only the philosophical study of humanity but also support of the WC. This hybrid we may call the "organic humanistic intellectual," organic to the working class. Such an intellectual can be organic to any of the other classes, too, as in the case of a technical intellectual.

However, everyone does not automatically become a bureaucrat or official, or an organic intellectual in other capacities. Many remain "unattached" or "free-floating." A humanistic intellectual can remain unattached to any of the other classes; she may only be interested in, for example, studying social life and disseminating her knowledge to anyone who wants to listen. We call this type the "unattached humanistic intellectual," or in Alfred Weber's terms, *socially unattached intelligentsia* (quoted in Mannheim 1936:155). Similarly, those interested only in technical puzzles or in disseminating scientific and technical knowledge are "unattached technical intellectuals." These unattached intellectuals may not actively participate in political activity or express their political points of view, but this does not mean that they have no opinions.

There are also those who are politically critical of certain interest groups but not necessarily organic to any other group. They can also be culturally critical of society as a whole. These are the political and cultural critics. They include, for example, intellectuals from academia who engage in writings and speeches that criticize government policies, but who do not necessarily engage in the organization or advocacy of cultural and political protests. Another example of political and cultural critics would be the political dissidents in China. Hence, we have a category of "critical" intellectuals in addition to the organic and unattached.

To provide a more comprehensive framework that will make sense of the variety of Chinese intellectuals, we might use the following two typologies: First, two kinds of intellectuals based mainly on their professional orientations: *technical intellectuals,* or what Gouldner and others would call *intelligentsia,* who are mainly technical in orientation and engage in science and technology, and *humanistic intellectuals,* who are mainly cultural in orientation and engage in the humanities and social sciences. Second, three kinds of intellectuals based on their political attitudes and their closeness to, or distance from, a specific interest group, namely *organic, unattached,* and *critical intellectuals*. This book attempts to illustrate the second typology in contemporary China. Table 1.4 illustrates the typologies, in which I use only the Chinese intellectuals as examples.

Table 1.4 Typology of Intellectuals

	Humanistic	Technical
Organic	1. Some middle- and lower-level Party and state bureaucrats; ideologues; secretaries to Party and state officials; some managers of state- and privately owned businesses, or "Confucian businesspeople"; working-class organizers and advocates; entrepreneurs of an intellectual class	2. Most of the middle- and lower-level Party and state bureaucrats; ideologues; secretaries to Party and state officials; some managers of state- and privately owned businesses, or "Confucian businesspeople"; working-class organizers and advocates; entrepreneurs of an intellectual class
Unattached (professionals)	3. Popular fiction writers; college professors in humanities and social sciences; some journalists. They are not interested in politics; they are humanistic professionals.	4. Scientists; engineers; lawyers; doctors; college professors in the sciences. They are not interested in politics; they are technical professionals.
Critical	5. Political dissidents; cultural and social critics	6. Political dissidents; cultural and social critics

Thus we have a two-way classification or typology: a horizontal one of humanistic and technical intellectuals based largely on their professions (see cells 3 and 4), and a vertical one of the organic, the unattached, and the critical based on their political attitudes. The typologies intercut one another; and so we can have a humanistic or technical intellectual who is organic, as in cells 1 and 2; a humanistic or technical intellectual who is unattached, as in 3 or 4; or a humanistic and technical intellectual who is critical, as in 5 and 6.

Conclusions

In this chapter introducing a political sociology of intellectuals, we have examined their political roles in history, that is, revolutionary intellectuals in power, and organic, critical, unattached, and professional intellectuals. We have also discussed their ideological foundations, and the various ethical dilemmas they face, including the conflict between the ethic of responsibility and the ethic of ultimate ends, morality and power, *Dao* and *shi,* vocation and profession, and resultant dual and split personalities. Finally, we have come up with a typology of the Chinese intellectuals' relationship with the state, or the BRC, which we will further explore in the following chapters on contemporary intellectuals.

In conclusion, we would like to emphasize that the boundaries between the four kinds of intellectuals or the four roles are flexible. Throughout the history of the intellectuals' involvement in politics, we have constantly seen them switching back and forth from organic to critical to unattached/professional. Many of the traditional literati became unattached or critical after being deposed, and many critical intellectuals became part of the ruling class, or revolutionary intellectuals in power. Even the members of the Donglin Party, whom we categorized as critical, were also striving to become government officials (Mote 1999:736–8). In modern times, there was Ding Wenjiang, who alternated between being a politician and a scientist (Furth 1970; Y. C. Wang 1966:379–86). Deng Tuo, as we discussed earlier, played all four roles at one time or another, if not at the same time: revolutionary, organic, critical, and professional. In contemporary times, we have seen Wang Meng switch positions. He was an organic intellectual until 1957 when he became a Rightist for writing a novel and was criticized for it. Then he became a member of the BRC as the minister of culture in the 1980s. Now he is a critical intellectual again; he left the ministry in the aftermath of the 1989 massacre. One can find many other examples. As Coser (1965:320–3) says, although the honeymoon between the intellectuals and the policymakers may be nasty, brutish, and short, the union at least in the top administrative hierarchy is more enduring. But even there, the divorce rate is high. There is a constant flux.

Two points made by Mannheim may help us understand this flexibility. First of all, unlike other classes, intellectuals have the freedom to affiliate with any classes they wish (1936:158). Their diverse ideological dispositions help them move freely from their original category into any other they choose. An organic intellectual who may be deposed from office can choose to become critical or unattached. And a critical or unattached intellectual can become organic. It is this quality of being able to adapt to any point of view and class position that makes one an intellectual. It is important to have ideal types but we need to keep in mind that no one ever achieves the ideal: most people are in a state of flux. This constant change is crucial to the understanding of the formation of the intellectual complex.

Second, that intellectuals choose among classes and are identified with, or rebuffed by, them will "lead eventually to a clearer conception on the part of such intellectuals of the meaning and the value of their own position in the social order" (Mannheim 1936:159). In other words, in the process of switching roles and resolving various ethical dilemmas, intellectuals learn to perform their functions better. Nevertheless, no matter whether they are accepted or rejected, unattached, organic, or critical, as intellectuals they tend to strive to fulfill a watchman's mission, to achieve a "dynamic synthesis," a "dynamic mediation," or a forum "in which the perspective of and the interest in the whole is safeguarded" (pp. 159–62). That is the overriding sense of mission of the intellectual.

Chapter Two

From Uniformity to Fragmentation: Intellectuals in the Mao Era (1949–1976) and in the First Deng Period (1977–1989)

Things are changing now.
(Shiqing zhengzai qi bianhua.)
—Mao Zedong[1]

Before we explore the political development of various intellectual groups in the 1990s, it is important for us to examine intellectuals in the *Mao era* (1949–76) and in the *first period of the Deng era* (1977–89), for this is a critical time of transition from the Republican diversity to a high degree of Communist uniformity with only limited resistance, and then back to the contemporary non-Communist fragmentation resembling that of the pre-1949 times.[2]

The *Mao era* began with the founding of the People's Republic of China in 1949, and ended with Mao's death and the close of the Cultural Revolution in 1976.[3] This era saw continued efforts by the CCP to reform intellectuals who had formerly been either critical, unattached, or organic to the Party. These efforts include the thought reform movement; the movements against Feng Xuefeng, Yu Pingbo, and Hu Feng and his friends; the anti-Rightist movement (i.e., the Hundred Flowers Movement); and finally the Cultural Revolution. There was continued dissent, though, among the organic intellectuals, demonstrating their dual personality. Some outside the system even dared to criticize the Party. Both, however, met with continued reform movements, during which some even paid with their lives. Consequently, a high degree of "political uniformity" developed, at least on the surface.

The first period of the Deng era began in 1977 with Deng Xiaoping's reinstatement into the powerful positions he had held a year earlier: vice-chair of both the CCP and the CCP Military Affairs Commission, first deputy premier, and People's Liberation Army (PLA) chief of staff. Deng was now able to steer the wheel of Chinese history—always, of course, with the general consent of the octogenarian leaders of his own generation. After the Party Central Committee's Third Plenary Session of the Eleventh Congress in 1978, with Deng reigning, the Party shifted its focus from class struggle to economic development. Intellectuals were beginning to be viewed as part of the working class, and organic intellectuals' dissent met with less violent reactions from the Party, unlike those in the Mao era. In this more relaxed atmosphere, some transformed themselves, joining the critical intellectuals from outside the system. However, being critical and outside the system continued to be difficult; it could still land one in prison. Meanwhile, more opportunities became open to other intellectuals: they were bureaucratized and became new organic intellectuals, or bourgeoisified and professionalized to become unattached. Because of these developments, their politics became fragmented, as various groups took shape. This period ended with the 1989 massacre, which we will discuss in chapter 3 on critical intellectuals.

These two eras had one characteristic in common: intellectuals were still largely organic to the Party. The difference between the two lay in the expansion of the dissident movement in the latter era. There was dissidence from outside the system and loyal opposition from inside. Both were fairly restrained, although they could be intense from time to time, as more intellectuals pushed for an independent critical movement.

A High Degree of Uniformity with Limited Resistance: The Mao Era (1949–1976)

We have noted in chapter 1 that in the years before the 1949 Communist takeover, various intellectual groups had already developed. Some, like

Deng Tuo, Wu Han, and Ding Ling, joined the revolution and became either part of the leadership or organic intellectuals. Others, like Zhang Junmai and Chu Anping, remained critical of both the CCP and the GMD. Still others, like Lin Yutang and Qian Zhongshu, remained unattached. Once in power, the revolutionary intellectuals decided that there was a need to transform the very fabric of society in their own image, as the Jacobins did in eighteenth-century France. The various political movements they instituted in the Mao era were partly an effort to bring dissident intellectuals under the Party's tutelage. In this section, we discuss what political roles intellectuals played in the Mao era during the various thought reform movements, including the reforms of the early 1950s, the Hundred Flowers movement in 1957, and the Cultural Revolution from 1966 to 1976.

Thought Reform Movements in the Early 1950s

First of all, we will look at the Party's assessment of intellectuals. Back in 1939, Mao (1966:581), in his article "Absorb Intellectuals in Large Quantities," made a distinction between intellectuals who served the landlord and bourgeois class, and those who served the workers and peasants. In the same year and in a different article, he asserted that the majority of them could be classified as petit bourgeoisie (p. 604). In the 1942 rectification campaign, he claimed that many of the so-called intellectuals were actually very ignorant indeed. He said, "If we compare the unreformed intellectuals and workers and peasants, we will find that the intellectuals are not clean. The workers and peasants are the cleanest, even though their hands are dirty, and there is cow shit on their feet. They are still cleaner than the bourgeois and petit bourgeois intellectuals" (Mao 1966:808). One might argue with Mao over what it means to be "ignorant" or "clean," but his assessment was largely accurate in its political annotations. All intellectuals did not favor the revolution: some opposed it; others were mildly critical of the various practices of the Communists. Still others remained aloof or were simply fellow travelers. Mao knew that the Party needed the intellectuals. But before they could integrate into the Party and into the state apparatus, they needed to be reformed. A thought reform was called for: it was necessary to resocialize them. In other words, it was necessary to turn the critical and unattached intellectuals of the GMD Chiang Kai-shek era into organic intellectuals of the Communist Mao era.

This is not to say, however, that intellectuals did not agree with Mao. In fact, many also felt a need to learn new ideas and to adapt to the new system. Together with eleven other well-known professors, Ma Yinchu, the president of Beijing University, proposed a reeducation movement even before the official thought reform movement began (Wei Xiaodong 1996:123; see also Yang Jianye 1997).[4] The formerly critical intellectuals, like the editor Chu Anping and the sociologist Fei Xiaotong, also wrote about the need for intellectuals' reeducation. *The Observer,* the political journal of critical intellectuals, had been published between 1946 and 1948 under the editorship of Chu Anping. It was closed down by the GMD government. When it resumed publication in November 1949, with the support of the CCP government and with Chu again as the chief editor, its leading article called for criticism and self-criticism. "We love our motherland with all our heart and enthusiastically hope that she will become prosperous. But because we have not had the right education, we still unavoidably remain at the stage of bourgeois nationalism both ideologically and emotionally. Because we don't know well enough the CCP's policies and circumstances, we haven't really felt close to the Party. . . ." (quoted in Dai Qing 1990:208).

Like Ma, Chu seemed to call on the intellectuals to come close to the Party. The new "observer" truly admired Mao's ability, the PLA's discipline, and the Communists' hardworking spirit. The sociologist Fei Xiaotong wrote in *The Observer* about the need for intellectuals to remold themselves. This, he said, they should do by shifting their stand to the working class and getting rid of their individualism. Some of his aptly titled articles include, "What Does It Mean to Really Understand One's Thinking?" "You Will Lag Behind if You Don't Reform Yourself," "From Climbing Up to Helping Each Other," and "The Baggage Hindering One's Progress" (Dai Qing 1990:214).

The formerly unattached intellectuals agreed. Ji Xianlin (1994:238–40) was a returned student from Germany, and an accomplished scholar in Buddhism and Sanskrit. Ji remarked that he welcomed the Communists to Beijing although (echoing Chu) he did not know them that well. He felt sorry that he had not participated in the liberation movement, having focused only on his scholarship. He believed, in fact, that he needed to reform his thinking about his avoidance of politics. He also needed to change his erroneous attitude toward the former Soviet Union and its control over the CCP. As the reform movement ended, he was moved to tears when the Party was convinced that he reformed himself.

There is no doubt that this was the *honeymoon* between the CCP and formerly unattached or critical intellectuals such as Ji, Ma, Chu, and Fei. Their professed need for thought reform indicates that they had, or at least wanted to, become organic intellectuals, as some intellectuals in the literary circles had in the 1940s. Once their desires met with those of the Party's, the official Thought Reform Movement began in 1951.[5]

The movement was, as Frederick T. C. Yu (1964) rightly calls it, a "mass persuasion," which entails a full-scale mobilization of mass communications including, among other things, the national system of the press, radio, film, big character posters (i.e., critical essays written in big characters and posted on walls), and art and literature. Lifton (1961: 379–80) outlined four basic tasks of thought reform. Its first job was to turn intellectuals into sons of the Communist regime, loyal, self-disciplined, and always respectful of authority. Second, it was to get rid of the lingering, undermining effects of Western liberalism. Third, it was to guard against such transitional emotional chaos as cynical detachment, asocial self-seeking, or hollow despair. Finally, it was to build a new identity, the spirit of the good Communist.

Lifton also identified three typical stages in the completion of these tasks. First, the intellectual was reminded that he was sick and needed treatment. As Mao himself explained, "The first method is to give the patients a powerful stimulus, yell at them, 'You're sick!,' so that the patients will have a fright and break out in an over-all sweat; then, they can be carefully treated" (quoted in Lifton 1961:381). The second stage was the struggle phase. The intellectuals experienced the pain of psychological surgery, as they and their works were dishonored. They realized that what Mao had said was true, that they had lost their dignity and social standing. They realized that their individualism was selfishness, hypocrisy, and insincerity; their worshiping of Western culture was blind; and that only Marxism-Leninism-Mao Zedong Thought was the correct, scientific, and revolutionary truth. In short, their old knowledge of the world and of themselves had no value at all. The final stage was one of submission and rebirth indicated by a denunciation of themselves, and of their parents (pp. 380–5).

The most successful method, however, was "democratic discussion," which required "criticism and self-criticism." The intellectuals being reformed were supposed to write exhaustive and ruthless criticisms of their parents and of themselves (Hunter 1971:10–1). This was called "self-criticism." They were then told to express themselves freely

(p. 103). This actually meant that everyone had to pick flaws in everyone else's confessions (p. 112). This was called "criticism." Ji Xianlin (1994:240) observed that at Beijing University to participate in self-criticism was to "take a bath," in a small, medium, or large "bathtub," depending on how serious one's thought problem was. Since he was the head of the Department of East Asian Languages and Literature, and suffered only mild "popular indignation," he had only to draw up a self-criticism of himself in the department, a medium-size "bathtub." Having gone through the process, critical and unattached intellectuals would be reformed into good organic intellectuals.

The task seemed formidable, but intellectuals were cooperating. Statistics show that in the early 1950s there were about 2,000,000 intellectuals (i.e., anyone with a high school education or above), constituting 0.37% of the national population (Wei Xiaodong 1996:123). The number of intellectuals was thought to be about 5,000,000 by 1957 (Mao 1977:404).[6] In the end, among others, over 91% of college teachers, 80% of college students, and 75% of middle school teachers participated in the movement (Wei Xiaodong 1996:127). Intellectuals were arguably the most difficult social group to transform, given the ideological dispositions they had developed. Zhou Enlai himself made a speech to 300 teachers from institutions of higher learning located in Beijing and Tianjin. He spoke on the dire need for thought reform, using himself as an example of a reformed intellectual. He talked about where intellectuals stood in the class struggle, their attitudes, whom they would serve, their "thought" problems, knowledge, democracy, and criticism and self-criticism. The speech, though it lasted five hours, riveted the intellectuals, according to Ma Yinchu, the Beijing University president. Not only were they moved by Zhou's lecture, but also by his own example. From September 30, 1951 to October 26, 1952, about 200 well-known scholars published articles of criticism and self-criticism in two major newspapers alone: *People's Daily,* the Party newspaper, and *Guangming Daily,* a newspaper for intellectuals (pp. 125–31; Yang Jianye 1997).

The movement, which had begun in colleges and universities, then spread to the fields of art and literature as well as to other areas where intellectuals were concentrated. There the movement was led by the revolutionary intellectuals from the Yan'an years, including Hu Qiaomu, Zhou Yang, Chen Boda, Ai Siqi, Shao Quanlin, and Ding Ling. Their speeches and articles laid forth why intellectuals in art and literature needed to reform themselves, and they organized meetings of criticism and self-criticism (Goldman 1967:89; Wei Xiaodong 1996: 128). For example, the movie on Wu Xun, an educator, was used as a tool to remold intellectuals' thoughts. The Party charged that the filmmakers depicted an idealist who wanted to change China through education rather than through revolution. Everyone who praised this movie had to go through criticism and self-criticism (Goldman 1967:91–2).

How successful was the entire movement? Lifton (1961:400) believed that it was quite successful, at least in its early phase, for a number of reasons. They include "the immense appeal of nationalism, the reinforcement of thought reform by the Chinese Communist environment, the sense of belonging to a group within one's own society, as well as many of the other historical and cultural influences" (see also Schein, Schneier, and Barker 1961:57). Many intellectuals felt that they had become part of the revolutionary cause and were truly happy. That was what Fei Xiaotong's foreign guests discovered about him (Arkush 1985:186–8). They reported that in the early years of the 1950s, Fei seemed to be at his happiest. In an article published in an English magazine, Fei refuted the implication that he was brainwashed, saying that it was absurd to even assume that a person's mind could be controlled. Indeed, he said, some of his previous thoughts about revolution and social development were unrealistic. Liang Sicheng, arguably the most accomplished architect in China at the time, also claimed that the period from 1949 to 1959 was his happiest time after he had gone through various thought reforms (Xie Yong 1999a:126).

But other developments in the thought reform movement cast doubt on its success. In fact, the long-term effects of these developments seemed to signal the beginning of an end of the honeymoon period. The dichotomy between the East and the West, good and evil, proletarian and bourgeois, became extreme, and cracks appeared in the structure of the latest orthodoxy. In some universities, violent struggles broke out against professors (Wei Xiaodong 1996:132–3). The problem was that while many intellectuals tried sincerely to reform themselves, the extreme demands led many to find the Communists' performance far different from the slogans and promises before 1949. "[The Communists'] ruthlessness, totalitarian control, and use of violence have disillusioned millions who were once hopeful about what a change of regime might bring. The Communists have undermined the position and attacked the interests of groups making up a great majority of the population. They have undoubtedly alienated most of the peasantry by collectivism, the majority of businessmen by socialization, and many intellectuals by campaigns of 'thought reform'" (Barnett, quoted by Schein, Schneier, and Barker 1961:57–8). A student in Lifton's (1961:268–9, 294) research at first wrote letters to his father urging him to "surrender voluntarily most of his land holdings to the surrounding peasants and to cooperate fully with the Communists in the manner of an 'enlightened landlord.'" The student later turned from an avowed Communist sympathizer to a bitterly disenchanted opponent and escaped to Hong Kong, as many did, including all of Edward Hunter's and Lifton's interviewees. What happened to the *Ideologues* and revisionists was happening to China's organic intellectuals.

Even among loyal organic intellectuals, old or new, some dissent appeared again during the thought reform years of the early 1950s. Goldman (1967:100) commented that Ding Ling even "had a schizophrenic character in this period," or what we would call a split personality. The conflict between professional standards and Party standards had troubled her from 1942 on. On the one hand, she urged writers to produce revolutionary literature depicting the class struggle between the working class and its enemies. On the other hand, she urged them to be independent and creative, to appeal to a larger audience, rather than to write literature as propaganda and textbooks (pp. 100–4). In the early 1950s, while applauding thought reform, Liang Sicheng adhered to his own ideas about architecture in the various articles he published in professional journals. He insisted that "to make art to fit the construction material is to cut the feet to fit the shoes." His was an unconventional voice during thought reform (Xie Yong 1999a:125).

Other examples of dissent include Yu Pingbo, arguably the most authoritative scholar on the study of the classical novel, *The Dream of the Red Chamber* by Cao Xuegin; Feng Xuefeng, the revolutionary literary critic from the 1940s; and especially Hu Feng, also a member of the left-wing writers of the 1940s (Goldman 1967). Yu, in fact, was a "dispassionate scholar who remained aloof from the political conflicts of the time" (p. 115). On the one hand, he supported communism, went along with thought reform, and participated in the denunciation of his former teacher, Hu Shih. On the other hand, he openly disputed the Party's interpretation of *The Dream of the Red Chamber* as a novel about the decay of the whole society rather than an individual incident. The Party then launched a campaign to discredit his non-Marxist views (pp. 115–6). Feng Xuefeng had also changed after "liberation," no longer advocating independent literary groups or defining *za wen,* a form of essays, as "sharp jabs at the existing social and political system" (p. 120). He even became a vice-chair of the Writers' Union. But when he assumed the editorship of one of the most important literary journals, *Wenyi Bao,* he began to criticize the Party's lowering of literary standards, lamenting that literature had falsified reality and become pure propaganda. The campaign against Yu was extended to criticize Feng for his unorthodox thinking.

Hu Feng and his disciples represent the most telling examples of the fate of organic intellectuals, their dissent, and their resistance to ideological remolding. In the 1940s, as we saw in chapter 1, Hu was not quite following the Party line. By 1950, he was a fairly good organic intellectual, although he still maintained his individual views on literature. He believed that "Under the enlightened leadership of Mao, the progress and reform of our nation . . . will provide us with the basic road to everlasting peace" (Goldman 1967:129–31). Hu retained his faith in the Communist system despite his belief that the system was suffocating its intellectuals' artistic creativity. But eventually, he found that the CCP had gone too far. In a letter to the CCP in 1954, he argued that "If we go as far as to use Marxism as a substitute for realism, then we will block artistic endeavor and will destroy art itself." He defined socialist realism as a "concern with man, . . . the emancipation of man, . . . and the spirit of humanism." He opposed the Party's emphasis on "bright things" and de-emphasis on the elements of backwardness and darkness (pp. 141–2). Hu even advocated the establishment of independent writers' organizations, though still with the approval of the Party, but freely competing with each other on their creative work. These were the same ideas the later organic intellectuals would advocate in the first period of the Deng era.

Hu believed, though, that it was literary officials, like Zhou Yang, not Mao or the political system, who were responsible for the deviation from the right path of socialism and communism. The Party, however, later decided that it was not Zhou, but Hu himself who was deviant, in fact counterrevolutionary and anti-Party. Most well-known writers in China such as Ba Jin, Lao She, Ai Qing, Mao Dun, and Guo Moruo all participated in attacking Hu (Goldman 1967:148). Hu was arrested in 1955 and was set up as an example to all intellectuals not to deviate from the Marxist orthodoxy as interpreted by the CCP.

Indeed, as Goldman (1967:107) observes, "Politically, most intellectuals after the campaigns of 1951 and 1952 accepted party doctrine and used Marxist-Leninist frames of reference, but intellectually, they still tried to work as they had in the past, divorced from party supervision and utilizing methods learned from the West." In 1956, Zhou Enlai, the premier, also gave an estimate of the Chinese intellectuals after five years of reform. Theodore H. E. Chen (1960: 101) summarizes Zhou's analysis. About 40% were actively supporting the Party and the government. Another 40% or so had formed the "intermediate sector" who did whatever they were asked to do but were not active politically. Over 10% were backward and lacking in political consciousness; and less than 10% were counterrevolutionaries or other bad elements. The same breakdown describes the success as well as the failure of the thought reform movements. Intellectuals are by disposition, as we discussed in chapter 1, critical, rebellious, and autonomous. They believe in justifying their arguments by the consent of the audience rather than by the authority of the speaker: this is the culture of critical discourse. Although one may not fully agree with Zhou's assessment, it is probably fair to say that, with all those still in need of remolding, the success rate of thought reform is still high. Nonetheless, the intellectuals we have just discussed, both fairly unattached like Yu and Liang and organic like Hu and Feng, are further proof of the rebellious critical disposition that leads to the dual personality of intellectuals. They may, in fact, also predict more such thought reform movements, which we will now discuss. As we will see, even seemingly reformed intellectuals dissented in these later movements. Their values conflicted with those of the Party's.

The Hundred Flowers Movement (1956–1957)

Throughout history most honeymoons between intellectuals and powers that be were fragile affairs, whether in China or in the West. So it is not surprising that the honeymoon between the Chinese intellectuals and the Party did not last long. The initial reform might be successful, but intellectuals soon found out that they still needed to criticize the Party. They were organic, but they also wanted to be critical. They functioned as the "loyal opposition," an indication of their dual or conflicting personalities. The Hundred Flowers Movement is a good example.

The movement was launched by the CCP and appropriated by intellectuals and others who were critical of the CCP dictatorship. The events in Poland and Hungary in 1956 shocked the CCP. Haunted by the specter of a similar uprising in China, Mao believed that the Party should launch an open-door rectification campaign. Its purpose was to invite the public to criticize the Party, and thus eliminate the contradictions between it and the people. Liu Shaoqi, however, believed that the contradictions between the masses and the Party could be resolved by a more equal distribution of economic resources, such as fairer wages, housing, food, and transportation (MacFarquhar 1960:199; see also Meisner 1967:167–203). But Mao and his supporters persisted in wanting non-Party members, especially intellectuals in the small democratic parties, to help the Party rectify itself. Despite the objections of Liu and others, Mao declared, "Will it undermine our Party's prestige if we criticize our own subjectivism, bureaucracy and sectarianism [known as the three evils]? I think not. On the contrary, it will serve to enhance our Party's prestige. The rectification movement during the anti-Japanese war proved this." Furthermore, the campaign would be "a movement of ideological education carried out seriously, yet as gently as a breeze or a mild rain," according to the rectification directive (cited in MacFaquhar 1974:187, 212; see also Goldman 1967:188–9).

After initial hesitation at this radical new experience, criticism poured in not only from intellectuals but also from students, workers, peasants, religious personnel, civil servants, businesspeople, and national minorities. Most complained that they were being bullied by Party members. Scholars claimed that they were unable to express their points of view fearlessly. Others charged that human rights were violated in the 1955 campaign to suppress counterrevolutionaries. Still others claimed that Party supporters were eavesdropping on other people's conversations. Minority cadres complained that they did not have the same power as their Han counterparts, and Catholic sisters and fathers complained that they were being shouted at and called "running dogs of imperialism" (MacFarquhar 1960:91, 94, 98, 207, 250).

Criticism from a number of radical students was more trenchant. They charged that the proletarian dictatorship was the root of all the country's evils, and that the system was to blame. The democratic parties, they said, should be given an equal footing with the CCP. Some even suggested that another revolution was necessary. Some students rioted, workers went on strike, or peasants withdrew from the cooperatives, although these seem to have been isolated incidents (MacFarquhar 1960:142–54, 166–68, 215–43; see also Teiwes 1979:297).

What made the Party especially afraid, though, was the dissent from well-known intellectuals in the CCP as well as in the small democratic parties, who were supposed to have become organic intellectuals. In her *Literary Dissent in Communist China* (1967:167–8), Goldman examined some of these intellectuals. Huang Qiuyuan, an old leftist writer, expressed his pessimism about the existing socialism in China and called on the writers to expose the dark diseases of society. Qin Zhaoyang, the editor of one of the most important literary journals, *Renmin Wenxue (People's Literature),* had been the typical revolutionary writer; he had attacked Hu Feng according to the Party line just several months before. Now, however, he reversed himself and advocated Hu Feng's ideas. He wanted to do away with the ideological restrictions on creative writing (pp. 168–70). Zhu Guangqian, the aesthetician, said that he had not dared to write anything scholarly for several years now for fear of being criticized (pp. 173–4). Ai Qing lamented the fact that there was only one kind of flower in the garden and dreamed there would be more (p. 176). Liu Binyan and Wang Meng both wrote stories criticizing the Party bureaucrats (pp. 178–9). Liu Shaotang and Cong Weixi criticized the literary bureaucrats as practicing 'vulgar sociology,' the words Hu Feng utilized to criticize Zhou Yang (pp. 183–4). Liu even held that Mao's ideas on art and literature expressed in his talks from the 1940s had outlasted their usefulness (p. 195). Art and literature should reflect the good as well as the bad (pp. 195–6). Young intellectuals like Lin Xiling, a college student, even compared Hu Feng's case to the Dreyfus affair and called for a just trial (p. 197; see Xie Yong 1999b for a more in-depth discussion on Lin). However, writers were only questioning the Party's leadership in art and literature, not the Party's leadership in general.

Some members of the small democratic parties, however, began to question the role of the higher Party cadres and the general leadership of the CCP, although they in no way wanted to replace the leading role of the Party. Chu Anping, now the editor of *Guangming Daily,* the organ of the democratic parties, for example, titled his speech, "Some Suggestions to Chairman Mao and Premier Zhou." He believed that in addition to the "junior monks," the "senior monks" should hear others' opinions as well (see Dai Qing 1990:277–9 for the full text; see also Goldman 1967:198; Seymour 1968:116). Some of his suggestions included increasing the number of non-CCP members in high-level government positions and decreasing the Party's involvement where they were not experts. He maintained that while the Party was playing a leading role in the country, non-Party members were also masters of the country and should be allowed to make a contribution.

Zhang Bojun, a member of the Democratic League and Minister of Communications, and Luo Longji, Zhang's colleague from the League and Minister of the Timber Industry, also held that the contradictions came from the privileged position of the CCP as opposed to other parties (Goldman 1967:191). Zhang Bojun proposed the establishment of a "political planning council" to help rectify the proletarian dictatorship, that is, the Party's dictatorship (MacFarquhar 1960:288). He believed that the "democratic parties ought to penetrate the *xian* [county] level—only thus can they fulfill their supervisory role." He believed that the Party was in a dilemma as to where to go, and their Democratic League had the responsibility to help (p. 170; Teiwes 1979:300–6).

Most of the criticisms from both the Party members and non-Party members seemed to be quite beneficial. They had functioned as the loyal opposition, which was exactly what the Party said it wanted them to do. That seems to be characteristic of the criticism during the Mao era: intellectuals wanted the Party to succeed in building socialism. They did not want to see it undermined by ever-increasing corruption and bureaucracy. Even demands for more power for democratic parties and national minorities were meant chiefly to curb abuses by Party cadres. As Zhang Bojun later told his daughter, he had truly meant to study how to implement democracy under socialism (Ye Yonglie 1988: 76). They were trying to be good organic intellectuals, but intellectuals nonetheless.

What happened should have been expected. Mao found himself having made an error by not foreseeing the depth of the country's discontent. So, helped by Liu, Deng Xiaoping, and others, he turned the campaign against the Party's ills into a ruthless campaign against its critics. Zhang, Luo, and Chu, and several others were termed the biggest "rightists" in the country partly because of the positions they had held at the time. Many revolutionary writers, including Ding Ling, Feng Xuefeng, Qin Zhaoyang, Ai Qing, Liu Shaotang, Cong Weixi, Wang Meng, and Liu Binyan also were suddenly rightists. Ma Yinchu, the president of Beijing University, who at first advocated thought reform, was not degraded to rightist but was criticized as a rightist for his theory on population control. Student leaders in a rightist riot in Wuhan were executed. Although the Party simply removed the top-level dissidents of the small democratic parties, such as Zhang, Luo, and Chu, many more rightists were either imprisoned or sent to work in factories or to labor in the countryside. All told, 552,877 intellectuals, cadres, industrialists, and students were dubbed rightists, according to the official statistic released in 1978 (Zhang Dake 1996:155).[7] Another round of dissent was squelched, and a high degree of political uniformity imposed again, if only temporarily and on the surface. Figure 2.1 depicts the relationship between intellectuals and the Party.

Figure 2.1 Don't Be Unreasonable! *(Xiude wu li)*
Source: Ding Cong 1999 (Vol. 3), p. 162.

The Great Proletarian Cultural Revolution (1966 to 1976)

During the years between the anti-rightist repression of 1957 and the Cultural Revolution in 1966, perhaps the majority of intellectuals retreated into acquiescence and uniformity.[8] Certain groups of organic intellectuals, however, continued a stubborn dissent from Mao's Party line. The chief of these dissenting intellectuals were from the Beijing Party Committee, from the propaganda departments, and from academic circles. Goldman (1981) provides us with a detailed account of the organic, or what she calls "liberal," intellectuals just before and during the Cultural Revolution in her well-researched book, *China's Intellectuals*.

The intellectuals from the Beijing Party Committee were Deng Tuo, secretary of the Secretariat and editor of its theoretical journal, *Front Line (Qianxian);* Wu Han, vice-mayor of Beijing and a prominent historian; and Liao Mosha, director of the United Front Work Department. Most of their criticisms were published in Deng's essays titled "Evening Chats in Yanshan [another name for Beijing]," or the trio's "Notes from a Three-Family Village" published in *Front Line* from September 1961 to July 1964 (Goldman 1981:27). In his essays, Deng, who had been the head of the Xinhua News Agency in the 1940s and editor in chief of the *People's Daily* in the 1950s, criticized Mao, without naming him, for his "arrogant, subjective, dogmatic, and arbitrary" way of leadership, thus beginning the demystification of the Party and of himself (p. 29). Deng also criticized the Party's break with the former Soviet Union and called for closer contact with the United States (p. 32). Wu Han published a historical play called "The Dismissal of Hai Rui from Office," implicitly supporting upright officials like Peng Dehuai, the defense minister who criticized Mao and who was deposed from office in 1959. Wu also called for academic work to be independent of politics (pp. 34–5; see also Cheek 1986, 1997; Fisher 1986).[9]

Intellectuals in the Party's propaganda departments also criticized Mao's dogmatism. In previous thought reform movements, Zhou Yang had led the attack on intellectuals dissenting from the Party line. Now he "called for more creative and diversified styles and less ideological subject matter" (Goldman 1981:39). He downplayed class orientation, and advocated "a joint leadership of artists and the Party in creative enterprises, but with the artists controlling their own work" (p. 41). Tian Han, a playwright, wrote *Xie Yaohuan,* and Meng Chao, wrote *Li Huiniang,* both similarly using the past to comment on the present. Both also pleaded for better treatment of the peasants (pp. 42–3). *The Death of Li Xiucheng,* a play written by Yang Hansheng, praised Li for risking his life to challenge the leader of the Taiping Revolution in the midnineteenth century (p. 44). Other dissenting organic intellectuals among the Party's literary leaders include Xia Yan, Mao Dun, and Shao Quanlin (pp. 44–50, 101–3).

In academic circles, Feng Youlan, the philosopher from Beijing University, maintained that the Confucian concept of benevolence embodies a universal ethic, not just a class character (Goldman 1981:54). Jian Bozan, an accomplished historian, pointed out that it was class reconciliation rather than class struggle that improved peasants' lives (pp. 56–7). Ma Yinchu, the president of Beijing University, continued to advocate population control to advance modernization, and Sun Yefang, a Party member since the 1920s, emphasized the importance of guiding prices by production costs rather than by political norms (p. 59; Naughton 1986:131–7). Yang Xianzhen, the Party's leading Marxist theoretician, maintained that complementary opposites were an integral part of China's cultural heritage, implying a tolerance of diverse viewpoints and classes (Goldman 1981:97; Hamrin 1986:76–9).

If all of these organic intellectuals were now less organic, Mao was ready to develop other organic intellectuals to replace them. These are what Goldman calls "radical intellectuals." They include Zhang Chunqiao, an ideological theorist, and Yao Wenyuan, a literary critic, both from the Shanghai Party Committee's Propaganda Department. They also include Guan Feng, a philosopher, and Qi Benyu, an historian, both of the Chinese Academy of Sciences, as well as Wang Li, an ideological theorist and deputy editor of *Red Flag,* the Party's leading journal on theory. These intellectuals upheld Mao's ideological positions on class struggle in several ways. They launched attacks on the liberal intellectuals' positions regarding the common interests of the classes. They criticized the works we have been discussing. And, like Jiang Qing, Mao's wife, they used revolutionary Peking operas as propaganda (Goldman 1981:66–84; see also Ragvald 1978; Walder 1978).[10]

Although the radical intellectuals had not so far viewed the liberal intellectuals as anti-Party, this changed in 1966, the official beginning of the Cultural Revolution. The historian Jian Bozan and the economist Sun Yefang, to name just two among many, were criticized for their deviant work. And liberal intellectuals were not only criticized. They were purged, one after the other, beginning with the Beijing Party Committee members, Deng, Wu, and Liao. Deng committed suicide, Wu died of medical neglect, and those who did not die were made to stand with heavy boards hung from their necks in "struggle rallies," meetings to denounce the "capitalist roaders" or other "bad elements," vast public punishments often attended by thousands of people (Goldman 1981: 117–33).

Most of these liberal organic intellectuals were known for their Party loyalty, yet the violence escalated. Mao and his radical intellectuals mobilized millions of students to overthrow all of the academic authorities in colleges, universities, and other schools, even including the middle schools. At the same time they overthrew the Party bureaucracy at various levels and made these "capitalist roaders" stand criticism in front of the masses. In the initial years of the Cultural Revolution, there were mass book burnings, and many intellectuals and Party cadres committed suicide. Others were simply put into prison or forced into makeshift prisons at their work units after the "struggle rallies." The "rebels," the revolutionary cadres, and the PLA leaders now constituted the new revolutionary authorities at every level of government.

With the help of radical intellectuals, the revolution continued in the early 1970s, using various repressive campaigns. One technique was to criticize Confucianism and Lin Biao, Mao's designated successor, who had died in an escape to the former Soviet Union following a failed revolt against Mao. Another trick was to criticize the concept of bourgeois rights and to glorify the dictatorship of the proletariat. A third target was to criticize capitulationism, which Mao believed to have been displayed by rebel leaders such as Song Jiang and Lu Junyi, characters depicted in the classical novel, *The Water Margin* by Shi Naian and Luo Guanzhong. All of these campaigns were designed to further solidify Mao's ideological control. The class struggle was directed against dissenting cadres as well as against Party bureaucrats such as Zhou Enlai, who was trying to moderate the control in order to further economic production (Goldman 1981:160, 166–231).

It is important to emphasize, however, that even though intellectuals like Deng, Wu, Liao, Jian, Yang, and Sun were deemed anti-Party and antisocialism, they were, in fact, organic to the Party. Theirs was loyal opposition, loyal to the Party, although not necessarily to Mao. Indeed, that is how Wu Han defined the concept of loyalty: to the Party, not to a ruler, as did Deng Tuo (Cheek 1986:123; Goldman 1981:58). Wu's "outspoken condemnation of dogmatism . . . was a response to central Party initiatives. It is thus difficult to see him as a dissenter" (Fisher 1986:183).[11] Indeed, Wu closely adhered to the Party's directives in the various movements in the 1950s. He "used his power to help whip fellow intellectuals into line . . . [and] was particularly zealous in attacking Luo Longji. . . ." (Israel 1986:xiv). Deng Tuo saw no conflict between adhering to Mao's writings and maintaining his personal integrity and interests, and he believed, like every good Communist, that individuals should subordinate their rights to the rights of the group (Cheek 1986:96, 113).

Jian's historicism was meant to complement the Party's class view of history (Edmunds 1987:86–8). He was trying to incorporate certain objectivity into his historical scholarship while carefully accommodating the needs of the Party. Historians had, in fact, become little more than propagandists for the Party's goals and values (pp. 69–71). Yang Xianzhen's "two into one" was not negating Mao's "dividing one into two," as he himself insisted, just two sides of the same coin. And he also opposed Wang Ruoshui's argument for a humanistic Marxism (Hamrin 1986: 77–8, 91). Economists like Sun carried out studies of industrial management, supplying advice for government policy-making (Halpern 1987:53, 63; Naughton 1986). The same is true of other intellectuals. Zhou Yang and Shao Quanlin might have modified their previous positions on literature and art (Goldman 1981:40, 47), but their pledge was still to the Party. Even Yao Wenyuan's earlier criticisms regarded these conflicts as academic rather than political (p. 70).

Perhaps most telling is what Deng Tuo wrote before he died. In a letter to the Beijing Party Committee written just before he committed suicide, he asked the Party to further investigate the articles he had written, and expressed confidence that they were not anti-Party. Even if he was going to die, he said, his heart would "always be toward the beloved Party and beloved Chairman Mao." The letter ended with "Long live the great, glorious, and correct Chinese Communist Party! Long live our beloved leader Chairman Mao! Long live the victory of the great thoughts of Chairman Mao! Long live the world-wide victory of the great cause of socialism and communism!" (see Yuan Ying 1986:128). Even if the expression of loyalty to Mao was to protect his family, Deng's expression of loyalty to the Party was representative of organic intellectuals in general. They had tried to help the Party rather than sabotage it. The charges of anti-Party and antisocialism were simply Maoist playing of politics. These intellectuals were basically organic intellectuals of the Party.[12]

On the other hand, there were indeed critical voices, though limited and restrained, during the Cultural Revolution, but they came basically from outside the system. One of the most important voices was that of Gu Zhun (1915–74), an economist and former vice-director of finance in the East China government. He was termed a "rightist" in 1957, and spent the rest of his life laboring in the countryside. Gu's uniqueness lies in his persistence in looking beyond the revolution. He had always believed in the absolute correctness of revolutionary idealism. But when he saw it turn into reactionary despotism, he found himself turning to "complete empiricism and diversity" (Chen Minzhi 1997:340; see also Gao Jianguo 2000). He delved into the study of democracy and wrote *The Greek City System,* which was published posthumously in 1982. In the last two years of his life he wrote *From Idealism to Empiricism,* also published posthumously. The following quote gives us an idea of the conclusion he arrived at:

> The revolutionary may have begun as an advocate of democracy. But if he has an ultimate goal, and believes in this as the only goal , then he would sacrifice democracy and practice dictatorship to achieve it. Stalin was brutal, but his brutality may not have been solely to solidify his personal power. He might have believed that for the benefit of the public and to reach that ultimate goal, he simply had to be brutal. It was a tragedy for him to have meant well but to have done evil. (quoted in Chen Minzhi 1997:368)

He appears to be defending Mao's brutality, but his analysis was not only fresh at the time, in that he called a "spade a spade," but is still enlightening to this day. Why the Revolution turned so antiprogressive, and how totalitarianism could transform one-time revolutionaries like Mao, needs further investigation, but Gu has a very interesting point. Coser (1965) and Boggs (1993) have reached similar conclusions in their analysis of the Bolsheviks (see chapter 1 in our discussion of revolutionary intellectuals in power). The similarity between Gu and Deng Tuo is that both started as revolutionaries. The difference between them may be that Gu began to question the system fairly openly, whereas

Deng did not go as far. Gu set an example of the critical intellectual persisting in critical thinking under adverse circumstances. And yet his influence was not felt until the 1990s.

Yu Luoke (1942–68), a young worker turned intellectual, however, made a huge impact at the very beginning of the Cultural Revolution. The state, in fact, thought that his criticism was so threatening that he must be executed. His most famous work is "On One's Family Background." First published in a student newspaper, the article spread all over the country. In it, he questioned the then popular belief that if your family background is bad (capitalists, landlords, rich peasants, reactionary, rightist, etc.), you are bad, and if your family background is good (workers, poor peasants, and revolutionary cadres), you are good. His article spoke to the experience of many youths who were not able to go to college, find a good job, or join the army because their parents or grandparents were from one of the "bad" categories. In a sense, it questioned prevalent class theory (see also Xu Youyu 1999).

Yu was also able to publish an article in *Wenhui Daily,* criticizing Yao Wenyuan and his article, the "Dismissal of Hai Rui." (Yao's article was one of the chief events that started the Cultural Revolution.) By doing so, he was indirectly questioning Mao, for it was Mao who was behind Yao's article. And Yu was directly challenging Mao when he said that it was wrong to be against everything your enemy is for, and for anything your enemy is against (Yu Luoke [1966] 1999a:110). He also criticized Chen Boda, Mao's secretary, for promoting a personal cult of Mao; praised the play *Xie Yaohuan,* which pleaded for better treatment of the peasants; noted Mao's hypocrisy in disparaging others for referring to ancient emperors and generals while mentioning them himself, and observed that the Cultural Revolution was really a struggle between two groups of cadres rather than between classes, as Mao claimed (Yu Luoke [1966] 1999b:113, 116, 120). These were insightful observations, and it was daring for him to spread them around. He was executed for his ideas.

An article of influence comparable to "On One's Family Background" is Li Yizhe's "big character poster" of November 7, 1974. Li Yizhe is a pseudonym for *Li* Zhengtian, Chen *Yi*gang, and Wang Xi*zhe,* three disaffected students from Guangzhou (i.e., Canton). They criticized the autocracy, the despotism, and the personal cult of Mao, and called for legal guarantees of democratic and individual rights. To be sure, they were criticizing the Lin Biao system, not directly criticizing

Mao. But the message was threatening to the Party as a whole. The three were arrested and not released until 1978 (see Baum 1994:74; Goldman 1981:189–91).

Conclusions

First, in the early Mao era during the honeymoon between intellectuals and the Party, many unattached and critical intellectuals were eager to become part of the government's socialist reconstruction. Men like Ji Xianlin and Fei Xiaotong showed a willingness to reform themselves, and Chu Anping suggested that they be given a chance to contribute. In fact, unattached and critical intellectuals *independent* of government organizations ceased to exist, partly because every intellectual had to belong to a unit and partly because they began to believe in the Party line.[13] If the intellectuals were co-opted by the Party, that co-optation was in all probability mutual. After all, intellectuals also wanted to change China. According to Wang Yuanhua, former director of the Propaganda Department of the Shanghai Party Committee, they joined the revolution truly believing it was the only way to save China; whatever they did, they did out of that conviction (Interview with Wang 1994:1.1).

Second, while one group of organic intellectuals, like Zhang Chunqiao and Yao Wenyuan, steadfastly followed Mao and the orthodox Party line, another group of intellectuals was just like the Polish revisionists we discussed in chapter 1. Even if they became organic, as members of the CCP or of various small democratic parties, these intellectuals still spoke out when the Party deviated from what they believed to be the right path of socialism. Many may have accepted thought reform, but they refused to give up their professionalism and the culture of critical discourse. Even those who were largely educated after "liberation," like the writer Liu Shaotang, or who seemed to have been reformed, like the editor Qin Zhaoyang, could rise in opposition. Lu Dingyi, the Party's propaganda chief, summarizes it well: "[A]mong bourgeois intellectuals, there is a group which is very difficult to reform. Some even unto death are not willing to reform. . . . Some have joined the Party, but even though they have gone through Communist education for a long time, they cannot reform themselves" (quoted in Goldman 1967:240).

Third, these organic intellectuals focused their criticism on the Party bureaucrats, if they were writers, or the ways in which the Party governed, if they were democratic party members. Most were not questioning the leading role of the Party. The writers may have criticized Zhou Yang and his leadership for deviating from the humanitarian goals of Marxism, but very few would admit that they were anti-Party. They even made a point of not opposing the political system (Goldman 1967:140, 166, 173, 177, 212–4, 219). Indeed, at the end of his famous speech during the Hundred Flowers movement, Chu Anping said that he was just making suggestions, and that it was up to the Party to create an atmosphere of socialism in which everyone could have a place and be happy *(rongrong lele ge de qi suo)* (see Dai Qing 1990:279). Throughout the Mao era, most criticisms were from loyal opposition from organic intellectuals (see also White III 1986:108). Although they often tried to carve a niche within the confines of Party ideology, the political environment led most intellectuals to become good organic intellectuals: to support the Party, to conform to its politics, even to act as very good Party cadres and spokespersons. The loyal opposition was intended only to help the Party succeed. It was understandable that after years of turmoil, and of foreign aggression and colonization, intellectuals wanted socialism to work.

Fourth, these intellectuals demonstrated the qualities of the organic intellectual who follows an ethic of responsibility. They were willing to cooperate with the powers, hoping their help would contain the evil. For example, Hu Feng advised his followers to "find suitable quotations from Soviet leaders and Mao to bolster" their arguments, even if doing so might be troublesome. One of Hu's colleagues even advised him to join the Party (Goldman 1967:140). The Party, however, suspected what writers inside the Party were doing. As a *People's Daily* editorial commented in 1957, "The writers inside the Party do more harm than those outside. The easiest way to attack a fortress is to attack from within" (quoted in Goldman 1967:227).[14] The editorial was exaggerating, but it is true that organic intellectuals tended to believe that they could better change society by cooperating with the powers.

Fifth, their criticism clearly indicates their dual or split personality, as we saw in Deng Tuo and Wu Han. We see it also in non-Party organic intellectuals, like Zhang Bojun and many of the Rightists in the Hundred Flowers Movement. In other words, while we see organic intellectuals often functioning as deputies and spokespersons for the ruling class, following the ethic of responsibility, we also see them trying to remain true to the critical tradition of Confucianism, demonstrating an ethic of ultimate ends. Nevertheless, whether they criticized from inside or outside the Party, most intellectuals could not totally detach themselves from Party politics. (Even Yu Luoke had to use pro-Mao words in his articles against Mao's policies.) They were controlled not only by the Party's oppression, but also by their own desire to help socialism succeed. They could better change society by cooperating with the powers. Intellectuals like Deng Tuo seriously believed that they understood Marxism-Leninism-Mao Zedong Thought better than the Party leaders and could make the orthodox work (Cheek 1997). This inevitably created a conflict in roles. Recall also Mannheim's view, which we discussed in chapter 1: for intellectuals, one way out of the unattached status is to be affiliated with a class, especially a dominant class. The challenge is to fight devils without becoming devils themselves, as the ethic of ultimate ends would require. To criticize or to conform, that is the question. If one tries both, one is a dual or even a split personality in the making.

Sixth, although the demand for political uniformity led to severe suppression in the Mao era, criticism from outside the system did exist. These were the voices of largely nonorganic intellectuals like Lin Xiling, Gu Zhun, Yu Luoke, and Li Yizhe. Their criticism was fairly sharp and was suppressed quickly, but it represented a different intellectual tradition. We will see this critical tradition continuing to attract more intellectuals during the Deng era following the Cultural Revolution.

In sum, political uniformity dominated the Mao era, in spite of critical voices both from within and without the Party system. There was little room for the critical and the unattached intellectual (see figure 2.1). As Huang Ping (1994) points out, intellectuals' bodies belonged to the work units, and their minds were being unified as well. The Party purges, ranging from executions and imprisonment to ostracism, were often more than enough to deter intellectuals from voicing criticism. This heavy-handed suppression taught intellectuals some very sharp lessons. When even the mildest criticism was "counterrevolutionary," only the most extraordinary would speak against the state. If they did, it was chiefly, and not always safely, as the loyal opposition (Fogel 1987b: 24). (How much greater, then, were the dangers to a true critic like Yu Luoke?) Whether or not they shared a true faith in communism, intellectuals learned to suppress their opinions and to function as cogs and screws in the revolutionary machine. Many wrote about workers, peasants, and soldiers; others worked in different ways for the education of the masses in the revolutionary struggle (see also Wagner 1987:192).

However, although there is no way of knowing what they actually thought, beneath the surface of political uniformity intellectuals might have been increasingly dissatisfied. Goldman (1967:242) observes that "The anti-rightist movement widened the gap still further between the Party and the intellectuals. Having once had their hopes aroused and then drastically shattered, the disillusionment of the intellectuals undoubtedly was more acute than ever before." The Cultural Revolution heated this dissatisfaction even further. This, then, was the politics of the intellectual in the Mao era. There was a high degree of uniformity, but with much dissent in the form of loyal opposition and some beginning criticism directed at the system itself.

The Beginning of Fragmentation: The First Deng Period (1977–1989)

If the uniformity of intellectuals in the Mao era is characterized by both a physical confinement to a work unit and ideological conformity to the Party line, the fragmentation in the first period of the Deng era is characterized by both the physical and ideological loosening of the ropes *(song bang)* on intellectuals. Some have described it as a "thaw in the spring." Other characterizations include *China Wakes,* the title of the popular book by Nicholas D. Kristof and Sheryl WuDunn (1994); "The Mandate Shaken," a chapter title in Harrison E. Salisbury's (1992) *New Emperors;* X. L. Ding's (1994) *The Decline of Communism in China;* and Richard Baum's (1994) *Burying Mao*. These titles imply what it was like in the Mao era, and vividly capture the essence of the Party policy between 1976 and 1989.[15]

The political economy was changing. As we mentioned earlier, the Third Plenum of the Central Committee of the Party's Eleventh Congress in 1978 shifted its focus from class struggle to the economy. To support the shift, the Party had to liberate its mind. Riding the tide, intellectuals again questioned the orthodox Marxist-Maoist beliefs, and even practices adopted since Mao (in addition to the authors we cite in the next section, see also Calhoun 1991).[16] A larger group of independent critical intellectuals emerged, such as Wei Jingsheng of the Democracy Wall movement and Hu Ping of the 1980 elections. Meanwhile, a number of organic intellectuals began to confront the Party line, and to take the first steps in becoming independently critical. It is important to note, however, that this political change in the organic intellectuals was not yet an obvious break from the Party line by a sizable group. That break did not come until the spring of 1989. At the same time, other organic intellectuals rose up to defend the traditional Party line, especially the four cardinal principles: the Party's leadership, socialism, the proletarian dictatorship, and Marxism-Leninism-Mao Zedong Thought, which in 1957 Mao (1977:462) had already outlined for the antirightist movement as crucial issues. Other fragmenting changes include the bureaucratization, bourgeoisification, and professionalization of China's intellectuals.

Critical Intellectuals Outside the System

Several political movements following the critical tradition outside the system are important in the transformation of intellectuals' political roles in this first period of the Deng era. They are the April 5 movement in 1976, the "wounded literature" and "obscure poetry" movements, the Democracy Wall movement at the end of the 1970s and the election campaign in 1980, as well as the student demonstrations from 1986 to 1987. Intellectuals involved in these movements began to deviate from the organic tradition and to criticize the system from the outside. Unlike the few voices of Lin Xiling of the Hundred Flowers Movement or Yu Luoke and "Li Yizhe" of the Cultural Revolution, these voices signaled the beginnings of a concerted group of independent critical intellectuals during the Communist era.

The April 5 movement in 1976 started as a protest against the radicals in power: Wang Hongwen, Zhang Chunqiao, Jiang Qing, and Yao Wenyuan. "The Gang of Four," as they were later called, was charging that Zhou Enlai, the premier who had died in January, was a capitalist roader. But as Baum (1994:33) points out, "As much as for Zhou Enlai, the people seemed to be grieving for themselves and their country." Understandably, the articles and poems at the time were not anti-Party, but anti-Gang of Four. It is also significant that the criticism came from below, rather than from established organic intellectuals in the Party leadership or from academic or literary circles. These voices continued a tradition of criticism started under the Communist regime among educated youth such as Lin Xiling, Yu Luoke, and Li Yizhe.

If the April 5 movement was still to some extent pro-Party, the "wounded literature" that started in 1977 was less complimentary. As the term implies, this was a literary movement in which young writers "depicted the pain, violence, injustices, and destruction of the Cultural Revolution" (Goldman 1994:32). Love, which used to be a forbidden zone in literature, was again portrayed as being a human emotion. Individuality was restored. There were also a great many novels depicting the lives of the educated youths sent down to the countryside, the "negative impact of the ultra-leftist lines on every aspect of the young people's lives, as witnessed by the educated youth's depression and perplexity" (Ma and Ling 1998:107). A new literary genre, "obscure poetry" (*menglong shi,* or misty poetry*),* such as that of Bei Dao, Shu Ting, and Gu Cheng, expressed the poets' critique of the absurdity of the Cultural Revolution, the pain of the transition period, and their anxiety about the future (p. 105; see also Su and Larson 1995). Overall, "wounded literature" and "obscure poetry" may be viewed as movements that exposed the follies and tragedies of the Mao era. They make one question the legitimacy and efficacy of the political system. Their practitioners tended to be from outside the system, not the usual organic intellectuals.

The critical tradition culminated in the Democracy Wall movement after the fall of the Gang of Four.[17] In 1978 and 1979, democratic debates took the form of big character posters on the walls along Chang'an Street in Xidan, Beijing. Baum (1994:70) summarizes two major themes of the posters: criticism of those who believed in whatever Mao said, and the challenges to Mao's judgments in using Lin Biao and the Gang of Four. The criticism then moved on to question the system itself. The best-known is Wei Jingsheng's article on "The Fifth Modernization," which called for democratizing Chinese politics so as to avoid repeating the tragedies of the Mao era (see also Leys 1985: 224–39). Underground journals sprang up calling for democratization and for voicing public dissent, including *Beijing Spring, April Fourth Forum, Enlightenment, Exploration, Today,* and *Masses' Reference News* (Baum 1994:74).

At first, Deng supported a forum where people could air their dissatisfactions. This was partly because he needed their support in repudiating the Gang of Four. He also needed help against the Maoist Party leaders who, instead of liberating cadres like himself, deprived them of power under Mao's directives. But now he was back firmly in his old positions, and criticism of the system would endanger his own power. He decided in 1979 that he could no longer tolerate a freedom of speech that "slanders Mao Zedong and proclaims that 'proletarian dictatorship is the source of all evil.'" He still favored democracy, but he would "link democracy for the people with dictatorship over the enemy, and with centralism, legality, discipline, and leadership by the Communist Party" (see Baum 1994:81). People, said Deng, must adhere to the four cardinal principles. As a result of this change in thinking, Fu Yuehua, a democracy activist, was arrested in early 1979; other activists were rounded up, including Wei Jingsheng, Ren Wanding, Huang Xiang, and Liu Qing (pp. 77, 81; Goldman 1994:41–46).

Although the Democracy Wall movement was suppressed, it seemed to have started a movement toward autonomy among critical intellectuals. In 1979, a completely new Electoral Law was adopted, providing for competitive elections: there could be more candidates than places to be filled in any election. The next year, 1980, students in Beijing University launched an election campaign with a number of students running for a position in the Haidian District People's Congress (Hu and Wang 1990). A number of sensitive issues were raised and debated. The candidates called for freedom of speech; freedom of the press; separation of the Party and the government; and division of power among the legislative, executive, and judiciary branches. They criticized Mao's role in the antirightist movement, the Great Leap Forward, the Cultural Revolution, and various other policies devised after "liberation." Sixteen student candidates ran for the position and each expressed his or her opinion on various issues, including evaluations of Mao and Wei Jingsheng. Many of these activists, such as Hu Ping, Wang Juntao, and Fang Zhiyuan, have since become leading figures in the democracy movement.

The significance of the election campaign, as Hu Ping points out, lies not in whether any one of them could have been elected or what they could have done after election, but in the process itself (Hu Ping and Wang Juntao 1990:15). Other Democracy Wall activists also won seats, including Chen Ziming of Beijing, Fu Shenqi, a worker from Shanghai, and Liang Heng of Hunan Teachers' College, although they were not allowed to take their seats (Goldman 1994:79). The election itself, however, was unprecedented. It was an effort by young critical intellectuals to seek political autonomy. Like Wei Jingsheng in the Democracy Wall movement, these young people continued the critical tradition started by earlier democracy advocates. They also paid a price. Although advocates like Hu Ping and Wang Juntao were not arrested, they nonetheless could not find jobs after they finished their graduate studies at Beijing University.

The new activism was continued by the student demonstrators of late 1986 and early 1987, and broke out even more strongly in the democracy movement of 1989, which we will discuss in chapter 3. These efforts differed from the movements of dissent among organic intellectuals both in the Mao era and in the Deng era in that they not only questioned the system but questioned it from *outside* the system. They represented the growth of the *independent* critical intellectual. These intellectuals were directly involved in social movements of one sort or another, were openly critical of the regime, and were fast becoming independent.

There were, however, groups of intellectuals who were critical but less politically engaged, who were also *largely* outside the system. Edward X. Gu (1999) describes three such groups: (1) the editorial committee of the *Toward the Future* book series; (2) the International Academy of Chinese Culture (Zhongguo wenhua shuyuan); and (3) the editorial committee of the *Culture: China and the World,* another book series.[18]

The first group gathered such intellectuals as Jin Guantao, Bao Zunxin, Chen Yueguang, Tang Ruoxin, Jia Xinmin, Liu Qingfeng, Fang Hongye, Le Xiucheng, Wang Qishan, Wang Xiaoqiang, He Weiling, and Wang Junxian. In addition to the books they wrote individually, the group published translations of such important international scholars as Max Weber, Robert Merton, Kenneth Arrow, Janos Kornai, Cyril Black, Alex Inkeles, and Joseph Levenson.[19] Advocating scientific rationalism, economic reform, and cultural enlightenment, the group was more critical culturally and economically than it was politically.

The second group brought together well-known scholars both at home and abroad, including Liang Shuming, Feng Youlan, Tang Yijie, Ji Xianlin, Zhang Dainian, Li Zehou, Pang Pu, Bao Zunxin, Tu Weiming, Chung-ying Cheng, Yu-sheng Lin, and Frederic Wakeman Jr. They published dozens of books on traditional Chinese culture. They organized conferences, seminars, symposia, and short-term training courses on various cultural issues (Edward X. Gu 1999:411). This group was critical in that they typically "abandoned a variety of then-accepted doctrines of the official Marxist-Leninist ideology, drew much of [their] intellectual nourishment from Chinese traditional thoughts or western Marxism, or both, and developed their own Chinese neo-Marxist cultural theories" (p. 413).[20]

The third group drew together Gan Yang (editor in chief), Su Guoxun, Liu Xiaofeng, Li Yinhe, Chen Pingyuan, Chen Lai, Hu Ping,

Xu Youyu, Qian Liqun, Yan Buke, Liang Zhiping, among others. These scholars published dozens of translated works, including those of Martin Buber, Jean-Paul Sartre, Martin Heidegger, Max Weber, and a host of other Western thinkers. One can only imagine the impact these Western classics would have had on a Chinese mind trained in Confucian and Marxist traditions.

Criticism and Defense of the Party Line: Organic Intellectuals Divided

Organic intellectuals within the system, on the other hand, were beginning to be fragmented. Some leaned toward a more independent critical stance, others toward a position more organic to the Party line. Goldman (1994) calls the first group the "democratic elite"; we will call them "critical organic intellectuals." She calls the second group "radical intellectuals," who upheld orthodox Marxism and resisted the changes proposed by the first. We will call them "orthodox organic intellectuals." These terms will be used interchangeably. The distinction between critical and orthodox organic intellectuals is important because the term organic intellectuals is not a monolith. It is a variable responding to changes in the political climate; it has at least two subcategories.[21]

At the end of the 1970s, the critical organic intellectuals, or the democratic elite, enjoyed an alliance with Deng Xiaoping and Hu Yaobang, as Goldman (1994:47) observed. They might have sympathized with the main tenets of the previous democracy movements, and with the call for a new interpretation of Marxism and some institutional reform. But they rejected the advocacy of Wei Jingsheng and others for radical changes in the political system. They "still believed in Marxism and socialism and had faith that the Deng leadership and reforms would ultimately bring China into the modern world" (p. 47). The developments in the 1980s, however, left them more and more alienated from the Party. They thus distinguished themselves from the more orthodox organic, or radical, intellectuals. This is one of the most important developments during the first Deng period, and it grew out of the following events.

Debates on Practice Criterion, Alienation, and Humanism

In 1979 and 1980, the Party called on the country to "emancipate its mind." This was an effort by the new leadership, headed by Deng Xiaoping and Hu Yaobang, to offset the influence of Mao and his successor,

Hua Guofeng, who advocated following whatever lessons Mao had taught (Ma Licheng and Ling Zhijun 1998). The goal for the new leadership (to liberate themselves and their comrades) coincided with the goal of intellectuals to find out what had gone wrong in the Cultural Revolution (see also Link 1992:147–9).[22] Critical organic intellectuals, as did the Democracy Wall intellectuals, began to reflect aloud upon the Cultural Revolution and upon the Party's policies in the Mao era. With Hu Yaobang's support, they first began to pave the way for a climate that tolerated more questioning, an effort to overcome Mao's dogmatism.

Thus came the debate asking, "Is actual practice the sole criterion for examination of truth?" A number of such intellectuals participated in writing an article asking that question. They included Hu Fuming, a philosophy teacher from Nanjing University; Sun Changjiang of the Central Party School; Yang Xiguang, the editor of the *Guangming Daily;* and Wu Jiang, also from the *Guangming Daily* (Goldman 1994: 36; Hu Fuming 1999 [1998]:107–8; Sun Changjiang [1998]1999:98–105;). The debate soon spread to other areas; for example, economists began to dwell on the theories of a market economy under socialism (Fang Gongwen [1998]1999:115–20). From May 10, 1978, when the "practice criterion" article was first published, until the end of the year, provincial-level newspapers and journals published six hundred and fifty articles on the topic. Various provincial level cadres and military leaders expressed support for the principle. With the help of this group of critical organic intellectuals, Deng and Hu won the debate and forced Hua and his followers to suffer through self-criticism. The debate led to the firm establishment of Deng's and Hu's position in the Party. It also guaranteed the government's shift from class struggle to the economy, a policy established in December 1978 (Ma and Ling 1998:46–90).

Another group of critical organic intellectuals, however, again with Hu's support, were contemplating a more radical political shift at the end of the 1970s. Yan Jiaqi, who in 1985 was to become the first director of the Institute of Political Science of the Chinese Academy of Social Sciences (CASS), recommended limited terms for political leaders. Li Honglin, a former deputy of the Theory Section of the Propaganda Department, urged an end to life tenure for Party officials (Goldman 1994:52). Li "was one of the first in the country to draw a distinction publicly between the nation and society on the one hand and the Party and the political system on the other" (p. 57). Guo Luoji, a philosopher, openly defended the Democracy Wall movement and called for "the full emancipation of the mind" (p. 52). Su Shaozhi, who in 1982 would become director of the CASS Institute of Marxism-Leninism-Mao Zedong Thought, was advancing a concept he called "the primary stage of socialism," toward which, he said, China was moving (p. 53). Human rights issues, which had been debated during the Democracy Wall movement, were once again discussed in scholarly journals (p. 59).

Among the most controversial issues at the beginning of the 1980s was the debate on alienation under socialism, and the emergence of Marxist humanism. Wang Ruoshui, the deputy editor of *People's Daily,* identified three kinds of alienation under Chinese socialism (Goldman 1994:75–6). One was ideological: the leader, like Mao, became the god who laid down the law for the people. Another was political: leaders of the society became masters rather than servants of the masses. The third kind of alienation was economic: the rules of economics were ignored and the bureaucratic will took priority (see also Brugger and Kelly 1990; Kelly 1987: 159–61). Together with Zhou Yang, the rehabilitated cultural czar, and other high-profile intellectual cadres, Wang began to promote a new school of thought. Since the current brand of socialism has produced alienation, a socialist humanism should be promoted. According to them, humanism is, in fact, a characteristic of Marxism (Kelly 1987:173).

If critical intellectuals, including some of the organic ones, were beginning to deviate from the orthodox Party line, other intellectuals rushed to its rescue. Famous poets of the old school such as Ai Qing, Zang Kejia, and Tian Jian criticized the "obscure poetry" for its incomprehensibility to workers. The writer Liu Shaotang, who had been critical of the Party line in 1957, and who was then labeled a "rightist," now criticized Liu Binyan for exposing the Party's abuse of power; he urged him to stay away from politics. Ding Ling was willing to support the orthodox Party line even though she had suffered from it ever since 1957. Liu Baiyu, the head of the Cultural Department in the General Political Department of the People's Liberation Army, led the army's criticism of Bai Hua, an army writer who had written a script titled "Unrequited Love." Published in 1979 and made into a movie in 1981, its most famous line is, "You love the country; but does this country love you?" Bai was criticizing the Party's and the government's treatment of intellectuals, and the Party was not happy with his script. Huang Gang, the editor in chief of the *Contemporary Reportage (Shidai de baogao)* joined Liu in criticizing Bai (Goldman 1994:84–7, 88–95; Kelly 1987:219; Kraus 1986).[23] See figure 2.2 for an illustration of the debates in the 1980s.

Figure 2.2 The Picture of [A Hundred Schools] Contending *(Zhengming tu)*

Source: Ding Cong 1999 (Vol. 2), p. 31.

Campaigns Against Bourgeois Liberalization and "Spiritual Pollution": Further Push of Intellectuals to Be More Critical

The orthodox criticism culminated in the Party's campaign against the bourgeois liberalization of 1981. Hu Qiaomu, the former political secretary to Mao and now the president of the Chinese Academy of Social Sciences, represented the concern among both Party elders and orthodox organic intellectuals. He remarked that "a wrong ideological trend [like that expressed in "Unrequited Love"] with a widespread social influence . . . will spread like an epidemic and will harm the spiritual health, stability and unity of the whole society" (cited in Goldman 1994:99–100). Huang Gang charged that Zhou Yang and Xia Yan were Bai Hua's "behind-the-scenes backers." Some of Zhou's former colleagues from the Yan'an era, such as Lin Mohan and He Jingzhi, also joined the denunciation of Bai and the move toward bourgeois liberalization (p. 100).

Other writers criticized in the campaign for deviance from the Party line included Sun Jingxuan, a Sichuan writer, who rejected the view of absolute obedience to the Party; Ye Wenfu, a writer, who called on the military and Party officials to reform and live up to their professed high ideals; Wang Ruowang, who wanted the Party to do more by doing less, a Daoist idea; and Liu Binyan who exposed the Party cadres' abuse of power (Goldman 1999:103–8). A division seemed to be developing between the critical and orthodox organic intellectuals. The former were supported by reform-oriented officials like Hu Yaobang, and the latter by Deng Xiaoping, who was reform-oriented in the economy but much less so in politics.

The same paths were later traveled by organic intellectuals in the years leading to the 1989 spring democracy movement. After the first round of campaigning against bourgeois liberalization, and with Hu Yaobang's support, critical organic intellectuals revived their call for greater autonomy in cultural and political activities. Li Honglin even suggested establishing other political parties to curb the autocratic rule. Zhou Yang called for giving writers' associations more autonomy to avoid alienating intellectuals from the Party and also to promote humanism. Again, alienation and humanism governed the debate. Wang Ruoshui of the *People's Daily* wrote articles defending socialist humanism, and Su Shaozhi again advocated a reinterpretation of Marxism. This led the Party in 1983 to campaign against "spiritual pollution," with Hu Qiaomu and Deng Liqun leading the charge. They were joined by Xing Bensi, the director of the Institute of Philosophy and a vice president of CASS, and by Wang Meng and Ding Ling.

The campaign succeeded, but only in some ways. The Party's hardliners were able to remove Wang Ruoshui from his job. Hu Jiwei, Ba Jin, Xia Yan, and Wang Ruowang were also publicly criticized. But rather than blunting it, this campaign only accelerated the critical organic intellectuals' drive toward reform. Faced with this irony, the playwright Wu Zuguang complained that the Party seemed to have forgotten its promise never to engage in campaigns again (Goldman 1994: 114–32). Meanwhile, more radical revisions of ideology and political procedures by critical organic intellectuals were on the way.

The most radical of the changes this time around was the democratic election of its own leaders by the Fourth Congress of the Chinese Writers Association in 1984. Those who were criticized in the previous campaigns—Ba Jin, Bai Hua, and Liu Binyan—were elected as chair (Ba) and vice-chair (Bai and Liu), whereas those who had criticized them, like Liu Baiyu and He Jingzhi, lost their positions as vice-chair (Goldman 1994:142–3). Although the change was not duplicated in other organizations, "demands for more autonomy and freedom in academic research, publication, and comment were heard from virtually all professional organizations" (p. 147). Demands for even steeper political and institutional reforms were raised. Hu Jiwei revived his efforts to draft a journalism law to protect journalists,[24] and Yan Jiaqi described the current political system as "a machine without a brake and [a machine that] cannot function properly (p. 173).

Thus in the mid- and late 1980s, we see these organic intellectuals of the Party transforming themselves from a critical group *inside* the system to one *outside* it. Indeed, the critically organic intellectuals still supported the Party and believed that the Party could transform itself. They had faith in the Hu and Deng leadership and believed that reforms would work. That is why most of them stayed away from the Democracy Wall movement, with few exceptions such as Ge Yang, the editor in chief of the journal *The New Observer,* and Wang Ruoshui, Yan Jiaqi, and Guo Luoji (Goldman 1994:47). While Bai Hua was criticized, he also received an award for a poem written in 1979 eulogizing the Party's new course after the Third Plenum of the eleventh Party Central Committee. He believed that the Party Central Committee and Hu Yaobang would finally help the writers overcome the obstacles on their way to more autonomy (pp. 94, 145). Ye Wenfu's criticism of the Party, like that of Liu Binyan's, was intended to help the Party to reform (p. 105). They wanted to improve the system, not to replace it. They criticized the shortcomings of the system, just as did some dissidents in the former Soviet Union, but they did not criticize the system itself.

As Wang Ruowang, one of the most vocal critics, said once, "We don't wish to eliminate Party leadership but to soundly change the Party's style of leadership" (Rubin 1987:237). Liu Binyan, too, viewed investigative journalists as "scouts" for the Party leadership, who would keep the Party leaders informed and keep them honest (Hamrin 1986: 288; Wagner 1987:197–203). Nor did the young intellectuals in their thirties and early forties see the need for a multiparty system (Hamrin 1987:302). Even the Party line proponents would say that those who wrote on alienation were their "own comrades" (Goldman 1994:125). Liu Binyan's characterization of Chen Shizong and Ni Yuxian in his reportage, *A Second Kind of Loyalty,* captures what intellectuals were doing at the time. Rather than blindly following the Party, they remonstrated with it so that it could transcend its flaws. "In the mid-1980s [Liu] still hoped that political reform would come from more enlightened Party leaders" (Goldman 1994:150). Like Hu Jiwei and others, he also advocated an independent judiciary and press to help the Party resolve its problems more effectively.

After repeated campaigns in the 1980s, however, they were not so sure that they could push for substantive reform while staying within the system. Wang Ruoshui's feelings expressed in a 1984 article may be typical of what his cohorts thought at the time: "I gradually discovered that reality was not as perfect and flawless as I imagined and that the new society had its maladies . . . I often had a feeling of oppressiveness" (Goldman 1994:129). Although he was talking about the Mao era, it certainly applies to the Deng era as well. It is true that most democratic elites did not advocate a multiparty system, believing that the internal reform in the Party would effect a systemic political change. But some of them began to envision intellectuals functioning as an interest group outside the system. One of them was Yang Baikui, who had run in the 1980 election in Beijing University and now worked in the Institute of Political Science of the CASS (p. 179).

In 1986, the small parties also began to assert themselves. They asked for a bigger role as checks and balances to the Party. They did not, however, want to function as opposition parties, as Fei Xiaotong said (Goldman 1994:180). This was the same request they had made in the Hundred Flowers Movement, and had much the same invisible effect. Liu Binyan, Wang Ruowang, and Fang Lizhi accelerated their criticism of the Party's lack of political reform. Fang totally rejected Marxism and socialism.[25] As vice-chancellor of the Chinese University of Science and Technology (Keda) in Anhui Province, he called on college students to take responsibility for their own rights and political future. Encouraged by Fang's words and frustrated by the slow pace of political reform, student demonstrations broke out in 1986 first in Keda and then in universities in Wuhan, Xi'an, Tianjin, Nanjing, Shanghai, and finally Beijing. They "called for more independent student unions and more control over student newspapers, in addition to more general demands for democracy, human rights, and freedom of the press" (pp. 191–203).

The 1986 year-end demonstrations prompted more suppression by the Party's hard-liners: Hu Yaobang was deposed from his powerful position as the Party's general secretary, and another round of campaigning against bourgeois liberalization began. Fang Lizhi, Liu Binyan, and Wang Ruowang were purged from the Party. Also asked to resign from the Party were Zhang Xianyang, a member of the Marxist-Leninist Institute; Su Shaozhi, director of the institute; Sun Changjiang, one of the writers of the "practice criterion" article; Wang Ruoshui, former deputy editor of the *People's Daily;* and Wu Zuguang, the outspoken playwright. Zhu Houze, the director of the Propaganda Department, was replaced by Deng Liqun's associate, Wang Renzhi. Writers who wrote novels that might have portrayed the Party in a dark light were also criticized, as in the case of Zhang Xianliang and Liu Xinwu. The "fifth-generation" movie directors who tried innovative styles and carried out symbolic criticism of the political system were criticized as well. Semi-independent papers, such as *Modern People's News (Xiandai ren bao)* in Guangzhou and *Society News (Shehui bao)* in Shanghai, were closed. The *World Economic Herald* came under pressure although it was spared the fate of its fellow journals (Goldman 1994:204–32).

However, those who were criticized in the campaign were not totally silenced. Fang, Liu, and Wang were able to publish their articles in one way or another, and they could give interviews to the foreign press. Fang and Liu could even travel abroad. Yan Jiaqi continued to advocate democratic reform. Su Shaozhi was busy guiding graduate students and writing articles for newspapers and journals. Most importantly, this group began to question whether enlightened leaders like Zhao Ziyang, who replaced Hu but also was in favor of more political transparency, and Deng could solve China's problems. The *World Economic Herald,* started by Qin Benli as an unofficial newspaper, in 1988 became a major forum for a discussion of democracy. Cao Siyuan, the head of a think tank established by China's largest computer company, Stone Group, also advocated democratic procedures to guarantee people's freedom of speech. Chen Ziming, the head of another nongovernmental think tank, was able to survey the deputies of the National People's Congress on their views on democracy (Goldman 1994:238–55). The new campaign against bourgeois liberalization thus only led to more dissatisfaction and more distance between the Party and the critical intellectuals still in the system, thus accelerating the transformation of the group.

Independent Activities of Critical (Organic) Intellectuals

The critical intellectuals' views may be best summarized in the documentary TV series *River Elegy* (1988), which, after reviewing China's past, expressed a sense of concern and anxiety over the present through the voices of experts and scholars. The only way, it said, to avoid the tragedies of the past was to modernize the country's politics, economy, culture, and ideology. This was the fifth modernization, once advocated by Wei Jingsheng during the Democracy Wall movement at the end of the 1970s. The only difference was that this time the speakers were professors, writers, and other professionals who had experienced ten more years of distress and frustration. They had had ten more years to think, and to understand the problem: the traditional culture and its resistance to Western civilization. The following paragraph may well represent the theme of the TV series:

> The Confucian culture may have given us various kinds of ancient and perfect "treasures" but it has failed to produce a kind of national aggressiveness, the legal system, and the mechanism that can help our culture rejuvenate itself. On the contrary, as it declines, it has left us an awesome suicidal mechanism that has destroyed the nation's own quintessence, killed its own life-promising elements, and throttled generation after generation of its best people. . . . Only when the blue sea wind [Western civilization] has changed into rain water and moistened this yellow and dry land, can [the vitality it brings] which only bursts out in spring festivals be able to make the massive yellow plateau regain its vigor and life. (Su Xiaokang and Wang Luxiang 1988:104)

Su Shaozhi, after being purged by the Party, again condemned its campaigns against spiritual pollution and bourgeois liberalization, charging that intellectuals like Li Shu, a historian, Yu Guanyuan, an economist, and Wang Ruoshui suffered unfair treatment. Hu Jiwei and Yu Guangyuan (1989) edited a collection of essays, entitled *The Moment of Awakening,* as part of the "Democratic Studies" series. The democratic elite had a series of symposia and continued to write articles discussing human rights, political reform, and freedom of the press. Small parties again wanted more power. Deng Weizhi, a vice-chair of the Association for the Promotion of Democracy criticized one-party dominance in Chinese politics. Others talked about small parties' independence from the CCP.

The debate on political reform finally centered on two views: those who were in favor of a pluralistic political system, and those who were in favor of a new authoritarianism, which was the current system. The latter views were represented by Wu Jiaxiang, a researcher in the General Office of the Central Committee, and Xiao Gongqin, a history professor at Shanghai Normal University. They believed that an authoritarian state was better able to enforce the economic reform that was needed in China. And the market in turn would produce a middle class in favor of democracy. Understandably, Zhao and Deng supported this view: that was what they thought they were doing anyway. But the democratic elite were vehemently opposed to it, believing that an enlightened authoritarian leader would either turn into a despot or be overthrown by the entrenched bureaucracy (Goldman 1994:263–82; X. L. Ding 1994:174–90). This debate seems to have further pushed one group of intellectuals into critical confrontation with the regime and the other group into a compromising alliance with the Party.

The confrontation accelerated when intellectuals organized various activities to push for their agenda. Wang Yuanhua, the scholar and former director of the Propaganda Department of the Shanghai Party Committee, established a nonofficial journal, *New Enlightenment*. Critical intellectuals, in or outside the system, also organized a series of seminars without Party authorization to discuss political modernization. Salons outside Party control had become a common sight in universities, institutes, and cities all over China, and they became refuges where intellectuals could debate political matters.

In the beginning of 1989, intellectuals took more specific actions. Fang Lizhi first wrote to Deng Xiaoping calling for Wei Jingsheng's release, which was China's equivalent of the Dreyfus case. Then three petitions were signed by intellectuals from various fields, started respectively by Bei Dao, an obscure poet; Xu Liangying, a physicist from CASS; and Dai Qing, a *Guangming Daily* journalist. The signers include not only many members of the democratic elite, such as Yan Jiaqi, Su Shaozhi, and Wang Ruoshui, but also well-known writers such as Su Wei and scientists like Wang Gangchang. Some cultural intellectuals who were never interested in politics also put their names on it. They demanded not only the release of political prisoners, but also the basic rights of citizens supported by political reform. University students also organized salons and invited intellectuals to come and make speeches on those issues as well as issues concerning educational reform: raising the salaries of professors and investing more in education (see Goldman 1994:284–95; Link 1992:260–1; Edward X. Gu 1999:424).[26]

The situation was now ripe for a major storm, which would occur when Hu Yaobang died on April 15, 1989 (Goldman 1994:284–301). At the same time, many of the critical organic intellectuals finally jolted themselves out of the system, both by outside forces and by their own volition. The ranks of the independent critical intellectuals swelled. We will discuss the June 4 massacre and its impact in chapter 3.

This independence movement, however, involved still only a limited number of mostly humanistic intellectuals. The technical intellectuals were more likely to be bureaucratized, bourgeoisified, and professionalized. They might be interested in the cause of the humanistic intellectuals; for example, one of the petitions of 1989 was signed mainly by well-known scientists. But the majority of technical intellectuals appeared to have little interest in these movements, either because they did not want to jeopardize their political and economic status or simply from a lack of organization. In addition, relatively few humanistic intellectuals participated; the petitioners were for the most part well-known writers, journalists, and scientists. Those who participated, both humanistic and technical intellectuals, were exceptional. We will now look at what happened to the majority of them.

Bureaucratized Intellectuals: A Different Kind of Organic Intellectual

As we have already noted, in December 1978, after many years of Maoist revolution and its consequent economic stagnation, the Party decided to focus on economic development. In the ensuing decade, the country went through massive and unprecedented economic restructuring and growth. Among some leading indicators: by 1988, the average per capita income of urban residents had shot up 3.5-fold (from 316 yuan in 1978 to 1,119 yuan, with about eight yuan equal to one U.S. dollar) and per capita peasant income had quadrupled (from 134 yuan to 545 yuan). Over the same decade, foreign trade also expanded fourfold, from U.S. $20.6 billion to $80.5 billion (Fewsmith 1994:3). Such unimaginable growth was made possible through a series of fundamental economic reforms on a scale never before seen in socialist states.

First, the "responsibility system" in the rural areas dismantled the communes. Peasants were now becoming independent farmers. They were allowed to specialize, diversify, hire their neighbors in either agricultural or small-scale industrial production, and produce food at market prices for urbanites. Second, in the urban areas, the Party decentralized control over China's 390,000 state-owned enterprises by granting them a high degree of self-management. They could, for example, retain profits for reinvestment or to hand out as bonuses.

But these sensible policies alone could not go far to increase agricultural and industrial production. Greater mechanization and technical skills were needed for rural development, while expert knowledge in management became more important in urban development (McCord and McCord 1986:209–11). These scientific and technological skills could only be provided by intellectuals. But first the Party had to loosen the ropes that had hog-tied them during the Mao era. And it did. As Simon (1987:130) points out, "the leadership in Beijing recognizes that, without an adequate pool of qualified [scientific and technical] intellectuals and more strategic placement of these individuals, the country's goal of closing the economic and technological gap between itself and the West will be largely unattainable."

So intellectuals were rehabilitated. Wronged during the Anti-Rightist period that followed the Hundred Flowers Movement, hideously mistreated during the Cultural Revolution, they were now, said the Party, part of the working class. Record numbers of intellectuals, mainly technical experts, found themselves promoted to bureaucratic positions in universities, research institutes, hospitals, and industrial enterprises (Simon 1987:141–2). Think tanks came to play an important part in the formation, development, and propagation of new, reformist rural as well as urban policies. The Chinese Rural Development Group was one example. It was founded by former educated youths such as Chen Yizi, He Weiling, and Deng Yingtao, but was supported by Deng Liqun, who was the deputy head of CASS and the head of the Party's Policy Research Office (Edward X. Gu 1999:407; Fewsmith 1994:34–7). We might call this incorporation of intellectuals into the Party apparatus as a 'bureaucratization' process.

These changes, however, were *déjà vu*. Already in the early 1950s, the Party had tried technical organization, introducing into industry a scientific system of management. As Schurmann points out, men were placed in positions because of their knowledge and skills (1968:231–3). Then came the Great Leap Forward of 1958. Partly scared by the potential for subversiveness as demonstrated in the 1957 Hundred Flowers Movement, the Party reversed its policy of relying on intellectuals. Instead, it introduced human organization, this time relying on ordinary workers. People worked very hard, but without the skills of the technicians, the country was met with one of its biggest failures in both agriculture and industry. Thus, what we witnessed in the early 1980s was a second effort to bureaucratize intellectuals, especially technical intellectuals, and to incorporate them into the state apparatus for economic purposes. This would create a large body of organic intellectuals with a technical background.

Bourgeoisified and Professionalized Intellectuals: A Renewed and Unattached Breed

Meanwhile, economic privatization had begun. Intellectuals were actually allowed to resign from their state-controlled jobs and look for new ones (Simon 1987:152). Beginning in 1982, scientists and technical personnel could hire themselves out usually on a part-time basis or even for a fee for service (p. 142; White III 1986:222). According to one estimate, by 1988 about 15 percent of the ten million academics and professionals had taken up second jobs full-time or part-time (Anita Chan 1991:110). Many were retained as advisors or instructors in work units in scientific research, teaching, public health, and industrial and agricultural production. They could even, if they so wished and had the capability, start their own businesses. They were also allowed to commercialize their scientific and technological knowledge and expertise. This they did in various ways, from selling patents to providing consulting services. For the first time, they no longer had to share their earnings with the work unit, as had been the case at the beginning of the reform. This we might term as a *bourgeoisification* process.

Furthermore, from 1977 on, the higher education entrance examinations were restored and graduate programs were established in various universities. Degrees such as bachelor's, master's, and even doctoral were awarded, and all intellectuals, outside or inside universities, acquired formal classification titles such as physician, engineer, professor, researcher, and technician. A new system of education and credentialing had been established, and the *professionalization* process had begun (Simon 1987:152; White III 1986:219). Upon graduation, students were beginning to be able to choose where they worked. They could follow their preferences into the public sector, private sector, or into joint ventures, instead of being allocated a job somewhere where they might not want to go.

One area of the intellectual complex that benefited from the economic and educational reforms was the legal profession. As Feinerman (1987:113) commented, "the Chinese officials negotiating with businessmen from developed countries—accompanied in almost every meeting by legal advisors—would have felt themselves at a disadvantage without their own legal counsel." With the growth of international transactions, China needed more lawyers. Lawyers were needed, too, when the Party and the government wanted to put on a more legitimate appearance: an accused criminal had the right to representation by counsel. Although political criminals were another story (pp. 114–5), it now became possible for those accused of nonpolitical crimes to be represented in court. And this necessitated the expansion of the profession. A third development that gave further impetus to the growth of the profession was the reordering of the economic structure. "The reliance upon contracts, governed by recently promulgated law, has required that Chinese peasants and other individuals seek the assistance of lawyers and notaries in the drafting and execution of contracts, among state enterprises and between state entities and collectives" (p. 115). The legal profession was beginning to be established.[27]

Thus, we see intellectuals, particularly technical intellectuals, beginning to be *bourgeoisified* and *professionalized* on a massive scale. They might have to serve the interests of the economic powers, but at least they were moving away from the rigid ideological bonding they had suffered in the Maoist years. Now there was, at least, the possibility for intellectuals to be detached from the ruling Party. We will treat both the bourgeoisified and professionalized intellectuals as unattached intellectuals, meaning unattached to the Party, not in the way organic intellectuals are attached.

Conclusions

The main characteristic of the Mao era is its political uniformity, which was achieved by the various thought reform movements, including the antirightist movement and the Cultural Revolution. Although one might say that the state co-opted intellectuals, both technical and humanistic alike, the fact is, intellectuals, as we have seen, *wanted* to be co-opted.

The co-optation was thus mutual. Unattached intellectuals were almost nonexistent. The Party was able to build one of the strongest political and organizational controls in the two millennia (Israel 1986:xi). The honeymoon, however, did not last long, as is always true of honeymoons between intellectuals and the powers. As Wang Shiwei and Ding Ling found during the Yan'an period, organic intellectuals in the Mao era found that they had made too huge a compromise in their professionalism and conscience. Thus, they began to air their criticisms, which culminated in the Hundred Flowers Movement. More intellectuals began to criticize the Party for its dogmatism and dictatorship. Most of the criticisms, however, as we have seen, were still loyal oppositions. But since Mao's ideal revolution would not tolerate even the mildest challenges, suppression ensued. Nonetheless, intellectuals continued their loyal opposition, which led to their further persecution during the Cultural Revolution. This aggravated the frustration and alienation of intellectuals. A few critical intellectuals outside the system openly challenged Mao and his Cultural Revolution, in both the Hundred Flowers Movement and the Cultural Revolution, but they met swift punishment, imprisonment, and even execution.

Thus in the Mao era, a high degree of political uniformity was the order of the day, at least on the surface, with few daring to challenge Mao and the Party. Critical intellectuals existed mainly as loyal opposition, the second kind of loyalty, as Liu Binyan described it.

The first period of the Deng era, however, saw the fragmentation of intellectual politics, following the Party's need to shift its focus from class struggle to economic construction. First, more educated youths outside the system began to question the system. Second, the critical wing of the organic intellectuals began to reinterpret Marxism and to call for democratic reforms; exercising an ethic of responsibility, the concept we have explored in chapter 1, these intellectuals were able to help reform from the inside. Third, the orthodox wing of the organic intellectuals countered by adhering to the four cardinal principles and, with the help of Deng Xiaoping and the other octogenarian leaders, checked the democratic elite whenever they could. Fourth, while the two groups of organic intellectuals seemed to have parted ways, record numbers of intellectuals were promoted to leadership positions and became a new kind of organic intellectual, working to further economic reform.

Fifth, at the same time, unattached intellectuals were looking for their niche in the market economy. Whether bourgeoisified or professionalized, they were beginning to be detached from the Party apparatus. To be sure, most intellectuals, especially legal workers, still worked for the government. The law at that time still required legal workers to first and foremost preserve the interests of the socialist state (see also Feinerman 1987:118). But they also began to work for corporations. It is true that most high-level intellectuals—academics, writers, artists, doctors, scientists, engineers, lawyers, economists, and journalists—were still part of the official establishment even though they had not directly staffed the Party bureaucracy. While almost all of the institutions they worked in were controlled by the government (Goldman and Cheek 1987:2), the fact is that more and more intellectuals began to move away from state control of their livelihood. It should be noted that the state welcomed the trend that lightened its own burden.

In both the Mao era and the first period of the Deng era, we have observed organic intellectuals' dual or split personalities. Zhang Guangnian has always felt that the physical illness that killed Zhou Yang had much to do with his "alienated personality" (Zhang Guangnian and Li Hui, 1995:50). Intellectuals were torn between the commitment to the state and the commitment to their own interpretation of the ruling orthodoxy, between Marxism-Leninism-Mao Zedong Thought (Goldman and Cheek 1987:7) and their commitment to their own consciences. Thus, they were constantly faced with the dilemma of having to conform but wanting to criticize.[28]

The conflict would only lead to more fragmentation among organic intellectuals. They would either become more critical, retreat into other endeavors and become unattached intellectuals, or adhere to the Party orthodoxy, whatever that was at the time. Indeed, some critical organic intellectuals have later become independent critical intellectuals detached entirely from the Party apparatus. In X. L. Ding's (1994:43) words, "there was a consistent and remarkable growth in the collective self-consciousness of Chinese intellectuals as a politically awakened, independent social stratum with a unique role and responsibility." Others have left the public sector to work for corporations or to start their own businesses, or simply become professionals. Still others have stayed in the system, and more have become bureaucratized; the Party has certainly not been short of organic intellectuals. The re-formation of the intellectual complex along the same lines has accelerated since the June 4 massacre in 1989 and the rapid growth of the market economy after 1992, which we will discuss in chapter 3. What we have witnessed and will continue to witness is a return to the intellectual formation before "liberation," when organic, critical, and unattached-professional intellectuals each began to establish themselves in society. Thus, intellectuals as a whole were becoming fragmented.

Chapter Three

Critical Intellectuals

The army may be deprived of its general
but a man cannot be deprived of his spirit.
(Sanjun ke duo shuai ye, pifu bu ke duo zhi ye.)
—Confucius, *Analects* 9:26[1]

The tragic crackdown on the democracy movement in 1989 ended the first period of the Deng era and ushered in the second. In the 1990s, more and more intellectuals became politically alienated from the Party, and that alienation helped produce a number of independent cultural and critical movements. This period also saw an even more vigorous economic campaign by the government, starting in 1992, accompanied by even greater bureaucratization and professionalization of intellectuals. After further fragmentation and reorganization, various groups of intellectuals decided to backtrack, to consolidate their diverse orientations, and to continue their U-turn back to where they had started in the Republican era. In chapters 3–5, we discuss this process of fragmentation, reorganization, and consolidation of the political roles of critical, professional, and organic intellectuals. The second period of the Deng era ended when Deng died in 1997 and the Jiang Zemin era began thereafter. But Jiang still largely followed Deng's policies, both politically and economically. "The Jiang Zemin era" is not, therefore, essentially different from its predecessor.[2] Chapter 3–5 cover both of these eras.

In this chapter, we first discuss the social environment in the 1990s and beyond. We then examine where critical intellectuals stood in the debates on such great social issues as the humanist spirit, postmodernism, nationalism, democracy, and the direction of the economic and political reform. We show how the critical tradition has continued up to the present day, and how intellectuals have developed their independent critical stance as well as the group movements.

The Social Environment after 1989

The years following the June 4 massacre in 1989 saw, on one hand, the tightening of political control, especially concerning organized opposition to the Party's leadership, including Falun Gong, and on the other hand, the liberalization of the economy. These changes have created a political environment that is confusing and contradictory in many ways. But despite the Party's strong control over opposition parties, there are still many signs of political, social, and cultural relaxation (see also Perry and Selden 2000:6). By way of example, we will discuss the crackdown on the 1989 democracy movement, the rapidly changing political economy, and how both have affected the public space available for the development of the critical movements.

The Crackdown of 1989 and Its Impact on Intellectuals

As we discussed in chapter 2, the 1980s had seen the emergence of independent critical intellectuals; the division of organic intellectuals into the orthodox, the critical, and the bureaucratized; and the rise of a group of bourgeoisified and professional intellectuals who were unattached to the Party. They all shared one concern, political reform. Orthodox organic intellectuals like Deng Liqun and Hu Qiaomu were concerned about the Party losing its power; critical intellectuals were frustrated by the Party's campaigns to purge its critics, and were disappointed at the lack of democratic reform. The bourgeoisified and professional intellectuals, on the other hand, although also concerned, were afraid of losing their newfound power, political or professional, and the freedom to engage in private practice. Meanwhile, corruption continued to be rampant, and the Party did not seem to have an effective way to deal with it. Thus, the 1980s were full of anxiety and uncertainty on the part of intellectuals. It was at this moment that the 1989 democracy movement broke out, precipitated by Hu Yaobang's death that year.

As general secretary of the Party, Hu was most remembered as an enlightened leader, open to new ideas and willing to engage in political reform. In the 1980s, he promoted emancipation of mind, as well as the rehabilitation of Party cadres and intellectuals wronged during the Hundred Flowers Movement and the Cultural Revolution. He also effectively checked the campaigns against intellectuals, which were started by the Party elders and supported by the orthodox organic intellectuals. He was deposed in 1987 because of his sympathy toward the student movements at the end of 1986.

Thus, when Hu Yaobang died on April 15, 1989, intellectuals and students started a series of activities to mourn him and to call for the restoration of his name. These activities, which the Party termed as "anti-Party," soon evolved into demonstrations that quickly spread to other big cities all over China. It was much like the April 4 movement in 1976, when intellectuals wanted to restore Zhou Enlai's name while expressing their own anxiety over conditions at the time. In the 1989 demonstrations, students called for freedom of the press, the rule of law, direct elections, and extension of human rights (see Goldman 1994:305). Newspapers and journals such as *The World Economic Herald, The Science and Technology Daily,* and *The New Observer* published extensive and positive reports on these demonstrations. Other newspapers followed their line, including even the *People's Daily.* Journalists staged their own demonstrations calling for political reform. Entrepreneurs, insecure at best, supported the demonstrations because they wanted a democratic government that would be more stable (p. 315).

When rumors spread that the Party was going to use the military to suppress the demonstrators, intellectuals of all stripes signed petitions asking the Party to enter into a dialogue with the students and to avoid a military crackdown. When the crackdown was obviously imminent, intellectuals sought to persuade the students to withdraw from Tiananmen Square. However, as Goldman (1994:346) observes, by mid–May, the movement had already taken on a dynamic of its own. Nobody seemed to have much influence on where it would go (see also Saich 1990:ix).[3]

The unwillingness to compromise on the part of both the very young and the very old finally led to the bloody crackdown on June 4, 1989, when over a thousand were believed to have been killed by the People's Liberation Army (PLA) as they moved through the streets of Beijing onto Tiananmen Square. As part of the crackdown, some intellectuals were imprisoned, including Wang Juntao and Chen Ziming, democracy activists; Bao Tong, Zhao Ziyang's political secretary; and Dai Qing, the reporter, along with student leaders like Wang Dan and Liu Gang. Others escaped the country, including Yan Jiaqi; Su Shaozhi, part of the democratic elite, or the former critical organic intellectuals; Wan Runnan, the intellectual-turned-entrepreneur; and Su Xiaokang and Yuan Zhiming, two of the writers of *River Elegy.* Newspapers were purged of all those who sympathized with the demonstration. Intellectuals and students were asked to report to the Party their detailed whereabouts in those days; self-criticism and criticism of others was also required. Students in large universities were even subjected to a period of military training.

The ironfisted crackdown of 1989 has made China's intellectuals rethink and reshape their ties with the state. Many of the democratic elite who have escaped or exiled themselves from the country have become dissidents outside the system, joining the existing dissident movements overseas. They have organized alternative parties as a way to effect change in China from outside the country. Inside China, it has become almost impossible to advocate radical political reforms as critical intellectuals did before the June 4 crackdown, and the organization of opposition parties has met with constant repression.

While the critical (organic) intellectuals were suppressed or exiled, the orthodox organic intellectuals from the Yan'an era, such as Deng Liqun, Hu Qiaomu, Liu Baiyu, Lin Mohan, and Chen Yong, now took center stage immediately after the crackdown in 1989, helping the Party in another round of ideological remolding. Following the Party line, they again emphasized loyalty to the Party and patriotism to the Party-state, and criticized Western political culture (Goldman 1994: 329–32). This Old Left, however, fell out of favor after 1992 when Deng Xiaoping pushed for more vigorous economic reform. Along with the New Left, they have since become critical of both the liberal intellectuals and the Party for their capitalist economic reform. Meanwhile, the advocates of new authoritarianism have continued to call for a strong central government. They are now called "neoconservatives." As we will see later, however, their intellectual stance is still different from that of the Party's. Other critical intellectual trends include the debate over the humanist spirit and nationalism, as well as the postmodern critique.

One of the legacies of the June 4 crackdown is that "[t]he Party is no longer seen as the state representing all the people but simply as a political organization representing the particular interests of its members" (Brook 1992:209). It is time that each group looked out for its own interests. Following the leadership of Ba Jin (1987) and Hu Jiwei, Yu Guangyuan et al. (1989), and having taken a hard look at their relationship with the state,[4] critical intellectuals have begun to forge new ties with it and to find their own niches under the new circumstances. In the process, they seem to be evolving into various independent forces of and for themselves, either through the democracy movement or through other kinds of criticism. Organic intellectuals have also gone through their own fragmentation and reorganization. We will now discuss the second change in the social environment that has affected the intellectual politics. (For the post-Communist confession of Central European intellectuals, a similar reflection movement, see Eyal, Szelenyi, and Townsley 1998:107–12).

The Rapidly Changing Political Economy

After a temporary halt of about three years following the June 4 massacre, economic and social development picked up speed. Deng visited southern China in 1992 and assured the nation that he intended to continue with the economic reforms. These changes further prompted intellectuals to rethink their roles in society. While some have become more critical of the consequences of China's modernity, others have remained bureaucratized, bourgeoisified, and professionalized. Moneymaking has become a primary concern for many of them, which probably indicates a clear change in intellectual values. More and more intellectuals have simply become unattached, a trend that was impossible in the Mao era but that flourished in the 1980s and the 1990s. We will now further examine these macro-politico-economic developments in the 1990s, so that we can better understand the circumstances under which groups of intellectuals developed their new political roles.

One of the earlier summaries of the politico-economic changes in the first half of the 1990s is attributed to Deng Liqun, spokesperson for the orthodox organic intellectuals.[5] In one of his famous "ten-thousand character" articles (a nickname given to petitions to authorities), this one entitled "Several Factors Endangering Our National Security" (1996),[6] Deng summarizes these changes: in *economic ownership, class structure, social ideology,* and in *the Party.* We will look at them separately in this section. We will also see how intellectuals have involved themselves in these changes.

In terms of the changing *economic ownership,* Deng Liqun reports that from 1980 to 1994, the output of state-owned enterprises (SOEs) dropped from 76% to 48.3% of the national total.[7] At the same time, the output of private enterprise increased from 0.5% to 13.5%, and the output of collective enterprises (some of which were in fact private) increased from 23% to 38.2%. Yang Fan (1995) notes that the nonstate economy, meaning both private and collective, had already risen to close to 60% of the total industrial output. The private sector was growing at a surprising pace. By 1997, state-owned enterprises constituted a mere 26.5% of the industrial total (Deng Liqun 1998:6).[8] By 1998, township and village enterprises (TVEs) had shown remarkable increases, alone accounting for 60% of China's GNP (Christoffersen 1998:115; *Los Angeles Times,* June 7, 1998, Section D).[9]

Closely related to the privatization of economy was the change in *class structure.*[10] A new bourgeoisie had developed, and in size had already surpassed that of the national bourgeoisie when the People's Republic was founded in 1949 (Deng Liqun 1996). The increase had been remarkably rapid. In 1991, there were only 107,800 private enterprises with a workforce of 1.8 million, a modest increase of 9.9% and 8%, respectively over the previous year (Zhu Guanglei 1994: 339). By the end of 1994, notes the Research Group on Private Enterprises in China (1996), there were 430,000 private enterprises with about 5.6 million employees. By June 1995, according to Lu Jianhua (1996), the country had established 560,000 private enterprises employing 8.2 million workers. This steady rise was in addition to an increase, by 1995, in individual business entrepreneurs and households to 22.39 million, with a workforce of 39.58 million. The rise of the new bourgeoisie was accompanied by an increase in hired labor. By 1998, over 100 million workers had been hired by private enterprise (Deng Liqun 1998:3). By 2001, according to anther estimate, 1.6 million private businesses had already employed about 10% of China's 1.3 billion people (Ching-Ching Ni 2001).[11]

As might be expected, this increase in private ownership had opened up a vast gap between the rich and the poor. While the new entrepreneurs could now spend lavishly on food and clothing, 80 million people in the countryside and 12 million people in the cities remained mired in absolute poverty (Li Pingshe 1994). In 1994 the poorest 20% of households accounted for only 4.27% of the country's income, while the richest 20% accounted for 50.24%. This gap surpassed that of the United

States, where according to 1990 figures, 20% of the poorest and 20% of the richest households accounted for 4.6% and 44.3% of the national income, respectively (Deng Liqun 1998:7; He Qinglian 1995).

What interests us here is that a significant portion of this new bourgeoisie consisted of former intellectuals. Table 3.1, comparing figures for 1993 and 1995, shows the percentages of private entrepreneurs with various levels of schooling.

If we accept the conventional definition of intellectuals as those who have had at least a vocational school education, table 3.1 shows that in 1995, 27.7% of private entrepreneurs were former intellectuals. The last two categories increased slightly from 1993 to 1995. Nonetheless, the trend was steady, and a significant number of intellectuals had joined the new capitalist class. Note that we have not even counted the organic intellectuals who serve the private entrepreneurs, that is, their managers, engineers, attorneys, accountants, and public relations specialists. Once we include this group, we see a much larger number of intellectuals becoming part of the new bourgeoisie, although not necessarily part of the capitalist class.

More important, the aggressive new economic powers were starting to demand more representation in the political process. As one of them said,

> The reform in the political system will develop along with the development of the private economy and the enlargement of the private entrepreneurial ranks. A large number of private entrepreneurs will enter government positions at all levels. They can no longer be treated as part of the political rubber stamp in the National People's Congress or the Chinese People's Political Consultative Conference. (quoted in Deng Liqun 1996:41)

In some places, private entrepreneurs selected their own candidates to compete in local elections. In one place in Hebei Province, 21.3% of the

Table 3.1 Percent of Private Entrepreneurs with Different Levels of Schooling

	No Schooling	Primary School	Junior High	High School	Vocational Schools	Colleges and Universities	Graduate School
'93	1.0	9.9	36.1	26.3	9.6	16.6	0.6
'95	0.3	8.2	34.9	28.9	9.3	17.6	0.8

Source: Research Group on Private Enterprise in China. 1996. "1995 Chinese Private Enterprise Research," p. 203. See also Margaret M. Pearson. 1997. *China's New Business Elite*, p. 18.

local entrepreneurs had entered local government. They had also organized their own associations, journals, and newspapers. Deng Liqun (1996) noted that it would not be long before they demanded the right to establish their own political parties in competition with the Communist Party of China![12]

The third change was in *ideology.* On the one hand, as Deng Liqun (1996) observes, many advocated replacing today's socialist market economy with a modern capitalist market economy. They declared that the Party's sixty years of history had been dominated by leftist tragedies. Marxism, they said, is utopian; it should be replaced by postmodernism and popular culture. It was a continuation of the trend in the 1980s toward a multiparty and parliamentary political system.

On the other hand, according to Li Xiaojiang (1996), who is one of China's best-known scholars in women's studies, one important trend in the 1990s was actually the "de-ideologization" of people's thinking. This, we may assume, arose partly out of the high-handed suppression at the end of the 1980s. Rather than arguing ineffectually for a democratic movement, most intellectuals had turned to projects that were more doable and less ideological. Several cultural "crazes" characterize this trend: the revival of national learning *(guo xue);* the fever over Mao; the flap over the culture of the three graduating classes in the Cultural Revolution *(lao san jie);*[13] and the emotions raised by the culture of overseas students, by humanism, by the new commercial culture, and by nationalism. For all the heated discussion they now raised, these events no longer carried the heavy ideological freight that cultural events did before the 1989 democracy movement.

These changes came at a moment when the government was pushing in two opposite directions. Pressure against democratic activity was high after the June 4 crackdown. But the demand for a more vigorous market economy sprang up quickly after Deng's visit to the southern provinces. These two counterpressures left intellectuals at a loss in the early 1990s. They had been at the center of attention in all of the cultural and political upheavals of the 1980s: the movement against bourgeois spiritual pollution, "cultural fever," and the 1989 democracy movement. In the beginning of the 1990s, intellectuals suddenly felt that they were no longer relevant:

> Modernization is something that intellectuals have long dreamed of. But now when it shows up at their door as something real, they find it not as

> beautiful as they had expected. Along with the development of the economy and the secularization of society, morality has deteriorated, the intellectuals' ultimate concern is lost, and humanistic thinking arouses little attention. (Xu Jilin 1997b:5)

The traditional Marxist ideology had lost much of its appeal, and modern capitalist ways of thinking and doing seemed too far from what they had imagined. Intellectuals, especially humanistic intellectuals, were faced with the challenge of finding a place for their own discourse in a changing world. The various cultural crazes we have just mentioned were examples of those efforts. Indeed, some of those crazes are still alive, and are likely to last well into the twenty-first century. They will help us understand and redefine who intellectuals are and what they do.

Thus, on the one hand there are fewer and fewer ardent capitalist or socialist ideologues, and under Deng Xiaoping's influence, pragmatism is in full swing. On the other hand, intellectuals are still pursuing various beliefs, including humanism, liberalism, conservatism, nationalism, and postmodernism, as we mentioned earlier.

Finally, the *Party* itself had changed in the 1990s, as Deng Liqun (1996) remarks. It was no longer an iron fist controlling everything under the sun. It was fast becoming a decaying organization (Goldstein 1994:723, 730). In Deng's words, it had become blind and deaf in many places, unaware of the suffering of the millions of workers and peasants who lived in poverty. Some Party members had become a new bourgeoisie, and others had begun to believe in a peaceful transition to total capitalism. Furthermore, the corruption of Party cadres had become worse and worse. In 1993, 6,790 cases of embezzlement and bribery exceeding 10,000 yuan (with about eight yuan equal to one U.S. dollar)[14] were prosecuted, an increase of 210% over the previous year. There were also 1,748 cases of illegal use of public funds totaling over 50,000 yuan per case, an increase of 270%.[15]

Indeed, according to Wei Jianxing (1996:2), one of the highest officials in charge of fighting corruption both in the Party and the government,

> From January to November 1995, "commissions for disciplinary inspections" at various levels filed 122,476 cases of corruption, an increase of 5.1% from the same time last year; cases involving cadres higher than the county level numbered 4813, an increase of 6.5%; 102,317 cadres were disciplined, an increase of 7.5%. Among these, 3084 were cadres at the county level, 279 were cadres of the prefecture,

> and 24 were provincial level cadres, representing an increase of 29.2%, 43.8%, and 166.7% respectively."

In the same article, Wei reports that by October 1995, 1,760,000 enterprises and agencies had been involved in self-examination of their own financial accounts and another 210,000 were checked. Investigators found that 4 billion yuan had been illegally accumulated, 1.3 billion of which should have been turned over to the state government.

Other kinds of corruption among Party cadres included flagrant uses of public money for private purposes: to embezzle for education or flood relief, to buy cars for themselves, to hold lavish feasts, and to indulge in recreational travel at home and overseas. At the same time we see a consistent failure to pay teachers' salaries, production of fake and defective goods, indifference to the kidnapping and selling of women, persistent damage to the environment and depletion of natural resources, and so forth (Xie Xiaoqing 1995). And all this is undoubtedly only the tip of the iceberg.

As a result of this corruption, which parallels or sometimes exceeds that of the Guomindang (GMD) before 1949, the popular support the Chinese Communist Party (CCP) enjoyed during the revolutionary years, which was based on its appeal to equality, began abating fast in the 1990s. As Cheek and Lindau (1998:8, 23, 29) point out, the noncharismatic and wounded party now resembles Mexico's Institutional Revolutionary Party (PRI), that is, before it was voted out of the ruling party position in 2000.[16] Losing an ideological core, the CCP is becoming more a form of state corporatism than a state-party, or an *iron fist* in Deng Liqun's words. Many Party members became cadre-capitalists, and private entrepreneurs are joining the Party to strengthen its bourgeois side. Together they may form what Cheek (1998:235, 242) calls a new "socialist corporate" elite.[17] Cheek and Lindau predicted that the PRIs today could very well be the CCPs tomorrow.[18] Indeed, unless it starts to play modern and democratic politics, the CCP will find it more and more difficult to survive. And the PRI model before 2000 does not help in the long run. To remedy the CCP's woes, the elections being held at the local level in the villages are a good place to start.[19] The increasing role of the National People's Congress (NPC) in legislation and rule-making is another important step, despite the CCP's continued control over its agenda (see Potter 1998). Once the CCP has mounted the tiger of legal reform, it will be difficult to dismount it *(qi hu nan xia),* as Potter (1994a) earlier pointed out.

Faced with all of these changes in the political economy—the increasing privatization of economic ownership; further social stratification, with a widening gap between the rich and the poor; de-ideologization; and greater and greater corruption of the Party—many intellectuals have opted to "plunge into the sea" of commerce and to join the new bourgeoisie. Others, however, have begun to ponder the consequences of modernity and the solutions to its problems. Still others have continued to advocate bourgeois democracy. Let us now examine the more microsociopolitical environment in which critical intellectuals have operated since 1989.

The Public Space Available to Critical Intellectuals

The existence of critical intellectuals requires a certain degree of freedom of expression. As Sheldon Hsiao-peng Lu (1997:74) phrases it, "[Is] there any room for a relatively independent, critical space for the debate and dissemination of social and cultural issues?" In the Mao era, it was almost impossible for independent critical intellectuals to exist. In the first period of Deng, critical (organic) intellectuals met with constant suppression but they also experienced occasional freedom: letting go *(fang)* and tightening up *(shou)* alternated (Baum 1994:5–9). What has it been like since then, especially with the further development of the market economy since 1992? Understanding the extent to which intellectuals dare to be publicly critical will help us to appreciate how much they have or have not been able to achieve in their critical discourse.

Brook's (1993) discussion on the late-Ming gentry as a society inhabiting the public sphere is very illuminating. The public sphere, according to Habermas ([1990] 1999), was formed in Europe as the abstract counterpart of public authority (see also Brook 1993).[20] Here the bourgeoisie developed a critical awareness of, and a conscious resistance to, state interference. In late-Ming gentry society, commerce grew and private markets emerged, as was also happening in Europe. And "the core dynamic of the public sphere—*private* people relating to each other as a *public*—was present. . . . The local gentry of the late Ming was [thus] moving into a public realm that was still under construction" (Brook 1993:26–9). In the early twentieth century, a public institutional sphere was again being developed in China. In Zhejiang Province, for example, according to R. Keith Schoppa's study, "specialized public institutions sanctioned or sponsored by the government, but created and controlled by local elites" were already seen "as important supervisory, mediational, and interest organizations in local affairs" (cited in Brook 1993:338). That public sphere was greatly diminished under Mao before it had chance to fully develop.

Today in China sociopolitical circumstances seem to be echoing those of the late Ming, early European capitalism, and of the early twentieth-century China itself. Is Chinese society then moving into another phase of the critical public? If so, what is it like? Is it yet "an intermediate arena of interaction between state and society in which the two sides meet and which neither can claim as completely its own" as Rankin defines the public sphere (cited in Brook 1993:26)? This interesting transition, if transition it is, we will explore now, especially as it pertains to critical intellectuals.

In chapter 2, we discussed the changes between 1976 and 1989 and the public spaces intellectuals enjoyed (see also Edward X. Gu 1999). In general, critical intellectuals from the 1992 onward have again benefited from a certain easing of the environment. Sheldon Hsiao-peng Lu (1997:74–5) notes that there are two kinds of public space for critical intellectuals: the space of commercialized popular culture and the mass media, and the "relatively autonomous critical public spaces . . . constituted by critical journals, avant-garde literary works, art exhibits, academic symposia, and the classrooms in some institutions of higher education." (See also Goldman 1996:50–1.)

In one of his most discussed articles on contemporary Chinese thought and modernity, Wang Hui ([1997] 2000:115–6) lists a number of unofficial and semi-official journals that have appeared since 1989. The unofficial publications include *Xue Ren (*The Scholar*),* edited by Chen Pingyuan, Wang Shouchang, and Wang Hui; *Zhongguo Shehui Kexue Jikan (*Chinese social science quarterly), edited by Deng Zhenglai; *Yuan Dao* (Original Dao), edited by Chen Ming; and *Gonggong Luncong* (Public forum), edited by Liu Junning, Wang Yan, and He Weifang. To that list, we should also add *Shijie* (Horizons), edited by Li Tuo and Chen Yangu. Most of these journals have been funded by overseas private foundations in Japan, Hong Kong, or the United States. Foreign capital has already invested in some media organizations and is expected to take a more active role in shaping Chinese civil society once China enters the WTO (Xia Xinruo 2001).

Semi-official journals include *Zhanlue yu Guanli* (Strategy and Management), edited by Qin Zhaoying, Gao Chaoqun, and others, past editors including Yang Ping and Li Shulei; and *Dongfang* (Orient), edited by Zhong Peizhang and Zhu Zhenglin in the 1990s but Wei Qun in 2001 with Wang Ying as the director. There is also the widely celebrated intellectual journal *Dushu* (Reading), edited by Huang Ping and Wang Hui, with Dong Xiuyu as the chief editor. It is officially sponsored by the State News and Publication Bureau. Added to the list are yet two more journals: *Tianya* (Frontiers), edited by Jiang Zidan and Li Shaojun, sponsored by the Hainan Writers' Association, and *Shuwu* (Home of Books), edited by Zhou Shi and Wang Ping, sponsored by the Hunan Publishing Bureau. (Both Zhou and Wang, however, were replaced by the authorities in 2001 for their nonconformist editorial policies.)

Chinese Central TV's programs have also provided intellectuals with some public space. Most popular among them are *Jiaodian Fangtan* (Focused interviews); *Dongfang Shikong* (Time and Space in the East) (see Jing Yidan 1998, who is also the host of both programs); *Shi Hua Shi Shuo* (Tell It as It Is) (see Cui Yongyuan 2001, also the host of the program); *Jinri Shuofa* (Law Today) (see Yin Li 2001, Vols. 1–4; Yin is one of the producers of the program); and *Xinwen Diaocha* (News Probe) (see Liang Jianzeng, Sai Na, and Zhang Jie 2001, Vols. 1–2, all producers of the program).[21] This is in addition to such provincial radio programs as Shanghai's *Shimin yu Shehui* (Citizens and Society, a call-in show Bill Clinton visited in 1998) or newspapers such as *Nanfang Zhoumo* (South China Weekend), one of the few newspapers in China that dare to take a critical stance (see Xu Lie 2000).

As Lynch illustrates in *After the Propaganda State,* commercialization, globalization, and pluralization of thought work have brought forth an increasing number of newspaper and magazine publishers, television stations, and individuals with access to telephones, fax machines, and modems. For example, in 1996, more than 80 percent of Chinese households owned a television set, and about a billion people regarded themselves as regular viewers of programs produced by 880 licensed television stations (1999:141). "Internet messages, faxes, shortwave radio broadcasts, television programs, films, videotapes, and even books and periodicals" from the United States, Hong Kong, and Taiwan have found their way into the Chinese market (p. 105). And it is increasingly difficult for the Party-state to effectively control either the content of the mass communication or its venues. Consequently, "Beijing's domination of the circulation of political information is itself eroding as part of the overall crumbling of the propaganda state" (p. 9).[22]

As a result of this larger social environment, intellectuals have been able to express their opinions on many issues on radio, and television, and in newspapers, journals, and books. Once banned authors like Li Shenzhi, a retired vice president of CASS and now a renowned liberal democratic intellectual, can now publish his call for political reform (see Li Shenzhi 2000b). And issues such as the legitimacy of the CCP's rule in China are sometimes discussed (see Zhang Jian 2000). Other critical intellectuals who have published their books include Deng Weizhi (1993, 1998), He Qinglian (1999[1998], 2001), Lin Xianzhi (1999), Xie Yong (1999a, 1999b), and Yu Jie (1999).[23] While the government is tightening its ideological control, a series of books on intellectuals reflecting their relationship with the Party have been published, as we mentioned earlier.

Even if they are discussing a very sensitive issue, they can generally find some roundabout ways to do it. For example, a collection of editorials and signed articles from the CCP newspapers in the 1940s has been published recently. These articles advocate freedom, democracy, and human rights, and are sharply critical of the one-party dictatorship (Xiao Shu 1999). It reminds the CCP painfully of what they had promised half a century ago.[24] Books banned by the government, such as Wang Lixiong's *Yellow Peril*,[25] can occasionally even find their way onto bookstore shelves and street vendors' carts as pirated editions, and their authors may not be punished. This intellectual freedom, though limited, has benefited from the less strict personnel system. For the first time since the revolution, intellectuals do not have to belong to a specific work unit. A very few can even make a living by writing.

The public space is, therefore, expanded compared with the past and yet still restricted compared with what it ought to be. There is potential for the emergence of a Chinese civil society, but it is not there yet, as Lynch (1999:230–8) points out. The Party line remains strict for some issues, and nobody can publicly deviate from them. These issues include the Taiwanese and other minority independence movements and the Falun Gong movement, a semireligious organization.[26] Dissenting opinions are off limits for both the Chinese intellectuals and foreign researchers or reporters (Brookes 2000; Lawrence 2000; Postiglione 2000; Rosen 2000).[27]

On one hand, various intermediate groups have been established and they do form a public discourse space. He Qinglian (2001:31–4) reports that these organizations range from various study groups to associations of alumni, lawyers, accountants, and private entrepreneurs. By 1996, national organizations numbered 1,800, and local ones 200,000. Goldman (1999:708) reports that altogether the number was over 1,000,000 by 1998. Although these organizations do not participate in the government's decision-making processes, they still form a discourse space that has the potential for political influence.[28] On the other hand, however, dissident organizations are out of the question. In 1998, Wang Youcai, Qin Yongmin, Xu Wenli, and their colleagues organized the China Democracy Party, but they were soon arrested and sentenced to prison for eleven to thirteen years, although the organization still continues to exist in other forms. The China Development Union, an association concerned with environmental issues, was also disbanded and one of its leaders, Peng Ming, was arrested. The Falun Gong members have continued to stage protests against the government's suppression but their protest leaders have been constantly arrested and put into prison.

Indeed, according to Xiao Gongqin (Interview 1996:2.40), an advocate of neoconservatives in the 1990s, there does exist a line in the minds of the government. As long as you do not cross this line, they will restrain themselves. Do not organize political activities challenging the government, and you are safe. Xu Jilin (Interview 1996:2.20) seemed to agree with Xiao. When the Party line does not specify what intellectuals can or cannot do, local authorities determine the extent of deviance. Our interviewees reported some of those restrictions in the 1990s. For example, even at public meetings of colleagues at their work units, intellectuals had to be careful about what they would say. One of our interviewees talked at a meeting about the difficulties intellectuals had in merely surviving, and he was warned not to do so again by both the school authorities and the State Educational Commission. The department, however, protected him, asking him just to be careful in the future (Interviews with Chen Yichi, Fu Ji, Gong Haiyang, and Yan Yang 1994: 1.52, 60–62).[29]

Our interviewees also reported a great many restrictions on scholarly research in the 1990s. Deng Weizhi, a sociologist and member of the city Academy of Social Sciences, mentioned the restrictions on intellectuals' research into the conditions of the working class (Interview 1994:1.68).[30] That restriction, however, was relaxed toward the end of the 1990s, as the ordinary workers' conditions became more of a concern for the government. Another sociology professor commented, "There are certain topics you cannot do research on. Once our students wanted to do some research on the promotion system, looking into who was promoted and who was not and why. They were not allowed to do it" (Interview with Cheng Guan 1994:1.36).

Local TV stations may face more restrictions than the Central TV stations. As one of our interviewees reported, "The city TV station is much more constrained in what they can report than Central TV. For example, they cannot do critical reports on legal, medical, or educational issues (which may make the city look bad)" (Interview with TV journalist Yan Zhaowei 1996:2.5).

No matter where, however, programs and journals can be suspended if they deal with certain sensitive issues. This happened to one of Central TV's programs, *Shi Hua Shi Shuo* (Tell It as It Is), and journals such as *Jiao Dian* (Focus) and *Dongfang* (Orient). They were admonished and temporarily suspended by the government for having published or wanting to publish articles commemorating the Cultural Revolution (*World Journal,* October 21, 1996; Interview with Zheng Yefu 1996: 2.4). This has happened to many other journals and newspapers (Hua Damin 2001), although it does not seem to deter even more new endeavors (Nan Yu 2001). After all, the mass media is still supposed to produce and disseminate the official ideology. As another journalist, Jiang Zhexin, reports,

> You have to be careful in what you say. Be a little bit careless, you step on a land mine. We are always told by the propaganda departments what to say and what not to say. The story of Zhou Enlai's foster daughter was one of those land mines. Those news agencies which had reprinted the story had to go through self-criticism and self-discipline *(zi cha zi lu).* (Interview with Tian Zhaoyun and Jiang Zhexin 1994:1.56–7)

A journalist's account may be representative of the general conditions of freedom and constraints of the press:

> There are fewer restrictions on interviewing people now. There is more transparency *[touming du]*. When I first began to work as a journalist, the leaders would check on many of the articles I wrote. Now they check mostly on speeches by authorities. But we also have to be careful in our reporting; we could be punished for what we say. There are always one or two things a year that you want to report but cannot. For instance, there was a case involving a Taiwanese merchant selling fake jewelry and another involving murder by a city cadre. The city government

> stopped journalists from further probing into the cases. If you persist in reporting enough cases they don't like, you will be out of a job. We are living between a rock and a hard place *[jiafeng zhong shengcun]*. (Interview with Ge Shannon 1994:1.3)

Similar freedom and constraints apply to the Internet. As some have observed, the Internet has become China's "virtual Democracy Wall" (see Goldman 1999:708). It is estimated that there are at least 2,000 forums in Chinese (*Press Freedom Guardian,* May 19, 2000). A Web-site of Chinese sociology (http://www.china-avenue.com/wash) used to have a forum where readers debated social issues ranging from corruption and education to the roles of intellectuals. Some of them were frank about their criticism of the one-party dictatorship, although they did not mention the Party per se. In a series of discussions on education in China, for example, Ma Zhiyong commented that the acquiescence of intellectuals is a result of the rulers' bullying (March 15, 2000). The forum contained articles by well-known critical intellectuals such as Xu Jilin, Xiao Gongqin, and Wang Yuanhua from Shanghai. Readers could obtain articles from somewhere else and post them onto the Web. Li Shenzhi (2000a) wrote an article criticizing the Party on the fiftieth anniversary of the founding of the People's Republic. He found it posted on the Web without his knowing it beforehand.

But the government is able to exert some control over the Internet through monitoring devices, or "fire walls." A platform of the dissident China Democratic Party was posted on March 27, 2000 on the sociology web-site, but it was taken down one day later. The owner of the sociology forum declared on April 4 that the Web-site they had used had a filter system, which would refuse messages containing sensitive words. More extreme measures can be used to deal with the "virtual democracy wall." In 1998, the government arrested the owner of a computer software company for supplying E-mail addresses to dissident publications overseas. Several bulletin boards were closed for hosting critical political discussions; as a result, chat rooms tend to actively police themselves (Human Rights Watch, February 2000). For example, the sociology forum solicited comments on the 2000 Taiwanese presidential election on the day of the election in March 2000, but the next day, not only were there no comments at all but the solicitation ad was gone as well. Figure 3.1 may illustrate the forces facing intellectuals trying to score a point.

Thus, it is not always clear exactly how much room there is; policies

“老将们跑不动，又不肯退出，都要当守门员。”

Figure 3.1 The Senior Members of the Team Can No Longer Run Fast Enough But They Don't Want to Retire. They All Want to Be Goalies. *(Lao jiang men pao bu dong, you bu ken tuichu, dou yao dang shoumenyuan.)*

Source: Ding Cong 1999 (Vol. 1), p. 60.

can change from time to time and from place to place in spite of the general relaxation. In 1995, the prohibitions apparently extended to cover questionnaire surveys on any intellectuals. (We had done our limited survey on technical intellectuals in 1994.) When our joint research project was finally suspended in 1995, we learned later that all similar projects had been suspended because some research on intellectuals had become too sensitive. A training course on statistics given by American professors was suspended, and the foundations sponsoring joint research projects were investigated. Even the job of a United Nations officer who was helping the poor in Sichuan Province was cut short. At times, obviously, the political control could be really tight. Other times, it could be very relaxed. Still other times, it could just be bureaucratic tangles rather than political controls (Interviews with Huang Ping 1996:2.38; 2001). In

2001, Li Shaomin and Gao Zhan were arrested, sentenced, and expelled from China. Their crime: obtain internal documents and pass them onto someone else (see Hu Ping 2001; Li Shaomin 2001). The catch, however, is that it is not always clear what is classified as "internal."

Political dissent, as we said, is strictly forbidden and violators can wind up in prison. However, if the dissenter is a well-known intellectual, there is a tendency to go easy on him:

> Persons writing anonymous letters can be easily found out, and phone talks are constantly tapped when the authorities believe something suspicious is happening. Any dissident activity will lead to the arrest of the persons doing it. However, those who are nationally and internationally well-known are relatively safe. A prime example is Wang Ganchang, the physicist who signed the petition in 1989 to the National People's Congress calling for political reform and signed another one in 1994 for political lenience. The fact is, the government dares not touch Wang. (Interview with Cheng Guan 1994:1.36)[31]

The varying levels of treatment applies also to dissidents in prison: better-known dissidents receive better treatment than lesser-known dissidents. For example, Zhang Xianliang had no books to read or paper to write on, while Wang Dan not only had books and paper but could play Ping-Pong with his jailers (Zhang Boli's interview with Zhang Xianliang 1997; Wang Dan 1998).

Because of the restrictions, critical intellectuals have to find roundabout ways to express themselves. But because of the existence of roundabout ways, many intellectuals seem to be able to find a form to express themselves in. As Xiao Guimei said, "When writing articles, we play little games [net ball, or *ca bian qiu*]. My articles are all about social problems, but I cannot be too direct or detailed. Otherwise, my words would be crossed out by my editor. But people understand what I mean. They think it is well said" (Interview 1994:1.6).

And a talk-show host echoed Xiao:

> We play little games in our programs on social problems. You have to learn to say things in certain ways. You can discuss things the central government is concerned about. But when sensitive topics come up, you have to know how and where to channel them. It can be dangerous, but we've made it. I am talking about state affairs, and you are too. We are not contradicting each other. (Interview with Zuo Anliang 1994:1.7)

To sum up, there have been various restrictions as to what critical intellectuals can or cannot do, but the public space is much freer compared with the first period of the Deng era. It is possible to engage in some criticism if the critics avoid naming names (especially the names of current leaders) and do not organize opposition parties. The Internet is so widely used that it is becoming easier for intellectuals to communicate such criticisms. Many articles critical of the Party and state first appear on the Internet although some may remain there for only a short period of time.[32] Although there is a ban on opposition parties, over one million nongovernmental organizations, most of which deal with intellectual, social, and cultural issues, were established by 1998.

This public space for intellectual discourse since 1989 indicates a more profound interaction between the different political forces within the state, and of the social and economic forces between the state and the society (see Wang Hui [1997] 2000: 116–7). There have been restrictions and relaxation. We might even call it a civil society in the making. Although socialist corporatism and traditional clientelism are still the dominant mode of the state-society relationship,[33] civil society may be operating more than just around the edges as Pearson (1997:43) has observed in her study of the business elite. A civil society has not emerged, but "there is much that goes on in China" (Christoffersen 1998:121). Our discussion on various schools of thought and their critical intellectuals will further illustrate this point.

The Critical Intellectual Discourses

Along with the continuing, highly vocal overseas democracy movement, intellectuals inside China have engaged in debates on the humanist spirit, postmodernism, nationalism, national learning, and a variety of other critical areas. The intellectual discourses in the past decade indicate that Chinese intellectuals have gone further on a road to an independent critical movement, not paralleling, because of the political suppression in China, but maybe resembling the critical intellectuals before 1949. The rest of this chapter will examine the various critical intellectual discourses, the democracy movement, and criticisms by those who are not often noticed.

Dongfang and the Critical Intellectual Discourse: A General View

First, let us look at a tabulation of the articles published in *Dongfang* (Orient), a journal best-known among socially and politically conscious intellectuals. The contents of these articles give us an overview of issues of concern by critical intellectuals. Table 3.2 shows us the kinds of articles *Dongfang* published in 1995.

Table 3.2 Number and Percent of Various Articles in *Dongfang,* 1995

Types of Articles	Number of Such Articles	Percent of Total
Women's issues: gender gap, equality, psychological liberation, women's NGO's, comparative studies on women, women in ancient times, post-colonialism and feminism, etc.	23	15.2%
Cultural Critique: articles on music, mental labor, "-isms and problems," academic thoughts, the culture of the "three old classes" graduated from the cultural revolution, literary critique, humanism and the real world, philosophy, the academy and the world, on Wang Meng	22	14.6%
Miscellaneous Thoughts: remembering Xia Yan, history, East and West, Japan, Brussels, reform and moral deterioration,education, social progress, the 1960's, anti-corruption, the Poles and WWII, on "the wisdom of not arguing," intellectuals' dilemma	20	13.2%
Oriental Forum: values, spirits, social justice, national learning, the humanist spirit, law, morality, on science, information superhighway, progressiveness and conservatism, escape from reality	15	9.9%
Social Observations: stocks, law, movies, people, Christianity in China, genealogy in the countryside, sports, group interests, clans and entrepreneurs, state-ownership, reform in the countryside, wealth and poverty, independent writers	13	8.6%
World Affairs: Confucianism in the world culture, universal values, Chinese in American movies, NGO's, the UN, what is happening in Europe and America, sales revolution, Sino-US relations, transnational corporations	12	7.9%
50th anniversary of anti-Fascist war: reflections, refusing to forget, war and peace, fascism, Nuremberg trials	7	4.6%
Painting: Chinese, Indian, Korean paintings, women (in) painting	6	4.0%
Special Articles: on economy, social and cultural thinking, intellectuals' loss of discourse, Asian values, general social tendencies	5	3.3%
Environment: China's environmental issues, ecology, the humanist spirit and environmental protection, social and economic development	5	3.3%

Table 3.2 continued

Types of Articles	Number of Such of Total	Percent
People: Fei Xiaotong, Rao Zongyi, Xiong Wei, Hai Rao, Lu Zhengxiang	5	3.3%
History of thinking: on Hu Shih, Nationalist Revolution, dictatorship and democracy	5	3.3%
Interviews: with Wang Yuanhua, Zhang Guangnian, Sheng Hong	4	2.5%
Academic fields: National studies, sciences, social sciences, freedom	4	2.5%
Corruption and anti-corruption: on social justice, the exchange between power and money, measures to fight corruption in modern civilizations	3	2.0%
Book reviews: sexuality and law, international politics	2	1.3%
	151	100%

Source: Dongfang. 1995.

Notes:

1. The classification of articles is not exact. Articles on women, for example, cut across several categories, but they are grouped here under women's issues.
2. In late 1999 and early 2000 *Dongfang* became very different from that of 1995. It lost the edge of social and political criticism and was more likely to focus on cultural issues. But since 2001 the journal has bounced back and resumed its 1995 critical edge: it has begun to publish more articles on corruption, human rights, and political reform (see *Dongfang* 2001 [Nos. 7 and 8]). The ups and downs of editorial policies in newspapers and journals seem to be another feature of the "socialism with Chinese characteristics."

The contents of the articles reflect issues concerned by critical intellectuals at the time. Although radical political reform was still taboo, there were many other social concerns intellectuals could discuss. As we will see in chapter 5, while almost 70 percent of the 1995 articles in *Qiu Shi,* the Party's journal on theory, were focused on how to build socialism with Chinese characteristics, and how to strengthen the Party leadership, none of the articles in *Dongfang* in the same year were about any of those topics. Rather, *Dongfang* articles covered a wide range of other social and political issues, which makes it difficult even to categorize them. Issues such as environmental protection, Asian values, learning the lessons of World War II, and corruption and anticorruption were termed "special topics," and women's issues were given the space of almost an entire issue, of which there were only six a year. Other articles focused on various social, cultural, and political issues. The authors here were by and large critical intellectuals writing fairly independently, while the authors in *Qiu Shi* were organic intellectuals, writing for the Party's cause.

The *Dongfang* writers are also intellectuals who had actively debated many of these issues in the 1990s. Those whose names appear at least twice in the 1995 issues include Chen Pingyuan, Chen Xiaoya, Ge Jianxiong, Lei Yi, Liu Bing, Liu Dong, Yu Guangyuan, and Zheng Yefu. Other well-known figures include Li Xiaojiang, Wang Lixiong, Wang Meng, Wang Xiaoming, Wang Yuanhua, Wang Yuechuan, and Zhang Guangnian. And this is only a brief list out of over a hundred writers. We will now look at the major trends of thought in the years after June 4, most of which are also discussed in *Dongfang,* not all of course in 1995.

The Humanist Spirit and the Critical Intellectuals' "Consciousness Raising"

One of the most important events among critical intellectuals in the 1990s was the debate over humanism, or "the humanistic spirit." It is important because it defines the reason for the existence of critical intellectuals. The debate began with Wang Xiaoming's article on literature and the crisis of the humanist spirit, published in 1993 in *Shanghai Wenyi* (Shanghai literature and art). It was, of course, related to the rapidly changing political economy. The discussion quickly spread to other journals such as *Dushu* and *Dongfang.* Many joined the conversation, which, in effect, attempted to clarify the reasons for their very being.

To be sure, there was disagreement on what exactly is humanism, whether there was ever a humanist spirit in Chinese history, and whether the humanist spirit needed to be constructed or reconstructed. As two of our interviewees asked;

> Should humanism, or the humanist spirit, be "reconstructed," implying that we had our system but new values had to be incorporated, or should it be "rekindled and strengthened," meaning that it had always existed but had been lost somewhere sometime in the past and now we had to regain it and strengthen it. Or maybe we had never had it in our system at all, and the humanist spirit had to be "constructed." (Interviews with Tian Zhaoyun and Jiang Zhexin 1994:1.56–7)

Wang Meng (1994), the former Minister of Culture, is one of those who has questioned the very existence of humanism in Chinese intellectual history.

But Xu Jilin (1997b:231), a professor of history from Shanghai and one of the most important scholars on intellectuals, explores the humanist spirit in the Chinese traditional culture of the eight principles *(ba tiao mu)*. These are:

1. investigating things *(gewu)*
2. acquiring (or extending) knowledge *(zhizhi)*
3. having sincere intentions *(chengyi)*
4. rectifying the mind *(zhengxin)*
5. cultivating oneself *(xiushen)*
6. putting one's house in order *(qijia)*
7. governing the country *(zhiguo)*
8. bringing peace to the world *(ping tianxia)*[34]

They can be condensed into three intellectual traditions, according to Xu. The first, *Dao Tong,* is ideology, defined as the principles of good faith, sincerity, uprightness, and cultivation of oneself. *Zheng Tong* is politics, that is, putting one's house in order, governing one's country, and pacifying the world. *Xue Tong* is scholarship, the study of things, and the acquisition of knowledge (see also Cheek 1992; Tu Wei-ming 1993b).[35] The humanist spirit in the Chinese tradition is embodied in *Dao,* the perfection of the individual. In the new era, China may need a new *Dao,* a new "ideology" with multiple meanings. That is, a *Dao* that can mean different things in different contexts: attention to human beings as life's central subject; a protest against, and reflection on, political dictatorship; and a concern for the meaning in human life (Xu Jilin 1997: 234). It would be a transformation and transcendence of the old *Dao Tong.* Xu comments that obviously it is difficult to say what the humanist spirit is. We can much more easily say what it is not; for example, it is not dictatorship, poverty, material greed, or total control by technology.

Xu does not want to tie humanism down to a specific definition. Nevertheless, the examples of what he considers the humanist spirit direct our attention to the concern for human values as a basic aspect in one's intellectual consciousness. That, he is saying, should be the intellectuals' new *Dao,* or ideology. This focus on human beings is echoed by other critics. Wang Meng (1994:46), for example, believes that the humanist spirit really should mean simply a concern for human beings *(yizhong duiyu ren de guanzhu)*. He believes that the discussion on the humanist spirit should not be politicized, and we should not build another repressive value system for intellectuals to follow. According to Wang Meng, the humanist spirit should recognize human beings' differences as well as their similarities, their strengths as well as their weaknesses.[36] Wang Shuo and Wu Bin, both "Confucian businesspeople," are also concerned about the possibility of another oppressive system that might suppress differences (see *Dushu* 1994, No. 7).

So far, however, their definitions seem still too broad. They welcome anyone, politician or businessperson, as a humanist. By extension, then, everyone should be considered an intellectual since everyone has at least some knowledge. The discussion by the two Wangs and Wu on the merits of the market economy and of secularized literature broadens our understanding of the humanist spirit. But it does not help us understand the humanist spirit as a *special pursuit of critical intellectuals*. The concept of the humanist spirit has to have more concrete meanings than they have given it, although what these thinkers say is certainly of crucial importance.

Xiao Tongqing's (1995:20) definition is more specific. Humanism, he says, is the human being's understanding and grasp of his or her own life. It is even more. It is a concern for the meaning of life in general: its values, its dignity, and its defense of the rights of humans. It is a process of seeking to understand life and death, pain and freedom from pain, happiness and suffering, and so on. Xu Jilin (1997:234–5) also acknowledges that although it is hard to say for sure what the humanist spirit is, for it is many things, still the main subject of the humanist spirit is the human being. The main process of humanism is reflection, social criticism, and emphasis on spiritual concerns.

As the discussion shows, scholars have tended to agree that humanism, or the humanist spirit, can be defined as the *belief* that the human being is the central subject in social interactions. That belief is embodied in a *spirit* that seeks to understand the most profound of human concerns, and by a *spirit* that uses social criticism to reshape political and academic issues according to those human emotions. This humanism descends from the Chinese cultural tradition of self-perfection. Inspired by that tradition, and confirming Xu Jilin's vision of a synthesis, this form of humanism emphasizes the interaction between itself, politics, and scholarship. It covers the traditional *Dao Tong, Zheng Tong,* and *Xue Tong*. But it has also developed a modern component, for it has made room, as we have seen, for the Western humanist concepts of human rights, democracy, freedom, and individualism.

In China, today's humanism validates the independent existence (Wu Xuan et al. 1994) of critical intellectuals. This is because the critical intellectual represents the same belief, that human beings are the subject of social interaction, and the same vocation, the wish to understand human existence, and to make social criticism, which is of course their social responsibility. The new humanism recognizes the multiple layers of human existence (Wang Meng 1994). It is the reestablishment, the reincarnation of a belief, a concern, a worldview, and a practice (Wang Xiaoming 1995).

Defining the humanist spirit is defining the consciousness of the critical intellectual. Indeed, the question of the humanist spirit was raised in 1993 when critical intellectuals found that they had suddenly become irrelevant to what was happening in China. High-handed political oppression and the rapid development of the market economy meant that there was little space for the discussion of political democratization, and there was little interest in what intellectuals had to say unless what they said could make money. Critical intellectuals found themselves marginalized, unlike the situation in the 1980s. During those tumultuous years, they had been at the center of great cultural and political events: the "cultural fever," "Marxist humanism," and the many democracy movements (Chen Shaoming 1995). Now they were concerned about the loss of traditional values and about moral deterioration. They wondered what their roles were in this rapid social change (Dong Ping 1995.) The discussion of the humanist spirit has helped them redefine who they are and what they can do. That is the importance of this development of the 1990s. The debates and experiments we discuss in the next section will help us understand the meaning of the humanist spirit, and most importantly, the intention, or the consciousness of the critical intellectual.

Postmodernism, Postmodernity, and the Diverse Critical Intellectuals

Postmodernism has many meanings, many interpretations, and many applications in different fields (Ross 1988:x–xi). Postmodernism may include questioning the established assumptions of the modern age, as in Jean-Francois Lyotard. It may involve decentering the current dominant discourse. It may mean examining the specifics of power and its relation to knowledge, as in Michel Foucault. It may involve opposing the binary opposites of truth/falsity, unity/diversity, or man/woman, as in Jacques Derrida (see Parpart 1993). All of these are attempts by postmodern theorists to explain development in the West. China is *not* in most senses a developed country. But it has achieved a bureaucratic authoritarian domination, and the market economy is taking hold. For these reasons, postmodernism appeals to those Chinese intellectuals who see their mission as one of social criticism. For postmodernism is subversive of the dominant official discourses, both political and economic. In other words, if the humanist spirit provides critical intellectuals with a consciousness, postmodernism provides them with a tool of critique.

According to Wang Ning (1997), postmodernism was introduced into Chinese literary circles in the early 1980s. Postmodern thinking and practice developed as more and more translations of theoretical works by scholars from the West poured in, bolstered by visits from some of the authors in the 1990s. Translations included Fredric Jameson's *Postmodernism and Cultural Theories* and *Approaching Postmodernism,* a collection of essays edited by Douwe Fokkema and Hans Bertens. These and other postmodern authors, such as Ihab Hassan, Jonathan Arac, Ralph Cohen, and Terry Eagleton not only visited China but were invited to give lectures. All of this happened, of course, within the more open space of discourse facilitated by the atmosphere of globalization, modern technology, and consumer culture.

We will now examine postmodernism's effect on Chinese literary and cultural circles. We will discuss the postmodern phenomenon in literature, the arts, music, and the movies.[37]

Writers

Wang Ning (1997) describes the 1990s postmodern trends in literature and culture in his article, "The Mapping of Chinese Postmodernity." Wang identifies six versions of Chinese postmodernity in the literary and cultural spheres. First, a kind of avant-garde fiction *(xianfeng xiaoshuo)* and experimental poetry *(shiyan pai shige)* has cropped up. The authors recognize no forbidden areas of artistic expression, and some have sought to combine writing for the sake of literature with writing for the market. Second, the new realist school *(xin xieshi pai)* has challenged the avant-gardists by describing their characters' real states of mind and by evoking an atmosphere of reality. Third, a "Wang Shuo

Phenomenon" oriented toward the mass market has arisen in which writers have challenged "high" literature (e.g., the orthodox socialist works) by satirizing it. Wang Shuo also calls his works a literature of royalty bargaining *(yijia wenxue),* meaning that they are written for a negotiated price. Others have written just for popular consumption, since the mass media pay them big money. Some simply call themselves persons piling up characters *(ma zi de ren),* as in men laying bricks. Fourth, there are those who write historical novels, retelling stories of historical figures. Fifth, literary critics use postmodern theories to decode Chinese literature. Sixth, "postcolonial discourse" has entered into the critics' lexicon to describe both Western influences and domestic totalitarianism.

It may be argued that trends like commercialized literature are not necessarily evidence of postmodernism. But the wide variety in the writing in the past decade definitely constitutes a postmodern phenomenon, or, at the least, a form of postmodernity. To Wang Ning's list of literary trend-makers, one may also add Zhang Chengzhi, Liang Xiaosheng, and Zhang Wei. These writers use their works to reprimand intellectuals and others for their deteriorating morality under the influence of the market economy (Dong Ping 1995; see also Min Lin 1999). But Wang Xiaobo (d. 1997), a novelist and essayist, criticized them as being moralistic, a problem Chinese intellectuals share (Barmé 2000: 206). One may also add Jin Yong, the most popular writer on *gongfu,* or martial arts. Indeed, according to Wang Meng (1998), a random sample revealed that readers in Shanghai liked Jin Yong first of all, Lu Xun next, and third Wang Shuo. The literary world does seem varied! One thing is certain: the center, the once dominant official discourse, has been seriously challenged, although not completely replaced. The "literary" works of the Party's model cadres and workers, so warmly praised in *Qiu Shi,* the Party journal, which we will discuss in chapter 5, are nowhere to be found on these lists. It is in this sense that we may consider Wang Ning's writers as critical intellectuals.

However, if these writers lose their critical ability and do nothing more than follow orders from some higher power, political or economic, they would cease to be critical intellectuals. Remember that we are talking about ideal types. Whether one is or is not a critical intellectual depends on the preponderance of evidence. For example, Wang Shuo is a critical intellectual in that his writing makes fun of anything serious, and it becomes a gadfly to the official discourse. If there were no official discourse, if he then began writing only to make money, he could no longer be considered a critical intellectual. Analyzing cultural phenomena is not enough. One has to criticize the phenomena, actually express social criticism, in order to be called a critical intellectual. Otherwise, one is an unattached/professional intellectual, the category we will discuss in chapter 4. (We will discuss the "dissident writers" in the section on the democracy movement.)

Artists

According to Sheldon Hsiao-peng Lu (1997), postmodern art since 1989 has taken two directions. One is the explosion of Political Pop. The other includes installation, performance, body, video, and mixed-media art. Andrews and Gao (1995) and Solomon (1993) also show us some of the Political Pop works, and introduce us to various other avant-garde movements such as Cynical Realism and the Current of Life.

According to Solomon, along with the Democracy Wall movement in 1979 came the avant-garde movement. This was initiated by the Stars group, named to reflect their individuality. The Stars had flourished before 1989. After 1989, they opted for Cynical Realism and Political Pop. A typical example of Cynical Realism is photo-perfect figurative painting. Fang Lijun, for example, paints a man in the midst of an enormous yawn. Napoleon is quoted as saying, "When China wakes, it will shake the world." In Fang's rendition, China may have wakened, but it is certainly still very sleepy. Fang likes to paint idle characters sitting or swimming or walking around with utter lack of purpose, or what he calls "the absurd, the mundane and the meaningless events of everyday life" (Solomon 1993:48). Liu Wei, another artist, sheds more light on our understanding of Cynical Realism:

> In 1989, I was a student. I joined the democracy movement, like everyone else, but didn't play an important part in it. After June 4, I despaired. Now I have accepted that I cannot change society: I can only portray our situation. Since I cannot exhibit in China, my work cannot be an inspiration here, but painting helps to relieve my own sense of helplessness and awkwardness. (p. 49)

Indeed, Cynical Realism arrived, one art critic says, after people finally realized that "extreme resistance" only proved the power of one's opponent. At that point, humor and irony took over. However, as Solomon points out, isn't portraying a cynicism that society denies a form of idealism (pp. 48–9)?

A typical piece of Political Pop portrays Mao on the left applauding one of his own principles and Whitney Houston on the right applauding her own music, both copied from actual photos. Another example paints black-and-white images of idealistic young people in Tiananmen Square. Still others use brand names such as "Band-Aid," "Marlboro," or "Benetton" to identify idealized young soldiers and farmers in Mao caps. One painter explains that he worries that commercialism will destroy people's ideas, perhaps even their ability to *have* ideas. But is there any real difference between the craze for Coke or Marlboro and the craze for the Little Red Book of Chairman Mao's quotations? Another artist portrays the hypocrisy, shallowness, and cruelty of government campaigns through a video entitled "The Correct Procedure for Washing a Chicken." In it a poor chicken is repeatedly lathered with soap, rinsed down, and laid on a board. As one can imagine, after such an ordeal, the chicken is no longer its old self (Solomon 1993:49–51). Li Shan once portrayed Mao as a Shanghai hooligan, at another time as a bisexual. Some of these artists' portraits sold for $15,000 or more in the Hong Kong markets (*World Journal,* August 24, 1994).

In the second phase of the avant-garde movement, Sheldon Lu (1997) reports that artists claim to be creating *international* postmodern art, rather than playing the domestic political card as do artists of the Political Pop. Zhang Hua, for example, had his own naked body bound to a horizontal bar and had a doctor draw 250 milliliters of his blood, which would then drip slowly onto a heated plate three meters below. This was his vision of the condition of life and art in China. Wang Luyan built a bicycle that moves backward when the rider peddles forward. Like much of life in China, it defies common sense. Xu Bing placed a female and a male pig in their high breeding season into a pen with scattered books. Printed all over the pig were unreadable English words, and all over the sow, nonsensical Chinese characters. The two pigs mated after a brief courtship. The original title of the underground exhibition was *Rape or Adultery?* But it was later changed into *A Case Study of Transference,* also known as *Cultural Animals.* According to the artist, he wants the spectators to ponder the relationship between China and the West.[38]

These works of art show us how intellectuals articulate their criticism of society and of the Communist system as a whole, as Andrews and Gao (1995:235, 256) point out. While Political Pop could make a man rich, installation art is by its nature uncollectible, and therefore noncommercial. Indeed, as Lu (1997) reports, many installation artists had no institutional affiliation, belonged to no work units, and were the most marginal and displaced class in China. They were often subject to police harassment. On July 2, 1993, the mayor of an artists' village in Beijing was brutally beaten by the police. The artists decided not to swallow the pain: they signed a petition, a lawyer took up the case, and they proceeded to bring a lawsuit against the police. A number of journalists agreed to publicize the suit. The lawyer stated, "Whether we win or lose, I hope we will make people realize that they can protest, that they can find a way to stand up for what they believe, so that they can live as human beings" (Solomon 1993:72). Unfortunately, in 1995, the protesters were forced out of the village entirely (*World Journal,* December 20, 1995). Their work, and the *way* in which they work, are both critical of, and rebellious against, the dominant paradigms, and they paid the price. Toward the end of the twentieth century, however, the avant-garde movement seemed able to coexist with the official arts, and the works of both were exhibited in the same gallery in Shanghai's 2000 art festivals (Gu Zheng 2001).

Popular Musicians and Artists

Shortly after the June 4 massacre, a fad sprang up (and was inevitably banned) for "cultural T-shirts" (see also Barmé 1999:145–78). Some of the more memorable imprints were as follows:

> "I am annoyed; don't bother me."
>
> "I am so tired."
>
> "Money is what life is all about."
>
> "Be an honest person."
>
> "Some things are like this: if you take them seriously, they do become serious."

"I have nothing."

"I have only one weakness."

Below the four character title, *La Jia Dai Kou,* meaning "having a big family to raise," you see "Licenses, Work Unit ID, Personal ID." The T-shirts express exactly the worry, the boredom, the frustration, and the anger of ordinary folks. (See Yang Dongping 1994b:552–3; *World Journal,* July 30, 1991, August 8, 1991; *China Spring,* January 1992.)

The popular rock 'n' roll singers were also considered subversive. Cui Jian's "All Over Again" includes the following cynical lyrics:

I am more and more skilled in talking nonsense,
I am more and more skilled in keeping silence,
And more and more skilled in pretending not to know anything.

In "Saying One Thing but Thinking Another," Cui writes;

My anger is no longer shame and regret,
My firmness is no longer hypocrisy,
My courage belongs to me myself,
And my freedom belongs to the heaven and earth.

Here is "The Last Gunshot," which he wrote out of his rage following the June 4 massacre:

If this is the last gunshot,
I am willing to accept this greatest honor,
Oh, the last gunshot; Oh, the last gunshot.

After the performance, Cui asked the audience twice what the title of the song was. When the audience told him twice, he said, "I hope the gunshot I heard last time is really the last gunshot" (See *China Spring,* October 1991). All this was shortly after the June 4 massacre. The words say it all. Note, however, that they are *nowhere* openly against the Party rule.

In his album, "Eggs Under the Red Flag," Cui Jian voices a cry from the anchorless youth of China for direction (*Overseas Chinese Daily,* August 15, 1999; Pickowicz 1995:200–1). He sings, "Money is fluttering in the wind. We have no ideals." And,

The time is now,
But who knows what we should do?
The red flag is waving,
It has no clear direction.
Revolution is ongoing;
The old men are still in power.

Or

Dreamed 'bout livin' in modern city space,
Now it's hard to explain what I face.
Skyscrapers poppin' up one by one,
But let me tell ya, life here is no fun.

Obviously rock 'n' roll lyrics and "cultural T-shirts" can become critical voices, just like novels and paintings. Such artists do present a problem for our synthesized typology, though: like Wang Shuo, they may not have had any college education. Nevertheless, with no diplomas in hand, these people are fulfilling important intellectual functions. The same applies to actors and actresses. And it especially applies to the movie directors we will meet next.

Movie Directors

The movie industry's so-called fifth-generation film directors, the generation that grew up in New China, went through the Cultural Revolution, and benefited by learning about Western culture after the economic reforms began. They and their movies were nominated for or won foreign awards, such as the Oscars or awards at the Cannes Film Festival. These films include Zhang Yimou's *Raise the Red Lantern* (1991), *The Story of Qiuju* (1993), *To Live* (1994); Chen Kaige's *Farewell My Concubine* (1993); and Tian Zhuangzhuang's *Blue Kite* (1992). All of these depict life and death in China, particularly under the Communist rule. Human rights and democracy are never mentioned but are always there by implication. As Xudong Zhang (1997:208) notes, these films tend to present "exotic spectacles, a melodramaticized epic, and a standard denunciation of the Cultural Revolution." Indeed, the "New Chinese Cinema" is actually a "political effort to disengage the existent social discourse embodied by the state in general and the extant field of filmmaking in particular" (p. 206). Their films "could be interpreted as expressions of individual criticisms of the current regime" (Pickowicz 1995:205). This is true not only in the motif and the content of these movies, but in their cinematic techniques and other aesthetic breakthroughs. Although they are by no means dissidents, their works do "chip away at the foundation of state socialism" (pp. 217–8).

Most of the group's movies were funded at least partly by Hong Kong and Taiwan producers, and some have been so successful abroad that they have been banned at home. In 1994, Zhang Yimou was forced to suspend the shooting of his new movie, *The Rules of the Gang,* because he had entered his movie *To Live* at the Cannes Film Festival (*World Journal,* September 28, 1994). While these films were commercial successes internationally, we are more concerned with what they say and how they were made. In both aspects they defy the official model.

Like the writers Zhang Chengzhi, Liang Xiaosheng, and Zhang Wei, there are movie makers who are particularly concerned about morality. Chen Jialin, for example, discussed the principles he follows in making movies. He was talking to a reporter in Shanghai about his new forty-episode TV series *Emperor Tang Ming Huang,* which made no money, and on which his cast worked hard for very little pay. Specifically, he followed five principles of moviemaking: nationalism, patriotism, collectivism instead of individualism, heroism, and humanism (Zhang Qunli, 1993). Chen seems to be quite idealistic. He says that artists should have a sense of both historic responsibility and national responsibility. They should leave something worthwhile to their offspring; their artistic conscience should not be drowned in today's sea of commodities. In fact, he is frankly disgusted with commercialism, which makes him one of the few voices raised against the current tide of consumerism.

Amid the postmodern phenomena are the Chinese postmodern theories and national learning. We will explore them in the following section on nationalism since they tend to be considered as part of the effort to define China's national identity.

The Great Debate on Nationalism

The 1990s proved to be a time of ferment for nationalism. In the first place, economic reform was making big strides, and the Chinese seemed about to realize their dream of a strong nation. Many found a sense of pride in their socialism, with its Chinese characteristics, especially in light of the economic failures in Russia. The Soviet failures seemed to justify the 1989 crackdown: had China followed Russia in political reform, they thought, it would have faced the same social and economic chaos.

In the second place, a number of incidents between China and the United States in the 1990s made many Chinese intellectuals believe that the United States was following a policy of containing China. This reaction was especially strong following the Harvard political scientist Samuel Huntington's (1993) article, "The Clash of Civilizations?" Huntington argued that a clash between the Confucian culture of the East and the Christian culture of the West was unavoidable. The biggest threat, he claimed, to Western civilization was the Islamic and Confucian cultures (see also Suisheng Zhao 1997:740). In the eyes of Chinese intellectuals, his arguments justified the conflicts between China and the United States in the following years.

Here are some of the conflicts. In 1993, China failed in its bid to host the 2000 Olympics. To many Chinese, this snub was the result of U.S. obstruction, rather than bribery of Olympic officials by Sidney and the poor human rights record in China (Friedman 1999). Also, China had failed in its application for membership in the World Trade Organization (an agreement with the United States was not reached until the end of the 1990s). Throughout the 1990s, the United States maintained a yearly review of China's Most Favored Nation status in trade. In July 1993, the United States insisted on inspection of the Chinese freighter *Yinhe,* though by a third party under U.S. supervision, for chemicals believed to be bound for Iran. The inspection found nothing suspicious on board, and the United States had to apologize for the inconvenience.

Then, in 1995, Lee Teng-hui, the president of the Republic of China, who was pro-Taiwanese independence, was allowed to visit the United States. In May 1999, the U.S.-led NATO bombing of the Chinese embassy in Belgrade, which many Chinese intellectuals believed to be intentional, further intensified the tension. But that was not all. In the same month, Congress published the Cox report accusing China of stealing U.S. military secrets, an accusation that lacked substantial evidence in support. In fact, many in the United States believed that Lee Wen-ho, the scientist who was accused of passing nuclear secrets to China, was accused chiefly because he was Chinese. In the same year, Lee Teng-hui declared that the relationship between Mainland China and Taiwan was a "special state to state" relationship. Some in Congress, even the Republican candidates for the 2000 presidential election, including the chief candidate George Bush Jr., supported a U.S.

involvement in defense of Taiwan should Mainland China strike. Many Chinese considered this interference with China's internal affairs. All of these events further fanned Chinese anti-American sentiments. Thus, in the 1990s, despite a few dissident voices, Chinese intellectuals came to view the United States as doing its best to contain China.

Amid this barrage of events between China and the United States, which stirred the nationalist sentiments of the Chinese, there emerged two major trends of nationalism in the 1990s. One is represented by the tele-series *A Beijing Man in New York* (1993), and books such as *China Can Say No* (1996), *China Can Still Say No* (1996), both by Song Qiang et al., and *Behind the Demonization of China* by Li Xiguang et al. (1997). This trend was characterized by anti-Westernism, especially anti-Americanism. Some intellectuals criticized this trend as being too radical and too crude. The other nationalist trend was, arguably, characterized rather by the modern Chinese tradition of criticism and self-criticism than by anti-Westernism. Postmodernism and the "national learning" are two examples of this second trend. Both aspects of nationalism provided intellectuals with more space for independent criticism, pushing them further along the way to an independent critical movement. But they were also viewed as part of the conservative trend in the 1990s. We will explore the intricacies of these thoughts in the following sections. The various intellectuals involved in each of these movements, including its critics, have demonstrated the extent to which intellectuals exercised their criticism. Let us now further examine the two trends of nationalism.

Anti-Westernism and Its Criticism

In his article "To Screw Foreigners Is Patriotic" (1996), Geremie R. Barmé, an Australian expert on China, lists a number of intellectuals and events that he thinks represent nationalism in China. His major example is the tele-series *A Beijing Man in New York* (perhaps since *China Can Say No* was not yet in print). Barmé begins his article with a scene from the drama in which the protagonist Wang Qiming thrusts himself onto a white, blond, and buxom New York prostitute, showers her with dollar bills, and makes her cry out repeatedly, "I love you." Barmé writes, "Reportedly, this was an extremely popular scene with mainland audiences, in particular with the Chinese intelligentsia" (p. 183). For some Chinese students and for a group of other Chinese Mainlanders in

Australia, the phrase "to screw a foreign cunt is a kind of patriotism" was a familiar idiom (hence the title). In addition, Barmé seems to agree with one critic who sums up the theme of the series in one line: Screw you, America *(Meiguo, wo cao ni daye).* Here are other examples of Chinese nationalism Barmé has identified (the words in quotes are taken directly from Barmé):

> There is "a growing disenchantment with the West and its allies," with intellectuals realizing that the 1989 upheaval might have brought on the kind of turmoil that now troubles Russia. (p. 187)
>
> There is "an underlying sentiment that the world (that is, the West) owes China something." (p. 187)
>
> The popular Mao cult in the early 1990s "had a perceptible *anti-foreign* edge to it." (p. 187. Italics mine)
>
> China's Olympic bid in 1993 was a "demand for better treatment from the international community." (p. 187)
>
> Yuan Hongbing, a political dissident, "condemns those who seek from the West a solution to China's problems. . . ." and indulges in "what could be called 'Sino-fascism'," calling for purifying the Chinese cultural "ugliness" through fire and blood. (p. 203)
>
> *A Beijing Man in New York* belittles Western capitalism by depicting its horrors. At the same time it takes what is useful for China by "affirming the positive dimensions (rags-to-riches) of the Western market economy." (p. 206)
>
> The new generation of Chinese with power and money "are resentful of the real and imagined slights that they and their nation have suffered in the past, and their desire for strength and *revenge* is increasingly reflected in contemporary Chinese culture." (p. 207. Italics mine)

Thus, "Having been 'shaped by defunct Party propaganda,' the 'new mythology of East Asian material strength and spiritual worth . . . feeds into the century-old Chinese dreams of national revival and *supremacy*' and will likely survive into the future" (p. 208. Italics mine).

Antiforeign sentiments, lust for revenge, and feelings of racial supremacy seem to characterize Chinese nationalism, according to Barmé.

Indeed, the nationalism represented by *A Beijing Man in New York* and *China Can Say No* does express a cultural nationalism that borders on cultural superiority. Some of the headings and subheadings from *China Can Say No* can give us an idea of the sentiments of these young intellectuals: "The Blue Sky Must Die; the Yellow Sky Must Rule," "The U.S. Foreign Policy Is Both Dishonest and Irresponsible," "Burn Down Hollywood," "Only a Fool Does Not Understand What America Wants to Do," and "The U.S. Has No Rights to Criticize China Over Human Rights" (Song Qiang et al. 1996). Liu Kang and Li Xiguang, two of the major authors of *Behind the Demonization of China,* stated, "in the 1990s, Chinese intellectuals ought to . . . liberate themselves from 'modern' Western speech and thought patterns, and acquire a new understanding of modern nationalism and nativism. . . . " (quoted in Suisheng Zhao 1997:735).

Guan Shijie, a scholar from Beijing University, even stated that "the time has come for the West to learn from the East. The West should switch positions and the teacher should become a student. The Confucian concept of universal harmony will be dominant during the next century, which will be one of peace and development" (quoted in Suisheng Zhao 1997:736). Guan certainly sounds both arrogant and vindictive. Wang Xiaodong, a researcher at the China Youth Research Center and one of the most ardent nationalists, believes that the nationalism in the 1990s is a reaction to the reverse racism *(nixiang zhongzu zhuyi)* in the 1980s (cited in Chen Dabai 2000; see also Wang Xiaodong 2000b). At that time, intellectuals belittled themselves and their race by admiring the West. Wang thinks that this world indeed is dominated by powers that are by no means just, and that China needs to strengthen itself so as to compete with them.

Other intellectuals, however, have criticized the nationalist sentiments of works such as *A Beijing Man in New York* or *China Can Say No.* Liu Xiaobo (1997:32) criticizes the former as grossly distorting Western civilization, and Xu Jilin (1997b:328) believes the play advocates a "hooligan culture." Many have noted the crude and slipshod quality of *China Can Say No* and its sequels *China Can Still Say No* and *Behind the Demonization of China* (1997). Chen Ming (1997) points out many of the inaccuracies in *Behind the Demonization of China.* In the book's description of the *New York Times* reporters Nicholas Kristof and Sheryl WuDunn, Chen finds an unfortunate racism. Xu Jilin (1997b:290) thinks that *China Can Say No* indicates a return to "the

Boxer Rebellion spirit in the time of the World Wide Web." He considers it so absurd that it deserved none of the sound and fury it roused (see also Lin Mu 1997a). Fei-ling Wang (1997) thinks the book simply reveals the authors' ignorance, arrogance, and ultranationalism. For Chen Dabai (2000), nationalism like that of Wang Xiaodong's is like a "drug addition" and needs to be overcome. He Jiadong (2000a) criticizes Wang Xiaodong (2000b) point by point and concludes that the nationalist medicine to cure China's illness is nothing but poison.

Ling Zhijun and Ma Licheng (1999:264–326) have made one of the more level-headed criticisms of such radical nationalism. They point out that rather than "containing China," the U.S. government's policy has been to engage and cooperate with China. Moreover, multinational corporations have lobbied long and hard for permanent normal trade relations for China. In their view, expecting the words of a few to represent America's China policy is simple-minded to say the least. They also challenged the exaggerated supremacy of Asian values as seen in the financial crises and racial conflicts of 1998. They remark that radical nationalism of this sort would only lead to stagnation of China's modernization, increased separatist tendencies in China's minority areas, and hostility between China and her neighbors and with the United States.

Xu Jilin (1997b:294) also points out that this anti-Westernism is dangerous because it can be, and is easily used by, radical intellectuals and those of the ruling class who resist modern social change. This vulgar, emotional, irrational, and racial nationalism could become a real concern once China has fulfilled its "dream of a strong national power." These "superpatriotic, anti-American" intellectuals also tend to be "antidemocratic and antihuman rights," as Friedman (1999:537–8) remarks. They pose a danger especially because they are part of the educated elite and as such appeal strongly to the populace. After the NATO bombing of the Chinese Embassy in May 1999, this nationalism reached its peak. Some even claimed that they were willing to risk a war with the United States. Even Xiao Gongqin (1999, 2000a, 2000b), the neoconservative who has long advocated a new nationalism, saw a danger: this "indignant nationalism" could lead China back to closing its doors, a reflection of the radical left.

Undaunted amid such criticisms, Fang Ning, Wang Xiaodong, Song Qiang, and their friends published another sequel to *China Can Say No*. Their new book is entitled *China's Road in the Shadow of Globalization*

(Quanqiu hua yinying xia de Zhongguo zhi lu), and it is a collection of articles. Both the front and back covers of the book are provocative. They show a map of China divided into five parts: the PRC (People's Republic of China), Tibet, Manchuria, East Turkestan, and Inner Mongolia. The caption says; "This is a map the Western media have overzealously published in their papers." In the book, the authors reiterate their nationalistic sentiments: "the U.S. wants to prevent the third world from developing" (p. 4), "most people in the U.S. hate the People's Republic of China" (p. 139), "the U.S. is the most unfriendly country in the eyes of China's youths" (p. 92), and so forth.

In one of his articles in the collection, Wang Xiaodong claims that those intellectuals who criticize him and his colleagues are unfortunately misguided and selfish. For example, they are only concerned with learning from the West. They ignore the West's problems and avoid criticizing the United States because they and the social stratum they are organic to have too many private interests there (Fang Ning et al. 1999:51). In addition, Wang lashes out at what he calls the reverse racism *(nixiang zhongzu zhuyi)* of the liberal intellectuals and hails the return of the normal nationalism *(zhengtai minzu zhuyi huigui)* (pp. 82–90). The authors of the book pride themselves on belonging to the "say no" club *("shuo bu" jule bu)* (p. 2).

With all of their defects, and the fact that most of them are far from being at the level of scholarship and they lack substance, these nationalistic works represent the beliefs of a sizable group of intellectuals, whom we may call radical critical intellectuals.[39] Their unusual appeal to the populace is partly because they also make some pertinent points about America's China policy (Suisheng Zhao 1997:741). They point out that the United States fears China's strength but also its weakness, its wealth but also its poverty, and its stability but also its chaos. Moreover, there is a hegemonic attitude on the part of the American government toward China, which it makes no effort to hide. This is the observation of Chen Feng, one of the authors of another best-seller, *A Depiction of Trials of Strength Between China and the United States* (cited in Suisheng Zhao 1997:741). Wang Xiaodong (2000a, 2000b) makes similar arguments.

Many intellectuals were involved in the debate (see the article on Wang by Zhang Xiaoxia 2001, Vol. 5). In addition to the ones we have just cited, other Mainland Chinese scholars also published books and essays in 1997 debating the popular nationalism. For example, Shen

Jiru (1998) of CASS published a book entitled *China Doesn't Want to Be "Mr. No"* arguing that the writers of *China Can Say No* are clearly misguided themselves in their judgment. This surge of nationalism and its criticism have certainly provided critical intellectuals with a forum where they could debate important and sensitive issues that help define the Chinese identity.

Meanwhile, both the American and Chinese governments have made efforts to improve their relations, including Jiang Zemin's visit to the United States in 1997 and Bill Clinton's visit to China in 1998. Even Huntington, as well as Bernstein and Muro, who have often raised the specter of conflict between China and the United States, now say that they mean only to alert people. Their aim is to urge both sides to work toward greater cooperation and the benefits that would bring them (cited in Ling and Ma 1999:275, 300). Both China and the United States have continued efforts to improve their relations, working in such areas as trade (e.g., the WTO deals), arms control, and lessening the conflicts between Taiwan and Mainland China.

Liu Xiaobo (1997) believes, however, that it is the particular nationalism of China's scholars, as seen in national studies and postmodernism, which deserves the greatest attention. For nationalism cloaked in scholarship represents the moral deterioration of the intellectuals, their failure to fulfill their social responsibilities. Is he right?

"Self-Loathing" and "Self-Approbation," Postmodernism, and National Learning

What is the scholarly nationalism, then? Here again, Barmé seems to have provided us with an interesting picture. Most of his analyses in this area focus on the discussions of self-hate and self-approbation by Chinese intellectuals. According to Barmé, Tan Sitong, Lu Xun, Li Ao, Bo Yang, and Liu Xiaobo, have all expressed their disgust with China's generations of tyrannical rulers. Many feel that China has fallen from the grace of "five thousand years of history." What they see are myriad social and political problems, for which they simply hate themselves (1996:194–5). Another example Barmé gives of this self-loathing is Wang Shuo. Wang comments that foreigners are naive since their spiritual culture consists simply of smoking dope. But the sophisticated Chinese really know how to get their kicks: out of self-annihilation. A third example is *River Elegy (Heshang)* which "equated older civilizations

(China, Egypt, Africa, and so on) with decadence, non-competitive economies and backwardness" and showed great frustration and hopelessness (p. 197). A fourth example is the students in the 1989 movement who were disgusted with the slow pace of political reform.

Along with the self-loathing there is also self-approbation. A newer tele-documentary, *The East,* depicts the cultural integrity of the Chinese rural world, which teaches that "'the peripheral world' should succor the spiritually depleted 'center' of the mainstream culture" (Barmé 1996:198). As another example, in 1993 Cui Jian, the rock musician, claimed that the "northern Chinese can produce a robust, positive and socially progressive type of music that is quite different from the negative and decadent rock of the West" (pp. 201–2). In comparison, these Chinese seem to have a lot of confidence in themselves.

The "self-hate and self-approbation" among scholars and writers of popular culture, however, seem to be quite different from the anti-Westernism we have just discussed. The main focus may be a kind of "self-belittling," self-criticism and self-evaluation, a very different kind of nationalism. But rather than practicing "reverse racism," as Wang Xiaodong charges, the intellectuals who mercilessly criticize and dissect their own culture may be taking the first step toward building a new one, as they did with the debate on the humanist spirit. Lu Xun, for example, remained an idealist and humanist in spite of his deep skepticism. To move toward a democratic society similar to that of the West's is still the goal of China's modernism.

Then there are the postmodern scholars, who may be Liu Xiaobo's real targets, along with the scholars of national learning. While critiquing the West's dominance and its modernist expansion, the postmodern scholars at the same time are hoping to combine the East and West, rather than exclude the West entirely. For example, after discussing the historic relationship between China and the West, Zhang Yiwu (1994: 108–9) concludes that the current constant reflection and critique on modernity suggest a new way of development and a new cultural strategy. The new world will be characterized by pluralism, and intellectuals will have to find a way of retaining their national identity while participating in global social and cultural advances. Sheng Hong (1995:98) too emphasized China's responsibility to respect other civilizations and to follow the international principles of free trade.

Still, like Liu Xiaobo, some intellectuals see a real danger: that postmodernism will be co-opted by Chinese conservatives and by the lowest level of nationalists (Barmé 1996:191–2). Zhao Yiheng warns that postmodern studies in China validate the commercial culture and clearly show intellectuals escaping from their critical roles. Xu Jilin cautions against a cultural cold war, and Wang Hui cautions against the alliance of postmodernism and extreme nationalism. In fact, in the article Barmé cites, Wang Hui goes further. He emphasizes that nationalism is a two-edged sword: it can unite a nation, but it can also destroy it. He believes there must be something transcending nations and cultures that can form the basis of world harmony (Wang Hui and Zhang Tianwei 1994: 19–20; see also Zhao Yiheng or Henry Y. H. Zhao 2000:355–6).

To be sure, in both Zhang and Sheng, as in the scholars cited by Barmé, there is much criticism of Western modernity, some of which is clearly misguided. Sheng Hong, for example, believes that the test of a nation's strength is its military power, which seems to him the only measurement of a civilization. But anti-Westernism as a prejudice does not seem to be typical of these scholars. After all, their fields of study are out and out Westernism, as Xu Jilin (1997:284) comments. Both postcolonialism and analytic Marxism are Western theories. As for their intellectual background, most of these scholars are actually returnees from schools in the West. Rather than anti-Westernism, then, it is criticism of radical nationalism and anti-Westernism that characterizes these intellectuals. Chen Xiaoming (1998:65–6), one of the most quoted postmodernists in China, has criticized antiforeign sentiments in the strongest terms:

> I want to point out that this way of pitting China against the world (as in *China Can Say No* and *Behind the Demonization of China,* etc.) poses the greatest danger. Beneath the surface of the emphasis on multiculturalism is "self-isolationism" and "closing the country to the outside" *(bi guan suo guo);* it is a crazy yearning for the old way of doing things.

A far cry from crude nationalism is today's *national learning*. As is explained by Zhang Dainian, a major figure in the field, national learning refers to the study of China's traditional culture: philosophy, Confucianism, history, political science, military science, and the natural sciences, as well as religion and art (cited in Chen Lai 1995). Its purpose is to make a critical evaluation of the traditional culture. Since 1989, national learning has developed at a faster rate: over a dozen journals have sprung up and many scholarly books, as well as new editions and translations of classics, have been published. *Xue Ren* (The Scholar), for example, focuses on modern scholarly history and Western cultural studies, and *Xueshu Jilin* (Scholarly Works) takes "free spirits and independent thinking" as its motto. The following titles also demonstrate the tendency of national learning scholars: *Wenhua de Chongtu yu Ronghe* (The conflict among and integration of different cultures), a collection of articles commemorating Zhang Shenfu, Tang Yongtong, and Liang Shuming, written by Zhang Dainian et al. (1997); and *Ruxue yu Ershi Yi Shiji Zhongguo* (Confucianism and twenty-first century China), a collection of articles on how to construct and develop "contemporary neo-Confucianism," edited by Zhu Ruikai (2000). These are in direct conflict with the antiforeignism we just examined.

In fact, neo-Confucianism draws on the success stories of East Asian countries, and asserts that "a revived neo-Confucianism, with its emphasis on the group, authority and education, could provide the intellectual and cultural underpinnings for China's rapid economic development while helping it avoid the immorality and individualism of Western capitalism" (Goldman 1999:704; see also Jing Wang 1996: 64–78). This intellectual current was influenced by the neo-Confucianism of Tu Wei-ming, the well-known Confucian scholar from Harvard University.

But, of course, the national learning movement started in the late Qing dynasty, in the early twentieth century, when a group of intelligentsia (the "national essence," or guocui group), faced with the pressure of Western-style modernization, took upon themselves the task of *defining, protecting, and perpetuating* Chinese culture. The movement boasted such well-known scholars as Zhang Binglin (or Chang Ping-lin, i.e., Taiyan, 1869–1935), Liu Shipei (or Liu Shih-p'ei, 1884–1919), Liang Shuming (1893–1988), and Xiong Shili (or Hsiung Shih-li, 1884–1968) (see Furth 1976; Bernal 1976; Alitto 1976; Tu Wei-ming 1976). National learning took a beating in the May 4 era and during the early parts of Communist rule, except for a brief surge in 1935 when ten professors signed the "Declaration of the Construction of a China-based Culture (Edward Wang 2001:152–60).[40] When the school was revived in Taiwan and in Hong Kong in the 1950s, it had added a New Confucianism spearheaded by Zhang Junmai, Mou Zongsan (Mou Tsung-san, 1909–93), Tang Junyi (Tang Chun-I, 1909–78), Qian Mu (Chien Mu, 1895–1990), and Xu Fuguan (Hsu Fu-kuan, 1904–82) (Hao Chang 1976; Tu Wei-ming 1993b; Edward Wang 2001:200). The tradition has continued with such scholars as Tu Wei-ming, Yu Ying-shih, and Lin Yu-sheng, all living in the United States but traveling extensively in the Chinese world.[41]

It should be noted that the movement at its start was not unrelated to the late Qing reformer Zhang Zhidong's advocacy of "Chinese learning as essence and Western learning as functions" (Schneider 1976:58–64). Zhang is reminding us that the traditional national learning school has never been in favor of a total rejection of Western learning.[42]

To be sure, the CCP government has had a hand in the newest national learning movement, in much the same way when GMD endorsed the ten professors' declaration in 1935. In the 1980s, as we discussed in chapter 2, the Party endorsed the establishment of the International Academy of Chinese Culture, and sponsored various lectures and symposia (Edward X. Gu 1999:409–10; Jing Wang 1996: 70). It is true that national learning emerged on a large scale after 1989, when the government was actively engaged in criticism of Westernization (Chen Lai 1995). It is also true that Zhang Dainian related national learning to the government's task of patriotic education. National learning received a warm welcome from *People's Daily* in 1993, obviously for political purposes since the government was then campaigning for patriotic education. And it was attacked by critics of government like Liu Xiaobo for fostering a radical nationalism. As we just mentioned, Barmé and Xu also considered national learning as a way of promoting radical nationalism.

But it might be ideologized by both the government and the critics of government. And to put it on the same level with *China Can Say No* or *Beijing Man in New York* is far-fetched. This "crude nationalism" may be forced upon the national learning scholars, and it would hardly be of their own making. In fact, they are very much aware that their specialty could be appropriated by ideologues at both ends of the political spectrum. Tang Yijie, yet another well-known, influential scholar in Chinese traditional cultural studies, warned in 1994 that there were two directions in which national learning could go (cited in Chen Lai 1995:25). First, it could put Chinese traditional culture in touch with world cultural developments and connect the true spirit of Chinese culture with the requirements of modern times. Second, it could deviate from true scholarship and become ideologized. Tang even suggested that it was not a good time to advocate national learning. Although the neo-Confucians might have also participated in the rising tide of nationalism in the

1990s (Goldman 1999:705), this awareness among national learning scholars tells us that they may deserve more credit than they are given for not fanning a crude nationalism.

Xiao Gongqin (1994c) summarizes it well: while we can draw upon the many resources in the traditional Chinese culture to build a new one, people should not worry that the traditional oppressive relationship between the rulers and the ruled will make a comeback. For the benefits that people have experienced from the market economy and from social pluralism it will be virtually impossible to return to the old repression.[43]

A New Nationalism in the Making?

A question arises here. If there is, in fact, an independent nationalism in national learning, or for that matter, in postmodernism, and it is different from the nationalism of *China Can Say No,* what kind of nationalism is it? Hu Shih delineates three kinds or levels of nationalism. At the lowest level, nationalism is an antiforeign sentiment or a push for foreign exclusion *(pai wai)*. At the middle level, nationalism refers to the protection of one's national culture. At the highest level it reflects the most difficult task of all: building a national state (cited in Luo Houli 1998).

On the first level, we might place *China Can Say No* and the like, a crude statement of anti-Westernism, or what Li Shenzhi, the former vice president of CASS, calls a vulgar *(cubi de)* nationalism, which calls for revenge and conflict rather than reward and cooperation (cited in Suisheng Zhao 1997:744). National learning and postmodernism are more likely to be on the second and third levels, substantiating and building a national culture within the context of world cultural development. Both national learning and postmodernism represent the crisis Xu believes is currently facing China's intellectuals: the negotiation of a Chinese cultural identity. The "complete Westernization" of the 1980s and the "anti-Westernization" of the 1990s are good examples of that crisis. Once China's intellectuals are able to overcome their binary thinking and to address the complex cultural problem directly, they may be able to move from that crisis to achievement, and to carve out a national identity. National learning and postmodernism are good places to begin. That there are two different levels of nationalism is important, although at times the line can be blurred.

As Lucian Pye points out, China's nationalism has not yet substantiated itself. It lacks basic building blocks such as the American-style *Declaration of Independence, a Universal Declaration of Human Rights,* a sacred constitution, or a complete set of rules and regulations governing the behavior of political parties, as in the parliamentary system in Britain (cited in Xu Jilin 1997b:292–3). Pye's following observation is also poignant:

> [B]etween the two extremes of either nihilistically denouncing Chinese civilization or romanticizing it, most Chinese intellectuals and political leaders have consistently failed to do what their counterparts in the rest of the developing world have tried to do, which was to create a new sense of nationalism that would combine elements of tradition with appropriate features of the modern world culture. (cited in Suisheng Zhao 1999:744)

But that is just what Chinese intellectuals had been struggling with in the 1990s. Moreover, it is a continuation of the struggle by Sun Yat-sen, who invented and tried to implement the Three People's Principles *(San min zhuyi)* of nationalism, democracy, and socialism. To make democracy work in the Chinese pursuit of a national identity is a doable task (Friedman 1995:311–43). The debate on nationalism in the 1990s seems to be a good example of the critical intellectuals' continual work on the issue of national identity and modernity. A new nationalism resembling Sun's Three People's Principles may be in the making. Whatever its form, this new nationalism, or neonationalism, will need "to strike a balance between the extreme position of xenophobia and that of total Westernization" (Min Lin 1999:177). Cultural transcendence is the key (see also Edward Wang 2001:206–8). We will now examine more critical intellectuals' discourses in the same question of identity and modernity.

The Great Debate Between Liberal Intellectuals, Neoconservatives, and the New and Old Left over China's Modernity

The crackdown in 1989 silenced some *critical organic intellectuals* (the democratic elite in both Party and government) and sent others abroad. Many who did not leave, however, continued to advocate democratic reforms in the system. Goldman (1999:706–7) described a number of such intellectuals. Liu Ji, a vice president of CASS and an adviser to Jiang Zemin, sponsored books advocating political reforms, following motion Jiang made in the Fifteenth Party Congress in 1997. Dong Fureng, an economist and adviser on state industry reform, also called for political reforms to deal with various social problems such as corruption, unemployment, widening income gaps, and environmental pollution.

There have also been a group of *liberal democratic intellectuals.* Fang Jue, a provincial reform official turned businessperson, drafted a platform for democratic reforms. Li Shenzhi, the retired vice president of CASS, advocated political and civil rights of ordinary citizens and criticized the regime publicly for not carrying out political reforms. Indeed, to Fang and Li, we should also add the intellectuals in the democracy movement. We will, however, leave the discussion of the whole group to the next section on the democracy movement. Their criticisms aroused the government's strong reaction, as other democracy movements would do. Fang Jue was sentenced to four years of prison in 1999, ostensibly for illegal business practices (*Press Freedom Guardian,* June 18, 1999). In the first months of 2000, Li Shenzhi and three other *liberal intellectuals* became the targets of another new round of criticism. Li was criticized for his article commemorating the fiftieth anniversary of the founding of the People's Republic. In the article, Li (2000a) criticized Mao for his errors, Deng for his crackdown on the 1989 movement, and Jiang for covering up the previous errors. Mao Yushi, a researcher, and Fan Gang, an economist, both originally from CASS, were criticized for spreading economic liberalism. Liu Junning, a political scientist from CASS, was criticized for spreading doubts about collectivism and socialism (*Guanming Daily,* March 29, 2000). He was fired from his CASS position in March 2000.

What interests us most are the *liberal intellectuals* and the *neoconservatives,*[44] who are different from the *liberal democratic* intellectuals in that they emphasize the market economy rather than democracy as Li Shenzhi and Fang Jue do. These intellectuals have been locked into a debate with the New Left intellectuals over the issues of China's modernity. Let us now have a look at their points of view.

According to Xu Youyu (2000:413–30), who is a philosopher with CASS, *liberals* like himself take as their top priority personal freedom, by which they mean a person's political and legal freedoms. They therefore believe in the protection of personal property and a balance of administrative powers. They know that capitalist production produces inequality and alienation. However, Wang Dingding (2000:362–8), a liberal intellectual who is also an economist at Beijing University, insists that such imbalance is a sacrifice a society must make in order to reach a freer world. Liberals, according to Xu, also believe in a democratic system, but not until the market economy is fully developed. The latter development is a necessary condition for democracy, although it is not a sufficient condition. Their version of democracy is characterized by freedom of speech, by freedom of the press to offset governmental power, by diversity in religious and other values, and by equality before the law. They are not talking about national or even provincial elections.

If the liberal intellectuals appear to be focused on defending the market economy, *neoconservatives* seem to focus on defending the political system. Neoconservatism in the 1990s refers to "a body of arguments calling for political stability, central authority, tight social control, and a role for ideology and nationalism" (Feng Chen 1997:593). It is, in fact, a new name for the new authoritarianism of the 1980s. Back in the 1980s, a few scholars like Xiao Gongqin and Wang Huning from Shanghai advocated a strong authoritarian state to enforce economic reform. They were supported by the then Party General Secretary Zhao Ziyang, but criticized by liberal democratic intellectuals, who argued that in any case there probably was no correlation between Confucian authoritarianism and economic success (Suisheng Zhao 1997:733).

Neoconservatism still emphasizes state control for the purpose of social stability. Immediately after the 1989 democracy movement, He Xin, a scholar from CASS, wrote on the importance of stability over everything, following the Party line and defending the crackdown. Then in 1992, a group of intellectuals published a widely read article entitled "Realistic Responses and Strategic Choices for China after the Disintegration of the Soviet Union." In it they advocated strict policy and even the establishment of Party-owned assets to consolidate Party power (Baum 1994:328–30; Suisheng Zhao 1997:733–4). Xiao Gongqin again warned against the dangers of a weak central government. It is not surprising that this neoconservatism became popular, after the chaos and instability following the reforms in the former Soviet Union and Eastern Europe. Neoconservatism became even more popular as China's difficulties mounted: corruption, crime, large numbers of migrant workers in the cities, urban unemployment, and income disparity (Feng Chen 1997:596).

Neoconservatives, however, do not see radical political reform as a way out of these difficulties. Xiao Gongqin criticizes those who assume that China's problems lie in the old system and want to solve them by eradicating it. He believes that radical social change, including democratic changes, will only bring about chaos. Li Zehou, a well-known philosopher, also argues against radicalism along with Liu Zaifu, a literary critic. Li and Liu (1997) favor gradual change rather than revolution. Wang Shan, the author of two popular books, *Looking at China Through a Third Eye* (1994) and *Looking at China Through a Fourth Eye* (1996), flatly denies the feasibility of a democratic system in China, claiming that the Chinese people do not have the capacity to govern themselves. As for intellectuals, they only know how to engage in irresponsible criticism, according to Wang. For the neoconservatives, the success of the market economy requires that the ideal social equality and democracy be sacrificed (cited in Wang Sirui 2000:410–14; see also He Jiadong 2000b, 2000c for his criticism of neoconservatism, especially Li and Liu's theme on the "good-bye revolution").

What is to be done, then? Xiao Gongqin favors tough control in the political domain and leniency in social, economic, and cultural affairs, the latter part echoing the liberals. In other words, China should follow the East Asian authoritarian model. Wang Shan, too, advocates a technocratic authoritarianism. Neoconservatives advocate a strong central government that has the economic and political resources to lead development in the provinces. But to achieve this, some neoconservatives believe, the government can no longer rely on the omnipotence of the Party. Nor can it count on the elimination of dissent at various levels, in an effort to achieve structural stability. Rather, the government needs to incorporate a variety of interests into the system, under, of course, the leadership of the Party. Ideologically, neoconservatism calls for a return to the traditional culture, where resources can be found to develop a nationalism that will bind the country together (Feng Chen 1997:598–610; Baum 1994:330).[45]

Neoconservative thought "gives the Communist Party [i.e., the bureaucratic ruling class] a rationale for aggrandizing its power" (Forney 1997). Jiang Yihua (2000:67–73), a historian from Fudan University, criticizes that with its emphasis on stability, order, and efficiency, neoconservatism will actually lead to a system that is unstable, disorderly, and inefficient. For absolute power only covers up the unstable elements that could have been easily resolved through some little disturbances (caused by democracy). When these elements are not taken care of, unrest and even violence will occur, according to Jiang. However, although neoconservatism may serve to legitimize the Party rule, it differs from the official ideology (Feng Chen 1997:611), as liberalism does. Neoconservatism criticizes liberal democracy for its possible destabilizing effect, but the official ideology criticizes it for its potential to overthrow the CCP. Like the liberals, the neoconservatives are not opposed to democracy. They argue for a strong authority only as a means to an end, not the end itself, in the same way that the market economy is a condition for democracy, as the liberals argue. Their opposition to revolution is also at odds with the Party, which came to power through revolution.[46] As Xiao Gongqin (2000a) claims, they have no quarrels now with the liberal intellectuals who favor a gradual change. We do see a lot of convergence between the liberals and the neoconservatives, especially their difference with the Party.

Nonetheless, we can still say that neoconservatism has teamed up with nationalism, liberalism, national learning, and, to some extent, postmodernism to form a conservative bloc, a coalition to protect the current political and economic system however unjust it may be. Nationalism characterized by patriotism and by a strong defense of national interests is the *keystone* of this conservative trend. Neoconservatism is its *political* aspect, national learning its *cultural* aspect, and postmodernism is its *useful tool* (see Wang Sirui 2000). One can even say that liberalism is its *economic* aspect. On the other hand, the New Left endorses nationalism and criticizes liberalism, using postmodernism and postcolonialism as its tool. Its critique of neoconservatism and national learning is, however, much less salient.

We will now look at the New and Old Left, comparing their points of view in their debate with liberals (and sometimes with neoconservatives) over China's paths to modernity. Developed in the 1990s, the *New Left (xin zuoyi,* sometimes called *xin zuopai)*[47] is a large group of intellectuals who have questioned the fairness of the market economy and the lack of popular participation in the political process. Like China's liberals and neoconservatives, they are also troubled by the problems plaguing their country. They are especially concerned about the disparity between the poor and the rich. But they believe that this is a result of world capitalist development, that is, globalization (see Wang Hui [1997]2000:122).

Han Yuhai (2000:227), a professor of Chinese at Beijing University and one of the champions of the New Left,[48] charges that global capital oppresses and exploits Third World nations by imposing on them its own rules of the game. Global capital seeks, for example, to restrict the working class' right to strike. He accuses the liberals of failing to understand this. Wang Shicheng (2000:407–12), a professor of Chinese at Jinan Normal University, also criticizes the liberals. He sees them as the representatives of the newly rich, or at least the new middle class. Their enthusiasm for the market economy prevents them from criticizing its corruption. Their longing for freedom is thus harmed by the lack of democracy. For Wang, freedom will never occur without democracy. Xudong Zhang (1998:129–30), too, criticizes the liberal intellectuals as acting in an "elitist" fashion toward "the society sanctioned by the bureaucracy," fundamentally lacking "any serious commitment to democracy," and paying "only sporadic lip service to civil rights."

The New Left may criticize, but does it provide its own platform for democracy? In a few cases, the answer may be yes. For example, Cui Zhiyuan, a political scientist from MIT, advocates combining Mao's commune system with the village autonomy, the Great Leap Forward with township enterprises, the Cultural Revolution with campaigns against bigwigs, and the Angang Constitution with Fordist economic democracy.[49] In Cui's view, a reconfiguration of these various factors would provide China with a unique model of modernization (cited in Suisheng Zhao 1997:737). He believes that as long as there is democracy at the lower levels, there is no need for multiparty politics at the state level (Cui Zhiyuan 2000:528–38). For Xudong Zhang (1998:130–1), means such as the Angang Constitution and "neocollectivism" would provide us with "new possibilities for political participation and democracy within the residual socialist framework." Their solution, then, is not more capitalism under a centralized state, as the liberals and neoconservatives would have, but more socialism. Since they are not totally opposed to the market economy and Western-style democracy, they propose, in a sense, a third way, a new path between the capitalist and socialist systems (Wang Hui [1997] 2000:122–3).

In 1996, some Chinese students of the New Left established an overseas electronic magazine called *China and the World*. Since then, scholars from both home and abroad contributed articles (see http://www.chinabulletin.com/). The Web-site stated its mission thus:

> We hope that through our forum, *China and the World,* we can promote a deeper understanding of the global capitalist system. We want to reflect seriously on the experiences and lessons of Chinese and world socialist

> movements, so that we can find a Chinese way that transcends Western capitalism. We hope this journal will help us regain our historical critical perspective against both capitalism and imperialism. Finally, we hope it will rekindle the enthusiasm and idealism with which we seek a different way. This is our basic mission and understanding.

It is clear that the New Left intellectuals are nostalgic about the old days and critical of the new, but they still hope to bridge the two. Again, they are very critical of the liberal intellectuals. For example, some of their articles lashed out at Li Shenzhi for his criticisms of Mao, Deng, and Jiang in his widely circulated article we just mentioned. They also lashed out at Wang Yuanhua, the Shanghai-based writer and former director of the Shanghai Party's Propaganda Department, for his views on political reform (http://www.chinabulletin.com/, March 13, 2000).

The New Left may be vehement, but they are just as vehemently criticized by other intellectuals. Neoconservatives like Xiao Gongqin (2000a) comment that the New Left has romanticized Mao's China, especially the Cultural Revolution. Without actually going through the Cultural Revolution, these intellectuals are designing a system based on idealized history rather than on practical experience. Xiao predicts that such a system, if put into practice, would be a monster. He observes that many of his New Left friends are full of conscience and enthusiasm, but their "cultural romanticism" is like an opiate they use to overcome life's difficulties.

One member of the New Left, however, replies with witty innocence:

> We don't understand this. On the one hand, people who are sympathetic to the disadvantaged majority and concerned about their feelings and interests are viewed as unrealistic, their heads in the clouds. On the other hand, those who intentionally or unintentionally create theories helping the powerful, wealthy minority protect its interests and status are viewed as realists with their feet on the ground. We don't understand.[50]

It is fair to say, though, that the New Leftists are making an effort to find a new way to solve China's problems, just as the neoconservatives do, however romantic and unrealistic some of them may be.

However, by setting up this new path, according to Tao Dongfeng (2000:444–6), a professor of Chinese from Capital Normal University, the New Left emphasizes more their criticism of capitalism and liberalism, but less than their criticism of socialism as they have experienced it. The fact is, says Tao, that there is in China too little of either liberalism or capitalism. That is why there is so much political and cultural dictatorship, and so much corruption among government officials. For Tao, the New Left's criticism, derived as it is from postmodernism, postcolonialism, neo-Marxism, world-system theories, dependency theories, and so forth, might be useful in a critique of Western capitalism, but for China today, it is a bit far-fetched. Xu Ben makes a similar criticism of postmodernism for its failure to criticize the oppression at home (cited in Xudong Zhang 1998:126).

Ren Jiantao (2000:200–7) summarizes all this very well. The New Left is commendable in its critique of the social problems in China, but it fails to provide an alternative that will make the current market economy work. Nor does it suggest a political system that can accommodate this market economy. The New Left's insistence on popular participation like that of the Cultural Revolution is a dangerous solution, as Xu Jilin points out (in Xu Jilin et al. 2000:324; see also He Qinglian 2001: 234–42). This can also be seen from the play *Che Guevara* some New Left intellectuals wrote and directed in 2000.[51] Both the play and its writers, directors, and performers demonstrate a strong sense of pro-violence, pro-Castro's Cuba, and anti-American imperialism (see *Shi Jie* 2001). Actually, the lack of democratic political reform may be a problem for both the New Left and the liberals. Luo Gang (in Xu Jilin et al. 2000:315–6) observes that both sides want to rely on the state to provide a space for public political participation. But both fail to clarify how the highest and lowest classes can be equally represented in the political process. One of them focuses on the middle class, and the other on the working class. Neither tries to accommodate both.

The problem of the New Left is similar to the problem of the *Old Left,* represented by Deng Liqun, the retired director of the Party's Propaganda Department, and his followers. We referred to them in chapter 2 as orthodox organic intellectuals. Now, however, they are being squeezed out of the power structure and are becoming more critical of the current regime's efforts at economic reform, like the New Left. Indeed, their forces are so strong that they publish a number of journals and have challenged the reformers and their liberal intellectual supporters. Their journals include *In the Middle of the Current* (Zhong liu), implying that they may be against the tide, *Contemporary Trends in Ideology* (Dangdai sichao), and *The Pursuit of Truth* (Zhenli de zhuiqiu), The first journal is edited by Lin Mohan and Wei Wei, both orthodox revolutionary intellectuals, the second published by The Association for

National History of the People's Republic of China (Zhonghua renmin gonghe guo guo shi xue hui). Deng Liqun is the leader, but the journal is edited by Duan Ruofei and Jiang Huanhu. The third journal is edited by Yu Quanyu, Sun Yongren, and Chen Tanqiang. Immediately following the crackdown on the democracy movement in 1989, the Old Left raised its voice again through the Propaganda Department and the media. However, since the opening of the new economic campaign in 1992, they have again been marginalized, as we mentioned earlier. Nevertheless, they have been able to promote their discourse through their journals.

What is the main position of the Old Left? In several of their "ten-thousand word" statements, and in numerous articles published in their journals, they show grave concern over the decline of state industries and the lamentable conditions of the working class (Goldman 1999: 703; Zhao Huaquan 2001), as the New Left does. We have discussed one of Deng Liqun's articles in a previous section, in which he describes the changes in class structure caused by the changes in the economic structure. A tally of the articles on this subject in *Contemporary Trends in Ideology,* in 1998 alone, gives us a snapshot of the issues that concern the Old Left. The order is arranged by the journal itself:

- 1 leading article by Deng Liqun on the current economic situation of the country
- 1 on the correct understanding of Deng Xiaoping's thoughts
- 1 on the importance of the practice criterion
- 3 debating the ideas in *Crossing Swords,* a book arguing for radical economic reform
- 5 on the contemporary relevance of the *Communist Manifesto*
- 6 on the importance of getting water from the South to the North
- 10 on the reform of state-owned enterprises
- 1 on labor relations in the enterprises owned by foreign capital
- 6 on the Party's history, theories, and the PLA
- 3 on the Asian financial crisis and globalization
- 4 on the lessons from the former Soviet Union and Eastern Europe
- 3 criticizing American hegemony
- 3 on computerization, the culture industry, and modernism and postmodernism
- 8 on the study of traditional Chinese thoughts

The Old Left has challenged the current regime to honor its promise to follow its professed socialism. They have challenged the Party's lack of leadership in protecting workers' interests. They attack the Party's policy of not asking whether a reform is socialist or capitalist, saying that this failure is not what Deng Xiaoping had in mind. And they attack the government, especially local government, in selling state-owned enterprises to private owners. To privatize is to deprive labor of the power and status, for which it has struggled over several generations, according to Deng Liqun (1998:10; see also a collection of ten years of such articles from *The Pursuit of Truth,* two volumes edited by Yu Zheng 2000). In 2001, the Old Left directly challenged Jiang Zemin's call to invite private entrepreneurs to join the Party (see Zhang Quanjing 2001); *The Pursuit of Truth* is now suspended at the time of the writing.[52]

However, while the Old Left may have some sharp observations on all this, their solution is to go back to Mao, or to Mao's socialist democracy, and to let Marxists rather than "rightist opportunists" hold Party power. (Indeed, the journal is full of Mao quotations, in the articles and, it seems, in every available space.) Ordinary people must have power and must participate in the superstructure, says Deng Liqun (1998:12). His arguments certainly coincide with that of the New Left, but he does not say *how* to get power to the people. He is certainly not arguing for a general election, where everybody has a vote, as the New Left sometimes argues for lower-level participation. So his grand statements become mere propaganda, as did Mao's about people power.

Nonetheless, the Old Left does represent the concerns of many ordinary people about the consequences of privatization. Although the pace of reform of state-owned enterprises has been slow, it does indicate that the regime is addressing the concerns expressed by the Old and the New Left. In effect, both the Old and New Left have become the watchdog of the regime, making sure that the latter does not deviate too much from its professed socialist ideals. They have become a force to be reckoned with by the regime (see also Feng Chen 1999:466).

The Old Left has also become a force for the liberal intellectuals to reckon with as well. For example, its members have launched a battle against two journalists from the *People's Daily,* Ma Licheng and Ling Zhijun, who wrote the book *Crossing Swords*.[53] The book attacks the Old Left for their opposition to economic reform. The Old Left responds by saying that the authors advocate abolishing public ownership of state properties in favor of capitalist restoration. Peng Jianpu (1998:52–5), a teacher from the Dalian Navy Political Institute and one of the young theorists of the Old Left, criticizes the book's stance on not debating whether a reform is socialist or capitalist. He says that liberals refuse to debate the issues just so they can sell capitalism. The journal *In the Middle of the Current* has also published a number of articles attacking the book, following the same arguments. Peng states that people like himself became socialists and communists after the victory over bourgeois liberalization following the events in 1989. Replying to one of his supporters, Peng (1999:60) maintains that there is indeed anti-Marxist thought in *Crossing Swords,* and many believe in it. History, he says, dictates that people like him will bear the heavy responsibility of spreading the truth and carrying on the tradition of the Russian Revolution.

In short, how do the Old and New Left compare and contrast? Neither of them seems to have a full-fledged program of reform, so the comparison here will be sketchy. Although the Old Left believes in socialism just as the New Left does, their versions may be different. While the New Left may advocate utilizing some of the Maoist practices of social and economic organization, the Old Left does not seem to have any concrete suggestions for checking the negative consequences of capitalism. For example, they are against selling state-owned enterprises. But they do not know how to improve the latter's performance other than relying on the masses and the Party. But they know the Party is corrupt, so they advocate people's democracy. Yet they do not say how democracy can be implemented. In addition, people's democracy might upset the Party leadership in which they believe. In short, they may have legitimate concerns, but they are limited by the Party's conventional ways of dealing with them, which fall far short of their expectations. Besides, both the Old and New Lefts' discourses smell too much of Maoism, and Maoism lacks appeal to many who believe in Western-style democracy and Western economic practice. Even the reformist Party leadership has been warning for a decade against leftist tendencies to obstruct reform. As Peng (1999:60) himself acknowledges, history dictates that people like him will suffer *(shounan)* in an uphill battle.

Nonetheless, both the Old and New Left have played important roles in reminding the leadership, as well as the populace, of the conditions of the working class. The sufferings of the workers, they say, violate the regime's professed socialist ideals. Although one may fault their Maoist nostalgia, it would be hard to ignore their criticism. They seem to have become a very important voice and exerted some influence in the political arena. Many from the Old and New Left teamed up in the nationalist surge against the United States after the crisis in Kosovo and the NATO bombing of the Chinese embassy in Belgrade (Xiao Gongqin 1999:136). As we just mentioned, the government is showing restraint in privatization, which could be viewed as a response to pressures from the Left. The Left has always been a force to be reckoned with by both the government and liberal intellectuals, and it will continue to be so.

So far, we have examined social critics, writers, artists, musicians, movie directors, and scholars in national learning and postmodern studies in the 1990s. We have also examined various kinds of nationalists, the liberal democratic intellectuals, the neoconservatives, the liberals, and intellectuals of the New and Old Left.[54] We call them critical intellectuals because their criticisms were largely independent of the official discourse. The debates in the 1990s over the humanist spirit, nationalism, and Chinese modernity between the left-wing and right (liberal)-wing intellectuals have provided the critical intellectuals with a space to ponder the Chinese identity in the current waves of globalization. One can see a convergence between China and the West in that intellectuals clash in their different paths to modernity or postmodernity. And some have been looking for a third way. We will come back to this topic in chapter 6 when we discuss the roles of the intellectual class.

The Democracy Movement

What has happened to the liberal democratic elite since 1989? We just mentioned Li Shenzhi and Fang Jue. In this section, we examine more intellectuals in the democracy movement both inside and outside the country. We will first, however, examine *Beijing Spring,* one of the dissident journals published in the United States, which will give us an idea of the concerns of the Chinese democracy movement and the intellectuals involved in it.

Beijing Spring and the Democracy Movement in General

The best-known dissident journals include *Beijing Spring, China Spring,* and *Democratic China,* all of which are published in Chinese in the United States and on-line. *China Spring* was started in 1982 by a group of Chinese scholars in the United States, and *Beijing Spring* was started in 1993 by a group of scholars who were unhappy with the operation of

China Spring. Democratic China was started by the democratic elite who escaped China after the crackdown in 1989. It began in regular print but is now only on-line because of financial constraints. There is also a dissident biweekly newspaper, *Press Freedom Guardian,* published in California. I will examine in table 3.3 only *Beijing Spring.* It will show us the focus of the Chinese democracy movement.

Table 3.3 Number and Percent of Various Articles in *Beijing Spring,* No. 1–9, 1997

Types of Articles	Number of Such Articles	Percent of Total
Articles on Political and Economic Events and Personages in China: on Deng Xiaoping, Jiang Zemin, Zhao Ziyang, Chen Xitong, other Chinese leaders, political reform, election, repression, legitimacy of CCP rule, defining China, Deng's death, officialdom, mass media, economic reform, social justice, diplomacy, relations with Russia	61	20.8%
Democratic Movement Activities in the U.S.: collections of news reports on various activities, "100 days in a simulated prison," Wu Hongda's and Hu Ping's speeches, conference notes, messages, comments on events, strategies, on publication of Wei Jingsheng's book, *The Courage to Stand Alone.*	32	10.9%
Hong Kong Issues: the return of Hong Kong, its implications, law, the mass media, Zhao Ziyang	31	10.6%
Articles Commemorating the 8th Anniversary of June 4th: reflections, remembrance, declarations, letters, poems	23	7.8%
Declarations, Letters, Speeches, Newsreleases: by Wang Xizhe, Wu Xucan, Ding Zilin, Zhao Ziyang, Tong Yi, Yang Jianli, Lin Mu, various organizations, including a workers' organization in China. There are protest letters, petitions, position declarations concerning June 4th, Deng's death, or other specific issues.	16	5.5%
Nationalism in China: on radical nationalism, criticism and evaluation of nationalism, relation to democracy, its being exaggerated	15	5.1%
Democratic Movement in China and the World: democracy and human rights, US elections, Diaoyu Island confrontations	14	4.8%
Literature and Democracy: stories, poetry	13	4.4%
On Law and Human Rights: the anti-revolutionary law, law on bankruptcy, law reform	12	4.1%
On the Cultural Revolution and the Anti-Rightist Movement: defense of Liu Shaoqi, underground reading movement, books on the cultural revolution, workers' movement, Beida in 1957,Mao and the movement, recollections by Xu Liangying	12	4.1%

Table 3.3 Continued

Types of Articles	Number of Such of Total	Percent
Book Reviews: on Hitler, Mao, democracy, China and the West, *Tian Nu (Heavenly Rage),* on Cheng Kuide's collection of essays,on Wang Juntao's escape from China, on *China Can Say No,* on *Study in the U.S.*	12	4.1%
Personal Interviews with Fu Shenqi, Chen Jun, Qi Mo, Zhang Xianliang, Ni Yuxian, Lu Siqing, Sheng Xue, Zhao Hongzhang, Tang Boqiao, Tong Yi, Zhong Weiguang, and Jiang Qisheng. Most interviews were done by Ya Yi	12	4.1%
Collections of Letters to the Editor	9	3.1%
Cultural Forum: on the independent personality, Gu Zhun, freedom, Asian values	7	2.4%
European Support of Human Rights in China: awards to Wei Jingsheng, to Gao Yu, support from Denmark and Sweden	6	2.1%
Personal Histories: on Hu Ping, Fan Zhili, Wang Xiaobo	5	1.7%
On Democratic Figures: defense of Wang Dan, on Liu Nianchun, on Wei Jingsheng	5	1.7%
Tibetan Issues: independence, the Dalai Lama	5	1.7%
Workers in China: independent workers' movement, unemployment	2	0.7%
Taiwan and Mainland relations	1	0.3%
	293	100%

Source: Beijing Spring 1997 (Nos. 1–9).

Note: The classifications are not exact; for example, the poetry commemorating June 4 is grouped with articles in that category rather than in the category of literature and democracy. Also, the actual total is about 1 percent less due to rounding.

Several observations are worth noting. First, almost none of these articles can be published in China. Thus, a journal like *Beijing Spring* is an invaluable outlet for opinion on the democratic movement, one of the most important issues engaging China's critical intellectuals. It is where critical intellectuals involved in the democratic movement can exchange and disseminate ideas and rally support. Since all of these dissident journals as well as the newspaper are on-line, one can expect some mainland Chinese to have access to them in one way or another. Without this forum, even readers in the West would find it difficult to know what is happening with China's democratic movement. One would be unable to read, for example, the letters from Ding Zilin about her efforts to locate parents who lost their children during the June 4 massacre. One is likely to miss the protest letter of Lin Mu, the former assistant to Hu Yaobang. Lin's house was searched in 1995 and again in 1997 for any evidence of his dissident activities (Lin Mu 1997b).

In addition, the journal does give the reader a fair picture of what critical intellectuals are doing in the democratic movement. From this tabulation, we can see that over 30% of its articles are political and economic critiques of events and people in China, and of democratic activities in the United States. The return of Hong Kong in 1997 and the eighth anniversary of June 4 both have significant implications for the democracy movement: 10.6% and 7.8% of the articles are devoted to those issues, respectively. Several authors also joined the debate on nationalism, since it relates closely to how activists in the democratic movement want to define themselves. Personal interviews always seem to get around to democratic movement figures; they put a personal touch on what seems to be impersonal political organizing.

To be sure, there is occasional sloganeering in some of the writings and one wonders whether it serves any useful purpose. For example, in an open telegram by Wang Xizhe (1997:14) and others, Jiang Zemin was accused of wanting to be chair of the Party, rather than general secretary. This was viewed as following Yuan Shikai's empire-building. But the telegram does not support its accusation except for some overused slogans and trite phrases: If we can tolerate this, is there anything we cannot tolerate? *(shi ke ren, shu bu ke ren),* or Look at tomorrow's China; it will be Jiang's family empire *(shi kan ming ri zhi zhong guo, bi shi Jiang jia zhi tian xia).* Most of the articles, however, are quite informative. The interviews especially are almost always sincere and convincing.

Most of the people who appear in the journal are active in the democracy movement. How do we describe these intellectuals? First of all, there is no doubt that they are critical intellectuals since they are aiming to change the current political system in China. Second, they are working in a different context than the critical intellectuals we have analyzed earlier in this chapter. To use Eyerman and Jamison's (1991:98) term, they are *movement intellectuals.* These are intellectuals "who through their activities articulate the knowledge interests and cognitive identity of social movements . . . [and who] create their individual role at the same time as they create the movement, as new individual identities and a new collective identity take form in the same interactive process." Our question, then, is, What are their identities, both in the movement and individually?

Zhang Xianliang, a dissident from Shanghai, was interviewed by Zhang Boli (1997). The former articulates the eight goals he and his Shanghai dissident colleagues seek. Zhang Boli agrees that these are also the goals of the overseas democracy movement. The eight goals are

1. freedom of speech;
2. freedom of press;
3. abolition of counterrevolution as a crime, abolition of "labor reform," and protection of human rights;
4. release of all political prisoners;
5. overturn of the verdict on June 4;
6. designation of June 4 as the Day of Chinese Democracy;
7. revision of the constitution to get rid of the Four Cardinal Principles and the one-party system;
8. welcoming the overseas Chinese and the exiled political dissidents to participate in reform in China.

In fact, the realization of even one of these goals would mean that the others could be realized at almost the same time. How they think they can get there is, of course, the big question. These goals, however, do represent the guidelines of the democratic movement both inside and outside China. At the time of the interview, the activities of dissidents in Shanghai, according to Zhang, were focused on releasing those who were still in prison, and on helping their families. (Zhang himself was released in 1997 after three years in prison and came to the United States.)

This should give us an idea of what the democracy movement does and who the critical intellectuals are. Let us look more specifically at the democratic activities taking place inside and outside China and the intellectuals involved in those movements.

Democracy Movement Inside China

Given the tight control of political activities, any opposition would be difficult. Still there have been some careful efforts, and here are some examples.

First, petitions to the government for a more open political atmosphere. Perhaps best-known over the years are Zhao Ziyang's repeated petitions for the overturn of the June 4 verdict, as well as petitions from

Ding Zilin and other families of the June 4 victims. In addition, a number of dissident intellectuals launched a campaign of petitions to the National People's Congress in 1995, and they made sophisticated arguments for promoting and protecting human rights (Sullivan 1995:37–8). They called for investigations of government corruption, an end to the abuse of human rights by the police, and the development of a spirit of tolerance. They demanded a democratic system that protected individuals holding differing political or religious points of view. The signers of the petitions include former *People's Daily* editors such as Wang Ruoshui and Wu Xuecan; prominent political dissidents such as Chen Ziming, Xu Wenli, and Liu Xiaobo; and a number of magazine editors, sociologists, legal scholars, university professors, and writers, as well as former student leaders. Wang Ganchang, the premier nuclear physicist who designed the country's first atomic bomb, again joined the petitioners. It is noteworthy that especially since the military crackdown in 1989, intellectuals from different categories have continued to try to coordinate their efforts and act as groups on Mainland China, although with only limited success.

Second, efforts to organize independent movements. In the 1990s, dissidents inside China wanted to organize movements, as they tried to do in the 1970s and 1980s. For example, Tang Boqiao from Hunan organized the China Private Organizations Autonomous League *(min zi lian)* (Ya Yi 1997e). Their strategy was to make friends in order to disseminate ideas, but not to organize any other activities. After a failed effort by Shen Tong in 1992 to connect with league members, some were arrested, some interrogated, and others escaped to the West. Tang himself escaped to the West in 1991.[55]

In mid-1998 Wang Youcai, Qin Yongmin, Xu Wenli, and others began to organize the China Democracy Party as an opposition party, recruiting members from Beijing, Shanghai, and at least eight other provinces (see also Minxin Pei 2000:28). In July, Wang Youcai was arrested for starting the party. By December, the leading members were being sentenced to prison terms of over ten years (Human Rights Watch 2000). At first, when Wang was detained, 136 dissidents from twenty-one provinces coordinated a protest letter to Jiang Zemin and Zhu Rongji, calling for his release (*Press Freedom Guardian,* August 14, 1998). But their efforts were eventually suppressed. Other intellectuals who were interested in political and environmental reform organized the China Development Union. But again their leader, Peng Ming, was sentenced to eighteen months in prison in 1999.[56] Yu Xinjiao, a poet, started a movement to revive Chinese literature and art (*Zhongguo wenyi fuxing yundong*) in 1993, and later the Chinese National Revival Party (*Zhongguo minzu fuxing dang)* in Hongzhoug, Zhejiang, in 1997. He was arrested and sentenced to seven years in prison in 1999. Several members of the movement, including Ma Zhe and Wang Yiliang, were also sentenced to prison terms (Wang Dan 2000). We mentioned earlier about Fang Jue's imprisonment for spreading democratic reform ideas. The government suppression is severe, but the democratic movement intellectuals are persistent.

Since 1999, Falun Gong, the semireligious meditation and exercise movement, has also met with severe oppression, with its protest leaders arrested and imprisoned, as we mentioned earlier. As a social movement, Falun Gong serves democratization in that it strives for the people's freedom to practice what they believe in.[57] Other organizations such as Corruption Watch, an NGO, as well as peasants' and workers' protest movements have continually emerged and have been continually stifled (Human Rights Watch 2000). It is likely that these movements will keep popping up whenever conditions are right. These organized movements pose a threat to the CCP monopoly, but the CCP's refusal to share power with other social groups will likely stimulate more resistance, as the one posed by Falun Gong and by other democratic movements.

Third, work on the overturn of the verdict on the June 4 movement. Profs. Ding Zilin and Jiang Peikun, who lost their son in the June 4 massacre, compiled a list of the victims, and have ever since been investigating the current conditions of their families, providing whatever help they could, with both financial and moral support from overseas. Of course, their efforts have been constantly obstructed by the police. On the occasions when foreign donations were not intercepted, they were afraid to receive them for fear the authorities would think they were making an "organized" effort (see *World Journal,* December 14, 1994). Lois Wheeler Snow, the widow of the American writer Edgar Snow who publicized the Chinese revolution in the West, tried to visit Ding and to bring some money and a book to her in April 2000, but the security blocked the meeting from taking place (Mann 2000). Nonetheless, the professors continue their efforts.

Fourth, lawsuits against the Party and the government. Under similar harassment, some intellectuals tried to sue the Party and government officials for violating their civil rights. William P. Alford (1993) documented five of the most important cases at the beginning of the 1990s. In 1991, Wang Meng, the novelist and former minister of culture, sued both *Wenyi Bao* (The literature and art gazette), which is sponsored by the Ministry of Culture, and the author of an article it ran, for denouncing his short story "Thin, Hard Gruel," which they interpreted as an attack on Deng Xiaoping. Dai Qing, a well-placed journalist, sued the newspaper she worked for, the *Guangming Daily,* for accusing her of being a "pawn of reactionary forces in and out of China" during the June 4 movement. She was termed "a reporter intent on creating turmoil." Guo Luoji, a professor of philosophy, sued the Nanjing University Communist Party Committee and Director Li Tieying of the State Education Commission for depriving him of his right to teach because his politics differed from the Party line. Wang Juntao and Chen Ziming, two of the most celebrated political dissidents, both of whom were imprisoned several times for their political activities, brought their own lawsuits. Wang's wife Hou Xiaotian, on Wang's behalf, sued the jailers for negligence in allowing her husband to contract hepatitis B, and both Wang's and Chen's families sued newspapers that accused them of playing a reactionary role in the June 4 movement.

All of their suits were rejected. But the fact that they were able to sue at all shows how much the consciousness of their rights and power and independence has been heightened among politically critical intellectuals. There is no doubt that litigation also heightens the consciousness of their political allies and arouses the attention of a larger audience, both domestic and foreign. Guo Luoji (1997) points out that his experience with the litigation makes him further believe that it is important for the democracy movement to use legal means to achieve their goals: only by suing will you know what problems the legal system has and know what you need to do to change it. He views the efforts to change the legal system as one of the most important means to achieve democratic ends.

Fifth, dissident writers. These include, for example, the novelists and poets as described in the book *Dalu Yijian Zuojia Qun* (The group of dissident writers in Mainland China), edited by Liu Dawen (see Zheng Yi 2001). These writers have made a point of criticizing the one-party dictatorship and various kinds of political, economic, and social corruption under the Communist rule, especially in the 1990s. Among eighty such writers are Can Xue, Chen Ran, Er Yue He, Gao Xingjian (who won the 2000 Nobel prize in literature), Han Shaogong, Huang Xiang, Liu Suola, Liu Xinwu, Mo Yan, Shi Tiesheng, Shu Ting, Su Xiaokang,

Wang Anyi, Wang Lixiong, Xu Mingxu, Zhang Jie, Zhang Kangkang, and Zhang Xinxin. Zheng Yi is also one of such writers, although like Su Xiaokang and Xu Mingxu, he is now forced to settle in the United States (Interview with Zheng Yi 1997).

But the most daring dissident writer and poet in Mainland China probably should be Liao Yiwu (or Lao Wei), who published several books directly challenging the dominant official discourse (see Shen Lizhi 2001). These include *Chenlun de Shengdian* (1999) (The degraded temple), which is a study of the "obscure poetry" and other underground literature in the 1980s, and *Zhongguo Diceng Fangtan Lu* (2001) (Interviews of the underclass in China), which is a description of the most disadvantaged people both politically and economically. Even though they were banned two to three months after publication, these books had enjoyed tremendous popularity among intellectuals during their short time of existence. (The most serious consequence so far at the time of the writing is that the director and chief editor of Xinjiang Youth *(qingshaonian)* Press, which published the first book, were deposed, so were the editors of *South China Weekend,* or *Nanfang Zhoumo,* which published an interview of Lao Wei on the second book. See Shen Lizhi 2001.)

Those are some examples, mainly inside China, of the intellectual movement's activities. Although only a limited number of intellectuals have been involved in those activities, one can safely assume that they are appealing to many more. There is indeed an emergence of "a new kind of intellectual" (Goldman 1996). Given the political repression in China today, their activities are already quite provocative. They do not seem to produce very concrete results, but they certainly have forced the government to keep political reform on its mind. They have helped teach the democracy advocates what may be the best means to achieve further democratic reform.

Overseas Democracy Movement (ODM)

The democracy movement in exile, largely in the United States, shows some interesting characteristics. First, Chinese political dissidents and democracy advocates overseas have continued to reflect on the June 4 movement, trying to understand what happened and why. Their chief emphasis, however, is on research for a democratic Chinese future. Hu Ping, an activist in the 1981 student election movement at Beijing University, and Yan Jiaqi, Guo Luoji, and Yu Haochen, part of the democratic elite in the 1980s, for example, have done a great deal of theoretical work on democracy in China. Hu has written about his own transformation and his reflections on the Chinese democracy movement. Yan writes about a hundred articles per year and they are published in Hong Kong, Taiwan, and the United States. Many of his works are on freedom of the press, constitutional reform, and party building. Along with others, Yan has presided over a research project on constitutional reform in China and has published a journal devoted to that subject.

Chen Yizi, part of Zhao Ziyang's think tank in the 1980s, and Wang Juntao, a democracy advocate at the time, has each established a research group. They serve as democratic think tanks and put out research on political and economic reform in China. By 1997 Wang Juntao's research institute had published a dozen issues of their journal, and Chen Yizi's research center published a journal on an irregular schedule. Wu Hongda has established the *Laogai* (Labor reform) Foundation, exposing the inside workings of the prison system. There is also the Democratic Education Foundation, which commends those who have made contributions to the democracy movement (Interviews with Hu Ping 1997:3.4 and Yan Jiaqi 1997:3.3.)

Chen Kuide, a philosopher who was actively engaged in the emancipation movement in the 1980s, is now the chief writer of *Democratic China,* an editor of *Beijing Spring,* and a program host at Radio Free China. Gao Xin, another democracy activist, has written a number of popular books about Chinese government officials. Su Shaozhi, the former director of the Institute of Marxism, presides over the research on Chinese issues at the Princeton (University) China Initiative, which is doing cultural studies as well. Many of their articles are published in the dissident journals, including *China Spring, Beijing Spring,* and *Democratic China.* These journals have continued to circulate throughout the world; some are even smuggled into China. The development of the Internet in China also provides some help. Numerous books have been written on the movement as well (Interviews with Chen Kuide 1997: 3.7, Su Xiaokang 1997:3.9, and Su Shaozhi 1997:3.11).

Second, a number of political organizations have sprung up since 1989. Before the June 4 massacre, there was only one Mainland Chinese dissident organization in the United States, that is, The Chinese Democratic Alliance, established by overseas Chinese students, and they published *China Spring*. After 1989, the Federation for a Democratic China was founded, composed mainly of those who had fled

China after the June 4 massacre. They published *Democratic China*. The Chinese Freedom and Democracy Party is composed of intellectuals who have broken away from the Chinese Democratic Alliance. There is also the Independent Federation of Chinese Students and Scholars, a semipolitical organization whose aim is to carry on activities Mainland students could not because of Party suppression. The organization also includes as one of its aims to help students and scholars in the United States. After several unhappy encounters with the other democratic movement figures, Wang Ruowang decided to start his own organization, The Chinese Democratic Party (Interview 1997:3.2). At the time of the interview, Wang was also publishing a journal entitled *Tanshuo,* or The quest. David Ma and others have established The China Rights Party, which is also fairly active.

All of these organizations advocate democracy in China and favor a pluralistic political system. However, each has its own principles and strategies. For example, Ni Yuxian, one of the examples of Liu Binyan's *Second Kind of Loyalty,* and his Chinese Freedom and Democracy Party aim to overthrow the CCP, while others believe in a gradual reform of the Party (Ya Yi 1997b). Ni advocates action as a kind of direct threat to the CCP. Otherwise, he feels the government will continue to dismiss the democratic movement as "powerless and not worth their attention," or *bu cheng qihou, bu zu wei huan* (Interview 1997:3.1).

Despite their differences, however, these groups have coordinated activities on occasions such as the death of Deng and the transfer of Hong Kong, and they have organized conferences on democracy in China. But as Liu Qing points out, dissident organizations still have to find more effective ways to influence politics in China (Interview 1997: 3.6). For example, it is difficult for demonstrations in the United States to have much impact on the Chinese government. Largely this is because little connection exists between what the dissidents think and what Congress does in its China policy. So Hu himself has taken little part in demonstrations lately (Interview with Hu Ping 1997:3.4). There has been more coordination of activities since Wei Jingsheng of the 1979 Democracy Wall movement was released from prison in 1997 and exiled to the United States.

Third, many individual dissidents have become devoted activists in the democratic movement. We will now have a general look at some of them, then take a more detailed look at others. First, a selected profile of some activists:

Wu Hongda: A well-known activist who works on China's labor reform system, and who published *Lao Gai: The Chinese Gulag (*1992*).* In 1995, he secretly went back to China to videotape human rights abuse in prisons, but was found, detained, and only released after U.S. intervention. He is dedicated to human rights in China.

Han Dongfang: A labor organizer engaged in workers' welfare and other movements. Han is one of those who have chosen to remain in Hong Kong after its return to China. He publishes *The China Labor Bulletin,* which is distributed to factories across the border, and speaks on Radio Free Asia. (Farley 1997)

Sheng Xue: Now a Canadian citizen living in Toronto, she is the director of the June 4 Investigative Committee. She and her colleagues are compiling a list of victims and their families, raising funds to help the disabled and the victims' families, and investigating what actually happened at the time. For her work, she was denied entry into China in 1996. (Ya Yi 1997d)

Lu Siqing: A democracy activist presiding over the China Human Rights and Democracy Movement Information Center in Hong Kong, which provides to the world much of the information about what is happening to dissidents in China. The center also "smuggles" democracy movement materials like *Beijing Spring* into China (Ya Yi 1997c).

Wu Renhua: The editor of *Xinwen Ziyou Daobao (Press Freedom Guardian),* a dissident newspaper based in Alhambra, California. In 1998, the newspaper had a circulation of 1,500, larger than either *Beijing Spring* or *China Spring.* Since May 1998 it has also been on-line. Two months after it went on-line, 4,000 people had already read it in China. In addition, as of 2001, 40,000 people in China had received the newspaper via E-mail, according to Wu Renhua. Furthermore, the paper had on hand an additional one million E-mail addresses from China, which it could send its paper to if the owners do not object (Interview with Wu Renhua 1998, 2001).

Let us now look at some of the movement intellectuals in more detail.

Liu Qing heads Human Rights in China, an organization based in New York. Here is how he articulated what his organization does:

> Human Rights in China mainly works to support the dissidents in China, publicizing their work and providing humanitarian support. For example, we informed the international community of what dissidents like Wei Jingsheng, Guo Luoji, Liu Nianchun, and others were doing either in or out of prison, and how they are treated if and when in prison. We are one of the most reliable sources for international organizations and state governments concerning human rights in China. We help dissidents find lawyers and pay for the legal service. Much of this work, however, has to be done despite the strict suppression of the Chinese government on these activities. We also lobby the international community for the support of human rights in China, by activities such as testifying in Congress and meeting with government officials. In addition, we spread the idea of human rights by publishing a journal, speaking on VOA (Voice of America), Radio Free Asia, etc. (Interview 1997:3.6)

Su Xiaokang's change of heart since June 4 has been tremendous (Interview 1997:3.9). He has reflected on his own criticism of the Chinese culture in his well-known documentary *River Elegy,* where he now says he and his cowriters made a large number of unsound comments. Indeed, these comments were also criticized by Yu Ying-shih and Lin Yu-sheng, two Chinese-American historians of high repute, at Princeton University and the University of Wisconsin at Madison, respectively. Yu and Lin saw the ideas represented by *River Elegy* as too radical; connected, in fact, to the radical tradition carried from Sun Yat-sen down to the Communists. Su says that he used to see all things Western as good for China, and always discredited China's traditions. He now believes that since China clings to its own cultural traditions, much has to be changed before Western democracy can take hold. There are many other conditions, such as the modernization of man as well as economic modernization, which have to be met. He thinks he was too immature in his conclusions in the documentary.

Su says that now he has given up the idea of enlightening the public. He does not believe he can influence anyone in anything. This very unaggressive attitude is entirely different from that of the critical intellectual tradition. Su now writes about his own experiences on life and death. He has also been editing *Democratic China,* and writing about the development of Taiwan and its impact on Mainland China. He still doubts, however, whether his work would have much impact on his native country. (Recognizing one's limitations may be the light that the Su phenomenon sheds on the path of the critical intellectual.)

Su Shaozhi (Interview 1997:3.11) was the director of the China Initiative at Princeton University at the time of our interview and was researching issues on China such as the transition from dictatorship to democracy. His articles are published in Taiwan, Hong Kong, and the United States, mainly in the Chinese media. He has also attended international conferences on China, such as the conference on the country's ethnic problems. Su Shaozhi believes that he has had some influence in China, largely because the journals such as *Cheng Ming,* in which he writes articles, can be read by mainland politicians as well as by academicians. He found that he could say things that people inside the country could not say. His criticism of a TV series on Deng Xiaoping, for example, won applause from his friends in China, since he said what they wanted to, but could not possibly, say publicly. Su believes that a comment on him and his work that appeared in one of the books describing Chinese men of culture fits exactly what he does, *zhi kai feng qi bu wei shi,* that is, "he blazes a trail but does not want to be a teacher."

At the time of the interview, Liu Binyan and his wife were publishing an English journal on China (Interview 1997:3.10). They collected excerpts of important news articles concerning current events in China and arranged interviews with those who had just come from China. The couple did all of the writing and compiling but would ask others to translate their work into English. This was their way of keeping in touch with developments in China. Liu has already written a number of books, including his autobiography.

This Chinese dissident movement is active not only in the United States but in other countries as well. We have mentioned Sheng Xue and her activities in Canada. Qi Mo and his groups in Germany are another example (Ya Yi 1997a). According to Qi, one of the chief organizers, these organizations are more grass roots, with few "stars" and little infighting. And they have extensive contacts with academia, the mass media, the federal government, Congress, the Ministry of Foreign Affairs, and the local governments. Qi himself participated in a European research project on China's culture and economy. Qi's groups hold regular meetings with various organizations in Germany and solicit their support on China's human rights issues. They also publish their own journals.

The Political Roles of the ODM

Andrew Nathan (1992:323) summarizes the roles of the Overseas Democracy movement well. First, it "reminds the world that China is not an exception to the human yearning for freedom." This should deflate the self-confidence Huntington (1993) and Bernstein and Munro (1997a) have about the clashes and confrontations between civilizations.

Second, the ODM has helped to publicize the human rights abuses in China. Indeed, political prisoners have been released thanks largely to the movement's efforts and to the international organizations and foreign governments that acted upon that information. The ODM has thus helped develop the consciousness of human rights in China, a concept that has been gradually, if grudgingly, accepted by the Chinese government. China signed the International Covenant on Social, Cultural, and Economic Rights in 1997, and the International Covenant on Civil and Political Rights in 1998. This would not have been possible without the efforts of the democratic movement both in and outside the country.

Third, the ODM has become a sophisticated political lobby. The democracy organizations have developed fairly good contacts in the United States and elsewhere in the world. They will function as a bridge between China and the world whether they stay overseas or go back to China.

Fourth, and most important, according to Nathan (1992:324), is the fundamental intellectual work the ODM does in building a workable democratic creed and practice. For example, "can a workable version of democracy be built on the foundations of the existing culture or do democrats have to try to reconstruct these cultural orientations as well, obviously a very difficult job?" In addition, factionalism, competitive fund-raising, corruption, and so forth within the ODM have taught the democrats the perils they confront.[58] They have been forced to learn to deal with the devils, which may provide valuable lessons for future political reform in China.

As Chen Kuide (Interview 1997:3.7) observes, we are no longer living in the time of Sun Yat-sen. The future of China depends on the outcome of the struggle among various social forces within China today. However, echoing Nathan, he believes that the ODM is useful in a very special sense: with the availability of all kinds of information, the overseas intellectuals can do more in-depth studies of China's future in an atmosphere of free discussion. Chen notes that the Chinese government is watching the ODM very closely, which proves their usefulness. In addition, the movement serves as a spiritual force to balance the pressures of the Chinese government. It is the first dissident movement the CCP has difficulty controlling. No organization in the

People's Republic of China has objected to CCP politics as openly as this movement does now.

In the past twenty years, 300,000 students and scholars have come to study in the West, and so far about 90,000 have returned (Zhongguo Gaodeng Jiaoyu, or *Chinese Higher Education* 1999:6). If only a small percentage of them are interested in the ODM, that can translate into quite a number of people. Add the old *huaqiao,* the earlier expatriates, and those in the West who sympathize with democracy in China, and one can see the ODM persist in the twenty-first century.

Other Social Critics: Some Examples

Critical intellectuals are not just scholars involved in various discourses and movements. Many of them are ordinary people doing extraordinary work under difficult circumstances. In this section we examine a group of intellectuals who also perform social criticism, albeit in some very different, yet no less important ways. The misfortune of this group is that it tends not to get heard when scholars discuss critical intellectuals. It includes not only the less visible critical intellectuals, but also those who have been termed 'professional' and 'organic' yet still 'critical.' We discuss them here because the critical aspect of their personalities can often take precedence over their official tasks. We should note that they all show a humanistic concern over the problems of ordinary people. The humanist spirit, as we have seen, is a characteristic of critical intellectuals.

A graduate student in Marxism critiques life in the countryside and shows his concern for state affairs, using his own example and generalizing the conditions of the peasants:

> Life is very difficult there. I was a middle school teacher and wanted to go to graduate school. But there were obstacles at all levels *(ceng ceng she ka),* and I had to give presents, beg authorities and cultivate connections to get permission to take the entrance exam. It took me so much time and energy that it caused me great psychological suffering. But that is how things get done. (Interview with Li Yishun 1994:1.49)

According to Li, the social environment in the countryside is getting worse for everyone, especially for the peasants. The village heads are like local despots, doing anything they please. Political reform is lagging far behind economic reform. The environment is threatening the very survival of China's ordinary peasants.

An administrator in a county education bureau criticizes the astonishing corruption in the countryside and the abuse by the cadres:

> The local officials would use every possible means to punish those who had more than the accepted number of births. They would fine them or put them in make-shift jails if they could not pay. They would tear down their houses. The policy was to get money by all means possible, and they did not care if those people lived or died. As they would say, "We will give you a rope if you want to hang yourself; and we won't take away the bottle if you want to drink pesticide from it," i.e., *shang diao gei ni sheng, he yao bu duo ping*. What did they do with the money they got? They would construct buildings for the county government. And 20% of the fines would go into their own pockets as commissions, 20% of the fines. (Interview with Tian Xufeng 1996:2.12)[59]

A lawyer criticizes what it is like to practice law, or *zhi fa huanjing:*

> There is too much administrative interference. The county governor can decide whether a defendant can or cannot be detained and imprisoned, even when the person has been found guilty by a court of law. If the defendant happens to be the brother of the governor, it will be even more impossible. If the lower court decides, under administrative pressure, not to prosecute a case or deliberately delay action, the higher court can do nothing about it. And corruption is not limited to the lower levels. As the doggerel goes, *fan fu bai, fan fu bai, fu bai jiu zai zhu xi tai. Zhongdian jiu zai qian san pai.* (Interview with Wang Lixiang 1996:2.23)

In English, Wang's quote says,

> Fight corruption,
> Fight corruption,
> But corruption is right here on the rostrum.
> And the culprits are in the first three rows.

Cadres of higher levels always sit in the front rows. In another saying, "Big corruption leads small corruption to fight corruption." Oftentimes, it is the courts and police themselves who are corrupt. The judgment has already been made even before the trial, and the lawyer is useless and powerless. And since judges take bribes, the outcome may depend on whether the plaintiff or the defendant has more graft to give.

Furthermore, Wang says,

> Many times, there is no way for common folks to seek justice. The mass media, newspapers or TV stations, may take up a case sometimes. But there are so many cases out there that you need some kind of connections with the newspaper authority in order for your case to be heard. Many people actually kneel in front of the courthouse (the traditional gesture of appealing to an authority figure), hoping that somebody will take their cases. But they are rarely successful. Coming together and going to appeal to the higher court *(jiti shangfang)* is not allowed. It is very difficult for ordinary people to find justice in the system.

Here is a journalist with nine years' experience explaining how she concerned herself with the life of ordinary people:

> I work for a women's newspaper in Beijing. I am stationed in this city. I report whatever happens here, such as the 100 days after they enacted the law against reaping staggering profits. I exposed KTV, a karaoke night club, for exploiting customers. I reported on the status of young nannies/housekeepers from the countryside *(xiao baomu)* and young girls from elsewhere looking for a job in this city. These are the *wai lai mei* who are said to bring problems to the city such as out-of-wedlock pregnancies, marriage without love, etc. But at the same time, they are doing jobs the city people don't like to do, such as work in textile factories, and they are exploited terribly: they work 50–70 hours a week, especially in privately-owned factories. The state-owned factories have started a "peasant-worker school," which I reported on. My report was published on the front page of our paper. The city is leading the way in dealing with the problem. I also report other events like children's art festivals, etc. (Interview with Ge Shannon 1994:1.3)

Also as a lawyer, she enjoyed working on civil and criminal cases and felt a sense of having helped someone:

> I feel a sense of mission to help others, to save people, like Lei Feng (the

icon from the 1960s). These cases won't bring you much money, unlike economic cases. I received only 200 yuan [about eight yuan equals one U.S. dollar] in a recent case of robbery for defending a retarded person involved in robbing others. In a case of divorce, I ran from one real estate agency to another to help find appropriate housing to settle a dispute involving housing. I received only several hundred yuan for the work, but it was immensely rewarding. After many years, the woman still invites me for dinner. I find happiness in helping those in hardship. No other job can compare with this one in this regard. (Interview with Ge Shannon 1994:1.3)

Here is the story of another journalist. On one trip we had an opportunity to visit a radio talk show program. We sat in the room where incoming calls were screened, and watched the show's host in the other room as he talked with his guest and callers. They were discussing a recent deal made by the producer of a TV series with a corporation. Short of money, the producer allowed the corporation manager to buy the copyright of the story, make himself the actor, and hire a former female convict named Ying as the actress. Ying had been imprisoned for hiding criminals wanted for robbery and murder, but she had served her time and now lived a quiet life. Hers had been a case that shook the city, so the corporation hoped to use her on the TV series for her promotion value. That, at least, is what was argued.

The guest was a professor from a well-known university who had just written an article criticizing the corporation for using the notoriety of an individual for its own publicity. He believed that it went against the traditional value of "punishing evil and fostering good." Some callers believed that Ying had the right to do whatever she liked. The host even cited the example of Olympic ice-skater Tonya Harding, who cashed in on her fame after her boyfriend attacked her competitor Nancy Kerrigan. But most callers objected to the attitude of the corporation, and both host and guest were unmistakably on their side for the same moral reasons. "Social consequences and social responsibility" were the issues, they said.

The host told us that he was writing a book commending talk shows. They were, he said, the voice of democracy, since they provide a place for ordinary folks to air their views; occasionally they even promoted exchanges between officials and the masses. His program, for example, focused on social issues that concerned ordinary people in the city, such as traffic, living conditions, the electricity supply, and the food supply.

When he heard that certain businesses wanted to cut down the trees lining one of the two chief commercial streets because they were hiding business signs, he organized a program that allowed ordinary folks to air what they thought. Most, of course, were against the move even though it was supported by the city government. Even if efforts like these do not always succeed, they at least make policymakers think twice before they leap. Indeed, as some analysts speculate, China's call-in shows may be "on the verge of evolving into an electronic, liberal public sphere, in which citizens critically discuss political and social problems in a serious way, generating a societal public opinion that state leaders must recognize as a legitimate and important input into the policy making process" (Lynch 1999:193), in spite of the existing censoring and screening processes.

TV journalists have also made great strides. In June 1994, Channel 8 of Shanghai TV started a program named *News See-Through,* in which reporters report what happens live from the scene. Reporters had never done anything like this before in the Mao era or the first period of Deng, yet now they were dealing with sensitive issues involving social criticism. In the month following its debut, the program succeeded in reporting such events as the death of several people on a sidewalk caused by the negligence of construction contractors. In this case, the vice-director of a city tax bureau, who was passing by, could have helped the injured by simply offering his government-owned and chauffeured car. He refused, and he was punished (Wang Jinyuan 1994).

That kind of reporting has made this one of the city's most popular programs. Other journalists have also begun to voice the concerns of the public. *Jiaodian Fangtan* (The focused interviews), started by the official national network, Central TV, in April 1994, does investigative reporting on all kinds of social issues, including official corruption, business scandals and youth problems, and important international and national events (see Yuan Zhengming and Liang Jianzeng 1999). It too has become very popular. Its producers say they take tremendous responsibility and risk in choosing what to report. But they feel the pressure is worth it, for the sense they have of success, of contributing to people's welfare. Again, journalists like these are fulfilling a calling (*Wenhui Movie Times,* July 9, 1994). As we mentioned earlier, such popular programs developed in the late 1990s also include *Shihua shishuo* (Tell it as it is) (see Cui Yongyuan 2001); *Dongfang shi Kong* (Time and space in the East) (see Jing Yidan 1998); *Jinri shuofa* (Law

Figure 3.2 Exposure *(Bao guang)*

Notes: At the upper left hand corner is written "Focused Interviews." The words on the bag are: fake and inferior commercial products.
Source: Ding Cong 1999 (Vol. 3), p. 93.

today) (see Yin Li 2001, Vols. 1–4); and *Xinwen diaocha* (News probe) (see Liang Jianzeng, Sai No, and Zhang Jie 2001, Vol. 1–2). Figure 3.2 illustrates what *The Focused Interviews* does, but it may apply to what critical intellectuals generally do.

These journalists, like other critical intellectuals throughout the country, tread a very thin line. There are rules they must follow: for a radio talk show host, "don't touch politically sensitive issues; find ways to get around them if callers raise them." A city-level radio station should be careful not to criticize senior city officials. They are, however, pretty free to attack lower-level ones like those of the districts (boroughs), or lower-level agencies and institutions. By the same token,

Central TV, as an agency of the central government, can criticize provincial agency heads but not high-level officials. As people often say, they play games. Or, put it another way, they play net ball, that is, what Lynch (1999:96–8) calls "edgeball journalism." Numerous such journalists "are seriously committed to exposing the country's deep-rooted social problems in an engaging way without, at the same time, deploying hackneyed communist jargon" (p. 96).

A sociologist also finds her own way of exercising social responsibility. Xiao Guimei was a prolific writer and appeared on various TV and radio shows. Her interests included medical sociology, sociology of gender and sexuality, sexual behavior, family, marriage and divorce, and women's issues in general. She felt her work made a lot of impact and she felt very fulfilled. She also worked in AIDS prevention. "We are economically poor but spiritually fulfilled," she said (Interview 1994:1.6).

Here is how Wang Xiaoming, the literary critic, viewed his work:

> As literary critic, I need to be sensitive to what is happening in society so that I can comment on what popular novelists like Wang Shuo are saying. I need to feel the pulse of the city and smell the flavor of its life. Especially when the mass media are the mouthpiece of the government, you have to go and find out for yourself what is happening in the city. (Interview 1994:1.11)

Wang was an editor of several journals of literary criticism such as *Wenyi Lilun Yanjiu, Xue Ren,* and *History of Literature*. One of their major focuses at the time was the humanistic spirit and ultimate concern for the quality of human life *(renwen jingshen he zhongji guanhuai).*

A professor in the sociology of education performs a moral role in his classroom. I attended the first class Professor Zhang taught to three of his students, two MA's and one Ph.D. He emphasized five relationships. First, the relation between scientific research and ethics: it is more important to learn to be a good person than to be a good researcher. That is a critical approach, given the context of commercialization. Second, one has to be both a generalist and a specialist. Third, theory has to be combined with practice: positivist research is to be emphasized. Fourth, we have to emphasize both the connection with the world *(yu guoji jiegui),* or internationalization, and the focus on our native land *(ben tu hua),* or nationalization. Fifth, students have to absorb knowledge, and publish what they have learned (Interview 1994:1.35).

Professor Zhang's class lasted *five hours* in the dead heat of summer in a deserted classroom (it was vacation time), with no air conditioning or electric fans. And he was on the eve of his departure to take a position in Guangzhou. The main theme of his lecture was how to become a good person. He talked about the relationship between scientific studies and personal morality. Education is more a matter of teaching young students to become good persons than teaching them specific knowledge or technical skills, he said. Students have to be able to compete in the world. He is a very strict teacher, who requires students to read a long list of books in a very orderly way, in addition to the heavy burden of learning to become a good person. And he requires his students to report to him if they want to go into business or other sideline work to make money.

These examples are brief illustrations of the generally "unheard critical intellectuals." Studies of intellectuals are more likely to focus on the relatively few who set trends of intellectual thoughts, such as the democratic elite, liberal or conservative intellectuals, and the Old or New Left. The intellectuals we have just met are more numerous, but are generally ignored. They certainly add to the scope and quality of intellectual criticism, and may very well form the mass base of China's critical intellectuals.

Conclusions: The Politics of Critical Intellectuals

As we have seen in this chapter, critical intellectuals, like other intellectuals, are very diversified. The social critics are quite different from one another: there are the intellectuals of the largely overseas movement in *Beijing Spring,* the ardent nationalists, postmodernists, liberal intellectuals, neoconservatives, the Old and New Left, and the social critics in other walks of life. While the movement intellectuals' major concern is democracy, and they are free to criticize the Party and government from overseas, the social critics inside China have to play a different ball game. In the debate on the humanist spirit, critical intellectuals not only differ on what it means, but also differ on what it should encompass. Wang Meng and Wang Shuo strongly oppose any dominating ideology that may be imposed on intellectuals. It nonetheless is a very important exercise and it did achieve some purposes. In the debate on nationalism, the nationalists, postmodernists, and national learning scholars are on the defensive when other critical intellectuals attack them as conservative. Even the neoconservatives clash with the Old and New Left over nationalism, although they both support a strong central government. Those in literature and art, and music and the movie industry seem to follow their own paths, breaking new ground as they go. Indeed, the picture of critical intellectuals seems to be fragmented. And this fragmentation may lead to the fragmentation of their politics. But will it? What is politics anyway?

Politics in General and What Influences the Politics of Critical Intellectuals

Politics, from Aristotle on, has been seen as the art of controlling and reconciling the diverse interests within a state (Scruton 1982:361). According to Weber, "a state is a human community that (successfully) claims the *monopoly of the legitimate use of physical force* within a given territory . . . [It is] a relation of men dominating men, a relation supported by means of legitimate (i.e., considered legitimate) violence" (1946:78). Politics thus is defined as the striving by diverse interest groups to share or influence such a state power. If we define the current Chinese state, that is, the Chinese "domination of men by men," as being monopolized by the CCP, but with an increasing share going to the new bourgeoisie, then the politics in this state fits the definition: different interest groups striving to share power. The intellectuals' politics will thus be their endeavors to share that power with the state, using their intellectual arts to control and reconcile the diverse interests within China. Politics can be confrontational, as with some movement intellectuals, or reconciliatory, as with other movement intellectuals and the neoconservatives. In chapter 1, we learned that critical intellectuals follow an ethic of ultimate ends by exercising criticism no matter what. The question now is: How does that definition of critical intellectuals' politics fit into the picture of critical intellectuals in the 1990s and beyond?

In addition, as we will also see in chapter 4, intellectuals' professional positions may influence their politics. In a similar way, their "academic" positions may affect their politics. By that I mean positions they adopt such as postmodernism or national learning. When the postmodernists were attacked as cooperating with the government *(yu guanfang hemou)* by promoting commercialism, Chen Xiaoming (1998) cautioned against not seeing the difference between the name *(ming)* and the reality *(shi).*

In other words, we should not confuse one's scholarship with one's political attitudes. We have also argued in this chapter that much of the nationalist politics perceived to be that of the postmodernists may be imposed upon them. But doesn't one's scholarship inevitably inform one's politics? What is the scholarship of some of the critical intellectuals?

The Humanist Spirit and the Politics of the Critical Intellectuals

We discussed in this chapter the fact that many intellectuals participated in the discussion on the humanist spirit, and that this discussion has provided critical intellectuals with a consciousness. What does that actually mean about their politics and their relationship with the state? Xu Jilin maintains that the humanist spirit should have an authority equal to financial and political power. He is saying that critical intellectuals should play a role as important as the Party and the bourgeoisie. The humanist spirit, however, should remain in the realm of "spiritual utopia." By this he means that once people allow the humanist spirit to be politicized, once they use the humanist spirit to reform society, they will betray its spirit and this can lead to tragedy (1997b:235–6). *Dao* used to be the principle that governed "politics," and "scholarship" existed to support and extend *Dao.* Xu believes that the reconstruction of the humanist spirit involves the reconstitution not only of *Dao,* but also of the relationship among the three traditions. Rather than governing the other two, the new *Dao,* or the "humanist spirit," will only deal with systems of meaning and rules for communication and will interact with, but not govern, politics and scholarship (p. 233).

However, this seems to take away the activist role of the humanist spirit. Is he wrong? Perhaps this new humanist spirit should indeed govern politics and scholarship. Politics and scholarship may be inseparable from *Dao,* as the Confucian tradition tells us (see Tu Wei-ming 1993b:6). Maybe *Dao* is indeed the foundation for politics, society, and culture (Bol 1992:176).[60] To insist on humanist values and to make efforts to realize them in both politics and scholarship can be emphasized as the critical intellectuals' "calling," or *tian zhi.* Applied in the democracy movement, the critical intellectuals' politics would then be to make sure that state power is controlled by a representative government, representing especially the oppressed and the disadvantaged. They may do this through a democratic movement, writing novels, making movies, pursuing a postmodern or other social critique, advocating national learning or even a neo-authoritarianism, or teaching. *But* the starting and ending point of their criticism must be the humanist spirit. That can and should be the politics of critical intellectuals who adhere to a humanist spirit.

The critical intellectual's politics is different from that of the organic intellectual in one vital way. The organic intellectual serves mostly the interests of a certain social group, most likely, the powerful, whereas the critical intellectual serves mainly the interests of the disadvantaged, no matter what kind, and does not refrain from criticizing the group it serves if necessary. The critical intellectual's politics is also different from that of the professional (the unattached intellectual), who serves largely his own professional interests. But as we have repeatedly emphasized, these categories are only ideal constructs. In reality, there are no *pure* organic, critical, or professional intellectuals. Individual intellectuals often change from one category to anther, thereby altering their politics.

When the young literary critic, Hu Heqing, committed suicide by jumping off a building in 1994, some commented that it symbolized the critical intellectuals' existence. "Before he died, he was a question mark; when he died, he was an exclamation mark; after he died, period. The fox mourns the death of the hare; like grieves for like. We all feel the pain and reflect on how we should live our lives" (Interviews with Tian Zhaoyun and Jiang Zhexin 1994:1.56–57). The death of Hu Heqing might not have been a social protest, as his friend Wang Xiaoming commented (Interview 1994.11). But it so shocked the literary and art circles in the city that the city government instructed all the mass media not to carry articles of remembrance. Protest or not, his death does pose a question: What do critical intellectuals live for? They must find a reason.

The answer seems to lie in their independent existence. Many have commented that critical intellectuals need to become an independent social force. Wang Yuanhua notes that intellectuals need to *bai tuo yibang*—"to get rid of dependence on anyone or anything." They have reached the end of Mao's theory of skin and hair. "I believe that intellectuals . . . should have their own independent personality, with independent consciousness and points of view" (1990:99). Many seem to have found their consciousness in the humanist spirit, which can give them an independent personality or existence and inform their politics and their points of view. The humanist spirit may explain why critical intellectuals are concerned about human rights and the full development of human beings. It also explains why they may be in conflict with the powers that be.

The Political Roles of Critical Intellectuals

This discussion of the politics of the critical intellectuals and their relationships with the state points to their political roles. What are they? According to Gouldner, the culture of critical discourse (CCD) "claims the right to sit in judgment over the actions and claims of any social class and all power elites" (1979:59). Although all intellectuals have CCD, critical intellectuals make the most use of it. Critical intellectuals concern themselves with the various modernization issues, from *Dongfang* journal's coverage of environmental and women's issues to *Beijing Spring*'s coverage of the democracy movement inside and outside China.

Therefore, the critical intellectuals' role is to analyze and criticize. That is, to comment on social issues, to criticize corruption, and to debate the best paths of development. They are supposed to "expose the lies of governments, to analyze actions according to their courses and motives and often hidden intentions" (Chomsky 1969:324). As Apter (1987:112–3) suggests, intellectuals in modernizing societies play a critical role in seeking solutions to particular problems, creating public meaning, and identifying the interconnections and directions of change. The regime that can heed intellectuals' social criticism helps its own cause.

Indeed, as we have demonstrated in this chapter, critical intellectuals both inside and outside China play a pivotal role in finding the meaning of development, and in devising ways to achieve a national identity and modernization. Xu Jilin's and Zheng Yefu's book titles capture what they do: *Looking for Meanings (Xunqiu Yiyi)* (1997b) and *Getting Out of the Prisoner's Dilemma (Zouchu Qiutu Kunjing)* (1995). The critical intellectuals no doubt face formidable obstacles in China. Considering the pressure they are under, as we discussed before, Chinese critical intellectuals have already achieved a great deal, and they are posed to achieve more.

The Politics and Ethics of Critical Intellectuals

As we have discussed in this chapter, the relatively open environment made it possible for critical intellectuals of different shades to emerge, such as democracy activists, postmodernists, nationalists, and humanists.

But the relatively closed atmosphere also created an environment for the emergence of neoconservatives and the New Left. The former mostly follow the ethic of ultimate ends, while the latter the ethic of responsibility. The different ethic they follow defines a different relationship with the state, or a different way of influencing the state politics, although they are all critical.

Like the nineteenth century Abolitionists in the United States and the Dryfusards in France, the Chinese movement intellectuals have persisted in their efforts to promote democracy in China, largely following an ethic of ultimate ends. Even faced with arrests and prison terms, many have continued to do so. They have made it their goal in life, although they know it may take a long time to realize that goal. As we mentioned earlier, their job is to keep burning "the flame of protesting against the injustice of the social order" (Weber 1946:121). Most of them do not expect to obtain a seat in the current regime, or even become part of its think tank, but they wish to prick the conscience of those in power, as Coser (1965:208) says about critical intellectuals. The same applies to the ardent nationalists who criticized the Chinese government for weakness in the face of American aggression. Xiao Gongqin (1999:137) observes that these intellectuals are following the tradition of *qingliu pai,* a group of critical *shi,* or "intellectuals," who, because they are not in power, have adopted a moral and idealistic stance in their criticism of the pragmatic officials who are in power. Xiao seems to align himself with those in power and can see things from their perspectives.

Indeed, neoconservatives like Xiao resemble organic intellectuals in that they follow an ethic of responsibility: viewing and accepting a strong central government as a necessary evil in dealing with the social problems on hand, and willing to compromise with the powers by not instigating greater radical reform. However, the neoconservatives also follow an ethic of ultimate ends when they do not compromise with the powers. They do not always accept the government's stance on social, political, and economic issues, and they say so. They are not, therefore, always liked by the regime. They are, in fact, afflicted with the dual personality we have discussed earlier.

Postmodernism poses another challenge for our model of ethics. In the West, it is criticized by feminists as lacking theorized agency and strategies of resistance corresponding to their own. Its focus on difference "is leading to political fragmentation and the dissipation of feminist consciousness and activism" (Parpart 1993:442). In China, this politics of difference may have undermined the Party's domination in all spheres—political, economic, and cultural—but it may also have undermined the intellectuals' efforts to pursue democratic changes. The postmodernists follow the ethic of ultimate ends when they undermine the Party's dominance, and an ethic of responsibility when they undermine the democratic efforts.

In his article "Post-Ism and Chinese New Conservatism," Henry Y. H. Zhao argues that there is a powerful buildup of a new conservatism in Chinese postmodernity. It is characterized by refutation of the political engagement of intellectuals in the 1980s, endorsement of the popular commercial culture, and dismissal of internationally acclaimed films by Zhang Yimo and Chen Kaige and of memoirs such as *Wild Swans* by Jung Chang or *Life and Death in Shanghai* by Nien Cheng, all of which have clear political messages. Having undermined its supports, Zhao then claims that "postmodernism has actually turned itself into a conformist theory in China which serves to justify the institutionalized mainstream culture" (1997:42).

Obviously, since it stands for decentralizing power and recognizing the legitimacy of all competing players, political or cultural, postmodernism has to recognize the legitimacy of the commercial culture and the ruling power as well. As the feminists would charge, that takes away the agency for change and dismisses the activism of the democracy movement. Postmodernism does have that potential, as Zhao has also charged. But it does not have to go in that direction. Chen Xiaoming (1998:66) has reminded us that "Postmodern critique has multiple layers: linguistic challenges, deconstruction of the ideology, and the creation of a new system of discourse and expressive strategies. They can all be considered as criticism *(pipan xing).*" However, in the current political context in China, Chen's summary may be as far as the postmodern critique can go. Postmodernism certainly does lack the feminist consciousness of active participation in changing society, and it certainly does not deal with the agency of social change.

Thus, we could say that postmodernists do have the potential to be on the conservative side of the political line. We could say the same of national learning scholars for that matter: recall Tang Yijie's comments that national learning can be appropriated by conservative forces. The same can be said about the New and Old Left. They all seem to follow the ethic of responsibility and comply with the state by not demanding a multiparty system. But these intellectuals, as we said, do not have to take that line. They can also follow the ethic of ultimate ends and be very critical. In order not to blunt its critical edge, these intellectuals need feminism as its political conscience (Kipnis 1988). In China, however, since feminism is still at its inception, the humanist spirit as we defined it earlier might serve as the consciousness of critical intellectuals in general.[61]

We thus see that critical intellectuals may move between an ethic of ultimate ends and an ethic of responsibility. Moreover, they may be afflicted with a dual personality because of it. Kraus (1995:191) describes China's artists as moving between plan and market, and it is hard to locate intellectuals "within an uncomplicated scheme of state-flatterer or state-dissident." Pickowicz (1995:206) portrays filmmakers as operating in "velvet prisons": they might not see themselves as collaborators, but they "were conscious of the fact that they engaged in self-censorship virtually every day." They maintained basic loyalty, and they chose the ethic of responsibility. But they were nonetheless critical and contributing to undermining state socialism. That may be typical of the politics of China's critical intellectuals.

To sum up, from humanists to nationalists and postmodernists, from democracy advocates to neoconservatives, from the Old Left to the New Left, and from popular artists to filmmakers, critical intellectuals are widely diversified in their orientations. They nonetheless are all very concerned about the conditions of ordinary people, and they all claim to strive for democracy, however each defines it. These concerns are indications of the humanist spirit. Most importantly, although they engage in self-censorship most of the times, their criticism is still largely independent of the official ideology, which indicates a movement of intellectuals toward becoming independent forces and playing independent political roles. They are all at odds with the regime in one way or another, following different ethics. But they can be characterized as critical intellectuals.

If intellectuals moved from a high degree of uniformity in the Mao era to the beginnings of fragmentation in the first period of Deng, then in the 1990s and since, they have solidified their positions and are well on their way to independent criticism. We will see further evidence in our discussion on professional and organic intellectuals in chapters 4 and 5.

Chapter Four

Bourgeoisified and Professionalized Intellectuals

Science and technology is a productive force,
and the first productive force at that.
(Keji shi shengchan li, erqie shi diyi shengchan li.)
—Deng Xiaoping, *Collected Works of Deng Xiaoping*[1]

In chapter 1, we described the development of unattached-professional intellectuals. In premodern China, unattached intellectuals were the *yinshi,* a group of the literati who kept their distance from officialdom and from organized political activities. In the Self-strengthening movement of the nineteenth century, a sizable group of technical intellectuals emerged when the Qing government felt a need to learn foreign technology so that it could survive in an aggressive world, but these intellectuals largely worked in government enterprises.

The Republican era saw more intellectuals going into professions, this time not necessarily "attached" to the government. Some became outstanding professionals and scholars, such as Zhan Tianyou, Qian Zhongshu, and Shiing-shen Chern. Of those who went into business and became bourgeois, T. V. Soong and H. H. Kung stood out above all, although they later both served the government as ministers of finance. In the Mao era, it was impossible to be a *yinshi,* or unattached professional, for virtually everybody was politicized, as we saw in chapter 2. In the 1990s, however, with the government's emphasis on science and technology, and the commercialization of the whole society, a bourgeoisification and professionalization process began; intellectuals now continued what they had begun in the Republican era. This chapter focuses on the further development of businessmen and women as well as professionals after 1989.

By professionals, we refer to teachers, engineers, doctors, lawyers, and journalists. We also refer to them as intellectuals, though *unattached* intellectuals. They constitute the majority of the intellectual complex, other groups being critical and organic intellectuals. Table 4.1 gives us an idea of the number of professionals in state-owned enterprises and institutions in 1997. Although there are inadequacies and inconsistencies in these statistics, it is not too wrong to estimate the number of professionals in the public sector to be close to 21 million in 1997, including some working in news organizations. (A small number of them may also be critical or organic intellectuals.) It is impossible to know the exact total number of professionals, but it would far exceed 21 million if we include those in the private sector.

Indeed, based on the 1990 census, the total number of intellectuals, which would also include those in government agencies (organic intellectuals) and a small number of independent critical intellectuals, was 33.04 million (*People's Republic of China Yearbook 1998:* 1104). Among them, there were 6.14 million people with four years of college, 9.62 million with three years of college *(da zhuan),* and 17.28 million graduates of professional schools. However, out of the 1.13 billion people in China in 1990, intellectuals constituted only about 2.9%, including some without a college education.

By the end of 1995, according to one count, there were already 44.65 million intellectuals (Qin Yan 1999:35). And the numbers, of course, increase each year, with more and more students enrolled and graduating. In 1998, for example, professional schools enrolled 1.67 million students, with an increase of 47,200 persons from the year before. Colleges and universities enrolled 1.16 million (including postgraduate students), with an increase of 83,200 persons from the previous year. Adult higher educational institutions enrolled 1 million, with a decrease of 2,200 persons from the previous year (Ministry of Education, 1999). That was close to 4 million students enrolled in 1998 alone, which would translate into a sizable number of graduates each year if the trend remains steady. The change in the number of intellectuals from 33.04 million in 1990 to 44.65 million in 1995 indicates a net increase of

Table 4.1 Number of Intellectuals/Professionals in State-Owned Enterprises and Institutions in 1997

Categories	Numbers of Intellectuals
Teachers in	
Institutions of Higher Learning	405,000
Secondary Schools	4,186,000
Primary Schools	5,794,000
Technical Professionals	
Industrial Engineers	5,719,000
Agricultural Engineers	611,000
Scientists	303,000
Medical Professionals	3,214,000
Lawyers	110,000
Total	20,342,000

Sources:

1. Zhongguo Tongji Nianjian 1998 (the *China Statistical Yearbook 1998*), p. 681, Zhongguo Tongji Zhaiyao 1998 (*A Statistical Survey of China 1998*), p. 149, both by the State Statistical Bureau, and Zhonghua Renmin Gongheguo Nianjian 1998 (*The People's Republic of China Yearbook 1998*), p. 208.
2. The number of journalists does not appear in these yearbooks, but according to *The People's Republic of China Yearbook 1998*, p. 807, there were 2,149 newspapers and 7,918 magazines in 1997. It is fair to assume that the number of journalists working in each news and journal organization can normally range from several to several hundred. Judy Polumbaum (1992) estimates the total number of "real" journalists to be 50,000, including those who collect, write, and edit the news. Considering the expansion of the mass media later in the 1990s, the number of journalists should far exceed that figure now.
3. The conventional definition of intellectuals, or professionals, includes those who have had a professional school education (equivalent to senior high school but with professional training) and above, and who have at least a junior professional title.
4. Medical professionals include both doctors and nurses.
5. Although the private sector produces most of the state's industrial output, the public sector still employs the largest number of professionals. However, many professionals work in both sectors.

about 2 million intellectuals each year. A more recent statistic shows that the percentage of those with a higher education rose from 1.42% in 1990 to 2.53% in 1997 (Zhang Yi 2000:292), assuming the number includes all those with at least three years of college.

Most probably, at least three quarters of the total number of intellectuals, that is, over 30 million in 1995, in both public and private sectors, can be considered as unattached professionals, as compared with organic and critical intellectuals. There were 12.6 million cadres in 1991

(Zhu Guanglei 1994:226). By 1997, most of the cadres were already intellectuals. We will discuss these organic intellectuals in chapter 5. Critical intellectuals, on the other hand, have always been a small number, although they play no less important roles, political or otherwise, than the other two groups of intellectuals.

This chapter traces the bourgeoisification and professionalization of intellectuals in the 1990s. We concentrate on professors and engineers in state-owned institutions and enterprises, the focus of our 1994 research, although we will also touch on other professionals. Specifically, we examine how some intellectuals became entrepreneurs, and we study the swing of the intellectuals' interest toward moneymaking. We then describe professionals' work, their living conditions, their continued professionalization, and their politics.

The Bourgeoisification of Intellectuals

We noted in chapter 3 that many intellectuals threw themselves into the critical movements of the 1990s, propelled by the crackdown on the 1989 democracy movement as well as by the rapidly changing political economy. Others, however, became more bourgeoisified. Xiao Gongqin, the neoconservative of the 1990s, notes that the market economy made social values mundane and the quest for ideal values less important. The former worship of isms and beliefs now evaporated. The June 4 events further accelerated the process and destroyed what romanticism still remained (Interview 1994:1.2). For example, if many journalists still had a sense of mission *(shiming gan)* at the time of the June 4 massacre, only a few admitted to such idealism in the 1990s (Interview with Ge Shannon 1994:1.3.11). Cheng Guan, a sociologist, concurs. He says, "Intellectuals feel that politics is an effort wasted and that it is no use being 'affectionate' about it without the other party [the Party and the government] feeling the same (or *zi zuo duo qing*). So many turn to money-making activities, such as trading stocks, selling television sets, tutoring pre-college students, etc. although very few actually have made much money" (Interview 1994:1.36).

Indeed, many intellectuals have shifted their focus to moneymaking in the past decade, some successfully. Maurice Meisner (1997:268) notes that slogans such as To Get Rich Is Glorious, Some Must Get Rich First, and Smashing the Iron Bowl have sanctified acquisitiveness, entrepreneurship, inequality, and the abolition of any guarantee to the right of subsistence. Attitudes like these have social and psychological effects on the intellectuals as well. One effect is that moneymaking has become a primary concern for intellectuals from all walks of life. Many have felt their livelihood threatened, and decided they had better forget their scruples and get rich by all means necessary. (For the bourgeoisification of intellectuals in post-Communist Central Europe, see Eyal, Szelenyi, and Townsley 1998.)

Entrepreneurial Intellectuals

This mentality breeds new entrepreneurs of all kinds. We observed in the beginning of chapter 3 that a large number of the new entrepreneurs were intellectuals when we discussed the social environment in the past decade. Let us now look at some figures and examples of intellectuals who have left the public sector and joined the private business world (Liu Zeming et al. 1993):[2]

> 1. In 1992, 80% of the professionals who came to the Beijing Personnel Exchange Center *(rencai jiaoliu zhong xin)* looking for jobs were from state-owned enterprises (SOE's). Private enterprises absorbed over 90% of the job seekers. (p.186)
>
> 2. At Shanghai Radio Factory Three, 100 out of 470 of the technical personnel had left. (p. 187)

At the same time,

> 3. A township enterprise in Yantai, Shandong Province, received 8,000 applications within two weeks after they advertised for certain positions. Many of the applicants were cadres, professors, and experts in various fields. (p. 187)
>
> 4. Another township enterprise in Zhejiang Province hired over 100 high-level experts as their technical advisors and 120 technical personnel. Most of them were from SOE's and government agencies. (p. 187)

Professors have established money-making enterprises in their fields:

> 5. Forty professors at the East China College of Chemical Industry started 15 enterprises at the college and departmental levels, using their knowledge of high-level science and technology. (p. 210)

6. Professor Xue Wenguan of Tongji University started a construction company that renovated well-known commercial buildings in Shanghai. He made a yearly profit of a million yuan. (p. 210)

7. A survey indicated that 40% of the professors in Beijing's 10 institutions of higher learning engaged in second jobs outside their colleges. (p. 211)

Humanistic intellectuals have also found their niche in the market economy:

8. A law professor from a university in Beijing was the legal counsel to three companies. He said, "I have lived over 40 years now, and only today do I feel that I am a full individual *(hun chu ge ren yang lai)*." (p. 230)

9. Hu Wanchun, a well-known Shanghai writer, started two bookstores and an exhibition and sales store in Hanoi, Vietnam, dealing with products from Shanghai. (p. 248)

10. Wang Shuo and a number of colleagues started the Sea Horse Company. It helps writers who sell to TV stations, movie studios and publishing houses to protect their intellectual rights. (p. 271)

These examples give us an idea of the extent to which intellectuals have been bourgeoisified and the ways in which they have been bourgeoisified. The examples in 1, 3, 4, and 8 show that intellectuals have started to *work for private corporations* as technical experts or advisors, while 5, 6, 9, and 10 show them as *bosses of their own enterprises*. (Some enterprises like these may be considered as collectively owned.)

A playwright reports that his theater group had its own businesses to support the theater: a restaurant, clothing store, and cultural development company. "We are afraid that some day we 'won't have bread to eat.'" [This is comparable to the pun in the film *Lenin in 1918,* "there will be bread"] (Interview with Yang Wei 1994:1.4). This is true with other institutions where intellectuals work. To supplement their advertising revenues, for example, news organizations also have begun to run hotels, apartments, stores, and other enterprises (Lynch 1999:74). Some have transformed their profession into businesses when they could:

Since to write books is not as profitable as publishing them, and to publish them is not as profitable as selling them, the mentality of humanistic

> intellectuals *(wen ren)* is collapsing and intellectuals themselves are corrupted. They begin to write popular and pornographic books. They write ads for businesses. I wrote for Hong Kong publishers, imitating another writer without using my own name. This is to serve as a "professional killer" *[zhiye qiangshou]*. To make a living, you have to do something like this. (Interview with Yang Wei 1994:1.4)

His story is corroborated by Zhou Weiwan. Discussing her writer-husband, Zhou said he had kept aloof, writing for the sake of art. But he could not make much money; readers had lost their interest in pure art. While some writers shared his dedication, many had joined the ranks of businesspeople. One of the well-known poets from her province was doing business with the Russians, and other writers were buying and selling stocks. Those who did not engage in business often led a lonely life, with little money, or perhaps faced a family crisis, as had one of her friends (Interview with Zhou Weiwan 1996:2.35).

Intellectuals can be innovative in making money. Journalists, for example, would use their stories as a way to increase their incomes:

> When businesses open, these reporters will attend the openings *(gan changzi, or zou xue)* and later write glowingly about them. In return they will be given envelopes containing money; even the editor, who had not been there, will receive a gift. To go to the "press conferences" of businesses and write them up in news releases has now become a profession. These reporters can "produce" *(zuo)* news even when there is none to produce. They earn a great deal of this "gray income." Journalists for TV stations, especially Central TV, make the most money, or *zui fa*. But a mission-oriented person would never stoop to this. (Interview with Ge Shannon 1994:1.3)

For these people, journalism has become an entrepreneurial enterprise rather than a professional job. (See also Lynch 1999:61–4). Indeed, the problem has persisted into the twenty-first century—so much so that the central government is still calling on journalists to adhere to their moral principles and to ban news for money, or paid news *(you chang xinwen)* (*Overseas Chinese Daily,* March 29, 2000). Lawyers tend not to deal with divorce cases because there is little money to be made there. They are willing to handle only economic cases, where they could earn tens of thousands of yuan. When they have a good relationship with the judge, that money could multiply (Interview with Ge Shannon 1994:1.3).

College professors have joined the business ranks as well. Here is what a lecturer in English has to say about teachers as well as about students of English:

> Many college teachers don't take teaching seriously. They have little time to prepare their classes or read students' homework. They are busy teaching outside the college or working at other businesses. . . . Many spend their time translating works of pornography, *gongfu,* detective stories etc. to make money. Many people who have studied literature have gone into business. Few students now want to major in literature. Out of 30 graduate students, only three or four do. (Interview with Shan Junyi 1994:1.34)

While some of these intellectuals have detached themselves from their original intellectual and professional jobs, others are doing business *and* their professional jobs at the same time. For example, Chen Zhangliang, the president of the College of Biological Engineering at Beijing University, was also president of the Biological Engineering Company he founded (Shi Jian 1996:74–5). Zhang Xianliang was the president of several companies, but he still wrote novels (pp. 231–3). According to Liu Zeming and his colleagues (1993:249–53), many writers from the Guangdong Writers' Association had second jobs in business. Hu Wanchun, a writer-turned-businessperson, still wrote novels and essays. Zhou Li, the author of *A Chinese Woman in Manhattan,* and Cao Guilin, author of *Beijiners in New York* were both in business. Both books were popular in China. Cheng Naishan and Liang Fengyi were also writing and doing business at the same time.[3]

Professor Wan in citobiology is another example of intellectuals doing business while engaging in their profession (Interview with Wan Yaofa 1994:1.18). After he graduated from college in 1957, Wan worked on a variety of projects: treating sheep skin to extract its oil to lighten army coats, treating polluted water, producing antibiotics, creating cosmetics to resist the aging of the skin, using Chinese herbal medicine to prevent coughs, and experimenting on various drugs to treat heart and other diseases. In our interview, he talked at length about his inventions and even used his herbal medicine on the spot to show how effective it was. At the time, he had already put some of his inventions into production; others were still being negotiated, such as a drug to treat myocarditis. The following is part of the saga of one of his new drugs:

> The government controls drug production very strictly. The university doesn't have the economic power to produce it, and factories think it is too much trouble. A couple of factories, one in Suzhou and the other in Lianyungang, wanted to buy the right to produce it once for all, but we were reluctant to do so *(bu she de.)* A corporation in Dongguan, Guangdong, will come next month to negotiate a deal with us. (Interview 1994: 1.18.6)

College students, too, are busily engaged in money-making professional and entrepreneurial activities. Many work as "family teachers," tutoring elementary or middle school students, office workers, or buying and selling stocks. Those who major in Chinese, philosophy, or history are pursuing lucrative second majors. At the time of the interview, two Ph.D. students in history believed they had a real chance to go into business after graduation. They commented that perhaps when they had money, or influence over people who had money, they would be able to help with other people's academic studies. "There is an obvious difference between a Ph.D. in history who doesn't have enough money to raise his children and an entrepreneur who can afford to waste ten thousand yuan on luxury meals in a fancy hotel," they commented (Interviews with Yan Hongyu and Chang Youde 1994:1.50–1). See figure 4.1 for an illustration of this trend of bourgeoisification.

Changing Intellectual Culture

The economic changes in China have directly altered the social organization of the production, distribution, and rewards of knowledge. The resultant bourgeoisification of intellectuals has thus led to changes in the meaning of intellectual work, in intellectuals' views of themselves, and in their commitment to social responsibility. It poses a dilemma for intellectuals; How can they adhere to their social calling while still making a living? We will now examine the value changes in the intellectual culture in this bourgeoisification process: what was changing, what was lost, and how intellectuals learned to cope with it in the 1990s.

The Shifting Focus: To Moneymaking from Intellectual Work and Ideology

The playwright we cited earlier explains that while they understand their responsibility to society, intellectuals find it difficult to retain such a sense of mission. "It is hard. In the past, we had a sacred cause. Right

Figure 4.1 We Want Professor, Not . . . *(Yao jiaoshou, bu yao . . .)*
Source: Ding Cong 1999 (Vol. 3), p. 34.

now, we do our 'work' first, we try to complete a task, and we try to make it more educational. But, then, we have to make money because of the market economy, which has made an impact on both the rank and file and the leadership. People look to material gains rather than the arts" (Interview with Yang Wei 1994:1.4).

Money is apparently more crucial than ideology:

People are more concerned with keeping alive than keeping their faith. People would say that something is wrong with you if you still believe in communism. When negotiating a writing contract, the first thing people talk about is money, which was not the case in the past. I offered a photographer 250 yuan to work on one episode of a TV series. He was furious. He asked me whether that was how much I thought he was worth.

> How was I to know that he used to be paid 300 yuan? So I gave him the 300 yuan instead. (Interview 1994:1.4)

Shen, a lecturer in Chinese, is anther case in point. At the time of the interview, he had already published a dictionary of Western holidays, a translation of Lin Yutang, the Republican era writer, and was working on a dictionary of slogans. His specialty was linguistics. He taught two to three courses a semester, but he did not want to work much harder in his specialty because it could not earn him a living. "You cannot make a living by pursuing a legitimate profession *(zhengdang zhiye)*. I would be doomed if I only did linguistics. Now I only do things that will earn me money. I am not interested in anything else" (Interview with Shen Yahong 1994:1.33). He wrote popular books, taught Chinese to foreign students, and ran a translation agency to make money. He said that he was a language peddler *(yuyan fanzi)*.

These intellectuals use their predecessors as their reference point. Shen commented that his graduate professor had saved only about 3,000 yuan in his entire life, and he himself did not want to work that hard and end up with so little. Shen's picture of his professor is echoed by that of the playwright in the following example:

> People in our field are afraid. The majority of them are having a tough life, especially the playwrights, directors, choreographers, song writers. One of our first-rate song writers is still living in a one-room dorm, sharing toilets with other families. He has been working for 40 years now. When I see him, I see my future. It is scary. I have to do something else. Indeed, some writers have begun to write popular songs. Today you don't find children's songs like we had in the past, such as those in *The Flower of Acanthaceous Indigo* (Malan Hua), or another song named *The Small Bamboo Raft* (Xiaoxiao Zhubai). For a children's song like that you will earn 300 yuan, but for a popular song, you can earn several thousand. (Interview with Yang Wei 1994:1.4)

College students, too, see their professors as role models. According to Du, the professors in his department, international finance, led a very good life. In addition to teaching, they worked for companies that not only paid them salaries comparable to the best around, but even bought houses for them. The students conceded, however, that while some professors were lured by these financial enticements, the more virtuous were not. These remained dedicated to their teaching, feeling that they might lose their freedom as thinking human beings *(renge ziyou)* (Interviews with Du Yanbing and Ni Dan 1994:1.58–9).

Shen also contrasted himself with his classmates who had gone into business, and found that he was being shortchanged. "The contrast with my classmates is huge. They may not have the same ability I have, but they work for advertising companies and can earn 1000 yuan a month" (Interview with Shen Yahong 1994:1.33). In 1984 when he began his graduate studies, he wanted to do research. Since then, the market economy has apparently made a major change in his thinking. "We used to be slaves of politics. Now we are all influenced by the economy. The pressure is huge: lack of one penny can make a hero surrender himself *[yiwen qian bidao yingxiong han],*" Shen said.

The same is true from an engineer's perspective:

> The technical personnel are the poorest. You hear about intellectuals dying at the prime of life. I personally know someone who died at the age of 46. Newspapers praised him for his hardworking spirit, but what's the use? Now when college graduates look for a job, they want to go where they can get the most pay. It does not matter whether the work they do has anything to do with what they learned at school. (Interview with Yan Huiren 1994:1.39)

The market economy has really tilted the values of intellectuals, says an engineer and administrator. They feel off balance psychologically. Some even ask for sick leave just so they could work outside the factory (Interview with Yu Junjie 1994:1.42).

Indeed, a sociologist feels that intellectuals need to turn their knowledge into money:

> During the '50s and '60s workers, soldiers, and cadres had the highest prestige *(chi xiang)* politically and economically. Nobody wanted to be a peasant. College teachers still enjoyed relatively high prestige because we still revered our thousands of years of tradition. Even when they were criticized during the Cultural Revolution, intellectuals would still be consulted for their expertise. They commanded respect in private. But now nobody cares about them. Intellectuals need to turn their knowledge into money; otherwise, people will look down upon them. Economics, the earning of money, is the only standard now by which people measure others. (Interview with Cheng Kejiang 1994:1.8)

This change in the consciousness of China's intellectuals—from creative to economic—is also a reflection of the change in society in general. As Yang Wei observes, a writer is no longer admired:

> When I was young, I believed that a writer was even more prestigious than an engineer. An artist would be even more exalted. But now people ask, "Is a writer as big as a boss?" People's eyes brighten *(yanjing yi liang)* when they hear the word "boss," but when they hear the word "writer," they say, "So what?" The prestige of a writer has become something from a distant past. People are willing to buy a dress for 500 yuan but not to see a play for five yuan. Our theater art is in a desolate situation. (Interview 1994:1.4)

Culture has become simply a commodity:

> Culture has lost its purity in the traditional sense of opera, books, etc.; it has become a commodity. When people say culture, they put more emphasis on dining elegantly, touring, etc. There is little pure literature now; much of it is commercialized popular literature written for entertainment. You have to have connections to have your works published. Works can even go to auctions. If you have a good relationship, or *guanxi,* with a businessman, he will put up a higher bid for your work. A work can be bought even before it is written. It is hard to say whether this is good or bad. The novel *Ruined Capital* by Jia Pingwa can tell us something about the corruption of intellectuals. (Interview with Yang Wei 1994:1.4)

This emphasis on commercial values has apparently also affected children:

> I spent a month writing a ten-episode TV series for children and about a year producing it. It was aired on Central TV but few children bothered to see it. Children don't even watch children's plays nowadays. They want to study a foreign language, or electronic piano. You wonder how you can realize your values. (Interview with Yang Wei 1994:1.4)

A group of students, most in Ph.D. programs, tell of their encounter with people who thought studying law was much more valuable than studying history. One of them says, "I study *lishi,* i.e., history. When I said to people that I studied *lishi,* their eyes brightened because they thought I was saying *lushi,* meaning law or lawyer. Their attitude changed as soon as I corrected their misunderstanding" (Interviews with Chang Youde, Fu Ji, Sun Zhongxin, Yan Hongyu, and Yu Xilan 1994:1.50–4). A graduate student in Marxist philosophy provides another example. "When you interact with people, their eyes shine when they hear that you are learning economics; but their eyes become dim when they hear you study philosophy" (Interview with Li Yishun 1994:1.49).

College students, who are trained to be intellectuals, want majors that promise a good income. Here is what some young teachers and students in history and literature have to say:

> Students don't want to study history for it does not bring them money. They want to study foreign languages, business, and finance. (Interviews with Chang Youde, Fu Ji, Sun Zhongxin, Yan Hongyu, and Yu Xilan 1994:1.50–4)

> College students in Chinese literature are enthusiastic when they first enter college. A year later, 90% of them lose the enthusiasm and want jobs to make money. (Interviews with Chen Yichi, Fu Ji, Gong Haiyang, and Yan Yang 1994:1.52, 60–2)

Students no longer want to work hard in academics. As one of the lecturers observes, "In the 1980s, students would fight each other for a seat in the classroom. Now the classrooms are almost empty *[kongkong dangdang]*" (Interview with Quan Ming 1994:1.30). Quan, a lecturer and researcher, provides a reason. "Humans live to pursue happiness. I can be happy doing research, and I need this. But money provides another kind of happiness" (Interview 1994:1.30).

Money also enhances one's social status and opportunities for personal development, as some M.A. students in international finance and economics comment (Interview with Du Yanbing and Ni Dan 1994: 1.58–9). Du had been a middleschool teacher, but found his life unbearable. There was no opportunity for upward mobility; he was near the bottom of the ladder in income, housing, and other infrastructure. He would have gone mad if he had stayed in the countryside. These students were not concerned about politics except as it affected their own economic well-being. Their concerns were to maximize their opportunities and to make more money. They had not thought much about how others were doing, such as workers and peasants. They considered themselves to be minor intellectuals, but idealistic and neither vulgar nor philistine (Interviews 1994:1.58–9). Two Ph.D. students, one in psychology and another in geographic information, had no interest in politics either (Interview with Chang Chunli and Lu Xin 1994:1.63–4). Among many intellectuals and young students, there indeed was a movement toward making money rather than making democracy, more oriented toward individual development than collective progress.

What Have They Lost?

The intellectuals may have gained much in their emphasis on economics, but many believe something has been lost at the same time. What have they lost, in addition to their sense of mission? For Yang, the first loss is the *worth of intellectual labor*. He gives us an example: "The playwright who wrote the famous play *The Flower of Acanthaceous Indigo* made 400 yuan in the '50's and makes 800 yuan now. Even with a special allowance, his living standard is even lower than that of an ordinary worker" (Interview with Yang Wei 1994:1.4).

Shen gives us another example: "We published a book of maxims and we earned only 1500 yuan, which is the price of a beeper. Is our book worth only a beeper? How can they be compared? Even though the salary level of college teachers has been raised, professors still feel they live in poverty" (Interview with Shen Yahong 1994:1.33).

For others, it is *the humanistic spirit* that has been lost. For Tian, a lecturer, and Jiang, a journalist, the humanistic spirit is the most valuable aspect of our society, and it is being destroyed by the market economy (Interview with Tian Zhaoyun and Jiang Zhexin 1994:1.56–7). Many are trying to live in two worlds at the same time: a commercial world, and the intellectual world, that is, as Confucian businesspeople *(ru shang)* (Interviews with Du Yanbing and Ni Dan 1994:1.58–9). This may point to an even bigger loss, that is, the freedom to produce what may be more valuable than profits. One is tempted by the market, and moneymaking becomes a major goal in life. And it is what Le Guin ([1973] 1977) calls the "censorship by the market." The market now becomes the Stalin in the soul.[4]

According to Professor Fan who teaches chemistry, another loss is the *sense of equality* and *innocence* people used to have in the revolutionary years:

> People are more concerned about hierarchies now. In conference hotels professors can have two-person rooms but others have to be in three-person rooms. Professors travel in cars; others travel in buses. People

> used to be modest and cooperative before the Cultural Revolution, but now they would do anything to get promoted, including quarreling, stirring up trouble, crying *(chao, nao, ku),* etc. Very few people would talk about style *(fengge)* or sacrifice *(fengxian).* The slogan now stresses "public as well as private interests" *(da gong you si)* instead of "public interest only" *(da gong wu si).* (Interview 1994:1.12)

The loss of values can also be seen in academic work. Some books have been published to expose various kinds of corruption in the academia: plagiarism, vicious attacks on others, huge numbers of errors in printed books, fake study centers set up for profit, sloppy translations, and so forth (see Dongfang Shanba 1999, Xu Linzheng 2001, Yang Shoujian 2001). People's eyes are on the money they can make in such practices rather than on academic standards. The word *business* has gained enormous prestige. Cheng Guan, a professor in sociology, comments that the word *business* used to have a negative connotation; now it has the most positive meaning, although many consider this an abnormal phenomenon in the transformation of our society (Interview 1994:1.36).

Indeed, some believe that intellectuals who have abandoned their academic work and plunged into business have sold themselves *(chumai ziji)* to the world of the powerful. These people, they say, are more concerned with making money than making democracy, or dealing with any other of China's social problems. Such concerns, of course, are not new. Two quotes from Zhang Tao, a sixteenth-century scholar-official, commenting on the commercial atmosphere in the late Ming dynasty are very illuminating:[5]

> Those who enriched themselves through trade became the majority, and those who enriched themselves through agriculture [let's say "culture" for people today] were few. The rich became richer and the poor, poorer. Those who rose took over, and those who fell were forced to flee. It was capital that brought power. . . . Trade proliferated and the tiniest scrap of profit was counted up. Corrupt magnates sowed disorder and wealthy shysters preyed. . . . Purity was completely swept away. (cited in Brook 1998:153)

> One man in a hundred is rich, while nine out of ten are impoverished. The poor cannot stand up to the rich who, though few in number, are able to control the majority. The lord of silver rules heaven and the god of copper cash reigns over the earth. Avarice is without limit, flesh injures

> bone, everything is personal pleasure, and nothing can be let slip. In dealings with others, everything is recompensed down to the last hair. The demons of treachery stalk. (cited in Brook 1998:238)

These contemporary intellectuals are echoing what Zhang said five hundred years ago.[6]

Do they still consider themselves intellectuals? The change of focus of their work and ideology has also led to the change of *their views on themselves as intellectuals,* and eventually to the *loss of the strict definition of the intellectual.* Li Gang (Interview 1996:2.28) was one of the deputy managers of a private company producing alarm systems; he was in charge of production. The company was composed mainly of people like himself, recent college graduates and engineers who had quit their jobs in state-owned enterprises. He had worked in a radio factory but he believed that he could not make full use of his ability there and decided to "plunge into the sea." Asked whether he would consider himself an intellectual, Li believed that it did not matter whether people like him were intellectuals or not. He felt confident about himself. That was more important. Although it is unclear how many intellectuals felt the way Li did, there is no doubt that intellectuals are changing their focus of work and their views of themselves.

There is another consideration. If too many intellectuals escape to lucrative jobs, academic and scientific fields needed for modernization will face *a shortage of personnel.* A professor is concerned about his graduate students "plunging into the sea" of business rather than pursuing the academic professions they were trained for.

> How to deal with the impact of the market economy is the issue. For example, should graduate students be allowed to choose their own professions? How to guarantee that some less glamorous disciplines, such as mining, agriculture, etc. will have the manpower they need? Two or three out of twenty to thirty of my students have gone to corporations such as an advertising company, a stock trading company, and a film-dubbing studio. (Interview with Xu Tianxiang 1994:1.15)

Going Against the Tide or Compromising?

Indeed, intellectuals faced a serious dilemma: to pursue a nonlucrative profession or simply to "plunge into the sea." Xia, a dedicated physicist, is afraid that many talented physicists no longer felt at ease pursuing science as a vocation:

> This is not good news for basic physics. We are not looking to find a chunk of gold but to find a view in the world of physics. Young people no longer have the will and perseverance to do so, although they don't lack the talent. For example, one of my Ph.D. students makes only 400–500 yuan a month. His wife is sick and cannot work. He has to ask his father-in-law for help. In contrast, his middle-school classmate who did not pass the college entrance exam is now making big money. How can you blame him for wanting to do applied physics so that he can make ends meet? Furthermore, our university does not provide its own graduates with even a one-room home; whereas if they go to a different university, they will get at least a two-bedroom one. Some go into joint ventures, or into sales, or translation agencies etc. to better themselves economically. The world outside the university is larger *[chuqu tiandi da]*. We are at a turning point, moving from more basic to more applied research under the pressure of the market economy. But the problem is that basic research will be weakened, which may not be a blessing. (Interview 1994:1.32)

Xia Hairong is not influenced by money. But she is probably an exception. "Personally, I would like to do more basic research. Others say that I do this because I have been abroad and now have jolted myself out of poverty *[tuo pin le]*. But it is mainly because I like it" (Interview 1994:1.32).

Xia raises the issue of how professionals can survive as intellectuals without going into private business. Some have tried compromising. We mentioned some intellectuals who tried to work in their professions and in business at the same time. Others who were in business tried to maintain an intellectual's sense of social responsibility. Zhang Xianliang, presiding over his three companies, still wrote in order to show the tragic lives of the past, so that people would not repeat them (see Shi Jian 1996:234). He seemed to have a strong sense of social responsibility. Zhang Jinjiang, a professor from Shanghai University, used the money he earned to help publish the work of a senior writer, Ha Hua, who had died believing that his autobiographical novel would never see the light of day (Liu et al. 1993:249). While doing business, Li Ping continued to do research and teach (Interview 1996:2.29). She too had a strong sense of social responsibility.

Duan Qihua is another example of the intellectual entrepreneur who retains his sense of social responsibility. He resigned from his law firm in the United States in 1992 and started his own firm in Shanghai, one of the earliest private law firms in China. He said, "To do good works in my own country and devote all I have learned to my motherland is the passion that I have always cherished in my mind" (Tang Qinmei 1997). Duan's Shanghai law firm dealt with many international cases. It represented not only corporations but also Chinese laborers. One of the cases Duan told us he would never forget was when he won compensation for a peasant family whose son had died in a sea accident, but who had no way to sue a foreign company. One of my lawyer interviewees also expressed her excitement over winning cases for those who needed her help but could not afford it (Interview with Ge Shannon 1994:1.3). Intellectuals such as these have become bourgeois in a less crass manner.

But could there be a tension between the businessperson whose primary goal is to make money and the same person who, as an intellectual, is supposed to function as the conscience of society? In other words, does the split personality present itself in the "Confucian businessperson?" Not according to Zhang Xianliang. When the interviewer asked him whether doing business affected his writing, he said it was a positive influence: by broadening his perspectives he understood better the tragic past he was writing about (see Shi Jian 1996:231–4). He did not believe that doing business would affect his personality. He believed his personality had always been that of a businessperson.

Zhang Hua, an accomplished writer of investigative reports and a former college lecturer, started the Beijing Aidier Advertisement Consulting Company in 1992. His colleagues were mainly professors and students from the Beijing Foreign Languages Institute and they did business chiefly with foreigners. He comments that there is one thing that his three personalities—teacher, writer, and businessperson—have in common: they are all human beings. They all have to learn how to be a good person (Meng Xiaoyun 1997). Indeed, Wang Hong (1491–1545) a merchant in the Ming dynasty already made the same argument. He believed that "gentry and merchants pursue different methods but share the same commitment" (cited in Brook 1998:143). Merchants should not be regarded as inferior to gentry. The two Zhangs and one Duan here are arguing the same.

Conclusions[7]

A bourgeoisification process has unquestionably occurred among intellectuals, from college students to veteran scholars. Some intellectuals have the luxury—and the tenacity—to pursue their academic and social endeavors without having to worry about making ends meet. But a far larger number have been lured into entrepreneurship by necessity, or by their own changing ideology. As some of our interviewees comment, intellectuals from the 1990s on have experienced a number of value changes, including their views on themselves, their social responsibility, their sense of mission, their humanist spirit, and their sense of equality. Many feel that without money there is no status. There has been a shift in the social construction of status from *wenren* (the scholar) to *shangren* (the businessperson). The old belief in scholarship as the loftiest ideal of an individual has been torn apart. There is no doubt that many intellectuals are moving on the road to bourgeoisification, as their predecessors did in the Republican era. As a result of this movement, intellectuals are afflicted with a dual personality.

However, it is not easy for intellectuals to make a complete change of values overnight. Many try to strike a balance between business and intellect. But when they do so, our bourgeoisified intellectuals may experience many built-in stresses. They do spend a good deal of their time doing business. This, of course, means that they have less time for their professional and intellectual jobs. Even more importantly, there is a conflict between morality and the single-minded pursuit of profit, as *Shanggu Xingmi* (or Bringing Merchants to Their Senses, a seventeenth-century moral guide for merchants) would tell us. It is true, as the prominent Huizhou scholar Wang Daokun (1525–93) would argue, that commerce was not in contradiction with scholarship and often funded it (see Brook 1998:215–8). But the primary focus of businesses is to make money, and the means to make money could very well be controversial. Even if the goal is to fund scholarship, or inform scholarship as Zhang Xianliang would argue, will the end justify the possibly dubious means? This is a tension that may cause dual personality, and it is a conflict that Confucian businesspeople have to constantly strive to manage. There is no denying the possible conflict such men and women feel between their moral/intellectual and business sides. The fact that they talk about it is an indication of the conflict.

The two-way pull facing the bourgeoisified intellectual is similar to that faced by organic intellectuals who follow an ethic of responsibility.

However, compared with their dilemma our current dilemma is much easier to deal with. The bourgeoisified intellectual tends to have more freedom of expression. This may be because the pull of business is traditionally less strong than that of officialdom. It is thus easier to get out of business than out of politics.

At any rate, there is a degree of tension shared by various stripes of unattached as well organic and critical intellectuals. This is a general pattern, that is, the ubiquity of split or dual personality for all sorts of intellectuals as they try to negotiate their relationship to both *knowledge* (truth, beauty, and understanding) and *power* (security, wealth, status, and social efficacy). How they manage this tension determines the extent to which they can effect social change. The contradictory class locations of these intellectuals, which we will discuss in chapter 5, may throw more light on this conflict. In the next section, however, we will focus on the professionals.

The Professionalization of Intellectuals

While some intellectuals are becoming bourgeoisified, others are going through a process of professionalization. In this section, we first examine what professions, professionalism, and professionalization mean in the Western context. For, after all, professions, or the technical functions of the intelligentsia, emerged with capitalism, and large-scale capitalism developed first in the West. Professional skills were not valued as much as humanistic ones in the Chinese tradition, as we explained in chapter 1. After the examination of these concepts, we go on to discuss the making of Chinese professionals and their politics.

Professions and Professionalization

Professions generally refers to occupations whose practitioners, or *professionals,* have received a certain amount of education and credentialing in their specific fields, and who enjoy a great deal of autonomy in their work. According to Talcott Parsons (1968:536), the core criteria for a profession should include (1) formal technical training and credentialing indicating the mastery of a generalized cultural tradition; (2) some skills developed to use that tradition; and (3) institutional means to put the skills to socially responsible use. Typical professions include medicine, law, engineering, and education. Colleges provide the training in skills within a certain intellectual tradition, and professional agencies license the professionals. Hospitals, industrial and government agencies, law firms, and colleges provide means for their practice.

Modern professions arrived with the development of capitalism. The minute division of labor, or the "occupational principle" implied in the work of Durkheim (Freidson 1973:19), makes professions necessary. (Modernism also gives rise to the administrative hierarchy, which is explicated by Max Weber, and that we will discuss in chapter 5 in our analysis of organic intellectuals). Understandably, with the development of Chinese capitalism, professions in China have followed, though not without ups and downs.

The arrival of the professions is accompanied by an ideology, *professionalism,* "which is said to include such attitudes as commitment to one's work as a career so that one's work becomes part of one's identity and emphasis on public service rather than private profit" (Freidson 1970:70). It is packaged with "claims to knowledge, expertise, service, and autonomy" (Hoffman 1989:204). These values and beliefs, taught to developing professionals, provide them with a label that brings them power and prestige, and that helps them retain their class (professional) status (Larson 1977:156; Montagna 1977:202–7). This process has been called "market closure" (Collins 1990).

Professionalization, on the other hand, is the *process* of achieving the professional status manifested in professionalism. As Abbott (1988:16) summarizes, it is a process through which professions are organized for association, for control, and for work, and through which they legitimate their control by attaching their expertise to rationality, efficiency, and science. In essence, professionalization serves to achieve a *professional autonomy* "in selecting the economic terms of work, the location and social organization of work, and the technical content of the work" (Freidson 1970:44). This professional autonomy is largely a result of negotiations with the state and society in general, since it is the state that licenses the professionals and society that approves or disapproves their practice. Generally, it is the professional associations that conduct the negotiations with the state and society.

China's Professions and Professionals: A Historical-Comparative Perspective

In the Chinese context, professions *(zhuanye)* and professionals *(zhuanye renshi)* are weak concepts, compared with the term 'intellectuals.' The evolution of the terms resembles that in Poland and Russia. In these two countries, the term 'intelligentsia' used to refer to an educated stratum that distinguished itself by a set of "psychological characteristics, manner, style of life, social status and, above all, value system" (Gella 1976:13). Professional skills did not come into the picture. Things changed with social and economic development. In Poland, for example, a professional model emerged in the 1970s. While the *traditional model* of the intelligentsia would call on the intellectuals from various fields to actively engage in a common political effort supporting oppressed workers, a *more professional model* would call on the intellectuals to use their technical expertise to suggest concrete reforms in social, economic, and health issues. No wonder Polish sociologists have already referred to intelligentsia as "specialists with higher education," or "professionals" (Kennedy and Sadkowski 1991:175–6).

The term intellectuals in the Chinese context shares many characteristics with the traditional Eastern European intelligentsia. Intellectuals in China are supposed to be concerned about injustice and inequality in society, and about how to save the country and its people *(jiu guo jiu min)*. However, with the development of a market economy, as we have seen, many intellectuals have focused on how to make use of their technical expertise, and their political enthusiasm has dwindled. They have become more like the West's professionals. An intellectual model of professionals similar to that of the Polish is fast developing. In addition to the bourgeoisified intellectuals, these professionals are the unattached intellectuals of modern times.

The first group of technical intellectuals, who most resembled the Western professionals, came into being during the Self-Strengthening movement of the late nineteenth century, as we discussed in chapter 1. But as we have pointed out, the technical intellectuals, given the political and social circumstances, inevitably succumbed to the powerful tradition of the scholar-official. Nevertheless, professions continued to develop. Fei Xiaotong pointed out in a 1948 essay that with the demise of the Qing dynasty and the development of industrialism, the traditional intellectuals in China had already been replaced by professionals, or "intellectuals with technical knowledge" (cited in Jin Yaoji 1987:76). The slogan letting experts run the country *(zhuan jia zhi guo)* has been around since the Republican era. Thus in many fields, professionalization was well on its way in pre-1949 China, with an increasing number of Western-trained lawyers, doctors, engineers, teachers, journalists, and businesspeople.

However, intellectuals had no chance to be professionalized in the Western sense. After the Communist takeover, the Chinese government made early efforts to Westernize education: it overhauled universities and colleges in 1952 to drastically decrease the number of general universities and to increase the number of specialized colleges, following the Soviet pattern (Yang Dongping 1994a). Even during the Cultural Revolution, after several years of suspension in college enrollment, Mao originally restored only colleges of science and technology, showing much less interest in the humanities and social sciences.

Nonetheless, in the Mao era efforts at creating a professional stratum were developed along the lines of "red" and "expert," and intellectuals did not achieve much autonomy. Rather, they were deprofessionalized (see also Miller 1996:185). As we discussed in chapter 2, intellectuals had to conform to the Maoist ideology and serve the Party's political goals. Even in their own technical fields, intellectuals were constrained by the Party objectives. A Party secretary, with or without a professional background, was installed in each working unit, and became the authority over technical issues, dictating what could and could not be done. As in the case of the French Revolution (Siegrist 1990), the Chinese Revolution resulted in a *civil-egalitarian laity model* for professions, in which the laity could become judges, and peasants with little training could become doctors as long as they were socially and politically reliable. Chinese intellectuals were thus deprofessionalized, stripped of what little professional standing they had enjoyed. This happened despite the Party's efforts in 1952 to restructure the universities, and its repeated calls to utilize the intellectuals and their expertise during the first decade of the People's Republic.

In the first and second periods of the Deng era, as we have seen in chapters 2 and 3, the Party loosened its political control over the intellectuals. The educational system was reformed to train new professionals, and no one could perform duties in medicine, law, engineering, or teaching without credentials. Now the professionalization process has been renewed and intellectuals have achieved a certain professional status. They carry formal technical and academic titles, and they can even set up private practices in medicine, law, engineering, or education, although on a very limited scale. The situation resembles that of the Consulate and the first French Empire under Napoleon: a mixture of state control and a liberal market economy. Siegrist (1990:197) terms this model *the entrepreneurial professional*. Clearly, a professional stratum has come into being. Under this second model, however, the state still monopolizes the system of education and determines the economic and working conditions of the intellectuals. Intellectuals still cannot form their own independent associations to bargain over social and economic issues, including their pay, their working conditions, or their role in society. We have just seen some evidence of these entrepreneurial professionals.

It is not clear, though, whether or when these Chinese intellectuals, these unattached professionals, will enter the contemporary Western model. This is the model of *the organized and to some extent autonomous profession*. Here, its members would bargain with other social agents over issues that matter to them: the production and reproduction of their ranks, their professional autonomy, and especially their economic conditions (Siegrist 1990:197). In this model, the professionalism we just described is grounded in the general social thinking, and professionalization becomes a standard part of social life.

That is a brief review of the development of the Chinese intellectual we call the professional, as opposed to the critical and organic. We have covered various models of professional development. But it remains to describe the unattached intellectuals' work, their general perception of politics, and their working and living conditions in terms of income and housing, funding for research, problems with technical intellectuals' research equipment, and promotion. We will see how little control professionals have over their working and living conditions in the 1990s, which would in turn inform their politics. We will see that even if, for one reason or another, they have kept their distance from politics, like the *yinshi* of the past, these intellectuals, or professionals, are still more politically charged than, say, the working class. They are articulate about their group interests, and aware of their potential ability to bargain with the state for more professional autonomy.

Professionals' Work and Politics: Lack of Autonomy

We have learned so far that, although some intellectuals became critical, bureaucratized, or bourgeosified, most became professionalized and refrained to some extent from politics. These unattached professionals could be either technical or humanistic intellectuals.[8] In our case analysis, however, we will focus on technical intellectuals. Specifically, we will examine engineers, researchers, college professors, doctors, and lawyers.

The work of the Research Institute, at a state-owned TV factory we visited in 1994, fell into three areas: imitation of, and improvement on, foreign technology; joint design with foreign companies; and development and incorporation of its own new technologies. At the time, a number of reforms in the management of the factory were under way. An important change gave the Institute greater freedom to allocate a lump sum to salaries for the whole year *(quan nian gongzi zonger chengbao).* Another divided the company into three parts: one for joint ventures, one for developing service enterprises *(san chan),* and one to continue production of TVs in the original factory (Interview with Zhong Yanchu 1994:1.43).

Their products were sold to other parts of the world as well, including South Africa, Russia, Eastern Europe, and the United States. The export models were conventional products (Interview with Chen Xiang 1994:1.40.9). However, the designer's work could be creative. As one of them said, "I am in charge of the external design of our TV sets. Much of my work is creative. Unlike the assembly workers who don't have to be concerned about their work outside the eight hours here, I often have to think about how to resolve a design issue even on my way home" (Interview with Zheng Zhongqi 1994:1.41).That is intellectual work. Their concerns are primarily about that work. Here is what another of them has to say:

> I do research on new products such as picture phones, car monitors, and a medical instrument. But these are for research purposes only. There is no money for production. We can copy and improve other people's technology and use different parts to replace the ones we cannot produce. But the factory does not want to take the risk of putting new products on the market. They'd rather produce more conventional TV sets. They don't think much about the future. (Interview with Yan Huiren 1994:1.39)

Here we see an intellectual describe not only her work, but also her vision for the future and her criticism of the way in which money is allocated for professional work. Another engineer comments that production decisions are made by factory management based on how well the items would sell on the market. Engineers do not generally have a say in matters like this (Interview with Cheng Xiang 1994:1.40).

An engineer in charge of the external design of TV sets explains why they are restricted in trying new designs:

> We are not as bold as Japanese companies in our external designs. We do try new designs, but we are restricted. First, can people in the workshops make the required changes? Second, what if something goes wrong? What if the workmanship is poor, or a certain part does not work well? We have to bear the responsibilities. We have to stick to known designs that meet the market's needs. As long as they do, we are better off not making any changes. (Interview with Zheng Zhongqi 1994:1.41)

An engineer and an administrator also comment on the problems of a system that does not encourage the development of their own technology:

> The problem is that when we import things like an integrated circuit from Japan, we don't get their newest. As a result, we will always lag behind. It is true that we needed to import when we were at the initial stage of development, but it now becomes important for us to develop our own. We do have the ability. In fact, we have a joint venture with an American company to develop software and certain delicate instruments. Also, the products using our own technology are generally cheaper and even of better quality. But the leadership has to support such research that will yield sure results only later. . . .
>
> Out of twenty new products each year, we do have about two that break some new ground. The leadership is excited, but then there is no follow-up. (Interviews with Gu Sihong and Cheng Meidi 1994:1.37, 69)

A junior engineer expresses the same concern. She believes that this "copying," or *zhao ban,* will leave them far behind current international levels (Interview with You Xiaming 1994:1.38.4).

Obviously, these intellectuals have plenty of complaints about the nontechnical authorities governing their work. They would certainly like to exert more influence on how research relates to production, but they could not. If there is such a thing as intellectual politics, this is where it will focus.

And what about their politics concerning social issues? All of them focus on their own work, rather than on social problems. Again that does not mean that they are not concerned with social politics, but only as it affects their personal work. Here is the reaction of one who worked in a research institute that was affiliated with the Ministry of Electronics: "Intellectuals should have their own ways of thinking and play a political role in society. But many cannot fulfill these requirements even if they are viewed as intellectuals" (Interview with Zhang Xiaoyu 1996:2.34).

Take Zhang himself for example. He had his own views about society. But he was not very much concerned about what was happening to others; he did not want to involve himself politically. That had not always been the case, though; he said his sense of political participation dwindled after 1989. This could be partly because intellectuals have lost confidence in conventional politics after the repeated failures of the democratic movements. A researcher and lecturer in environmental studies comments, "I don't have much interest in talking about or participating in politics, or what they call *'can zheng yi zheng.'* Nothing would change even if I did participate" (Interview with Yu Liqun 1994:1.17).

A lecturer in biology echoes Yu:

> Unlike people in the humanities and social sciences, we don't talk much about social problems. I used to, but not now. I used to be a hot-blooded youth, believing in *pifu you ze* [i.e., everybody has a responsibility in state affairs]. But now I feel it is foolish. You cannot solve anything unless you are in a leadership position. You might as well do something real. It is no use talking that much. . . . My husband, a painter, used to draw pictures with political themes. Now he is doing pure art, unrelated to politics. (Interview with Quan Ming 1994:1.30)

Shan Junyi is another who demonstrates how little interest conventional politics holds for unattached intellectuals. A lecturer in English, he taught composition and linguistics and had done research in English and American poetry. Very few of his composition assignments asked students to write about politics. Most questions were about nonpolitical issues such as descriptions of places or discussions of music and art. Yet in describing his views of the current reforms in China, he had many important things to say. He predicted, as we reported earlier, that the flagrant corruption would make the rule of law necessary (Interview 1994:1.34).

These personal examples provide us with an overview of the unattached intellectuals' characteristics, work, and politics.[9] We see that they do have control over their own immediate tasks, but they do *not* have control over policy issues. They certainly cannot control their salaries. They may be interested in politics, but that interest is limited to armchair discussions.

We will now move a little closer to our professionals, looking at their living and working conditions in the 1990s. We will see that in the process of professionalization, there are some real issues to be resolved. The more autonomy they achieve in the process, the more easily these problems will be solved. Specifically, we want to discuss income, housing, funding for research, funding for equipment, and promotion.

Income and Housing

In 1994, we conducted a survey of a purposive sample of 101 technical intellectuals, all state employed, in a major Chinese city.[10] The survey included 29 intellectuals with higher professional titles (i.e., full and associate/assistant professors and senior engineers); 40 with middle-level titles (i.e., lecturers and engineers); and 31 with lower-level titles (i.e., assistant lecturers and assistant engineers). One respondent did not indicate any title. Table 4.2 shows the distribution of their monthly incomes.

The average salary in the city in 1994 was about $80 (640 yuan) a month, and we see that about 42% of our sample earned about that much or less. The majority, 77%, earned about $100 or less. The salary level of teachers was indeed "lower-middle" (Interview with Xu Tianxiang 1994:1.15).

It is true that the income system was such that basic salary formed

Table 4.2 Income Distribution of Technical Intellectuals

Monthly Income		% of People Receiving Listed Income
RMB Yuan	US$ Equivalent	
1100–1500	$138–$188	3%
900–1099	$113–$137	20%
700–899	$88–$112	35%
500–699	$63– $87	28%
300–499	$38– $62	14%
		100%

Source: The Research Group on Scientific and Technical Personnel. 1994.

Notes:

1. The research group was composed of researchers from three teaching and research institutions in China and in the City University of New York. The respondents included professors, lecturers, and engineers from two institutions of higher learning and one research department in a factory.
2. Efforts were made to represent intellectuals from different academic and professional disciplines.

less than one third of the total income received at the end of the month. The major part of it consisted of various allowances or bonuses depending on one's position and workload. Unfortunately, people did not always know how much they would get in bonuses, so their incomes were not always predictable. Whatever they earned was considered a pittance in one of the largest cities in China, one with one of the highest standards of living.

Indeed, when asked how they felt about their salaries, 53% said "very unsatisfactory" and "quite unsatisfactory" and 39% said "average." Only 9% said "fine," and no one said "very satisfactory." It seemed to be a fact that intellectuals generally earned only an average salary, and there was a common perception among intellectuals that they were unfairly treated by the state.

Some personal accounts should help us further understand the depth of their concerns over income. We have already met Cheng Xiang, an assistant engineer at the Research Institute of his factory. In 1994 Cheng was living with his wife, child, and parents in one and a half rooms. With his limited income, he did not feel that he could afford to support his parents, especially because his father had rectal cancer and medical care was very expensive. He felt that his father would probably have to stop using the medicine he was taking, given Cheng's own financial situation. He did not want to leave the factory. But he did not exclude the possibility of leaving later if the factory did not change its policy and start raising salaries for technical intellectuals (Interview 1994:1.40).

Professor Gui, a computer scientist and a former worker-peasant-soldier-student, had studied and taught abroad twice. He was now teaching graduate courses and was working on the design of multimedia technology, computer-aided management (i.e., management information systems), the information highway, and a data bank for the navy (Interview 1994:1.31). He made this comment: "I was able to support my family only because I have savings from my work abroad. Otherwise, it would be impossible for our four-person family to make a living" (Interview 1994:1.31).

Indeed, as a lecturer in chemistry commented, "Some scholars have returned and are able to stay just because they have been abroad and have earned enough to improve their living conditions. They are using the money they earned or saved in a foreign country" (Interview with Bao Chuping 1994:1.19).

Bao said that was one of the chief factors that made it possible for him to stay and work here. He had earned enough money abroad to maintain a comfortable standard of living. He now owned a washer, a color TV, and a refrigerator, amenities he otherwise would not have been able to afford.

Another example of the stresses on income: the university had just put up a new residence building. Let us say you were a lecturer and it was your turn now to have an apartment. You had been on a list for years, and had met various stringent requirements. You would now get a one-bedroom apartment. But if you could put up 15,000 yuan of your own money, you could get a two-bedroom apartment:

> Money can buy you qualifications. And I bought a place in the front. Otherwise, I would get only one dorm room of 11.8 square meters for the whole family of three. [One foot equals 0.3048 meter.] Right now I have 30 square meters instead. If I hadn't had extra income from some other sources, I wouldn't have had a chance like this. (Interview with Bao Chuping 1994:1.19)

But were they being fairly paid for their professional contributions, their research? Bao Chuping said that first of all it was difficult to get funding. Second, even if a project was funded with the maximum amount (around 50,000 yuan), individuals involved in the project could only get 12 percent of the money for their labor, and that might mean around 1,000 yuan for a year, which would contribute little to the purchase of a home (Interview 1994:1.19).

In fact, technical intellectuals were already in line for better income and housing than humanistic intellectuals. This was because the need for technology in the country's economic development made jobs available outside the university or research institute. With no economic or technical skills to offer, humanistic intellectuals tended to have a harder time. Prof. Xiao Gongqin, an historian, commented that his colleagues all smoked cheaper brands of cigarettes, for example, Flying Horse or Peony. Once in awhile he would bring a pack of Yun cigarettes, one of the best in China, and everybody would be very anxious to share one with him (Interview 1994:1.2).

One humanistic intellectual found the gap between what he earned and what his trainees would earn unfair. He trained secretaries, who would earn about 1,000 yuan after graduation, whereas he was earning only 500. "Many of us don't have gray [under the table] incomes, and our mere survival is a miracle," said one of them (Interviews with Chen Yichi, Fu Ji, Gong Haiyang, and Yan Yang 1994:1.52, 60–2).

The intellectuals in the countryside lived in even harsher conditions. Middle schoolteachers were typical examples. In Shanxi province, in a school with eight faculty members, only the principal was a full-time teacher *(gong ban),* who was paid about 500 yuan by the county government. Five of them were also full-time but were paid only about 200 yuan by the *xiang* (the government of several villages), and were therefore *min ban,* that is, supported by the lower-level governments. Full-time or not, they had their farmwork to do, and that waited for the weekends. Finally, there were two substitute teachers, who were paid even less (Interview with Hao Huiling 1996:2.36).

The situations were improving, though slightly. In 1998, according to official statistics, 802,900, or 13.8%, of the 5,819,400 primary schoolteachers were *min ban,* which was a 5.33% drop from the previous year (Ministry of Education 1999:167). In junior high schools, 1.8%, or 65,800, of the 3,094,300 full-time teachers were *min ban,* a drop of 1.55%. This school in Shanxi province, however, had a much higher percentage of *min ban* teachers than the national average, judging from what we learned.

This was one of the constant themes in our interviews: the intellectuals, especially the young ones and those in the humanities and social sciences, believed that they were being shortchanged in income and housing. They had only to compare themselves with people of their age working in joint business ventures, who might get five to ten times their salary. Furthermore, our interviewees on the whole believed that those who worked with their brains should earn more than those who worked with their hands. This was a traditional belief they inherited from Mencius, who said that those who work with their brains should *govern* those who work with their hands. The principle was overturned by the Communist Revolution. Now they felt that the tradition should be restored. In terms of income, *nao ti dao gua,* that is, the "reversal to body over mind," was simply not right. *Nao ti dao gua* was on the lips of almost every intellectual I talked to, and it was a great source of alienation.

Nevertheless, unattached intellectuals believed they were still doing a very good job under the circumstances. Professor Fan, the chemist, whose department was at the cutting edge of electrochemistry, added, "intellectuals are reasonable *[tong qing da li]*. They treat their work very seriously even though they feel that they are short-changed *[sixiang bu pingheng]*" (Interview 1994:1.12.3).

Let us now look at housing conditions in more detail. According to our survey of 101 intellectuals, 16% did not have permanent housing, that is, they were living either in dorms or in other people's homes; 7% lived in one bedroom with their spouse and more than one child; and only 9% had a separate study of their own. Table 4.3 shows the living space per person.

If we assume that one room is about 10 square meters, which is already quite small, we see that well over 90% had less than one room of their own. It was not surprising then that when asked how they felt about their housing conditions, 44% of them said "very unsatisfactory" and "quite unsatisfactory" and 33% said just "average." Only 1% said "very satisfactory," and 23% said "fine."

Professor Wan of cytobiology lived in a small apartment with two bedrooms, one 9.8 square meters and the other 7.8 square meters. With him were his wife, daughter, and a grandchild. He had earlier lived in one of his brother's two rooms. When his brother returned from outside the city, Wan had to give up the room and get an apartment at the university. According to the planned economy, he, a full professor, should have been given a three-bedroom apartment. The university asked him to move into a two-bedroom apartment first and promised that he would be given a three-bedroom apartment later. But a month later, the university ruled that he would be given no more because the room he used to have at his brother's house was now considered part of his apartment,

Table 4.3 Living Space Per Person

Living Space in Square Meters	% of Intellectuals' Family Occupying the Space Per Person
4–5	17%
6–7	27%
8–9	24%
10–11	12%
12–15	2%
16–20	2%
No stable housing	16%
	100%

Source: The Research Group on Scientific and Technical Personnel. 1994. See Notes for Table 4.2.

even though it was no longer available to him and was in fact miles away. He commented that even if one took into consideration both homes, he was not getting the square footage he was entitled to. As a consequence, he worked only at his lab, bringing his own lunch, and went home only for dinner and to sleep. His apartment did not even have space for his Encyclopedia Britannica (Interview 1994:1.18).

Shen Yahong, a lecturer in Chinese, lived with his wife in a small one-room dorm, and there was only one bathroom, without a bath, on the entire floor. As a condition of her employment, his wife could not get housing from her workplace in her first four years (Interview with Shen Yahong 1994:1.32). Another newly hired lecturer was asked to share one room with a Ph.D. student (Interviews with Tian Zhaoyun and Jiang Zhexin 1994:1.56–7). The housing situation, obviously, was really tight.

What Perry Link discusses in his *Evening Chats in Beijing,* though uncomplimentary, applies to the living conditions of intellectuals in other cities as well:

> The kitchen is a dirty gas burner and sink, located in the public hallway of the dormitory-like building and shared with several other families. The communal toilets are down the corridor. The passageway also serves as everyone's pantry, laundry room, and storage space. It is cluttered to near-impassability with boxes, clotheslines, cooking equipment, bicycles, and other things. (1992:90)

It should be noted, though, that toward the end of the 1990s and into the beginning of 2000, various reforms have been discussed and some implemented in improving intellectuals' income and housing. For example, the dorm-like buildings have been gradually transformed into apartments, each with its own kitchen and bathroom facilities. In addition, both universities and industrial employers are gradually phasing out their responsibility for providing employee housing. In the past, housing was an expected part of the benefits for workers at a university or in a company. Now the authorities encourage people to buy their own homes, and the work unit will in some way subsidize the purchase (Li Tongxian 1999:29–30). Most importantly, at the end of 1999, the government decided to subsidize professors' yearly incomes at nine different levels, that is, 3,000; 5,000; 8,000; 12,000; 17,000; 23,000; 30,000; 40,000; and 50,000 yuan, respectively (*World Journal,* February 6, 2000). Considering that in the mid-1990s the majority of professors earned much less than 15,000 yuan a year, as our survey indicates, the new policy would mean an increase of at least 20% for most of them. For some of them, it would mean an increase of severalfold.

In fact, some surveys show that in 1999, professors in Beijing were already earning an average annual salary of 15,852 yuan, surpassing the average 13,500 yuan earned by city workers (see *Overseas Chinese Daily,* February 18, 2000; http://www.sina.com.cn November 24, 1999). Nationally, however, professors' salary levels were still below average. Most professors in developed areas, especially along the coast, might earn a yearly salary of over 10,000 yuan, but they earned less than 10,000 yuan in the heartland, and less than 8,000 yuan in the West (Ministry of Education 1999:20). Since the end of 1999, Qianghua and Beijing universities have been implementing the new subsidy policy, and other colleges and universities are following suit. The government is determined to increase professors' salaries to above the national average that will certainly help improve housing.[11]

On the other hand, these increases in salary and improvements in housing have been government initiatives, rather than the result of organized bargaining on the part of the professors. Furthermore, the improved income and housing carry a heavy penalty. Professors are losing their tenured status: they can be let go if the authorities deem that they are excessive. All of these changes raise an important question of professional autonomy, which we will discuss later in the chapter.

Funding for Research

The professors had another burden to carry in the 1990s: overall, it was difficult to get money to do research, whether social, scientific, or technological. Professor Xu was from the university's Department of Higher Education Administration. He described for us the funding situation in the mid-1990s. The central government funded just a hundred key labs in the entire country. Each received one million yuan a year (about $125,000). There was only one such key lab in the local university, the Research Lab of River Mouths and Sea Shores. The lab was also one of the five key national specialties in the university, the others being basic mathematics, statistics, basic theory of education, and the history of education (Interview with Xu Tianxiang 1994:1.15).

This meant that all the other research labs had to make do with even more limited funding from the state, or to find their own financial sources. The state did fund universities, but as Professor Fan, chemist and former provost of the university, commented with understatement, the state funding did not seem enough. For example, in the 1980s the state's contribution for research equipment for his institution was 1,800,000 yuan, but now it was only 1,200,000 yuan. At the same time, the university had expanded from 13 departments to 25 with 48 specialties. This money did not even seem to be enough for the maintenance of equipment, much less for new projects (Interview 1994:1.12).

How to support scientific research, then? Most researchers depended mainly on three sources of funding: the Chinese National Science Foundation (NSF), the city government, and industrial corporations. The NSF money was not only small in amount, 30,000 yuan (or $4,000 for three years per person at most) but it was administered by the Chinese Academy of Sciences (CAS). If an institution did not have a member of CAS on their side, it was very unlikely that its professors could win academy funding. The local university, for example, did not have one single member of CAS at the time of this research in 1994.

City money generally went to projects initiated by the city's own research institutes. The city did not want its money to flow into pockets other than its own attached institutes. That is, *fei shui bu liu wai ren tian,* or "we must see that our rich water does not flow into other people's fields." So the city Bureau of Environmental Protection, for example, would give the project to its own research institute, with the bureau head as the research director—a convenient source of research credentials for her promotion.

Where did that leave nongovernment researchers? When we asked a group of professors about their immediate concerns, a professor of environmental science complained that he could not find money for his projects, even though he was well qualified, having presided over a dozen projects and been further trained for two years in the West (Interview with Gui Yongji, Quan Ming, Xu Yaotong, Ye Jianong, and Zhong Wei 1994:1.26–30).

As for support from industrial corporations, the professor of environmental science commented that there were fewer projects available now from industrial sectors, that is, "horizontal projects," or city-level alliance with businesses. Corporations tended not to concern themselves with long-term goals of environmental protection. As a result, he and his colleagues had to take on engineering projects that were neither on the frontiers of scientific research nor even within their specialties. As Lecturer Bao of the Instrumental Analysis Lab commented, "horizontal projects" were chiefly for money and were not necessarily always to their liking (Interview 1994:1.19).

Since the chances of getting research money were so slim, most researchers did not have enough to support graduate students and therefore could not take on graduate teaching. Nor did they have enough even to travel to academic conferences. You could do nothing even if you had the most wonderful proposals; often you had to stop in the middle of a project for lack of money. Professor Wan of cytobiology, for example, used the China NSF money to start a project on cytosociology: the impact of noncardiac muscle cells on cardiac muscle cells. But he could not continue the project because he could not raise 50,000 yuan (about $6,000) to buy a certain piece of equipment (Interview with Wan Yaofa 1994:1.18).

Younger people have even more difficulty getting funded. Quan Ming recently received her Ph.D. in biology. She said that she applied to a foundation that funded young scholars, a foundation aptly named *Qi Ming Xing,* or "Venus, the morning star." Quan's project was considered so original and so important it won the recommendation of a member of CAS. But since she had graduated only three years before, and since there was no one on the committee from her university to speak on her behalf, the grant never materialized. She felt that she was wasting her life by doing nothing, or *langfei shengming, yi shi wu cheng* (Interviews with Gui Yongji, Quan Ming, Xu Yaotong, Ye Jianong, and Zhong Wei 1994:1.26–30; Interview with Quan Ming 1994:1.30).

Most worrisome, if full-time researchers could not generate funds for their projects, their positions would be eliminated and they would have to be transferred to teaching jobs or find employment elsewhere. As a lecturer in environmental sciences commented,

> In fact, each research position allocated to the department must make enough money to pay three thousand yuan a year to the school, quite an excessive burden. Otherwise, the position would be eliminated. When a research person is abroad, those who remain have to pay for the person's position as if he or she were here to make money for the department. [This may not be the case with other universities.] That's one of the reasons why researchers hold grudges against those who don't return. They have to think of their own survival all the time. (Interview with Gui Yongjie 1994:1.28)

Gui commented that she herself was in the worst position: if she did not get a research project soon, she would have to find something else to do.

What about funding in the humanities and social sciences? According to Professor Wu, there was even less money for these disciplines (Interview with Wu Dong 1994:1.13). To begin with, there were only a few foundations available, and they funded only about 20 percent of the applications. For lack of money, those who taught in colleges had a hard time going to conferences, buying books, and obtaining decent housing. Another sociologist commented, "I do have some funding, but since professional conferences charge a great deal of money, I dare not go. . . . The university says publicly that if you don't have funding, don't go to professional conferences. So the majority of professors don't go" (Interview with Cheng Guan 1994:1.36).

Professor Cheng noted another problem: "You might be able to get funding from corporations, but you will be constrained by what the companies want." And school authorities were not always supportive of researchers' efforts. He was invited to attend a conference in South Korea and applied for funding from the university. When he asked the university president, the president asked in return, "If I give you money, and then everybody else expects it too, where do I get it?" (Interview 1996:2.41).

Mathematicians were also constrained by the need for funds. "It is difficult to organize academic conferences, for people don't have the money to travel to them. The state used to give us some money in the 1980s, but very little now. It is not that the state does not have money; they just don't give us much. We don't need a lot of money, anyway" (Interview with Cao Yihua 1994:1.16.3).

The sociology institute of a provincial academy of social sciences did not even have a fax machine; researchers had to go elsewhere to send or receive faxes. The only way they could afford a fax machine, say, or an air conditioner, was to use the research money from a joint project with Israeli and Dutch sociologists that was supported by an Israel-Holland foundation (Interview with Qi Xi 1996:2.21). However, the lack of money for social sciences does not apply to pet projects of the Party and the government. "The Foundation of Marxist Academic Works has more money than applications" (Interview with Wu Dong 1994:1.13).

To sum up, in addition to income and housing problems, unattached intellectuals of the 1990s faced other serious problems. If the government

Figure 4.2 Why Don’t You Start Running? *(Zenmo bu kuai qipao?)*

Notes: The arrow points to “The New Long March,” and beneath the man’s shoes are written: living conditions, and working conditions.

Source: Ding Cong 1999 (Vol. 1), p. 56.

fails to increase its funding for research, intellectuals will be forced to rely on private funding. Either way, unattached professionals have no right of collective bargaining over their living and working conditions. In addition, if they pursue either source of funding, they are likely to become organic intellectuals unless they can transcend the roles they are expected to play, which is not easy. With limited funding possibilities and no bargaining power, not only the quality but the variety of their research will be even more strictly limited.[12]

There are more factors that illustrate the limitations of their work. See also figure 4.2.

Problems with Research Equipment

For unattached technical intellectuals in the 1990s, the problems did not stop with income, housing, or funding for research. They also faced constant problems with equipment. It was either defective, took endless complex procedures to obtain, or was simply unavailable. When we asked our respondents about their experience with their research equipment, 21 percent said that the equipment did not meet their needs, and 45 percent said it met their needs only partially. Only 1 percent said it did meet their needs, 28 percent said fine, and 5 percent were "don't knows."

As Professor Gui commented,

> It is difficult to get institutional support. You have to do everything yourself, running from the equipment department to the finance (business) department. The department office secretary does not even want to take care of the faxes that come in and go out. I sometimes have to use services elsewhere in the city. (Interview 1994:1.31)

At one of the universities we researched, a serious concern for scientists was the lack of logistic support from the university's equipment department. As a researcher, if you needed, say, a steel cylinder, or a certain liquid, you had to apply first to your own department. If it did not have what you wanted, you had to get permission to go to the equipment department. You could not apply efficiently by phone because there were forms to be filled out and they had to meet you in person. The equipment people would then see whether they had it in stock. If not, they would buy it—but later, of course, at their own convenience. So you could wait ten to twenty days for something you needed immediately.

What was worse was that they might not even buy what you needed. So you would have waited in vain. Or they bought more than you ever asked for. Dr. Quan said that once she wanted one type of liquid and they bought her another kind (Interview 1994:1.30). And they would not change it for her. Another time, Lecturer Gui wanted six tube stands, but they bought her sixty (Interview 1994:1.27). Furthermore, they always paid more for less quality. One of the reasons why the equipment department insisted on doing everything themselves was that it allowed them to negotiate kickbacks, a form of bonus that increased their monthly income.

Sometimes you might be made to wait for some time, and then they suddenly asked you to go out yourself and buy what you needed. When you came back, you had to go through your own department, through the equipment department, and through the finance department to be reimbursed. If the person in charge was not there, you simply had to come back later. Some interviewees commented that it would take you a month to do in China what you could accomplish in a week in an American or Japanese research institution.

Professor Ye of chemistry compared what happened here and his own experience in the United States. He said that in the United States, if you needed a steel cylinder, you made a telephone call and by the second day it was at your front door. Here you would call the equipment department and they would say, "We have several but we don't know which are full and which are empty. You'll have to take your own measuring instrument and come and look for it" (Interviews with Gui Yongji, Quan Ming, Xu Yaotong, Ye Jianong, and Zhong Wei 1994:1.26–30).

Lecturer Bao said that in the Japanese lab he had worked in, they would not only bring you the steel cylinder the second day but would hook it up for you and at the same time say, "Sorry we delayed your work." Such consideration was unthinkable here (Interview 1994: 1.19.9).

A graduate student in the instrumental analysis lab commented that their research was world-class but their made-in-China instruments were far from that. All ten of the machines they had bought not long ago, which had cost them 5,000 to 6,000 yuan each, had broken down almost immediately. He recently returned eight of them to the manufacturer in northern Jiangsu province, but when he brought them back after repair, he found that three had been further damaged on the bus ride home and two went down after he plugged them in. Because of the enormity of the problem, they had to spend unusual lengths of time getting tests done (Interview with Jiang Han 1994:1.67).

Poor equipment support and inadequate funding affected not only their research but their teaching ability as well. Lecturer Zhang Wen of computer science told us that he taught a course in computer networks, but the students could only imagine how they worked because there was no computer for them to work on. Professor Cai of physics said that in their physics lab, only the teachers handled the instruments. Students could not touch but only watch. You could not afford to let students touch them because once they were broken, you either had to repair them yourself or find the money to do it. Professor Wu of biology said that many experiments had been canceled because they could not afford to buy the liquids they needed (Interviews with Cai Beibei, Ding Lingen, He Pinggan, Wu Xianrong, Zhang Hefeng, Zhang Wen, 1994: 1.20–5).

As Professor Fan commented,

> Our research facilities cannot compare with those of the West. You have to cut a lot of red tape to buy instruments. And you may not even be able to find them in this country. Even if you can, they may not meet your quality expectations. And it takes eight months to a year to buy a piece of equipment. When instruments break down, it takes several days to get anyone here to fix them, whereas in the West, you can have it done in a day. (Interview 1994:1.12)

Professor Xu, who was also an administrator, believed that it was a matter of money. "Our equipment cannot be renewed because of the lack of money, especially computers. Key labs are doing fine, but most disciplines are having a hard time" (Interview 1994:1.15).

If the equipment issue so seriously impairs the ability to do high-quality research and teaching, and thus threatens their survival, as Yu Liqun (Interview 1994:1.17.4) put it, what recourse do they have? Prof. Wan Yaofa (Interview 1994:1.18) suggested that they needed to set up alliances with various social organizations, including government agencies, hospitals, research institutes, and businesses. As an example, he said that at one time he himself was able to raise funds from a combination of the State Education Commission (50,000 yuan), the Chinese Academy of Sciences (20,000 yuan), the State Commission on Family Planning (20,000 yuan), and several industrial corporations (40,000 yuan). The effort allowed him not only to continue certain projects but to renovate his labs. He was also able to gather further resources for his projects by cooperating with other research institutes.

In other words, unless you become "organic intellectuals" and do projects that meet the needs of state and business, you will not have enough money for your research. That, as we have seen, seems to be the only way out for unattached intellectuals. The problem, however, is that there are not enough jobs for all unattached intellectuals to become organic.

Currently, colleges and universities are trying to privatize or reorganize their service departments, including faculty and student housing, equipment, and food, or what they call *gaoxiao houqin shehui hua,* that is, "let various social venues take on these tasks." In Shanghai, for example, under the direction of the city government, two companies have been set up to function as a private corporation in providing these services (Zhang Ying 1999). Colleges and universities would contract these services to them. These companies would also compete with companies outside institutions of higher education. All of these changes would be completed in all of Shanghai's colleges and universities by 2000, according to the city government's directions (p. 13). With the development of competition mechanisms, one can expect some improvement. However, there is still a possibility that these companies will become monopolies. Barring professionalization—organized efforts by intellectuals to negotiate with the powers that be—it is not clear whether the problems we have discussed can be effectively resolved.

Promotion

In addition to income, housing, research, and equipment problems, another issue that bothered unattached professional intellectuals in the 1990s was promotion. Under the planned economy, there had always been a connection between one's titles, income, and housing. A senior professor, for example, could have a monthly income of over 1,000 yuan and a three-bedroom apartment. An assistant/associate professor had an income of 600 yuan and a two-bedroom apartment. A lecturer, with an income of 400 yuan, had one bedroom in a dorm building with no private bathroom or kitchen. Incomes varied from person to person, from department to department, and from university to university, but our figures were accurate in general at least to the mid-1990s. (They do not, however, include the miscellaneous incomes people earn in ways other than teaching and research.)

Thus, promotion was required for both income and housing opportunities. According to Professor Fan, however, there were many problems in the promotion system. For example, once promoted, professors had to be given the right kind of housing and salary, which the state or the university did not always have. A parallel problem was that since the state did not emphasize the importance of education, it did not invest enough money in it. According to Prof. Fan, "If anyone should get rich first, it should be the intellectual. If the Japanese can begin revitalizing their country by revitalizing education, why cannot we?" he asked (Interview 1994:1.12).

Because of the relatively low investment in education, the number of professorships allocated to the departments limited the number of people who could be moved up. This meant that qualified people—usually younger people—were less likely to be promoted and thus were locked into lower incomes and poorer housing. For example, Mr. Bao of instrumental chemistry pointed out that he would probably not become Professor Bao very soon because his department had four or five senior lecturers of no less ability waiting for advancement (Interview 1994:1.19). Even if he understood the reason, and knew it was not his fault, he nonetheless continued to feel that he was lagging behind his peers. The lab authorities might consider advancing him sooner as a special case, but he felt that his chances of that were slim.

Because of the limited number of available professorships, authorities as well as faculty members suffered when the time came for evaluation. Lecturer Gui's personal story is illuminating. A former worker-peasant-soldier, she graduated college in 1977. In the year after graduation, she taught one semester and did research in the other. She had published four articles and developed a textbook. She had participated in a number of research projects including the study of water plants in Dianshan Lake, water pollution in the upper reaches of Huangpu River, and air pollution in the city. And the department had always assigned her a full teaching load. She applied for promotion but was rejected. She believed that her chances were hindered first by her worker-peasant-soldier background, and second, because she did not have an M.A. degree. She requested opportunities for retraining or studying for an M.A., but she never got further than a few graduate courses at the university. At one point, there was an opportunity for her to pursue an M.A., but her child was too young for her to leave. She never got another chance. On the other hand, when the cadres wanted similar opportunities to study for promotion, the authorities would create training sessions for them (Interview 1994:1.27).

Others listening to Gui agreed that it was just because there were too many qualified people and too few professorships assigned to the department. There were quotas; in addition, those who had worked in the department longest had to be considered first. She felt that she could not bear it anymore and she could not hold back her tears at the group interview (Interviews with Gui Yongjie, Quan Ming, Xu Yaotong, Ye Jianong, and Zhong Wei 1994:1.26–30).

Indeed, the process of promotion was far from fair. As Bao pointed out, it depended a lot on what your superiors thought of you, and in fact, being promoted did not necessarily mean that you were better (Interview 1994 1.19). However, as Gui commented, "I know that promotion does not necessarily indicate one's level of achievement. But when you see those who are not as good promoted while you are not, you feel a psychological imbalance *[xinli bu pingheng]*" (Interview 1994:1.27).

Promotion depended on many things: quotas, political balance, academics, interpersonal relationships, and especially one's relationship with the committee members (Interview with Shan Junyi 1994:1.34). One eye doctor complained that even if she met the requirements, she would not be promoted because she did not want to bribe the authorities (Interview with Luo Xiuming and Hao Linan 1996:2.30). You had to befriend the committee members and give them gifts. Otherwise, you had little hope.

But let us say you are promoted. Your problems with housing may well be insurmountable. We have already given the example of Professor Wan. The woes of another professor are equally illuminating. Professor Gui, an internationally known computer scientist in multimedia technology, ran into trouble with the housing bureaucracy at his university (Interview 1994:1.31). In 1993, he was winding up his third trip abroad. Just before he returned from Germany, where he had been teaching and doing research for two years, his department promised him a professor's housing and his wife a job at the university. A year had passed and he still was crowded in a one-room apartment with his wife, son, and mother. He still did not have telephones either in his room or in his lab. He had applied for one a year before, but somehow he still had not received it. At the time of the interview, he was in the process of negotiation with the state Ministry of Weaponry over a multimillion yuan project. Yet he could not afford a beeper for a thousand yuan, and was wearing a borrowed one.

Lecturer Li of literary criticism believed that the system of promotion was the central problem (Interview 1994:1.5). He felt it was the teacher's right to be promoted when he or she reached the level required; that promotion should not be given as a favor, as was very often the case. Promotion should be based on one's ability and achievement, not on one's seniority. As a group of engineers commented, "When a capable junior person is promoted, the authorities justify it by saying that they are trying to 'break the rule (of seniority.)' The rule should not be there in the first place" (Interviews with Gu Jin, Lu Zhesong, Wang Juhai, Wu Jiaping, and Zhang Chaoling 1994:1.44–8).

But in Li's case, the situation was more complicated. Despite his fine teaching, his research record, and his seniority, he was refused promotion; almost certainly this was because he had been involved in the June 4 movement and had been imprisoned for nine months thereafter. That he had regained his teaching position was a miracle. Anyone else might have chosen from then on to play it safe. But Li broke into, yes, literally broke into, a dorm room and occupied it until the time of our interview just so that he could have a place of his own to live in. He was not seriously challenged for his "audacity," but it was clear that being critical of the authorities made life for him even more difficult than it was for others. Li's example reflects the working and living conditions of critical intellectuals as well, although few would have his will to tough it out.

In sum, since promotion clearly determines income, housing, and other opportunities, it has become one of the most contentious issues for intellectuals. As some of our interviewees pointed out, the government's inadequate investment in education is one of the key problems, as is the university's favoritism and mismanagement. Quite obviously, the system in general needs to be reformed. That brings us to our next discussion in the final three sections: professionalization, professional roles, and the politics of unattached intellectuals as our conclusion.

The Possibilities of Further Professionalization

We have seen, first, that these unattached professionals, and for that matter, critical intellectuals as well, have faced serious problems in their working conditions. Second, they also face a long struggle before they can achieve professional autonomy, the right to determine their own economic conditions. The 1990s saw the first consciousness in that direction; a degree of professionalism has already been developed. Let us first examine some further models of professionalization, especially those concerning the relationship between the state and the professions. We will see more clearly where these unattached professionals might be going.

First of all, let us examine the current Chinese model. How do Chinese professionals go about seeking both professional working conditions and economic security? As we have observed, formal independent professional associations are out of the question. Every professional association is controlled by the Party in one way or another. Our interviews show that the only real way to address their professional concerns is through individual effort. They have only one recourse: to talk with their work unit authorities about their own income, their own housing, and their own promotion and research problems. What is even worse, they can only protest to their immediate bosses, and so, as in the former Soviet Union, "[t]heir professional interests are reduced to labor matters, or are coterminous with the orientation of the bureaucratic unit" (Cleaves 1989:62). Another example: the Party secretary of the research institute we visited would go to the factory meeting of representatives to ask for higher pay for his engineers. But everyone was aware that there was little chance he would get it.

Of course, there is always a last alternative: to wait for the authorities to come up with reform measures such as the Shanghai model of "privatization."

How much professional autonomy *do* intellectuals have? To be sure, they have some control over the content of their research, or at least the techniques they use. But they have no control over supportive services such as the equipment department, which they depend on for their research. They may have a great deal of control over how they are going to conduct a class on national politics, but they have little control over what they can say about the Chinese political system. The decisions on all of these issues—income and housing, conditions of work, promotion, and policy issues in their work—are based, not on the professional's authority or recognized expertise, but on the authority of the administrative office. The same applies to journalism. Yet true professionalization requires a certain amount of autonomy in decisions like these (Freidson 1973:25–6). In the Chinese model, to sum up, intellectuals are still constrained by a strong state despite the fragmentation of the propaganda system of control of thought work as discussed in Lynch (1999). Professionals continue to fight for more autonomy but they constantly meet with resistance from a state that still feels uncomfortable loosening its grip on professional and intellectual issues.

Even if they were legal, would formal professional associations work? Not according to the Mexican model. Those associations, Cleaves (1989:59) says, "are not appropriate social organizations to protect the interests of the profession as a whole, and rarely have a direct effect on advancing individual careers." Lindau (1998) also observes that independent groups and movements in Mexico actually have less influence than are commonly supposed. Rather, the Mexican professionals resort to groups linked to political parties, networks of individuals, university alumni associations, labor unions, and interest groups within state agencies (Cleaves 1989:62). True, the Chinese professionals also rely on their networks to protect their professional interests, but again these involve mainly labor matters. Besides, China has no independent organizations or parties. The Mexican professionals seem to have more avenues for protest than do their counterparts in China.

Finally, let us examine the Western model. The ideal professional associations in Britain and the United States, says Cleaves (1989:61), limit their lobbying efforts to matters directly concerning their professions, such as certification, support for graduate education, income, and professional autonomy. We have already noted that Western groups do a fair job in promoting professionalism and professional autonomy, thus protecting their monopoly in the field in terms of regulating the marketplace, defining the boundaries of knowledge in the field, and broadening employment opportunities. It is not clear whether and when Chinese professionals will follow this route.

The Roles of the Unattached Professionals

Development in the economy often means a shift of emphasis from the primary sector to the secondary and tertiary sectors. The primary sector refers to the exploitation of unprocessed resources, such as agriculture, fishing, mining, and oil extraction. The primary sector engages 60%-80% of the population in the Third World, as compared with 3% in the United States (Lewellen 1995:88). The secondary sector, or manufacturing, requires money, a market, and more techniques and competent management. The tertiary sector, or the service industry, refers to clerical work, retailing (commerce), health care, law, restaurant work, finance (banking), security, data processing, information, journalism, education, research and science, the military, government jobs, and nonprofit jobs (Bell 1980:151–3; Lewellen 1995:93; McMichael 1996:184).

As one can see, as society moves from primary to secondary to tertiary sectors, it needs more and more professionals. This applies in all spheres, private, public, and nonprofit. These experts, usually independent, may have their own professional practices, working on a fee-for-service basis, or they may work for private employers, or for national or multinational corporations. Public employers, such as institutions of education, medicine, and law, employ a large chunk of professionals (see also Burrage, Jarausch, and Siegrist 1990).

Obviously, as the market economy develops, more professionals will go into private practice. But a substantial number will remain in the public sector. The state will need more professionals in social welfare. It will need more professionals to regulate the professions and to deal with the crises, especially those involving environmental protection and economic restructuring. It will need to consult with the professionals in these fields, since only they know, or are supposed to know how the various environmental and economic systems work.[13]

Wherever they are, the more freedom to practice and the more autonomy professionals have, the more likely it is that they will organize to protect their own interests. This professionalization process will lead to conflict between the professions and their clients, or users, which will force professionals to politicize themselves. They will have to negotiate with other social players, with the state, with private employers, and with individual clients or their organizations, for the conditions of their existence. The failures and successes of journalists, as we discussed in chapter 3, for example, is a result of the reporters' interaction with the Party, the businesses, and the readers and audiences. This can also be seen in Yuezhi Zhao's (1998) detailed account of media, market, and democracy in China. The amount of their autonomy depends on that interaction. As we pointed out earlier, that is mainly where their politics will be, a politics of professionalization, of self-preservation.

Given the history of professional association or party-building among intellectuals,[14] it is not unthinkable that there will one day be professional organizations or even political parties representing professionals in China. In fact, it is reported that with the permission of the central government, physicians are in the process of organizing their own professional association, which will "function as the bridge between the government and the two million practitioners," according to the head of the Ministry of Health. It will be an organization that will regulate the trade and protect the interests of its members, the report says (*Zhongguo Daily News,* July 29, 1999).

If China follows the pattern we have described, as it shifts from the primary to the secondary and tertiary sectors, more and more professionals will be needed in both the private and public sectors. That is where their professional roles will be. But their professionalization will lead them to organize for their own interests, which will then lead to their involvement in the country's developmental issues. At that point they will be playing political roles. For example, they will be asked what they think as professional groups about environmental issues, or about education, or about social inequality. They will no longer play merely professional roles. They may very well become policy *makers* rather than just policy takers.

We live in a time dominated by expert systems of "technical accomplishment or professional expertise that organize large areas of the material and social environments. . . ." (Giddens 1990:27). In this environment professionals do have a great deal of potential power. The problem is, "the power of the technical intelligentsia depends on its *awareness* of the power realities of the political system and on its *consciousness* of its own potential power" (Cleaves 1989:89). Nor will that power come to them automatically.

Conclusions: The Politics of the Professional and Bourgeoisified Intellectuals

We have described the unattached professional intellectuals' work, reported their lack of concern for politics, and looked into their working and living conditions. We know what professionalization can achieve and what roles professionals may play. Although, as Israel (1986:xv) comments, "most intellectuals are, presumably, content to confine themselves to their areas of expertise and to leave politics to politicians," they may not be able to escape politics. And for many in the social sciences, humanities, and arts, Israel points out, it is not always easy to draw the line between the professional and the political.[15] Now, how can we summarize the politics of the professionals and the bourgeoisified intellectuals? If they do have a political outlook, what kind is it? In what way is it different from that of the critical intellectuals?

First, unattached professionals do have political views. Listen to the conclusions some of them drew from our discussions, and we will have a clear idea of their politics. A group of researchers and lecturers were articulate about what colleges should do, and what policies they endorsed. One of them summed it up well:

> The colleges should clarify what they are doing. They should focus on teaching, creating and applying knowledge. Since the government does not give us enough money, we have to learn to make our own. We have to learn to turn our knowledge into money. It is like a poor meal: we are only half full with what we are fed by the authorities. They need to adopt a policy that lets us provide for ourselves. There have to be ways for us to do our jobs—to educate and train people—and also to provide

> for ourselves. (Interviews with Gui Yongji, Quan Ming, Xu Yaotong, Ye Jianong, and Zhong Wei 1994:1.26–30)

Professor Fan Yuzhi, the scientist and chemistry professor, observed on law-building, "We have lagged too far behind in our building of laws. For example, we have laws on teachers, but not on education. We will have to pay dearly for our lack of effort in our system reform" (Interview 1994:1.12).

One professor from a group of professors, lecturers, and engineers in the natural sciences departments also commented on system reform:

> Much reform is needed in our systems. We need to change our ways of thinking. How is it that we don't have a single Nobel prize winner in a country of more than a billion people? Equipment is one problem, but the way of thinking is another. How come the Chinese don't seem to show as much ability *[benshi]* when they live in China as they do when they are abroad? It is our ways of thinking. (Interviews with Cai Beibei, Ding Lingen, He Pinggan, Wu Xianrong, Zhang Hefeng, and Zhang Wen, 1994:1.20–5)

The professor believed that the system was too rigid. For example, you could not change your field of study once you entered the university. In fact, people have debated for years whether the development of a student's individuality should be included as part of the curriculum.

Concerning their work, one professor commented,

> The university should allow departments to determine the lab teachers' workload. If the lab class is not counted towards their workload, there will be no incentive for them to put effort into it. Those who *do* take the labs seriously are only following their conscience *[ping liangxin zuo zhi],* which is not incentive enough. (Interviews with Cai Beibei, Ding Lingen, He Pinggan, Wu Xianrong, Zhang Hefeng, and Zhang Wen, 1994:1.20–5)

It is apparent that when unattached intellectuals discuss income at work and housing at home, they are not just concerned about themselves. They also believe that these are issues about the *system.* To many of them, it is the system that needs to be changed (Interviews with Gu Jin, Lu Zhesong, Wang Juhai, Wu Jiaping, and Zhang Chaoling 1994: 1.44–8). This criticism reflects intellectuals' alienative disposition and culture of critical discourse. This aspect of the unattached intellectuals' politics also applies to bourgeoisified intellectuals (see Pearson 1997 and chapter 5 in this volume).

Second, when the unattached intellectuals ponder the system, they are dealing with the politics of professionalization and thus democracy. If the professionals want to achieve autonomy, professional organizations are needed, professionalism has to be promoted, and professions have to negotiate with other political forces. Professions, in fact, need to become interest groups, lobbying to advance their aims and to protect their interests when policy is being made. In other words, rather than waiting to *be given policy,* they need to be able to *make policy*. First and foremost, they need to work with the state, because they need the state. As Freidson (1973:29) points out, it is the power of government that grants the profession the exclusive right to use or evaluate a certain body of knowledge and skill. Once granted the exclusive right to use knowledge, the profession gains power.

Thus, it is necessary for professions to be intimately connected with the formal political process in the course of professionalization, whether it involves establishing professional associations, setting up professional registration or licensing, or maintaining and improving the profession's position in the marketplace. For all this they have to work with the government.

On the other hand, the state needs the professions. The two are dependent on one another (Johnson 1982).[16] As Halliday and Curruthers point out,

> Professions are integral to state power and operations. The modern state depends on a certain concept of citizenship, on the satisfactory solution of economic and political problems, and professions are integral elements of such statehood, whether they are formally lodged inside the state or outside it. Professions identify social problems which become objects of state action and they frequently provide the technical apparatus to implement policy responses. (1991:3)

Indeed, we already know that Chinese economists are playing a crucial role in China's economic reform (see Fewsmith 1994:137 and chapter 5 in this volume). The projects our interviewees were involved in, such as development of new products or research on environmental issues, and above all teaching future professionals to deal with economic and social issues, are certainly an integral part of the state's goal of economic and social development. The professionals' technical advice is often useful in helping a country define its projects, plans, and approaches to its national development (Cleaves 1989). The government does appoint professionals to public sector posts. That is the power of "science" (Aronowitz 1988) and intellectuals have scientism as one of their most important dispositions. That is power for the professional, at least potential power. The bourgeoisified intellectuals have power parallel to that of professionals, if not more.

Out of this interdependence between professionals and the state comes the interplay leading to a dynamic relationship between intellectuals and the state. Indeed, the Chinese intellectuals' emphasis on scientism in the 1980s was an effort to define more sharply their relationship with the state. In the process, they have contributed to democratization. A sociology of science recognizes that "[S]cience is a language of power, and those who bear its legitimate claims, i.e., those who are involved in the ownership and control of its processes and results, have become a distinctive social category equipped with a distinctive ideology and political program in the post-war world" (Aronowitz 1988: 351). In China particularly, that political program has included and will still have to include democracy. Mr. Science and Mr. Democracy have not really been separated since the May 4 period, at least not in the minds of many an intellectual (see Miller 1996). In their effort to carve out their own identities and shape their relationship with the state, professionals as a group have become powerful players.

The problem is, professionals, or unattached intellectuals, may not realize that they have a lot of power or influence. Once more of them gain an awareness of such professional power, it may become possible for them to assert their interests, and to demand that professional associations protect their interests, and increase their autonomy. In so doing, they are also advancing democracy. That is the "professional" view of politics.

Third, generally speaking, most unattached intellectuals' concern about politics probably stops right there, indicating a "professional model" that is new to the intellectual tradition. Professionals, or unattached intellectuals, may want the Party to lift its heavy hand on intellectuals. They may want it to pull its Party chiefs from institutions of education, law, health, journalism, and so forth.[17] They may want the right to freely organize into unofficial groups. They may welcome a multiparty system. Indeed, some may even want to establish an opposition party. But those who do will become revolutionary or otherwise critical intellectuals, or organic intellectuals to their own class, such as Yu Guanyuan, Qian Xuesen, Xu Liangying, Wang Ganchang, and Fang Lizhi (see Miller 1996). Most, however, will not be active in advocating political or even educational reform. Their involvement in politics is limited to the protection of their personal professional interests. It is in this sense that they differ from organic and critical intellectuals.

But that may be what unattached intellectuals, or professionals, are all about. Alvin Gouldner (1979:48) distinguishes between intelligentsia, whose "interests are fundamentally 'technical,'" and intellectuals, "whose interests are primarily critical, emancipatory, hermeneutic and hence often political." (See also the appendix on defining intellectuals.) We argue that the development of Chinese intelligentsia, or technical intellectuals, began with the Self-Strengthening movement, when a new group of intellectuals emerged, who emphasized the use of modern professional knowledge rather than traditional Confucian teaching.

That is the trend ruling Chinese professionalism and it is probably going to gather strength. In the United States, as Brint (1994:37) points out, with the development of capitalism, especially after the 1960s, *expert professionalism* began to dominate the scene, a professionalism that emphasizes "instrumental effectiveness of specialized, theoretically grounded knowledge" and "comparatively little concern with collegial organization, ethical standards, or service in the public interest." Increasingly, applied science occupations, such as engineering, have become subordinated to entrepreneurial and large-scale businesses, and social science occupations have separated themselves from reform-oriented services in the name of "scientific" objectivity. *Social trustee professionalism,* which demonstrated "a commitment to the public welfare and high ethical standards combined with a claim to specialized authority over a limited sphere of formal knowledge" (p. 36) is under attack, and authority (in specialized fields), autonomy (freedom from political influence), self-interest, and self-serving have become the chief characteristics of the professions.

In China and in the United States professionalism is moving on parallel tracks. As we have demonstrated, the commercialization of society in China has brought greater freedom from political influence in scientific and technological work. In spite of this new freedom, many intellectuals seem to be more interested in the mundane making of money than in living up to democratic ideals.[18] This is in fact a continuation of the professionalization of intellectuals that began with the Self-Strengthening movement. (This again applies to the bourgeoisified intellectuals as well.)

However, it is only since the development of the market economy that a professional model of intellectual development has gathered strength. This professionalization further weakens the tradition that made the intellectual the conscience of Chinese society, concerned with the social welfare of the masses. Again, this parallels the way in which expert professionalism has weakened social trustee professionalism in the United States. The current Chinese educational system, still largely based on the Soviet model, has already had disastrous results. First, China has one of the lowest rates of students in the humanities and social sciences in the world (about 10 percent). Second, the scope of students' knowledge is woefully narrow, seriously impairing their chance of well-rounded intellectual development (Yang Dongping 1994a). That is the downside of the professionalization of intellectuals in China.

China's brand of conflict between social trustee professionalism and expert professionalism, or between a traditional model and a professional as well as a bourgeois one, is evidence of the conflict between morality and power, *Dao* and *shi,* vocation and profession, and the ethic of ultimate ends and the ethic of responsibility. The former would likely require that the intellectual be concerned about social welfare, and the latter would emphasize instrumental effectiveness. The conflict continues in the twenty-first century.

Fourth, even were there no professionalization movement, there are intellectuals who have been and always will be interested only in their own professional development, stubbornly avoiding political involvement. For example, technical intellectuals "often wish nothing more than to be allowed to enjoy their opiate obsessions with technical puzzles," convinced their "social mission [is] to revolutionize technology continually" (Gouldner 1978:48). As we have shown, their only "politics" is to resist obstacles that hinder them from advancing technology. In fact, this is true not only of technical intellectuals, such as the engineers we interviewed, but of certain humanistic intellectuals as well. Qian Zhongshu,[19] a literary critic and writer, and Chen Yinke, an historian, are good examples. Hu Houxuan is another, whose interest in revealing the secrets of the "ancient scriptures," *jia gu wen,* is his main obsession. These intellectuals are following the ideological tradition of autonomy and self-groundedness and are relishing in their freedom to connect with the world in their own ways. There is no denying that the chief interest of these intellectuals is *not* political action involving the social welfare of society in general. That is why we term them unattached intellectuals.[20]

To sum up, the unattached intellectuals, bourgeois or professional, do have a political outlook, albeit a different one from that of the critical or of the organic intellectuals. While the bourgeoisified intellectuals' politics is oriented toward moneymaking and can go counter to the dominant intellectual tradition, the professional intellectuals' politics is mainly oriented toward professionalization, and generally stops there. In both groups, politics represents a break, to some extent, from the mainstream traditional model of intellectuals, who are supposed to *xiu qi zhi ping,* that is, to "perfect oneself and serve the country." It represents an intellectual politics nonetheless, an expansion of the bourgeois and professional models of Chinese intellectuals themselves.

But they also share many of the intellectual traditions with other groups and they cannot escape the various ethical conflicts other intellectuals face. These shared traditions and their tough resistance to obstacles in the path of bourgeois and professional development can make these people a vital social force that other intellectual groups can tap into. Indeed, even though most may remain unattached, some bourgeoisified and professionalized intellectuals may become so actively engaged in politics that they become critical intellectuals, or organic intellectuals to other classes or to the professional stratum of the intellectual class, as we will discuss in chapter 5.

Chapter Five

Social Class and Organic Intellectuals

Okay. I am going to work in the government.
(Nuo. Wu jiang shi yi.)
—Confucius, *Analects* 17:1

Reply to Yang Huo when he asked whether it is benevolent for someone not to use his talents when the country needs them, and whether it is wise to miss opportunities to create meritorious services.

Typically, bourgeoisified and professionalized intellectuals keep their distance from officialdom, and are less likely to view themselves as the conscience of society. Critical and organic intellectuals, however, generally follow the ancient tradition of *xiu qi zhi ping,* consciously or subconsciously, and in some very different contexts from the traditional. They see themselves as socially responsible, closely concerned with worldly affairs. In chapter 3, we discussed one of the two groups, the critical intellectuals. This chapter focuses on organic intellectuals, who are politically engaged but in a different way. They function as *advocates* of a certain class rather than as its *critics,* whether it be Party and government or some other class. In fact, Confucius might well be saying, "I'll work for the peasants."

Class and the Class Structure in Formation

Before we discuss organic intellectuals, and so that we will know who they are organic to, we need to explain what we mean by class. We also need to describe the class structure of China as it has been forming at the turn of the twenty-first century. This structure features the *cadre class* of the Party and state, *private entrepreneurs,* the *middle class,* the *working class,* and the *peasants.* While the cadre class of the Party and state is well developed, other classes are still in the process of defining themselves. Organic intellectuals are instrumental in the formation of all of these. (I would like to emphasize that mine is not a full-fledged analysis of class transformation in China in the 1990s, although much space in this chapter is devoted to it and some class literature is used to couch our discussion in the larger—capitalist and/or statist—social context. A full-fledged analysis deserves another book. Rather, I am describing the main social groups and their relationships with intellectuals.)

Class and Class in Formation

Somehow, Karl Marx was not able to give us a formal definition of *class,* although he was the most enthusiastic advocate of the term. As Engels tells us, "the manuscript [suddenly] breaks off," two short paragraphs after Marx, in the last chapter of the last volume of *Capital* (Marx [1892] 1981:1026), declares that he is going to define class. Nevertheless, Marx and Engels do go on with their analysis. They generally view "class" from the economic standpoint, as the bourgeoisie's control over the means of production and exploitation of the working class. In their famous declaration in the *Communist Manifesto,* they say, "Society as a whole is more and more splitting up into two great hostile camps, into two great classes directly facing each other: Bourgeoisie and Proletariat" (Marx and Engels [1888] 1978:474).

Marx and Engels, of course, were not able to foresee what class structure would be like in a Soviet-type society. Here we may profit from Eric Olin Wright's (1985) Marxian analysis of the class structure in three systems. Wright compares the class situation in the capitalist system, the statist system (Soviet-type societies like China before the communist reform), and the socialist system as he defines socialism. Part of his table on class relations is reproduced here in table 5.1. We will discuss statist and capitalist relations.

Based on Wright's model of class structure, there are at least two classes in statism. On the one hand, there are the managers and bureaucrats who use their organizational powers to appropriate surplus value created by the working class. On the other hand, there is the nonmanagement working class whose surplus labor is appropriated. Wright is, in effect, drawing a picture of the Mao era. In capitalism, there are two classes, capitalist and worker, the same division Marx and Engels accept in the *Communist Manifesto*. Because of the mixed economy (both socialism and capitalism) in the Deng era, there has emerged a complex class structure, which we discuss in the next section. Wright's class based on the kinds of assets owned and the means of exploitation is useful for our analysis of China's class structure.

It takes more, however, to make a class than assets and the relations of production. Effective organization of the class itself is even more important. For example, in *The 18th Brumaire of Luise Bonaparte,* Marx does not seem to consider exploitation the sole criterion of class. Here is Marx:

> In so far as millions of families live under economic conditions of existence that separate their mode of life, their interests and their culture from those of other classes and put them in hostile opposition to the latter, they form a class. In so far as there is merely a local interconnection among these small-holding peasants, and the identity of their interests begets no community, no national bond and no political organization among them, they do not form a class. (Marx [1852] 1978:608)

In defining a class, Marx moves beyond exploitation to include economic conditions, mode of life, interests, culture, community, and organization. Peasants, for example, can be a class if there is sufficient common interest, consciousness of the possibility of change, and organization toward that change.

Weber's definition does not seem dissimilar to that of Marx. For Weber (1946:181), class refers to any group of people who share "a specific causal component of their life chances . . . [which is] represented

Table 5.1 Assets, Exploitation, and Classes

Type of class structure	Principal asset unequally distributed	Mechanism of exploitation	Classes
Statism	Organization	Planned appropriation and distribution of surplus based on hierarchy	Managers/bureaucrats and non-management
Capitalism	Means of production	Market exchanges of labor power and commodities	Capitalists and workers

Source: Eric Olin Wright, *Classes,* 1985, p. 83.

exclusively by economic interests in the possession of goods and opportunities for income . . . under the conditions of the commodity or labor markets." Indeed, the unequal access, not only to goods, but to economic opportunities such as property and education, is what grants people in the market different life chances. Thus, we see the relationship between economics and culture.

However, existence in one community, or in the same class situation, does not automatically create a class. Communities merely form a base for communal action. As Weber points out, class is born only when there is "communal" or "societal action" organized through "rational association," not just "acts of intermittent and irrational protest" (Weber 1946:184). Marx seems to agree with Weber. Commenting on the French nation in the mid-1800s, Marx says that the masses in a community are simply a sum of "homologous magnitudes, much as potatoes in a sack form a sackful of potatoes" (Marx [1852] 1978:608). That is why he emphasizes organization as well. Weber and Marx see eye to eye on this one. Following Marx's and Weber's arguments, for a class to exist, it must be organized and taking communal action; otherwise, it merely forms a community.

But when does a class become a class? Is there a process of class formation? And how can we recognize it? Here the British sociologist Anthony Giddens's model of two societies may help. According to Giddens (1981:105–8), there are two kinds of societies, "class societies" and "class-divided societies" (see also Webster 1990:135). In the former, represented by advanced capitalist societies, class relations are expressed through the political framework of the state. In other words, the state becomes a vehicle through which classes organize and struggle for their interests both economically and politically. In such societies, classes are by and large well-regulated and well-organized, meeting both Marx's and Weber's requirements.

A class-divided society exhibits distinct economic classes as well. But here, class interests are not expressed at the national level, and, in fact, are poorly integrated.[1] Each such class seeks to realize its interests through local measures. Webster (1990:135–7) reminds us that in Third World countries, where capitalism is still weak, economic relations are generally inadequately developed. Factions defend their class interests in nonclass terms. Political support of their interests is "bought through a system of *patronage* and *clientelism.* That is, privileged social groups may use ties of kinship, ethnic or regional loyalties, etc. to ensure that the political and bureaucratic administrations of the state develop policy—such as the provision of large commercial grants—that serve their interests. In return, the patronage buys the support of the 'client' groups" (pp. 133–4). Multinational corporations, too, become the clients of the state, seeking their own interests through local rather than national means, or through what Marx calls "a local interconnection."

If we accept Giddens's and Webster's definition, China is largely a class-divided society. Chinese social groups are merely communities that seek to realize their interests through individual negotiations with the state and local governments, rather than through group "societal actions." Professionals are a good example, as we have discussed in chapter 4. Class relations are not well-developed; there are communities, which could form a base for class action, but a class structure is only just emerging. It is certainly not yet formed in the fullest Marxian or Weberian sense. The picture in China, in fact, is one of *classes in formation.*

During the Republican era, a class structure had begun to emerge, with the CCP instrumental in its class formation. It raised the consciousness of the working class. It overthrew the emerging capitalist and landlord classes and abolished the nationalist state that largely represented their interests. Thus after 1949, there were only the cadre class of the CCP with its organizational assets on the one hand, and on the other hand, the working class and peasants, whose labor the cadre appropriated. Since 1978 economic reform has created an emerging class structure that harks back to that Republican era. Its classes, however, are still so rudimentary that we can best refer to them as "emerging classes," or "classes in formation" in a class-divided society. We will discuss the instrumental role of the intellectual in that process.

China's Class Structure in Formation

Zhu Guanglei (1994), a political scientist from Nankai University, has constructed an elaborate model of the class structure in China. This includes the working class in state-owned, collective, and private enterprises; the peasantry; intellectuals; cadres; cadres, and intellectuals in the countryside; private entrepreneurs working on their own *(geti laodong zhe, or geti gongshang hu);* private entrepreneurs with enterprises of their own *(siyin qiye zhu);* soldiers; college students; and the underclass composed of migrant laborers, beggars, and prostitutes. Other writers have also described these various classes (see Qin Yan 1999; Jin

Ye 1998; Liang Xiaosheng 1997; So 2000b). It is interesting to note that Zhu uses the term 'social stratification' rather than 'social class.' There is a very important distinction between the two. Stratification fails to convey what group relations are like. "Class" at least suggests some relationship, in which some classes might be dominant and others subordinate.

The facts of domination and subordination are more accurate in describing the social structure in China, so we will use "class" rather than "stratification" in our discussion. Although in the Party's rhetoric the working class are the "masters of the country," in essence, the CCP is the ruling or dominant class, and a well-developed one at that. Private entrepreneurs are the emerging new bourgeoisie, and with their economic muscle, they are becoming a powerful social group, albeit not yet a fully developed class. Workers and peasantry as a class are not fully developed either; what is worse, they have always been, if not powerless, certainly the least powerful.[2] In the following discussion, we will briefly describe the major classes, or social groups, namely, the Party and the state cadres, the private entrepreneurs, the middle class, the working class, and the peasants or peasant farmers.

The Cadre Class of the Party and the State

Modernity, which is in full swing in China, is based on two major principles. First, the occupational principle suggested by Durkheim's division of labor—hence the emergence of professionals, some of whom we discussed in chapter 4. Second, an administrative principle implied in Weber's rationalization of society—hence the bureaucracy (cited in Freidson 1973:19). For the moment we will focus on the second principle.

Weber is chiefly concerned about the modern bureaucracy that dominates both pubic administration and the private economy. Bureaucracy, he says, is characterized by rules, regulations, means, ends, and matter-of-factness. But he also points out the continuing existence of a traditional Chinese bureaucracy, alive since the time of Shi Huangdi and still maintaining its strong patrimonial and prebendal elements (Weber 1946:438–44).

To understand who these bureaucrats are, we need to understand what the state is. Weber's definition of the state is summed up succinctly by Lewellen (1995:133): the state is "an organization composed of numerous bureaucratic agencies coordinated by an executive authority that makes the binding rules for all people in the country, using force, if necessary, to implement those rules." In the case of China, the state, or the state bureaucracy, consists of the various levels of government led by the Party. The Party cadres are chosen largely from the sixty million Party members. These cadres not only represent the Party; they will tell you, flatly, "I am the Party." They constitute the overwhelming majority of government administrators at every level of government. In other words, the Party is the state, and the state is the Party. In the past two decades, there have been efforts to separate the two, but without much success. According to Zhu (1994:228), this team of Party and government cadres is composed of the following levels, in hierarchical order. Every cadre falls into one category or another:

State President and Premier level: the members of the Politburo, the President and vice-presidents, the Premier and vice-premiers, the members of the state council, the chairman and vice chairpersons of the standing committee of the National People's Congress, the chairman and vice chairpersons of the Chinese Political Consultative Conference.

Ministerial: ministers of various central and state government agencies, provincial Party and government heads, directors of companies at this level, and the members of the central secretariat of various other CCP-authorized parties and organizations.

Ting ju (a high level department): directors of the central and provincial government departments, the Party and government heads of the prefectures, cities at this level, companies, factories and agencies at the same level.

Chu (a middle level department): such department heads in central and provincial governments, heads of counties, of cities and companies and agencies at this level.

Ke (a lower level department): heads of various departments at the county level, and Party and government heads of the Xiang (lower than the county). Also companies and agencies at the same level.

At the lowest level are the members of the *ke,* who deal with everyday affairs from the central government down.

The Chinese army is organized along the same lines, with titles corresponding to the above levels.

It is important to note that China is in transition from the traditional "cadre" bureaucracy to the more modern one, with an emerging system of civil servants, or *gong wu yuan*. In fact, cadres are beginning to be called the less militant *gong wu yuan*. Since 1993, the state has used public examinations to choose expert civil servants for the central government, provincial, prefecture, county, and even down to some *xiang* governments. By 1997, after four years of practice in administering the examinations, the government had put 700,000 applicants through their paces, and 80,000 were recruited. Among all the bureaucrats, 5.33 million were scheduled to be examined every year, and 98% were actually tested. In four years, 5,500 were found not fit to work in the government and were let go (*People's Republic of China Yearbook 1998:* 373). However, compared with the total of at least over 12 million cadres (Zhu Guanglei 1994:226), the numbers recruited and replaced are still too small to be consequential. And the new recruits will most likely conform quickly to the bureaucratic conventions as well.

In addition, officialdom at all levels is largely patrimonial: Party membership is still the chief ticket to a leading position. (That is why it makes sense to continue calling them "cadres," which we will.) To become a cadre, one needs first of all to have both *de* (politics and morality) and *cai* (talent). Here Party membership is the most important criterion of *de* (Zhu Guanglei 1994:238). It is no surprise, then, that surveys at the end of 1990s found that between 10 percent and 20 percent of the students in certain key universities, such as Beijing, Wuhan, Jilin, and Nanjing, had joined the Party by the time they graduated. A larger percentage, 40–50 percent, expressed interest in joining. The majority of those who joined the Party, 70.1 percent, thought that Party membership was a bargaining chip that could increase one's chances for finding a good job (Rosen 2000:25).

These results are further evidence of the importance of Party membership. Party leadership, one of the four cardinal principles, demands that Party members constitute the majority of administrators, or cadres, especially the CEOs at various levels of government, as well as in state-owned enterprises (SOEs) and collective enterprises. According to some reports, even foreign companies investing in China favor Party members (Rosen 2000:25), at least for public (or private?) relations purposes. It is fair to say that the Party and its affiliated bureaucracy are thus the ruling class in China. Indeed, Party leadership is the first of the four cardinal principles the current regime trumpets, followed by socialism, a people's democratic dictatorship, and a blend of Marxism-Leninism-Mao Zedong thought.

That is China's power elite, what Milovan Djilas (1957) calls the "new class" (we perhaps should exclude members of the *ke*). Modestly, its members insist that the working class are the ruling class. In truth, what makes this class distinct is not only the power it wields in making the rules and regulations of the state through its organizational assets, but the benefits and privileges its members enjoy. In addition to money allowances in rent, food, books, baths and haircuts, fuel, and other bonuses, they enjoy the special privileges of their official positions. Zhu Guanglei (1994:232) calls it the value of gold *(han jin liang)* in a position. How much "value of gold" there is in an official position depends on the level of the office and whether and how the official uses his or her office. They may divert the assets and profits of state enterprises into their own hands by converting SOEs into private ones or collectively owned enterprises (see So 2000b). The way in which high officials travel, live, and spend their vacations can be envied even by a wealthy private entrepreneur. For example, a county *(chu)* level official can enjoy a three-bedroom apartment, government cars with drivers to carry him to and from work, and the use of public funds for installing telephones at home. In addition, he may receive gifts, gratuities, and other forms of compensation. The cadre class does indeed, as Wright's model indicates, use its organizational assets to appropriate the surplus labor created by the working class.

Understandably, the power elite have a vested interest in keeping their positions, and in watching others line up for the chance to join their ranks. In 1991, Zhu (1994:226) reports, the 12.6 million cadres were more than double the number in 1981, when there were 5.6 million. (Interestingly, the ratio between officials and the Chinese population is 1:100, about the middle level compared with other nations, according to Zhu.)

To be sure, as market transition theory (Nee 1996) predicts, the shift to the market mechanism reduces the state socialist redistributive power of the cadre class and therefore their income, in relation to the power and income of other economic actors. However, entrepreneurs still depend on the state "for government contracts, the ability to buy and sell land, to develop land, to control local product markets, and to gain access to capital" (Fligstein 1996:1076). The power elite will always find ways to remain on the top (Szelenyi and Kostello 1996:1095). The cadre class will in all probability remain as the most powerful class for a long time.

It is important to also note that the cadre elite are the successors to the revolutionary intellectuals who took over China in 1949. They are also largely intellectuals, albeit revolutionary intellectuals. Recall that six of the seven Politburo standing committee members of the Fifteenth Congress are engineers, and one has an M.B.A. Educated Chinese have provided over 90 percent of the provincial cadres, as well as the cadres of *Ting* and *Ju* (the next lower-level departments). They have provided 80 percent of the county level cadres (Wang Xiaohui 1997).[3] Although the revolutionary intellectuals in power now are less dogmatic than their predecessors, they are still constrained by the intellectuals' ideological belief that the truth is in their own hands. Their monopoly of political power makes it difficult for them to accept alternative ways of government. Unfortunately, perhaps, as the bureaucratic ruling class, the members of the Party are the only well-organized class in China.

The Private Entrepreneurs

There are two kinds of private entrepreneurs: those who work on their own (or with family members) in industrial or commercial endeavors *(geti gongshang hu, or geti laodong zhe),* hiring no more than eight workers, and those who own enterprises, hiring an average of 15 to 16 workers *(siying qiye zhu)* (Zhu Guanglei 1994:324, 345; Zhang Houyi 1999:482–91).[4] By the end of June 1998, according to Zhang Houyi (1999:482, 487, 489), there were 28.51 million *geti gongshang hu* with a workforce *(congye renyuan)* of 54.73 million, while there were 2.25 million *siying qiye zhu* in 1.04 million registered enterprises, with a labor force of 14.58 million. (Enterprises owned by foreign capitalists, including those from Hong Kong, Taiwan, and Macao, had a labor force of 5.81 million.) By the end of 1997, together with other kinds of enterprises, the private sector had already employed 155.64 million workers. The Fifteenth CCP Congress in 1997 stipulated that economic ownership in China would be primarily public ownership, but there would be development of other kinds of ownership at the same time. In addition, foreign capital is playing a more and more important role in China. One can assume that the ranks of private entrepreneurs will only expand.

However, do these two groups form a class? They do own the means of production, and they do continue to appropriate the labor of the working class. According to Margaret M. Pearson's (1997:6–8, 139–40) analysis of the business elite (chiefly managers of foreign and private sectors), they also possess "property rights" and have relatively high incomes and a higher educational level,[5] all of which have translated into greater social prestige. "They are imbued with 'modern' technocratic values of efficiency and rational management. Their lifestyle, too, is cosmopolitan when judged by Chinese standards." But they operate in what Pearson calls the "hybrid state-society relations of clientelism and socialist corporatism." And so they have "failed to transform [their economic and social] position into political power because [they are] uninterested in doing so, because there is viable clientelist option, and because the socialist corporatist strategy of the state is designed to prevent it" (1997:141). They are, thus, not yet a class in themselves. Let's be specific about the state-society relations of clientelism and socialist corporatism.

Under clientelism, private entrepreneurs rely on personal relations with selected offices and officials to influence policy making. For example, they cultivate *guanxi* (connections) with those at the top who control the use of land and grant various permits, or those in the state-owned enterprises who are more likely to have in their possession the materials private entrepreneurs need for their production. With the help of these state patrons, they are able to not only get access to the market but also avoid various labor regulations regarding pension schemes, health and welfare insurance, and environmental protection facilities (So 2000b). They establish *guanxi* through marriage, hiring the children of the powerful, giving them free shares of the enterprise. They oil these relations with various other gifts, favors, and monetary bribes (Qin Yan 1999:99–102, 143; Zhu Guanglei 1994:331; Pearson 1997:107). They donate money for public works and activities, and for activities initiated by the local government or local People's Congress, hoping that their economic string-pulling will influence government policies (Zhu Guanglei 1994:347–8, 359). You pave your own road with money *(jinqian pu lu),* as people say (Jia Ting and Qin Shaoxiang 1993:38). That's what Pearson (1997) calls "vertical clientelism."

Under the socialist corporatism, the state preempts the emergence of more autonomous associations (business or otherwise), "recognizes the legitimacy and limited autonomy of certain social interests," and devolves limited power to groups, some of which are outside the party-state, but controls their leadership selection and interest articulation.[6]

And these associations have to work in "the context of huge existing bureaucracy and weak societal institutions" (Pearson 1997:117).[7] For example, *geti laodong zhe* or *gongshang hu* have local associations of their own, but no independent national organizations, unlike the CCP. The larger entrepreneurs, the *siying qiye zhu,* are more politically conscious, but their associations are also local and sporadic, except in the case of the China Association for Enterprises with Foreign Investment (pp. 122–31). There is, indeed, the All-China Federation of Industry and Commerce *(gong shang lian),* a national association of industrial and commercial workers, and there is the Self-Employed Laborers Association *(geti laodong zhi xiehui)* of small entrepreneurs (pp. 133–5). These organizations are supposed to represent their interests. In fact, their main function is to assist the government in regulating the businesses, educating them to be patriotic, hardworking, and law-abiding (*aiguo, jingye,* and *shoufa)* rather than its professed aims to protect members' interests and to help them improve quality and standards (see also Solinger 1993:256–74; Pearson 1997:131). The government's aim is self-serving; it does not make much effort to advance the interests of professionals or entrepreneurs in the private sector (Qin Yan 1999:64–6, 134–40).

Some private entrepreneurs have made some headway into the power structure, but not yet in a real political sense. For example, they may be selected by the Party to join the National People's Congress (NPC) or the Chinese People's Political Consultative Conference (CPPCC) as members, and even as vice-chairs. But when they are thus honored, they are usually responsible to the Party rather than to the private entrepreneurships of which they are members (see Qin Yan 1999:139–42; Pearson 1997:111). Moreover, the small parties or groups that invite them are themselves under the leadership of the CCP. Some invitees have joined the CCP, but very few, since official policy used to stipulate that the Party generally did not recruit *siying qiye zhu.* Others have even become village heads, *xiang,* and county heads, though the higher the level of local leadership, the fewer such possibilities exist. However high the position, it does not accord them as much power as the CCP leadership.

Nonetheless, the longing to participate in policy-making power structures is strong. Indeed, one provincial survey found that 15.7% of the *geti laodong zhe* and *siying qiye zhu* wanted to join the Party, 5.3% wanted to join one of the small democratic parties, and 77% wanted to join the local industrial and commercial associations (*Guangdong Shehui Kexue* or *Guangdong Social Sciences* [1996]1999:283). Yet these ways of influencing politics do not seem to be successful since the CCP still controls the decision-making processes and the number of "Communist private entrepreneurs" (an oxymoron indeed!) is negligible. That seems to be changing now. As we discussed in chapter 3, the Party's door is being opened now for private entrepreneurs according to Jiang Zemin's speech commemorating the eightieth anniversary of the Party (see *People's Daily,* July 2, 2001 at www.people.com.cn; Ching-Ching Ni 2001).

They may have influence in terms of the taxes and fees they pay and in the number of people they employ, but the fact is, their enterprises concentrate on the service and construction industries, rather than in energy, finance, transportation, and foreign trade. The rights to the use of land and natural resources also belong to the Party and to the state, or at least to the bureaucratic ruling class. Private entrepreneurs may wield some influence, but it is still very limited, although when enough of them bribe officials, one can expect some change in policies, as Qin Yan (1999:143) predicts. These ways of asserting one's interests are typical of a class-divided society, where classes are still in formation since they have few ways of influencing government policies.

As we have shown, and as most researchers observe, China's private entrepreneurs are not yet a class (Yi Cheng [1999] 1998:290–2; Pearson 1997:140). They do own their means of production, dominate in certain production processes, and employ and exploit labor. But they have been in existence for only a short time, and their economic base is still fragile. Most importantly, they have yet to develop class consciousness, and they have not yet built the national organizations needed to effectively represent their interests in the power structure. In China, private entrepreneurs are still a capitalist class in formation.

The Middle Class

Qin Yan (1999:27–8) lumped together in his picture of the middle class a number of social groups, including all of these private entrepreneurs. In our analysis, however, we will treat as the middle class only those private entrepreneurs, over 28 million of them, who work on their own as individuals or as a family *(geti gongshang hu, geti laodong zhe, or geti hu),* and who hire less than eight workers. One note: It makes sense to treat *siyin qiye zhu* as a different class since they have average enterprise assets of 323,000 yuan and household assets of 204,000 yuan. Some have assets worth millions and millions. Most importantly, they own their own capital, hiring an average of fifteen workers. They are, therefore, upper-class private entrepreneurs rather than middle-class ones.

The middle class, then, includes *small* private entrepreneurs as well as the various white-collar professionals listed in Qin Yan's (1999:27–8) study. These can be highly paid employees in sales companies, in financial institutions, and in real estate companies, both public or private (some of the latter are foreign-owned). They are also managers of private companies or certain state-owned enterprises.[8] Some may contract with the state to manage these corporations and companies. Middle-class entrepreneurs may also be brokers in stocks and bonds, lawyers, accountants, cosmeticians, chefs, masseurs and masseuses, professional sports players, actors and actresses, popular singers and dancers, talk-show hosts, fashion models, agents and designers of various kinds, family tutors, as well as public speakers. The tutors and public speakers are likely to be intellectuals from colleges, research institutes, and government offices. The middle class may also include what Glassman (1991: 52–5) calls "the petite bourgeoisie." They are peddlers and vendors selling a variety of wares and foods on city streets, those who operate small repair shops, private restaurants, and inns in the cities. They also include the small entrepreneurs who are engaged in food processing, trade, commercial, and transportation businesses, and even run medical and educational facilities in the countryside.

A sizable percentage of the private entrepreneurs, especially in the cities, both from the middle class and the major entrepreneur class above it, is composed of intellectuals. We showed in chapter 3 that 27.7 percent of the private entrepreneurs attended professional schools in 1995. Another survey in 1996 found that in Beijing, 57 percent of the group also went to professional schools, compared with 1.9 percent in 1987 (Qin Yan 1999:31). In addition to entrepreneurs, many intellectuals have also become managers of both private- and state-owned enterprises and thus find themselves in the middle class. Others have become technical experts to this class, earning quite a high-level salary. That is further evidence of the bourgeoisification of intellectuals (see chapter 4). These intellectuals can also be viewed as organic intellectuals to the Party if they are in the public sector, and of the new bourgeoisie if they are in the private sector. We will discuss this aspect of the entrepreneur's personality later in the section on organic intellectuals.

Typically, the middle class does not own much in the way of means of production. Its members hire little labor or none, so most have little if any chance to exploit others. Or at least their exploitation is of a different kind. For example, lawyers, freelance writers, Internet café owners, actors and actresses, and singers and dancers, differ from the large-scale private entrepreneurs in the amount of means of production they own and, therefore, in the extent to which they can exploit workers. We will further explore this aspect of the middle class when we discuss some middle-class intellectuals' contradictory locations.

The new middle class, however, does develop a different set of beliefs and lifestyles. Rosen (2000:13) reported a survey of women white-collar workers in 1995. It found that they prefer to choose mates who are, in the order of preference: businesspeople (31.9 percent), scientific and technological personnel (16.8 percent), lawyers (9.7 percent), managers (5.9 percent), those in foreign trade (5.4 percent), cadres in offices (4.3 percent), doctors (2.7 percent), those in art and literature (1.6 percent), those in private economy (1.1 percent), those in the military (1.1 percent), and teachers (0.5 percent). While it does not add up to 100 percent, we have a glimpse of the reputations of various occupations in the eyes of young women professionals. The popularity of shopping guides and glossy fashion or lifestyle magazines for young women also indicates how much disposable income they have.

Like private entrepreneurs, the middle class does not have national associations. Because of the diversity of their professions, it is difficult to form a common class consciousness. The associations of industrial and commercial workers *(gong shang lian)* and of self-employed workers are not doing much to represent their members' interests, as we discussed earlier. Even among the members of the class itself, there is little communication or mutual investment. To use Pearson's (1997:108) words, the "horizontal ties" to each other are weak. In fact, those who come from an intellectual background look down upon the nouveaux riches. The professionals and managers in the public sector, on the other hand, are controlled by the Party and by the state. Thus, the middle class is fragmented, although its numbers are expanding and effective local organizations may be emerging. We will, however, explore in chapter 6 how intellectuals, many of whom are in this group, can form a functional class.

The Working Class

By the working class, we mean workers in both the public and private sectors. Table 5.2 tells us the number of those who work in, or have retired from, various enterprises.

It is important to note that the numbers of workers in SOEs are decreasing and that the numbers in private ones are increasing. If statistics show that at the beginning of the 1990s, there were 103.46 million, or about half of all workers, in SOEs, by 1997, the number declined to 40.40 million (Xu Xinxin and Li Peilin 1999:21). Another researcher sets the latter number at 46 million (Zhu Yong 1999:140). In contrast, at the beginning of the 1990s, there were only 107 million workers in the broader private sector, that is, companies owned by foreign and Chinese capital as well as township enterprises, most of the latter privately owned. By the end of 1997, that sector claimed 155.64 millions (Zhang Houyi 1999:487). Indeed, out of the 10.70 million workers who were laid off by the third quarter of 1998, 7.14 million were from SOEs, which constituted 66.7% of the total (Li Peilin 1999:327). Obviously, SOEs were in general not doing well. For example, by the end of the first quarter of 1998, only 6 out of 32 provinces and cities directly attached to the central government made money with their SOEs. They were Heilongjiang, Yunnan, Guangdong, Shanghai, Fujian, and Shandong (Zhu Yong 1999:137).

The living conditions of the working class can differ greatly from one place to another. For those in the public sector, life depends on how well the specific work unit does. If it does well, the workers may enjoy

Table 5.2 The Distribution of Workers in Enterprises

Kind of Enterprises	Number of Workers (in millions)
State-owned companies in industry, construction, mining, energy, transportation, and commerce	103.46 as of the end of 1990
Collectively owned factories and companies in townships	35.49 as of the end of 1990
Companies owned by foreign capital, or jointly by foreign and Chinese capital	3.00 as of the beginning of the 1990s
Private companies owned by Chinese	4.00 as of the end of 1989
Township companies	100.00 as of the beginning of the 1990s
Retired workers	23.01 as of 1990
Total	268.96

Source: Zhu Guanglei. 1994. *Great Division and New Organization,* pp. 53, 126. Most of Zhu's data were from the *Chinese Statistical Yearbook 1990.*

a steady income and adequate health care. That seems to be the case of, for example, Baoshan Steel Works in Shanghai, which was able to downsize but at the same time find employment for the laid-off workers within its own system. As a result, both productivity and workers' wages have increased (Freund 1998).

But since most SOEs are not doing well, most workers do not have steady incomes and face the constant threat of being laid off. Indeed, in the state-owned industrial and commercial enterprises alone, one third of the 46 million workers are surplus labor force (Zhu Yong 1999:140; Ching Kwan Lee 1999). In 1997, 12 million workers were laid off from both industrial and commercial enterprises as well as from administrative organizations. However diligently they searched for work, usually in the private sector, only about 26 percent found new jobs, according to a survey at the end of 1997 by the China Statistical Bureau and the Ministry of Labor (Mo Rong 1999:235). There are subsidies for unemployed workers, but payments amount to only 60–70 percent of their original salaries and last only for 12 to 24 months depending on their previous length of employment (Li Peilin 1999:330).

Joblessness in China carried the usual penalties. The families of those out of work face increasing hardships. A 1998 survey of unemployed workers in Tianjin, one of the largest industrial cities in China, shows that their average family income was only 866 yuan, half of the city level. Two percent of the families surveyed lived in poverty, with an income of less than 185 yuan; 40 percent of these had two members without work. The families tended to have no decent durable consumer goods, had had no new clothes for years, and had no health care for the sick. Of all the city's families living under the poverty line, 54 percent had family members laid off (Yan Yaojun et al. 1999:258–9). A 1998 survey of unemployed workers in Changchun, another big industrial city in northeast China, found that 79.3 percent of workers attributed their layoffs to social factors, expecting the state to help them resolve the problem. Of all the workers surveyed, 13.7 percent said they were willing to join in some collective action, such as collectively presenting their case to higher authorities *(jiti shang fang)*. That translates into 15,000 of all the 110,000 laid-off workers (Song Baoan and Wang Yushan 1999: 282).[9] Figure 5.1 describes the situation of the state-owned enterprises and the life of the retired workers and their families affiliated with them, as compared with the "new" enterprises and those who may be affiliated with them.

Figure 5.1 The Poor Old Ox! *(Kelian de lao niu)*

Notes: The words on the side of the cart read: old enterprises, meaning state-owned enterprises, and the words on the side of the truck read: new enterprises, mostly private ones. Hanging over the heads of the people in the cart are "the life, work, health care, housing, etc. of the retired workers and their family members."
Source: Ding Cong 1999 (Vol. 3), p. 154.

The private sector, on the other hand, has been expanding, as we have noted, and producing a greater and greater share of the national industrial output. In Chongqing, for example, by June 1998 the total output of production in the private sector had increased 61.7 percent from the previous year. As of today, the private economy constitutes 60 percent of all retail sales of consumer goods and 30 percent of the taxes paid (Zhang Houyi 1999:486). For the first time, there are more workers in the private sector, perhaps because they can earn more money than in the public sector. For example, in 1989, the average yearly salary of employees in state-owned enterprises was 2,055 yuan, whereas the joint ventures paid 29.9 percent more, corporations owned by overseas Chinese (including Hong Kong and Taiwan capitalists) paid 45.7 percent more, and foreign companies paid 73.6 percent more (Zhu Guanglei 1994: 105). There was a price for this generosity.

Let us now have a more detailed look at the work environment this class endures. In the state-owned enterprises, while workers in such companies as Baoshan Steel Works may be less alienated, other workers face harsh management control. Zhao and Nichols (1998:75, 90, 96) studied three state cotton mills in Henan province. They find "a work system that includes quota increases and speed-ups; longer working hours, the adaptation of socialist labor emulation to production for profit, new draconian controls over labor attendance; and the use of monetary sanctions and penalties to control labor." For example, the system refuses workers' time off for holidays and restricts their sick leave. Such controls are exercised in the name of "scientific management." The leaders say flatly that they have purposely introduced a sense of uncertainty and risk so that workers can work more efficiently.

Millions of workers in the private as well as the public sectors are peasants migrating from the countryside to cities looking for work, who face even harsher working conditions.[10] Dorothy Solinger (1995, 1998) describes their employment channels as construction workers, marketers and craftspeople, garment processors in cottages, factory hands, nursemaids, and vagrants, and presents their plight as second-class citizens. They are what Maurice Meisner (1997:265) calls "a functional underclass, [who tend to] do the work that permanent residents of the city wish to avoid and, like their counterparts in other capitalists countries, serve to make life comfortable for the well-to-do." As Meisner describes them, they

> encounter the harsh conditions of early industrialization, and they do so on the most massive scale in world history. In many areas, 12- to 15-hour workdays are common and low wages are universal; living conditions are primitive, often in unhygienic factory dormitories; overtime work is usually mandatory; many workers are young teenagers and, along with female laborers in general, are pitilessly victimized by owners and managers; working conditions are hazardous, resulting in many thousands of deaths annually in industrial accidents and fires; and workers are often preyed upon by greedy bureaucrats demanding payment of newly invented fees. While there are national and local laws limiting the length of the workday and prohibiting abuses such as child labor, the laws are rarely enforced. (p. 267)

Sweatshop conditions abound especially in privately owned enterprises, and industrial accidents are frequent. In 1993, for example, industrial accidents more than doubled from the previous year, killing and maiming thousands of workers. About 500,000 child laborers were among the 8 million transient workers in Guangdong alone (Tyler 1994a). In 1994, fires killed dozens of workers in Shenzhen and Zhuhai in Guangdong, either because there were no exits or because exits were padlocked to prevent theft by workers. Deaths caused by accidents at work totaled 3,300 in the first quarter of 1995 alone (*World Journal,* December 25, 1995; see also Jin Ye 1998: 302–4, Hessler 2001 for more examples of the lives of those who work in the cities).

One study found that in 217 jointly owned or entirely private enterprises in Guangdong province, most workers put in ten to twelve, sometimes even fourteen, hours a day, but were paid only monthly wages (Xu Zhijie 1994). In addition, 95 percent of the enterprises studied in Qingdao, Shandong Province, had no labor protection procedures. The official City Workers' General Union survey shows that 73 percent of the enterprises wrote no safety regulations into their labor contracts. Thirty-three percent of these businesses maintained deplorable working conditions. In Zhuhai, Guangdong, seven of the enterprises investigated emitted poisonous gases at a rate eight to ten times higher than the state standard. In one of the foreign-domestic-joint-capital ceramic factories in Tianjin, dust in the workshop was at a level 274 times above the state standard. In a foreign-capital enterprise in Xiamen, Fujian province, 39 out of 400 workers had hands crippled by labor accidents. Scolding, hitting, and corporal punishment of workers occurred frequently.

Even when peasant workers are employed in the state sector, they tend to do the hardest labor, with none of the benefits given to their state-affiliated coworkers (Solinger 1998:22–3). For example, in the textile industry, it is the rural workers who are assigned to the spinning and weaving workshops where "the environment is particularly poor, deafening, dusty, and debilitating, with its intolerable clatter, high heat and humidity." Since they are temporary workers, the company offers no health insurance, and crowds its workers into cheap housing with half a dozen or more squeezed into one dorm room. In addition, the factory escapes paying for child care or child education since it requires these workers to be unmarried and childless.

Moreover, workers have very little freedom to negotiate these conditions with capital or with state enterprise managers. The All-China

Federation of Trade Unions (ACFTU) is the only workers' organization that is supposed to represent the workers' interests. But as O'Leary points out (1998:67), it is still dominated by Party authority and is in essence a component of management. Although Chinese law stipulates that there must be labor unions in every enterprise, in 1992 only 30 percent of privately held companies were unionized. In most of these cases, the head of Human Resources was also the head of the labor union (Zhu Guanglei 1994:107). In other words, the labor union was managed by and represented management, as in the state-owned enterprises (see also Ching Kwan Lee 1999:58). Union members thus had no way of asserting their interests. To be sure, as we see in Anita Chan's (1998) study on labor relations, workers may have decent representation by the labor unions in such joint ventures as the Beijing Jeep Corporation. But in private enterprises, especially in overseas Chinese-owned enterprises, even when unions are set up, they are there to help better manage the workers (Zhu Guanglei 1994:139). Especially in the south, abuses of workers abound; some overseas Chinese-invested enterprises still refuse to set up unions.

No matter where they are, in joint ventures or in other private enterprises, unions remain under the Party's thumb and cannot do anything "in contradiction to the nation's emphasis on economic development" (Chan 1998:136; see also Ching Kwan Lee 2000:55). Collective bargaining on behalf of the workers is not the Party's priority. Jude Howell's (1998) study on trade unions in China discusses similar dilemmas.

Workers in both the public and private sectors are increasingly frustrated with the deepening social inequality and economic exploitation, layoffs, unpaid wages, cadre corruption and abuse, maldistribution of resources, pollution, taxes, relocation, and so forth. Since labor unions either do not exist or do not function as unions, people resort to other means. One recent example is the riots in February 2000 by miners in the Yangjiazhangzi mine, Liaoning Province in Northeast China, which involved 20,000 workers. They were laid off when the mine, which produced molybdenum used in alloys for the aerospace industry, was declared bankrupt. The workers were not satisfied with the subsidies they were going to get. With the town's economy dependent on mining, workers did not see a way out; more difficult still, the cadres were offered jobs elsewhere. Large numbers of police had to be called in to stop the rioters from smashing windows and blocking roads. As one of the workers said, "What can we do? There is no organized effort to lobby for our interests" (Xu Feng and Wu Yiyi 2000; *Press Freedom Guardian,* April 7, 2000). Such closings have occurred very often in places like Shanxi province, which produces the largest share of the country's coal. Since less is needed with today's technology, protests have become common, although riots on the scale of Liaoning's still seem rare.

Given all the ferment and disorder among workers, we can only say that the working class is also a class in the making. Compared with the private entrepreneurs, they may have a better chance of unionization since after all China has a socialist tradition and there exists an official trade union. ACFTU can be instrumental in fostering a sense of workers' rights and stimulating independent trade unions in the future. Only then can we say that the working class is a mature class, an important player in the national political scene. Right now, it is a restive working class in the making, as Ching Kwan Lee (2000:57) observes. We will discuss the organization of the working class in this chapter when we discuss its organic intellectuals.

The Peasants or Peasant Farmers

With 866.37 million people, the rural population constituted 70.31 percent of China's total population in 1997. Among them, 347.30 million were engaged in agriculture, that is, 49.9 percent of the total labor force in China, or 70.31 percent of the rural workforce (Fan Ping 1999:452). With the change from collective farming to the family responsibility system, both production and the peasants' incomes have increased tremendously compared with the prereform days.

There are three different strata of farmers, according to Zhu Guanglei (1994:159). The first are the private entrepreneurs in agriculture, who can make a great deal of money from contract farming. Indeed, some large-scale farming has emerged, with "landlords" hiring farmhands from outside their villages. For example, statistics show that in 1995 in Xiaoshan county in Zhejiang province, 3,599 landlords possessed 100 to 1,000 acres of land and hired farmhands to commute to their fields (Jin Ye 1998:319). The landlords are fast becoming commercial farmers, and the farmhands a social group of agricultural laborers (see also Meisner 1997:267). The second peasant group consists of subsistence farmers, who may occasionally have a little surplus for sale. Finally there are those so mired in poverty that they need help from the government. Most of this last group are in the far southwest and northwest of

China. In 1998, there were still 50 million Chinese peasants in absolute poverty, although this figure had dropped by 10 million from the previous year according to official statistics (Tang Jun 1999:401). Some estimates put the number of peasants in poverty at 200 million (Liang Xiaosheng 1997:395).[11]

The pace of improvement in peasants' living conditions is very slow; in fact, since 1997, the actual incomes have declined (Fan Ping 1999; Lu Xueyi 2001; see Ash 1991 for the conditions of the agricultural sector in the 1980s). Rural productivity in general is increased but peasants' incomes are low due to the cost of production, low prices for farm products, heavier taxes, and so forth. Furthermore, there is an increasing amount of surplus labor in the countryside due to mechanization and other improvements in the farming methods, and more peasants are going to the cities to look for jobs, competing with the laid-off workers there. Many find that it does not pay to do farmwork (see also Liang Xiaosheng 1997:403).

Corruption in the countryside does not help at all. There is almost no cadre in the villages who does not take bribes (see also Liang Xiaosheng 1997:403). The more serious offenders embezzle money that is supposed to help refugees from famine, flood, or other disasters. They also put into their own pockets money for dam construction meant to prevent floods. They control the buying and selling of seeds, fertilizer, and pesticides, demanding kickbacks and bribes from peasants who depend on these materials (Wen Shengtang 1999:177). One of my interviewees comments that in his rural area, where there is not much money to make anyway, every village head will have amassed at least several hundred thousand yuan of personal wealth before he retires (Interview with Yue Ziming 2000).

Facing so much corruption in the countryside, peasants resort to various means of protest. In the 1990s, rural cadres often found their homes firebombed, their ancestral graves destroyed, fruit trees felled, and crops destroyed. Some of them were even injured or killed by angry villagers (Li and O'Brien 1996:36–7). In August 1997, riots in the township of Beixiang, affiliated with Lechang City, Guangdong Province, resulted in the severe beating and injury of the township Party secretary and several of its security personnel, followed by the arrest of over 100 peasants for looting 100,000 yuan in cash and smashing windows and doors (*World Journal,* August 26, 1997). According to the May 1998 issue of *Cheng Ming Monthly,* from January to March of 1998 alone, in the cities as well as in the countryside, over 3,000 protests and demonstrations occurred, including almost 400 riots (*Press Freedom Guardian,* June 5, 1998). The situation has not abated.

Thanks partly to the Organic Law of Villagers' Committees, there is now more room in peasants' lives for organized legal action although most peasants still remain passive (Zhang Ming 2001).[12] Li and O'Brien (1996) delineate the peasant movements in the countryside in a very interesting and informative article, "Villagers and Popular Resistance in Contemporary China." They describe three kinds of peasants: the compliant villagers *(shunmin),* the recalcitrants *(dingzihu),* and the policy-based resisters *(diaomin).* (The Chinese names have negative connotations but they are used by the authors as neutral.) The compliant villagers are inactive for various reasons, chief of which is the belief that they are powerless to make any changes. This is the majority of peasants. The recalcitrants put up individual resistance against such injustices as extreme measures used in imposing birth control, funeral reform, or new fees and taxes. The extreme measures used by local cadres include tearing down the peasants' homes, seizing their grain, or confiscating their appliances.[13]

The policy-based resisters, however, "use laws, policies, and other official communications to defy local leaders" (Li and O'Brien 1996: 40). To combat the corrupt cadres, they even withhold taxes and fees until the township government has removed or disciplined the leaders. Most interestingly, when they find procedural violations of the election law, they lodge complaints against the township government and demand a new election. Writing to newspapers and magazines and lodging collective complaints have become popular forms of protest and political participation. Many times they succeed. (See Cao Jinqing 2000 for an ethnographic study of the conditions in the countryside, and Zweig 2000 for more discussions on rural conflict and resistance.)

Still, as Li and O'Brien (1996:54) point out, the policy-based resistance movements are local and parochial, rather than national and autonomous. "[T]hey generally do not claim more general civil and political rights to association, expression, and unlicensed participation . . . [although their activity] attests to the presence of an incipient civil society. . . ." If the workers have at least a national official trade union to represent their interests, peasants do not have such organizations. The peasants are only a rural class in the making. It will take much longer for a mature peasant class to occur than it does for the urban working class.

In sum, classes can be viewed as having different assets, whether

1. **The Cadre Class**:
or the BRC,
1% of the population

2. **The Big Private Entrepreneurs**;
some are Party members;
0.25% of the population.

3. **The Middle Class**:
small entrepreneurs, managers, commercial farmers, and professionals; **8.75%** of the population.

4. **The Working Class**:
urban workers, migrants, and workers in rural industries;
20% of the population.

6. **The Peasant Farmers**: 800 million or about **70%** of the population, who lack the benefits and privileges of the urban population. Most are independent farmers subject to exploitation by means of taxes, rents, unpaid labor, and unfair terms of trade. Their working and living conditions, and their political and economic power are generally even less favorable than those of migrant workers. Some of becoming agricultural laborers and may finally join the working class.

Figure 5.2 The Basic Class Structure in Today's China

Sources: Zhu Guanglei (1994:53, 126, 226) and Zhang Houyi (1999:482, 487, 489).

organizational capital or money capital, and enjoying different statuses, especially in the relationship between domination and subordination. The emerging class structure in China resembles a perfume bottle, with the cadre class, 1 percent, larger than the big private entrepreneurs, 0.25 percent, the middle class about 8.75 percent, the working class 20 percent, and the peasants 70 percent. The higher the social class, the more political and economic power. (See Figure 5.2.)

To function in a class society, classes not only must form communities but must also engage in national communal pressure through well-organized collective action. In China, the Party cadres, certainly the dominant class, are very well organized. Private entrepreneurs are not organized nationally, although locally they are beginning to assert their power, using local organizations and various other means, including bribery, to influence government policies. The middle class, the working class, and the peasants are still in the process of class formation: they have yet to organize nationally in order to function as fully developed classes. Thus, China today is still a typical Third World class-divided society rather than a class society in a fully developed capitalist structure. The rest of this chapter will examine the intellectuals organic to these various emerging classes.

Organic Intellectuals

Marx and Engels fail to clarify the roles of intellectuals and their status in class relations, although they do imply that most intellectuals are attached to one or another of the two hostile camps: the bourgeoisie and the workers. As we just mentioned, there are in fact more classes than the two basic ones, and intellectuals can be organic to any one of them. We will also discuss the intellectuals organic to the Party and state, as well as to private entrepreneurs and the working class. We will briefly mention organic intellectuals to the middle class as well as those to the peasants.

Barbara and John Ehrenreich's (1979:12) construct of the professional-managerial class (PMC) will be very helpful for us here. The PMC consists of "salaried mental workers who do not own the means of production and whose major function in the social division of labor may be described broadly as the reproduction of capitalist culture and capitalist class relations." Although the Ehrenreichs are talking about capitalism, their description also helps us understand organic intellectuals in statist systems as well, or what many call China's socialist corporatism. These intellectuals do not own either the means of production or the organizational assets that could move them into the dominant classes. But they do help these classes in their reproduction of culture and class relations. Many of the Party's theorists, journalists, researchers, scholar-cadres, and the private entrepreneurs' managers and technical personnel are part of the PMC. So are the labor organizers or advocates. We will now look at some of the members of this PMC. (Since intellectuals constitute a large part of the middle class, we will explore how they might become an independent class in chapter 6, in particular how they might develop their own organic intellectuals.)

Organic Intellectuals to the Party and the State

Which Party cadres can be considered as organic intellectuals is not always clear. Take Hu Qiaomu for example. He served as ghostwriter for Party leaders such as Mao and Deng, but he had a great deal of power over cadres whose ranks were lower than his. In the Rectification Campaign in 1942, Mao criticized Wang Shiwei and it was Hu who talked with Wang conveying to him Mao's criticism (see Dai Qing 1994:35). In the 1980s, he ordered Zhou Yang to undergo self-criticism for his views on Marxist humanism and alienation under socialism. He was both *part* of the ruling elite and one of the organic intellectuals who *served* the ruling elite (see Schoenhals 1992; Ye Yonglie 1994).[14] Many organic intellectuals enjoy similar situations, which resemble those of the scholar-officials in premodern China.

As we discussed in chapter 2, since the reform after the Cultural Revolution more and more intellectuals have become part of the cadre organization. This is because of the policy of promoting younger and more knowledgeable individuals to cadre positions. They become the managers of various local governments as well as of state-owned enterprises and organizations. By the end of 1991, cadres who had graduated from professional schools and beyond constituted 71 percent of the ranks (Zhu Guanglei 1994:242–3). By 1998 an estimated 80 percent to 90 percent of the cadres, that is, the overwhelming majority of the state government, were intellectuals as we define them.[15]

Other intellectuals are part of the establishment but as its advisers and advocates. In a book series of eight volumes, Zhang Xiaoxia (2000, 2001) describes seventy-nine such intellectuals (see table 5.3). The series is aptly entitled *Those Who Have Affected the Development in Contemporary China.*

As Zhang Xiaoxia (2000, Vol. 1, p. 3) herself points out, although most of these intellectuals were not regarded as high-level Party and state leaders, their achievements in advising the latter cannot be underestimated. Their roles are clear: to help promote the Party's drive to the four modernizations. But most of the times, their roles are subsidiary: they have the political authorities' ears, but they do not have their power in decision making.

This section will discuss such organic intellectuals, who may be part of the state apparatus but whose main job is to support the state functions. They are Party theorists, journalists, economists, and researchers in institutes like the academies of social sciences. There are a few small democratic parties. And finally there are the new scholar-officials, who may have some power and may even be considered part of the ruling class. In Gramsci's words, these people perform the function of ideological hegemony and direct domination on behalf of the dominant class (1971:12), which in our case is the Party. If we keep in mind the example of Hu Qiaomu, it is not always clear who is in the ruling class and who is simply a Party functionary.

Table 5.3 Those Who Have Affected the Development in Contemporary China

Vol. 1	Vol. 2	Vol. 3	Vol. 4
Wang Daohan	Wang Huning	Cao Jianming	Wang Mengkui
Liu Ji	Xiao Zhuoji	Ma Hong	Gong Yuzhi
Wu Jinglian	Long Yongtu	Mao Yushi	Liu Liying
He Xin	Xin Qi	Liang Dingbang	Gao Shangquan
Li Yining	Tong Dalin	Ai Feng	Yan Xuetong
Hu Angang	Zhang Hanlin	Du Gangjian	Bai Chunli
Wei Jie	Tang Shubei	Ye Wenhu	Liu Guoguang
Zhong Pengrong	Zhang Zhaozong	Xue Muqiao	Wang Dingding
Cao Siyuan	Lin Yifu	He Weifang	Chen Huai
Liu Wei	Sheng Hong	Yang Fan	Yi Gang
Fan Gang	Fang Shen		
Vol. 5	**Vol. 6**	**Vol. 7**	**Vol. 8**
Dong Fureng	Liu Hongru	Teng Wenshen	Zhao Qizheng
Li Zhaoxing	Xu Kuangdi	Shen Guofang	Li Jiange
Lu Yongxiang	Chen Yunlin	Dai Xianglong	Su Ge
Wang Shaoguang	Wang Shan	Zhou Ruijin	Shi Meilun
Zhang Shuguang	Han Deqiang	Hong Hu	Qiao Zonghuai
Wang Yizhou	Qiao Liang	Wang Qishan	Zheng Bijian
Du Runsheng	Shi Yinhong	Wang Jisi	Niu Wenyuan
Chen Yuan	Zi Zhongyun	Chi Fulin	Xu Xiaonian
	Sun Jin	Gao Xiqing	Zhu Chenghu

Source: Zhang Xiaoxia. 2000, 2001. *China's High Level Advisors* (Vols. 1–8).

Party Theorists and Journalists

To give us an idea of how they think and what they do, let us look at what the Party theorists and scholar-officials write. Table 5.4 is a summary of the subjects published in 1995 in the Central Committee's biweekly journal *Qiu Shi,* or *Seeking Truth,* the former *Red Flag*. Party committees at all levels were supposed to subscribe to the journal. The articles in it were written either by intellectual cadres holding various government positions, or by organic intellectuals who spoke for the government on current political and economic issues. According to Xing Bensi, the editor in chief, the primary task of the journal is to help build the socialist market economy by arming Party cadres with an arsenal of theory: Marxism-Leninism-Mao Zedong Thought, and Deng Xiaoping's ideas on building socialism with Chinese characteristics (see *Qiu Shi*—the journal—1995:673–4).

Table 5.4 The Number and Subjects of Articles Published in *Qiu Shi, 1995*

Kinds of Articles	Number of Articles	Percent of the Total
On improving Party leadership and government work. Education of cadres on anti-corruption issues	69	24.4%
On economy. Reform of economic ownership and SOE's. Reform in the countryside	67	23.7%
On how to build a socialism with Chinese characteristics. Socialist morality, thought education, patriotism, education of cadres, etc.	49	17.3%
On education in science and technology, humanities, physical education, etc.	35	12.4%
On how literature and art help improve image of Party cadres and Party's course	29	10.2%
On history of the Party. History of the anti-Japanese war	12	4.2%
On diplomatic affairs	6	2.1%
On laws governing ownership, education, physical education	4	1.4%
On the work of *Qiu Shi*	3	1.1%
On ethnicity, religion	3	1.1%
On relying on the working class	3	1.1%
On women	2	0.7%
On the peasantry	1	0.4%
Total	283	100%

Note: Articles follow the magazine's own classifications, plus a few adjustments I made according to the central idea each article conveys.

The articles published in the twenty-four issues of just one year show us the focus of the Party's concerns. Obviously, the writers do indeed follow the Party line; they certainly reflect the agenda of the day. The first three categories, on improvement of Party leadership and government work, economic reform, and building a socialism with Chinese characteristics, constitute 65.4 percent of the articles. As a means to achieve these goals, education in science and technology makes up a bit over 10 percent; so do literature and art. Not surprisingly, discussions of the rule of law are limited to only 1.4 percent of the articles.

In two other articles discussing corruption, the best cure the authors can suggest is to *strengthen the supervisory organs* in and outside the Party (without saying precisely how) and to ask the Party cadres to *supervise themselves* (Chang Guangmin 1995; Wang Jinshan 1995). Less than 2 percent of the articles are focused on workers and peasants.

Economic reform and the improvement of both Party and government work are obviously the center of attention for the Party and its organic intellectuals. There is little mention of reform of the political system or of the rule of law, reflecting the actual lack of emphasis on these issues in the Party line. A look at other examples may tell us more about the organic intellectuals' mission and their dilemma.

In a series of books entitled *China's Problems,* Xu Ming, a researcher from the CASS and the series editor, writes about the opportunity to publish such books:

> We should treasure this historic opportunity to help the socialist reform started by Comrade Xiaoping and inherited by the third generation of collective leadership, headed today by Comrade Jiang Zemin. We will protect its healthy development. This is the common understanding of the writers of this series. In current China's generous atmosphere for open discussion, and among its many different shades of opinion, we do not hide the fact that we are socialist reformers, or reform socialists.

> At the time of organizing the book our beloved Comrade Deng Xiaoping passed away. . . . We will try our best to study and interpret thoroughly the problems we encounter in the way of our country's advancement. We will give ordinary people *[lao bai xing]* "a way of understanding" *[shuo fa],* and provide the comrades in leadership positions with some opinions for reference in their decision making—this is the best way to commemorate [Deng]! (See Xu Ming 1998)

The first quote tells us who they are: "reform socialists." The second quote tells us what they do: help the Party and government in their decision making, although it also includes informing the masses. Both probably apply to the *Qiu Shi* writers as well, judging from their output. One book in the series, *Jiaofeng,* or *Crossing Swords* (Ma and Ling 1998), shows Deng and his followers over the past two decades fighting the leftist wing in the Party. After three encounters, Deng finally won, and nailed down his socialist reform. The first such "confrontation," or "thought liberation," came in 1978, with the defeat of the "two whatevers," that is, "whatever policies Chairman Mao formulated we will resolutely protect; and whatever instructions Chairman Mao gave us we will carry through" (p. 23). The second confrontation happened in 1992, when Deng successfully fielded Party members' doubts over whether the current reform was socialist or capitalist. And the third thought liberation occurred in 1997 when the Party's Fifteenth Congress declared victory over those who questioned whether the current reform was for the good of the "public" or for "private" and individual interests.

There is an interesting parallel at work. Although they discuss thought liberation, Ma and Ling (1997:425) have basically ignored political and legal reform, as have the *Qiu Shi* writers, until the very last few sentences of the book. They wonder when the next thought liberation will arrive; they assume it will be when the Party carries out its promise to "'further develop the reform of the political system' as promised in the political report of the Party's 15th Congress." Even when they discuss political reform, they make sure to mention the Party line. Ma and Ling are both editors of *People's Daily,* and they are skilled at propelling the Party's course and at the same time exercising some intellectual freedom. In addition, they do not, and cannot in the political atmosphere, mention the waves of the democracy movement.[16]

The practice is followed by many other journalists. A leading reporter and the administrator of the city government-sponsored daily newspaper, whose circulation is a strong one hundred thousand, made the following comments on their jobs and how they dealt with sensitive issues:

> Since the newspaper is affiliated with the city Party committee, it has to carry news about or reflect the policies of the city government. The readers look to the newspaper for policy implications and guidelines for their daily work. News we carry about other parts of China is fed to us by the Xinhua News Agency. We focus on the city news. Because of our official nature, we don't have as much freedom as the city's Evening News. They enjoy greater scope and depth in their coverage, such as publishing investigative reports on corruption or problematic business practices. People traveling to higher courts to appeal their cases are not to be reported. Important legal cases cannot be reported if they are not yet solved. Even when they are reported, you report only the successful cases and only their positive side. Negative things should be written with a more positive view, and exposure of negative things should be written from various angles. (Interview with Chang Zongmiao and Wu Ji 1996:26–7)

Yet another example is *Jiaodian Fangtan* (Focused Interviews), one of the most popular programs of investigative reporting by Central TV, similar to *20/20* and *60 Minutes*. Started in 1994, it has exposed corrupt officials in various provinces, fraudulent practices in businesses, and it has given ordinary people an opportunity to air their views, as we discussed in chapter 3. People even call it Jiao Qingtian, or "the upright official named Jiao" (Zhong Huai [1998] 1999:254–5). However, as Liu Jianming (1998:192) asks, What if the corrupt officials or fraudulent practices are from the Central government? Can it still practice its supervisory and critical role? Very unlikely. In other words, news organizations at different levels are controlled by the governments at those levels: provincial TV cannot criticize provincial government, so Central TV cannot criticize the Central government. Indeed, as we hear from the chief program producer of *Jiaodian Fangtan,* Sun Yusheng, their programs represent the Central TV, and the Central TV represents the Party and state (cited in Yan Shi [1995] 1999:271). So they have to follow the Party's policies, advocate them, and criticize those who violate them. This pledge of allegiance dictates that their programs must foster socialism and patriotism, promote Party causes such as combating crime and controlling inflation, and criticize corruption and environmental pollution.

To be sure, there are a lot of opportunities for the reporters; that is why the program is so popular. And with commercialization, a substantial number of news organizations have gained financial independence, and journalists' reports are beginning to be geared toward the needs of the masses. There is a crack in the propagandist model, as we discussed in chapter 3 (see also Yuezhi Zhao 1998:50, 156). Still, there are lines reporters cannot cross.

These journalists do have to meet the requirements of the Party, for instance, to advocate Jiang Zemin's thoughts, and they do seem to view that as their obligation, something critical intellectuals need not worry too much about. At the same time, however, journalists would also like to be more critical, to have leeway to broadcast or publish, as often as they wish, cases or articles that their listeners and readers enjoy. They know that their audiences judge them quite as severely as do Party officials, believing as they do that they too are intellectuals. The Chinese intellectual tradition requires that they be "eyes, ears, and mouthpiece" of the people as well while they serve the party-state in those functions (Polumbaum 1994a:212).[17] Under such restraints, it is difficult for journalists to avoid the dual personality, the lot of all organic intellectuals. We will learn more about that effect in the next section.

Young Economists

If writers and reporters are helping both to create the Party ideology and to get it across to their audiences, economists are helping craft the Party's economic policies. Back in the 1980s, even when some intellectuals began to deviate from the orthodox Party line, others diligently served in the government's economic reform program. These were mainly economists in Zhao Ziyang's think-tanks, for instance, the so-called "three institutes and one association," namely, the Chinese Institute for the Study of Economic Reforms, the Chinese Institute for the Study of Rural Development, the Institute for the Study of International Affairs, and the Beijing Association of Young Economists (Edward X. Gu 1999:407; Fewsmith 1994:135–8). While some economists, like Chen Yizi and Zhu Jiaming, fell along with Zhao Ziyang whose think-tanks were disbanded in 1989, the government was not hesitant to reassemble others in the powerhouse.

In the 1990s, some young economists especially had substantial influence on the government's policies. The Central TV program *Sons and Daughters of the East* or *Dongfang Zhi Zi* (Shi Jian 1996), interviewed some of these young up-and-comers. They included Fan Gang of the CASS; Lin Yifu of Beijing University; Qiu Xiaohua of the State Statistical Bureau; Li Xiaoxi, a researcher and inspector of the Council of the State; Zhou Shijian from a research institute affiliated with the Ministry of Foreign Trade; He Yang, a researcher and entrepreneur; and Wang Haijun of the State Commission on Reform of the Economic System. They advise various state agencies and corporations. They also write profusely on economic issues such as the reform of economic ownership (Fan), ways to suppress inflation (Lin), the macro-economy (Qiu), price structure (Li), international trade (Zhou), reform of SOEs (He), and comparative economic systems (Wang). Their research reaches the Party and government decision makers.

They are not always successful in influencing the government's policies, though. Hu Angang, another well-known economist, suggested the abolition of the special economic zones. He did not win his point, although the debate lasted on and off for more than a year (Ma and Ling 1997:293–9). But Hu at least had some freedom of expression. He in fact enjoyed the debate and was supported by provincial officials. He was excited to be able to start a debate that could potentially affect one of the most important policies of reform. But that the debate led nowhere probably tells us the limits within which organic intellectuals can exercise their power. Li Xiaoxi, the researcher from the State Council, tells us another limitation: although they were free to do research, when it came to publishing their results, they had to be careful because they were speaking for the government (1996:134). This may be a good cause of the dual or split personality.

New Scholar-Officials

We have looked at scholar-cadres in *Qiu Shi,* at journalists and at economists all as organic intellectuals. As we discussed in chapter 2, the Party's new cadre policy has made it possible for more and more intellectuals to enter leadership positions. For example, from 1985 to 1993 scientific and technical personnel made up a bit over half the workforce of 120,000 environmental workers (Lotspeich and Chen 1997:52–4). One can also assume that the majority of the managers are scientific and technical professionals. What about these new scholar-officials or the PMC of the Party as people? What do they say about their work? The president and the vice president of a judicial school can give us some idea of the new generation of cadres from an intellectual background. Both said they were intellectuals promoted to leadership positions. They observed how intellectuals made a difference in government:

> Intellectual cadres have made a lot of changes in reforming the political and administrative management. They make better use of the loans from the World Bank for education, and they arrange the promotion of other intellectuals to important positions. They bring with them a new way of thinking. The major cadres of our provincial government, for example, are all intellectuals. While they may look as though they are following the tradition, they are in fact doing something quite different. (Interviews with Chang Zhanjun and Li Jizhang 1996:2.32–3)

This is echoed by another Party cadre, the president of a city Party school:

> Large numbers of intellectuals have taken leadership positions, due to the government policy of promoting younger people with professional knowledge. They bring with them new ways of thinking and of doing

> things. They are quite different from the worker-peasant cadres in their leadership styles. Compared with the former president of the school, I emphasize punctuality, rules and regulations, efficient use of time at meetings, and systemic reforms. (Interview with Qi Ruisu 1996:2.24)

We hear clearly Weber's emphasis on formal rationality in modernity. At the TV factory I visited, the Party secretary of the Research Institute told me how he worked to reduce tension and dissatisfaction among his engineers. He had at times been successful, an example of Weber's substantive rationality:[18]

> I act as a bridge between the engineers and the directors of the institute. In order to better serve the rank and file engineers, I have moved my desk from the director's office to an office across the hallway so that I can have some privacy for meeting with other engineers. The directors decide how much each engineer is going to get in bonuses and I deal with any discontent that may arise and try to find a balance. When I go to the Conference of Factory Workers' Delegates, I always raise the consciousness of the workers about the value of the intellectuals in my institute and call for better pay and better housing for my engineers. (Interview with Yu Junjie 1994:1.42)

While there do seem to be many advantages to intellectuals becoming administrators, Chang and Li also commented that some intellectuals had alienated themselves from the masses once they were in leadership positions. As administrators, these intellectuals could be much worse than the worker-peasant cadres in the past; they knew much better how to persecute other intellectuals. Chang and Li, however, did not want to give specific examples. Those feelings were also reflected in the following remarks by a journalist (Interview with Zuo Anliang 1994: 1.7): "Intellectuals have a double character: they either possess an independent personality or they depend on certain political forces. Once they merge with the bureaucracy, they can make life even more miserable for the rank-and-file." Power can indeed corrupt, no matter how much expertise one can boast in his or her field.

Chang and Li believed they themselves were following the intellectual tradition of uprightness and fairness. For example, because they were not afraid of losing their leadership positions, they could speak their minds whenever they wished. They did not consider themselves first when new housing was allocated; they would wait in line with other faculty. They cited other cadres who actually put up housing complexes for their own use!

Chang and Li were confident that the Chinese political system was being transformed from a feudal to a democratic one. They had high hopes that an electoral democracy was not too far away. One of them, for example, was recommended by the majority of the teachers to be the president of the school and was confirmed by the Party. But they also believed that the pace of political reform was lagging far behind economic reform. This affected the way in which the school operated. They pointed out, for example, unequal opportunities available to graduates depending entirely on whether or not they had connections. In the building of faculty housing they had to resort to dubious measures to get the work done. It meant spending 10,000 yuan bribing the people in charge in order to save hundreds of thousands. These were among the things they had to do even if they disliked doing them.

This last point is interesting since it touches on the issue of the dual personality. While the *Qiu Shi* articles give us the impression of organic intellectuals strictly following the Party line, the presidents of the judicial school present a picture of the everyday problems facing an official. Most importantly, their examples show us the dilemmas they confront when caught between what they believe is the right thing to do and what they *have* to do. The lack of articles in *Qiu Shi* on the rule of law and more meaningful political reforms does not necessarily mean that its writers did not believe in them. It simply shows what they were required to write at the time. Regardless of their beliefs, however, organic intellectuals do perform Party and government functions and create the Party's ideology, as the *Qiu Shi* articles show.

We have met a cross-section of organic intellectuals, from those in leadership positions to journalists, economists, and other theorists. There are also think tanks that are supposed to help the government in making decisions. Two organizations are most notable: the democratic parties and the academies of social sciences. We will examine them at both the national and provincial levels, and discuss the problems that hamper their efforts.

Members of the Democratic Parties

In China today, there are seven democratic "parties" and a number of other non-Communist groups, whose members are all intellectuals and professionals. They are, however, under the leadership of the CCP. Some of their members, including chairs and vice-chairs, are also CCP members (Seymour 1992:289, 307–8). Together with the CCP, they form the Chinese Political Consultative Conference, or the United Front. Their participation in, and discussion of, politics *(can zheng yi zheng)* are limited largely to research on various issues concerning the country's social and economic development. At the time of the founding of the People's Republic of China (PRC), the minor parties had already abandoned the thought they once had of functioning as an independent political force and they had already begun to work as think tanks of the CCP (Mazur 1997:57, 64–5). As Fei Xiaotong (1992:312) of the China Democratic League (DL) says, the democratic parties are supposed to provide "intellectual support for decision-making." Of course, it is the Party that is the decision maker. The Association for the Promotion of Democracy (APD) is composed of intellectuals in education, culture, and publishing. The chair wants the organization to do a good job as a think tank *(zhi nang tuan);* to that end, they have made numerous proposals for educational reform (Li Dejin 1997). Zhigong Party is composed of overseas Chinese who have returned home, and they focus on research for the government and suggestions to the CCP concerning overseas Chinese and foreign exchange (Li Dejin and Liu Quan 1997). Jiusan Xueshe is a party of intellectuals in science and technology, and their research focuses on reforms in the systems of science and technology as well as the reasonable use of China's vast lands (Liu Quan and Li Dejin 1997).

We learned in chapter 1 that decision makers in the government follow different principles than do organic intellectuals. In fact, government decisions are based more often on politics than on research, at least in the social sciences, as Hu Angang's example shows. So, while some of the suggestions from intellectuals are adopted by the government, many of their suggestions go nowhere. Professor Fan provided another example. Fan himself was, at the time of our interview, on the faculty of the chemistry department. He had just completed a ten-year term as the provost of the university. Even more importantly, he had been serving as deputy director of the Education Commission of the City Political Consultative Conference. The conference commanded a great deal of respect. It advised the government on issues such as housing reform, health care, tax reform, and environmental protection. The university also held a meeting every two months to ask its members for their recommendations on college affairs. However, as to the percentage of the opinions adopted, Fan could only add that it was hard to say (Interview 1994:1.12). Obviously, the situation was not optimistic.

As for the political involvement of the democratic parties, Fei Xiaotong, the sociologist and former chair of the DL, put it in a "humble" way when he was asked why an independent party had to be under the leadership of another party:

> This is a Chinese characteristic. We democratic party members, especially those of the Democratic League, are researchers in our own fields, and some are professors and teachers. But we have one thing in common, that is we all hope that our country will be prosperous. We participate in politics, but do not do politics. My own humble opinion is that participation means to help the CCP, but not for the purpose of replacing the CCP to govern the country. We don't have the means of running the country. We are teachers, and don't have the ability to take care of state affairs *[qu guan guojia da shi guan bu lai de].* (1996:104)

Fei's remarks seem to explain the present function of the democratic parties, but his reason for not wanting to replace the CCP seems to be unconvincing. Certainly, the DL's aim was "to do" politics when it was founded in the 1940s. At that time, it was actively and openly competing with the CCP and Guomindang (GMD) (Xu Jilin 1997b:42).[19] Nor was it so humble during the Hundred Flowers Movement, when its members wanted to find a democratic way to govern the country (Ye Yonglie 1988:76). As one of the founding members of the party, Fei knew better than anyone else what its aims had been. One could sense in his reply the tension between the democratic parties and the CCP, a tension that erupted during the Hundred Flowers Movement. Fei probably exhibits most acutely the issue of the split personality.[20]

Yet there is no denying that these high-level technical or humanistic intellectuals can sometimes show a great sense of social responsibility, even if they may at times yield to the powers that be. Fei Xiaotong (1995) recalled that when at his birthday party somebody asked him what he had wanted to do all his life, he said without hesitation, *zhi zai fu min,* "to make our people rich." We cannot say he did not have a sense of social responsibility. Wang Ganchang, a nuclear physicist, had said in 1961 that he would devote all his life to the invention of a nuclear bomb if he was called on by Mao and Zhou Enlai to do so (Zhang Heping and Zhong Peiji 1997). They called, and he responded. Yet, in 1995, he joined other intellectuals in signing a petition to the government for more tolerance toward those involved in the democratic movement of spring 1989.

How do we evaluate these intellectuals? The argument has many sides. One might argue that they could do more but choose not to. Liu Binyan observes that when he was in the United States in 1982, someone asked him how much freedom the Chinese intellectuals had. He answered that it was difficult to say. Some had 50 percent freedom but they were able to stretch it to 70 percent; others were given 70 percent of freedom but would voluntarily reduce it to 30 percent. Until 1994, Liu Binyan believed that the intellectuals were being suppressed. Later on, however, he changed his opinion. He now believes that since the Cultural Revolution, the status of intellectuals has risen. They are no longer the "stinky ninth," following eight other classes including landlords, rich peasants, reactionaries, capitalists, rightists, and other "bad eggs." Instead, they have become a group that has benefited from the reform: They have become famous and have been given various freedoms, rights, and benefits. Those who have been absorbed into managerial positions have shown a particularly high level of contentment and have actually begun to parrot the regime in their own speeches, according to Liu. These include Li Zehou, Zhang Xianliang, Wang Meng, Liu Xinwu, Han Shaogong, and Liu Zaifu. Zhang Xianliang, for example, belittled Wei Jingsheng and other democratic movement figures in his Hong Kong speeches. Liu remarks that the Chinese government probably did not ask him to make those statements, although it no doubt appreciated them. But there are also many intellectuals who try to speak with different voices, their own voices, like Bai Hua, Ye Wenfu, and Jiang Zilong (Interview 1997:3.10).

The reason for the existence of the volunteer mouthpieces of the regime, according to Liu Binyan, is that these intellectuals have benefited from the reform and are no longer in touch with the reality that engulfs the workers and peasants. Zhang, for example, is the manager of three companies, although he is still considered a dissident in the West. Wang Meng and Li Zehou are in similar easy circumstances. In Liu's eyes, they have become obstacles to democratic reform rather than the advocates they once were (Interview with Liu Binyan 1997:3.10).

But Liu Binyan may well be exaggerating the loyalty of these intellectuals to the Party. For example, Li Zehou was an establishment intellectual who honestly tried to work within the system. Nonetheless, he was critical in believing that the arts of human creativity are the real motor of history rather than Marx's material labor (see Cheek 1999: 116; Cauvel 1999). He was critical as well when he advocated *xi ti zhong yong*. By saying, "Western learning as the essence, and Chinese learning for practical purposes," Li did not mean to put Western culture over Chinese, but rather he sought to challenge the traditional culturalist conceit exemplified by Zhang Zhidong's *zhong ti xi yong,* that is, *Chinese* learning as the essence, and *Western* learning for practical purposes. As Li's books on Chinese aesthetics and traditional philosophy show, he finds traditional Chinese learning relevant to, but not a replacement for, contemporary thought in both the East and West. He also believed that the Chinese enlightenment had come to a premature end because of the concern for foreign aggression (see Chong 1999:120). All of these beliefs put him into the critical camp. As we follow his perhaps sometimes conflicting behavior, we should always keep in mind the dual personality suffered by most intellectuals.

Furthermore, as Cheek (2001) points out, "The slur against Wei Jingsheng is just as likely based on intellectual arrogance [which we identify generically in chapter 6 as the flaw of the intellectual class] as on being the unwitting mouthpiece of the regime." Li Zehou, on the other hand, is "much more likely an organic intellectual to the middle class with a dual personality tension to make a big cultural contribution . . . while sustaining a decent life in Boulder, Colorado."

First of all, not all of the intellectuals are organic to the Party. Neoconservatives, for example, are not, even though they may appear to speak for the Party. Second, even if they are organic intellectuals, many have a sense of social responsibility and do attempt to function as the conscience of society. We also discussed some of them in chapter 4 in our discussion of critical intellectuals. This applies to our "mouthpieces," as well as to Fei Xiaotong and other democratic party members, and to economists, reporters, writers, and scholars in general. However, our description demonstrates that their efforts are hampered by the official positions they are in. That is further proof that the dual or even split personality is hard to avoid and difficult to deal with.

Researchers in Academies of Social Sciences and Other Research Organizations

There is another formal group of organic intellectuals: those who work at the academies of social sciences and at other research institutes and organizations affiliated with the government. Their job is to help the government research and design economic and social reforms. Chinese Academy of Social Sciences (CASS) publishes yearly reports on the social, political, and economic conditions of the country to help the government in its decision making. Some of our data in the section on class formation are taken from their reports. In fact, researchers from other government departments are increasingly joining in the effort, as some of the authors we cited demonstrate. For example, while Zhang Houyi, Fan Ping, Li Peilin, and Xu Xinxin are from CASS, Zhu Yong is from the State Council's Center for Research on Development, Yan Yaojun and Wang Jie from the Tianjin Academy of Social Sciences, Mo Rong from the Research Institute of Labor Science of the Ministry of Labor and Social Security, and Wen Shengtang from the General Bureau of Anti-Corruption and Anti-Bribery of the Supreme People's Procuratorate.

One group of sociologists from a provincial academy of social sciences, for example, was researching the cultural markets in the provincial capital. They found that the factors leading to the development of the city's dance halls included traditions of engaging in sex and pleasure *(sheng se quan ma),* spending the flexible money available to factory managers, and bringing in large numbers of unemployed women from other provinces such as Hunan, Jiangsu, and those in the northeast. The group's research was designed to help the provincial government control the "cultural" market in the city (Interview with Wang Youhao 1996:2.22).

Another sociologist, Professor Wu, had similar success. He has been actively involved in the development of a new financial district in the city. His contributions include devising social welfare programs for the elderly and writing textbooks on a pioneer course in social work. In the 1990s, he organized an annual conference of the Chinese Sociological Association in the city, arranging to have it funded by the Development Bureau. The funding permission came with a condition, however. The only theme of the conference must be social and economic development in the city. That may be another example of the limitations organic intellectuals suffer carrying out their research (Interview with Wu Dong 1994:1.13).

A city government policy researcher, Liu Xiang, reported that the research office, which was supposed to have twenty-five researchers, had only seventeen at the time. Their work was not as formal as that of the academy of social sciences, but their research topics had more direct relevance to what the government was trying to do. Topics included the responsibility system for industrial enterprises; problems arising from buying land from peasants for industrial development; housing, and construction. They also did surveys, largely on economic issues, although sometimes they added research on social problems. Some of their findings were circulated among government officials. According to Liu's own estimate, the city government adopted about half of their proposals. Researchers were permitted to publish their findings in the mass media, but only under their own names. They could not claim to speak for the government (Interview 1996:2.31). In any case, as another sociologist reported, with the number of journals dwindling it was getting more and more difficult to publish their findings (Interview with Zhou Weiwan 1996:2.35).

Sociologists in another city reported other problems. They said that most of their research projects were assigned by the authorities, but the city simply did not provide enough funding for the work they asked for. So most researchers just got by. The subjects of their research did not take it seriously either. These sociologists lived in the hope that someday there would be more freedom and more financial support, so they could produce really meaningful research (Interviews with Xiao Guimei and Cheng Kejiang 1994:1.6, 1.8).

As one of them commented,

> Our institute helps the government with some policy research. But after a while, you feel it is pointless. It looks as if it is very important, and if one or two points are adopted, you are very happy. But they [the government] don't look at it that way. Besides, there are many constraints, and they don't give you much funding for the projects either. It is difficult to get even several thousand yuan. (Interview with Xiao Guimei 1994:1.6)

There you have another example of the dilemma faced by organic intellectuals. They get paid to work on government assignments, but they still long to do meaningful independent research. Unfortunately, since government decisions are influenced by politics more often than by their research, frustrated sociologists, as well as other organic intellectuals, frequently fall prey to a split personality.

There have been some interesting developments concerning the status of the academies of social sciences. So far they have functioned as the think tanks of the state and provincial governments. And they are still employees of the state and are getting paid by the state. But recently there has been talk about letting them earn their own living. Take CASS for example. It is a national-level professional research organization *(guojia ji zhuanye yanjiu jigou)*. It does not belong to the State Council, but the state appoints a high-status official to be its head. Although one would think that CASS is a think tank of the state, it seems that with the exception of a few institutes like the Institute of Taiwan Studies, the researchers often seek their own funding and do their own investigation, fairly independently. Since the state does not seem to be always humored by their research, it is possible that it will develop into an independent think tank in the future.

Organic Intellectuals to Private Entrepreneurs

We discussed the bourgeoisified intellectuals in chapter 4. Although they tend to be unattached to the Party and state, many of them can be considered organic to the bourgeoisie, helping to build the bourgeois class. Some have even become part of the class of private entrepreneurs, including writers like Zhang Xianliang, Wang Shuo, and Hu Wanchun, and scholars like our interviewee Li Ping. But most, like Cheng Hong and Li Guan, have worked for the bourgeois class as its managers, researchers, or other kinds of representatives.

The Old Left charges that the private entrepreneurs have even developed a group of theorists and economists who advocate privatization for the class (Cong Ming 1999 [1994]:323). These specialists have become the class representatives and have gotten hefty fees for their work. They become what the Old Left calls *dakuan lilun jia* (wealthy theorists) and *dakuan jingji xue jia* (wealthy economists). Although the Old Left's charge is overly exaggerated, the private entrepreneurs do appear to have won support from many intellectuals, who have become, as a result, organic intellectuals advocating their interests.[21] (See figure 5.3 for an illustration of intellectuals changing positions.) When professors and other experts apply to work in township enterprises, they probably work for private entrepreneurs. When they are hired as technical experts or legal counsel in a company, they work for private entrepreneurs as organic intellectuals. In a sense, the liberal intellectuals we have discussed in chapter 3 in the section on critical intellectuals can be seen as working for private entrepreneurs but only from a distance and to a much lesser extent.

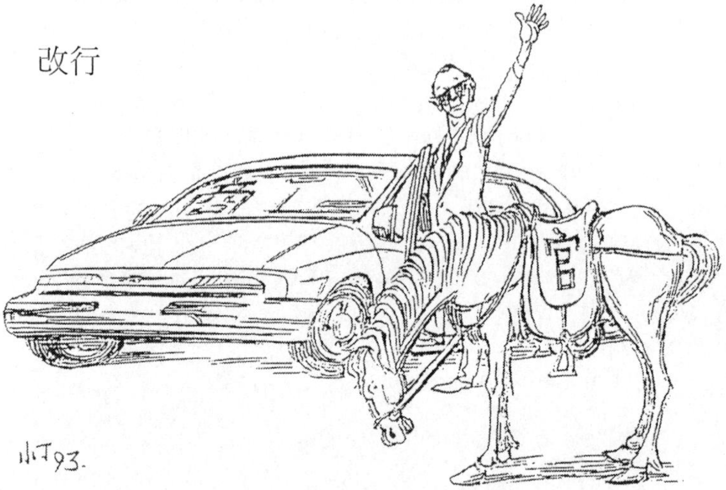

Figure 5.3 Changing Jobs *(Gai hang)*

Notes: On the horse is written "officialdom," and on the car is "business." Intellectuals do, however, become organic to other classes as well.

Source: Ding Cong 1999 (Vol. 3), p. 59.

The most important group of intellectuals organic to the private entrepreneurs, however, are the professional-managerial class. By definition, the PMC manages daily business and production activities, just as Cheng and Li do. And they manage the relationship between labor and capital as well. Above all, they manage the enterprise's relationship with the state. However, as we have seen, private enterprises are clients of the socialist corporatist state. In their relationship with the latter, private entrepreneurs and their PMC are not Western-style interest groups and do not have real political and economic autonomy. Typically, then, the PMC in China is not politically inclined. In advancing their interests, they adopt individualist strategies rather than collective schemes, just as their bosses do (Pearson 1997:4, 101, 108).

This does not mean, however, that they are ignorant about politics, or lack the desire for more prominent roles in the push for more political and economic reforms. Most of Pearson's interviewees, for example, believed that the new business elite as a group will have more power in the future. They cited the example of Shanghai Mayor Xu Kuangdi, who had been a member of the PMC. Some did favor greater democratization

(Pearson 1997:92–5, 105–6). In fact, although it is unlikely that the PMC and the private entrepreneurs will become the primary agent for a more progressive form of state-society relationships, they may ally with other social forces, such as liberal or even critical intellectuals, as well as organic intellectuals to the party-state. This joint pressure for more political democratization and economic liberalization would further change the state and society relations (pp. 160–5).[22]

It would also be interesting to trace the development of professionalism among the PMC, including technical experts or legal counsels who work for private companies. Further research on this and other issues concerning organic intellectuals, including the PMC is needed. We will, however, touch on these issues when we discuss their contradictory class locations, their dual or split personalities, and their politics in general at the end of this chapter.

Organic Intellectuals of the Middle Class

Theoretically, every class could develop its own organic intellectuals. Since a large part of the middle class consists of intellectuals, for instance, professionals such as lawyers, doctors, professors, and journalists, it might be more fruitful for us to talk about whether such intellectuals can form a class, and if so, who might be their organic intellectuals. That will be our major topic in chapter 6.

Organic Intellectuals of the Working Class

What about organic intellectuals of the working class? In what way are they involved in solving the social and political crises in the daily lives of the working class? They help workers form a collective consciousness, thus challenging the dominant class, the Party cadres, and the emerging entrepreneur class. When one considers the revolutionary tradition of China's working class and their sheer numbers, one can see why working-class independence is an explosive topic. Such movements are not allowed to exist; they cannot even be discussed openly inside China. Still, some have tried.

During the 1989 movement, Han Dongfang and others organized the Beijing Workers' Independent Union, and Li Jinjin, a Ph.D. law student from Beijing University, helped by writing its manifesto and serving as its legal advisor (Ya Yi 1993; for workers' involvement in the democracy movement, see Walder 1991). Li was later sentenced to prison for two years. Zhou Guoqiang, a lawyer and poet, engaged in dissident activities and even organized a workers' strike after the June 4 massacre. In 1994, Zhou was sentenced to three years in prison for further dissident activities (*Xingdao Daily,* December 23, 1994). Han Dongfang is still operating from Hong Kong, as we discussed in chapter 3.

Many are still trying to organize independent workers' movements, although they are in constant danger of imprisonment. In 1997, immediately after China signed the International Covenant for Economic, Social, and Cultural Rights, Xu Wenli and Qin Yongming tried to organize a workers' union in Beijing but were stopped. In January 1998 in Shanxi, Li Qingxi was arrested for trying to organize a workers' union (*Press Freedom Guardian,* January 30, 1998). In July 1998 in Hunan province, Zhang Shanguang was taken away by the police for the same effort. In Xiangtan, Hunan, some dissidents who were merely discussing organizing an unemployed workers' rights league were detained. In the same month, Fan Yiping of Canton was sentenced to three years in prison. His sins: helping Wang Xizhe, another dissident, escape China, and supporting an independent workers' movement (*Press Freedom Guardian,* July 31, 1998).

As Li Jinjin points out, the chief goals of this Chinese free union movement will be to protect the workers' interests and to negotiate between labor and capital. Before they can unionize, however, they will have to fight for and win the right to do so. Since the CCP constantly prevents them from organizing, the free union movement necessarily becomes a fight-for-democracy movement as well (see Ya Yi 1993). It is quite likely that the workers' movement will develop its own organic intellectuals.

History has already taught us a lot about the relationship between intellectuals and the working class. In chapter 1, we discussed the efforts of Communist intellectuals like Liu Shaoqi, Deng Zhongxia, and Zhang Guotao to organize labor movements in Republican China. They became labor leaders. In this chapter we have noted that today the All-China Federation of Trade Unions (ACFTUs) has real potential for unionizing Chinese workers. Back in the 1950s, Liu Shaoqi actually proposed that union and Party cadres join striking workers as a way of regaining worker sympathy (Perry 1997:237). At that time, the ACFTU leaders in Beijing and the labor leaders in Shanghai were, at the very least, sympathetic to the striking workers. The director of the ACFTU once said, "A so-called disturbance (or *suowei naoshi)* arises only because of *something* disturbing *[jiushi yinwei youshi cai naoqilai]*" (p. 247). Besides, if the Women's Federation can stand up and protect women to some degree from the onslaughts of the market economy, as we see in Wang Zheng's (2000) report, an organization like the ACFTUs should not be totally helpless. They may also become labor leaders.

On the other hand, it is possible that workers may stand on their own, as many of them did in 1957 when they organized their own *strike waves:* staging protests, sit-ins, demonstrations, and so on without the help of the intellectuals (Perry 1997).[23] Workers may even organize their own labor unions, as some did in 1989. As Ching Kwan Lee (2000: 55–7) also reports, in the post-Tiananmen years, a number of underground labor organizations and initiatives have also sprung up.[24] Despite some efforts by workers to act without intellectual guidance, the alliance between the two groups remains a natural force. This is especially true when there is a *general strike* involving issues of wider scope. Indeed, dissident intellectuals already account for the majority of the organizers of today's labor movements, according to Lee. In such cases, intellectuals may become either labor leaders or organic intellectuals. Independent movements like these, if allowed, may become an important balancing power in the Chinese polity.

Thus, in a future class society labor unions may become representatives of workers, and knowledge workers may become their organic intellectuals. If that happens, organic intellectuals will inevitably experience dual and split personalities. In the 1950s, intellectuals in the labor unions in the United States complained that they were there just for window dressing. "Economists, publicists, editors, education directors, fair practice representatives and (less often) engineers, lawyers—all in their candid moments—define their functions or those of their colleagues as 'just for show,' 'just fashion,' 'we're there for front'" (Wilensky 1956:35). As we mentioned in chapter 1, dual and split personalities are the perennial lot of intellectuals, caused by value differences with the union officials as in the example we cited, in the United States. Nevertheless, organic intellectuals do their jobs, performing important functions such as building legal cases for labor movements, mediating relations between unions and the outside world, and helping with internal control. They may even influence a labor boss without her ever realizing it (pp. 104–5, 195, 238–9). It will be interesting to investigate how the dynamics play out between organic intellectuals and the labor leadership. For now, it is simply interesting to see how and whether the former can become the latter.

Organic Intellectuals of the Peasants

Do peasants have organic intellectuals? Sometimes, peasants do find experts to help them with their social movements. In Xi'an, Shaanxi, for example, Ma Wenlin, a legal counsel, volunteered to help five thousand peasants from the Tuoerxiang *xiang* (the administrative district below the county) of Zizhou County in 1999. Representing the peasants, he appealed to the Beijing authorities for less taxes and for punishment of cadres who physically abused peasants. He was sentenced to prison for his advocacy, but legal experts in Shaanxi are appealing his case (*Press Freedom Guardian,* February 28, 2000). It is possible that the peasants will both produce their own political entrepreneurs, as we already discussed in this chapter, and develop their organic intellectuals, or movement intellectuals. For now, not too many intellectuals can be found speaking for the peasants. A member of the China Peasants' and Workers' Democratic Party, one of the democratic parties and groups (DPGs), lamented that peasants, who constitute 80 percent of the population, simply do not have representatives or organizations speaking for them (*Zhongguo Jingji Shibao* or China Economic Times [1996] 1999:318). In fact, the relationship between intellectuals and the workers and peasants is not an easy one.[25]

An Uneasy Relationship: Intellectuals vs. Workers and Peasants

There are in fact reports of this uneasy relationship between intellectuals and the workers and peasants. Perry and Fuller (1991:669), in their article "China's Long March to Democracy," recorded that workers who participated in the 1989 movement felt alienated by the students' elitism. Kelliher (1993:388–9), in his article, "Keeping Democracy Safe from the Masses," also points out that some democracy activists in the 1980s wrote off workers and openly disdained peasants. Wang Dan, for example, thought that democracy must be absorbed by students and intellectuals before it could be spread to workers. Many movement intellectuals equated the evils of the Party to peasant consciousness *(nongmin yishi):* "blind worship of leaders, self-importance and self-pity, suspiciousness and pettiness, short-sightedness, manipulation of power for personal ends, and intolerance for anyone with an independent point of view." Some, like Wang Shan, the author of *Di San zhi Yanjing Kan Zhongguo,* or *Viewing China through the Third Eye* (1994), even saw the peasantry as a potentially destructive force driven solely by a "get-rich" mentality (Liu Kang 1996:217).

A quote from Fang Lizhi is telling: "If you really go into the villages and take a look around, you'll find a class of people with no culture, who have never received any education—all those peasants subject to the influence of tradition. With their mentality, you'll find it awfully hard to give them any democratic consciousness" (quoted in Kelliher 1993:389; see also Calhoun 1991:121).[26] Confucianism, of which intellectuals are inheritors, is predicated on the principle of inequality as not only a social necessity but also conformity to a natural order of things (Grieder 1981:5–7). Although it also emphasizes the importance of the people, Confucianism does not in substance value them as equals. Intellectuals have inherited this cultural tradition. The elitism shown by intellectuals in their ambivalence toward workers and their hostility toward peasants may make success for the democracy movement more difficult, although as we have seen in Li and O'Brien (1996), the peasants' democratic movements may have a lot to teach intellectuals.

One point is indisputable: intellectuals and the working class, that is, workers and peasants, will eventually find that they need each other. This is especially true of the democracy movement. The Western experience shows that "no progressive social change is possible without the participation of a vital, powerful, and inclusive labor movement," as Foner (1997:56) points out in his article, "Intellectuals and Labor." Labor, on the one hand, relies on studies by some scientists of unemployment, underemployment, poverty, old age, and working conditions. It certainly needs more organizers who can interpret these studies, articulate labor's interests, and form successful strategies. Intellectuals, on the other hand, need to overcome their elitism and participate in the working-class movements. The CCP successfully organized workers and peasants in its revolution. The contemporary intellectuals have yet to learn to do the same, but on an equal basis, so as to avoid the eventual appropriation of the working-class movements. Some will have to serve as their organic intellectuals, rather than as the CCP did, taking over as their leaders.

Like their counterparts with the Party and the bourgeoisie, these organic intellectuals will also experience split personalities. On the one hand, they are expected to be, and in fact they are needed as, advocates of the working class, but on the other hand, they are also self-important intellectuals (see also Montagna 1977). If history is any guide, the Chinese intellectuals' experience in organizing peasants and workers, with Mao and his colleagues as the latest example, will affect the future of worker and peasant organizations.

Conclusions: Contradictory Class Locations of Organic Intellectuals

In this chapter, we have discussed the formation of classes in China today, including the cadre class of the Party and the state, the class of private entrepreneurs, the middle class, the working class, and the peasants. We have also discussed the intellectuals organic to these classes. We have touched on the different politics of these intellectuals. In this concluding part, we will look at some common characteristics of organic intellectuals, including what Wright (1985) calls their "contradictory class locations," the kind of ethics they follow, and their "dual and split personalities."

China has developed a multi-economic system that is a mixture of state-owned and private economies. The combination yields two systems of production: statist and capitalist, according to Wright's model, or socialist corporatism, as we discussed earlier in this chapter. The multi-economic system has further produced a multilayered class structure. As we saw in chapter 1, it is a basic characteristic of the intellectual to want to choose among organic, critical, and unattached positions. Furthermore, as we have shown, intellectuals are free to affiliate with any class they choose (Mannheim 1936:158). Here a challenge arises for these intellectuals. Their intellectual traits or ideological dispositions can be so different from that of the class they choose that they face various ethic conflicts. They want to follow the ethic of responsibility, and they have joined the class to help effect social change. They find in practice that they frequently have to compromise their integrity. Yet, they still want to be there. Organic intellectuals are a professional-managerial class in contradictory class locations.

The PMC's contradictory class location: on the one hand, it is employed by the Party and/or by capital, with authority to manage and control labor. It is, therefore, 'objectively antagonistic' to the working class, to use the Ehrenreichs' (1979:17) term. On the other hand, the PMC's reformist ideas may be blocked or modified by their bosses, who may feel their own interests threatened (p. 22). However, to remain in the power structure, following the ethic of responsibility and hoping to effect social change, these intellectuals have to sacrifice at least some reformist ideas and integrity. This conflict may lead to a dual or split personality. The PMC member is the boss, yet not the boss. We saw this clearly in some of our interviewees, such as the manager of the alarm equipment factory, and our journalists, who must weigh what they can and cannot say in their news reports. But it can be detected even in those who have become integrated into higher levels of bureaucracy, such as Wu Han and Deng Tuo of the former Beijing Communist Party Committee, and Tian Jiaying and Zhou Yang, whom we met in chapter 2 on intellectuals in the Mao and Deng eras.

If the Ehrenreichs (1979) view the PMC in the relationship of domination, Wright views them from the perspective of exploitation. We know that the bureaucratic ruling class exploits the working class through planned appropriation of its production, and through its distribution of surplus to recipients on the basis of hierarchy. A prime example is the privileges and benefits enjoyed by the cadres. The principal asset of the cadre class is organization, or the coordination of productive activities within and across labor processes (1985:79–80). The capitalists, in comparison, exploit the workers through the market exchanges of labor power and commodities. Their principal asset is wealth, that is, the means of production.

As professionals and working managers, organic intellectuals are also *exploited* by the bureaucratic ruling class (BRC) or capital because they lack organizational and capitalistic assets. But they also do their own *exploiting* because they have skill assets and they use them to exploit those who do not have them (Wright 1985:87). That is why they are in contradictory class locations. Think of the sometimes huge benefits technical intellectuals get from working for government or corporations: high salaries, expensive houses, cars, and so forth. On March 9, 1992, three technical intellectuals were each given an award of several hundred thousand yuan and an Audi car for their technical and scientific contributions to the development of Zhuhai City, Guangdong Province. It was the highest cash award ever given to intellectuals. The recipients, of course, said that they had never dreamed of anything like this and that they were the luckiest of all Chinese intellectuals. "The time has come for thousands upon thousands of Chinese intellectuals and technical personnel to develop their full potential," they said, while surrounded by reporters and news cameramen (Liu Zeming et al. 1993: 140–4). The money had to come from somewhere and somebody had to pay for the Audis. You can be sure it wasn't the bureaucrats. These organic intellectuals are apparently in Wright's contradictory class locations: exploiting and being exploited at the same time.

To dominate and to be dominated, to exploit and to be exploited: that is the contradiction of the organic intellectuals. It makes their politics anything but simple. Resolute support of today's economic policies is understandable since they are the direct beneficiaries of the reform; that is where their interests lie. But they may also want a more level playing field so that they can compete more fairly. That means they may support some sort of political reform. The authors of the book *Crossing Swords,* Ma Licheng and Ling Zhijun, are a good example of this mental conflict. This would also apply to most of the journalists, economists, scholar-officials, democratic party members, researchers attached to CASS, and other organic intellectuals discussed in this chapter.

The contradiction also leads to their dual or split personality. As intellectuals, they want to be the conscience of society, yet they are constrained by the positions they are in. They want to order, but they have to follow orders. They can withdraw from their positions close to the power, but the latter's pull is just too strong for them to do so. They end up with a dual or split personality.

Organic intellectuals do not just work for the Party and the new bourgeoisie. They may also work for the working class, that is, the workers and peasants, and for the intellectual class itself. As both the Nationalist and Communist revolutions show, Chinese intellectuals do have a long tradition of merging with workers and peasants in their *social* movements. Despite the sometimes uneasy relationships, they do form what Perry and Fuller (1991:680) call "cross-class alliances." Since the working class and peasants do not yet have the support of organic intellectuals, we need not go into detail at this level. We can still assume, however, that they are served by some kind of professional-managerial class, albeit only in their social movements. These intellectuals are also subject to the dual or split personality.

They may also be organic to other popular movements, such as feminist movements and environmental movements, by helping these groups articulate their interests, goals, and identities. Once they become organic intellectuals to a certain class or movement, their *politics,* too, will merge with the politics of that class or movement. When that happens, they may be following an ethic of responsibility, but they have put themselves into a contradictory class location as well, where they may well risk the dual or split personality.

To sum up, intellectuals organic to the political and economic elite help these dominating classes dictate where the country goes and how it deals with its modernization crises. But they are helpers only. They play important political roles, but they seldom play *independent* political roles. Hu Qiaomu was dubbed "the pen of the CCP Central Committee," or *zhong gong zhongyang yizhi bi* (Ye Yonglie 1994:2). It was meant as a compliment; he was filling an indispensable role. But for most of Hu's life, he was just that, no more and no less.[27]

In an open society, the political role of the organic intellectual is so important that the battle of discourses may seem to be largely among organic intellectuals representing various classes and movements, and its outcome will inevitably be reflected in changes in political procedures. The debate between the New Left and the liberals on modernity, which we discussed in chapter 3, is a good example, with one leaning toward the working class, the other toward the dominant classes. Obviously the path of China's development, and the ways chosen to solve its crises of modernization, depend largely on that battle. The critical intellectuals such as Xu Jilin and his comrades, on the other hand, will be likely to function as the referees or mediators, and the professionals will be a reservoir of resources on which both critical and organic intellectuals can draw.

Chapter Six

Intellectuals as a Class

> If a craftsman wants to do his job well,
> he has to sharpen his tools first.
> *(Gong yu shan qi shi, bi xian li qi qi.)*
> —Confucius, *Analects:* 15:10

So far, we have examined the three strata of intellectuals, critical, unattached (bourgeoisified and professional), and organic. Fragmented as they are, can they be a class? In chapter 5, we described the various classes and pointed out that with the exception of the cadre class of the Party and state, all classes are in the process of formation. That is especially the case with the intellectual class. This chapter will examine first the arguments for and against intellectuals as a class. We will then elaborate the ways in which Chinese intellectuals can form a class. Finally, we will see why it is bound to be flawed, but a class nonetheless.

Are Intellectuals a Class?

Arguments Against "Intellectuals as a Class"

Parsons (1968, 1969) believes that intellectuals have performed chiefly normative functions in the past. He cites the efforts of the Chinese literati to systematize and canonize both their cultural view of the world and the rules of behavior for both ruler and ruled. Today's intellectuals have evolved into functional professionals because modernity requires that intellectual disciplines in the humanities, sciences, and social sciences develop applied professions that can be incorporated into and serve capitalist (re)production. In his essay entitled "Professions and Social Structure," Parsons (1954) emphasizes the common elements between professions and business in terms of rationality (scientific investigation and normative standards), specificity of function (professional authority that recognizes technical competence in a limited field), and universalism (standards and criteria independent of particular social relationships).[1] By emphasizing the normative functions of intellectuals and their universalism, Parsons also denies them politically independent status. He does not admit that they may one day play an active political role and even contend for power with other classes in society, even though he does acknowledge that the professional complex "has begun to dominate the contemporary scene in such a way as to render obsolescent the primacy of the old issues of political authoritarianism and capitalistic exploitation" (Parsons 1968:549).

Parsons's understanding of the context of intellectual formation echoes Weber's (1946:299) understanding of modernity, which is characterized by the domination of instrumental rationality. Stable and exhaustive rules, laws, administrative regulations, office hierarchy, and impersonality all characterize the modern scene, where expertise plays a key role. While he believes there is a close connection between the prestige of culture, symbolized by intellectuals, and the prestige of power (p. 448), as in the relationship between professionals and the rational legal power, Weber, like Parsons, stops short of saying that intellectuals as a group can play an *independent* political role. Class situation is typically determined by markets: the labor market and the commodity market. The educated strata form a status group that is characterized by social honor and styles of living, and also by their economic opportunities (pp. 300–1). But intellectuals are not an independent political power that may contend, for example, with the moneyed class. Weber's analysis of the Chinese literati clearly illustrates this point (pp. 416–44).

Neither Parsons nor Weber seems to imply that intellectuals can form a class. Daniel Bell does not agree that an intellectual class yet exists, but he does understand the genesis of the idea. In his article entitled "The New Class: A Muddled Concept," Bell (1980:149–55) delineates four historical changes that gave rise to the idea of the New Class. First, with the collapse of major right-wing, reactionary, and protofascist influences after World War II, a *liberalism* focusing on issues such as equality, racism, and imperialism became the dominant tone in the intellectual community. Second, *postindustrial values,* such as "a concern for environment, pollution, and the like" (p. 150), emerged with the socioeconomic changes of the years after 1945. These socioeconomic changes include (1) a shift from a goods-producing to a service economy; (2) expansion of a white-collar and professional-technical occupational force, rather than, as Marx had predicted, an industrial proletariat; (3) the rise of an information economy, or knowledge industries; and (4) the expansion of the nonprofit sector. The third historical change was that *education* had become one of the largest industries, and those with higher education tended to be more "liberal" on noneconomic issues and more independent in opinion. And fourth, an *adversary culture* grew, whose adherents with their subversive intention were sufficiently large to be called a class.

Despite all of these postindustrial changes, favorable though they are to knowledge workers, there is still a lack of the social structure and the *community* of interests and ideology that could make an intellectual *class*. In terms of community, Bell (1980:157–8) identifies six groups of knowledge workers in the postindustrial age. They are (1) *the intellectuals and knowledge creators* (scientists and scholars, mathematicians and economists, research physicians, and law professors); (2) *creators of culture* (novelists, painters, musicians, and critics); (3) *transmitters of culture and knowledge* (cultural and intellectual periodicals, museums, publishing houses, and libraries); (4) *news and entertainment workers* (reporters, journalists, broadcasters, filmmakers, and people in show business); (5) *appliers and transmitters of knowledge* (engineers, physicians, lawyers, teachers, and social-service workers); and (6) *managers and administrators* (in economic enterprise, public bureaucracies, and nonprofit institutions). He concludes, "there are few institutional arrangements that bring these groups together, in structural terms, as a coherent class" (p. 158).

In terms of the *interests* of knowledge workers in the postindustrial age, Bell (1980:158–9) identifies four *functional interests*—scientific and scholarly, technological (applied skills), administrative, and cultural (artistic and religious); and five *institutional ones*—economic enterprises and business firms, government (bureaucratic-administrative, and judicial), universities and research organizations, social complexes (hospitals, social service, and community organizations), and the military. He concludes, "it is not clear what the common interest of the diverse 'information and knowledge' occupations would be."

For Bell, even culture cannot make much difference in class formation. He says, for example, that cultural attitudes in the United States make not a class but a mentality: "the dominant cultural mentality in the Western world . . . is the idea of the antinomian self: the individual, not an institution, is the source of moral judgment; experience, not tradition, is the source of understanding" (1980:161). The individuals of the "new class" make up a "cultural phenomenon that mirrors the breakdown of traditional values in Western society . . . [and they are] the endpoint of a culture in disarray" (p. 162). Although Bell does not go into the issue of class consciousness or ideology, his discussion on the dominant culture seems to indicate that there is not much of the intellectual ideology or consciousness required by class formation. For the antinomian self goes in all directions. Thus, Bell concludes, there is no New Class, at least not in the United States.

Brint has studied the "new class" using quantitative data. He reports in his book *In an Age of Experts* that there has been a steady movement from social trustee professionalism to expert professionalism. We have noted Y. C. Wang's (1966) similar analysis of China's intelligentsia. Brint (1994:85–6) concludes that with the commercialization and privatization of professions, professionals are more likely to merge with businesspeople and less likely to form a new class of their own. In terms of politics, professionals are "moderately conservative on issues having to do with business, labor, and the welfare state," although they are "relatively skeptical about moral certainties and tolerant of diversity." As if to corroborate Bell, Brint says that this professional middle class does not seem to be a politically coherent stratum. He seems to agree with Bell that a new class has not yet been born.

Arguments for the "New Class"

Other scholars, however, seem to be more positive about the existence of a new class.[2] Or perhaps an "intellectual class" is both a matter of definition and one of historical development. As Aronowitz and DiFazio (1994: 179) suggest, "If they are able to constitute a community that shares a common discursive space that leads them to identify with each other independently of their subordination to capital, the designation 'intellectual' connotes a collective that is in the process of 'class' formation. They can identify independent interests and demand to share economic and political power with the conventional contending classes." For Aronowitz and DiFazio, culture is central to class formation in addition to organizing for communal action. (We discussed the importance of organization in class formation in chapter 5.) They emphasize "the centrality of culture within the formation and reproduction of class—to demonstrate that class is a project in the making and not just a form of reification . . ." (p. 292).[3]

If culture is the key to class formation, how does it affect class formation among intellectuals? Gouldner (1979:22–5) outlines two theoretical foundations of the New Class, cultural capital and the culture of critical discourse. The concept of cultural capital was first developed by Pierre Bourdieu, a French sociologist. For Bourdieu (1977:186), cultural capital refers to academic qualifications, which are "inserted into the objective relations between the system of economic production and the system producing the producers." In those relations, Bourdieu (1984: 301–4) implies, cultural capital is subordinate to economic capital. For example, he notes that the profits accrued by executives and engineers are at least partially appropriated by the economic capital. Furthermore, the political position of knowledge workers is ambivalent at best. They want to maintain a distance from ordinary workers, and in fact anxiously search for integration into the dominant class. At the same time, they feel "meritocratic indignation at being treated" by economic capital as just ordinary workers. (This reminds us of the contradictory class locations of organic intellectuals we discussed in chapter 5.) For Bourdieu, culture functions as both capital and symbolic domination (see also Eyal, Szelenyi, and Townsley 1998:60–2; Martin and Szelenyi 1987).

Following Bourdieu, Gouldner (1979:22) defines culture as an "object whose public goal is increased economic productivity but whose latent function is to increase the incomes and social control of those possessing it. In this perspective it is plain that education is as much capital as are a factory's buildings and machines." In other words, capitalization of cultural skills acquired through education provides incomes to those possessing them through wages, royalties, patents, copyrights, or credentialing. But it also provides tools for social control. Cultural capital, therefore, has an autonomous grounding. The most convincing example he gives is technical intellectuals, whose cultural capital has become as important as money capital and whose work and services capitalism cannot do without. For the postindustrial ideology "holds that productivity depends primarily on science and technology and that the society's problems are solvable on a technological basis, and with the use of educationally acquired technical competence." This ideology has provided the technical intellectuals with the power to bargain with the moneyed class and therefore power of the New Class (pp. 24–5).[4]

Gouldner's second foundation for a new class is the culture of critical discourse (CCD), which we mentioned in chapter 1 when we discussed the ideological foundations of the intellectual. CCD requires that intellectuals justify their assertions by eliciting voluntary consent, not by invoking authorities or status in society. The self-groundedness or autonomy of this new class is thus further solidified. This is the deeper structure that advances the intellectuals' candidacy as a new elite. Gouldner disagrees with Shils' proposition that intellectuals are simply disrupting social solidarity, breaking with established tradition, and opposing constituted authority (1979:32–4). Instead, he says, CCD provides the new class not only with an independent *class status* but also with a *common ideology,* and a *common interest* in preventing or opposing all censorship of its wide-ranging speech. Along with cultural capital (education), this community of ideology and interest binds intellectuals and intelligentsia together and also separates them from other classes.

To take it a step further, we can add that cultural capital and CCD also form a common bond among the intellectuals in our typology: the unattached (i.e., the professional), the organic, and the critical intellectuals. Since they possess the same foundations, it is possible for them to form a class. Table 6.1 illustrates how CCD and cultural capital can both unite the intellectual class and separate it from other classes, and how the degree of CCD and organicity can both unite and differentiate among the organic, unattached, and critical intellectuals.[5]

As we discussed in chapter 1, BRC here refers to the bureaucratic ruling class, MC, the moneyed class (private entrepreneurs), and WC, the working class. A plus sign indicates the presence of a certain quality; the more pluses, the more of that quality. A minus sign shows little or none of that quality.

Intellectuals in all categories generally possess the greatest amount of cultural capital, including even those who have become part of the bureaucratic ruling class, the moneyed class, and the working class. On the other hand, many members of the latter three classes may have little or no education, or cultural capital.

CCD, along with organicity, makes the difference between organic and unattached/critical intellectuals, since the more organic a person is,

Table 6.1 Cultural Capital, CCD, and Organicity of Intellectuals Compared with Those of Other Classes

	Any One of the Classes: the BRC, MC, or WC	Organic Intellectuals	Unattached/ Professional Intellectuals	Critical Intellectuals
Amount of Cultural Capital	– to +++	+++	+++	+++
Amount of CCD	– or +	– or +	++	+++
Organicity	NA	+++	+	–

the less CCD she or he is going to have. As Mannheim (1936:38) comments on intellectuals involved in political parties, "The more intellectuals became party functionaries, the more they lost the virtue of receptivity and elasticity, which they had brought with them from their precious labile situation." Thus the bureaucratized and bourgeoisified as well as their organic intellectuals will have only one + or none, the least CCD, whereas the unattached/professional intellectuals will have ++ CCD, and the critical intellectual will have +++ CCD. Organicity can be measured by such indicators as one's interest in the cause of a major class, or to be more specific, the amount of time and energy one spends in promoting the cause of that class through papers written or specific work done for the cause. Organic intellectuals naturally possess +++ organicity, while unattached or critical intellectuals possess a little or none of it. The BRC, MC, and WC obviously do not need to be organic to themselves.

Cultural capital and CCD are indeed the basis of class formation in the various categories of intellectuals. The fact that organic intellectuals (including those who have become part of the ruling classes) still have plenty of cultural capital and some CCD makes it possible for us to consider them as from the same class. The amount of their CCD does differ, but CCD, as we said, is present in all intellectuals. The split personality is caused by their inability to carry CCD to the extent they would like. The so-called three confrontations (over whether practice is the sole criterion of truth, over capitalism vs. socialism, and over public vs. private) are examples of organic and critical intellectuals practicing their CCD.[6] The democracy movement indicates the dissident/critical intellectuals practicing their CCD.

There is another factor to consider in determining whether intellectuals can form a class: alienation. To be or not to be able to fully practice CCD is a major source of intellectual alienation. Such alienation fosters a common consciousness and togetherness. Because of their specific qualifications, aspirations, expectations, and status, intellectuals face a different kind of alienation from that of the working class. Instead of the loss of control over the means of production and over the process of production, Gouldner (1979:57–73) identifies five ways in which intellectuals may be alienated: (1) the blockage of their CCD, their right to judge the actions and claims of any social class and of all the power elites; in other words, intellectuals are deprived of their right to use their cultural capital to achieve status and to earn an income; (2) the blockage of both upward mobility and access to the media, which is in a sense to rob them of the market for their cultural products and therefore also prevent them from using their cultural capital to earn an income; (3) a status disparity between their high degree of culture and their low incomes and limited political influence, which naturally grows out of the first two obstacles; (4) the disparity between their belief in maintaining the harmony of society and their inability to do so, which is a psychological frustration grown out of the political; and (5) the blockage of their technical interests by the power elite, which again is to deprive them of their means to make a living.

While the extent of intellectual alienation in the West may be debatable, it seems quite real in the Chinese context, as we have discussed earlier. This alienated feeling can result from the fact that intellectuals are not permitted to express certain social criticism that helps define political and academic issues. Censorship is discouraging, frustrating, and alienating (see also Schoenhals 1992:105–7, 121–4). Under such conditions, the humanist spirit, or the consciousness that defines critical intellectuals, may atrophy. Another specific cause is their inability to become professionalized and therefore their inability to control their work processes and their incomes, that is, their inability to use their cultural capital for political and economic gain. As we discussed earlier, professionalization is associated with autonomy, and its absence inevitably creates alienation. Among organic intellectuals, the dual or split personality is a direct result of this alienation.

If we talk about consciousness or interests, what could be more important than alienation in bringing together intellectuals who feel and resent limitations on their interests and political power? Psychologically, intellectuals need to feel good and to get public acknowledgment of their moral good. They are not immune to the addiction to wealth, power, and prestige (see Weber 1946:180–95). Historically, the alienation of intellectuals in the May 4 period led to the establishment of the CCP, although the estrangement of scholars like Chen Duxiu and Li Dazhao was of a somewhat different kind, as Meisner (1967:35–6) observes. They were alienated from their own culture and tradition, but they were alienated from the state nonetheless.[7] The contemporary intellectuals' inability to use their cultural capital or CCD for political, psychological, and economic gain contributes to the development of a sense of an independent consciousness, one of the most important steps in the formation of a class, certainly of a new class. This alienation is itself a kind of social position in society. It creates a new definition of intellectuals' interests and class consciousness.

To sum up, Gouldner proposes that cultural capital makes it possible for intellectuals to access a space in public life, a structural location, at a time when, as Bell suggests, knowledge work moves to the center, and the working class as the agency of "universal human emancipation" is losing importance. In addition, the CCD gives these intellectuals an ideology. The cultural capital and CCD also unite different kinds of intellectuals, forming the basis of their solidarity. Alienation further strengthens the bond between them. As Aronowitz and DiFazio point out, in the United States the defunding of education, science, and the arts, the attacks on "political correctness," and the proletarianization of intellectuals all threaten the CCD and thus foster a class consciousness. This class has the potential of becoming its own lobby, its own political agency, identifying its own interests and demanding to share economic and political power with the conventional contending classes (1994:152, 179, 188).

Thus, in the United States at least, intellectuals may indeed be a class in the making. Life in the United States may be different from the days of Parsons and Bell, and intellectuals may be doing more than what the two theorists would allow. To be sure, intellectuals still perform normative functions, as Parsons observes. They are status groups with different lifestyles and economic opportunities, as Weber would say. And they may be scattered in different communities and have different functional and institutional interests, as Bell tells us. Nevertheless, intellectuals do possess common cultural foundations and face the constant possibility of alienation due to changes in their life chances.

Foucault's (1980:126–33) observation also helps us understand the differences and commonalities among intellectuals. He says that it is true that intellectuals may take different class positions, "whether as petty-bourgeoisie in the service of capitalism or 'organic' intellectual of the proletariat" (p. 132), and they may have different conditions of life and work. But their local, specific struggles "can have effects and implications which are not simply professional or sectoral. The intellectual can operate and struggle at the general level of that regime of truth which is so essential to the structure and functioning of our society" (p. 132). In other words, part of the nature of professional work transcends its local interests, and in that sense, the "specific" intellectual is also a "universal" intellectual who is concerned with the politics of truth and justice. That gives intellectuals of different stripes a common ground. Foucault's point reinforces Gouldner's conception on how CCD unites intellectuals.

As Schumpeter's (1976:146) comments,

> Intellectuals are not a social class in the sense in which peasants or industrial laborers constitute social classes; they hail from all the corners of the social world, and a great part of their activities consist in fighting each other and in forming the spearheads of class interests not their own. Yet they develop group attitudes and group interests sufficiently strong to make large numbers of them behave in the way that is usually associated with the concept of social class.

Thus, intellectuals do have the *potential* to form a class, despite the fact that some are either organic intellectuals to other classes, or are unattached. In fact, they can form "the spearheads of class interests" of their own class as well. For Gouldner and others, they can even form a class of their own, since they have the requirements for a class. But it is also a class in formation. Meanwhile, intellectuals act like a class (see figure 6.1 for an insight of intellectuals as a class).

Chinese Intellectuals as a Class

In the study of traditional as well as modern intellectuals, there have been references to intellectuals as a class. In his study of imperial China in the 1800s, Frederic Wakeman Jr. (1975:31), for example, describes the local gentry as a class. By 1850, while the upper gentry who received a *jinshi* (metropolitan) degree would be assured of administrative posts in the government, *juren* (provincial) or *shengyuan* (prefectural) degree holders would be more likely to serve as lower-level

Figure 6.1 Mr. King of All Animals. It's My Turn Now. *(Da wang, gai jiaoban le)*

Notes: The year of the tiger is going to be replaced by the year of the rabbit.
Source: Ding Cong 1999 (Vol. 3), p. 179.

functionaries in local governments. They would mediate legal disputes between peasants; supervise local schools, academies, and irrigation works; recruit and train local militia; and help collect taxes. They not only appeared to be a class. They were identified with the landlords who were deeply involved in urban real estate and usury in the Qing dynasty (p. 25). They were, in fact, the "organic intellectuals" of the time.

In the Republican era, Schwarcz (1986a:187) observes, intellectuals were viewed by some as just a collection of artists, teachers, and scientists rather than an intellectual class. If, however, they could acknowledge their ideological commonality and "take up the lofty task of discovering truth, elevating thought, and promoting beauty," these intellectuals, mostly critical ones, would then have an opportunity to become a class. With the rise of new professions, however, the interests of the intellectual group were no longer confined to politics or morality. Occupational excellence rather than public affairs became a new concern (Y. C. Wang 1966:397). Thus, we saw the rise of a professional-managerial class (Jin Yaoji 1987; Wen Chonyi 1989). Using Konrad and Szelenyi's criteria of an intellectual class, Mok (1998:173, 202–3) finds that China's intellectuals in the 1990s did not form a class. Konrad and Szelenyi laid down as criteria able and willing agents occupying a new socioeconomic class position, and a new consciousness.

In each of these cases, intellectuals were mentioned as a class but only in specific forms: organic, critical, or professional-managerial, and then only in a limited sense. This leads to a broader question, Can intellectuals of different kinds form one class? Based on the arguments we have already made, we can say that China's intellectuals do have the potential to form a class. They may not have the financial capital or the organizational assets of the private entrepreneurs and Party cadres, but they have cultural capital and a variety of skill assets. Above all, they have CCD and a perennial sense of alienation. They may occupy contradictory class locations, but they may also have a class location of their own, such as a middle class, a professional-managerial class, or simply an intellectual class. Even if they are in different class locations, retaining characteristics of their classes, they are united as long as they share a national discourse prompted by CCD and organize nationally. Thus, in addition to cultural capital, CCD, and alienation, intellectuals have the potential of organization. (As we emphasized in chapter 5, organization is central to any class formation.) The humanist spirit, which we discussed in chapter 3, on the other hand, may provide them with the political consciousness. Our answer to the question, then, is: As with most other classes in China, the intellectual class is in the process of formation. We will now explain how. We will discuss the economic (cultural capital), ideological (CCD), political (the humanist spirit), and organizational factors that may form China's own intellectual class. While discussing those factors, we will touch on the role of alienation.

Formation of an Intellectual Class: Cultural Capital as Its Economic Base

Using education, or one's cultural capital, to claim income has a long tradition in China. To become a scholar-official was never simply a routine effort. Weber (1946:420) says, "As a rule, the Chinese literati strove for princely service both as a source of income and as a normal field of activity." As we discussed earlier, even when they did not become officials, the gentry would still work for the government, mediating local disputes, supervising local schools, academies, and irrigation works, recruiting and training local militia, and collecting taxes. For each of these functions, they would be paid fees, wages, and salaries (Wakeman Jr. 1975: 31), in addition to gaining the power of social control.

Confucius was a good example of the scholar-official. He was an official for part of the time and a teacher at other times. Either way, he used his cultural capital to claim an income as well as a status as the currency of authority in the "regime of truth" and in CCD. On the one hand, he upheld the principles of the gentleman: the scholar devoted to truth is not embarrassed by his poor food or clothing *(bu chi e yi e shi)* (*Analects* 4:9); he did not even have to eat his fill or live in the most comfortable of houses *(shi wu qiu bao, ju wu qiu an)* (1:14). On the other hand, he said, "I'll teach anyone as long as he voluntarily gives me ten pieces of dry meat" *(zi xing shu xiu yi shang, wu weichang wu hui yan)* (7:7). Meat was a greeting gift in his day and Confucius claimed at least the minimum income. In addition, by formulating the dominant ideology through his educational efforts, he exercised his power of social control and acquired his status as the model teacher for generations to come *(wan shi shi biao)*.

We have already discussed how intellectuals did economically in the 1990s. While the unattached professionals might be having a hard time compared to the bourgeoisified intellectuals, they were economically much better off compared to an ordinary worker or a peasant. In fact, intellectuals tended to earn more than people with less than a high school education. According to Zhu Guanglei, the income ratio between those with primary school education and those with professional school education or higher was 1:1.2 in 1990, and 1:1.5 in 1996. The gap was increasing in favor of the intellectuals (1998:3), although intellectuals often claimed that their income was less than that of the less educated. *Nao ti dao gua,* or the "reversal to body over mind," was probably more a perception than reality. Anita Chan (1991:109–11) also notes that academics were doing better financially than the ordinary worker and the influence of the intellectuals had greatly improved since the 1980s and beyond. As one of our interviewees, Sun Zhongxin, summarizes, the intellectuals' status in general was not low. First of all, their status also depended on how other social strata thought about them; they still commanded a lot of respect from workers and peasants. Second, they tended to have lots of gray income. Third, the fact that many of them were hired by businesses and given high salaries indicated their high status (Interview 1994:1.54).

On the other hand, the feeling of alienation was indeed true among some intellectuals, especially the unattached and critical. The following is a reflection of their inability to use their cultural capital to advance their economic interests.

> Sometimes when you go out with friends, they say, "You're a college teacher. Let me pay for the dinner." And young teachers each have only one dorm room for the whole family. Even for that one room, you have to wait for a long time. Now you feel your status. . . . When I decided to remain in academia, I said I did not care about money. Now I feel its importance. You need the money to buy things you like. And you need several ten thousands to buy a house. You can't afford it at all." (Interview with Yu Liqun 1994:1.17)

We should note that they were comparing themselves with their friends who probably had become part of the bourgeoisie. They were not comparing themselves with the unemployed and underemployed workers, nor with the mass of peasants in the countryside or the migrant workers in the cities. They simply believed that their education made them worth more pay. In fact, as we discussed in chapter 4, college professors were beginning to get larger salary increases at the end of the 1990s than they had had in the mid-1990s. Nevertheless, today's alienation is real.

In sum, cultural capital certainly enables some bourgeoisified and bureaucratized organic intellectuals to make large salaries. Unattached professionals and critical intellectuals are catching up. Some critical intellectuals, for example, write frequently for newspapers and magazines, which brings them a great deal of gray income. For others, however, the improvement in their income may depend on the professionalization process. And that process will also enable them to have more social control and acquire higher social statuses, as we discussed in chapter 3. At any rate, the tendency is for intellectuals' cultural capital to bring them more income compared with ordinary workers and peasants, and it legitimizes their claim to higher pay and more social power. Cultural capital does form an economic base for all intellectuals. This base is strengthened, not weakened, by their feeling of alienation, of not being able to make good their claims.

Formation of an Intellectual Class: CCD as Its Ideological Base

Let us first look at CCD in the traditional intellectual culture. It seems paradoxical but Confucianism, although strict in its patriarchal and authoritative claims, does have an aspect of CCD. (The authoritative claims, however, may be a problem inherent in CCD itself.) Confucius advocates *wu yi, wu bi, wu gu, wu wo,* meaning "do not indulge in wishful thinking, absolute assertion, stubborn insistence, or self-righteousness" (*Analects* 9:4). Another of his famous sayings, *san ren xing bi you wo shi yan,* means, literally, "in a crowd of three, there must be one who can teach me" (7:22). The gist here is that one should always keep an open mind to others' opinions and be prepared to learn from them. Thus, even though Confucianism is noted for its rigidity, it does teach intellectuals to be modest and to question their thoughts and behavior. As Zeng Zi, one of Confucius' disciples, says, "I examine myself and reflect on what I do several times a day," or *wu ri san xing wu shen* (1:4). We may consider this self-examination, auto-critique, and openness to different ideas, as the first part of the Chinese intellectuals' CCD.

Mencius himself upholds the so-called *hao ran zhi qi,* meaning a "will and spirit that are on a grand scale, strong and upright" (*Mencius* 3:2). He also says that a *da zhang fu,* or a "gentleman," is not to be bewildered by wealth and honor, shaken by poverty and humbleness, or ready to bend before authority and force *(fugui buneng yin, pinjian buneng yi, weiwu buneng qu)* (6:2). One frequently cited example is the late philosopher Liang Shuming, who, although a supporter of Mao for a long time, was one of the most outspoken critics of his policies. When colleagues asked how he felt at being criticized for months for "contemning Lin Biao but not Confucius," although he was required to consider both, he quoted a line from Confucius, "The army can be deprived of its commander-in-chief, but a person cannot be deprived of his will and spirit" (1987:459–65). His colleagues were stunned at his defiance. Here again we have a Confucian saying that critical intellectuals have believed in for thousands of years. This is the concept of the indomitable will and spirit in the face of power and wealth, and in defense of one's ideas. We may consider this toughness as the second part of the Chinese intellectuals' CCD.

The third part of the Chinese version of CCD we may consider is *shi shi qiu shi,* or "seeking truth from facts." (The last two Chinese words are actually the title of the Party journal, *Qiu Shi* or "seeking truth.") The saying was first used by the historian, poet, and biographer Ban Gu (32–92) of the East Han dynasty in his biography of Liu De. The principle was developed by Yan Shigu (581–645) in his teachings and by Gu Yanwu (1613–82) in his philosophy of practicality in studies. Zeng Guofan (1811–72) carried it even further in his version of practicalism: he advocated combining Chinese studies and Western learning in the Self-Strengthening movement. Mao adopted the theme as the motto of the CCP's way of thinking (see Wang Shubai 1990:59). Mao says,

> "Facts" are all the things that exist objectively, "truth" means their internal relations, that is, the laws governing them, and "to seek" means to study. We should proceed from the actual conditions inside and outside the country, the province, county or district, and derive from them, as our guide to action, laws which are inherent in them and not imaginary, that is, we should find the internal relations of the events occurring around us. And in order to do that we must rely not on subjective imagination, not on momentary enthusiasm, not on lifeless books, but on facts that exist objectively; we must appropriate the material in detail and, guided by the general principles of Marxism-Leninism, draw correct conclusions from it. (Schram 1967:131)

In following this principle, Mao and his colleagues, although adhering to Marxism, defied Marx's belief that a Communist revolution can only succeed on a world scale among the most industrialized societies. The Sinification of Marxism led to the triumph of Marxism-Leninism-Mao Zedong Thought, which provided an ideological foundation for the Chinese revolution.[8] The same principle led Deng and his colleagues to launch their reform in the economic field, defying Maoism, but to pull their punches in the political field, that is, capitalist measures with Chinese characteristics, as Solinger (1993) terms it. As a further example, there was Chen Yun, one of the founders of the Chinese revolution. He called on the Party cadres to avoid blind obedience either to the authorities or to the written word. Instead they were to seek truth from practice *(bu wei shang, bu wei shu, zhi wei shi)* and to compare, exchange opinions with others, and to continue to do this even after decisions had been made *(jiao huan, bi jiao, fan fu)* (Chen Yun [1947]

1995; Xu Wenze 1995). In short, they were to try with open minds to find the best way to achieve socialism. But how the Communist Party has used CCD for its political purposes is another issue, which we have discussed in chapter 1 and will further discuss in the section on the flawed class.

These three aspects of their CCD not only define China's intellectuals but unite them as well. CCD is their ideology. It sets a standard for all intellectuals, be they organic, unattached, or critical. To practice or not to practice CCD is an internal struggle for every intellectual. The degree of CCD one possesses and how each demonstrates it may vary according to time and structural location. But there is no denying that CCD is integral to the intellectual ideology. The ability or inability to speak one's mind has long been the focus of the battles between intellectuals and the rulers of government, including the CCP and the Guomindang (GMD). These battles constantly cause the alienation of intellectuals. One damaging result, which we have examined, is the split personality. It is caused by the self-censorship, the watch-your-mouth psychology forced on intellectuals by political oppression. There is the urge to express themselves, to debate issues, but if they yield to it, they must constantly and fearfully look over their shoulders. Today, with the modernization movement, a professionalism characterized by autonomy or self-groundedness, as Gouldner (1979:34) calls it, is gaining strength and is likely to become one of the intellectuals' ideological weaponry, a part of their CCD.

To sum up, although there have been many changes in the intellectuals' values, including bourgeoisification and professionalization, the typical intellectual still needs space for free inquiry. CCD is representative of intellectuals' ideological foundations we discussed in chapter 1. It is the sociological nature of the intellectual that he or she upholds the principle of justifying one's assertions by voluntary consent of the audience, not by invoking authorities. Otherwise, the intellectual would have lost his or her reason for existence. In other words, intellectuals need to follow a CCD that requires them to keep an open mind, seek truth from facts, and not to bend before external forces of authority or wealth. This form of CCD is a vital need for, or vested interest of, intellectuals of various categories: critical, professional, and organic. They strive for it and fight to protect it. Complementing cultural capital, CCD gives them more autonomy and thus power for social control.

Formation of an Intellectual Class: The Calling and the Humanist Spirit as Its Political Base

In chapter 1, we discussed what we termed the "calling" of intellectuals in the traditional Chinese culture: the principles of *xiu qi zhi ping.* That is, in ascending order, one must cultivate and perfect oneself, get one's family in order, guide or govern one's country in the right course, and finally, help achieve peace in the world. The tradition also calls on intellectuals to *li de, li gong,* and *li yan,* that is, set themselves up as moral examples, perform meritorious services, and write great books, or what Tu Wei-ming (1993b) terms the *way, learning,* and *politics.* In chapter 3, in our discussion of critical intellectuals, we also analyzed the humanist spirit, the belief in human beings as the chief subjects in social interaction, a belief embodied in striving to understand human conditions and practicing social criticism. The present chapter has discussed the alienation caused when intellectuals are unable to use their cultural capital and CCD to advance their economic conditions and their political goals.

The calling and the humanist spirit constitute a collective political consciousness that underscores an important fact: intellectuals have been part of every ruling class in China's history, from feudal kings and emperors down to the Communist and Nationalist regimes. And while part of the ruling class, they are often critical of it. Han Yu, Fan Zhongyan, Ouyang Xiu, Wang Anshi, Sima Guang, Su Shi, and Cheng Yi, all great intellectuals of the eleventh century, are good examples of literati who, following the calling and the humanist spirit, strove to excel in the way (morality), learning (scholarship, culture), and/or politics (the transformation of the sociopolitical order through institutional activism) (see Bol 1992:5). So is Zhang Tao of the early seventeenth century (see Brook 1998). We have mentioned many other such examples in chapter 1.

The Republican China saw the May 4 intellectuals follow the calling and the humanist spirit and engage themselves in the advocacy of Mr. Democracy *(de xiansheng)* and Mr. Science *(sai xiansheng).* Among them are Chen Duxiu, Hu Shih, and Li Dazhao. The more radical organized political parties and attempted modern politics, as we will discuss in the next section. It is the literati tradition and the May 4 tradition that have brought forth the Leninist cadre tradition in Communist intellectuals like Deng Tuo (see Cheek 1997) and Wu Han (see Mazur 1996). The foreign values are nicely meshed with tradition in the realm of humanist spirit and intellectual vocation. Together, these traditions provide the resources for the vocation of Chinese intellectuals in the 1990s.[9]

Democratic liberalism and ideal Marxism have thus survived flawed "actual existing" versions in Chiang's GMD and Mao's CCP, and provided a political base for today's intellectuals. We see a number of the Party's organic intellectuals who have been very critical of the Party since the earliest days of its history. It is this critical stance that makes them part of the intellectual class. This political consciousness also explains why professionals want more autonomy so that they can perform more meritorious services. This certainly explains why many critical intellectuals are so obsessed with the democracy movement in China and so alienated by the Party.

The political consciousness, characterized by the calling and the humanist spirit, that is, the political base of the new class, will, along with cultural capital and CCD, help make the intellectual class more coherent. Alienation simply proves the necessity for the mission. Intellectuals who treasure tradition will follow the calling and the humanist spirit. It will not matter whether they are professionals, organic intellectuals, or critical ones. Thus, political consciousness will become one of the defining characteristics of the whole range of intellectuals, as well as their vested interest.

Formation of an Intellectual Class: Communities and Parties as the Organizational Base

As we discussed in chapter 5, Marx and Weber emphasize, and other theorists agree, that one of the most important indicators of class formation is the existence of communities, *and* class members take communal action guided by communal organization. Modern intellectuals are familiar with political parties as action communities. Indeed, many entered politics through party building and party politics of some kind. In the twentieth century, intellectuals displayed class action by helping workers to organize unions and peasants to organize associations. The GMD started by Sun Yat-sen at the turn of the century continued to hold power until the beginning of the twenty-first century; the CCP, started by Chen Duxiu and Li Dazhao in 1921 and later led by Mao until his death in 1976, is still in power. In fact, these two parties were so successful that their intellectual members were largely transformed by the parties rather than the other way around. Both parties later lost many of their intellectual characteristics, and descended from idealism into the use of violence to suppress opposition, although some democratic liberalism and ideal Marxism seem to have survived.

Intellectuals tried to start other organizations and to build other parties in the twentieth century as well. The few years following World War II witnessed a "participation explosion" by intellectuals, as Xu Jilin points out. First, there was a great increase in the number of newspapers and journals. In 1946 in the GMD area, there were 1,832 such media organizations, some started by liberal intellectuals. *Guancha Zhoukan* (The observer), edited by Chu Anping, declared its purpose to be "freedom, democracy, progress, and reason" (1997b:42; Dai Qing 1990:176), as we mentioned in chapter 1. The journal attracted many intellectual readers and for some time swayed national public opinion.

In the second aspect of the "participation explosion," there was an enormous increase in the number of opposition parties operating outside the GMD and CCP. Nearly a hundred new parties emerged. Many were intellectuals' parties, and some have persisted to this day. (How they did so we will discuss in the next section.) These include the China Democratic National Construction Association, the China Association for the Promotion of Democracy, the September Third Study Society, and the National Socialist Party by Zhang Junmai and others (see Jeans 1992, 1997 for more discussion on the third force, and Kong Fanzheng 2001 on the various efforts of third parties for democratization). The Democratic League, established in 1941 by liberal intellectuals, was close to becoming the third largest party (Xu Jilin 1997b:42).[10]

Yet, as Jeans (1992:10–19) points out, these parties failed for a variety of reasons. They could not survive the inhospitable environment created by the GMD dictatorship and by the violent struggles between the GMD and the CCP. They refused to take up arms against the bloody oppression because they could not believe that "political power grows out of the barrel of a gun." Their membership and audience were limited, since, as professors and journalists, they had no idea how, or did not want, to mobilize the masses. In addition, there were other problems such as a lack of adequate funds, inadequate organizational structures, factionalism, failure to unite with other opposition parties, single-issue movements, lack of a supportive civil society, and moderate personalities in an extremist environment. The results were inevitable. Worst of all, the oppositionists themselves were in some cases corrupt, brutal, protofascist, or simply not practicing what they preached.

How are the remaining small parties doing today? In chapter 5, we characterized their members as organic intellectuals. Indeed, as we mentioned in chapter 5, the minor parties had already been functioning as think tanks of the CCP at the founding of the PRC (Mazur 1997:57, 64–5). Today these democratic parties and groups (DPGs) have continued to do little more than act as support groups of the CCP, and have often been belittled as "flower vases," or "second-class rubber stamps" (Seymour 1992:298). For example, according to media reports, their central committees tried to outdo one another in support of the CCP after the June 4 massacre, although they knew they might not be representing their members in doing so. Neither the CCP nor the people in general know or care much about these DPGs.[11] Some surveys show that three quarters of the respondents and the majority of CCP members were unable to make any informed comments about them (pp. 300–5).

However, as small and organic as they are, the DPGs can rise to the occasion when the political environment permits, according to Seymour. The first such period came in the 1956–57 Hundred Flowers movement, when members of the democratic parties and groups constructively criticized the CCP at the urging of Mao and other CCP leaders. The second period of activity came in the reform era under Zhao Ziyang, when the CCP was seriously considering making the democratic parties and groups independent. Deng Weizhi, a vice-chair of the Association for the Promotion of Democracy (APD), urged the groups to act like real parties, selecting their own platforms and candidates (1992:290–3). The majority of group members favored a more open press. One democratic party luminary even stated that inasmuch as "the truth is on our side, so long as we clearly reason things out with the masses, we will earn the support of the masses. Do not fear attacks of hostile elements. Let the public judge opposing points of view. Trust their conscience" (p. 299). During the spring democracy movement in 1989, many of these small democratic parties declared their support for the students' patriotism.

At the Annual Convention of the APD in 1994, Vice-Chair Deng Weizhi called on the CCP to improve one of its policies toward the democratic parties. He said that "long term coexistence" seemed to be doing fine but "mutual supervision" had to be improved, although he did not say how (Deng Weizhi 1994; Interview 1994:1.68).[12] Those two factors were the United Front strategies that the CCP stipulated for its "equal relationship" with the small democratic parties. Unfortunately "equal relationship" has never lived up to the Party's promises. This longing by the small parties for more power dates back to the earlier days of the CCP rule; it culminated in the Hundred Flowers movement, and has since been brought into discussion repeatedly though without much success (*Press Freedom Guardian,* December 8, 1995). Although their numbers are still small, each organization having a membership of 10,000 to 50,000 in the early 1990s (Seymour 1992:306), it is not unthinkable that when the political environment changes in their favor, they will again rise to the occasion as the CCP's critics and competitors.

Other than these parties, there are various professional organizations, but they lack any independent political orientation. These include, for example, the Chinese Writers' Association, the Chinese Journalists' Association, and the Chinese Sociology Association. There are also the various local associations organized around activities such as painting, calligraphy, and the study of such subjects as environmental science or the United Front theory (Wang Ying, Zhe Xiaoye, and Sun Bingyao, 1993).[13] None of these can be independently political, and they must follow the CCP Party line while doing their professional work. This does not mean they can do nothing politically other than support the Party. They can when opportunities arise. In the 1989 democracy movement, one thousand journalists from the Chinese Journalists' Association signed a petition seeking a meeting with the CCP Central Committee.

While non-Communist parties and associations are important intellectual communities, other levels of intellectual community abound: universities, hospitals, and research institutes as well as newspapers and magazines. The overwhelming majority of these are state owned, although some are almost entirely independent or semiautonomous. Here are some examples of the latter. In the 1980s in Beijing, there were Chen Ziming and Wang Juntao's Social and Economic Sciences Research Institute, the Huaxia Institute of Legal Culture, the Capital Iron and Steel Legal Research Institute, the Stone Institute of Social Development, and Chen Ziming's Chinese Institute of Political and Administrative Sciences (Sidel 1995; X. L. Ding 1994; Bonnin and Chevrier 1991). Other such groups were organized around book series and journals (Edward X. Gu 1999; X. L. Ding 1994:65–76). In addition to the ones we discussed in chapter 2, there was the journal *Economic Weekly,* sponsored again by Chen Ziming. Various student associations and cultural salons also appeared in the 1980s (Wasserstrom and Liu 1995). Although these organizations were largely disbanded in the aftermath of the 1989 upheavals, numerous magazines emerged in the 1990s and survive today, some of them highly intellectual and critical in orientation. They focus on Chinese culture, economic reform, literature, the social sciences, and on and on. As we reported in chapter 3, there were 2,149 newspapers and 7,918 magazines in 1997, according to *The People's Republic of China Yearbook 1998* (p. 807).

These newspapers and magazines have also become congregating venues for intellectuals, although, as may be expected, different journals attract intellectuals of different convictions. Xiao Gongqin summarizes the phenomenon succinctly (1994b; Interview 1994:1.2). Since the mid-1990s, groups of policy intellectuals *(guo ce pai)* have clustered around *Strategy and Management (*Zhanlue yu guanli*).* Many of them are economists, sociologists, and political scientists, who seek to provide policy suggestions for, and to cooperate with, the government toward a gradual reform. That is where many of the neoconservatives published their articles. Academics *(xue yuan pai)* researching modernization and civil society, many of whom are social scientists, gather around the *Chinese Journal of Social Sciences (Zhongguo shehui kexue jikan).* Humanistic intellectuals (*wen ren pai)* who are worried about the negative consequences of the market economy and concerned about the independence of intellectuals write for *Reading (Dushu)* and *The Orient (Dongfang).*[14]

According to Xiao, Dissident intellectuals *(shehui pipan pai)* on the "right" who advocate freedom and human rights have turned to activities within the law such as advocating the rights of labor. They cannot publish their own magazines, though, for labor issues are still very sensitive. Xiao reports that the representative journal of the left, later called the New Left, is the *Journal of Chinese Development (Zhongguo fazhan zazhi).* Toward the end of the 1990s, however, many left-wingers' articles can be found in *Dushu, Tianya, and Shijie.* The Old Left, as we mentioned in chapter 3, cluster around *Midstream (Zhongliu), Pursuit of Truth (Zhenli de zhuiqiu),* and C*ontemporary Thoughts (Dangdai sichao).*[15] (See also Ma Licheng and Ling Zhijun 1998).

Venues thus do exist for intellectuals to develop some degree of common consciousness and to organize for communal actions. So far, however, they are more like Marx's potatoes in a sack (Marx [1852] 1978: 608), who form nothing more than a sackful of potatoes. They do not even have the intellectual space they had in the 1940s, harsh as it was at that time. With independent political organizations strictly forbidden, there is still a long way to go before China's intellectuals can act as effective interest groups. Nonetheless, the organizations just discussed help mold China's democratic development and facilitate the formation of China's civil society.

Can the intellectual organizations outside the country do any better? Communities of intellectuals outside of China can be classified into two kinds: political parties or organizations, and economic and professional associations. We have already delineated the extent and dimensions of the overseas democratic movements in chapter 3. On the issue of their consciousness about party building, Sheng Xue observes that overseas democratic organizations cannot function as opposition parties when both their constituencies and the party they oppose are in China (Ya Yi 1997d). As a result, they can do very little about coordinating ideology, emotions, and means. All they can do is study the democratic systems in the West and learn how to build their own democratic organizations. Then they can talk seriously about forming opposition parties if and when they are allowed back in China.

But even then, they will have to adjust to a new political environment. They will be competing with all of the other new parties in China. They will face the same evils that democratic parties faced in the 1940s. In fact, the overseas democratic organizations have already been fighting the same devils that haunted China's democratic parties in the 1940s. They are facing the still-hostile environment created by the CCP's one-party dictatorship, as well as by limited membership and audience, lack of funds, factionalism, failure to unite with other opposition movements, and lack of a supportive civil society in their mother country. There is a radical wing in the overseas movement that advocates the option of armed struggle, and there is no lack of extreme personalities. But having experienced the consequences of radicalism in the twentieth century, people seem wary about what radicalism may bring them in the twenty-first century. Furthermore, as in the 1940s, the oppositionists themselves may be corrupt, refusing to practice what they preach.

All of these issues bedeviling the overseas democratic organizations are discussed regularly in journals and newspapers such as *Beijing Spring, China Spring, World Journal,* and *Ming Pao Monthly.* They turned up as well in my interviews with democratic activists such as Hu Ping, Chen Kuide, Liu Qing, Su Shaozhi, Zheng Yi, Liu Binyan, Yan Jiaqi, and Wang Ruowang (1997). Nonetheless, like the democratic parties in China now, the democracy organizations overseas do have a great deal of potential, as we saw in chapter 3.

Then there are the numerous professional organizations composed of overseas Chinese students, scholars, and professors of science and technology; and business, engineering, economy, sociology, political science, and so forth. Some of them in the United States include the Chinese Association of Science and Technology (CAST), the Association of Chinese Political Studies (ACPS), the Association of Chinese Professors of Social Sciences (ACPSS), the North American Chinese Sociologists Association (NACSA), the Detroit Chinese Engineers Association (DCEA), the Chinese Economic Association of North America (CEANA), and the Chinese Economists Society (CES). The major purposes of these associations are to promote social, economic, and political communication and exchange with Mainland China, and if possible to help each other establish themselves in the United States. The bylaws of CES, for example, states that

> The aim of the Chinese Economists Society (CES) is to promote scholarly exchanges among its members and contribute to the advancement and dissemination of economics and management sciences in China. For these purposes, The CES sponsors annual meetings, conferences and publications (http://china-ces.org).

These organizations are largely academic and are almost never politically dissident, at least not openly.

There are few connections between the political and professional organizations in the United States. And the relationship between the political organizations in the United States and those in China is also minimal. As we have seen, the overseas dissident organizations have tried to smuggle newspapers and magazines into China. They have organized activities to support dissidents in China. They have also tried to help the families of those who have been imprisoned or who have suffered after the June 4 massacre. Their efforts, however, are often hampered by the authorities, so that, important as they are, they cannot really make a substantial difference. The economic and professional organizations are anxious to do business with China and are therefore in constant contact with government and professional organizations in the homeland. Some of them have started their own businesses with the help of these contacts. They tend to have very good relationships with officials from the

Chinese embassy and from consulates in the United States. These officials are often courted for their support by factions engaged in power struggles within the organizations.

To sum up, even if opposition parties and organizations are impossible in China now, intellectuals do cluster around certain kinds of parties, associations, publications, and other intellectual communities. But since they are not politically independent, they are not the political arms of interest groups in the full sense. On the other hand, a large number of political and professional organizations have been established by Chinese intellectuals overseas, which provide a forum for possible political and business dialogues. These communities sustain the intellectual consciousness by formulating and revising their own professional and political policies.

In this section, we have analyzed how cultural capital forms the *economic* base of China's intellectual class, CCD its *ideological* base, the calling and the humanist spirit its *political* base, and communities and parties its *organizational* base. Each of these foundations constitutes an interest common to the entire intellectual class. Intellectuals thus share economic, ideological, political, and organizational interests, each of which affects the others. Anything that prevents them from achieving their goals obstructs one or more of their interests. These *common interests,* like the common bases, help China's intellectuals form a group. The organizational base, however, is still so precarious that we cannot claim that a *class* already exists, but we can say that it probably is in the making.

Organic Intellectuals of the New Class

What about organic intellectuals of the intellectual class? We have shown that Chinese intellectuals in various categories share economic, ideological, political, and organizational bases. But because of a lack of a discursive national party or parties, plus the lack of clearly defined interests and consciousness, intellectuals are still largely ineffective. More concrete organizing is needed from the intellectual entrepreneurs, that is, the organic intellectuals of the intellectual class. Like the teachers' unions in the United States, they must articulate their interests, disseminate ideas, and organize and coordinate intellectual activities. Those may be the most important roles for the organic intellectuals of the intellectual class.

Organic intellectuals to the intellectual class may also suffer from dual and split personalities, as is the case of their counterparts to the dominating classes and the working class. Whatever the special interests of the groups they represent, these organic intellectuals are not and cannot be neutral. They may not agree with all their targets say or do. But their CCD requires them to judge honestly and advise objectively regardless of their target's authority or position. Like other organic intellectuals, organic intellectuals to the intellectual class play a pivotal role in advancing the interests of the class.

The Elitist Flaw of the Intellectual Class

We have shown how and why an intellectual class in China is a real possibility. Now let us suppose that such a class *is* formed, with intellectual parties representing various factions or interest groups, what will this class of intellectuals be like?

Gouldner refers to his New Class as flawed because of its members' *elitist nature.* They believe that they alone know the rules and theories for practicing CCD, and are therefore superior to other classes. There is a certain insensitivity to the feelings of others, and CCD thus breeds a kind of political brutality. "The New Class sets itself above others, holding that its speech is better than theirs. . . . Even as it subverts old inequities, the New Class silently inaugurates a new hierarchy of the knowing, the knowledgeable, the reflexive and insightful. Those who talk well, it is held, excel those who talk poorly or not at all" (1979:85). This broadens what Mencius has said: "Those who work with their minds govern those who work with their hands." "The CCD is alienating and even radicalizing because it demands the right to sit in judgement over all claims, regardless of who makes them" (Gouldner 1985:30). It is a contradictory class, and that is why, though its power is growing, its future success is not inevitable. From this standpoint alone, the New Class is badly flawed and in need of transcendence.

How is this flaw demonstrated in the various constituents of the intellectual class?[16] Apparently, all of these groups tend to look down on other classes or on other groups of intellectuals, or both.

Let us see, first, how critical intellectuals show elitism toward one another. Chapter 3 discussed the debate over China's modernity among the liberals, the Old Left, and the New Left. We also discussed nationalism in the 1990s. While some, like Xu Jilin, have shown a great amount of even-mindedness,[17] many others have demonstrated the usual flaws: insensitivity to opponents' feelings and inability to value opponents' views. For example, the liberals tend to discount the problems of the market economy, while the New Left tends to stress only its problems. Like the Old Left, both of them see the importance of authoritarianism but largely ignore the evils of one-party rule.[18] To be fair, they all look for ways to create a more equal society. But this is a commonality they do not grant one another. They spend their energies largely on hostile strategies of development, and they view their opponents as either all good or all evil. If each faction could empathize with the others, the debates among them would be much healthier. Indeed, the pros and cons of the market economy do need to be evaluated and appropriate solutions do need to be found. But if they explicitly or even implicitly treat these debates as between good and evil, with one side totally right and the other totally wrong, there is only one future in sight: rectifications, purges, and eventually civil wars.

Similarly, if the ardent nationalists like Wang Xiaodong and Sheng Hong could see that strengthening one's country requires respect for different cultures and differing opinions, they would seek humility and cooperation. But if they see dissidents and minorities at home and Americans abroad only as enemies, who keep them from unifying and modernizing China, they will move to build a strong military, ready to fight all enemies, real or imaginary.[19]

It is frightening to see how far this elitist flaw of CCD can take the critical intellectual. We have seen how far revolutionary intellectuals like Mao, Deng, and Jiang Zemin have traveled along this route.[20] When the Party undertakes to seek truth from the facts, it believes it has found the one and only "truth," and believes that all other positions are misguided. There can be only one truth, it is in *their* hands, and unbelievers need to be purged. Konrad and Szelenyi (1991:352) point out that the New Class's CCD has a *moralizing quality* that intimidates others and prevents them from airing their views. For example, conservatives in the 1970s complained that they could not discuss the need for U.S. involvement in South East Asian politics: they were silenced on moral grounds. But CCD can do much more harm than that in a totalitarian or authoritarian system as well as under China's current socialist corporatism and clientelism.

Second, if critical intellectuals are elitist toward their own, professionalized intellectuals may be even more so. Their emphasis on science may easily lead them to believe that everything that is different from *their* "science" is untrustworthy. For example, the revolutionary intellectuals we have discussed in chapter 1 believed that their socialism was based on science and must therefore dominate China's future. They refused to consider anything else.[21] We have seen that Fang Lizhi's criticism of Chinese socialism was also based on science (see Williams 1990, 1994; Calhoun 1991). Marxism, as Yu Ying-shih (1989), Fang Lizhi (1991), and others have proclaimed, is outdated. Fang saw Chinese communism as representing China's feudal heritage, in other words its outdated tradition. "Since physicists pursue the unity, harmony and perfection of nature, how can they logically tolerate unreason, discordance, and evil" (cited in Calhoun 1991:123)? Communism would of course represent unreason, discordance and evil, because it is not science. Even more specifically, it is not physics. Only something like physics can be trusted.

Following the same logic, those who know, the professionalized and scientific intellectuals, will govern those who do not know, the workers, peasants, soldiers, and other intellectuals.[22] The former have to teach the latter what is democracy and when to practice democracy. For the latter do not have the requisite knowledge, and they probably do not have the ability to develop that knowledge on their own because they are not scientists (see Calhoun 1991 on Fang's elitism).[23] The teaching of the untaught is what China's revolutionary intellectuals have done. This is also what Mencius would tell them to do. Ironically, those who are against tradition may in fact be following tradition, and a problematic one at that.

Much like the critical intellectuals, the professionals distain not only other "lesser" classes, but also the dissidents among themselves. Aronowitz (1990:44) points out that technical intellectuals are paradigm-bound: "Those challenging the dominant paradigm are consigned to the margins of the communities or, more routinely, completely excluded." Like critical intellectuals, professionals frequently use their dominant position to stifle dissident opinions, and in fact any opinions that they feel are less scientific. This applies especially to the opinions of workers or peasants. What is more, they feel that it is their responsibility to do so.

Third, and finally, we come to the organic intellectuals. They, too, are afflicted with this flaw of CCD. The professional-managerial class (PMC) of the party-state and the bourgeoisie, including small democratic parties, government economists, journalists, many scholar-cadres, and managers of private businesses, tend to feel that the only way to change China is to work within the system. On the other hand, many intellectuals organic to the democracy movement like Liu Binyan, would say that these people are being co-opted by the powers. The PMC of the bourgeoisie may think that scientific management is the only way to increase production, but intellectuals organic to the working class may think that they are using science to help their bosses further exploit workers. All of these are right to some extent, but none holds the total truth, since truth, never clear-cut, always falls somewhere between good and bad. Thus, among organic intellectuals, especially those of the party-state and the bourgeoisie on the one hand and of the working class on the other, there is enormous distrust, each believing the other is misled by untruth or immorality.[24] The same splits may occur also among one kind of organic intellectuals. For example, the dissident organizations, or organic intellectuals to the same social movement, each tend to believe that their group alone holds the truth. For this reason it is always difficult to coordinate their actions.

Overcoming this elitist flaw of CCD places certain demands on Chinese intellectuals. It requires them to acknowledge their tendency to judge others according to their own views. It requires that they accept the value of differing opinions. It demands also that they accept alternative ways of modernizing China, and hence different intellectual praxes: critical, organic, professional, and anything in between. They will have to realize that none of the isms, not Confucianism, Marxism, communism, socialism, nor capitalism marks the ultimate truth. More importantly, intellectuals must accept the fact that they are not superior interest groups; instead, they are as a class only one among many equals. As equals, they must be willing to ally with other classes in furthering their causes. In chapter 7, on the future of Chinese intellectuals, we will further discuss the transformation of the intellectual class and the transcendence of their flaws.

Conclusions

In his essay "On Intellectuals," Aronowitz outlines three conditions of cultural class formation: "(1) the occupation of a common structural space; (2) a common discursive (cultural) position that, however, is not

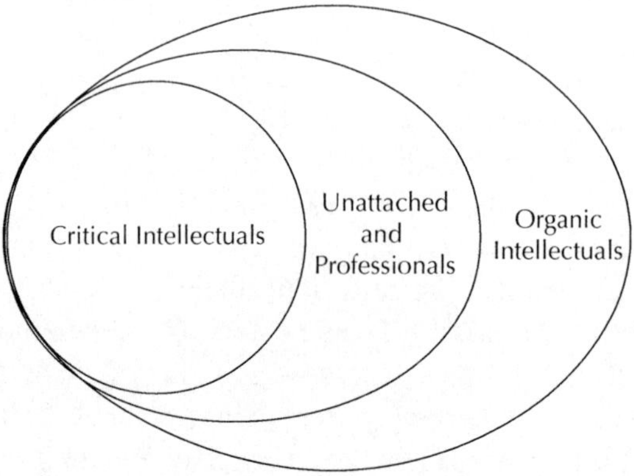

Figure 6.2 The Class Formation of Chinese Intellectuals

presupposed by structural unity; and (3) political organization exemplified by political parties and national trade unions that also function discursively" (1990:8). Konrad and Szelenyi also emphasize new socioeconomic positions, which correspond to Aronowitz's structural space, and consciousness, which may correspond to Aronowitz's common discursive position, as conditions of class formation. While Konrad and Szelenyi also require "agents" to be willing to occupy a new class position (1991:358), Aronowitz emphasizes political organizations. All of these class elements are emphasized as well by the other theorists we have quoted: Marx, Weber, Bell, Barbara and John Ehrenreich, Giddens, and especially Gouldner.

As we have explained, intellectuals in China share cultural capital that puts them in a certain occupational structure or structures; this is their economic base. They have a version of CCD that provides them with a discursive position, or ideological base. The calling and the humanist spirit constitute their political consciousness. Moreover, the political parties or professional associations they now have can be their organizational base. China's intellectuals thus have all the makings of a cohesive class with distinct economic, ideological, political, and organizational foundations and interests. What then is their problem? They lack a national political party or parties that can function discursively—*and publicly*—throughout the country. Chinese intellectuals, however, are struggling against the odds for the right to establish such parties. Once they have overcome these obstacles, they will be on their way to class power (For a discussion of the "new class" project in Central Europe, see Eyal, Szelenyi, and Townsley 1998:160–4).

But even if the political system is such that they can establish their own parties, intellectuals still face the challenge from their own culture, the flaw of CCD. Unless they can transcend their flaw, the future success of the intellectual class is still in doubt. Nonetheless, a class formation is still possible. And it can still be a cohesive class, with critical intellectuals at the core, unattached professionals next, and organic intellectuals in the periphery, as figure 6.2 indicates.

In addition, the flaws, divisions, and infighting among intellectuals are no more serious a threat to the intellectual class than they are to the working class. As Gouldner (1979:31) points out, "the working class itself has also been said to be too internally divided into different craft, industrial, and wage groups, sharply segmented by education, sex, race and age, and prey to nationalism and chauvinism; yet this has not aborted the rise of powerful working class political parties, trade unions, and movements . . . [And] as Marx said, each capitalist destroys many others." A largely cohesive and unitary class is far more likely if the intellectual class realizes its own flaws and strives to transcend them.

Chapter Seven

Summary and Conclusion: The Future of China's Intellectuals

Crises are opportunities.
(Weiji jiushi zhuangji.)
—Chinese proverb

This chapter summarizes the changing politics of China's intellectuals from the Mao era to the present. We will also explore certain directions in which intellectuals as a class may have roles to play in easing China's crises of modernization.

The Changing Politics of China's Knowledge Workers

In this section, we will first review the political sociology of knowledge workers as we have developed it in these pages. Then we will summarize the political transformation from the Mao era (1949–76) to the Deng era (1977–97), the further development of critical, unattached, and organic intellectuals in the 1990s and beyond, and intellectuals as a class.

A Political Sociology of Intellectuals

Although researchers may choose to analyze intellectuals according to the work they do, such as the humanities or science, or to categorize them as humanistic or technical intellectuals, we have followed a politico-sociological approach. We also adopt a broader than usual definition of knowledge workers. We include not only those who have followed the critical tradition, but also those who have been educated at a conventionally defined level and who perform certain cultural and social roles. We identify four types according to the political roles they play: revolutionary intellectuals, organic intellectuals, unattached intellectuals (both bourgeoisified and professionalized), and critical intellectuals.

When they are in power, *revolutionary intellectuals* become entrapped in the power structure they have created, and inevitably turn into irrational bullies and dictators. This is what happened to the Jacobins in eighteenth-century France as well as to the Chinese Communists in the twentieth century. At a lower level, the *organic intellectuals* serve the powers that be, as did the *Ideologues* under Napoleon's France, and the Fabians in England in the 1880s. Chinese intellectuals have a long tradition of serving kings and emperors, and later on the Party and the Communist state. Moreover, they can be organic to the bourgeoisie, the working class, the intellectual class, or a particular social movement. The third group of intellectuals remains *unattached* to officialdom; it includes the leisure class in traditional China and the professionals who arose in the Republican era. Finally, there are the *critical intellectuals,* who are concerned about social inequalities and who criticize the people in power, but largely from outside the system. Examples include the Abolitionists of nineteenth-century America and the Dreyfusards of nineteenth-century France. Again, Chinese history abounds with intellectuals who defy the authorities.

Intellectuals' political roles are based on various ideological foundations. Some of these include revolutionary orientations, distrust of authority and tradition, the culture of critical discourse (CCD), alienation, populism, anti-intellectualism, and scientism. Although they may emphasize certain traits, different intellectuals share at least CCD and alienation. As we discussed in chapter 5, Chinese intellectuals have their own traditional version of CCD. Combined with democratic liberalism *(de xiansheng),* scientism *(sai xiansheng),* and ideal Marxism (revolution to save China—*geming jiu guo*) of the May 4 tradition, the Chinese CCD provides the intellectuals with a foundation on which they can build their political and intellectual careers in the 1990s and beyond.

In playing their roles, intellectuals face various ethical dilemmas. They tend to follow either an ethic of responsibility or an ethic of ultimate ends. For example, intellectuals tend to be concerned about the social inequalities in the world. Some find that the best way to deal with the problem is to follow an ethic of responsibility and to join the government as organic intellectuals, thus fulfilling the vocation as espoused in the Confucian classic, *The Great Learning.* But in doing so, they have to compromise their integrity. They soon find that the decision makers do not share their values. These intellectuals need to be near power, but they feel frustrated because they cannot always freely criticize their bosses or the system. If they remain inside the government, they become just like other revolutionary intellectuals in power: using dubious means to achieve their goals. The bourgeoisified intellectuals face a similar set of conflicts, although what challenges their integrity is money or profits rather than political authorities. Critical intellectuals follow the ethic of ultimate ends, refusing to compromise and keeping the flames of protest burning. So do unattached and professional intellectuals who refuse to compromise their principle of keeping a distance from politics. They want to focus on their intriguing academic and technical puzzles.

No matter what roles they play, intellectuals also face the dilemmas between Dao (values and morality) and shi (power, political or economic), and between vocation and profession. Intellectuals gravitate toward power, or the powers that be, but they also maintain a different set of values, beliefs, and norms. Dao and shi therefore often conflict. They also face a hard choice between politics as a vocation and academic pursuits as their profession (as in the case of Liang Shuming), or intellectual pursuits as a vocation and business or politics as a profession (as in the case of Wu Han), because they tend to be interested in both. Yet, they cannot do both equally successfully.

In other words, intellectuals face the choice of working mostly inside the government as effective history movers but enduring constant frustration, working mostly outside the government as critics or onlookers, doing what they can to influence history, or trying to do both. There is no best way to do it. It all boils down to the trade-off between intellectual autonomy and social efficacy. The ways in which they manage this conflict determine the extent to which they can effect social change.

All of these dilemmas between the ethic of responsibility and the ethic of ultimate ends, between *Dao* and *shi,* and vocation and profession, lead to intellectuals' dual and sometimes split personalities. That is the perennial lot of intellectuals. To be an intellectual is to be afflicted with this lot, but to understand it may help intellectuals cope with the ache and find what they believe to be the best they can do at the time to effect social change.

Despite their different political roles and ethics, intellectuals have the potential to become a class. This is because of their commonalities, which include the possession of cultural capital (an economic base), CCD (an ideological base), the calling, and the humanist spirit (a political base); they may even share membership in local-level organizations (an organizational base). Their inability to achieve the goals in these aspects creates alienation, which will further solidify the basis of the intellectual class. But as is the case with most other social classes in China, intellectuals are not yet a class since they lack effective discursive national parties. Moreover, even if they form a class, it will be a flawed class because of its elitism.

Finally, intellectuals switch freely among categories and between roles, and our ideal typical characterization, for the sake of clarity, is based on their primary orientations. One can be organic at one time and critical at other times; many such switches took place before and after the June 4 massacre, and before and after the Cultural Revolution. Furthermore, although one may be predominantly, say, unattached, one can be critical and organic at the same time, though to a lesser extent. An organic intellectual can be critical but again to a lesser degree compared with the typical critical intellectual. (An exception: By definition, an organic intellectual can be a professional but cannot be unattached.) A critical intellectual may be in favor of the powerful in some respects, but criticism of the powers that be, whether the dominant classes or simply repressive tradition, occupies his or her main attention.

The freedom to affiliate with any class or choose any position to the intellectual's liking is one of the most important aspects of our political sociology of intellectuals. Mannheim (1936:158) observes that the ability to decide whom to serve and the ability to switch freely between positions is one major characteristic that distinguishes intellectuals from other classes: "they and they alone were in a position to choose their affiliaition. . . ." As Lipset (1963:334–5) says about American intellectuals, "either commitment to and support of existing institutions or a critical detachment from them are equally possible and [are] legitimate positions for the contemporary American intellectual." Because of these shifting affiliations, our classifications must necessarily be ideal types.

From Mao to Deng: The Transformation of Intellectual Politics

The Mao era (1949–76) was characterized by a high degree of conformity to the Party line. This was achieved by a series of social movements launched by the Party, including chiefly the Thought Reform movements in the early 1950s, the Hundred Flowers movements in the late 1950s, and the Cultural Revolution beginning in the mid-1960s, which did not end until 1976. Most intellectuals willingly participated in the Thought Reform movements, believing that they needed to learn more about the Party and about socialism so that they could better contribute to a worthy cause. In other words, they wanted to be organic intellectuals to the Party and to the state. As things turned out, however, intellectuals found that many of their basic values were endangered, including freedom of artistic creation, the right of social criticism, and the professionalism they had developed pre-1949. When writers and scholars like Hu Feng and Yu Pingbo were criticized, intellectuals were made keenly aware of what they could and could not do.

While a few kept asking questions, as in the later Hundred Flowers movement, many chose to conform to the Party line to avoid the social consequences. Moreover, those who did ask questions, for instance, the democratic party figures Zhang Bojun and Chu Anping, did not essentially challenge the system. Most of them merely expressed a loyal opposition. This was even more true for critics within the Party. Examples from just before the Cultural Revolution included Deng Tuo, Wu Han, and Liao Mosha.

Deterred by severe punishments, there was little criticism outside the Party, for example, from Lin Xiling during the Hundred Flowers movement and Yu Luoke during the Cultural Revolution. Even so, the muted criticism from the outside did signal a true critical tradition, one that was different from that of the organic intellectuals. And Yu is an example of those who paid with their lives for their not so severe criticism. Whether they tried to express their criticism as organic or critical intellectuals, or whether they did not criticize at all, the conflicts intellectuals suffered led to dual and split personalities, as we showed in chapter 2.

The first period of the Deng era (1977–89) witnessed the beginning of the fragmentation of intellectual politics, accomplished by a high degree of openness. First of all, the critical tradition outside the system expanded. Various movements emerged to challenge the Party leaders, Party ideology, and even the system. Some of these include the April 5 movement in 1976, the "wounded literature" movement, the "obscure poetry" movement, the Democracy Wall movement at the end of the 1970s, the election campaign in 1980, as well as the student demonstrations from 1986 to 1987. This critical growth culminated in the 1989 democracy movement. From all of these movements emerged a formidable group of critical intellectuals that included Xu Wenli, Ren Wanting, Wei Jingsheng, Liu Qing, Hu Ping, Wang Juntao, Chen Ziming, Wang Dan, and Wang Youcai.

In a second instance of fragmentation, among the organic intellectuals within the system there developed a group of advocates of democratic reform, such as Zhou Yang, Wang Ruoshui, Yan Jiaqi, Su Shaozhi, and Liu Binyan. Like the Polish revisionists, they were instrumental in exposing the problems of the system, including alienation, and called for various democratic reforms that would express Marx's humanism. But there was little or no communication between the two groups of intellectuals, those in and those outside the system. Within the system, orthodox organic intellectuals like Hu Qiaomu and Deng Liqun fiercely defended the Party line, helping the government in minicampaigns designed to purge bourgeois liberalization, "spiritual pollution," and other democratic tendencies within the Party and within the government.

Meanwhile, economic reform in Deng's first period necessitated the recruitment of intellectuals, especially technical intellectuals, into the Party and the government. Their skills were needed in various organizations, including local and state governments as well as state-owned enterprises. Thus, a bureaucratization process began. But these new organic intellectuals were different from the old ones. They were more likely to be recruited for their technical expertise, which was immediately put to work.

The economic reform also released the energy of many intellectuals who went on to become private entrepreneurs. So the process of bourgeoisifying intellectuals began, and with it came a new kind of organic intellectual, who would serve the private entrepreneurs. In addition, intellectuals were fast becoming professionalized. A credentialing system was developed and intellectuals who wished to practice law, medicine, education, or engineering had to earn their titles. Intellectuals were beginning to detach themselves from politics and morality as their predecessors had in the Republican era.

The Further Development of Critical, Unattached, and Organic Intellectuals

In chapters 3, 4, and 5, we discussed the further development of the three kinds of intellectuals in the 1990s: critical, unattached, and organic. The 1989 crackdown on the democracy movement greatly constrained intellectuals' democratic discourse, but the revived economic campaign of 1992 created a more open public space for discourse on other themes. Almost anything could be openly discussed as long as it did not challenge the one-party dictatorship. Prohibited were democratic activities such as independent party-building, ethnic independence movements, or some religious and semireligious organizations like the Falun Gong movement. The June 4 massacre and the subsequent economic reform served as a watershed signaling a change in the intellectuals' political involvement. Some continued to be just as, if not more, critical of the Party and social inequalities, while others simply detached themselves from politics and became bourgeoisified and professionalized. Still others stayed in the system, helping the Party with further reform. These continued to endure constraints on their freedom of expression.

In the first of the developmental changes, critical intellectuals have embarked on their way to independent criticism. This criticism is embodied in a number of ways.

First, from writers (e.g., Wang Shuo); artists (e.g., the avant-garde painters and installation artists); and musicians (e.g., Cui Jian); to movie makers (e.g., Zhang Yimou and Chen Kaige), intellectuals are experimenting with various ways to express their social criticism. This is what we have termed as a spectacular 'postmodern phenomenon' in the sense that it is defying and decentering conventional authorities and breaking new grounds in exploring and examining modernity.

Second, intellectuals have engaged in debates over the humanist spirit (e.g., Wang Xiaoming and Xu Jilin); nationalism (e.g., Wang Xiaodong and He Jiadong); and the consequences of modernity (e.g., Wang Hui and Gan Yang). The debate on the humanist spirit has helped intellectuals to form their consciousness and to clarify their roles, which is of crucial importance at a time when the entire society is rapidly becoming commercialized.

Third, the intense relationship between China and the United States in the 1990s has stimulated strong anti-Western sentiments among some intellectuals (e.g., Wang Xiaodong and Sheng Hong), but these sentiments have been criticized by other intellectuals (e.g., Xiao

Gongqin and He Jiadong) as radical and irrational. Although post-modernists (e.g., Chen Xiaoming) and national learning scholars (e.g., Zhang Dainian and Chen Lai) have also been involved in the debate, their efforts are more toward nation-building than toward anti-Westernism as some have charged. Nationalism has been a driving force in the Chinese revolution, and it will continue to affect Chinese politics in the future. The challenge before critical intellectuals is whether they can channel the nationalistic feelings in ways that will help define a Chinese national identity and facilitate racial and ethnic harmony—reconciling conflicts and promoting cooperation—within the country and between China and the world.

Fourth, the debate over modernity is a step in that direction. The specific question here, however, is how to view the modern transformations of Chinese politics and economy. The liberals (e.g., Xu Youyu and Wang Dingding) and neoconservatives (e.g., Xiao Gongqin and Wang Huning) applaud the market economy and want to postpone democracy until the time when conditions are ripe for it. They believe that rapid democratic reform should be avoided. The New Left (e.g., Han Yuhai and Xudong Zhang) criticizes them as failing to see the hardships caused by the market economy, and they want to develop grass-roots democracy to check government corruption and capitalist greed. Neither of them has, however, directly tackled the problems of the one-Party dictatorship or the effective ways to reform the CCP. The Old Left (e.g, Deng Liqun and his followers), while also seeing the problems of modernity, is lagging far behind in finding a solution. Still, the debate has provided space for critical intellectuals to ponder the paths of China's development, and it is largely independent of the Party's influences.

Fifth, there are intellectuals in China and abroad who strive for a political change. These are the democracy movement intellectuals (Wang Youcai, Xu Wenli, Wei Jingsheng, Liu Qing, Yan Jiaqi, Liu Binyan, etc.). They have persisted in spite of the government's arrests of their leaders and constant threat to those who dare to start any independent dissident movements. Their voice will become more and more important as China's modernization problems deepen.

Critical intellectuals in the 1990s and beyond have displayed tremendous potential for influencing public opinion on the current reform in China. In fact, they are on their way to reaching the level of political criticism against the Guomindang (GMD) that existed before the 1949 Communist takeover. Seeing what happened to the GMD in 1949 and again in 2000 when it lost its election in Taiwan, the CCP seems more determined than ever to suppress any organized activities that might challenge its control in China. Intellectuals are severely constrained in those terms, but other than that, there is still much room for social criticism. With the flourishing of newspapers and magazines as well as Internet sites, it is safe to assume that there will be, slowly but steadily, more and more room for criticism. Critical intellectuals seem to be ready for it. And they are not alone: there are other social critics in society, whom we do not always hear, as we discussed in chapter 3.

In the second of the developments in the 1990s and beyond, intellectuals are fast becoming bourgeoisified and professionalized. This was caused both by the crackdown of the 1989 democracy movement and by the economic campaign set forth in 1992. Moneymaking has now become a primary goal for many intellectuals. The environment is such that only if you have money can you be considered successful. So some have either started their own companies or begun to work for private entrepreneurs. In this bourgeoisification process some intellectuals seem to be quietly abandoning the traditional values of scholarship and concern over social inequalities. There remains, however, a built-in strain between the intellectual's business side and his or her scholarly side.

The vast number of intellectuals, it should be noted, do not become either critical or bourgeoisified intellectuals. They are professionals working as lawyers, doctors, journalists, teachers, engineers, and so forth. For most of the 1990s, while some did well in the market economy, others had to struggle for a decent living. We described the difficult conditions of college professors and engineers in chapter 4. Since the end of 1999, however, at least professors' incomes have been increased. But since they do not have their own professional organizations that could serve as advocates for their interests, the improvement of their living and working conditions—income, promotion, housing, and funding for their research—depends on the mercy of the state. They are waiting for the state to hand down a policy rather than forcing the state to accept a policy that would be conducive to their work.

The latest increase in salary beginning in 1999, following the increase in the mid-1990s, was not a result of their advocacy. It was a result of the state's belated realization that it needs, and must therefore pay for, the productivity of its professionals. With the development of professionalism, intellectuals are likely to become more assertive, especially since they know the state needs them. On the other hand, the move toward professionalism means a move away from the traditional morality of intellectual politics. Like the critical intellectuals, professionals are also making a U-turn to where they were in the Republican era.

The third and one of the most interesting developments in 1990s is the change in the organic intellectuals. In chapters 1 and 2, we saw the CCP develop its own organic intellectuals like Zhou Yang, Ding Ling, and even Wang Shiwei from the Yan'an era. We saw more and more intellectuals flock to the Party after 1949. At the same time more intellectuals became disenfranchised, from Wang Shiwei of the Yan'an era to Hu Feng, Feng Xuefeng, and then Ding Ling in the 1950s. In the Cultural Revolution, while the Party developed more organic intellectuals such as Zhang Chunqiao and Yao Wenyuan, it also purged numerous others, such as Deng Tuo, Wu Han, and Liao Mosha.

More of this took place in Deng's reformist era, though on a much smaller scale. Many of the democratic elite in the Party were thrown out, while the orthodox organic intellectuals held steady and even helped the Party to carry out its purges. Some of the orthodox organic intellectuals, for instance, Deng Liqun and his followers, however, have since become uneasy with the reform, and begun to criticize the Party for ignoring the workers' plight. They, too, seem to have become critical intellectuals as did the democratic elite, although of a different kind. Meanwhile, the Party has gathered around itself a larger number of theorists, economists, official democratic party functionaries, journalists, researchers in the academies of social sciences, and new scholar-officials. With the help of these organic intellectuals, the Party is now able to carry out its own political as well as economic agendas.

More interestingly, other classes have also been developing their own organic intellectuals. Again, because of the development of the market economy, a private entrepreneurial class, a middle class, working class, and peasant class are all taking shape. Intellectuals find themselves working for these various classes. We mentioned earlier that many intellectuals have become bourgeoisified, starting private companies, with their own organic intellectuals as managers or technical experts. Some intellectuals have also tried to organize laid-off workers or to start independent unions in private enterprises. Some peasants, too, have tried organizing themselves, thus developing their own organic intellectuals. Although the professional middle class has yet to find its own voice, we already see some professional associations achieving a level of autonomy.

However, these social classes are still in the process of formation, since the CCP forbids independent organizing. Thus, their organic intellectuals are only being formed. As China evolves from a class-divided society to a class society, one can see more and more organic intellectuals developed by these different classes. The contradictory class locations of these organic intellectuals, especially those from the Party and from the private entrepreneurs, will inevitably subject them to dual and split personalities. The ethic of responsibility they tend to follow will require that they compromise their intellectual integrity. Nonetheless, they are playing crucial roles in national politics. If there is a battle of discourses, it will almost surely be between these organic intellectuals and the various critical intellectuals.

Chinese Intellectuals as a Class

Finally, we have discussed the possibility of intellectuals forming a class. Traditionally, sociologists have not viewed intellectuals as a class either in China or in the West, although they have often been mentioned as though they were a class. Indeed, there are plenty of arguments against such a proposition, from Weber, Parsons, Bell, and Brint, as well as from Mao himself. But there are also plenty of arguments for a new class, especially in a postindustrial era when more people have higher levels of education and when the knowledge industries, science, and technology, become increasingly important. Gouldner is the most important advocate of the new class theory, and Aronowitz and DiFazio may be called his "disciples."

In the case of China, even with all of the fragmentation among critical, unattached, and organic intellectuals, there are also many commonalities. The cultural capital can be their economic base, the culture of critical discourse their ideological base, the calling and the humanist spirit their political base, and intellectual communities their organizational base. Of course, because the CCP forbids national discursive parties no intellectual class has yet emerged. It remains a possibility, though, for intellectuals do have the potential to form a class and they have been preparing for it. It will, however, be a flawed class because of the elitist nature of the intellectual.

The Future of China's Intellectuals

With its fast-paced market economy and its slow political development, the crises of China's modernization seem to be deepening. In this section, we will begin by describing these crises. We will then explain some possible future directions open to intellectuals as a class, always taking into account what we know about each group's concerns.

The Crises of Chinese Modernity

To be fair, China has made tremendous progress both economically and politically in the past decade. The per capita income of rural households increased from 133 yuan in 1978 to 922 yuan in 1993, and that of urban households, from 316 yuan to 2,334 yuan (Lam and Mok 1997:465). The corresponding figures for 1998 were 2,150 yuan for rural residents and 5,454 yuan for urbanites. These figures indicate increased living standards since prices for consumer goods have been decreasing since 1995 (Zhu Qingfang 1999:353, 356). So far, inflation has not been a problem. Ordinary families are able to "reduce their expenditures on basic necessities (e.g., food) [and] spend more on fashionable clothes, durable consumer goods and leisure" (Lam and Mok 1997:466).

Politically, although repression of dissidents is still severe, 50 percent of the villages in the countryside have successfully established their own governments through democratic elections, although many problems in the election process have still persisted (Cao Jinqing 2000; Zhang Ming 2001).[1] Another 40 percent of the villages have gone through the drill, though real elections have yet to occur (Bai Gang 1999:180). To the credit of the villages, efforts are being made to correct these problems.[2]

With all of the progress China has made so far, problems still abound. There are still 50 million people in absolute poverty in the countryside and another 15 million in the cities (Tang Jun 1999:401). The heavily polluted environment does not show much improvement in spite of the government's efforts, corruption is still rampant, and plural politics has yet to arrive. Indeed, a national survey of 50 cities in 1998 ranked corruption as their first concern, followed by unemployment (and underemployment), the possibility of inflation, environmental deterioration, social inequalities, law and order, and so forth (Xu Xinxin 1999:84–7; see also He Qinglian 1998 for other socioeconomic problems). We will briefly examine the problems of modernization in the following areas: first, the *ecological* crisis; then the *social and political* crises, including nationalism and quasi-nationalism, corruption, conditions of the working people, social unrest and the crisis in the spiritual sphere; and finally the *educational crisis*.

The Ecological Crisis

In China, as everywhere else in the world, people must seriously consider whether the species is "already pushing against the carrying capacity" of its own habitat (Lewellen 1995:191). The danger in China may be more serious than anywhere else. As Smil delineates in *China's Environmental Crisis* (1993), the Chinese are facing increased population (another 200 million by 2025 on top of today's 1.25 billion); water pollution and shortages; soil erosion and desertification; air pollution causing respiratory morbidity and mortality in large urban areas; and so on. We will take air and water problems in the 1990s as an example.

Air pollution. Solid fuels, primarily coal, provide China with 77 percent of her commercial energy, compared with 33 percent for the United States and 30 percent for the world. As one of the major sources of pollution (Lotspeich and Chen 1997:34; Mou Guangfeng 2000:318), they have had disastrous effects, especially in the north, where air pollution tend to exceed the World Health Organization standard by five to six times. Beijing's air, for example, is about seven to eight times as bad as the air quality in New York City. And Beijing is not even the most polluted city in China. Lung disease, which is one of the leading causes of death in China, climbed 18.5 percent in the major cities from 1988 to 1993. For several years, peasants around Chongqing saw onions, potatoes and vegetables wither, unripe fruit fall off the trees, and forests die from a formerly unfamiliar insect attracted to the sulfur-polluted leaves (WuDunn 1993a; Tyler 1994c; Lotspeich and Chen 1997). About a third of the country is still suffering from acid rain, increasing from 1,750,000 square kilometers in 1985 to 2,800,000 square kilometers in 1993, according to Xie Zhenhua, head of the State Environmental Protection Agency (*Overseas Chinese Daily,* January 7, 1995; see also Mou Guangfeng 2000:318). In 1991 alone, acid rain caused "$2.8 billion in damage to farm crops, forests and buildings across the nation. . . . And factories are expected to pump an increasing amount of sulfur dioxide into the air, from 15.5 million tons in 1991 to more than 1.4 billion tons projected for the year 2000 if pollution is not controlled" (WuDunn 1993a).

Water shortages and pollution. In the mid 1980s, statistics showed that "90 percent of urban groundwater resources were contaminated" (Lotspeich and Chen 1997:41). While 300 out of 500 of the nation's cities had water shortages, factories kept dumping industrial waste into the

Figure 7.1 The Dangerous Signs *(Weixian de xinhao)*

Note: The Chinese on the left reads: "the index of air pollution," and on the right, "the air quality levels."

Source: Ding Cong 1999 *Cartoons of Satire.*(Vol. 3), p. 169.

country's waterways. In 1993 alone, 35.5 billion tons of sewage and industrial wastes were discharged into the country's rivers, streams, and coastal seas. According to the State Environmental Protection Agency, about 80 percent of the 52,500 polluting factories had been closed by October 1996, but it would be difficult to insure that they do not open again (*World Journal,* October 13, 1996). The problem still continues (Liu Bing 1999: 416–7). Furthermore, as the U.S. Embassy reported, "Solid wastes piled outside of cities have leaked toxins into the ground water, and the water in many rivers does not meet the standards for bathing much less drinking" (Tyler 1994c). Indeed, people have long since begun to buy bottled waters. And worse yet, sample examinations in 1993–95 by government agencies found that 50 percent of the so-called spring water contained germs in excess of the numbers allowed by national standards (*World Journal,* January 5, 1997). According to Liu Bing (1996:259), 333 incidents of fish contamination, some quite serious, were reported in 1994 alone in twenty provinces, an increase of 142.3 percent over the previous year.[3]

Social and Political Crises

First, the country faces numerous *divisive forces* of nationalism and quasi-nationalism: the independent-minded Taiwanese, the challenging Hong Kongese, the unhappy Tibetans, the Xingjiang (Uygur Autonomous region) and the Inner Mongolian minorities. These restless areas may also be joined by deep-rooted regional particularisms. Some scholars suggest that Guangdong province, for example, might team up with Hong Kong and declare autonomous political status. Their common interest, language, and family ties, as well as their geographic closeness and their vast distance from Beijing make this scenario possible. Together they may ask for political and economic autonomy from the Beijing government. Indeed, the democracy movement in Hong Kong is setting an example not only for Guangdong but for other more developed regions in the country such as Shanghai (Siu 1993). Hong Kong is neither a capitalist paradise nor a timid Special Administrative Region of China (So 2000a). The fragmentation scenario is very unlikely, though, for it would be too costly, given the Central government's military power over the provinces (Baum 1996). But regional power is certainly growing. It will pose a strong threat to centralized governance, and before a balance can be achieved, some kind of chaos may be a real possibility (see also Starr 1996).[4]

Second, *corruption* is rampant despite the government's constant efforts at control. This includes bribery of and by Party and government officials, extortion and racketeering, graft and embezzlement, and negligence in carrying out their duties, causing grave loss in human lives and public money. It includes inquisition by torture, illegal appropriation of or simply taking as one's own relief funds for natural disasters, smuggling, money laundering, selling public property for one's private benefit, doctoring or destroying accounts to avoid taxes, and spending public funds on banquets and foreign tours (Wen Shengtang 1999; Tian Yuchuan 1999; Jin Ye 1998). All of this and more happens at every level of government. No wonder corruption has been the people's number one concern for so many years. Corruption continues unchecked today, despite the Central Committee's repeated efforts at sanctions. The committee repeatedly warns that if things go on like this, the Party is going to lose its power to control the country and may even lose its legal right to govern.[5]

Third, the conditions of the working people and their protests are equally distressing. In chapter 5, we discussed the conditions of laid-off workers from state-owned enterprises, as well as migrant workers from the countryside. Many have to work long hours for little pay in private or public companies. Unemployment and underemployment are becoming more and more serious. In the countryside, the actual incomes of peasants have also declined since 1997 (Lu Xueyi 2001). The increasing gap between the rich and the poor has now become a concern for many. As a result, social unrest is on the rise. For example, collective protests in 1998 numbered 5,000 throughout China according to official reports (Minxin Pei 2000:25). The total strikes nationally numbered 480 in 1992; 1,870 in 1995; and 1,740 in the first nine months of 1996 (Ching Kwan Lee 2000:49).[6]

Fourth, there is a lack of ideological backing to help tide people over these crises. Although there has been some revival of the traditional ideologies of Confucianism, Taoism, and Buddhism, what seems to be taking hold in the Chinese mind today is the "spirit of capitalism" but without the "Protestant ethic." Marxism has been used, abused, and almost refused, as is almost all socialism, except among the left-wing intellectuals. The Communist or communitarian spirit developed during the Chinese revolution has been put on hold. Deng's ostrich policy, still carried out by Jiang Zemin, says, "do not ask whether it is socialism or capitalism," and discourages and sometimes bans outright all discussion of ideologies when it comes to the political implications of the economy. This only creates ideological confusion and exacerbates the ideological crisis. Falun Gong, as we discussed in chapter 3, is a result of this crisis. It claims to have hundreds of thousands of believers and has left the government so panic-stricken that Beijing has labeled it illegal and banned its existence.

This is partly a result of what many Chinese as well as American intellectuals call a "morality vacuum." Public civility is at issue. Indeed, China faces as its central problem morality, propriety, and public service—the "core" that used to define China and Chineseness as an example to the world. With the advent of the market economy, the Chinese have yet to figure out what is proper behavior and what makes China the distinctive example many Chinese intellectuals believe it should be, however vaguely. China and its intellectuals are faced with the task of preventing a Chinese core ethic from eroding in the "universal solvent of modern commercial culture" (Link 1993:194, 203). We will discuss this issue in more detail later when we discuss the roles of intellectuals as a class.

Educational Crisis

The level of educational attainment for the vast majority of Chinese has always seemed to contradict its world-renowned literary tradition. Currently, the rate of education lags far behind what is needed for social and economic development. Although the number of college openings had doubled to 2.5 million by 1994 (Brauchli 1994), it had drifted back to 1.8 million by 1998 (Ministry of Education 1999:168). Table 7.1 shows the rate of advancement from primary to upper schools at various levels.

If we start with 100 children of primary-school age, 11 cannot go on to junior middle schools.[7] Only 27, that is, 30.2 percent, can go on to senior middle schools or middle-level professional and technical schools *(zhong zhuan);* 62 are left behind. Out of the 27 only 11, or 39.8 percent, can go to a college of some kind, leaving 16 behind. In other words, if the enrollment level at various schools remains at the 1993 level, only 11 percent of college-aged young people have an opportunity to go on to some tertiary education. This includes high-level professional and technical schools *(da zhuan)* that require two to three years of schooling, as in American community colleges. (There have been new schools built, especially private ones, but they are so few that they do not affect the general trends.) In contrast, in the United States, 75 percent of high school students have some tertiary education (Brauchli 1994). By 1997, only 2.53 percent of the general population had a college education (Zhang Yi 2000:292), as we mentioned in

Table 7.1 Advancement Rate to Secondary and Tertiary Level Education in 1993

	From primary to junior middle school	From junior to senior middle school	From senior middle school to college
Percent of students moving on	89.0%	30.2%	39.8%
Number left behind out of a total of 100 to begin with	11	62	16

Source: Statistical Year Book of China. 1994, ed. by State Statistical Bureau, PRC, p. 562.

chapter 4. Thus, China's educated population is so small that China's ability to modernize itself *and* at the same time deal with attendant problems is seriously impaired.

Furthermore, the market economy is dictating college curricula. Students tend to choose majors that they hope will help them economically. A survey of college students in seven universities in Hubei Province found that 57 percent of the respondents would like to engage in business or business management, while only 8 percent would choose to be teachers or agricultural engineers (*World Journal,* January 5, 1997). Some researchers have already cautioned against the negative consequences of market-driven education. Individual development and perfection, qualities cherished in the traditional Chinese education, are in danger of being swept away by the emphasis on technical and practical training (*Guangming Ribao,* June 19, 1994). Humanities and social science courses are pushed aside in the mistaken belief that science and technology alone can solve all modernization problems. The humanities and social sciences are neglected or intentionally avoided partly because of their political nature. Enrollments in sociology (already small in number) were actually temporarily suspended in the aftermath of the June 4 massacre.

To exacerbate this already deplorable situation, many young college professors and primary and secondary school teachers have opted to go abroad or to enter businesses. Chinese colleges face a serious shortage of motivated younger teachers. In 1992, 40 percent of the professors were over 61 years old, 40 percent were between 56 and 60, and 11 percent were below 35. The situation was even worse in 1994 (Brauchli 1994). Almost all of our interviewees from institutions of higher education in the three cities we visited said that their departments lacked faculty aged between 30 and 45. The older professors wondered whether their departments, or even the universities, would survive their retirement. A survey by the Chinese Academy of Sciences of 43 research institutes showed that 38 percent of those with graduate degrees and 27 percent of those with college degrees had left. In some institutes, the loss rate of young researchers reached 80 percent (Bai Zang 1994). The president of Beijing University reported that 60–70 percent of newly recruited college teachers leave every year (Yang Dongping 1999:382).

The exodus of university teachers was paralleled by the exodus of middle school and primary schoolteachers, creating a crisis of primary and secondary school education that affected the quality of university students. Reports show that in 1992, China lost a total of 450,000 teachers to private businesses. Shanghai lost 2,300 primary schoolteachers, and Beijing lost 6,300 from 1990 to 1993 (*World Journal,* June 10, 1994).[8] In a country where there are two hundred million illiterate people, these losses only aggravate the problem.

One of the chief reasons for the exodus was the teachers' low income and, worse, uncertainty that they would be paid. In 1992 over seven thousand schoolteachers went unpaid for seven months in a county in Sichuan. In cases like this, teachers had to depend on family and friends to help them survive. Over one hundred school principals submitted their resignations in that same county. As a result, the junior high school dropout rate in the county rose to 50 percent (*World Journal,* December 25, 1992).[9] The problem has persisted (*Overseas Chinese Daily,* June 13, 1998),[10] although university teachers' situation has been vastly improved since the end of the 1990s. Another report shows that over 100 townships in eight counties in Hainan province owed cadres and teachers 49 million yuan, and about half of that money was owed to primary school teachers (Yang Dongping 1999:388). The loss of schoolteachers will obviously result in the further loss of students. This is apparently a more difficult problem to deal with than the exodus of college teachers.

Some suggest that China is facing mounting problems with a waning capacity to deal with them, either environmentally or politically (Starr 1996). What are some of the political roles intellectuals as a class can play to alleviate such crises in the twenty-first century or, even better, to turn the situation around? In the remainder of the chapter, we will discuss their roles in seeking alternatives to the current political and economic systems, in social movements, in education, and in transforming themselves.

Looking for an Alternative

As we discussed in chapter 3, liberals, neoconservatives, and the New and Old Left have been locked in a battle of discourses on which way China should go in modernizing itself. Although the regime has made an effort to suppress discussion on the question of whether China is practicing socialism or capitalism, especially concerning the change in the political system, the issue is still debated. In fact, the Old Left has raised the issue again and again in their journals, such as *Zhongliu*

(Midstream), and *Dangdai Sichao* (Contemporary thoughts). What does the Party mean by "socialism with Chinese characteristics," an idea put forth at its Twelfth Congress in 1982? What is "the initial stage of socialism," another idea put forth at its Thirteenth Congress in 1987 (Wu Jianguo et al. 1993:525–7)? The great debate on modernity among intellectuals, independent of the Party's intentions, is an effort to clarify these issues. China's politico-economic stance is a tricky issue but obviously an important and legitimate one. It will continue to be one of the hot topics. One of the leading roles for intellectuals might be to look for an alternative between capitalism and socialism.

Indeed, inspired by Giddens's theory on the "third way," intellectuals are pondering a possible path between capitalism and socialism (Xu Jilin et al. 2000; Zhang Rulun 2000; Liu Kang 1996). But what is the "third way?" Giddens (1998:1, 3–4; 154–5) believes that with the collapse of "actually existing socialism" in Eastern Europe and the rise of free market philosophies, such as that of Friedrick A. Hayek, as well as the practices embodied in Thatcherism and Reaganomics in the 1980s, social democrats all over the world lost confidence in the future of social democratic politics. But in the 1990s, Thatcher's and Reagan's neoliberalism began giving way to the rise of New Labor in Britain, represented by Tony Blair, and America's New Democrats, represented by Bill Clinton. Indeed, the socialism that promises to generate more wealth than capitalism and then to distribute it equally is dead. Yet the values and ideals of socialism still remain intrinsic to a socially and economically good life. That is why social democracy can make a comeback. Nonetheless, Giddens thinks that for social democracy to remain on the political scene, there must be something solid behind it. So Giddens promotes the "third way."

By the "third way," Giddens (1998:viii; 2, 26) means "a framework of thinking and policy-making that seeks to adapt social democracy to a world which has changed fundamentally over the past two or three decades. . . ." It is "an attempt to transcend both old-style social democracy [represented by the collapsed socialism we just mentioned] and neoliberalism," or a "social democratic renewal." This means that one needs to know what sort of society to create and must have the concrete means to create it. For example, "third way" politics will take a positive attitude toward globalization, preserve a core concern with social justice, and look for a new relationship between the individual and the community, as well as a harmonious relationship between human beings and nature. Some of the prime dicta will include "no rights without responsibilities," and "no authority without democracy" (pp. 64–6). If this is the new thinking, it remains for social democrats to find out the means to accomplish its goals.

That is exactly what today's Chinese intellectuals are debating: the paths of development. As we discussed in chapter 3, critical intellectuals, concerned about the consequences of modernity, have been debating the advantages and disadvantages of the market economy, and whether and when China can establish a democratic polity. But liberals and the New Left do not seem able to reach common ground, and so cannot find a third way between capitalism and socialism (Xu Jilin et al. 2000:332–3). Intellectuals do not agree on how they should view globalization and free market forces, nor do they agree on how a society can preserve its social justice.

One possible direction China's third way, or "socialism with Chinese characteristics," could take would be to integrate Marx's humanism, embodied in socialism, and Weber's competitive political realism, embodied in capitalism. In the 1980s, there was much discussion on Marx's humanism by the democratic elite. But what *is* Marx's humanistic socialism? According to Bologh (1979:8, 239), Marx's socialism would be a form of life or system of production in which the individual would be free and social. They would be *free* because of the diversity of possible activities and relations open to them, which would contribute to their development as an individual. They would be *social* because they produce their own being in a community that collectively determines production. In contrast to this delightful picture, Marx would say that capitalism represents a divided object of the exchange value and use value of the commodity, and a divided subject of the proletariat and the bourgeoisie, which presents itself as internal conflict, that is, class struggle. In Marx's view of capitalism, individuals are neither free nor social.

However, Marx's socialism did not materialize either in the actual socialism of the former Soviet Union or in the late version of Chinese socialism. Again, individuals were neither free nor social. Weber would say that that was because socialism's planned economy weakens the incentive to labor, reduces formal calculatory rationality, fosters dictatorial administration, and requires a higher level of bureaucratization than does capitalism (Bologh 1984:179–80). But Weber is not happy with capitalism, either. Based on money calculation, capitalism privileges the wealthy, fosters a system of domination, develops a bureaucracy that may stifle private economic initiatives, and increases authoritarian constraint by controlling employment and unemployment (pp. 178–9).

What China faces is the dilemma of modernity, which, according to Weber, is characterized by the conflict between the instrumental, *formal rationality* (technical means, methods, and procedures) of capitalism, and the value-driven, *substantive rationality* (ethical ends, principles, and ideals) of socialism (Bologh 1990:134). Is there a solution to the dilemma? Weber is pessimistic. The two types of rationality give rise to two kinds of political dilemma: the *ethic of ultimate ends,* which is an ethic of brotherly love, and an *ethic of responsibility,* which urges one to act not according to an absolute value but according to consequences as well as to values. The end often does justify the means (Weber 1946: 120–8). Weber chose capitalism over socialism based on the ethic of responsibility. He is ambivalent about the consequences of capitalism, but as he says, "Here I stand; I can do no other" (p. 127).

But must it be so? According to Georg Simmel, individuals grow together into units that satisfy their interests, and association is one form in which they do so (1950:41). Sociability, a play-form of association, "creates an ideal sociological world in which the pleasure of the individual is closely tied up with the pleasure of the others. In principle, nobody can find satisfaction here if it has to be at the cost of diametrically opposed feelings which the other may have" (p. 48). There is one way to reconcile Weber's world of conflict and struggle with Marx's world of individual and community development. That way is a humanist socialism, or what Bologh (1990:284) calls a "feminist socialism," which

> as distinct from a masculine socialism [i.e., the actually existing socialism], would constitute an institutionalized commitment to sociability which explicitly acknowledges an inevitable internal tension between individual and community, differentiation and identification, separation and attachment, a tension that must be lived with and recognized rather than denied and repressed. Socialism as a mode of production characterized by people co-operating with and caring about each other and each other's needs, feelings and uniqueness requires a commitment to sociability if it is not to degenerate into coercion. Socialism must

> ground itself in sociability—a mutual play of difference between whole and part, community and individual, and between and among groups and individuals.

In other words, a humanist, or a feminist, socialism recognizes the differences and tensions between individuals and social groups or classes, but still strives to build a community in which each individual would have an opportunity to develop. No one can be happy if that happiness is achieved at the expense of others, as Simmel has just told us. To avoid that is the ideal on which a humanist socialism is based. That is a possible third way, which not only recognizes the validity of market forces but also the importance of social justice.

Can Chinese culture integrate such a humanist socialism, a socialism that is the result of interaction between Marx's humanist socialism and Weber's politically realistic capitalism? Can intellectuals find that "middle ground between total fidelity to the native heritage (be that Confucian or revolutionary) and unqualified admiration of the technological accomplishments of the West" (Schwarcz 1986b:253–4)? In the transformation of Chinese culture, intellectuals face the task of clearing up the current ideological and spiritual chaos by providing some *zhichi dian,* "some points of light," that is, a system that people can safely rely on (Link 1993:200). Discussions on alienation and Marxist humanism in the 1980s, on the transformation of Confucianism, a cultural China, national learning, postmodernism, the humanist spirit, and so forth, which we have discussed in chapters 2 and 3, are all part of that effort. This endeavor is joined by intellectuals not only in Mainland China but also in Taiwan, Hong Kong, the United States, and elsewhere.

Yin Haiguang (1982:73–116), for example, believes in an integration of Eastern and Western moralities by accommodation and adjustment. Confucianism, Buddhism, and Christianity are to be integrated around democracy and science, and each has to adjust to, and accommodate, the others. For example, Confucianism has to adjust by criticizing its own rigid hierarchical stratification, its exaltation of men over women, and its intolerance of differing views. It must also cultivate such virtues as trust, modesty, flexibility, and righteousness. Yin's is a new culture characterized by morality, freedom, democracy, and science. And creating this culture, he says, is the responsibility of intellectuals (Yin Haiguang 1980:150).

Tu Wei-ming (1991a, 1991b, 1993c) proposes creating a new meaning for the term "being Chinese," a new identity based on human concerns pregnant with ethical-religious implications such as Confucian humanism and democratic liberalism. Similarly, he advocates an "Asian modernity." The new Chinese identity, as part of the Asian modernity, will someday replace both the political-capitalist identity of the Taiwanese and the political-socialist identity of the Chinese. This identity will be the work of a "cultural China" composed of "three symbolic universes": (1) Mainland China, Taiwan, Hong Kong, and Singapore; (2) the Chinese communities throughout the world, including those in Malaysia and the United States—estimated to be 20 to 30 million individuals; and (3) scholars, teachers, journalists, industrialists, traders, entrepreneurs, and writers, who share an international discourse on cultural China (Tu 1991a). Tu declared, "The fruitful interaction among a variety of economic, political, social, and cultural forces at work along the periphery [China outside the Mainland] will activate the dynamics of cultural China" (p. 28).

However, how the periphery's discourse, that is, an integration of Confucian humanism and democratic liberalism, can be included in a debate on socialism and capitalism is not clear. If it cannot, its use may be limited. It is probably a bit too optimistic for Tu to say that the center (Mainland China) "no longer has the ability, insight, or legitimate authority to dictate the agenda for cultural China," and "the transformative potential of the periphery is so great that it seems inevitable that it will significantly shape the intellectual discourse on cultural China for years to come" (Tu 1991a:27–8). Yes, the periphery has played an important role in shaping cultural China, but the center remains pretty strong. The socialist discourse especially cast in the "third way" may be affecting the periphery as well. In fact, the success of capitalism in the West is partly based on its learning from the socialist critique from the East. The effect is reciprocal.

Furthermore, intellectuals on Mainland China have called on their peers to challenge themselves, to face a world that is in danger of becoming a "cultural and intellectual desert." They are to reevaluate their relationships with the ruling powers and to shoulder their cultural and moral responsibilities (Xiao Gongqin 1994a, 1994b; Qin Ling 1994; Zhang Rulun et al. 1994). This discussion on a humanist socialism, the debate about the humanist spirit, nationalism, and national learning, the exploration of modernism and postmodernism, and the investigation into a new cultural China, are all part of the effort to transform and transcend the traditional culture, the modern Chinese Marxist culture, and the Western culture that is imported into China. This is a sort of "creative transformation" as Lin Yu-sheng (2000) would call it. They all have political implications.

In fact, during the Republican era when Zhang Junmai and his minor-party colleagues advocated a third force between the CCP and the GMD, they were already in search of the middle way between democracy and dictatorship, between capitalism and socialism, or at the very least of some kind of transformation. That is why his party was called the "National Socialist Party": it promoted nationalism, democracy, and socialism (Jeans 1997:202).

Similarly, after the founding of the PRC, Liu Shaoqi was searching for a third way between substantive and formal rationality. He was more concerned with combining "efficiency with equality and order with revolution" (Dittmer 1974:285–93) while Mao remained preoccupied with class inequalities. In the policy and philosophy differences between the two, Liu was more likely to follow the ethic of responsibility, or what Dittmer (p. 193) calls "formal justice," or formal rationality, while Mao followed the ethic of ultimate ends, a kind of "substantive justice," or substantive rationality. Mao's line won, and China ended up with little inequality but a lot of poverty. The current debate on where China is headed is a continuation of these two debates between Zhang's third forces and the CCP and GMD, and between Liu's way and Mao's way. And Zhang's and Liu's way may very well spearhead the third way Giddens is talking about. As Dittmer (1998:227) observes, Liu "looms as the great but unsung founder of reform communism in China." The same may be said of Zhang.[11]

Indeed, a "third way" seems to be the goal intellectuals are seeking (see also Zhang Rulun 2000), although it may be somewhat different from other "third ways." Theorists in and outside China are already exploring what it should be like. This is one of the roles of intellectuals as a class. However, the exploration of a new society should be done not only by critical intellectuals but also by organic intellectuals and professionals, who occupy key positions in social life. Faced with modernization and its discontents, the role of the intellectual class is to "illuminate the historical choices that we collectively have" (Wallerstein 1996:24). These choices are not only economic (e.g., socialism or capitalism), but also political (e.g., democracy, totalitarianism, or authoritarianism; and ethnic and regional unity or separation), and social (e.g., equality and inequality).

Marx would assign intellectuals yet another role: not only to explain the world, but to change it as well. In other words, intellectuals still need to find the means to achieve the goal. This is the focus of our remaining three sections on social movements, education, and the transformation of intellectuals themselves, respectively.

Social Movements

One important way to deal with the crises of modernization and to strive for an alternative way of development is through social movements, of which intellectuals have almost always been the chief organizers. Flacks (1991:14) remarks that "university-based intellectuals searching for political connections must participate in social movements." But it is really a tool for all intellectuals, not just for those in universities. These social movements may include the democracy movement, a possible federation movement, workers' movements, the peasants' movements, the women's movement, the consumer movement, and the ecological movement. The jobs intellectuals perform include outlining theories and strategies, organizing peaceful social protests, and mediating social interests and conflicts, or to use Konrad and Szelenyi's (1991:354) term, functioning as referees or play-masters.[12]

By making use of social movements, intellectuals play a key role in establishing a liberal democratic polity and a more equitable market economy—that is, a humanist socialism, or social democracy. Intellectuals are not simply altruistic when doing so. It is in their own best interests, not only for the general public, but also for the intellectuals at the administrative and grassroots levels, to establish such a free, equitable political and economic system (see figure 7.2 for an idea of the difficulty of such a task). In this new system, each human being will be freer to express his or her own political views. Each individual will have greater room for personal development.

The resolution of the political, social, ecological, and educational crises depends to a great extent on the growing power of the social movements. They are part and parcel of the civil society that is required for a democratic polity, which goes along with a transformed and transcendent Chinese culture. All of these depend largely on the efforts of the intellectual class.

Figure 7.2 The Difficult Task *(Jiannan de renwu)*

Note: On the tree is written "corruption."

Source: Ding Cong 1999 (Vol. 3), p. 90.

Education

As we discussed earlier, education in China is also in crisis. It is in crisis not only for lack of teachers, but also for lack of students in the social sciences and the humanities. Perhaps most serious, it is in crisis because so many students have no opportunity for schooling at primary, secondary, or college levels. Yet education is the only venue through which the country can train the kind of professionals and the organic and critical intellectuals it needs. Education is a "central mechanism for social change that will contribute to increased economic productivity and enhanced understanding and remedying of population, health, and environmental problems as well as providing an intellectual foundation to foster democratization and to promote human rights and civil liberties" (Mennerick and Najafizadeh 1992:288).

Giroux (1988:127) observes that teachers as intellectuals shoulder the responsibility for educating active, critical citizens. Such an education is, in a sense, "a fundamental social project to help students develop a deep and abiding faith in the struggle to overcome economic, political and social injustices, and to further humanize themselves as part of this struggle." No other aspect of development is more important. Intellectuals play a pivotal role in it. In fact, education is the first and foremost way for intellectuals to make a difference by teaching critical thinking and by furnishing the state with trained experts (Etzioni-Halevy 1985:17–9).

Their role, however, is not limited to teaching. As our interviewees point out, they are involved in system changes. But how can they implement system changes? We are back to social movements, to politics. As Weber says,

> Politics is a strong and slow boring of hard boards. It takes both passion and perspective . . . [M]an would not have attained the possible unless time and again he had reached out for the impossible. But to do that a man must be a leader, and not only a leader but a hero as well, in a very sober sense of the word. And even those who are neither leaders nor heroes must arm themselves with that steadfastness of heart which can brave even the crumbling of all hopes. (1946:128)

In fact, to advance and reform education, intellectuals need not be leaders or heroes. What is needed is an ordinary worker who is working his hardest with passion and steadfastness. Educators like Zhang Renjie and Xia Hairong, two of our interviewees, are precisely that sort. They are heroes, too. Large-scale reforms, however, are also needed, and that takes a social movement. It takes the effort of all types of intellectuals.

Transformation of Intellectuals Themselves

If the primary agents of social change are intellectuals, as we have demonstrated in these pages, are they ready to shoulder the responsibilities? In chapter 6, we discussed the intellectual class as flawed because of the elitist nature of its culture of critical discourse and called for the transcendence of their flaws. We will now further discuss the possible transformation of intellectuals.

Intellectuals tend to believe that they are the leading class. However, the Marxist search for one universal class as the agent for social change in China has failed, as has the Maoist revolution and for similar reasons. History proves that just as the workers are not the universal agents, neither are the intellectuals. In fact, the workers and peasants in the Chinese revolution have never acted as a group; it was the intellectuals in their name and with their support who made the Chinese revolution.

But as Boggs (1993:185) comments on the Russian Revolution, when the radical intellectuals took over state power and constituted themselves a new ruling stratum, the contradictions within the system became explosive, as in any highly stratified society. The intellectual-led Communist Revolution "embellished the most grandiose of visions . . . assuming a unique convergence of state and civil society . . . [a dialectic which] sooner or later gave rise to the domination of the state over virtually everything else" (pp. 24–5). The failure of the Jacobins and the Chinese revolutionary intellectuals in power is further testimony to the truth of the statement. Intellectuals cannot be a dominating class because of their elitist nature. Intellectuals must be constantly reminded of their limitations and must work within those limitations.

If there is no universal agent for social change, will intellectuals accept an alliance with other classes? Intellectuals tend to look down upon other groups because they believe that they themselves are the best and most convincing speakers; this is how you judge others according to CCD. The uneasy relationship between intellectuals and the working class reflects the intellectuals' lack of confidence in any lesser being. Despite this hostility, this ambivalence, some intellectuals have begun efforts to organize the workers. It remains to be seen to what extent they can overcome their elitism and succeed.

Furthermore, the transformation of intellectuals requires them to keep an open mind about *other* intellectuals. For example, it is probably narrow-minded to think, as many critical intellectuals do, that they are the true intellectuals, and organic intellectuals and professionals are not. Critical intellectuals of different convictions, that is, humanists, postmodernists, neoconservatives, the Old and New Left, and so forth, have yet to recognize any common ground. They need to deal with their petty-mindedness, arrogance, and intolerance, as pointed out by a number of scholars. Here is Sha Xuejun:

> In collective activities, they [intellectuals] tend to be petty-minded and intolerant. They have scholarly knowledge but they may not have the vital ability to be leaders and to organize. They tend to be overly self-confident and self-respecting, lacking discipline and looking down on others. They become people who can neither order nor be ordered. (cited by Jiang Tingfu 1980: p. 57)

This arrogance, intolerance, and petty-mindedness certainly have been manifest in various intellectual movements, such as the Communist movement led by Mao, Zhu, Zhou, and Liu, and more recently in the overseas democracy movement. Another quote from Hu Feng concerning factional quarrels among the left-wing writers in the 1940s is also illuminating: "We do not realize how much 'struggle' there is over self-importance in literary circles. There are rumors filled with evil and sectarian quarreling. . . . This not only wastes valuable strength, it also harms proper theoretical criticism" (quoted in Goldman 1967:17).

However, the political intolerance may not be merely a flaw of CCD; it may also be a part of the traditional political culture, which "has not yet accepted the politics of compromise that are so vital to democratic governance" (Fewsmith 1996). Unfortunately, the educated elite does not seem to be more tolerant than the rest of the population. Tang Tsou (1994:64) observes that some of the elite are not only intolerant; they would use political means to suppress differing opinions. Nathan and Shi (1993:111–2) report in their study on Chinese political behavior and attitudes that the Chinese were the least tolerant among the seven nations they studied, the others being Australia, Germany, Great Britain, the United States, Austria, and Italy. For example, less than 20 percent of the Chinese respondents were willing to allow someone with a deviant point of view to express that view at a meeting, compared with 40 to 75 percent of respondents in other countries. One may say that since the survey was done in an especially repressive period, just after the June 4 massacre, the results may be skewed.

But the supposition that Chinese are less tolerant of deviant views is also supported by interpretive studies such as those done by Lucian Pye, who states that Chinese political culture knows no equals, only superiors and inferiors, and that Chinese politics perceives a sharp divide between friend and foe (cited in Nathan and Shi 1993:111). Another more recent survey found that 18.86 percent of the respondents did not believe that "a person's belief system is his/her own affair," meaning that society has a right to intervene, and 16.42 percent of the respondents did not know whether the statement was correct (Rosen 2000:23). Those are fairly large numbers.

In sum, to transform the culture and change the society, intellectuals have to transform themselves as well. They are, after all, the chief carriers of the culture they want to transform, and they are partly the product of this same culture. In addition, there is no universal class agent for social change, and intellectuals are only one of the many players, albeit a chief one. As a primary agency for social change, however, they have yet to learn to cooperate with other classes and status groups in pushing for social movements that can help resolve the modernization crisis (Goldman 1994:358). In carrying out successful social movements, intellectuals also need to do two things: develop a tolerance of differing political convictions, and find commonalities among their ranks.

Conclusion

In this postmodern era of decentering authority and globalization, intellectuals do have the potential to play political roles even more varied and powerful than any they have played so far. As the Chinese saying goes, crises also imply opportunities. Indeed, modernization may be heralding new opportunities for intellectuals to rethink their political roles and to regroup to bring about social change and social justice. While divided among themselves, representing different groups, and being elitist and thus flawed, intellectuals as a class are still "the most progressive force in modern society," and "the most internationalist and most universalist of all social strata." Contradictory as they may be as a class, intellectuals still play vital roles in society and constitute "a center of whatever human emancipation is possible in the foreseeable future" (Gouldner 1979:83). They will no doubt continue to influence China's modernization. The question is how and to what extent.

Appendix

A Note on the Concept of the Intellectual

There has been much confusion as to what constitutes an intellectual. An examination of the Chinese transition from literati to intellectuals and the Western transition from philosophers to intelligentsia will lead us toward some clarification. We will then define intellectuals from several perspectives: educational, professional, cultural, social, and critical, and explain why we adopt a broader definition of intellectuals that encompasses all of those aspects.

Transition from Literati to Intellectuals: The Chinese Story

Who is an intellectual? The answer differs in different places, at different times, and with different people.

In traditional China, people we might now call intellectuals were called *wen ren* (literati), *shi* (or *shih,* gentry) or another *shi* (or *shih,* scholar-official) (see Jin Yaoji 1987:61). But the terms generally referred to the same group: people who were well versed in literary and philosophical works and who aspired to become officials at a certain point in their lives as the reward for years of study and training. In Weber's (1946:428) words, they were the traditional literati who had been taught arts and literature, and who, to become officials, had to pass examinations that tested "whether or not the candidate's mind was thoroughly steeped in literature and whether or not [he] possessed the *ways of thought* suitable to a cultured man and resulting from cultivation in literature." Bol's (1992:4–5, 33–4) study on the intellectual transitions in Tang (618–907) and Song (960–1279) China further illustrates that tradition, although he also adds to the definition of *shi.* In other words, "office holding, pedigree, and learning were primary components in the corporate identity of the *shih.*" This intellectual tradition is definitely cultural and political, though sometimes hereditary.

Indeed, at the beginning of *The Great Learning,* one of the Confucian classics, Confucius lays down for the literati the principle of *xiu shen, qi jia, zhi guo, ping tian xia:* in short, *xiu qi zhi ping.* In other words, such a man was to perfect himself, get his family in order, guide or govern his country in the right course, and bring peace to the world. To perfect himself was to cultivate and acquire such virtues as love, benevolence, humanity, kindness, courtesy, magnanimity, good faith, diligence, loyalty, reciprocity, and to adhere to the golden mean, that is, not doing to others what one would not want done to oneself. He was supposed to put his house in order by applying these and other principles. Only then was he ready to go into politics to govern his country and to unify the world. At that time, of course, "the country" meant one's own state, and "the world" probably meant only China proper.

The other description of *xiu qi zhi ping* is *li de, li gong, li yan,* is to "achieve great virtues, to perform meritorious services, and to create great literary works" (see Tu Wei-ming 1993b). This is the "calling" that Chinese literati had followed for centuries in whatever they did, consciously or subconsciously (see also Wen 1989:70–4). Confucius and his disciples preached these principles not only in *The Great Learning* but in other Confucian classics: *The Golden Mean, The Analects,* and *Mencius* as well. These books taught the literati specifically how they could perfect themselves, put their house in order, govern their country, and pacify the world. Confucianism thus became the bible of the Chinese literati, so much so that anyone who aspired to office in premodern times had to be well versed in these doctrines.

Thus, the literati shouldered the responsibility of governance as well as cultural production and transmission. They were not only aspirants to political office, the scholar-officials (Yu Ying-shih [1987] 1999:3–11; Goldman 1994:5), they were the very conscience of society. They have been "the bearers of progress toward a rational administration and of all 'intelligence'" (Weber 1946:416). Zeng Guofan (1811–72), for example, was a late Qing politician, general, and diplomat. But he also wrote voluminously. To make sure that his works would be handed down to later generations, he made it a rule to have two copies made of all his diaries and manuscripts of his poems and essays, so that he could send one copy to his native home for safe keeping (Tang Haoming 1994:52). Li Hongzhang (1823–1901), the successor to Zeng, was proud of his calligraphy and of the fact that he could recite the classics by heart (Weber 1946:437). Xu Shichang (1855–1939), once president of China (1918–22), was a scholar who was also famed for his calligraphy. He would write wall scrolls or compose couplets for his guests and even their children (see Bodde 1991:48). If they were politically not very successful, the literati could at least hope to influence later generations with their scholarship, as did Liu Zongyuan (773–819), a major literary and intellectual figure in Chinese history (Jo-shui Chen 1992:83).

But as Bol (1992:5) points out, there is always a tension or contradiction "between individual cultivation and sociopolitical responsibility," which shows itself in the writings or political practices of many scholars. Some of the scholars Bol discusses include Han Yu, Fan Zhongyan (or Fan Chung-yen), Ouyang Xiu (or Ou-yang Hsiu), Wang Anshi (or Wang An-shih), and Sima Guang (or Suu-ma Kuang). Here we have again the conflict we discussed in chapter 1 on the tension between *Dao* (morality and culture) and *shi* (politics and power), which so often gives rise to the dual and/or split personalities suffered by many intellectuals.

These scholars are the typical *shi,* usually the most politically engaged *shi,* the major body of the group, who also tend to be the most closely studied. But there were other kinds of *shi* as well. These included *ceshi, youshi,* and *yangshi,* that is, vagrant "sophists," to use Weber's (1946:419) term, "floating" or unattached intellectuals, and those scholars who relied on the patronage of the wealthy for a living (Xu Fuguan [1980] 1996:38; Yan Buke 1996:12). They existed for the most part in the Warring States Period, several hundred years before Qin unified China in 221 B.C.E. We have discussed some of these *shi* in chapter 1 along with the reclusive *Daoist* (Taoist) *yinshi.*

Even among Confucian scholars, we find many who were less politically engaged. They were, in Brook's (1993:13) words, "providing essential extrabureaucratic services within local society rather than as a reserve army of bureaucrats." The Ming (1368–1644)-Qing (1616–1911) gentry, for example, engaged in extensive "liturgical" projects such as building schools, raising dikes, dredging lakes, erecting arches *(pailou)* in honor of local magnates, and building and restoring Buddhist monasteries (p. 19). They may even be mountain recluses. They were often literati, like Zhang Dai (1597–1689), who was a distinguished essayist and poet, a proficient amateur lutanist, a connoisseur of the subtle art of tea, an avid gardener and book collector, and a noted patron of the arts (pp. 40–50).[1] Some members of the gentry did become monks but continued to participate "in the gentry cultural sphere as lecturers, priests, poets, and painters, blending their previous activities as gentry with their subsequent vocation as clergy" (p. 119). This group was also part of the *shi*.[2]

That is a brief story of the literati. Where does the term 'intellectual' come from, then? Jin Yaoji (1987:61) thinks it is a borrowed from the West. But no matter where the word comes from, it does indicate a break with the traditional literati both structurally and ideologically. Hao Chang (1971:121–3) would put the date of the break in the 1890s when the new intelligentsia challenged Confucianism's basic morals and its concepts of social order. The break intensified with the abolition of the old examination system in 1905 and with the establishment of the new. The new system emphasized in its curricula a mixture of modern language, science, and history with the study of the traditional Chinese classics (MacKinnon 1980:144–5; Gasster 1969:vii-ix). The year 1905 may symbolically serve as a "dividing line between the traditional 'scholar' and the modern 'intellectual' because the latter was no longer linked to state power as the former was" (Yu Ying-shih 1993:143). Indeed, Li Zehou and Vera Schwarcz's (1983–84) definitions of six generations of *modern* Chinese intellectuals began with the generation of 1911.[3]

It is true that even though the state kept recruiting the educated elite for service, the criteria for that recruitment had certainly changed. The best example is the composition of the first full-fledged cabinet of the Republic established after the 1911 Revolution, as shown in table 8.1.

As we can see, almost all of the cabinet members had a formidable education, either traditional or modern. But above all, many had Western training. The last four were members of the Tongmeng Hui, the organization that spearheaded the 1911 Revolution. Their educational and revolutionary backgrounds clearly indicate that they were no longer the traditional literati, who were, as we know, immersed in traditional learning and getting ready to serve a monarch. Both the structure of education and the path to political success had changed.

The structural changes in the educational and political system brought

Table 8.1 The Composition of the Republic's First Cabinet

Name	Position	Education
Tang Shaoyi	Premier	English school in Hong Kong, later studied in Hartford, Connecticut, Columbia University and New York University, both in New York City
Duan Qirui	Minister of the Army	Beiyang Military Academy. Studied in Germany
Liu Guanxiong	Minister of the Navy	Royal Navy College, Greenwich, England
Zhao Bingjun[a]	Minister of the Interior	?
Xiong Xiling	Minister of Finance	A *jinshi* degree at the age of 24, member of the Beijing Hanlin Academy, worked with Tan Sitong and Liang Qichao for the One Hundred Day Reform in 1898
Lu Zhengxiang	Minister of Foreign Affairs	Studied French. Continued Western studies while in foreign service in St. Petersburg
Shi Zhaoji	Minister of Communications	A *juren* degree, then St. John's Academy in Shanghai and the Academy of Chinese Literature
Cai Yuanpei	Minister of Education	A *jinshi* degree, a scholar of the Hanlin Academy
Wang Chonghui	Minister of Justice	St. Paul's College and Queen's College in Hong Kong, studied classical Chinese with a tutor, continued at Tianjin's Beiyang University
Song Jiaoren	Minister of Agriculture and Forestry	Enrolled in the Kobun Institute in Japan but chiefly engaged in revolutionary activities, founding a journal, chief editor of Yu Youren's *Minli Bao*
Chen Qimei	Minister of Commerce and Industry	Modest education, apprenticed to a pawnbroker, later worked in a silk company in Shanghai

Source: Robert A. Scalapino and George T. Yu. 1985. *Modern China and Its Revolutionary Process,* pp. 352–7.

a. Scalapino and Yu probably had it wrong when they spelled Zhao's name as Zhao Bingzhun (1985: 353).

forth another group of intellectuals whose route to success was professional rather than political. Y. C. Wang (1966:378–9) observes the remarkable increase in the numbers of scientists and social scientists; essayists and novelists; engineers; lawyers (some 5,685 by 1932); Catholic and Protestant clergy (8,679 by 1932); and entrepreneurs and bankers. Obviously, the intellectual orientation of the educated elite had forever changed, and so had the role of intellectuals. Rather than depending on a political position in the government, intellectuals could find other means of making a living. This constitutes what Jin Yaoji (1987:81) calls the "new intellectual stratum," which, in addition to these professionals, includes professors and college students, reporters and editors, and people who engage in other cultural and ideological endeavors.

Intellectual values had also been transformed. Kang Youwei (1858–1927) and Liang Qichao (1873–1929), the reformists, failed in 1898 in their efforts to "rejuvenate Confucian thought and institutions and equip them for the modern age" (Gasster 1969:vii, 59–60). This, in a way, led to the 1911 Revolution, the success and failure of which further changed intellectuals' modes of thinking about reshaping the world. The May 4 movement in 1919 confirmed those thoughts: it sowed in the minds of the intellectuals the seeds of individual emancipation, scientific culture, and the prestige of democracy (Chow Tse-tsung 1960:365).

Some educated elite embarked on a crusade to save China through science *(kexue jiuguo),* thus the emergence of a professional stratum in the intellectual class. Others went even further. They wanted to distinguish themselves from both the old scholar-official class and the transitional 'intellectual class' *(zhishi jiejie)* by denouncing the latter's monopoly over knowledge and culture, and by limiting their own role in the emancipation of others. (This is certainly related to the founding of the Chinese Communist Party.) In the summer of 1927, some radical intellectuals began to call themselves *zhishi fenzi,* or 'knowledgeable elements' (Schwarcz 1986a:187–8). This was probably one of the first times when the term intellectual was used, and it did indicate an ideological break with the traditional literati.

The transformation of, and transition from, literati to intellectuals may be considered complete, at least symbolically by the end of the 1920s. For these structural and ideological changes do not mean that the modern intellectual is a different breed from the scholar-official, although he may have made the break between them. "The 'new intellectual' remained the keeper of the old as well as the bearer of the new. Skill in calligraphy, poetry, painting, and knowledge of the great Chinese literary classics remained the mark of the educated man" (Scalapino and Yu 1985:486). While they may have parted with tradition, modern intellectuals were still deeply rooted in it. Hao Chang (1987:3) concludes this after his exhaustive analysis of the writings and reforms of Kang Youwei (1858–1927), Tan Sitong (1864–98), Zhang Binglin 1869–1935), and Liu Shipei (1884–1919).

The same applies to later reformers and revolutionaries. The most revolutionary of all, Mao Zedong (1893–1976), was deeply immersed in traditional literature, loved calligraphy and poetry, and practiced traditional ways of ruling the country. Intellectuals have kept filling bureaucratic positions in every regime. They have simply expanded their roles by incorporating Western thinking. But this does warrant the transition of the name from "literati" to "intellectual," however much the latter may incorporate traits of the former (see also Grieder 1981:1). They are, in a sense, new "scholar-officials," new "principled critics," or new "Confucian businessmen and women." Things have changed, and things have not changed.

Transition from Philosophers to Intellectuals: The Western Story

Intellectuals in the West seem to have a very different tradition. Whereas the Chinese intellectuals since Confucius have usually emphasized both cultural production and public affairs, the Western intellectual tradition did not bring the two together until the Enlightenment in the eighteenth century. It used to be the Christian clergy who transformed societies, changed the rulers, and developed scholarship and education (Yu Ying-shih [1987] 1999:3–11). The ancient Greek philosophers contemplated the world, but as Marx ([1888] 1978:145) charges, they did not focus on changing it.

Nonetheless, the broader Western intellectual tradition began at about the same time as the Chinese tradition did. Parsons (1969:5–11) observes that the two steps of cultural evolution over the historic world are the development of written language, and the philosophical breakthroughs that occurred in Greece, Israel, India, and China. Greek philosophy, culminating in Socrates, Plato, and Aristotle, laid the foundations of Western civilization, including philosophy, science, and theology. Even the "Dark Ages" saw developments in theology, philosophy, art, science, and law, although the entire culture was set around the church.

Le Goff's work ([1957] 1993), *Intellectuals in the Middle Ages,* also describes the emergence of the intellectual whose job it was to write and teach. This intellectual, according to Le Goff, became identifiable in the twelfth century with the development of the medieval towns. Then the Renaissance saw the revival of learning in the classics, and the development of an independent art and a truly modern science. The modern university emerged as an offshoot of the monasteries. All of these, says Parsons, could not have happened without the Western cultural specialists, whom the Chinese would have called "literati," though they lacked much of the political function of the latter.

The term 'intelligentsia,' however, did not emerge until the 1860s, as we learned earlier. According to Gella (1976:13), the social stratum in Poland and Russia began at that time to distinguish themselves from other educated people of the upper and middle classes by "a specific combination of psychological characteristics, manners, style of life, social status, and above all, value system." This was demonstrated most conspicuously by their common calling to "serve their nation." In Russia, that meant to abolish Czarism, destroying the old state whether by peaceful or revolutionary means. In Poland, the calling was to abolish the emperors of the oppression and to rebuild an independent Polish state (pp. 14–15). Now we see the convergence between modern Chinese intellectuals and intellectuals in Russia and Poland.

When the term 'intellectual,' as a Westernization of "intelligentsia," was used in 1898 to describe those who protested the wrongful conviction and imprisonment of Capt. Alfred Dreyfus,[4] it kept the original meaning of a concern for social justice and an involvement in political affairs. In the following year, William James, referring to the role of the French intellectuals, claimed that the "intellectuals" in America must work to keep their precious birthright of individualism, and freedom from institutions such as church, army, aristocracy, and royalty (see Bell 1980:121). Thus, the term was used in America "in the context of just such a 'radical' utopian and anti-institutional statement of purpose," says Richard Hofstadter (see Bell 1980:121). Now we see the link between the intellectual traditions in Europe and in the United States, and we see the convergence between the West and China regarding the use and practice of the term intellectual.

So far we have focused only on the change from cultural (Parsons) to political (Gella and Bell) on the part of the Western intellectual. There is indeed at least one more change: the professional. As in the case of modern Chinese intellectual development, a professional stratum of the educated class emerged in the industrial and especially postindustrial eras in the United States. Bell (1980:157–8) lists at least six groups of knowledge workers:

Intellectuals and knowledge creators, e.g. scientists and scholars
Creators and critics of culture, e.g. novelists and painters
Transmitters of culture and knowledge, e.g. publishers
News and entertainment workers, e.g. reporters and movie makers
Appliers and transmitters of knowledge, e.g. engineers and teachers
Managers and administrators, e.g. bureaucrats in public, private and nonprofit institutions

Indeed, the rise of professions has certainly changed the intellectual milieu, which is true both in the United States and in China.

Definitions of the Modern Intellectual

The examination of the historical development of the term intellectual in China and in the West only tells us who intellectuals are in practice; it does not tell us who they are in theory. We will now explore the various categorizations of modern intellectuals. Each explanation depicts one or two aspects of the *abstract* intellectual: educational and professional, cultural and social, and critical.

Educational and Professional

First of all, intellectuals are those who have a certain level of education and a certain kind of profession. Our foregoing discussion on the development of the intellectual in China and in the West also testifies to that usage. The two are correlated: one's level of education usually determines the professions one can enter; on the other hand, each profession usually requires a specific level of education. Mannheim (1936:155) observes that education is a unifying sociological bond among all kinds of intellectuals, and it unifies in a striking way: "Participation in a common educational heritage progressively tends to suppress differences of birth, status, profession, and wealth, and to unite the individual educated people on the basis of the education they have received."

Because of the importance of education, those who have it are often regarded as intellectuals. And they normally pursue professions related to their education. *Ci Hai* (1999), one of the most authoritative encyclopedic dictionaries in Chinese, defines intellectuals *(zhishi fenzi)* by emphasizing both education and profession. Intellectuals are "mental workers with a certain amount of cultural and scientific knowledge, including people working in science and technology, literature and arts, teachers, doctors, editors, journalists, etc."

Many of the interviewees in our research on intellectuals also believe that a person's education and profession should determine whether he or she is an intellectual. Two journalists of a city government-sponsored daily newspaper, with a circulation of one hundred thousand, believe that its *editors, reporters,* and *administrators* are all intellectuals since they have degrees in journalism (Interviews with Chang Zongmiao and Wu Ji 1996:2.26–7). A *lawyer* says that lawyers are intellectuals since they are experts in the law (Interview with Wang Lixiang 1996:2.23). An *engineer* defines intellectuals in an educationally and professionally generic way: "Intellectuals work differently from our assembly workers. We are working all the time, at home, on the bus, and in the office, reading, writing and doing research. We work all the time" (Interview with Yan Huiren 1994:1.39).

Moreover, this group believes that only those in the *humanities* and the *social and natural sciences* are intellectuals. When one becomes a businessperson or bureaucrat, she is no longer entitled to be called an intellectual (Interviews with Chang Youde, Fu Ji, Sun Zhongxin, Yan Hongyu and Yu Xilan 1994:1.50–4). This will certainly raise problems with people in those positions who consider themselves to be intellectuals. According to this latter group, then, one's level of education determines whether she is an intellectual.

But can one's education alone make her an intellectual?[5] Can we de-emphasize professions in the making of an intellectual? It is possible, although how much education an "intellectual" requires is another issue of contention. Qi Ruisu, the president of a large city Party school, summarizes it well:

> Who is viewed as an intellectual also depends on where the person is. In the countryside, an elementary school teacher or a high school graduate will be considered as an intellectual. In our school, you have to have a college degree. The personnel department determines who is or is not going be treated as an intellectual based on their years of study. (Interview 1996:2.24)

In any case, one can be considered an intellectual if he has *some* education. Qi brings up another issue: government policies and cultural practice also determine who is an intellectual. In this context, education has been the most important criterion. But the level of education changes over time. At the time of the 1911 Revolution, those with a middle-school education may be taken as "intellectuals" (Li Zehou and Schwarcz 1983–84:46). In the 1950s, the Chinese State Statistical Bureau defined anyone with a high school education as an intellectual. In the 1980s, the state agency defined intellectuals as those with a professional school education or above (Jia Chunzeng 1996:242). This has been the definition used in meting out responsibilities, liabilities, and benefits in China ever since. As we can see, however, different organizations may still have different definitions as to *how much* education is needed.

In sum, although most would probably agree that education is a necessary condition for the intellectual, some may say that education is the only criterion. Others would argue for education *as well as for specific* professions. This would exclude bureaucrats and businesspeople from the intellectual complex. Still others, however, would say that the educational and professional criteria are necessary but not yet sufficient to define an intellectual. We will now look at those views.

Cultural and Social

The second aspect of the abstract intellectual speaks to the cultural and social functions of the intellectual. These functions are related to education and profession, but they are a more specific, narrower interpretation of the intellectual. Here is how Shils (1969:26) defines intellectuals:

> There is in every society a minority of persons who, more than the ordinary run of their fellow-men, are inquiring, and desirous of being in frequent communion with symbols which are more general than the immediate concrete situations of everyday life, and remote in their reference in both time and space. In this minority, there is a need to externalize this quest in oral and written discourse, in poetic or plastic expression, in historical reminiscence or writing, in ritual performance and acts of worship.

The cultural symbols that he refers to concern "man, society, nature and the cosmos," according to Lipset and Basu's (1976:119) interpretation. Thus, intellectuals are those who are interested in the more abstract meanings of this world, and who want to communicate what they have learned to ordinary people through spoken words, written works and other forms. They then provide models and standards, as well as the "expressive dispositions within a society" (Shils 1969:28). Or, as Mannheim (1936:10) points out, they "preach, teach, and interpret the world."

Weber and Parsons also emphasize cultural and social roles as the core of intellectuals' concerns. Weber (1946:176) defines intellectuals as "a group of men who by virtue of their peculiarity have special access to certain achievements considered to be 'cultural values,' and who therefore usurp the leadership of a 'cultural community.'"[6] Parsons (1969:3–4) emphasizes the cultural role of intellectuals and downplays their social role. He says, "I should like to speak of the intellectual as a person who, though as a member of a society in the nature of the case he performs a complex of social roles, is in his principal role-capacity expected—an expectation normally shared by himself—to put cultural considerations above social. . . ." These cultural considerations, he believes, concern meanings in symbolic systems, which are normative in nature and "specify what in some sense *should* be done and evaluate the actual performance accordingly, rather than either describing what in fact is done or predicting what will be."

Lipset too focuses on intellectuals' cultural and social roles. He defines intellectuals as

> all those who create, distribute and apply culture, that is, the symbolic world of man, including art, science and religion. Within this group there are two main levels: the hard core of *creators* of culture—scholars, artists, philosophers, authors, some editors of newspapers and some journalists; and the *distributors*—performers in the various arts, most teachers, most reporters. A peripheral group is composed of those who *apply culture* as part of their jobs—*professionals* like physicians and lawyers. (cited in Nettl 1969:97; italics mine)

In other words, the creators, distributors, and appliers of culture are all intellectuals. Work on culture indeed defines the intellectual. But compared with Shils's, Weber's, and Parsons's definitions of culture, Lipset's culture is more broadly defined to refer to any norms and beliefs such as law and medicine. Thus professionals such as lawyers and doctors can both be viewed as performing their cultural roles and are thus intellectuals. It is important to note, though, as Shui Binghe (1989:16) points out, that Lipset's emphasis is on the first two groups. He generally does not consider professionals in his analysis of intellectuals.

However, there is also an argument to adopt the broader cultural and social definition, by which even some businesspeople or administrators can be included as intellectuals, let alone engineers and lawyers. Gouldner (1979), for example, includes the technical intellectuals in the intellectual class when he discusses "intelligentsia." Another sociologist, Lewis Coser (1965:vii) does not include professionals in his analysis of "men of ideas," but he believes the wider definition "may have a number of practical advantages."

One of our interviewees, Li Ping (Interview 1996:2.29), is a good example of such "practical advantages." She continued to do research on ancient Chinese arts and crafts while doing related business in tie-dyeing. She also wanted to teach. Her business aim was to become wealthy; and to eventually invest in research and teaching. She wanted to be a person of culture, not an entrepreneur. At the time of the interview, Li was negotiating with the university to retain her teaching job; at the same time, she wanted to start a teaching and research workshop in the university on tie-dyeing. In addition, she believed she was doing something socially responsible: reviving an ancient tradition, much like the Japanese traditions of kimono designing, flower arrangement, and tea ceremonies. She emphasized that her sense of social responsibility had not lessened any because of her role change. She was more concerned with spiritual satisfaction than material satisfaction, and that, she said, was the distinction between intellectuals and nonintellectuals. When people talk about "Confucian businessmen or women," they are talking about this group of people who are engaged both in cultural and business activities. Li's example seems to indicate that intellectuals-turned-businessmen or women can still perceive themselves to be intellectuals. Indeed, they can *be* intellectuals if one considers their concerns for culture and their sense of social responsibility, instead of what they do. The same applies to administrators.

To sum up, work on culture determines whether one is an intellectual, as we can see from Shils, Weber, and Parsons. The social roles are implied in the cultural work, as we can see from Weber, Parsons, Lipset, Gouldner, and Li. This is a narrower definition of the intellectual than the educational and professional but it is broader than the following definition.

Critical

The third definition describes intellectuals as those who have a sense of social responsibility and the ability to criticize. For example, Wang

Yuanhua (Interview 1994:1.1), a well-known Chinese writer and a former "modern scholar-official," says, "You don't have to go to the demonstrations, but you have to be concerned. Otherwise, you are not an intellectual. It is your responsibility to be concerned. And one of those concerns is democracy." A group of young college teachers and students seem to agree. These young people believe that intellectuals need to be the conscience of society: they need to have a sense of social responsibility, and they should express their criticism on social issues. They have to be open to new ideas and new thinking. They must be able to think independently, not according to Party politics. They are, in fact, the balancing power in society because they are able to speak for those whose voice is not always heard (Interviews with Chen Yichi, Fu Ji, Gong Haiyang, and Yan Yang 1994:1.52, 60–2).

According to Yu Ying-shih (1988:94–5), the critical aspect of intellectuals is a manifest tradition in both the East and the West.[7] For example, Yu says, Michael Confino divides the characteristics of intellectuals into five areas: concern about public affairs; belief that the resolution of the country's problems is their responsibility; belief that political and social problems are morality issues; belief that it is their duty to find logical solutions to all problems; and belief in social justice. These characteristics correspond to those of the Chinese traditional intellectual who accepts the whole world as his responsibility *(yi tianxia wei ji ren)*. The concept is embodied in part of the couplet written by Gu Xiancheng (1550–1612) of the Donglin Academy, a group of critical intellectuals at the end of the Ming dynasty (1368–1644). It reads, "family affairs, national affairs, and world affairs, everything is of my concern."

Edward Said seems to follow the same line of argument. He says, "The intellectual's representations—what he or she represents and how those ideas are represented to an audience—are always tied to and ought to remain an organic part of an ongoing experience in society: of the poor, the disadvantaged, the voiceless, the underrepresented, the powerless" (1994:113). Said himself finds that what grips him is the spirit in opposition rather than the spirit in accommodation. He finds it romantic, interesting, and challenging to be "in dissent against the status quo at a time when the struggle on behalf of underrepresented and disadvantaged groups seems so unfairly weighted against them" (p. xvii). His involvement in Palestinian politics complements that attitude.

Thus, intellectuals, according to the critical approach, include only those who practice social criticism (Yu Ying-shih 1988:255). The atomic physicist is an intellectual only when he signs a petition against nuclear testing, according to Sartre (cited in Konrad and Szelenyi 1979: 8). In this sense, education, profession, and culture are no longer so important in defining intellectuals. Both technical and humanistic intellectuals can be critical or noncritical. Nor is there any problem in including businessmen and women or bureaucrats, as long as they have that sense of concern, the social responsibility, and the critical ability.[8]

Conclusions: Narrower and Broader Definitions of Intellectuals

As summarized by Xiao Gongqin (Interview 1994:1.2), the term 'intellectuals' in its *narrower* sense refers to those who have a spirit of social criticism, can think independently, and feel so strongly about social justice that their consciences force them to speak out. According to this narrower definition, it is the "duty" of intellectuals "to doubt everything that is obvious, to make relative all authority, to ask all those questions that no one else dares to ask" (Dahrendorf 1970:55). The critical definition of the intellectual is the narrowest. And the cultural and social definitions are narrow, too. On the other hand, intellectuals in a *broader* sense would include all those who have a higher education, since they would almost inevitably pursue some professional, cultural, and social, though not necessarily critical, roles.

In the contemporary Chinese scholarship on intellectuals, some follow the inclusive approach and maintain that as long as one possesses the educational, professional, cultural, and social aspects of the intellectual, he or she is an intellectual (Jia Chunzeng 1996:243; Liu Hongxia and Liu Guitian 1987:17). Others, however, follow the exclusive approach and maintain that those aspects are only secondary. The primary characteristic of the intellectual is that he or she has a sense of social responsibility and performs social criticism (Xu Jilin 1997b:212–3; Xie Yong 1999a, 1999b; Li Jie 1999). Some of our interviewees support the inclusive and broader definition, while others support the exclusive and narrower definition.

An argument has been raised that may support the narrower definition of the intellectual in both the cultural and the critical approaches. It calls for a clear distinction between "intellect" and "intelligence." Intellect, according to Hofstadter (1963:25), is "the critical, creative, and contemplative side of the mind. . . . It examines, ponders, theorizes, criticizes, imagines." Intelligence, on the other hand, "is employed within a fairly narrow, immediate, and predictable range; it is a manipulative, adjustive, unfailingly practical quality . . . [It] works within the framework of limited, but clearly stated goals, and may be quick to shear away questions of thought that do not seem to help in reaching them. . . ." It seizes "the immediate meaning in a situation and evaluate[s] it. Intellect evaluates evaluations, and looks for the meanings of situations as a whole." Therefore, "intellectuals" tend to be humanistic, whereas "intelligentsia" tend to be technical. That is indeed how Alvin Gouldner (1979:48–9) differentiates the two. The former are interested in criticism and emancipation, while the latter are obsessed with technical puzzles. The former are intellectuals, whereas the latter are less likely to be intellectuals because they tend not to be critical and emancipatory in their work. As we mentioned earlier, Louis A. Coser (1965) considers only the former as intellectuals in his *Men of Ideas,* believing that there is a qualitative difference between the two. So do theorists like Yu Ying-shih.

However, the distinction between intellect and intelligence does not hinder a more inclusive definition. Gouldner (1979), for example, considers both as intellectuals while acknowledging that there is a difference between the two. Gouldner believes that together they form the New Class of intellectuals, partly because they are both revolutionary, though in different ways.

Thus, the educational and professional aspects are certainly the most inclusive. Cultural and social aspects are less inclusive: only those who are engaged in fairly narrowly defined cultural activities are accepted as intellectuals. The critical aspect is the most specific and the most exclusive. Figure 8.1 shows the weightings among the three.

To be an intellectual, one has to have at least some education and a certain profession. In addition, one may also perform certain cultural and social roles. Furthermore, one may be critical of the powers that be or society in general. Look at the diagram, and we may be seeing different kinds of intellectuals, or we may also be seeing different aspects of any one intellectual. Timothy Cheek (1992:135) insightfully points out that in the study of China's intellectuals, "we must attempt to account for *all* their activities." Deng Tuo, the former member of the Secretariat of the Beijing Party Committee before the Cultural Revolution in 1966, was not only a "liberal" or "Marxian Confucian" who courageously

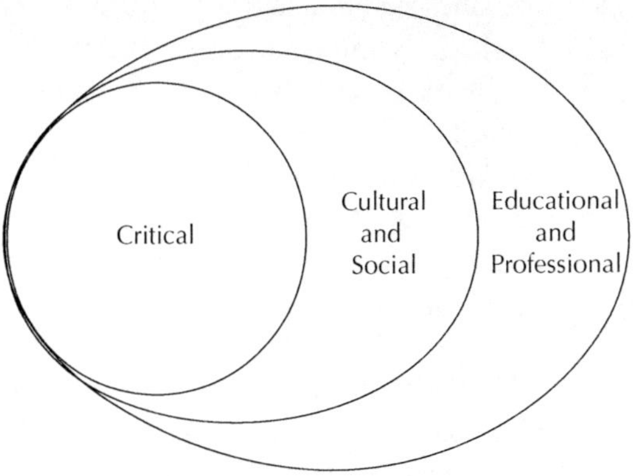

Figure 8.1 Defining the Intellectual

criticized the Party for its errors during the Great Leap Forward, as is noted in Western and Japanese studies of China. He was also a cultured man who was well-versed in aesthetics, poetry, Ming and Qing social history, and who collected antiques. He was also a professional journalist. Above all, he was a dedicated, loyal Party cadre (Cheek 1986; 1992: 135–6) Deng embodied all the aspects of the intellectual thus defined.

However, a person may possess one or more of these characteristics, or one characteristic at one time, and another characteristic at a different time. It is useful for our analysis to say that as long as he has at least two of these characteristics, we can consider the person an intellectual. Wang Shuo, the popular novelist, or Wei Jingsheng, the democratic movement advocate, might not have college educations, but they are performing very important cultural and social role. An engineer is a professional, but he or she has a certain level of education, and is creating or at least applying a culture.

In this work, we have adopted the broader definition: as long as a person has at least two of the characteristics, he is an intellectual. We include both *intellectuals* and *intelligentsia,* to use Gouldner's terms. To avoid any confusion, though, we refer to both as intellectuals. But when we need to make a distinction between the two, we refer to the former as "humanistic intellectuals" to mean mainly intellectuals in the humanities and social sciences, and the latter as "technical intellectuals" to mean intellectuals in sciences and in various technical professions.

We have chosen to follow the inclusive approach to intellectuals for several reasons. First, it is the customary definition in China. As we have seen, many of the educated elite, as well as the government itself, refer to knowledge workers as intellectuals (see also Calhoun 1991: 113–4; Hong Yung Lee 1991:190). Many scholars also see the advantages of being more inclusive.

Second, as we just mentioned, an intellectual's role varies from time to time and from place to place. One may be critical when he attends a political meeting in the evening but professional when solving a technical puzzle during the day. Intellectuals do migrate from one role to another fairly frequently. They are still doing intellectual work but they may not always be critical. We have already briefly examined Deng Tuo's case. For another example, if a sociologist does research on poverty objectively (if that is possible), and reports only the findings, she is still intellectual, but more professional than critical. "This is what we find. Do whatever you [the powers that be] want to do with it." But if the person does her report objectively, and then argues for a solution (left, right or middle), she is being critical, not just intellectual and professional. Professors and lawyers can be intellectuals or nonintellectuals depending on their attitudes toward the ideas they work with (Hofstadter 1963:27). The point is that they do switch from one attitude to another, as this sociologist may do. So it makes sense to call both of them intellectuals but to examine specifically what they do with their ideas.

Fang Lizhi, for yet another example, was a critical intellectual when he used his ideas on cosmology to advocate freedom of speech in the 1980s (Williams 1990), much as Andrei Sakharov (1921–89) did in the Soviet Union. But if and when democratic advocacy, including cultural critique, ceases to be one of the critical intellectual's main functions, he becomes a professional, or unattached, intellectual. This does not mean that he is no longer critical. It means that being critical is not now his chief characteristic, as it clearly was in the 1980s. It is true that no matter what kind of intellectual you are, you most likely will follow the culture of critical discourse. But the extent of one's criticalness can vary greatly. As we explained in table 6.1 in chapter 6, the professionals have less CCD than critical intellectuals. And less CCD is correlated with more organicity. Our definition needs to be inclusive; we want to miss no nuances and to capture every change.

Hence the third and most important reason: our study is chiefly political and sociological. We focus on intellectuals' political attitudes and roles rather than on their professions. Although one's profession influences one's political attitude, it is not the only variable. Neither are other distinctions, as between technical and humanistic, important for our purpose, although we touch on them. We call people with higher education intellectuals. They may be technical or humanistic, but our classifications are based on their *political* attitudes, on their actions or non-actions toward the powers that be. We may also mention their cultural productions, but only for their political impact. Since all intellectuals produce some kind of culture and adopt some kind of political attitude, it makes sense for us to employ a broader definition.

Notes

Notes to the Preface

1. In summarizing the empirical and theoretical implications of the book, I have benefited from the comments of a number of State University of New York Press reviewers, especially Professors Timothy Cheek, John Israel, and Richard Madsen.
2. For the writing of this section and indeed for my own methodological approaches to this book project, I have benefited greatly from a course I took with Prof. Robert R. Alford at City University of New York Graduate School in the early 1990s. His lectures now appear in his book, *The Craft of Inquiry* (1998).

Notes to Chapter One

1. Hereafter, translations from the Chinese are mine unless otherwise specified. The quote is taken from the silk editions *(bo shu)* of *Dao De Jing,* as interpreted by Zhang Songru. Written over two thousand years ago and excavated in 1973 in Changsha, Hunan, they are believed to be the oldest editions we have seen so far (1987:1–4). Unlike the later editions, they use *heng* to denote "eternal," rather than *chang*. This was because Liu Heng (reigned from 179 B.C.E to 156 B.C.E.) had become Emperor Xiaowen of Western Han (206 B.C.E.–A.D. 220). To use the personal names of emperors or one's elders was taboo. So the earlier *heng* was replaced with *chang* in later editions.

   Speaking of names, Chinese people will be referred to in the book by their last names. When both names are used, their last names will come first. Chinese American authors, however, tend to use their first names first and last names last. When in doubt, please check both in the bibliography.
2. Indeed, Gramsci even calls this distinction based on the intrinsic nature of intellectual activities "the most widespread error of method" (1971:8). However, he acknowledges the value of intrinsic analysis four pages later, as we just showed.
3. Coser (1965:227–43) also identifies a kind of intellectual who looks to other parts of the world for something lacking in his own country. For example, Voltaire praised the paternal authority in China and Russia, and many British and American intellectuals praised communism in the former Soviet Union. There was a parallel development in China, but our typology will not deal with these intellectuals as a separate category.
4. In an article written in 1947, Jiang Tingfu (1980) commented that 90 percent of the

bureaucracy were intellectuals. That should give us an idea of the involvement of intellectuals in the Guomingdang era.

5. Ji Xianlin (1994:238) recounted the discomfort he felt in the first few years of the revolution, when he had to don the Sun Yat-sen jacket and shout, "Long live Chairman Mao."
6. Even during the Yan'an era, many already viewed Mao as modest, warm, gentle, intimate, close to ordinary soldiers, and authoritative, although some also felt that there was "something of the tyrant about him" (Apter and Saich 1994:16, 89, 97, 165, 168). After his first talk with Mao in 1948, Wu Han, a vehement critic of Chiang Kai-shek at the time, was so impressed with Mao that he wanted to join the CCP (Mazur 1997:56).
7. According to Li Cheng's (2000:3) study on Jiang Zemin's successors, the fourth-generation leaders after Jiang are "more diversified than previous generations in terms of formative experiences, political solidarity, ideological conviction, career paths and occupational background." It does seem that they will be more technocratic and less career bureaucratic, just as defined. The most recent indication is to allow private entrepreneurs to join the Party, a controversial idea Jiang expressed in his 2001 speech to commemorate the eightieth anniversary of the Party. We will have to wait and see what the real story is, though. Like other classes in China, which we will further discuss in chapter 5, the BRC is constantly in formation and reformation (see also Kraus 1981:6). The BRC thus defined resembles X. L. Ding's (1994:12) "ruling elite."
8. Please note that the line between revolutionary and organic intellectuals, our next category, is not always clear. At any rate, some of the studies of these intellectuals include Lowell Dittmer's *Liu Shao-ch'i and the Chinese Cultural Revolution* (1974), which also has an illuminating chapter comparing Liu Shaochi and Mao Zedong; Dittmer's revised 1998 edition; Timothy Cheek's *Propaganda and Culture in Mao's China* (1997); Ma Zimei's (or Mary Mazur) *Shidai Zhi Zi: Wu Han* [A man of his time: Wu Han] (1996); Joshua A. Fogel's *Ai Ssu-ch'i's Contribution to the Development of Chinese Marxism* (1987a); Maurice Meisner's *Li Ta-chao and the Origins of Chinese Marxism* (1967); Andrew George Walder's *Chang Ch'un-chiao and Shanghai's January Revolution* (1978); Lars Ragvald's *Yao Wenyuan as a Literary Critic and Theorist* (1978); Ye Yonglie's biographies on Zhang Chunqiao, Yao Wenyuan, and Chen Boda (1999); Nick Knight's *Li Da and Marxist Philosophy in China* (1996); Song Jingming's *Li Da* (1997); Raymond F. Wylie's *The Emergence of Maoism* (1980); James H. Williams's *Fang Lizhi's Big Bang* (1994); Jerome Grieder's *Intellectuals and the State in Modern China* (1981); Carol Lee Hamrin and Timothy Cheek (eds.), *China's Establishment Intellectuals* (1986); Merle Goldman with Cheek and Carol Lee Hamrin (eds.), *China's Intellectuals and the State* (1987); H. Lyman Miller's *Science and Dissent in Post-Mao China* (1996); Daniel Lynch's *After the Propaganda State* (1999); Hung-Yok Ip's "Politics and Individuality in Communist Revolutionary Culture" in *Modern China,* vol. 23 (1997); Harold D. Lasswell and Daniel Lerner (eds.), *World Revolutionary Elites* (1965); Lucian W. Pye, *The Spirit of Chinese Politics* (1968) and *The Dynamics of Chinese Politics* (1981); Robert A. Scalapino (ed.), *Elites in the People's Republic of China* (1972); Frank N. Trager and William Henderson

(eds.), *Communist China, 1949–1969* (1970); Mary Backus Rankin, *Early Chinese Revolutionaries* (1971); and Benjamin Yang, *From Revolution to Politics* (1990).

9. Some Soviet revolutionary literature had a profound impact on the Chinese. The teenagers in the Long March were called "the little red devils," from a 1923 Soviet film by that title. The Chinese also claimed that their flag was painted red with the blood of the revolutionary martyrs, a phrase from another Soviet movie (see Kenez 1985:111, 205). In one of my postgraduate exams in the 1980s, when I was asked to write on the books that influenced me the most, I wrote down *Mother* by Maxim Gorky, and *The Real Man* by Boris Nikolaevich Polevoi.
10. Of course, whether the Soviet Union after Lenin, or China under Mao for that matter, was for the working class is another issue. "Ruling class" it was, no matter in the Soviet Union or China, but it was not the working class that was ruling.
11. Qian Mu ([1987] 1991:33), however, finds that Confucius' execution of Shao never happened.
12. According to Bol (1992:213–4), however, Wang's New Policies did carry the day in most of the five decades after Wang's retirement in 1076. And much of the debate between Wang and his opponents such as Sima Guang (or Ssu-ma Kuang 1019–86) was a reflection of their different approaches to government. But the case does speak to the pitfalls of politics. See also Mote (1999) for more on Wang and his reform efforts.
13. It was Lu Chia, a Confucian and enlightenment thinker in early Han (206 B.C.E.–C.E. 8), who first used the horseback metaphor when advising the founding father of the dynasty (Tu Wei-ming 1993b:18).
14. See a previous note for Lenin's and Stalin's views on the importance of organic intellectuals in the revolutionary movement.
15. Working in the GMD areas, for example, Wuhan and, later, Chongqing, were other Party theorists and writers like Guo Moruo, Tian Han, Xia Yan, Mao Dun, Lao She, Ba Jin, and Hu Feng (Holm 1991:43–4).
16. As Holm (1991:3) poignantly remarks, "if there was a literature of dissent in China, surely also there was a literature of assent—of works of literature and art that were produced under Party guidance and sponsorship, in accordance with Party guidelines, by artists who intended their work to serve as a contribution to the Chinese revolution."
17. Both the New Culture movement and the New Literature movement, which developed at the same time, can be seen as part of the May 4 movement in its broader sense. For a more in-depth description of the era, see Chow Tse-tsung (1960).
18. See John Israel (1998) for a description of liberalism at Lianda, a wartime university in the 1940s, of which Wen was a faculty member. The liberal professors' attitudes were in direct contrast with that of Hu Shih, although the latter was often viewed as the father of China's liberalism.
19. To "live for politics," according to Weber, means that one enters politics to strive for a "cause," whereas to "live off" politics means that one enters politics to strive for an "income" (1946:84–5). To be sure, those who live for politics mostly also make a living out of politics. And one who lives off politics can also strive for a cause. But the focus is different. In our discussion of intellectuals playing political

roles, we assume that critical and organic intellectuals, including revolutionary ones, mostly "live for politics."

20. It is interesting that Kong's first name "fu" means a fish stranded in a dry wheel track on the road, and is in dire need of help.
21. Among the labor organizers were also GMD intellectuals and other social elements like the Green and Red gangs (Perry 1993).
22. In Chinese: *mo wei shusheng kong yilun, toulu zhi chu xue banban.*
23. See Lu Xun (1973a) for a collection of his short stories published in *New Youth.*
24. In 1949, Zhang Junmai decided neither to go to Taiwan nor to remain in Mainland China, as most of his colleagues in minor parties did. A part of his own party accompanied the GMD regime into exile in Taiwan, while other third-force members such as Luo Longji, Zhang Bojun, and Zhang Dongsun chose to remain in Mainland China. Zhang eventually settled in the United States after two years in India (Jeans 1997:306).
25. Nobody knows when he died, how he died, or whether he has really died (Dai Qing 1990). But he disappeared in 1966.
26. Coser also talks about unattached intellectuals, but he means unattached to any institutions. That is a definition different from ours.
27. That is *guannian de chanshi* in Chinese.
28. See the appendix for further discussion on the Confucian gentry.
29. Gao Min (1994:2) simply defines *yinshi* as those who did not want to become officials. But it should be noted that these *Yinshi* had always engaged in a dialogue with Confucianism, explicitly or implicitly.
30. It is the often quoted saying, *fei Tang Wu er bo Zhou Kong*.
31. But the fact that in the past there was a technical side, though overshadowed, in China's humanistic intellectuals, or, to put it another way, that in individuals the professional and intellectual were more often intermingled than separated, demonstrates an interesting phenomenon. Were (or are) Chinese intellectuals more oriented toward universalism, while Western intellectuals are oriented toward particularism? Could it be part of the "gentleman ideal?" As Perry Link (1993:193) comments, if modern Western scholars of literature, ethics, sociology, and political science were to travel to the China of four hundred years ago (perhaps even to the China of today!), "they would be viewed as quaintly narrow specialists working on different aspects of the same thing." It may be that the humanistic and technical distinction was and still is a little blurred in China because of its philosophical underpinnings.
32. It was a difficult place, though. Hua Tuo, the doctor, was killed by Cao Cao (155–220) because he did not want to join his army.
33. That is, *yang wu yundong* or "foreign matters movement," hence "*yangwu* intellectuals."
34. To consider the capitalist movement as a professionalization movement is a little bit tricky. For the capitalists are a different class by itself, and the intellectuals who serve them are organic intellectuals. But since the capitalist class was still largely in formation at this stage, it might be plausible to treat the intellectuals who started it as unattached professional intellectuals. The same applies to the intellectuals in

the budding capitalist class in the 1990s. The bourgeoisification and professionalization movements are again discussed in the same chapter, that is, chapter 4.

35. See Pollard (1976) for an analysis of Zhou Zuoren the person and his works.
36. Indeed, Lu Xun "vehemently" implied his own distance with the CCP in this *zawen* (miscellaneous, short, witty, but often critical essays) where he lashed out at Liang.
37. In a sense, all intellectuals are public. As soon as one sets down words and publishes them, he or she has entered the public world (Said 1994:12). Intellectuals are also public in the sense that their services tend to be publicly oriented.
38. That's the thinking behind the rectification campaigns since 1942. See Dai Qing (1994:39) and Teiwes (1979). But, of course, Mao Zedong Thought is the result of the Sinification of Marxism, of his conflict with Wang Ming, and of the support of his colleagues such as Liu Shaoqi, Zhu De, Zhou Enlai, Wang Jiaxiang, Chen Boda, and a host of other intellectuals (Wylie 1980:158, 191, 207–8, 281–3; Ye Yonglie 1999).
39. See Mote (1999) for a more in-depth discussion on the history of the Jurchen state.
40. See also Bol (1992:295) for a discussion on Su Shi's divisions of cultural accomplishment, which also includes painting.
41. Criticizing the Americans, Wu Han had an entirely different view than Hu Shi, his professor at Qinghua University, on this issue (Mazur 1996:434).
42. * is used to denote *zhiye,* with the fourth tone on the first syllable, meaning vocation or calling.
43. Thomas Hayden, the former senior member of the California Senate, used to be a student-activist in the 1960s. Here is an example of an intellectual who became a politician, apparently believing that participation in government is a better way to effect social change.
44. In his analysis of the case of Bai Hua, a writer and military official, Kraus (1986: 194–5) shows an interplay between politics and culture in the Mandarin tradition, where "the artist has a responsibility to influence the political world according to his or her own ideas." In other words, art and politics are inseparable, as are morality and politics. Here both art and morality are *Dao.*
45. Apparently, the patronage of superiors was always important to scholar-cadres. Peng Zhen's support was critical for Deng and Wu of the Beijing Party Committee in the 1960s. In the 1980s, Xiao Hua's support of Bai Hua was vital. Xiao was the head of the PLA's General Political Department at a time when Bai was being attacked for his unorthodox critique of Mao and socialism (Kraus 1986). We will come back to these intellectuals in chapter 2.
46. See Shen Weiwei (2000) for a description of Wu's life.
47. In the 1920s and 1930s, for example, Ding served as the manager of a coal mine, director-general of the Port of Greater Shanghai under a warlord, economic consultant to the government, and secretary-general of the Academia Sinica (Furth 1970).
48. There are, of course, many reasons why a person commits suicide. But, as Durkheim would say, the most prominent reasons are sociological, located within much broader social processes. Chen killed himself just before Chiang Kai-shek's fall in

China, and Tian did so just after he was thrown out of the Zhongnanhai Compound for siding with the wrong people. Tian also complained to Li Rui (1998:357) about the difficulty to deal with Mao. It is probably safe to say that their suicide had to do with politics, although we are not 100 percent sure of it. See Sing and Kleinman (2000) for more examples of suicide as resistance in Chinese society. And see Li Ruoyu (1999) for examples of seventy-eight intellectuals in traditional China who suffered myriad vicissitudes in their lives. One could imagine the kinds of personalities they had developed.

49. For another example, Soviet sociology had a "split personality" when it had much autonomy in empirical work but was still constrained by Marxist and Leninist ideology (Jones and Krause 1991:236).
50. Merton (1968:277) also talks about value conflicts, but his focus is on specifics such as one's research findings being exploited by politicians for purposes against the researcher's values. That is not our main concern here, but his analysis greatly informs our discussion.
51. On the other hand, Li Da also participated in the partisan criticism of Fei Xiaotong, the sociologist, during the Anti-Rightist movement in the 1950s, but much of that criticism was based on his belief in Marxist sociology rather than on the need to follow the political tide, as Knight (1996:267) observes.
52. It should be noted that intellectuals also needed Deng's help, for example, to "dislodge Maoists from cultural positions if their own careers were to flourish" (Kraus 1986:199). It was a mutual need.
53. Another example is Hai Rui (1513–87), who first sent his family to their native home, purchased a coffin, and arranged for his funeral before he submitted a memorial strongly criticizing the emperor (Mote 1999:671).
54. It did not have to be that way. The value conflict experienced by organic intellectuals may have been inevitable, but the system could have provided a safe exit.
55. For the relationship between Yin Haiguang and Chiang Kai-shek, and Yin's involvement in the Lei case, see Wang Xingfu (2000).
56. See the appendix for a discussion of the difference between intellect and intelligence.
57. It is not known how many intellectuals committed suicide from 1949 to 1976, but it would likely amount to thousands. In his article on the study of suicides among intellectuals in this period, Xie Yong (2000) lists the cases of forty intellectuals, and reported on some others.

Notes to Chapter Two

1. This is the title of an article Mao wrote on May 15, 1957 for Party cadres to read concerning the so-called Rightists' "attack" on the Party. See Mao (1977:423).
2. For the summary of an eight-stage transition of intellectuals "from the independent critics of the May Fourth period to the bureaucratic-intellectual syncretism of the past quarter century," see Israel (1986:x–xii).
3. Historians tend to treat the Mao era as beginning from the Yan'an times when Mao secured his dominant position in the Party. Our division of time here is chiefly for

the convenience of our analysis, much of which, however, applies to the "Mao era" both before and after "liberation."

4. Ma was criticized in the following years for his ideas on population control, and he eventually lost his position.
5. It should be noted that official thought reform ended a year later, but waves of thought reform continued even after 1952. Indeed, the Anti-Rightist movement and the Cultural Revolution later should be viewed as thought reform movements as well.
6. Mao's exact words at a national meeting on propaganda in 1957 are, "There are no precise statistics on the number of intellectuals in China. Some estimate that there are about five million of them, including both higher and lower level intellectuals in various fields."
7. This figure far exceeds Mao's estimate at the time: three hundred thousand.
8. Lu Jiandong (1995:303) comments that in 1960, the dissenting intellectual two years ago was nowhere to be found. Most intellectuals willingly submitted their teaching notes to the Party and criticized their own bourgeois thoughts.
9. See Mote (1999:671–8) for a discussion of Hai Rui (1513–87) an historical figure.
10. Walder (1978:79), however, also showed us Zhang Chunqiao, the practical politician, who, during Shanghai's Cultural Revolution, reinstated labor discipline, redirected factional energies, sidetracked social grievances and economic demands, and suppressed incorrigible opposition. Ragvald (1978), on the other hand, showed us China's Zhdanov, Yao Wenyuan, in the making before the Cultural Revolution, posing to replace Zhao Yang.
11. As Fisher (1986:184) points out, Wu and his dissenting colleagues only became dissenting *retrospectively*.
12. Cheek (1986:93) comments that Deng Tuo was "a notoriously complex man who is virtually uncategorizable." The same, however, may be said of other intellectuals, considering the different political roles (critical, organic, and professional) they play often at the same time, as well as their dual orientations of politics and culture/profession, and their dual and split personalities. Some might even be considered more "notoriously complex" than others. Still, while acknowledging an individual's personal complexity, we should be able to identify his basic tendencies at a particular time in a his life using our typology.
13. In Mao's China, unattached intellectuals, formerly *yinshi,* could no longer exist. No one could be a *yinshi* and escape politics; everyone belonged to a unit. Chen Yinke (1890–1969), who refused to become an official if it meant he had to study Marxism and Leninism (Lu Jiandong 1995:102), was one of the very few who came close to being a *yinshi.* People like Chen were very rare. But even he remained under the care of the Party and government: he belonged to Zhongshan University in Guangdong Province, which even provided him with writing paper. When he died in 1969, Chen was still a member of the Standing Committee of the Chinese Political Consultative Conference (p. 491), although he probably did not participate in any of their activities. He was plagued by illnesses most of the time starting in 1949. We need to keep in mind, though, that unattached intellectuals are not unconcerned about politics. Whenever somebody visited him, especially high-level Party cadres, Chen would ask them questions about why the economy was so

bad, or why the Party policy constantly changed (pp. 281, 359). Those who visited him include Tao Zhu, the Party secretary of Guangdong Province, Zhou Yang, the Party's cultural czar, and Hu Qiaomu, Mao's political secretary.

14. This is the tactic used by Monkey King, the most famous figure in the classical novel *Journey West,* by Wu Chengen, to persuade his opponents or enemy to change their course.
15. For further analysis of the political changes, see Tang Tsou's *Cultural Revolution and Post-Mao Reforms* (1986).
16. Calhoun (1991) describes the political ferment before 1989 among scientists, social scientists, and literary intellectuals.
17. Recall that in chapter 1, we discussed some of the ideological and organizational resources for this critical tradition: Confucian remonstrance, the May 4 activism for democracy and science, and the populist and revolutionary stance advanced by intellectuals. Added to that tradition are also the Marxist-Leninist call to revolutionize society and Mao's call "to rebel is justified" in the Cultural Revolution. (Note: Prof. Timothy Cheek helped in pointing this out.)
18. They would like to be independent but given the political constraints at the time, they generally had to get permission from various government offices and be affiliated with some official organizations. Their affiliated organs are, respectively, the Institute for Youth Studies at the Chinese Academy of Social Sciences, the Beijing University's Study Society of Marxism-Leninism, and Sanlian Press (though loosely). The International Academy of Chinese Culture received special permission and welcome from Hu Yaobang, the Party chief at the time (see Edward X. Gu 1999:402; 407–10; 421–2 for nuances of the relationships, changes, etc.).
19. For a more complete list of the names of authors and titles of books, see Edward X. Gu 1999:401, 404–6. See also X. L. Ding (1994:65–76) for a more in-depth discussion of the book series, cliquish magazines *(tongren zazhi),* and other semi-autonomous professional organizations.
20. In the 1990s, the group was criticized as being conservative and in line with the government agendas of patriotic education of the masses. It certainly has the potential, but it does not have to be a tool of the government. We will further debate this point in chapter 3.
21. See also X. L. Ding's (1994) discussion on the larger social context in the 1980s in which the various debates took place. He characterizes the debates as largely between the ruling elite (orthodox organic intellectuals) and the counterelite (various other critical intellectuals).
22. This, of course, concerns not only the Cultural Revolution; it was just the latest disaster. Link (1992:147–9) asked Dai Qing why she wanted to write about Wang Shiwei, whom we discussed in chapter 1. One of the reasons, she said, is to find out what went wrong. "How did we end up in this mess?" Other questions intellectuals ask include "Had the party always been arrogant and cruel?" "Had it turned bad at some point?"
23. See Wagner (1987) for a more in-depth discussion of Bai's work.
24. See Polumbaum (1994b) for a full discussion of the issues surrounding China's draft press law.

25. For a full discussion of the making of a political dissident out of a scientist, see James Harley Williams's study, *Fang Lizhi's Big Bang* (1994). See also Fang's (1991) own writings on science, culture, and democracy in China. In addition, Craig Calhoun's (1991) insightful description of Fang's elitism must be read. His analysis highlights the complexity of Fang. See also Miller (1996) for the role of natural scientists and dissent.
26. Bei Ling listed dozens of unofficial magazines and books published in the reform era before and after 1989 in an article entitled "*Dangdai Zhongguo Dalu de Dixia Kanwu yu Dixia Chubanwu*" (Underground journals and publications in contemporary China). See *World Journal,* June 21, 1998.
27. For a more in-depth discussion of domestic law reforms in China, see Epstein (1994); Feinerman 1994; Polumbaum (1994b); and Potter (1994b).
28. See also Shu-Yun Ma's (1993) illustration of a patron-client relationship between Hu Yaobang, and Liu Binyan and Ruan Ming, two critical voices in the Party.

Notes to Chapter Three

1. For the quotes from *Analects* hereafter, see Huang Pumin et al. (eds.) 1990.
2. In 2001, a year before he planned to retire, Jiang did call on the Party to admit private entrepreneurs into its ranks. Although this was a significant step, it may have come too little and too late for him to leave a lasting imprint on Chinese politics. True, the term "Jiang era" is used by, for instance, Willy Wo-Lap Lam, and the era is characterized by the worsening corruption, the continuing Taiwain Strait conflicts, the Asian financial crisis in 1998, and so forth. Indeed, the title of Lam's book is *The Era of Jiang Zemin* (1999). The way in which Jiang deals with Falun Gong (more on this in the next section) also adds to his legacy. But however he tried, he never went much beyond Deng Xiaoping. A term coming into use now, "Jiang Zeming Thought," does little to add to his weight. No matter how generously we treat Jiang Zemin, he is no Mao Zedong or Deng Xiaoping. For the analytic purpose of this book, then, there was hardly a Jiang Zemin era. The term is used here chiefly to denote the difference in time.
3. Here is Saich (1990:ix): "Much of what happened on Tiananmen Square was spontaneous and the result of circumstance. Many of those who participated did so for vague reasons. Beyond the idea that things were wrong and should change, many had no concrete proposals for ideas of change. Once started, the movement gained its own momentum, and some joined in simply because it was fun to humiliate a bunch of old men locked up in their governmental fortresses."
4. For examples of such reflections in the 1990s, see the following works: collections of essays and diaries by Wang Yuanhua (2000, 2001) and Li Rui (1998); interviews by Li Hui and Ying Hong (1999) with twelve important intellectuals (Wang Yuanhua, Shao Yanxiang, Wang Xiaoming, Lei Yi, Zhu Xueqin, He Qinglian, Xu Youyu, Chen Sihe, Lin Xianzhi, Lan Yingnian, Li Rui, and Ruan Yisan); articles by twenty (mostly) intellectuals collected in Xiao Ke et al. (1998); a remembrance of Yu Luoke, including his diaries and articles, edited by Xu Xiao, Ding Dong, and

Xu Youyu (1999); a biography of Gu Zhun by Gao Jianguo (2000), as well as Gu's diaries and a number of remembrances and reflections edited by Chen Minzhi and Ding Dong (1997, 1998).

These also include Ye Yonglie's investigative work on what happened to intellectuals in the Anti-Rightist movement of 1957 and in the Cultural Revolution of 1966–76. Ye's achievements include, among others, his 1988 and 1997 books on the Rightists, and his 1994 and 1999 biographies of Mao's organic intellectuals Hu Qiaomu and Chen Boda, as well as his biographies of Zhang Chunqiao and Yao Wenyuan.

What Ye (1997:391–2) says may be typical of what other intellectuals think. He states that he began his project on intellectuals by interviewing those who were still alive and doing archival and library research on them. He did this because he was inspired by Ba Jin's own reflections. He believes, as Ba Jin does, that only when we keep in mind what happened in the past can we prevent it from happening again. While Ba Jin wanted to build a museum of the Cultural Revolution, Ye wanted to start an institute studying the period at the same time (p. 397). Although for obvious reasons none of these projects has materialized, Ye's and others' works may very well function as a virtual museum and all of those who study the period become part of a virtual institute. They all contribute greatly to the development of intellectuals as an independent force. See also He Qinglian's (2001:77–8) brief summary of the reflections of intellectuals in the 1990s.

5. See also Perry and Selden (2000) for a collection of essays on conflict and resistance in contemporary China.
6. Deng and his group have reportedly written several such articles called *wan yan shu* (ten-thousand character protest document). The main point is to criticize the current reform as deviating from socialism. See Ma and Ling (1998), Feng Chen (1999), or *Los Angeles Times,* September 10, 1997, Section A. As we will show here, their analysis is accurate, although their conclusions may be against the current reform.
7. For more information, see Zong Han (1994). He reports that SOE's constituted 1.2 percent of the total industrial enterprises, 35.5 percent of the labor force, 48.1 percent of the industrial output, and paid 62.5 percent of the taxes.
8. Indeed, despite sporadic stalling in the privatization process, the tendency remained steady in the 1990s. In 1997, it was reported, the Chinese government decided to reduce the 3,000 SOEs to 1,000, forcing the remaining 2,000 to find a way out on their own (*Los Angeles Times,* June 7, 1998, Section D). These operations would undoubtedly be forced to adopt some form of privatization.
9. Christoffersen's article discusses the political economy of Chinese civil society, comparing it with the cases of Russia and other East Asian countries, especially South Korea and Taiwan. He analyzes the roles of Chinese enterprise groups, TVEs, and SOEs.
10. See chapter 5 for a more detailed discussion on the formation of the current class structure in China.
11. It should be noted from the outset that the growth of the private and collective sector does not mean autonomy of the bourgeois class. As Christoffersen (1998: 115–7) points out, TVEs tend to be controlled by local government, and private

entrepreneurs also depend largely on the latter for various resources. We will come back to this state-society relationship in chapter 5.

12. Of course, entrepreneurs in local government does not necessarily equal democratization. See chapter 5 for more discussions.
13. That is, the graduates of both junior and senior high schools in 1966, 1967, and 1968.
14. About eight yuan equals $1, and 10,000 yuan in 1993 was equal to two years' salary for a junior professor.
15. According to the Attorney General of Guangzhou, from 1993 to 1997 the prosecutors there handled over 1,900 cases of corruption, involving 2,233 cadres and 439 million yuan. See *World Journal,* June 21, 1998.
16. Vincente Fox, the head of one of the opposition parties, the National Action Party (PAN), won the general election, ending the almost 80-year one-party rule by the PRI.
17. In his talk on July 1, 2001 commemorating the eightieth anniversary of the founding of the CCP, Jiang Zemin, the Party chief, said that although the core of the Party is still composed of workers, peasants, intellectuals, soldiers, and cadres, the Party should also admit into its ranks other excellent social elements. He is alluding to private entrepreneurs (see *People's Daily,* July 2, 2001 at www.people.com.cn; Ching-Ching Ni 2001). It is quite likely that "red capitalists" will become a major component of the Party. See Cheek (1998) for more discussions on the political culture in this socialist corporatism, "represented by a technocratic party, co-opted business associations, and the mutual benefit in local enterprises for entrepreneurs and state cadres" (1998:252). We will again discuss the socialist corporatism in chapter 5 in light of Pearson's analysis of it. Cheek is (or was?) pessimistic about the role of intellectuals in fostering a democratic opposition. However, while it is true that some intellectuals are functioning as the agents of hegemony for the sate (1997:248–52), more intellectuals than Cheek allows may be doing just the opposite, as we will show in this chapter.
18. They made this prediction before the PRI was replaced by its opposition, though. The Chinese Communists used to say, "the Soviet Union's today is our tomorrow." The dissidents would deride the current regime with the same saying when the former Soviet Union began its democratic reform in the 1980s. Now is the PRI's today the CCP's tomorrow? For more aspects of the comparison between Mexico and China, see the collection of ten essays edited by Lindau and Cheek (1998).
19. For a more in-depth discussion on corruption and the village elections, see the sections on peasants in chapter 5 and on social crises in chapter 7.
20. For more discussions on the various definitions and implications of the public sphere, see Wakeman, Jr. (1993), Rowe (1993), Rankin (1993), Madsen (1993), Chamerlain (1993), and Philip Huang (1993), all in Huang (ed.), *Symposium: "Public Sphere"/"Civil Society" in China,* a special issue of *Modern China* 19(2).
21. These books talk about the planning and contents of their programs as well as how they feel about what they do. These TV programs frequently invite intellectuals to participate in the planning stage or to appear on the programs as experts. *Tell It as It Is,* for example, has invited sociologists like Yang Dongping, Zheng Yefu, and Lu Jianhua to head the planning staff at one time or another (see Cui Yongyuan 2001:301).

22. Polumbaum (1994a:202) also observes that "China's media system is far more variegated, more informative and more subject to chance and human whim than the totalitarian model would lead one to suppose." The title of her article is telling: "China's Press—Forget the Stereotype." For a comparative study of the state propaganda in the PRC and in the former Soviet Union in the 1950s, see Julian Chang (1997). See also Peter Kenez (1985) for an analysis of the Soviet methods of mass mobilization in 1917–29.
23. To be sure, when a book is published, the most sensitive words, sentences, or even parts are already deleted (see He Qinglian 2001:51, 157). We will further discuss this in the next section. Still, the amount of criticism would be unthinkable in the past.
24. It is said, though, that the press was in trouble for publishing the book.
25. *Yellow Peril,* or *huang huo,* depicts a fictitious future for China when all fails and China is on the verge of war with the world.
26. William T. Liu (1999) defines Falun Gong as a special case, a "cult-like quasi-religious movement." It meets people's psychological and health needs to a certain extent, and it fulfills a spiritual vacuum. But it poses a threat to the government. In 1999, it staged a "siege" of Zhongnanhai, a sit-in demonstration at the CCP headquarters against the government's negative stance on the group. Its effective organization reminds the CCP painfully of Hong Xiuquan's Taiping Rebellion in the middle of the nineteenth century (John Wong 1999:16–7). Since then, the government has denounced Falun Gong as a cult.

    Although it has gone underground inside China, one still constantly hears about its protest activities as well as their continuing suppression by the government. Falun Gong has nonetheless established organizations and continued its practice and protests elsewhere in the world (see Tam Chen Hee 1999). In the United States, for example, one would often see its members practice or protest in front of Chinese consulates, at international airports, and periodically at local rallies. Worldwide, the number of its followers may be less than the 100 million its master Li Hongzhi claims, but more than 2 million the government estimates (John Wong 1999:10). Still, it is a social movement that is much more active than the conventional democracy movement.

    Falun Gong is also a form of *qigong,* or a health exercise that cultivates *qi,* one's bodily energy. Although the organization officially denies this charge, one often hears that it discourages people from seeking medical help if they are sick. That is one of the reasons why the government has labeled it a cult, a reason the government can put on the table. For more information, our readers may visit Falun Gong's own website at *http://falundafa.org*. See also Jian Xu (1999) for a more in-depth discussion of Chinese *qigong* and He Qinglian (2001:104–12) on Falun Gong's role in providing an opportunity for social participation.
27. At the Fifty-second annual meeting of the Association for Asian Studies (March 9–12, 2000), Stanley Rosen of the University of Southern California and Gerard Postiglione of the University of Hong Kong reported facing the same restrictions during research in China. Adam Brookes of BBC and Susan V. Lawrence of *The Far Eastern Economic Review* discussed similar difficulties in getting the information they wanted to know.

28. For more discussions on the various associations and their political roles, see chapters 5 and 6.
29. These were lecturers and recent Ph.D. graduates, a Ph.D. student, and a college student, all specializing in Chinese literature. In the citations of interviews, the numbers following the year of the interviews stand for the page numbers of my personal notes.
30. Indeed, the topic of intellectuals itself is a very sensitive one. In our research in 1994, the Chinese colleagues in our joint project told us that we could not do research on intellectuals in the humanities and social sciences. They would rather withdraw from the team than take the political risk. In fact, they said, they were already taking risks just by researching scientific and technical personnel. I ended up doing my research on other intellectuals on the side, independently of the project. Although there was no harassment of any kind from the police, I learned later that I had been watched and that my research had itself been "researched" by the "public security agencies."
31. Although there are many intellectuals with Wang's stature, few would dare sign their names to such a petition, an example of the split personality.
32. One intellectual I interviewed in 2001 commented that he would check certain websites every few hours for fear that he may miss something interesting.
33. See chapter 5 for more discussions on this relationship.
34. See also Hao Chang (1987:17).
35. There are some slightly different explanations of these traditions. In his discussion on types and roles of intellectuals, Cheek (1992:135) tells us how Tu Wei-ming understands them. For Tu, *zheng* is politics or governance, *xue* is learning or study, and *dao* is the "way," "an almost untranslatable ethical and religious term," which Cheek prefers "to think of as the search for 'transcendence." See Tu Wei-ming (1993b) for a more detailed discussion. Tu's book has also been translated into Chinese (2000).
36. See also Xudong Zhang (1998:121–2) for a more in-depth discussion of Wang's stance on humanism and his criticism of other humanists.
37. For a description and discussion of the popular culture in the 1980s and early 1990s, see also Huang Huilin and Yin Hong (1998).
38. For some more examples of this postmodern art, see also a special issue of *Social Text* (Summer 1998, Vol. 55) on *Intellectual Politics in Post-Tiananmen China,* edited by Xudong Zhang.
39. We call them critical intellectuals because their criticism is largely independent of the official ideology, although it may occasionally coincide with the official propaganda. Some do believe, though, that this popular nationalism was "officially tolerated and manipulated" (Barmé 1999:370). "Tolerance" may be true since the government did allow demonstrations against the bombing of the Chinese Embassy. But even the word 'tolerance' needs to be qualified: after the publication of *China Can Say No,* the Chinese government banned any discussion of it in the official media (Xudong Zhang 1998:138). The government's stance has been understandably ambivalent to say the least. They may not always know what they do. So "manipulation" may be doubtful.
40. See Chow Tse-tsung (1960) for a discussion of the May 4 era in general and

Q. Edward Wang (2001) for a discussion of the role of Hu Shih, Gu Jiegang, and so forth in the critique of Chinese culture. Among others, the professors who signed the declaration include He Bingsong (1890–1946) and Tao Xisheng (1899–1986). Theirs was an effort to build a China-based modern culture rather than returning to the past, according to He, although he later seemed to have veered toward Chinese culture supremacy (Q. Edward Wang 2001:156–7). See also Eastman (1976) for a discussion of the GMD conservative movement in the 1930s.

41. However, Yu is said to be determined not to return to China as long as it is under Communist rule.
42. See Schwartz (1976) and Miller (1996:244) for a discussion on conservatism in China. Caution must be exercised since the title given to a person, conservative or liberal, rarely, if ever, fits. For example, Chen Boda, a radical Communist who influenced Mao in his Sinification of Marxism in the 1940s, also advocated a balance between modernization and the preservation of a genuine Chinese character (Wylie 1980:123).
43. Quite different from Barmé's (1996) implication, Xiao is not really advocating "firm Party rule" and rejecting Western values.
44. Both liberals and neoconservatives are conservative in that they believe in the market forces, and they are authoritarian in that they believe in the strong government fostering the market forces. It is the New Left, which we will discuss in the next section, that is more like the liberals in the United States.
45. It is in this sense that neoconservatism joined the nationalist surge in the 1990s. But it seems to be doing more to rebuild the Chinese culture, to nurture the second- and third-level nationalism we just discussed, than it is simply being anti-Western, as Barmé (1996) would charge.
46. Some of their views are similar to those of the new Confucians who advocate a revival of Confucian values and a new cultural nationalism (Baum 1994:330).
47. Xu Jilin suggests that it is better to call the group *xin zuoyi* (new left wing) rather than *xin zuopai* (new leftists) since *zuopai* has a negative connotation in modern Chinese history (see Xu Jilin et al. 2000:308). Of course, Xu points out, intellectuals cannot be simply divided into two groups, liberals and the New Left. Some intellectuals' views fall on either end; others' views are simply too complicated to be classified. Huang Ping (2000) and Cui Zhiyuan (2000) are vehemently against the use of the term 'New Left.' They believe that intellectuals' thinking is so complex that the dichotomy will inevitably miss the shades of meaning. Still, as Xu Jilin insists, these terms can be used to help us identify different strands of thought as long as we understand that they are only ideal types, tools to help us in our thinking, and they cannot be simply applied to each individual thinker. One's thoughts tend to be more varied than what one or two labels can tell. But for the general trend of each thought, the labels we use here still apply. And we use the term New Left to refer to the New Left Wing.
48. Han himself is not humored by other people's calling him the New Left, though. In the interview article we cite here, he constantly avoids answering the interviewer's question of whether he thinks himself as a member of the New Left.

49. The so-called Angang Constitution of the 1950s emphasizes cooperation between managers, engineers, and workers in production, management, and technological innovation.
50. The quote is from an article by an anonymous author in response to Xiao Gongqin's comments, which I just quoted. The two appear to have been writing to each other. The article was posted on the web by Chang Ren the day after Xiao's article appeared. See (*http://www.netsh.com.cn/wwwboardm/540/* February 5, 2000)
51. One of the playwrights, however, denied that they belonged to the New Left. Neither did they belong to the Old Left since, as one of them said, none of the writers or performers was a Communist Party member although some of them were Communists (*Shi Jie* 2001:179, 183).
52. In his article commemorating the eightieth anniversary of the CCP, Zhang comments that the failure of the former Soviet Union started when they opened their party to everybody, implying that Jiang was just doing the same. Although the journal may be suspended, the Old Left has many venues to continue with their challenge to the Party.
53. They also wrote the book that we cited earlier concerning nationalism and other contemporary thoughts.
54. For more discussions of the intellectuals at various places of the political spectrum, see also Barmé (2000).
55. He helped Shen with his effort, but now regrets that he did so. In 1997 Tang organized the New York Concert to Commemorate the Eighth Year Anniversary of June 4. He has started a cultural and publishing company in New York. Through it he wants to promote press freedom in China and the right to associate with other independent organizations there.
56. See also Minxin Pei (2000:30) for more discussions of activities of Peng Ming, Qin Yongmin, and so forth. And see Jun Jing (2000) for more examples of environmental protests.
57. See note 26 for a more in-depth discussion on Falun Gong. Feuchtwang's (2000) article on religion as resistance in contemporary Chinese society, though not dealing with Falun Gong, shows us the potential of religious movements in diffusing the power of the Party-state.
58. As Barmé (1991:98) points out, "many famous exiles have given the impression that they are little better than the system they oppose."
59. See Tyrene White (2000) for examples of people's resistance against, and accommodation of, the one-child policy, including violence and threat of violence against birth-control officials and evasion.
60. Bol (1992) discusses fully the transformation of the *shi,* or the literati, in Tang and Song China, especially the development of the intellectual ethos of political activism and cultural attainment.
61. A last note: Postmodernism and feminism, or some other isms, may also give rise to new techniques of exploitation and oppression, which we need to be aware of (Ross 1988).

Notes to Chapter Four

1. See Deng's ([1978] 1983:82–8) talk at the National Science Conference. Citing Marx, he argued why science and technology is a primary productive force.
2. Their book, *The Chinese Intellectuals Who Have Stepped Down the Chancel* (1993), depicts how intellectuals went from what seemed to be higher social positions of intellectual labor to practical moneymaking jobs.
3. See more examples in Liu Zeming et al. (1993).
4. Le Guin is comparing intellectuals under the former Soviet rule and the intellectuals in the capitalist United States. Although there is no Zhdanov telling American intellectuals what to write, the market serves as the censor. The Chinese intellectuals, however, have both the external Stalin and the Stalin in the soul.
5. It is not clear when Zhang was born or died, but he received his *jinshi,* the metropolitan (higher than provincial *juren)* degree in 1586. He was magistrate and chronicler of Sheh county, the home of many Huizhou merchants (see Brook 1998:15).
6. While general feelings about the prospects ahead for intellectual work may have been pessimistic, there were some optimistic notes. Shan Junyi saw the bright side: money caused corruption, but it made the rule of law a necessity:

   > It is obvious that the country is on the road to a market economy and globalization. The world is becoming a place where money talks. It is good in that money is now bigger than bureaucratic power, which is a revolution against tradition. But money can also corrupt politics. Therefore, the rule of law will become necessary. (Interview 1994:1.34)

7. In summarizing my concluding thoughts for this section, I have benefited greatly from Prof. Timothy Cheek's comments on this part of the manuscript.
8. Hu Houxuan, an *historian,* is a good example of a humanistic intellectual who seems to have remained a professional, almost completely unattached to politics. He is one of a group of intellectuals whose stories are published in *The Chinese Intellectuals Series: China's Twentieth Century and I* (1994), a collection of autobiographies with Xu Ming as the chief editor. In his essay he described how, over several decades since he graduated from Peking University, he persisted in his research on ancient Chinese inscriptions unearthed on bones or on tortoise shells *(jia gu wen).* These were in fact specimens of the Chinese language, dating from three thousand years ago. He persevered in his work despite the difficulties caused by the Anti-Japanese War, the Civil War between the CCP and GMD, and the Cultural Revolution. By 1993 the series of books he published on *jia gu wen* had received five major awards. Altogether he has published over one hundred seventy books and articles on *jia gu wen* and on related topics. He is a professor in several universities and he holds office in various historical reserach associations (1994:299).

   Again we underscore the fact that Hu was able to concentrate on his work all through the turbulence of twentieth-century China. In his entire essay, he did not once say whether he participated in the Anti-Japanese War or in the Civil War. It is safe to assume, however, that he did not. Nor did he mention how he fared during the Anti-Rightist movement, or during the Cultural Revolution, which spared virtually no intellectual. Here, too, it is probably safe to assume that he was among the least affected. He never once spoke of the democracy movements or even of the economic reforms being attempted in China.

Of course, this was not total detachment from political forces. His work, after all, was underwritten by both the GMD and CCP governments. Nor does his inattention to political events in China mean that he does not have an opinion. But judging from his autobiography, politics is apparently not of grave concern to him, and has never been. Hu seems to follow the tradition of scholars and writers like Qian Zhongshu, Liang Shiqiu, and Lin Yutang in the Republican era.

9. We have not discussed separately the work of each profession, for we meant to speak about them in a general sense. But our discussion throughout the book will give the reader an idea of the work of other professionals. The following two short examples will also help.

   Here is how two eye doctors describe their work: "To earn some extra money beyond our usual salary of less than 700 yuan, each doctor has to see a certain number of patients and reach a certain rate of successful treatment. The quotas are determined by the average over the years. Being one of the major hospitals in the city, we are required to make a profit of 100 million yuan this year" (Interviews with Luo Xiuming and Hao Linan 1996:2.30).

   A playwright describes his work: "We are supposed to write a play each year with pre-approval of the plan by the theater. The theater puts on three new plays each year and goes on tours during spring and fall. Currently we employ only two playwrights, 40 actors, plus other workers, altogether about 100 people. We are not allowed to raise ticket prices since we are a nationally renowned theater for children's plays" (Interview with Yang Wei 1994:1.4).

10. Purposive sampling is a method of selecting respondents in such a way that major types of individuals will be included and studied in-depth. Our selection was based on intellectuals' academic rank.
11. These measures will also help stop the brain drain, which we discuss in chapter 7.
12. Jones and Krause (1991:234–5) discuss the relationship between the state and professions in several countries, including France, the former Soviet Union, the United States, and Eastern Europe. They point out that in the Eastern European system, any real bargaining power over work conditions, pay, and activities of the profession is a missing ingredient.
13. One more point: since it is the state that has the full power to allocate resources, and professionals are close to that power, it is the professionals who benefit most. What we say here does not mean, however, that the intellectuals working in the public or private sectors must necessarily become organic; they can remain unattached until they reach managerial jobs. To be organic requires more institutional dependency and loyalty, as we have shown before, although the demarcation is not always clear. But generally, once professionals make the upward move into managerial positions, either in the private or public sectors, they become part of the world of organic intellectuals. We need to keep in mind that intellectuals can be "organic" in either the public or the private sectors of the economy and polity. See the discussion on organic intellectuals in chapter 5.
14. See also Pearson (1997:48–55), for example, on the business guilds in late-Qing (1840–1911) and in the "golden age" of 1911–27. More in chapters 5 and 6.

15. Israel (1986:xv–xvi) is making a different point, though. He argues that it is possible to escape politics by obtaining professional autonomy. But what we are saying is that obtaining autonomy is the politics of professionals. These are two different kinds of politics, but they both are applicable here.
16. See also Bertilsson (1990) for a detailed discussion on the relationship between the welfare state, the professions, and citizens.
17. For similar development in the former Soviet Union in the years of its *perestroika,* see Jones and Krause (1991:240–1).
18. Krause (1992:10) compares the Egyptian profession of law with that of France and finds that "the change from pre-capitalist to more capitalist politics has brought with it a decreasing degree of activity of the bar in politics and a concentration on the goal of making money through the pursuit of corporate clients." The same seem to be happening in China as well, not only in the legal profession, but also in medicine, engineering, teaching, and so forth.
19. Qian said in his preface to *A Cadre School Life* (1982), "Our only boldness was a lack of enthusiasm for the endless movements and struggles we participated in. . . ." (cited in Schwarcz 1986b:247).
20. After all, as Israel (1986:xv) remarks, few have more than marginal interest in the crusade of critical intellectuals' pursuit of broader freedom, which is still a high-risk enterprise in China now. But even if the risk is reduced, probably not many more will join that pursuit. The majority of intellectuals, both technical and humanistic, Zhao Jialing (1989:5) observes, are not active in politics. Many of them believe that their individual value will be demonstrated in their achievement in their own fields. They are most concerned about things that affect their work. As long as they can concentrate on that, they feel they are home-free.

Notes to Chapter Five

1. Giddens (1981:108) defines a class-divided society as one "in which there are classes, but where class analysis does not serve as a basis for identifying the basic structural principle of organization of that society."
2. The best example I can think of, which may indicate some degree of working-class power, is their involvement in schools during the Cultural Revolution. They formed the Workers' and Peasants' Mao Zedong Thought Propaganda Teams, which went into schools to help restore order in uncontrolled student bodies. But they were simply following orders from the Party. Chen Yonggui, a peasant, became a vice premier at the time, but it hardly indicates peasant power, for he was picked by Mao, not by the peasants, to serve in the state government.
3. See also Li Cheng (2000) on the fourth generation of leaders in the PRC.
4. One might be tempted to view managers of both the foreign and private sectors as private entrepreneurs, and indeed, they overlap in many cases. But in our theoretical framework, managers are organic intellectuals, except when there is overlap between owner and manager. They are, then, what Ehrenreich (1979) calls "the professional-managerial class." (See Pearson 1997 and our discussion in the next section for an analysis of such managers.) But much of Pearson's analysis

of private managers applies to our analysis of private entrepreneurs as well, as we show in the next section.

5. See our discussion in chapter 4 on intellectuals as private entrepreneurs.
6. See Cheek (1998) for more discussion on the socialist corporatism. See also chapter 3 for a discussion on the public sphere, which is a micropicture of this socialist corporatism in other aspects.
7. In the 1980s, over 1,000 national-level groups and 100,000 local-level associations had been formed (Pearson 1997:118).
8. See Pearson's (1997) analysis of the managers in the foreign and private sectors.
9. For more examples and discussions of the jobless, see Li Wen et al. 1998. See Walder (1991) for a comparative view of the working-class conditions in the 1980s.
10. The number of migrant laborers who have left the countryside to look for jobs in towns and cities is estimated to be 100 million (Ching Kwan Lee 2000:44).
11. In a Gallup poll in 1997, respondents were asked to evaluate their lives on a satisfaction scale from 1 to 10, where 1 was the worst possible life one could imagine, 10 the best possible life. People living in the cities had an average score of 5.33, while people in the countryside averaged 4.93. When asked how they would have scored their lives five years earlier, the peasant respondents' average score was 3.58 (Fan Ping 1999:455). There was improvement, but the general level of satisfaction was still low, especially for the peasants.
12. Zhang Ming (2001) points out that many lack interest in the village elections because the cadres thus elected do little to solve their everyday problems. One of the reasons is that they are still responsible to the authorities at higher levels, for example, *xiang,* the "township," or the "county," not necessarily to those who elect them. See more on village elections in chapter 7.
13. One of our interviewees, Tian Xufeng (1996:3.12) reported on brutal actions used to impose birth control in Henan Province, which we related earlier. See also the stories told by Gao Xiaoduan, who appeared on *Nightline ABC,* and testified at a hearing of the House of Representatives' International Relations Human Rights Committee concerning extreme measures in Fujian province (*Nightline ABC,* June 10, 1998; *Los Angeles Times,* June 11, 1998).
14. Hu Qiaomu (1912–92) had some college education at Qinghua and Zhejiang universities. He joined the CCP in 1932 and was named in 1935 the general secretary of Shanghai's left-wing association of writers, playwrights, journalists, educators, musicians, artists, and Esperanto specialists, that is, Zhongguo Zuoyi Wenhua Jie Zong Tongmeng. He went to Yan'an in 1937 and became Mao's secretary in 1941. Some of the important positions he occupied since then include the director of Xinghua News Agency, the deputy head of the CCP's propaganda department, deputy secretary general of the CCP Central Committee, the director of *People's Daily,* and after 1975 the president of the Chinese Academy of Social Sciences.
15. As we mentioned earlier, this can be seen from the composition of the Party's Fifteenth Central Committee: 92.4 percent of the governing organ had attended university or technical school (*World Journal* and *Los Angeles Times,* September 19, 1997).
16. These include, for example, the Democracy Wall movement at the end of the 1970s and the student movements in the 1980s, as we discussed in chapter 2.

17. Polumbaum's (1994a) article analyzes the dynamics of the Chinese media and the role of the Party and tradition. See our discussion in chapter 3 on the public space available to intellectuals. Things may not be as bad as Marlane (1994) fears, though.
18. See chapter 7 for an explanation of Weber's notion of formal and substantive rationality. We introduce the idea when talking about the roles of intellectuals as a class in finding alternatives to both Chinese socialism and Western capitalism.
19. In chapter 6, we will discuss further the political roles of democratic parties in the 1940s.
20. Indeed, the comments of some critical intellectuals on technical intellectuals are especially revealing. One of them believed that these intellectuals had lost their political independence when they attached themselves to the power elite. "Three *qian* does not equal half a *liang,*" he said. (The Qians: Qian Xuesen, Qian Sanqiang, and Qian Weichang, are well-known intellectuals in contemporary Chinese history. In addition, *qian* and *liang* are also measurements of weight: ten *qian* equals one *liang*.) This very critical intellectual had already struck the Qian he knew out of his phone book! (Interview with Wang Yuanhua 1994:1.1.7–8). One could, however, also view *liang* as one of the humanistic intellectuals, Liang Shuming, who defied Mao in his policies after "liberation."

    Another critical intellectual observed, "When I first met the members of the Chinese Academy of Sciences, I felt very humble in front of them and full of respect for them. Then I hear that these people have their own weaknesses. First, they are like everyone else, gossiping around a lot, neighbor on the right, neighbor on the left, his third aunt, her sixth mother-in-law *(dong jia chang, xi jia duan, san gu liu po)*. Second, their legs shake when they see their leaders" (Interview with Wang Xiaoming 1994:1.11).

    He believed that the state had overemphasized the production of technical intellectuals. In fact, Mao had said during the Cultural Revolution, "Colleges should still enroll students, but I mean technical colleges." Wang believed that technical intellectuals might be useful tools, but lacked the critical spirit. Asking these "tools" to function as intellectuals in the real sense he thought would be very difficult.
21. Their roles, however, can be ambiguous. In 1998, some economists urged land speculation, which helped some private entrepreneurs but caused uneven development in real estate (He Qinglian [1998] 1999:345–6).
22. Pearson's book does not deal with managers of state-owned enterprises (SOEs) and collective township and village enterprises (TVEs). But one can imagine a great many similarities among these groups, the least of which is their organicity. One is organic to the party-state and the other to independent entrepreneurs, whether they are foreign, private, or collective. (Most TVEs are in fact controlled by private capital.) Furthermore, most of these managers are not politically inclined. If anything, the managers of the SOEs, protecting their own interests, may well be more conservative than those in the private sector when it comes to political change (see also He Qinglian 2001:220). As another example, one of my friends, a manager of a big SOE, ordered his workers to stay put during the June 4 movement; otherwise, they would not be paid. On the other hand, many managers in 1989 supported workers who went to Tiananmen (Walder 1991). Things do change, though.

23. According to Ching Kwan Lee (2000:43), there were thirteen hundred strikes in Shanghai alone between March and June 1957.
24. These include the Free Trade Unions of China, the League for the Protection of the Rights of the Working People, the Hired-hands Workers' Federation, and the China Development Union.
25. For a brief reference to the Central European intellectuals as organic to the working class and peasants, see Eyal, Szelenyi, and Townsley (1998:80).
26. However, as Calhoun (1991:122) observes, although Fang, being elitist like many of his colleagues, believed that democracy could be achieved only through intellectuals' education of the workers, peasants, and soldiers, he also made some good points in basic human rights and in the need to change from bottom to top.
27. For more examples of ghostwriters and their political life, see Schoenhals (1992).

Notes to Chapter Six

1. This reminds us of Foucault's (1980) term, *specific intellectual.* It has a similar meaning. And Foucault's "specific intellectual" is also related to the "universal." But Foucault allows intellectuals more independence in politics. We will come back to Foucault later in the next section.
2. Frank W. Heuberger provides us with a panoramic view of the New Class theories in his article, "The New Class" (1992).
3. See also Aronowitz (1988:297–8).
4. See also our discussion on the professional intellectuals in chapter 4.
5. See also Gouldner (1979:27) on how the possession of cultural capital unites the New Class and separates it from the working class.
6. See chapter 5 on a discussion of the confrontations. See also chapter 3 for more such debates.
7. Lu Xun's (1973a:7–19) short story, "The Diary of a Madman" shows a good example of such alienation. The story blames an insane society for the man's madness (see also Meisner 1967:44).
8. See Wylie (1980) for a full discussion of the Sinification of Marxism, and Apter and Saich (1994) for further exploration of the Yan'an era when this theoretical work was carried out.
9. In revising this section of the book, I benefited greatly from Professor Cheek's (2001) comments on the manuscript.
10. Many of the prominent members of the Democratic League were from Lianda, the wartime university in Kunming, Yunnan Province, including Wu Han, Wen Yiduo, and Fei Xiaotong (Israel 1998:351).
11. Seymour (1992:290) points out that Mao used to take them seriously, but not Deng and Jiang. Hu Yaobang and Zhang Ziyang were more like Mao.
12. When we met him in the office he shared with a dozen researchers, he at once began to criticize the authorities for neglecting the intellectuals' working conditions. He pointed out the broken chairs, and how difficult it was for us just to find a place to sit. He finally found two serviceable chairs and spread newspapers on the seats to protect our clothes.

13. During the movement of cultural studies in the 1980s, dozens of organizations were established focusing on the study of both Chinese and Western cultures (Edward X. Gu 1999:417).
14. Some of the magazines of the 1990s are financed by Hong Kong corporations, as we mentioned in chapter 3. When asked how a publication could maintain its independence if it was sponsored by businesses, Xiao Gongqin quoted another old Confucian motto, *cong dao bu cong jun,* meaning "one can work for the emperor but still follow one's own principles." While they may carry their backers' commercial ads, the editors largely control what will run in the magazine—as long, that is, as the content is not too political (Interview 1994:1.2).
15. We have discussed some of their articles in chapter 3. As we mentioned earlier, at the time of the writing of this book (August 2001), the first two were suspended by the government for their objection to Jiang Zemin's call for private entrepreneurs to join the Party. We should keep in mind that the editors of newspapers and journals may be replaced at any time by the authorities if the latter do not see the former doing the right thing.
16. Boggs (1993:17–27) identifies five kinds of Jacobinism, which is, in fact, a broader analysis of intellectuals' elitism. Here is my summary: (1) The *Platonic form,* as expressed in the work of Plato and Hobbes. Platonic Jacobinism is a vision of a sovereign order organized by intellectualized and knowledgeable politicians, or what Max Weber calls "responsible intellectualized politicians." That seems to be also the Confucian thinking of the rule of the sage-king (see Tu Weiming 1993b:50–1). (2) A *religious form,* as expressed in Catholicism and Protestantism. It sees state power exercised with a transcendental and spiritual underpinning. In traditional China, it is the interaction between Confucianism, Legalism, Taoism, and Buddhism, with the former two as the dominating beliefs, which formed the underpinning of the elitist dynastic governments. (3) A *Machiavellian form,* a strong, secular, creative, and intelligent government that resembles what we would call authoritarianism, which again we do not lack in the Chinese intellectual tradition. (4) A *scientific form.* Here intellectuals, as the vehicles of science and technology, would lead humanity to emancipation from oppression, alienation, fear, and superstition. Its elitism is very obvious here. Finally (5) A *Leninist form,* with intellectuals as vanguards who would seize all power and establish a Party-state. That is what China's revolutionary intellectuals have done. Boggs's analysis is more macro. In contrast, our analysis here will focus on some micro spheres of intellectual elitism.
17. See also Xu Jilin et al. 2000.
18. One may argue that this is because it is inconvenient to criticize the Party openly. But there are numerous other ways by which intellectuals can get their ideas across.
19. Again see Wang Xiaodong (2000a, 2000b), and Sheng Hong (1995). For opposing views, see He Jiadong (2000a, 2000b) and Xiao Gongqin (1999, 2000b).
20. It is important to remember, though, that this flaw is only one variable in determining what intellectuals do. As we discussed in chapter 1, structural factors, such as the political, social, and economic systems, are as important as intellectuals' culture in affecting their behavior. The various factors interact with one another, and they are inseparable.

21. As the revolutionary slogan goes, "Only socialism can save China," or *zhiyou shehui zhuyi cai nen jiu Zhongguo.*
22. So it is no incident that the overwhelming majority of the Politburo are engineers.
23. Indeed, democratization is not just a process of learning the textbook knowledge of democracy, but one of practicing that knowledge, that is, education through participation in the political activity (see Calhoun 1991:122). Those who know the knowledge, say the Chinese dissident organizations in the United States, do not seem to do much better than the peasant-farmers in China's countryside engaged in local elections. Democratization takes practice and time.
24. Interestingly but understandably, the conflict between intellectuals organic to the party-state and those organic to the bourgeoisie is minimal, or at least of a different kind. The market economy has brought them together.

Notes to Chapter Seven

1. As we mentioned in chapter 5, Zhang Ming (2001) observes that peasants lose interest in village elections when they see no real benefits in the practice. In the village where I am from, the election in 1999 was heavily influenced by clan relationships. Many people elected the village head simply because he is from the same clan. However, it is fair to assume that if villagers see their interests hurt by a less capable person, they will change their vote next time. It is true, though, that to fundamentally improve peasants' political and economic lives, the democratically elected village heads need more autonomy from the Xiang, or county authorities.
2. See also Perry's and Selden's (2000:6) assessment on the village elections. Other similar studies include O'Brien and Li (2000), Pastor and Tan (2000), and Oi and Rozelle (2000).
3. Mou Guangfeng (2000) and Jun Jing (2000) provide us with more data on the environmental crisis. See also Edmonds's article, "The Environment in the People's Republic of China 50 Years On" (1999).
4. See Bulag (2000) for more discussion on ethnic resistance.
5. See one of the warnings from Jiang Zemin at a meeting in June 1998 attended by high-level Party cadres (*World Journal,* July 5, 1998).
6. In her article, Ching Kwan Lee gives more examples of work stoppages, stikes, and other forms of protest in various parts of the country in the 1980s and 1990s. Some of the slogans found in their demonstrations include "We Want to Work," "Our Children Want to Go to School," "We Need to Eat," "Save the Factory, Save the People" (pp. 48–54).
7. Reasons that stop children from going to primary school or middle school can include the family need for help with housework or farmwork, or the lack of money to pay various fees. The reason for further advancement to high school and college is mainly the lack of such schools. Recently, however, alternative educational institutions have sprung up, providing various kinds of vocational and prepatory education. But most of the times they are private and costly, which again prevents many from getting more education.
8. Yang Dongping (1994b:530) reports that a survey of twenty-six institutions of

higher learning in Shanghai showed a loss of three thousand teachers in the ten years before 1994, or about 10 percent of the total.

9. The figures reported in the media tend to require more caution on the part of the reader. However, enough such reports in the media do tell us that the numbers are largely accurate.
10. According to the same article, the situation was at its worst from 1994 to 1995, and is still grave. The central government has been urging local governments to make efforts to guarantee the timely payment of teachers' wages. But the future is not promising, since many local government officials simply do not see it as a problem (*renshi bu dao wei).*
11. Indeed, the policies that Zhang and his colleagues set out for China in one of their journals can very well be used for China today. These include protection of human rights, improvement of the lives of the peasants and workers, opposition to unification through military subjugation, and opposition to class struggle and other social movements that hinder economic development (see Jeans 1997:103).
12. For the roles of Chinese intellectuals in social movements in Taiwan, see also Zhang Xiaochun (1989) and Zhang Maogui (1989).

Notes to Appendix

1. In the latter part of his life, Zhang did shave his head and become a monk, living in monastic seclusion. Like many others, part of his decision to become a monk was his reaction to the dynastic change from Ming to Qing (Brook 1993:50). There is, indeed, no lack of examples of secluded *shi* in Chinese history. One could always find a reason for becoming one.
2. See also Bol (1992:58–75) on the transition from bureaucrats to local elites.
3. The remaining generations include the May 4 generation, the 1920s generation, the generation of the anti-Japanese War, 1935–38, the liberation generation (the late 1940s and early 1950s), and the generation of the Red Guards.
4. We have discussed the Dreyfusards in chapter 1.
5. Gouldner (1979) even advances education to the status of capital, forming one of the foundations of the intellectual class, as we have discussed in chapter 6 on intellectuals as a class.
6. Interestingly, when Weber was about to further define intellectuals and the relationship between intellectuals, culture, and power, the manuscript breaks off (Gerth and Mills 1946: 448). The same happened when Marx was about to define class. Nonetheless, the terms they failed to define remained key concepts in their sociological analysis.
7. As we mentioned earlier, the only difference is that in the West the critical tradition was born with the Enlightenment in the eighteenth century, whereas in China it has been in existence for over two thousand years (Yu Ying-shih 1988:114–5).
8. It might be difficult, though not impossible, for these people.

Bibliography

Newspapers and Magazines

Asia Weekly 亚洲周刊 *(Yazhou Zhou Kan),* a magazine published in Hong Kong.
Beijing Evening News 北京晚报 *(Beijing Wan Bao),* an official newspaper in Beijing.
Beijing Spring 北京之春 *(Zhongguo zhi Chun),* a dissident journal based in the United States.
Cheng Ming Monthly 争鸣 *(Contend),* a magazine based in Hong Kong.
China Spring 中国之春 *(Zhongguo zhi Chun),* a dissident magazine based in the United States.
China Statistics 中国统计 *(Zhongguo Tongji),* published by the China Statistical Bureau.
Chinese TV News 中国电视报 *(Zhongguo Dianshi Bao),* a Chinese newspaper.
Dangdai Sichao 当代思潮 *(Contemporary Thoughts),* a journal of the old left.
Democracy and Law 民主与法制 *(Minzhu yu Fazhi),* a newspaper sponsored by the Chinese Association of Law.
Democratic China 民主中国 *(Minzhu Zhongguo),* a dissident magazine sponsored by Chinese intellectuals whoescaped after June 4, 1989.
Dongfang 东方 *(Orient),* a journal in Beijing sponsored by the Ministry of Culture, the People's Republic, and run chiefly by humanistic intellectuals.
Dushu 读书 *(Reading),* a magazine sponsored by San Lian Bookstore (Press) and run chiefly by humanistic intellectuals.
Frontline Monthly 前哨月刊 *(Qian Shao Yuekan),* a magazine published in Hong Kong.
Frontiers 天涯 *(Tianya),* a journal of the new left.
Guangming Daily 光明日报 *(Guangming Ribao),* an official newspaper of intellectuals, based in Beijing.
Horizons 视界 *(Shijie),* a journal of the new left.
Los Angeles Times, The
Min Jin 民进 *(Democratic Promotion),* a magazine sponsored by the Association for the Promotion of Democracy, one of the small "democratic parties."
Ming Pao Monthly 明报月刊 *(Ming bao yuekan),* a journal published in Hong Kong.
Magazine of Social Sciences 社会科学辑刊 *(Shehui kexue ji kan),* a magazine for the so-called academic intellectuals.
New York Times, The

Overseas Chinese Daily 侨报 *(Qiao Bao),* a Chinese language newspaper partly sponsored by the Chinese government but based in New York.

People's Daily 人民日报 (海外版) *(Renmin Ribao),* overseas edition, a Chinese newspaper sponsored by the Central Committee, Chinese Communist Party.

Press Freedom Guardian 新闻自由导报 *(Xinwen Ziyou Dao Bao),* a dissident Chinese newspaper in the United States.

Strategy and Management 战略与管理 *(Zhanlue yu guanli),* a Chinese magazine run by intellectuals in the social sciences.

Wall Street Journal, The

Wenhui Daily 文汇日报 *(Wenhui Ribao),* an official newspaper in Shanghai.

Wenhui Movie Times 文汇电影时报 *(Wenhui dianying shibao),* a newspaper in Shanghai.

Wenhui Reading Weekly 文汇读书周报 *(Wenhui Dushu Zhoubao),* a newspaper about writers and their books.

World Journal 世界日报 *(Shijie Ribao),* an overseas Chinese newspaper based in New York .

Xingdao Daily 星岛日报 *(Xingdao Ribao),* a Chinese newspaper based in Hong Kong with a New York edition.

Xinmin Evening News 新民晚报 *(Xinmin Wanbao),* a Chinese newspaper in Shanghai.

Zhengli de Zhuiqiu 真理的追求 (*Pursuit of truth*), a journal of the old left.

Zhougguo Daily News 中国日报 *(Zhongguo Ribao),* a Chinese newspaper based in Los Angeles.

Zhongliu 中流 (*Midstream*), a journal of the old left.

People Interviewed

(Note: Some were interviewed in groups, others individually. And the distinction is not made in the list between senior and junior professors and engineers.)

Name	*Field, Discipline*	*Date of Interview*
Bao Chuping	Lecturer in chemistry	July 14, 1994
Cai Beibei	Professor in chemistry	July 27, 1994
Cao Yihua	Professor in mathematics	July 16, 1994
Chang Chunli	Ph.D. student in psychology	July 19, 1994
Chang Youde	Ph.D. student in history	July 7 and 15, 1994
Chang Zhanjun	Administrator	July 5, 1996
Chang Zongmiao	Journalist and administrator	July 3, 1996
Chen Fong	Sociologist	June 15, 1994
Chen Kuide	Philosopher and democracy activist	June 30, 1997
Chen Hongchun	Manager of a private business	June 14, 1994
Chen Yichi	Professor in classical literature	July 19, 1994
Cheng Guan	Professor in sociology	July 6, 1994, June 29, 1996
Cheng Kejiang	Sociologist	July 18, 1994
Cheng Meidi	Engineer and administrator	June 30, 1994
Cheng Xiang	Engineer	July 24, 1994
Ding Lingen	Senior engineer	July 27, 1994

Deng Weizhi	Sociologist	July 12, 1994
Du Yanbing	M.A. student in international finance and economics	July 21, 1994
Fan Yuzhi	Professor in chemistry	July 10, 1994
Fang Huimin	Administrator	June 21, 1996
Fu Ji	Ph.D. student in Chinese	July 15 and 19, 1994
Gao Jiming	Banker	June 22, 1996
Ge Shannon	Lawyer and journalist	July 26, 1994
Gong Haiyang	College student in Chinese	July 19, 1994
Gu Jin	Engineer	July 24, 1994
Gu Qinnan	Professor in English	June 20, 1996
Gu Sihong	Engineer and administrator	July 15, 1994
Gui Junzong	Professor in computer science	July 14, 1994
Gui Yongji	Lecturer in environmental science	July 28, 1994
Guo Jiming	Writer and democracy activist	June 22, 1997
Hao Huiling	Schoolteacher	July 8, 1996
Hao Linan	Doctor	July 5, 1996
He Pinggan	Lecturer in chemistry	July 27, 1994
Hong Yang	Student advisor	July 15, 1994
Hou Junshi	Sociologist	June 20, 1996
Hu Ping	Political scientist and democracy activist	June 27, 1997
Huang Ping	Sociologist	July 14, 1996, July 2001
Jiang Han	M.A. student in chemistry	June 15, 1994
Jiang Shaoyu	Ph.D. student in sociology	June 17, 1996
Jiang Zhexin	Journalist	July 10, 1994
Li Guan	Manager	July 3, 1996
Li Jian	Literary critic	July 27, 1994
Li Jiming	Professor in English	June 20, 1996
Li Jizhang	Administrator	July 5, 1996
Li Ping	Entrepreneur	July 4, 1996
Li Rongling	Administrator	July 3, 1996
Li Yaxing	Professor in English	July 14, 1996
Li Yishun	M.A. student in education and Marxism	July 4, 1994
Liu Binyan	Journalist and democracy activist	July 1, 1997
Liu Jun	Sociologist	June 20, 1996
Liu Qing	Democracy activist	July 2 and 3, 1997
Liu Sicong	Professor in English	June 20, 1996
Liu Xiang	Researcher	July 5, 1996
Lu Xin	Ph.D. student in geography	July 17, 1994
Lu Zhesong	Engineer	July 24, 1994
Luo Guozhi	Sociologist and administrator	July 7, 1994
Luo Xiuming	Doctor	July 5, 1996
Ma Ran	Sociologist	June 17, 1996
Ni Dan	M.A. student in international finance and economics	July 21, 1994
Ni Yuxian	Democracy activist	June 26, 1997

Qi Jingxiu	Translator	June 22, 1996
Qi Ruisu	Administrator	July 3, 1996
Qi Xi	Sociologist	July 1, 1996
Quan Ming	Lecturer in biology	July 28, 1994
Shan Junyi	Lecturer in English	July 4, 1994
Shen Yahong	Lecturer in Chinese	July 2, 1994
Su Shaozhi	Writer and democracy activist	July 1, 1997
Su Xiaokang	Writer and democracy activist	July 1, 1997
Sun Mengji	Artist	July 30, 1994
Sun Zhongxin	Ph.D. student in sociology	July 13, 15, and 29, 1994
Tian Gusen	Professor in English	June 17, 1996
Tian Xufeng	Administrator	June 21, 1996
Tian Zhaoyun	Professor in literature and literary criticism	July 10, 1994
Wan Yaofa	Professor in biology	June 29, 1994
Wang Juhai	Engineer	July 24, 1994
Wang Lixiang	Lawyer	July 2, 1996
Wang Ruowang	Writer and democracy activist	June 26, 1997
Wang Xiaoming	Literary critic	July 11, 1994
Wang Youhao	Sociologist	July 1, 1996
Wang Yuanhua	Writer	July 22, 1994
Wei Deqi	Mayor of a medium-size city July 14, 1996	
Wu Dong	Sociologist	July 21, 1994
Wu Ji	Journalist	July 3, 1996
Wu Jiaping	Engineer	July 24, 1994
Wu Renhua	Editor	1998, and Sept. 16, 2001
Wu Xianrong	Professor in biology	July 27, 1994
Xia Hairong	Professor in chemistry	July 7, 1994
Xiao Gongqin	Historian	July 22, 1994, June 29, 1996
Xiao Guimei	Sociologist	July 25, 1994
Xu Jilin	Professor in history	June 28, 1996
Xu Tianxiang	Professor in education and administrator	July 6, 1994
Xu Yaotong	Professor in environmental science	July 28, 1994
Yan Hongyu	Ph.D. student in history	July 7 and 15, 1994
Yan Huiren	Engineer	July 20, 1994
Yan Jiaqi	Political scientist and democracy activist	June 28, 1997
Yan Yang	Professor in literary theory	July 19, 1994
Yan Zhaowei	Journalist	June 19, 1996
Yang Peishen	Translator	June 22, 1996
Yang Wei	Playwright	July 26, 1994
Yang Xiheng	Sociologist	June 20, 1996
Ye Jianong	Professor in chemistry	July 28, 1994
You Xiaming	Engineer	July 20, 1994
Yu Junjie	Engineer and administrator	July 15, 1994
Yu Liqun	Researcher and lecturer in chemistry and environmental studies	July 9, 1994

Yu Xilan	College student in education	July 15, 1994
Yue Ziming	Cadre in a middle-level city	June 26, 2000
Zang Shulin	Professor in English	June 21, 1994
Zhang Chaoling	Engineer	July 24, 1994
Zhang Diwen	Administrator	June 21, 1996
Zhang Fa	Ph.D. student in education	July 1, 1994
Zhang Hefeng	Lecturer in biology	July 27, 1994
Zhang Renjie	Professor in education	June 28, 1994
Zhang Wen	Lecturer in computer science	July 27, 1994
Zhang Xiaoyu	Engineer	July 6, 1996
Zhao Yaqin	Translator	June 22, 1996
Zheng Zhongqi	Engineer	July 15, 1994
Zheng Yefu	Sociologist	June 19, 1996
Zheng Yi	Writer and democracy activist	June 30, 1997
Zhong Qian	Journalist	July 30, 1994
Zhong Yanchu	Engineer and administrator	June 30, 1994
Zhong Wei	Professor in chemistry	July 28, 1994
Zhou Weiwan	Sociologist	July 6, 1996
Zuo Anliang	Journalist	July 18, 1994

Books and Articles Cited

Abbott, Andrew. 1988. *The System of Professions*. Chicago: University of Chicago Press.

Alford, Robert R. 1998. *The Craft of Inquiry: Theories, Methods, Evidence*. New York: Oxford University Press.

Alford, William P. 1993. "Double-edged Swords Cut Both Ways: Law and Legitimacy in the People's Republic of China." *Daedalus* 122 (2)45–69 (Spring).

Alitto, Guy. 1976. "The Conservative as Sage: Liang Shu-ming." Pp. 213–41 in *The Limits of Change: Essays on Conservative Alternatives in Republican China,* edited by Charlotte Furth. Cambridge: Harvard University Press.

Andrews, Julia F. and Gao Minglu. 1995. "The Avant-Garde's Challenge to Official Art." Pp. 221–78 in *Urban Spaces in Contemporary China: The Potential for Autonomy and Community in Post-Mao China,* edited by Deborah S. Davis, Richard Kraus, Barry Naughton, and Elizabeth J. Perry. Washington D.C.: Woodrow Wilson Center Press.

Apter, David E. 1987. *Rethinking Development: Modernization, Dependency, and Postmodern Politics*. Beverly Hills: Sage Publications.

———. 1995. "Discourse as Power: Yan'an and the Chinese Revolution." Pp. 193–234 in *New Perspectives on the Chinese Communist Revolution*, edited by Tony Saich and Hans van de Ven. Armonk, N.Y.: M. E. Sharpe.

Apter, David and Timothy Cheek. 1994. "Introduction: 'The Trial.'" Pp. xvii–xxxi in *Wang Shiwei and "Wild Lilies": Rectification and Purges in the Chinese Communist Party, 1942–44,* by Dai Qing. Armonk, N.Y.: M. E. Sharpe.

Apter, David and Tony Saich. 1994. *Revolutionary Discourse in Mao's Republic*. Cambridge: Harvard University Press.

Arkush, R. David. 1986. *Fei Xiaotong Zhuan* 费孝通传. (Fei Xiaotong and sociology in revolutionary China). Beijing: Shishi Chubanshe 北京时事出版社 (Current affairs press).

Aronowitz, Stanley.1988. *Science as Power: Discourse and Ideology in Modern Society*. Minneapolis: University of Minnesota Press.

———. 1990. "On Intellectuals." Pp. 3–56 in *Intellectuals: Aesthetics, Politics, Academics*, edited by Bruce Robbins. Minneapolis: University of Minnesota Press.

Aronowitz, Stanley and William DiFazio. 1994. *The Jobless Future: Sci-Tech and the Dogma of Work*. Minneapolis/London: University of Minnesota Press.

Ash, Robert F. 1991. "The Peasant and the State." *China Quarterly* 127:493–526.

Ba Jin. 1987. 巴金. *Suixiang Lu* 随想录 (Reflections). Beijing: Sanlian Press 北京三联出版社.

Bai Gang 白刚. 1999. "1998 1999 Nian: Zhongguo Cunmin Zizhi Buru Guifanhua Fazhan Xin Jieduan" 1998 1999 年: 中国村民自治步入规范化发展新阶段 (1998 1999: the new stage of development in normalizing the village autonomous government in China). Pp.179 91 in *1999 Nian Zhongguo Shehui Xingshi Fenxi yu Yuce 1999* 年中国社会形势分析与预测 (1999 analysis and prediction of social conditions in China), edited by Ru Xin 汝信, Lu Xueyi 陆学艺, and Shan Tianlun 单天伦, et al. Beijing: Shehui Kexue Wenxian Chubanshe 北京社会科学文献出版社 (Social science literature press).

Bai Zang 白臧. 1994. "Zhongguo Mianlin zhe Rencai Duangdai Weiji" 中国面临著人才断代危机 (China faces the danger of losing a generation of talents) *Press Freedom Guardian* 新闻自由导报 February 4, 1994.

Barmé, Geremie R. 1991. "Traveling Heavy: The Intellectual Baggage of the Chinese Diaspora." *Problems of Communism*. January-April:94–112.

———. 1996. "To Screw Foreigners Is Patriotic: China's Avant-Garde Nationalists." Pp. 183–208 in *Chinese Nationalism*, edited by Jonathan Unger. Armonk, New York: M. E. Sharpe.

———. 1999. *In the Red: On Contemporary Chinese Culture*. New York: Columbia University Press.

———. 2000. "The Revolution of Resistance." Pp. 198–220 in *Chinese Society: Change, Conflict and Resistance*, edited by Elizabeth J. Perry and Mark Selden. London: Routledge.

Baum, Richard. 1994. *Burying Mao: Chinese Politics in the Age of Deng Xiaoping*. Princeton, New Jersey: Princeton University Press.

———. 1996. "China after Deng: Ten Scenarios in Search of Reality." *China Quarterly* 145:153–75.

Bei Ling 贝岭. 1998. "Dangdai Zhongguo Dalu de Dixia Kanwu yu Dixia Chuban Wu" 当代中国大陆的地下刊物与地下出版物 (Underground journals and other publications in contemporary China). *Shijie Zhoucan* 世界周刊 (World Journal Weekly). June 21.

Bell, Daniel. 1973. *The Coming of Post-Industrial Society: A Venture in Social Forecasting*. New York: Basic.

———. 1980. *The Winding Passage: Essays and Sociological Journeys 1960–1980*. Cambridge: Abt Books.

Bernal, Martin. 1976. "Liu Shih-p'ei and National Essence." Pp. 90–112 in *The Limits of Change: Essays on Conservative Alternatives in Republican China,* edited by Charlotte Furth. Cambridge: Harvard University Press.

Bernstein, Richard and Ross H. Munro. 1997a. *The Coming Conflict with China.* New York: Knopf.

———. 1997b. "The Coming Conflict with America." *Foreign Affairs* 76(2)18–32.

Bertilsson, Margareta. 1990. "The Welfare State, the Professions and Citizens." Pp. 114–33 in *The Formation of Professions,* edited by Rolf Torstendahl and Michael Burrage. London: Sage Publications.

Blackburn, Robin, ed. 1991. *After the Fall.* New York: Verso.

Bodde, Derk. 1991. *Chinese Thought, Society, and Science: The Intellectual and Social Background of Science and Technology in Pre-Modern China.* Honolulu: University of Hawaii Press.

Boggs, Carl. 1993. *Intellectuals and the Crisis of Modernity.* Albany: State University of New York Press.

Bol, Peter. 1992. *"This Culture of Ours:" Intellectual Transitions in T'ang and Sung China.* Stanford, CA: Stanford University Press.

———. 1995. "Chao Ping-wen (1159–1232): Foundations for Literati Learning." Pp. 115–44 in *China under Jurchen Rule: Essays on Chin Intellectual and Cultural History*, edited by Hoyt Cleveland Tillman and Stephen H. West. Albany: State University of New York Press.

Bologh, Roslyn Wallach. 1979. *Dialectical Phenomenology: Marx's Method.* Boston: Routledge and Kegan Paul.

———. 1983. "Economic Problems and Proposed Solutions in the Mid-Nineteenth Century: Marx's Analysis and Critique." Pp. 246–61 in *Inflation through the Ages: Economic, Social, Psychological and Historical Aspects*, edited by Nathan Schmuckler and Edward Marcus. New York: Columbia University Press.

———. 1984. "Max Weber and the Dilemma of Rationality." Pp. 175–86 in *Max Weber's Political Sociology: A Pessimistic Vision of a Rationalized World*, edited by Ronald M. Glassman and Vatro Murvar. Westport: Greenwood Press.

———. 1990. *Love or Greatness: Max Weber and Masculine Thinking—A Feminist Inquiry.* London: Unwin Hyman.

Bonnin, Michel and Yves Chevrier. 1991. "The Intellectual and the State: Social Dynamics of Intellectual Autonomy during the Post-Mao Era." *China Quarterly* 127:569–93.

Bourdieu, Piere. 1977. *Outline of a Theory of Practice.* London: Cambridge University Press.

———. 1984. *Distinction: A Social Critique of the Judgement of Taste*, translated by Richard Nice. Cambridge: Harvard University Press.

Brauchli, Marcus W. 1994. "Wary of Education but Needing Brains, China Faces a Dilemma." *Wall Street Journal*, November 15, 1994.

Brint, Steven. 1994. *In an Age of Experts: The Changing Role of Professionals in Politics and Public Life.* Princeton, New Jersey: Princeton University Press.

Brook, Timothy. 1992. *Quelling the People: The Military Suppression of the Beijing Democracy Movement.* New York: Oxford University Press.

———. 1993. *Praying for Power: Buddhism and the Formation of Gentry Society in Late-Ming China.* Cambridge: Harvard University Press.

———. 1998. *The Confusions of Pleasure: Commerce and Culture in Ming China.* Berkeley: University of California Press.

Brookes, Adam. 2000. Talk at the roundtable "Covering China: A Dialogue between Journalists and Academics." The annual meeting of the Association for Asian Studies, San Diego, California, March 9–12.

Brugger, Bill and David Kelly. 1990. *Chinese Marxism in the Post-Mao Era.* Stanford, CA: Stanford University Press.

Bulag, Uradyn E. 2000. "Ethnic Resistance with Socialist Characteristics." Pp. 178–97 in *Chinese Society: Change, Conflict and Resistance,* edited by Elizabeth J. Perry and Mark Selden. London: Routledge.

Bullock, Mary Brown. 1996. "American Science and Chinese Nationalism: Reflections on the Career of Zhou Peiyuan." Pp. 210–223 in *Remapping China: Fissures in Historical Terrain,* edited by Gail Hershatter, Emily Honig, Jonathan N. Lipman, and Randall Stross. Stanford: Stanford University Press.

Burrage, Michael, Konrad Jarausch, and Hannes Siegrist. 1990. "An Actor-based Framework for the Study of the Professions." Pp. 203–25 in *Professions in Theory and History,* edited by Michael Burrage and Rolf Torstendhl. London: Sage Publications.

Calhoun, Craig. 1991. "The Ideology of Intellectuals and the Chinese Student Protest Movement of 1989." Pp. 113–142 in *Intellectuals and Politics: Social Theory in a Changing World,* edited by Charles C. Lemert. London: Sage Publications.

Cao Jinqing. 2000. *Huanghe bian de Zhongguo: Yige Xuezhe dui Xiangcun Shehui de Guancha yu Sikao* 黄河边的中国: 一个学者对乡村社会的观察与思考 (China by the Yellow River: a scholar's observations and thoughts on rural society). Shanghai: Shanghai Wenyi Chubanshe 上海文艺出版社 (Shanghai literature and art press).

Cauvel, Jane. 1999. "The Transformative Power of Art: Li Zehou's Aesthetic Theory." *Philosophy East & West* 49(2)150–73.

Chamberlain, Heath B. 1993. "On the Search for Civil Society in China." *Modern China* 19(2)199–215.

Chan, Anita. 1991. "The Social Origins and Consequences of the Tiananmen Crisis." Pp. 105–30 in *China in the Nineties: Crisis Management and Beyond*, edited by David S. G. Goodman and Gerald Segal. New York: Oxford University Press.

———. 1998. "Labor Relations in Foreign-funded Ventures, Chinese Trade Unions and the Prospects for Collective Bargaining." Pp. 122–49 in *Adjusting to Capitalism: Chinese Workers and the State*, edited by Greg O'Leary. Armonk, New York: M. E. Sharpe.

Chang Guangmin 常光民. 1995. "Dangfeng Lianzheng Jianshe he Fan Fubai Douzheng de Ruili Sixiang Wuqi" 党风廉政建设和反腐败斗争的锐利思想武器 (The sharp ideological tool in constructing a clean Party and fighting corruption). *Qiu Shi* 求是 6:23–6.

Chang, Hao. 1971. *Liang Ch'i-ch'ao: and Intellectual Transition in China, 1890–1907.* Cambridge: Harvard University Press.

———. 1976. "New Confucianism and the Intellectual Crisis of Contemporary China." Pp. 276–304 in *The Limits of Change: Essays on Conservative Alternatives in Republican China*, edited by Charlotte Furth. Cambridge: Harvard University Press.

———. 1987. *Chinese Intellectuals in Crisis: Search for Order and Meaning (1890–1911)*. Berkeley: University of California Press.

Chang, Julian. 1997. "The Mechanics of State Propaganda: The People's Republic of China and the Soviet Union in the 1950s." Pp. 76–124 in *New Perspectives on State Socialism in China,* edited by Timothy Cheek and Tony Saich. Armonk, New York: M. E. Sharpe.

Chang, Ren (posted). 2000. "Hui Xiao Gongqin." 回萧功秦 (A response to Xiao Gongqin). February 4. <*http://server12.hypermart.net/tursi/z/messages/22651.html*>.

Cheek, Timothy. 1986. "Deng Tuo: A Chinese Leninist Approach to Journalism." Pp. 92–123 in *China's Establishment Intellectuals*, edited by Carol Lee Hamrin and Timothy Cheek. Armonk, New York: M. E. Sharpe.

———. 1992. "From Priests to Professionals: Intellectuals and the State under the CCP." Pp. 124–45 in *Popular Protest and Political Culture in Modern China: Learning from 1989*, edited by Jeffrey N. Wasserstrom and Elizabeth Perry. Boulder, Colorado: Westview Press.

———. 1995. "The Honorable Vocation: Intellectual Service in CCP Propaganda Institutions in Jin-Cha-Ji, 1935–1945." Pp. 235–62 in *New Perspectives on the Chinese Communist Revolution*, edited by Tony Saich and Hans van de Ven. Armonk, New York: M. E. Sharpe.

———. 1997. *Propaganda and Culture in Mao's China: Deng Tuo and the Intelligentsia*. New York: Oxford University Press.

———. 1998. "From Market to Democracy in China: Gaps in the Civil Society Model." Pp. 219–52 in *Market Economics and Political Change: Comparing China and Mexico*, edited by Juan D. Lindau and Timothy Cheek. New York: Rowman & Littlefield Publishers.

———. 1999. "Introduction: A Cross-Cultural Conversation on Li Zehou's Ideas on Subjectivity and Aesthetics in Modern Chinese Thought." *Philosophy East & West* 49(2)113–9.

———. 2001. Comments on the manuscript of the current book.

Cheek, Timothy and Juan D. Lindau. 1998. "Market Liberalization and Democratization: The Case for Comparative Contextual Analysis." Pp. 3–31 in *Market Economics and Political Change: Comparing China and Mexico,* edited by Juan D. Lindau and Timothy Cheek. New York: Rowman & Littlefield Publishers.

Chen Dabai 陈大白. 2000. "Minzu Zhuyi de Zhongguo Daolu" 民族主義的中國道路 (The Chinese way of nationalism). *Zhanglue yu Guanli* 戰略與管理 3:98–104.

Chen, Feng. 1997. "Order and Stability in Social Transition: Neoconservative Political Thought in Post-1989 China." *China Quarterly* 151:593–613.

———. 1999. "An Unfinished Battle in China: The Leftist Criticism of the Reform and the Third Thought Emancipation." *China Quarterly* 158:447–67.

Chen, Jo-shui. 1992. *Liu Tsung-yuan and Intellectual Change in T'ang China, 773–819.* New York: Cambridge University Press.

Chen Lai 陈来. 1995. "Jiushi Niandai Bulu Weijian de 'Guoxue Yanjiu'" 九十年代步履维艰的"国学研究" (The difficult steps in the "national learning" of the 1990s). *Dongfang* 东方 224–8.

Chen Minzhi 陈敏之. 1997. "Gu Zhun Shengping he Xueshu Sixiang" 顾准生平和学术思想 (The life of Gu Zhun and his scholarship). Pp. 323–368 in *Gu Zhun Riji*

顾准日记 (The diaries of Gu Zhun), edited by Chen Minzhi and Ding Dong 陈敏之, 丁东. Beijing: Jingji Ribao Chubanshe 北京经济日报出版社 (Economic daily press).

Chen Minzhi 陈敏之 and Ding Dong 丁东 (eds.). 1997. Gu Zhun Riji 顾准日记 (The diaries of Gu Zhun). Beijing: Jinji Ribao Chubanshe 北京经济日报出版社 (Economic daily press).

———. 1998. Gu Zhun Xunsi Lu 顾准寻思录 (A record of reflections on Gu Zhun). Beijing: Zuojia Chubanshe 北京作家出版社 (Writers' press).

Chen Ming 陈明. 1997. "*Yaomo Hua Zhongguo de Beihou de Beihou*" *《妖魔化中国的背后》的背后 (Behind the book "behind the demonization of China"). Beijing Spring.* 北京之春4:86–91.

Chen Pingyuan 陈平原. 1999 [1991]. "Xuezhe de Renjian Qinghuai" 学者的人间情怀 (Scholars' human feelings). Pp. 413–20 in *Zhishi Fenzi Yinggai Gan Shenme* 知识分子应该干什么 (What intellectuals should do), edited by Zhu Yong 祝勇. Beijing: Shishi Chubanshe 北京时事出版社 (Current affairs press).

Chen Shaoming 陈少明. 1995. "Renwen Jingkuang de Guancha Yijian" 人文景况的观察意见 (Comments and observations on the humanist phenomena). *Dongfang* 东方 2:29–31.

Chen, Theodore H. E. 1960. *Thought Reform of the Chinese Intellectuals*. Hong Kong: Hong Kong University Press.

Chen Xi 陈曦. 1997. "Haiwai de Minzu Zhuyi Qingxu de 'Da Pipan'" 海外的民族主义情绪的 "大批判" (The overseas "great criticism" of nationalist sentiments). *Beijing Spring* 北京之春 1:55–6.

Chen Xiaoming 陈晓明. 1998. "Hou Xiandai Zhuyi Bushi Yiduan Xieshuo" 后现代主义不是异端邪说 (Postmodernism is no heresy). *Ming Pao Monthly*. 明报月刊 2:61–6.

———. 1999. "Renwen Guanhuai: Yizhong Zhishi yu Xushi" 人文关怀: 一种知识与叙事 (The humanist concern: a knowledge and narration). Pp. 362–70 in *Zhishi Fenzi Yinggai Gan Shenme* 知识分子应该干什么 (What intellectuals should do), edited by Zhu Yong 祝勇. Beijing: Shishi Press 北京时事出版社 (Current affairs press).

Chen Yun 陈云. [1947] 1995. "Zenyang Cainen Shao Fan Cuowu" 怎样才能少犯错误 (How can we make fewer mistakes?). *Qiu Shi.* 求是 10:2–4.

Chen Yung-fa. 1995. "The Blooming Poppy under the Red Sun: The Yan'an Way and the Opium Trade." Pp. 263–98 in *New Perspectives on the Chinese Communist Revolution,* edited by Tony Saich and Hans van de Ven. Armonk, New York: M. E. Sharpe.

Chesneaux, Jean. 1968. *The Chinese Labor Movement 1919–1927*. Stanford: Stanford University Press.

———. 1973. *Peasant Revolts in China 1840–1949*. Translated by C. A. Curwen. London: Thames and Hudson.

Ch'i, Hsi-Sheng. 1991. *Politics of Disillusionment: The Chinese Communist Party under Deng Xiaoping, 1978–1989.* Armonk, New York: M. E. Sharpe.

China Statistics. 中国统计 1998. "Wo Guo Gongye zhong Guoyou Jingji Zhanju Youshi" 我国工业中国有经济占居优势 (In China's industry, the state-owned sector dominates) *China Statistics.* Vol. 193. No. 2. Article by the Office of the Third

National Industrial Census and the Industrial Structure Research Group of the Economic Institute of the State Economic Commission.

Chomsky, Noam. 1969. *American Power and the New Mandarins*. New York: Pantheon.

Chong, Woei Lien. 1999. "Combining Marx with Kant: The Philosophical Anthropology of Li Zehou." *Philosophy East & West* 49(2)120–49.

Chow, Rey. 1991. *Woman and Chinese Modernity: The Politics of Reading between West and East.* Minnesota: University of Minnesota Press.

Chow Tse-tsung. 1960. *The May Fourth Movement: Intellectual Revolution in Modern China.* Cambridge: Harvard University Press.

Christoffersen, Gaye. 1998. "Socialist Marketization and East Asian Industrial Structure: Locating Civil Society in China." Pp. 95–123 in *Market Economics and Political Change: Comparing China and Mexico,* edited by Juan D. Lindau and Timothy Cheek. New York: Rowman & Littlefield Publishers.

Cleaves, Peter S. 1989. *Professions and the State*. Tucson: University of Arizona.

Collins, Randall. 1990. "Market Closure and the Conflict Theory of the Professions" Pp. 24–43 in *Professions in Theory and History,* edited by Michael Burrage and Rolf Torstendhl. London: Sage Publications.

Cong Ming. 1999 [1994]. "Yixie Tichu Siyouhua Guandian de 'Da Jingji Xue Jia' Cheng le Baofu Jituan de Daiyan Ren" 一些提出私有化观点的"大经济学家"成了暴富集团的代言人 (Some "big economists" who promoted the idea of privatization have become representatives of the newly rich). Pp. 323–4 in *Yanlun Zhongguo: Guandian Jiaofeng 20 Nian*《言论中国: 观点交锋 20 年》(Discourse China: debating ideas in the past twenty years), edited by Jing Wu 京伍. Beijing: Zhongguo Jiancha Press 中国监察出版社.

Coser, Lewis A. 1965. *Men of Ideas: a Sociologist's View.* New York: Free Press.

Cox, Roberth H. 1992. "After Corporatism: A Comparison of the Role of Medical Professionals and Social Workers in the Dutch Welfare State." *Comparative Political Studies* 24(4)532–52.

Cui Yongyuan 崔永元. 2001. *Bu Guo Ruci* 不过如此 (It's no big deal). Beijing: Hua Yi Chubanshe 北京华艺出版社 (China art press).

Cui Zhiyuan 崔之元. 2000a. "Hunhe Xianfa yu dui Zhongguo Zhengzhi de Sanceng Fenxi" 混合宪法与对中国政治的三层分析 (A mixed constitution and a three-tier analysis of Chinese politics). Pp. 528–38 in *Zhishi Fenzi Lichang: Ziyou Zhuyi zhi Zheng yu Zhongguo Sixiang Jie de Fenhua* 知识分子立场: 自由主义之争与中国思想界的分化 (The intellectual stance: the debate on liberalism and the division of Chinese thought), edited by Li Shitao 李世涛. Changchun, China: Shidai Wenyi Chubanshe 吉林长春时代文艺出版社 (Art and literature of the time press) .

———. 2000b. "Guanyu 'Dushu' yu 'Xin Zuopai' Guanxi de Shuoming" 关于'读书'与'新左派'关系的说明 (About the relationship between *Dushu* and the "new left"). E-mail from Huang Ping 黄平. July 6.

Dahrendorf, Ralf. 1970. "The Intellectual and Society: The Social Function of the 'Fool' in the Twentieth Century." Pp. 49–52 in *On Intellectuals: Theoretical Studies Case Studies,* edited by Philip Rieff. Garden City, New York: Anchor Books, Doubleday.

Dai Qing. 1990. Wode Ruyu 我的入狱 (My imprisonment). Hong Kong: Ming Bao Press. 香港明报出版社.

———. 1994. Wang Shiwei and "Wild Lilies:" Rectification and Purges in the Chinese Communist Party, 1942–44. Armonk, New York: M. E. Sharpe.

De Mauny. 1984. Introduction to *Ilya Ehrenburg: Revolutionary, Novelist, Poet, War Correspondent, Propagandist—The Extraordinary Epic of a Russian Survivor.* New York: Viking.

Deng Liqun 邓力群. 1996. "Ying Xiang Wo Guo Guojia Anquan de Ruogan Yinsu" 影响我国国家安全的若干因素. (Several factors endangering our national security). *Beijing Spring* 2:39–45.

———. 1998. "Guanyu Guoqing de Ruogan Jingji Fenxi." 关于国情的若干经济分析 (Some economic analysis of current situation of the state). *Dangdai Sichao* 当代思潮 (Contemporary thoughts). 6:2–15.

Deng, Weizhi 邓伟志. 1993. *Wo Jiu Shi Wo* 我就是我 (I am me). Shanghai: Sanlian Press 上海三联出版社.

———. 1998. *Ren Bi Que-er Lei* 人比雀儿累 (People are more tired than birds). Shanghai: Hanyu Da Cidian Chubanshe 上海汉语大词典出版社 (Chinese language dictionaries press).

Deng Xiaoping. [1978] 1983. *Deng Xiaoping Wenxun* 邓小平文选 (Collected works of Deng Xiaoping). Beijing: Renmin Chubanshe 北京人民出版社 (People's press).

Ding Cong 丁聪. 1999. *Fengci Hua* 讽刺画 1–4 集 (Cartoons of satire. Vols. 1–4). Beijing: Sanlian Press 北京三联书店.

Ding Dong 丁东 and Cai Zhongde 蔡仲德. 1999 [1992]. "Shi Renge: Yige Shiji de Huigu" 士人格: 一个世纪的回顾 (The personalities of the literati: reflections on the past century.) Pp. 309–19 in *Zhishi Fenzi Yinggai Gan Shenme* 知识分子应该干什么 (What should intellectuals do), edited by Zhu Yong 祝勇. Beijing: Shishi Chubanshe 北京时事出版社 (Current affairs press).

Ding Dong 丁东 and Xie Yong 谢泳. 1995. "Shichang yu Ziyou Zhuangao Ren" 市场与自由撰稿人 (The market and independent writers). *Dongfang* 东方 4:89–90.

Ding, X. L. 1994. *The Decline of Communism in China: Legitimacy Crisis, 1977–1989.* London: Cambridge University Press.

Dittmer, Lowell. 1974. *Liu Shao-ch'i and the Chinese Cultural Revolution: The Politics of Mass Criticism*. Berkeley: University of California Press.

———. 1998. *Liu Shaoqi and the Chinese Cultural Revolution*. Revised edition. Armonk, New York: M. E. Sharpe.

Djilas, Milovan. 1957. *The New Class: An Analysis of the Communist System*. New York: Praeger.

Dongfang 《东方》 (Orient) 1994. "Cu Qi Tan Wu Si: Ben Kan Zong Bian Fang Xia Yan" 促膝谈五四: 本刊总编访夏衍 (A heart-to-heart talk on May 4: the chief editor visits Xia Yan). 2:24–5.

Dong Ping 董平. 1995. "Shehui Sichao yu Wenhua Xianxiang Pingshu" 社会思潮与文化现象评述 (Comments on social thoughts and cultural phenomena). *Dongfang* 东方 1:7–10.

Dongfang Shanba 东方善霸. 1999. *Choulou de Xueshu Ren* 丑陋的学术人 (The ugly academician). Xi'an: Shaanxi Shifan Daxue Chubanshe 西安陕西师范大学出版社 (Shaanxi teachers' university press).

Dupuy, Alex. 1991. "Political Intellectuals in the Third World: The Caribbean Case." Pp. 74–93 in *Intellectuals and Politics: Social Theory in a Changing World*, edited by Charles C. Lemert. London: Sage Publications.

Eastman, Lloyd. 1976. "The Kuomintang in the 1930s." Pp. 191–212 in *The Limits of Change: Essays on Conservative Alternatives in Republican China*, edited by Charlotte Furth. Cambridge: Harvard University Press.

Edmonds, Richard Louis. 1999. "The Environment in the People's Republic of China 50 Years On." *China Quarterly* 159:640–9.

Edmunds, Clifford. "1987. The Politics of Historiography: Jian Bozan's Historicism." Pp. 65–106 in *China's Intellectuals and the State: in Search of a New Relationship,* edited by Merle Goldman with Timothy Cheek and Carol Lee Hamrin. Cambridge: Harvard University Press.

Ehrenreich, Barbara. 1990. "The Professional-Managerial Class Revisited." Pp. 173–85 in *Intellectuals: Aesthetics, Politics, Academics,* edited by Bruce Robbins. Minneapolis: University of Minnesota Press.

Ehrenreich, Barbara and John Ehrenreich. 1979. "The Professional-Managerial Class." Pp. 5–45 in *Between Labor and Capital,* edited by Pat Walker. Boston: South End Press.

Epstein, Edward J. 1994. "Law and Legitimation in Post-Mao China." Pp. 19–55 in *Domestic Law Reforms in Post-Mao China,* edited by Pitman B. Potter. Armonk, New York: M. E. Sharpe.

Etzioni-Halevy, Eva. 1985. *The Knowledge Elite and the Failure of Prophecy.* Boston: George Allen & Unwin.

Eyal, Gil, Ivan Szelenyi, and Eleanor Townsley. 1998. *Making Capitalism without Capitalists: Class Formation and Elite Struggles in Post-Communist Central Europe*. London: Verso.

Eyerman, Ron and Andrew Jamison. 1991. *Social Movements: A Cognitive Approach.* Pennsylvania State University Press.

Fan Ping 樊平. 1999. "1998 Nian: Zhongguo Nongmin Zhuangkuan Baogao" 1998 年: 中国农民状况报告 (1998: a report on the situation of China's peasants). Pp. 451–63 in *1999 Nian Zhongguo Shehui Xingshi Fenxi yu Yuce* 1999 年中国社会形势分析与预测 (1999 analysis and prediction of social conditions in China), edited by Ru Xin 汝信, Lu Xueyi 陆学艺, and Shan Tianlun 单天伦, et al. Beijing: Shehui Kexue Wenxian Press 北京社会科学文献出版社 (Social science literature press).

Fang Gongwen 方恭温. [1998] 1999. "Jingji Xuejia Men zai Zhenli Taolun zhong de Huodong he Zuoyong." 经济学家们在真理讨论中的活动和作用 (The activities and roles of economists in the discussion of truth criterion). Pp. 115–20 in *Yanlun Zhongguo: Guandian Jiaofeng 20 Nian* 言论中国: 观点交锋 20 年 (Discourse China: debating ideas over the past twenty years), edited by Jing Wu 京伍. Beijing: Zhongguo Jiancha Press 北京中国监察出版社.

Fang Lizhi. 1991. *Bringing Down the Great Wall: Writings on Science, Culture, and Democracy in China.* New York: Knopf.

Fang Ning 房宁, Wang Xiaodong 王小东, Song Qiang 宋强, et al. 1999. *Quanqiu hua Yinying Xia de Zhongguo zhi Lu* 全球化阴影下的中国之路 (*China's road in the shadow of globalization*). Beijing: Zhongguo Shehui Kexue Chubanshe 北京中国社会科学出版社 (China social science press).

Farley, Maggie. 1997. "China Dissident to Stay in Hong Kong." *Los Angeles Times*, June 6.

Fei Xiaotong 费孝通. 1992. *Xing Xing Chong Xing Xing: Xiangzhen Fazhan Lunshu* 行行重行行: 乡镇发展论述 (One trip after another: on the development of the townships.) Yinchuan, China: Ningxia Renmin Chubanshe 银川宁夏人民出版社 (People's press).

———. 1995. "Wode Dierci Xueshu Shengming" 我的第二次学术生命 (My second academic life). *Dongfang* 东方 (Orient) 2:32–4.

———. 1996. "Fei Xiaotong" 费孝通. Pp. 100–4 in *Jingshen de Tianyuan: "Dongfang zhi Zi" Xueren Fangtan Lu* 精神的田园: "东方之子" 学人访谈录 (The field of spirit and vigor: the interviews of scholars on *Sons and Daughters of the East*), edited by Shi Jian 时间. Beijing: Huaxia Chubanshe 华夏出版社 (China press).

Feinerman, James V.1987. "Law and Legal Professionalism in the People's Republic of China." Pp. 107–128 in *China's Intellectuals and the State: In Search of a New Relationship*, edited by Merle Goldman with Timothy Cheek and Carol Lee Hamrin. Cambridge: Harvard University Press.

———. 1994. "Legal Institution, Administrative Device, or Foreign Import: The Roles of Contract in the People's Republic of China." Pp. 225–44 in *Domestic Law Reforms in Post-Mao China*, edited by Pitman B. Potter. Armonk, New York: M. E. Sharpe.

Feng, Tongqing 冯同庆. 1996. "1995–1996 Nian Zhongguo Zhigong Zhuangkuang de Fenxi yu Yuce" 1995–1996 年中国职工状况的分析与预测 (An analysis and forecast of Chinese workers' conditions in 1995–96). Pp. 270–286 in *1995–1996 Nian Zhongguo Shehui Xingshi Fenxi yu Yuce*, 1995–1996 年中国社会形势的分析与预测 (The analysis of current Chinese society and forecast of its future: 1995–1996), edited by Jiang Liu 江流, Lu Xueyin, 陆学艺, and Shan Tianlu 单天伦. Beijing: Zhongguo Shehui Kexue Chubanshe 北京中国社会科学出版社 (Chinese social sciences press).

Feuchtwang, Stephan. 2000. "Religion as Resistance." Pp. 161–77 in *Chinese Society: Change, Conflict and Resistance,* edited by Elizabeth J. Perry and Mark Selden. London: Routledge.

Fewsmith, Joseph. 1991. "The Dengist Reforms in Historical Perspective." Pp. 23–52 in Contemporary Chinese Politics in Historical Perspective, edited by Brantly Womack. Cambridge: Cambridge University Press.

———. 1994. Dilemmas of Reform in China: Political Conflict and Economic Debate. Armonk, New York: M. E. Sharpe.

———. 1996. "Institutions, Informal Politics, and Political Transition in China." Asian Survey 3:230–67.

Fincher, John H. 1981. *Chinese Democracy: The Self-Government Movement in Local Provincial and National Politics, 1905–1914.* Croom Helm: Australian National University Press.

Fisher, Tom. 1986. "Wu Han: The 'Upright Official' as a Model in the Humanities." Pp. 155–84 in *China's Establishment Intellectuals,* edited by Carol Lee Hamrin and Timothy Cheek. Armonk, New York: M. E. Sharpe.

Fitzpatrick, Sheila. 1970. *The Commissariat of Enlightenment: Soviet Organization of*

Education and the Arts under Lunacharsky, October 1917–1921. London: Cambridge University Press.

———. 1999. *Everyday Stalinism: Ordinary Life in Extraordinary Times: Soviet Russia in the 1930s*. New York: Oxford University Press.

Flacks, Dick. 1991. “Making History and Making Theory: Notes on How Intellectuals Seek Relevance.” Pp. 3–18 in *Intellectuals and Politics: Social Theory in a Changing World,* edited by Charles C. Lemert. Newbury Park: Sage Publications.

Fligstein, Neil. 1996. “The Economic Sociology of the Transitions from Socialism.” *American Journal of Sociology* 101(4)1074–81.

Fogel, Joshua A. 1987a. *Ai Ssu-ch'i's Contribution to the Development of Chinese Marxism*. Cambridge: Harvard University Press.

———. 1987b. “Ai Siqi: Professional Philosopher and Establishment Intellectual.” Pp. 23–41 in *China's Intellectuals and the State: In Search of a New Relationship*, edited by Merle Goldman with Timothy Cheek and Carol Lee Hamrin. Cambridge: Harvard University Press.

Foner, Eric. 1997. “Intellectuals and Labor: A Brief History.” Pp. 46–56 in *Audacious Democracy: Labor, Intellectuals, and the Social Reconstruction of America,* edited by Steven Fraser and Joshua B. Freeman. New York: Houghton.

Forney, Matt. 1997. “China's New Big ‘Thought.’” *World Press Review*, February: 38–9.

Foucault, Michel. 1980. *Power/Knowledge: Selected Interviews and Other Writings 1972–1977,* edited by Colin Gordon. New York: Pantheon.

Freidson, Eliot. 1970. *Profession of Medicine: A Study of the Sociology of Applied Knowledge*. New York: Harper.

———. 1973. “Professions and the Occupational Principle.” Pp. 19–38 in *The Professions and Their Prospects*, edited by Eliot Freidson. Beverly Hills: Sage Publications.

Freund, Elizabeth M. 1998. “Downsizing China's State Industrial Enterprises: The Case of Baoshan Steel Works.” Pp. 101–21 in *Adjusting to Capitalism: Chinese Workers and the State,* edited by Greg O'Leary. Armonk, New York: M. E. Sharpe.

Friedman, Edward. 1993. “A Failed Chinese Modernity.” *Daedalus* 122 (2) (Spring).

———. 1995. *National Identity and Democratic Prospects in Socialist China*. Armonk, New York: M. E. Sharpe.

———. 1999. “Comment on ‘Nationalistic Feelings and Sports.’” *Journal of Contemporary China* 8(22)535–8.

Furth, Charlotte. 1970. *Ting Wen-chiang: Science and China's New Culture*. Cambridge: Harvard University Press.

———. 1976. “The Sage as Rebel: The Inner World of Chang Ping-lin.” Pp. 113–150 in *The Limits of Change: Essays on Conservative Alternatives in Republican China*, edited by Charlotte Furth. Cambridge: Harvard University Press.

Gao Jianguo 高建国 2000. *Chaixia Leigu Dang Huoba: Gu Zhun Quan Zhuang* 拆下肋骨当火把: 顾准全传 (Take off one's ribs and use them as torches: a complete biography of Gu Zhun). Shanghai: Shanghai Wenyi Chubanshe 上海文艺出版社 (Shanghai literature press).

Gao Min 高敏. 1994. *Yinshi Zhuang* 隐士传 (Biographies of yinshi). Zhengzhou, China: Henan Renmin Chubanshe 郑州河南人民出版社 (Henan people's press).

Gao Xinmin 高新民 and Zhang Shujun 张树军. 2000. *Yan'an Zhengfeng Shilu* 延安整风实录 (A record of Yan'an rectification campaign). Hangzhou, China: Zhejiang Renmin Chubanshe 杭州浙江人民出版社 (Zhejiang people's press).

Gasster, Michael. 1969. *Chinese Intellectuals and the Revolution of 1911: The Birth of Modern Chinese Radicalism.* Seattle: University of Washington Press.

Ge Xiaoyin 葛晓银. 1983. "Sheng Tang Shanshui Tianyuan Shiren" 盛唐山水田园诗人(Landscape poetry in the prosperous Tang dynasty). Pp. 57–64 in *Yuyan Wenxue Zixiu Daxue Jiangzuo* 语言文学自修大学讲座. (Lectures in language and literature by the self-study correspondence university). Vol. 12. Beijing: Dizhi Chubanshe 北京地质出版社 (Geology press).

Gella, Aleksander. 1976. "An Introduction to the Sociology of the Intelligentsia." Pp. 9–34 in *The Intelligentsia and the Intellectuals,* edited by Aleksander Gella. Beverly Hills: Sage Publications.

Gerth, H. H. and C. Wright Mills. 1946. "Introduction: The Man and His Work." Pp. 3–74 in *From Max Weber: Essays in Sociology,* edited by H. H. Gerth and C. Wright Mills. New York: Oxford University Press.

Giddens, Anthony. 1981. *A Contemporary Critique of Historical Materialism. Vol. 1. Power, Property, and the State*. Berkeley: University of California Press.

———. 1990. *The Consequences of Modernity*. Stanford: Stanford University Press.

———. 1998. *The Third Way: The Renewal of Social Democracy*. Cambridge: Polity Press.

Giroux, Henry A. 1998. *Teachers as Intellectuals.* Granby, Massachusetts: Bergin and Garvey Publishers.

Glassman, Ronald M. 1991. *China in Transition: Communism, Capitalism, and Democracy.* New York: Praeger.

Goldberg, Anatol. 1984. *Ilya Ehrenburg: Revolutionary, Novelist, Poet, War Correspondent, Propagandist—The Extraordinary Epic of a Russian Survivor.* New York: Viking.

Goldman, Merle. 1967. *Literary Dissent in Communist China.* Cambridge: Harvard University Press.

———. 1981. *China's Intellectuals: Advise and Dissent*. Cambridge: Harvard University Press.

———. 1994. *Sowing the Seeds of Democracy in China*. Cambridge: Harvard University Press.

———. 1996. "Politically-Engaged Intellectuals in the Deng-Jiang Era: A Changing Relationship with the Party-State." *China Quarterly* 145:35–52.

———. 1999. "Politically-Engaged Intellectuals in the 1990s." *China Quarterly* 159: 700–11.

Goldman, Merle and Timothy Cheek. 1987. "Introduction: Uncertain Change." Pp. 1–20 in *China's Intellectuals and the State: in Search of a New Relationship,* edited by Merle Goldman with Timothy Cheek and Carol Lee Hamrin. Cambridge: Harvard University Press.

Goldstein, Avery. 1994. "Trends in the Study of Political Elites and Institutions in the PRC." *China Quarterly* 139:714–30.

Gouldner, Alvin. 1979. *The Future of Intellectuals and the Rise of the New Class.* New York: Seabury Press.

———. 1985. *Against Fragmentation: The Origins of Marxism and the Sociology of Intellectuals*. New York: Oxford University Press.

Gramsci, Antonio. 1971. *Selections from the Prison Notebooks*. Translated by Quintin Hoare and Geoffrey Nowell Smith. New York: International Publishers.

Grieder, Jerome B. 1981. *Intellectuals and the State in Modern China: A Narrative History*. New York: Free Press.

Gu, Edward X. 1999. "Cultural Intellectuals and the Politics of the Cultural Public Space in Communist China (1979–1989): A Case Study of Three Intellectual Groups." *The Journal of Asian Studies* 38(2)389–431.

Gu Xin 顾昕 and Xue Yong 薛涌. 1989. "Yishi Xingtai de Chuangzao Zhe, Chuanbo Zhe he Weihu Zhe" 意识形态的创造者, 传播者和维护者 (The creator, advocator, and defender of ideology). Pp. 10–13 in *Xiandai Shehui yu Zhishi Fenzi* 现代社会与知识分子 *(Modern society and intellectuals),* edited by Liang Congjie 梁从诫. Shenyang: Liaoning Remin Chubanshe 沈阳辽宁人民出版社 (Liaoning people's press).

Gu Zheng 顾铮 2001. "Luo Kong de 'Shanghai Jingshen'" 落空的 "上海精神" (The still empty 'Shanghai spirit'). *Dushu* 读书 (Reading) 2:3–9.

Guangdong Shehui Kexue 广东社会科学 (Guangdong Social Sciences). [1996] 1999. "Siying Qiye Zhu Zuomeng Dou Xiang Canzheng Yizheng." 私营企业主 '做梦都想' 参政议政 (Private entrepreneurs wanting to participate in government even in their dreams). Pp. 283–4 in *Yanlun Zhongguo: Guandian Jiaofeng 20 Nian.* 言论中国: 观点交锋 20 年 (Discourse China: debating ideas over the past twenty years), edited by Jing Wu 京伍. Beijing: Zhongguo Jiancha Press 北京中国监察出版社.

Guo Luoji 郭罗基. 1997. "Feiqi 'Yibao Yibao,' Kaichuang 'Yifa Yifa'" 废弃 '以暴易暴', 开创 '以法易法' (Discard "using violence to replace violence" and begin "using law to replace law"). *Beijing Spring* 北京之春 8:51–4.

Habermas, Jurgen. (Habeimasi 哈贝马斯) 1999. *Gonggong Lingyu de Jiegou Zhuanxing* 公共领域的结构转型 (The structural transformation of the public sphere). Translated by Cao Weidong 曹卫东, Wang Xiaojue 王晓珏, Liu Beicheng 刘北城, and Song Weijie 宋伟杰 from German. Shanghai: Xuelin Chubanshe 上海学林出版社. See also the 1989 English edition, which has a subtitle, *An Inquiry into a Category of Bourgeois Society,* published by Massachusetts Institute of Technology Press.

Halliday, Terence C. and Bruce G. Carruthers. 1991. "The State and the Professional Division of Labor: Terrains of Struggle over Bankruptcy and Corporate Reorganization in the United States and England." Paper presented at the American Sociological Association annual meeting, Cincinnati, August.

Halpern, Nina. 1987. "Economists and Economic Policy-Making in the Early 1960s." Pp. 45–63 in *China's Intellectuals and the State: In Search of a New Relationship*, edited by Merle Goldman with Timothy Cheek and Carol Lee Hamrin. Cambridge: Harvard University Press.

Hamrin, Carol Lee. 1986. "Yang Xianzhen: Upholding Orthodox Leninist Theory." Pp. 51–91 in *China's Establishment Intellectuals,* edited by Carol Lee Hamrin and Timothy Cheek. Armonk, New York: M. E. Sharpe.

Hamrin, Carol Lee and Timothy Cheek (eds.). 1986. *China's Establishment Intellectuals*. Armonk, New York: M. E. Sharpe.

Han Yuhai 韩毓海. 2000."'Xiangyue 98', 'Gaobie 98'" "相约 98," "告别 98" (Hello 1998, good-bye 1998). Pp. 221–31 in *Zhishi Fenzi Lichang: Ziyou Zhuyi zhi Zheng yu Zhongguo Sixiang Jie de Fenhua* 知识分子立场: 自由主义之争与中国思想界的分化 (The intellectual stance: the debate on liberalism and the division of Chinese thought), edited by Li Shitao 李世涛. Changchun, Jilin: Shidai Wenyi Chubanshe 长春时代文艺出版社 (Art and literature of the time press).

He Jiadong. 何家栋 2000a. "Zhongguo Wenti Yujing xia de Zhuyi zhi Zheng" 中国问题语境下的主义之争 (The debate on isms in the context of China's problems). *Zhanlue yu Guanli* 战略与管理 (Strategy and management). 6:101–111.

———. 2000b. "Jinri Zhongguo Xin Baoshou Zhuyi" 今日中国新保守主义 (The neoconservatism in contemporary China). Pp. 273–91 in Zhongguo de Daolu 中国的道路 (China's road), by Li Shenzhi 李慎之 and He Jiadong 何家栋. Guangzhou, China: Nanfang Ribao Chubanshe 广州南方日报出版社 (South China daily press).

———. 2000c."'Geming' Bianzheng" "革命" 辨正 (The meaning of "revolution"). Pp. 423–62 in *Zhongguo de Daolu* 中国的道路 (China's road), by Li Shenzhi 李慎之 and He Jiadong 何家栋. Guangzhou: Guangdong: Nanfang Ribao Chubanshe 广州南方日报出版社 (South China daily press).

He Pin 何频. 1994. "A Visit with Professor Yu Ying-shih." 访问余英时教授 *Beijing Spring* 北京之春 3:6–10.

He Qinglian 何清涟. 1995. "Caifu yu Pinkun" 财富与贫困 (Wealth and poverty). Dong Fang 东方 5:43–8.

———. 1998. X*iandaihua de Xianjing: Dangdai Zhongguo de Jingji Shehui Wenti* 现代化的陷阱: 当代中国的经济社会问题 (The traps of modernization: contemporary China's economic and social problems). Beijing: Jinri Zhongguo Chubanshe 今日中国出版社 (Today's China press).

———. [1998] 1999. "Yao Jingti Lilun he Jinqian Jiemeng" 要警惕理论和金钱结盟 (Beware of the alliance between theory and money). Pp. 345–6 in *Yanlun Zhongguo: Guandian Jiaofeng 20 Nian*. 言论中国: 观点交锋 20 年 (Discourse China: debating ideas over the past twenty years), edited by Jing Wu 京伍. Beijing: Zhongguo Jiancha Press 北京中国监察出版社.

———. 2001. *Women Rengran zai Yangwang Xingkong* 我们仍然在仰望星空 (We are still looking at the sky). Guilin, Guangxi: Lijiang Press 广西桂林漓江出版社.

He Yimin 何一民.1992. *Zhuanxing Shiqi de Shehui Xin Qunti: Jindai Zhishi Fenzi yu Wanqing Sichuan Shehui Yanjiu* 转型时期的社会新群体: 近代知识分子与晚清四川社会研究 (New social groups during the periods of transformation: a study of modern intellectuals and the late Qing Sichuan society). Chengdu, Sichuan: Sichuan Daxue Chubanshe 成都四川大学出版社 (Sichuan university press).

He Zhaowu 何兆武, Bai Jinzhi 白金智, Tang Yuyuan 唐玉元, and Sun Kaitai 孙开太. 1980. *Zhongguo Sixiang Fazhan Shi* 中国思想发展史 (The development of Chinese thoughts). Beijing: Zhongguo Qingnian Chubanshe 北京中国青年出版社 (China youth press).

Hessler, Peter. 2001. "Boomtown Girl: Finding a New Life in the Golden City." *New Yorker*. May 28.

Heuberger, Frank W. (1992). "The New Class: On the Theory of a No Longer Entirely New Phenomenon." Pp. 23–47 in *Hidden Technocrats: The New Class and New*

Capitalism, edited by Hansfried Kellner and Frank W. Heuberger. New Brunswick, New Jersey: Transaction Publishers.

Hoffman Lily M. 1989. *The Politics of Knowledge.* Albany: State University of New York Press.

Hofstadter, Richard. 1963. *Anti-Intellectualism in American Life.* New York: Alfred A. Knopf.

Holm, David. 1991. *Art and Ideology in Revolutionary China.* New York: Oxford University Press.

Howell, Jude. 1998. "Trade Unions in China: The Challenge of Foreign Capital." Pp. 150–72 in *Adjusting to Capitalism: Chinese Workers and the State,* edited by Greg O'Leary. Armonk, New York: M. E. Sharpe.

Hsu, Immanuel C. Y. 1983. *The Rise of Modern China.* New York: Oxford University Press.

Hsuan Mo 玄默. 1973. *Zhong Gong Wehua Da Geming yu Dalu Zhishi Fenzi* 中共文化大革命与大陆知识分子 (Cultural revolution and Mainland intelligentsia). Taibei: Zhong Gong Wenti Yanjiu Suo 台北中共问题研究所 (Institute for the study of Chinese Communist problems).

Hu Fuming 胡福明. 1999 [1998]. "Zhenli Taolun Shiqi de cong 2:2 dao 3:1." 真理讨论时期的从2:2 到 3:1 (From 2:2 to 3:1 during the discussion of truth criterion). Pp. 107–8 in *Yanlun Zhongguo: Guandian Jiaofeng 20 Nian* 言论中国: 观点交锋 20 年 (Discourse China: debating ideas in the past twenty years), edited by Jing Wu 京伍. Beijing: Zhongguo Jiancha Press 北京中国监察出版社.

Hu Houxuan 胡厚宣. 1994. "Rensheng Manman Wei "Jiagu" 人生漫漫为甲骨 (My life's struggle for "Jiagu"). Pp. 282–301 in *Wo yu Zhongguo Ershi Shiji* 我与中国二十世纪 (China's twentieth century and I), edited by Xu Ming 许明. Zheng Zhou: Henan Renmin Chubanshe 郑州河南人民出版社 (Henan people's press).

Hu Jiwei 胡绩伟, Yu Guangyuan 于光远, et al. (eds.). 1989. *Mengxing de Shike* 猛醒的时刻 (The moment of awakening). Beijing: Zhongwai Wenhua Chuban Gongsi 北京中外文化出版公司 (Chinese and foreign cultures press).

Hu Ping 胡平. 2001. "Gao Zhan Fangtan Lu" 高瞻访谈录 (An interview with Gao Zhan). 北京之春 *(Beijing Spring)*. September, <*www.beijingspring.org*>.

Hu Ping 胡平, Wang Juntao 王军涛, et al. 1990. *Kaituo: Beida Xueyun Wenxian* 开拓: 北大学运文献 (To cultivate: documents on Beijing University's student movements.) Hong Kong: Tianyuan Press 香港天元出版社.

Hua Damin 华大民. 2001. "Roulin Chuanmei: 'Ru Shi' Qian de Zuihou Fengkuang" 蹂躏传媒: "入世" 前的最后疯狂 (Trampling on the mass media: the last madness before joining the World Trade Organization). *Qian Shao Yuekan* 前哨月刊 (Frontline monthly), October, pp. 70–4.

Huang Huilin 黄会林 and Yin Hong 尹鸿 (eds.). 1998. *Dangdai Zhongguo Dazhong Wenhua Yanjiu* 当代中国大众文化研究 (A study on the popular culture in contemporary China). Beijing: Beijing Shifan Daxue Chubanshe 北京师范大学出版社 (Beijing teachers university press).

Huang, Philip. 1993. "'Public Sphere'/'Civil Society' in China?: The Third Realm between State and Society." *Modern China* 19(2)216–40.

Huang Ping 黄平. 1994. "Tizhi Guifan yu Huayu Zhuanhuan: Wushi Niandai de Zhishi Fenzi Gaizao" 体制规范与话语转换: 50 年代的知识分子改造 (Normalization of the system and the change of discourse: the reform of intellectuals in the 1950s). *Dongfang* 东方 3:30–4.

———. 2000. "Jinlai guanyu Dushu's de Yixie Wenzi" 近来关于 "读书" 的一些文字 (Some recent writings/interviews on Dushu). E-mail from Huang Ping. July 10.

Huang Pumin 黄朴民, Lai kehong 来可泓, Yu Zhongxin 愈忠鑫, Zhu Hongjie 祝鸿杰, and Ye Bin 业斌 (eds.). 1990. *Baihua Sishu* 白话四书 (Confucius' four books in both classical and vernacular languages). Xi'an: San Qin Press 西安三秦出版社.

Huang Weijing 黄伟经. 1993. "Gubo Chong Qing" 古柏重青 (Old pine turns green: recollections on sociology Prof. Chen Da). Pp. 162–8 in *Choulaojiu, Suanlaojiu, Xianglaojiu* 臭老九, 酸老九, 香老九 (Smelly ninth, sour ninth, fragrant ninth), edited by Huang Weijing 黄伟经 and Xie Rixin 谢日新. Guangzhou: Huacheng Press 广州花城出版社.

Human Rights Watch. 2000. "China Human Rights Update." February.

Hunter, Edward. 1971. *Brainwashing in Red China: The Calculated Destruction of Men's Minds*. New York: Vanguard Press.

Huntington, Samuel P. 1993. "The Clash of Civilizations?" *Foreign Affairs* 72(3)22–49.

Hung, Chang-tai. 1985. *Going to the People: Chinese Intellectuals and Folk Literature 1918–1937*. Cambridge: Harvard University Press.

Israel, John. 1986. Foreword. Pp. ix–xix in *China's Establishment Intellectuals*, edited by Carol Lee Hamrin and Timothy Cheek. Armonk, New York: M. E. Sharpe.

———. 1998. *Lianda: A Chinese University in War and Revolution*. Stanford: Stanford University Press.

Jeans, Roger B. 1992. Introduction. Pp. 1–33 in *Roads Not Taken: The Struggle of Opposition Parties in Twentieth-Century China,* edited by Roger B. Jeans. Boulder, Colorado: Westview Press.

———. 1997. *Democracy and Socialism in Republican China: The Politics of Zhang Junmai (Carsun Chang), 1906–1941*. New York: Rowman & Littlefield Publishers.

Ji Xianlin 季羡林. 1994. "Wode Xin Shi Yimian Jingzi" 我的心是一面镜子 (My heart is a mirror). Pp. 218–48 in *Wo yu Zhongguo Ershi Shiji* 我与中国二十世纪 (China's twentieth century and I), edited by Xu Ming 许明. Zheng Zhou: Henan Renmin Chubanshe 郑州河南人民出版社 (Henan people's press).

Jia Chunzeng 贾春增. 1996. "Zunzhong Zhishi, Zunzhong Rencai" he Xinshiqi Dang dui Zhishi Fenzi de Zhengce" "尊重知识, 尊重人才" 和新时期党对知识分子的政策 ("Respect knowledge, respect talent" and party policy toward intellectuals in the new period). Pp. 238–273 in *Zhishi Fenzi yu Zhongguo Shehui Biange* 知识分子与中国社会变革 (Intellectuals and reform in Chinese society,) edited by Jia Chunzeng 贾春增. Beijing: Hua Wen Chubanshe 北京华文出版社 (Chinese language press) .

Jia Ting 贾铤 and Qin Shaoxiang 秦少相. 1993. *Shehui Xin Qunti Tanmi: Zhongguo Siyin Qiye Zhu Jiecen* 社会新群体探秘: 中国私营企业主阶层 (An exploration of a new social group: the stratum of Chinese private entrepreneurs). Beijing: Zhongguo Fazhan Chubanshe 北京中国发展出版社 (China development press).

Jian Jun 剑军. 1990. "Cong Si Wu dao Liu Si" 从四五到六四 (From April 5 to June 4). *China Spring* 中国之春 6:58–68.

Jiang Tingfu 蒋廷黻. 1980. "Man tan zhishi fenzi de shidai shiming" 漫谈知识分子

的时代使命 (On the historical mission of intellectuals). Pp. 53–8 in *Zhishi Fenzi yu Zhongguo* 知识分子与中国 (Intellectuals and China), edited by Zhou Yangshan 周阳山. Taibei: Shidai Chuban Gongsi 台北时代出版公司 (Times press company).

Jiang Yihua 姜义华. 2000. "Zhongguo Zouxiang Xiandaihua de Heping Geming yu Xin Lixingzhuyi" 中国走向现代化的和平革命与新理性主义 (Peaceful revolution and the new rationalism in China's modernization). Pp. 493–506 in *Zhishi Fenzi Lichang: Jijin yu Baoshou zhijian de Dongtang* 知识分子立场: 激进与保守之间的动荡 (The intellectual stance: between radicalism and conservatism), edited by Li Shitao 李世涛. Changchun, Jilin: Shidai Wenyi Chubanshe 吉林长春时代文艺出版社 (Literature and art of the time press).

Jin Guantao 金观涛 and Liu Qingfeng 刘青峰. 1989. *Tangsuo yu xin zhi* 探索与新知. (Exploration and new knowledge). Taibei: Fengyun Shidai Press 台北风云时代出版社.

Jin Yaoji 金耀基. 1980. "Zhongguo xin zhishi jieceng de jianli yu shiming" 中国新知识阶层的建立与使命 (The establishment and mission of the Chinese new knowledge class). Pp. 417–422 in *Zhishi Fenzi yu Zhongguo* 知识分子与中国 (Intellectuals and China), edited by Zhou Yangshan 周阳山. Taibei: Shidai Chuban Gongsi 台北时代出版公司 (Times press company).

———. 1987. *Zhongguo Xiandai Hua yu Zhishi Fenzi* 中国现代化与知识分子 (Chinese modernization and intellectuals). Taibei: Shibao Wenhua Chuban Youxian Gongsi 台北时报文化出版有限公司 (Taipai times cultural press publications).

Jin Ye. 1998. *Jieceng de Fubai* 阶层的腐败 (The corruption in various social strata). Zhuhai, Guangdong: Zhuhai Press 广东珠海出版社.

Jing, Jun. 2000. "Environmental Protests in Rural China." Pp. 143–60 in *Chinese Society: Change, Conflict and Resistance,* edited by Elizabeth J. Perry and Mark Selden. London: Routledge.

Jing Yidan 敬一丹. 1998. *Shengyin: Yige Dianshi Ren yu Guanzhong de Duihua* 声音: 一个电视人与观众的对话 (Voice: a dialogue between a TV person and her audience). Beijing: Hua Yi Chubanshe 北京华艺出版社 (China art press).

Johnson, Chalmers. 1997. "Soft Totalitarianism in China." *New Perspectives Quarterly* 14(3)18–20.

Johnson, Terry. 1982. "The State and the Professions: Peculiarities of the British." Pp. 187–208 in *Social Class and the Division of Labor,* edited by Anthony Giddens and Gavin MacKenzie. Cambridge: Cambridge University Press.

Jones, Anthony and Elliot A. Krause. 1991. "Professions, the State, and the Reconstruction of Socialist Societies." Pp. 233–53 in *Professions and the State: Expertise and Autonomy in the Soviet Union and Eastern Europe,* edited by Anthony Jones. Philadelphia: Temple University Press.

Joppke, Christian. 1995. *East German Dissidents and the Revolution of 1989.* New York: New York University Press.

Kelliher, Daniel. 1993. "Keeping Democracy Safe from the Masses: Intellectuals and Elitism in the Chinese Protest Movement." *Comparative Politics* July, pp. 379–96.

Kelly, David A. 1987. "The Emergence of Humanism: Wang Ruoshui and the Critique of Socialist Alienation." Pp. 159–182 in *China's Intellectuals and the State: In Search of a New Relationship,* edited by Merle Goldman with Timothy Cheek and Carol Lee Hamrin. Cambridge: Harvard University Press.

Kenez, Peter. 1985. *The Birth of the Propaganda State: Soviet Methods of Mass Mobilization, 1917–1929.* London: Cambridge University Press.

Kennedy, Michael D. 1991. "Easter Europe's Lessons for Critical Intellectuals." Pp. 94–112 in *Intellectuals and Politics: Social Theory in a Changing World,* edited by Charles C. Lemert. Newbury Park: Sage Publications.

Kennedy, Michael D. and Konrad Sadkowski. 1991. "Constraints on Professional Power in Soviet-Type Society: Insights from the 1980–1981 Solidarity Period in Poland." Pp. 167–201 in *Professions and the State: Expertise and Autonomy in the Soviet Union and Eastern Europe,* edited by Anthony Jones. Philadelphia: Temple University Press.

Kipnis, Laura. "Feminism: The Political Conscience of Postmodernism." Pp. 149–66 in *Universal Abandon?: The Politics of Postmodernism*, edited by Andrew Ross. Minneapolis: University of Minnesota Press.

Knight, Nick. 1996. *Li Da and Marxist Philosophy in China*. Boulder, Colorado: Westview Press.

Kong Fanzheng 孔繁政 (ed.). 2001. *Zhongguo Minzhu Dangpai* 中国民主党派 (China's democratic parties and groups). Beijing: Jiefang Jun Wenyi Chubanshe 北京解放军文艺出版社 (People's Liberation Army art and literature press).

Konrad, George and Ivan Szelenyi. 1979. *The Intellectuals on the Road to Class Power*. Brighton: Harvester Press.

———. 1991. "Intellectuals and Domination in Post-Communist Societies." Pp. 337–61 in *Social Theory for a Changing Society*, edited by Piere Bordieu and Jo Coleman. Boulder, Colorado: Westview Press.

Kraus, Richard. 1981. *Class Conflict in Chinese Socialism*. New York: Columbia University Press.

———. 1986. "Bai Hua: The Political Authority of a Writer." Pp. 185–211 in *China's Establishment Intellectuals*, edited by Carol Lee Hamrin and Timothy Cheek. Armonk, New York: M. E. Sharpe.

———. 1995. "China's Artists between Plan and Market." Pp. 173–92 in *Urban Spaces in Contemporary China: The Potential for Autonomy and Community in Post-Mao China*, edited by Deborah S. Davis, Richard Kraus, Barry Naughton, and Elizabeth J. Perry. Washington D.C.: Woodrow Wilson Center Press.

Krause, Elliot A. 1991. "Professions and the State in the Soviet Union and Eastern Europe." Pp. 3–41 in *Professions and the State: Expertise and Autonomy in the Soviet Union and Eastern Europe*, edited by Anthony Jones. Philadelphia: Temple University Press.

———. 1992. "State, Profession and Culture in the Third World: The Case of Egypt." Paper presented at the International Sociological Association Conference, "Professions in Transition." April.

Kristof, Nicholas D. and Sheryl WuDunn. 1994. *China Wakes: The Struggle for the Soul of a Rising Power*. New York: Random.

Kwan, Daniel Y. K. 1997. *Marxist Intellectuals and the Chinese Labor Movement: A Study of Deng Zhongxia (1894–1933).* Seattle: University of Washington Press.

Lam, Jermain and Ka-Ho Mok. 1997. "Economic Prosperity or Democracy: Dilemma of Development in Hong Kong and China." *Journal of Contemporary China* 6(16)461–86.

Lam, Willy Wo-Lap. 1999. *The Era of Jiang Zemin.* Singapore: Simon & Schuster

Larson, Magali Sarfatti. 1977. The Rise of Professionalism: A Sociological Analysis. Berkeley: University of California Press.

———. 1990. "In the Matter of Experts and Professionals, or How Impossible It Is to Leave Nothing Unsaid." Pp. 24–48 in *The Formation of Professions*, edited by Rolf Torstendahl and Michael Burrage. London: Sage Publications.

Lasswell, Harold D. and Daniel Lerner (eds.). 1965. *World Revolutionary Elites: Studies in Coercive Ideological Movements.* Cambridge: The Massachusetts Institute of Technology Press.

Lawrence, Susan V. 2000. Talk at the roundtable "Covering China: A Dialogue between Journalists and Academics." The Annual Meeting of the Association for Asian Studies. San Diego, California, March 9–12.

Lee, Ching Kwan. 1999. "From Organized Dependence to Disorganized Despotism: Changing Labor Regimes in Chinese Factories." *China Quarterly* 157:44–71.

———. 2000. "Pathways of Labor Insurgency." Pp. 41–61 in *Chinese Society: Change, Conflict and Resistance*, edited by Elizabeth J. Perry and Mark Selden. London: Routledge.

Lee, Hong Yung. 1996. "From Revolutionary Cadres to Bureaucratic Technocrats." Pp. 180–206 in *Contemporary Chinese Politics in Historical Perspective,* edited by Brantly Womack. Cambridge: Cambridge University Press.

Le Goff, Jacques. [1957] 1993. *Intellectuals in the Middle Ages.* Translated from the French by Teresa Lavender Fagan. Cambridge/Oxford: Blackwell Publishers.

Le Guin, Ursula. 1977. "The Stalin in the Soul." Pp. 11–20 in *The Future Now: Saving Tomorrow,* edited by Robert Hoskins. Greenwich, Connecticut: Fawcett Publications.

Lei Duqiao 雷度乔 (ed.). 1995. *Hundun Chukai: Laizi Dangdai Daxuesheng Xinling de Baogao* 混沌初开: 来自当代大学生心灵的报告 (The beginning of the earth: reports on contemporary college students'mentality). Guangzhou: Zhongshan Daxue Chubanshe 广州中山大学出版社 (Zhongshan university press).

Leng Chengjin 冷成金. 1997. *Yinshi yu Jietuo* 隐士与解脱 (Yinshi and escape from the world). Beijing: Zuojia Chubanshe 北京作家出版社 (Writers' press).

Leng, Hengmei 冷横眉. 1993. "Renshou Chu le Chen Sheng and We Guang" 仁寿出了陈胜和吴广 (Chen Sheng and Wu Guang emerged in Renshou). *Beijing Spring* 北京之春 7:63–5.

Lewellen, Ted C. 1995. *Dependency and Development: An Introduction to the Third World.* Westport, Connecticut/London: Bergin & Garvey.

Leys, Simon. 1985. *The Burning Forest: Essays on Chinese Culture and Politics*. New York: Henry Holt and Company.

Li Changli 李长莉. 1989. "Yangwu zhishi fenzi" 洋务知识分子 (Foreign matters intellectuals). Pp. 33–6 in *Xiandai Shehui yu Zhishi Fenzi* 现代社会与知识分子 (Modern society and intellectuals), edited by Liang Congjie 梁从戒. Shenyang: Liaoning Renmin Chubanshe 沈阳辽宁人民出版社 (Liaoning people's press).

Li Cheng. 2000. "Jiang Zemin's Successors: The Rise of the Fourth Generation of Leaders in the PRC." *China Quarterly* 161:1–40.

Li Chunqing 李春青. 1995. *Wu Tuobang yu Shi: Zhongguo Gudai Shiren Wenhua yu Wenxue Jiazhiguan.* 乌托邦与诗:中国古代诗人文化与文学价值观 *(Utopia and poetry: ancient Chinese literati culture and literary values).* Beijing: Beijing Shifan Daxue Chubanshe 北京师范大学出版社 (Beijing teachers' university press).

Li Dejin 李德金. 1997. "Can Zheng Zhi Xue Liangxiang Jiangu" 参政治学两相兼顾 (Scholarship and political participation: they do both). *People's Daily* (overseas edition) 人民日报海外版, December 3.

Li Dejin 李德金 and Liu Quan 刘全. 1997. "Tuanjie Jinqu Qiuzhen Wushi" 团结进取求真务实 (Unity and progress, seeking and doing solid work). *People's Daily* (overseas edition) 人民日报海外版, November 8.

Li Hongxi 李鸿禧. 1989. "Yuhui Chichu yu Tuizhan Zhongguo Minzhu Xianzheng de Daolu: Tao Baichun Shengya Zhiyie de Sumiao" 迂回踟蹰与推展中国民主宪政的道路:陶百川生涯职业的素描 (Trudging along the winding way of Chinese democratic constitutional development: life and work of Tao Baichun). Pp. 481–507 in *Zhishi Fenzi yu Taiwan Fazhan* 知识分子与台湾发展 (Intellectuals and the development of Taiwan), edited by Zhongguo Luntan Bianwei Hui 中国论坛编委会 (China forum editorial committee). Taibei: Zhongguo Luntan Zazhi 台北中国论坛杂志 (China forum magazine).

Li Hui 李辉 and Ying Hong 应红 (eds.). 1999. *Shiji zhi Wen: Laizi Zhishi Jie de Shengyin* 世纪之问: 来自知识界的声音 (The question of the century: the voices from the knowledge stratum). Zhengzhou: Daxiang Chubanshe 郑州大象出版社 (Elephant press).

Li Jie 李劼. 1999. "Zhongguo Zhishi Fenzi de Renge Chonggou he Ziwo Xuanze" 中国知识分子的人格重构和自我选择 (Chinese intellectuals' reconstruction of their personalities and self choice). Pp. 331–4 in *Zhishi Fenzi Yinggai Gan Shenme* 知识分子应该干什么 (What intellectuals should do), edited by Zhu Yong 祝勇. Beijing: Shishi Chubanshe 北京时事出版社 (Current affairs press).

Li, Lianjiang and Kevin J. O'Brien. 1996. "Villagers and Popular Resistance in Contemporary China." *Modern China* 22:28–61.

Li Peilin 李培林. 1999. "Ying Zhubu Shixing Shiye yu Xiagang Zhidu Binggui" 应逐步实行失业与下岗制度并轨 (To standardized the mechanisms gradually to cope with the issues of layoffs and unemployment). Pp. 326–36 in *1999 Nian Zhongguo Shehui Xingshi Fenxi yu Yuce* 1999 年中国社会形势分析与预测 (1999 analysis and prediction of social conditions in China), edited by Ru Xin 汝信, Lu Xueyi 陆学艺, and Shan Tianlun 单天伦, et al. Beijing: Shehui Kexue Wenxian Chubanshe 北京社会科学文献出版社 (Social science literature press).

Li Pingshe 李平社. 1994. "Guanyu Woguo Muqian Pinfu Chabie de Sikao" 关于目前我国贫富差别的思考 (Some thoughts on the current gap between the rich and the poor in our country." *Strategy and Management* 战略与管理 6:84–94.

Li Qingxi 李庆西. 2000. "Ziyou Zhuyi Zhishi Fenzi" 自由主义知识分子 (Liberal intellectuals). *Dushu* 读书 (Reading) 2:60–7.

Li Rui. 1998. *Li Rui Riji: Chufang Juan* 李锐日记: 出访卷 (Li Rui diaries: on foreign visits). Beijing: Zuojia Chubanshe 北京作家出版社 (Writers' press).

Li Ruoyu 李若愚. 1999. *Kuse Fengliu: Gudai Zhishi Fenzi Fuchen Lu* 苦涩风流: 古代知识分子浮沉录 (Bitter greatness: the vicissitudes of ancient Chinese intellectuals). Beijing: Beijing Daxue Chubanshe 北京大学出版社 (Beijing University press).

Li Shaomin 李少民. 2001. "Ziyou de Daijia" 自由的代价 (The price of freedom). 北京之春 (*Beijing Spring*). September, <*www.beijingspring.org*>.

Li Shenzhi. 2000a. "Zhongguo Wenhua Feng Yu Canghuang Wushi Nian" 中国文化风雨仓黄五十年 (Chinese culture in fifty years of storm) <http://www.netsh.com.cn/board.html> April 21.

———. 2000b. "Ye Yao Tuidong Zhengzhi Gaige" 也要推动政治改革 (We must also push for political reform). Pp. 371–4 in *Zhongguo de Daolu* 中国的道路 (China's Road) by Li Shenzhi 李慎之 and He Jiadong 何家栋. Guangzhou, Guangdong: Nanfang Ribao Chubanshe 广州南方日报出版社 (South China daily press).

Li Shulei 李书磊. 1999."'Renwen Jingshen' de Zhenshi Hanyi" "人文精神" 的真实含义 (The true meaning of the "humanist spirit"). Pp. 286–94 in *Zhishi Fenzi Yinggai Gan Shenme* 知识分子应该干什么 (What intellectuals should do), edited by Zhu Yong 祝勇. Beijing: Shishi Chubanshe 北京时事出版社 (Current affairs press).

Li Shuqing 李树青.1980. "Lun zhishi fenzi" 论知识分子 (On intellectuals). Pp. 9–22 in *Zhishi Fenzi yu Zhongguo* 知识分子与中国 (Intellectuals and China), edited by Zhou Yangshan 周阳山. Taibei: Shidai Chuban Gongsi 台北时代出版公司 (Taipei times press company).

Li Tongxian 李同宪. 1999. "Dangqian Gaoxiao Zhufang Zhidu Gaige Youdai Jiejue de Jige Wenti" 当前高校住房制度改革有待解决的几个问题 (Several questions remaining to be resolved in the current reform of the housing system in institutions of higher education). *Zhongguo Gaodeng Jiaoyu* 中国高等教育 (China's higher education.) 7:29–30.

Li Wen 李文, Li Jishen 李济深, and Wang Ruicheng 王瑞成. 1998. *Zhongguo Bu Xiangxin Yanlei: Lishi Jiang Xuanze Qiangzhe* 中国不相信眼泪: 历史将选择强者 (China does not believe in tears: history will favor the strong). Yanji, Jilin: Yanbian Daxue Chubanshe 吉林延吉延边大学出版社 (Yanbian University press).

Li Xiaoguang 李晓光. 1994. "Xianzai Jing You Zheyang de Qiyie" 现在竟有这样的企业 (We even have such kind of enterprises now). *Beijing Evening News*. 北京晚报. August 17.

Li Xiaojiang 李小江.1996. "Guanyu Zhongguo" 关于中国 (About China). *Dongfang*. 东方1:77–8.

Li Xiaoxi 李晓西. 1996. "Li Xiaoxi." Pp. 130–6 in *Jingshen de Tianyuan: "Dongfang zhi Zi" Xueren Fangtan Lu* 精神的田园: "东方之子" 学人访谈录 (The field of spirit and vigor: the interviews of scholars on *"Sons and Daughters of the East")*, edited by Shi Jian 时间. Beijing: Huaxia Press 北京华夏出版社.

Li Xiguang 李西光, Liu Kang 刘康, et al. 1997. *Yaomo Hua Zhongguo de Beihou* 妖魔化中国的背后 (Behind the demonization of China). Taibei: Jieyou Press 台北捷幼出版社.

Li Xiaofeng 李筱峰.1989. "Zhishi fenzi yu zhengzhi gexin yundong" 知识分子与政治革新运 (Intellectuals and political reform). Pp. 221–85 in *Zhishi fenzi yu Taiwan fazhan* 知识分子与台湾发展 (Intellectuals and the development of Taiwan), edited by Zhonghuo Luntan Bianwei Hui 中国论坛编委会 (China Forum Editorial Committee). Taibei: Zhongguo Luntan Zazhi 台北中国论坛杂志 (China forum magazine).

Li Zehou 李泽厚 and Liu Zaifu 刘再复. 1997. *Gaobie Geming: Huiwang Ershi Shiji Zhongguo* 告别革命: 回望二十世纪中国 (Good-bye revolution: a retrospective on twentieth-century China). Hong Kong: Tiandi Tushu Youxian Gongsi 天地图书有限公司 (Heaven and earth book publishers).

Li Zehou and Vera Schwarcz. 1983–84. "Six Generations of Modern Chinese Intellectuals." *Chinese Studies in History* 17(2)42–57.

Li Zehou 李泽厚 and Wang Desheng 王德生. 1994. "Guanyu Wenhua Xianzhuang Daode Chongjian de Duihua" 关于文化现状道德重建的对话 (Dialogue on contemporary cultural phenomena and the reconstruction of morality). *Dongfang* 东方 5:69–73; 6:85–7.

Liang Jianzeng 梁建增, Sai Na 赛纳, and Zhang Jie 张洁 (eds.). 2001. *Diaocha Zhongguo: Zhongyang Dianshi Dai "Xinwen Diaocha" Neibu Dangan* 调查中国: 中央电视台 "新闻调查" 内部档案 (Investigate China: Central TV's "News Probe" internal archives). Vols. 1–2. Beijing: Zhongguo Minzu Sheying Yishu Chubanshe 北京中国民族摄影艺术出版社 (China ethnic photography and art press).

Liang Shuming 梁漱溟. 1987. *Wo de Nuli yu Fanxing* 我的努力与反省 (My efforts and reflections). Guilin, Guangxi: Lijiang Press 广西桂林漓江出版社.

Liang Xiaosheng 梁晓声. 1997. *Zhongguo Shehui Ge Jieceng Fenxi* 中国社会各阶层分析 (An analysis of various social strata in China). Beijing: Jingji Chubanshe 北京经济出版社 (Economy press).

Lifton, Robert Jay. 1961. *Thought Reform and the Psychology of Totalism: A Study of "Brainwashing" in China.* New York: Norton.

Lin, Min with Maria Galikowski. 1999. *The Search for Modernity: Chinese Intellectuals and Cultural Discourse in the Post-Mao Era.* New York: St. Martin's.

Lin Mu 林牧. 1997a. "Bubi Jinghu Lang Laile" 不必惊呼狼来了 (No need to cry wolf). Beijing Spring 北京之春 8:55–8.

———. 1997b. "Lin Mu Zhi Jiang Zemin Qiao Shi Li Ruihuan Kangyi Xin" 林牧致江泽民乔石李瑞环抗议信 (A protest letter to Jiang Zemin, Qiao Shi, and Li Ruihuan). *Beijing Spring* 北京之春 9:31.

Lin Tongji (Tongqi Lin) 林同济. 1980. "Shi de tuibian" 士的蜕变 (The transformation of shi). Pp. 45–52 in *Zhishi Fenzi yu Zhongguo* 知识分子与中国 (Intellectuals and China), edited by Zhou Yangshan 周阳山. Taibei: Shidai Chuban Gonsi 台北时代出版公司 (Times press company).

———. 1993. "A Search for China's Soul." Daedalus 122 (2) (Spring).

Lin Xianzhi 林贤治. 1999. *Nala: Chuzou huo Guilai* 娜拉: 出走或归来 (Nora: leave or return). Tianjin: Baihua Wenyi Chubanshe 天津百花文艺出版社 (Hundred flower literature press).

Lin, Yu-sheng 林毓生. 2000. "Rujia Chuantong yu Xifang Renquan Sixiang de Duihua" 儒家传统与西方人权思想的对话 (The dialogue between Confucian tradition and Western ideas on human rights). *Ming Pao Monthly* 明报月刊 35(1)59–62.

Lin Yutang. 1939. *My Country and My People*. New York: John Day.

Lin Zhenguo 林振国. 1982. "Weiji de fanxin yu chaoyue: fang Zhang Hao jiaoshou" 危机的反省与超越: 访张浩教授 (Reflection on the crisis and transcendence: a talk with Prof. Hao Chang). Pp. 381–8 in *Wenhua chuantong de chongjian: Zhongguo wenhua de weiji yu zhanwang* 文化传统的重建:中国文化的危机与展望 (The reconstruction of traditional culture: the crisis of Chinese culture and its prospects), edited by Zhou Yangshan 周阳山. Taibei: Shidai Chuban Gongsi 台北时代出版公司 (Times press company).

Lindau, Juan D. 1998. "The Civil Society and Democratization in Mexico." Pp. 187–

218 in *Market Economics and Political Change: Comparing China and Mexico,* edited by Juan D. Lindau and Timothy Cheek. New York: Rowman & Littlefield Publishers.

Lindau, Juan D. and Timothy Cheek (eds.). 1998. *Market Economics and Political Change: Comparing China and Mexico,* New York: Rowman & Littlefield Publishers.

Ling Zhijun 凌志军 and Ma Licheng 马立诚. 1999. *Huhan: Dangjin Zhongguo de Wuzhong Shengyin* 呼喊: 当今中国的五种声音 (Calling out: five voices in contemporary China). Guangzhou, Canton: Guangzhou Press 广州出版社.

Link, Perry. 1992. *Evening Chats in Beijing: Probing China's Predicament.* New York: Norton.

———. 1993. "China's 'Core' Problem." *Daedalus* 122 (2) (Spring).

Lipset, Seymour Martin. 1963. *Political Man: The Social Bases of Politics.* Garden City, New York: Anchor Books.

———. 1994. "The Social Requisites of Democracy Revisited." *American Sociological Review* 59(1)1–22.

Lipset, Seymour M. and Asoke Basu. 1976. "The Roles of the Intellectual and Political Roles." Pp. 111–50 in *The Intelligentsia and the Intellectuals: Theory, Method and Case Study,* edited by Aleksander Gella. Beverly Hills: Sage Publications.

Liu Bing 刘兵. 1996. "Dangqian Zhongguo Shengtai Huanjing de Baogao" 当前中国生态环境的报告 (A report on the current ecological conditions in China). Pp. 257–69 in *1995–1996 Nian Zhongguo Shehui Xingshi Fenxi yu Yuce* 1995–1996 年中国社会形势分析与预测 (The analysis of current Chinese society and forecast of its future: 1995–1996), edited by Jiang Liu 江流, Lu Xueyi 陆学艺, and Shan Tianlun 单天伦. Beijing: Zhongguo Shehui Kexue Chubanshe 北京中国社会科学出版社 (Chinese social sciences press).

———. 1999. "Zhongguo Dangqian Shengtai Huanjing de Baogao" 中国当前生态环境的报告 (A report on the current ecological conditions in China). Pp. 411–26 in *1999 Nian Zhongguo Shehui Xingshi Fenxi yu Yuce 1999* 年中国社会形势分析与预测 (1999 analysis and prediction of social conditions in China), edited by Ru Xin 汝信, Lu Xueyi 陆学艺, and Shan Tianlun 单天伦, et al. Beijing: Shehui KexueWenxian Press 北京社会科学文献出版社 (Social science literature press).

Liu Hongxia 刘洪侠 and Liu Guitian 刘贵田 (eds.). 1987. *Zhongguo Zhishi Fenzi Wenti* 中国知识分子问题 (Issues on China's intellectuals). Shenyang: Liaoning University Press 沈阳辽宁大学出版社.

Liu Jianming 刘建明. 1998. *Tianli Minxin: Dangdai Zhongguo de Shehui Yulun Wenti* 天理民心: 当代中国的社会舆论问题 (The course of nature and the common aspirations of the people: the issue of public opinion in contemporary China). Beijing: Jinri Zhongguo Chubanshe 北京今日中国出版社 (Today's China press).

Liu Kang. 1996. "Is There an Alternative to (capitalist) Globalization? The Debate about Modernity in China." *boundary 2*. 23(3)193–218.

Liu Mengxi 刘梦溪. 1996. "General Preface" 总序. Pp. 1–76 in *Qian Jibo Juan* 钱基博卷 (Collections of Qian Jibo's Works), edited by Liu Mengxi. Shijiazhuang: Hepei Jiaoyu Press 石家庄河北教育出版社 (Hebei education press).

Liu Quan 刘全 and Li Dejin 李德金. 1997. "Xinren Lianzhe Qiwang" 信任连著期望 (Trust connected with expectations). *People's Daily* 人民日报海外版 (overseas edition). November 14.

Liu, William T. 1999. "A Sociological Perspective on *Falun Gong.*" Pp. 29–49 in *The Mystery of China's Falun Gong: Its Rise and Its Sociological Implications,* by John Wong and William T. Liu. Singapore: World Scientific and Singapore University Press.

Liu Xiaobo 刘晓波. 1997. "Jiushi Niandai Zhongguo de Jiduan Minzu Zhuyi" 九十年代中国的极端民族主义 (Radical nationalism in the China of 1990s). *Beijing Spring* 北京之春 No. 1.

Liu Xiuming 刘修明. 1997. *Rusheng yu Guoyun* 儒生与国运 (Confucians and the fate of the state). Hangzhou: Zhejiang Daxue Chubanshe 杭州浙江大学出版社 (Zhejiang university press).

Liu Zehua 刘泽华. 1987. *Zhongguo Chuantong Zhengzhi Sixiang Fansi* 中国传统政治思想反思 (A reflection on traditional Chinese political thought). Beijing: Sanlian Press 北京三联出版社.

Liu Zeming 刘则鸣, Zhang Fengyi 张凤义, You Zhanyong 游占永, Wu Liansheng 武连生, and Sun Kaimin 孙开民. 1993. *Zou xia Shengtan de Zhongguo Zhishi Fenzi* 走下圣坛的中国知识分子 (Chinese intellectuals who have stepped down from the chancel). Beijing: Junshi Yiwen Chubanshe 北京军事艺文出版社 (Military art and literature press).

Lotspeich, Richard and Aimin Chen. 1997. "Environmental Protection in the People's Republic of China." *Journal of Contemporary China* 6(14)33–59.

Lu Jiandong 陆健东. 1995. *Chen Yinke de Zuihou Ershi Nian* 陈寅恪的最后二十年 (Chen Yinke's last twenty years). Beijing: Sanlian Bookstore. 北京三联书店.

Lu Jianhua 陆建华. 1996. "Duoyuanghua Jincheng zhong Jiannan de Guifanhua Nuli" 多元化进程中艰难的规范化努力 (The difficult task of normalization in the diversification process). *Dongfang* 东方 (Orient) 1:11–4.

Lu, Sheldon Hsiao-peng. 1996. "Postmodernity, Popular Culture, and the Intellectual: A Report on Post-Tiananmen China." *boundary* 2. 23(2):139–69.

———. 1997. "Global POSTmoderiniZATION: The Intellectual, the artist, and China's Condition." *boundary* 2. 24(3):65–97.

Lu, Suping. "Nationalistic Feelings and Sports: The Incident of the Overseas Chinese Protest against NBC's Coverage of the Centennial Olympic Games." *Journal of Contemporary China* 8(22)517–33.

Lu Xueyi. 2001. "Nongmin Zhen Ku, Nongcun Zhen Qiong?" *Dushu* (Reading) 1:3–8.

Lu Xun 鲁迅. 1973a. Nahan 呐喊 (Crying out—a collection of short stories). Beijing: Renmin Wenxue Chubanshe 北京人民文学出版社 (People's literature press).

———. 1973b. Er Xin Ji 二心集 (Double heart—a collection of short essays). Beijing: Renmin Wenxue Chubanshe 北京人民文学出版社 (People's literature press).

———. [1927] 1999. "Guanyu Zhishi Jieji" 关于知识阶级 (On the intellectual class). Pp. 87–94 in *Zhishi Fenzi Yinggai Gan Shenme* 知识分子应该干什么 (What intellectuals should do), edited by Zhu Yong 祝勇. Beijing: Shishi Chubanshe 北京时事出版社 (Current affairs press).

Luo Gang 罗岗. 1995. "Er Ma Bing Chi: Zhishi Fenzi de Zhiye yu Zhiye" 二马并驰: 知识分子的职业与志业 (Two horses running head to head: intellectuals' profession and calling). *Dongfang* 东方 (Orient) 6:82–4.

Luo Houli 罗厚立. 1998. "Cong Sixiang Shi Shijiao Kan Jindai Zhongguo Minzu Zhuyi" 从思想史视角看近代中国民族主义 (Studying modern Chinese nationalism from the perspective of the history of thoughts). *Strategy and Management* 战略与管理 1:103–110.

Lynch, Daniel C. 1999. *After the Propaganda State: Media, Politics, and "Thought Work" in Reformed China.* Stanford: Stanford Univeristy Press.

Ma Hua 马华 and Chen Zhenghong 陈正宏. 1992. *Yinshi Shenghua Tanmi* 隐士生活探秘 (Exploring the lives of yinshi). Jinan: Shandong Wenyi Chubanshe 济南山东文艺出版社 (Shandong art and literature press).

Ma Licheng 马立诚 and Ling Zhijun 凌志军. 1998. *Jiaofeng: Dangdai Zhongguo Sanci Sixiang Jiefang Shilu* 交锋：当代中国三次思想解放实录 (Crossing Swords: a truthful report on the three thought liberation campaigns in contemporary China). Beijing: Jinri Zhongguo Chubanshe 北京今日中国出版社 (Today's China press).

Ma, Shu-Yun. 1993. "Continued Clientelism in Chinese Intellectual Politics." *Journal of Contemporary Asia* 23(4)465–83.

Ma Xiangyang 马向阳. 1997. "Fangzheng Rushuai" 方正儒帅 (The Confucian business chief of Fangzheng Corporation). *People's Daily* (overseas edition) 人民日报海外版. November 1.

MacFarquhar, Roderick (ed.) 1960. *The Hundred Flowers.* London: Stevens & Sons.

MacKinnon, Stephen R. 1980. *Power and Politics in Late Imperial China: Yuan Shikai in Beijing and Tianjin, 1901–1908.* Berkeley: University of California Press.

Madsen, Richard. 1993. "The Public Sphere, Civial Society, and Moral Community: A Research Agenda for Contemporary China Studies." *Modern China* 19(2)183–98.

Mann, Jim. 2000. "Heavy Hand Eclipses the 'Red Star'" *Los Angeles Times*, April 5.

Mannheim, Karl. 1936. *Ideology and Utopia: An Introduction to the Sociology of Knowledge*. New York: Harcourt.

Mao, Zedong 毛泽东. 1966. *Mao Zedong Xuanji* 毛泽东选集 (Selected works of Mao Zedong). Vols. 1, 2, 3, and 4. Beijing: Renming Chubanshe 北京人民出版社 (People's press).

———. 1977. *Mao Zedong Xuanji* 毛泽东选集 (Selected works of Mao Zedong). Vol. 5. Beijing: Renming Chubanshe 北京人民出版社 (People's press).

Marks, Robert B. 1984. *Rural Revolution in South China: Peasants and the Making of History in Haifeng County, 1570–1930.* Madison, Wisconsin: University of Wisconsin Press.

Marlane, Judith. 1994. "The World of Chinese Television." Pp. 214–22 in *China at the Crossroads,* edited by Donal Altschiller. New York: H. W. Wilson Company.

Martin, Bill and Ivan Szelenyi. 1987. "Beyond Cultural Capital: Towards a Theory of Symbolic Domination." Pp. 16–49 in *Intellectuals, Universities and the State in Western Societies,* edited by Ron Eyerman, Lennart G. Svensson, and Thomas Soderqvist. Berkeley: University of California Press.

Marx, Karl. [1852] 1978. "The Eighteenth Brumaire of Louis Bonaparte." Pp. 594–617 in *The Marx-Engels Reader*, edited by Robert C. Tucker. New York: Norton.

———. [1888] 1978. "Theses on Feuerbach." Pp. 143–5 in *The Marx-Engels Reader*, edited by Robert C. Tucker. New York: Norton.

———. [1894] 1981. *Capital*. Vol. 3. Introduction by Ernest Mandel and translated by David Fernbach. New York: Vintage Books.

Marx, Karl and Friedrich Engels. [1888] 1978. "The Mannifesto of the Communist

Party." Pp. 469–500 in *The Marx-Engels Reader,* edited by Robert C. Tucker. New York: Norton.

Mazur, Mary (Ma Ziemei). 1996. *Shidai zhi zi: Wu Han* (A man of his times: Wu Han the historian). Beijing: Zhongguo Shehui Kexue Press.

———. 1997. "The United Front Redefined for the Party-State: A Case Study of Transition and Legitimation." Pp. 51–75 in *New Perspectives on State Socialism in China*, edited by Timothy Cheek and Tony Saich. Armonk, New York: M. E. Sharpe.

McCarthy, John D. and Mark Wolfson. 1992. "Consensus Movements, Conflict Movements, and the Cooptation of Civic and State Infrastructures." Pp. 273–98 in *Frontiers in Social Movement Theory,* edited by Aldon D. Morris and Carol McClurg Mueller. New Haven/London: Yale University Press.

McClelland, Charles E. 1990. "Escape from Freedom? Reflections on German Professionalization, 1870–1933." Pp. 97–113 in *The Formation of Professions,* edited by Rolf Torstendahl and Michael Burrage. London/Newbury Park: Sage Publications.

McCord, William with Arline McCord. 1986. *Paths to Progress: Bread and Freedom in Developing Societies*. New York: Norton.

McMichael, Philip. 1996. *Development and Social Change: A Global Perspective.* Thousand Oaks, California: Pine Forge Press.

Meisner, Maurice. 1967. *Li Ta-chao and the Origins of Chinese Marxism*. Cambridge: Harvard University Press.

———. 1997. "The Other China." *Current History*. September, pp. 264–69.

Meng Xiaoyun 孟晓云. 1997. "Cong Xueren, Wenren dao Shangren" 从学人，文人到商人 (From scholar, man of letters, to businessman). *People's Daily* (overseas edition) 人民日报海外版. November 21.

Mennerick, Lewis A. and Mehrangis Najafizadeh. 1992. "Contemporary Issues and Future Challenges for Professionals in Third World Social Change: The 1990s and Beyond." Pp. 283–96 in *Development and Democratization in the Third World: Myths, Hopes, and Realities,* edited by Kenneth E. Bouzon. New York: Crane Russak & Co.

Merton, Robert. 1968. *Social Theory and Social Structure.* New York: Free Press.

Miller, H. Lyman. 1996. *Science and Dissent in Post-Mao China: The Politics of Knowledge*. Seattle: University of Washington Press.

Ministry of Education Personnel Department Research Team on Building Up Teaching Forces. 1999. "Yijiu Jiuba Nian Quanguo Jiaoyu Shiye Fazhan Tongji Gongbao." 一九九八年全国教育事业发展统计公报 (1998 national educational development statistical report). *Xinhua Wenzhai* 新华文摘 (Xinhua news digest). No. 8.

Mo Luo 摩罗. 1999. "Zhishi Fenzi: Ruoyin Ruoxian de Shenhua" 知识分子: 若隐若现的神话 (Intellectuals: a myth that comes and goes). Pp. 320–30 in *Zhishi Fenzi Yinggai Gan Shenme* 知识分子应该干什么(What intellectuals should do), edited by Zhu Yong 祝勇. Beijing: Shishi Chubanshe 北京时事出版社 (Current affairs press).

Mo Rong 莫荣. 1999. "1998–1999 Nian: Zhongguo de Jiuye Xingshi jiqi Fazhan" 1998–1999 年: 中国的就业形势及其前景 (The employment situation in China now and in the future). Pp. 231–42 in *1999 Nian Zhongguo Shehui Xingshi Fenxi yu Yuce* 1999 年中国社会形势分析与预测 (1999 analysis and prediction of social conditions in China), edited by Ru Xin 汝信, Lu Xueyi 陆学艺, and Shan Tianlun

单天伦, et al. Beijing: Shehui Kexue Wenxian Chubanshe 北京社会科学文献出版社 (Social science literature press).

Mok, Ka-ho. 1998. *Intellectuals and the State in Post-Mao China*. New York: St Martin's.

Montagna, Paul. 1977. *Occupations and Society: A Sociology of the Labor Market*. New York: Wiley.

Mote, F. W. 1999. *Imperial China 900–1800*. Cambridge: Harvard University Press.

Mou Guangfeng 牟广丰. 2000. "Gao Wuran, Di Kongzhi: Zhongguo de Huanjing yu Shengtai" 高污染, 低控制: 中国的环境与生态 (Heavy pollution and low control: China's environment and ecology). Pp. 316–36 in *2000 Nian Zhongguo Shehui Xingshi Fenxi yu Yuce* 2000 年中国社会形势分析与预测 (2000 analysis and prediction of social conditions in China), edited by Ru Xin 汝信, Lu Xueyi 陆学艺, and Shan Tianlun 单天伦, et al. Beijing: Shehui Kexue Wenxian Chubanshe 北京社会科学文献出版社 (Social science literature press).

Mu Ran 木然. 1998. "Zhongguo Siying Jingji Fazhan Xin Xingshi" 中国私营经济发展新形势 (New developments in the private economy). *Jing Bao Monthly* 镜报月刊 5:44–8.

Nahirny, Vladimir C. 1983. *The Russian Intelligentsia from Torment to Silence*. New Brunswick, New Jersey: Transaction.

Nan Yu 南瑜. 2001. "Chuanmei Jingzheng Da de Tou Po Xie Liu" 传媒竞争打得头破血流 (The media are engaged in a bloody competition). *Qian Shao Yuekan* 前哨月刊 (Frontline monthly), October, pp. 58–61.

Naughton, Barry J. 1986. "Sun Yefang: Toward a Reconstruction of Socialist Economics." Pp. 124–54 in *China's Establishment Intellectuals,* edited by Carol Lee Hamrin and Timothy Cheek. Armonk, New York: M. E. Sharpe.

Nathan, Andrew J. 1992. "Historical Perspectives on Chinese Democracy: The Overseas Democracy Movement Today." Pp. 313–27 in *Roads Not Taken: The Struggle of Opposition Parties in Twentieth-Century China*, edited by Roger B. Jeans. Boulder, Colorado: Westview Press.

Nathan, Andrew J. and Tianjian Shi. 1993. "Cultural Requisites for Democracy in China: Findings from a Survey." *Daedalus* 122 (2)95–123.

Nee, Victor. 1996. "The Emergence of Market Society: Changing Mechanisms of Stratification in China." *American Journal of Sociology* 101(4):908–49.

Nettl, J. P. 1969. "Ideas, Intellectuals, and Structures of Dissent" Pp. 53–122 in *On Intellectuals: Theoretical Studies/Case Studies*, edited by Philip Rieff. New York: Doubleday.

Ni, Ching-Ching. 2001. "Communists at Ironic Juncture." *Los Angeles Times,* A3. July 3.

North, Robert C. with Ithiel de Sola Pool. 1965. "Kuomintang and Chinese Communist Elites." Pp. 319–455 in *World Revolutionary Elites: Studies in Coercive Ideological Movements,* edited by Harold D. Lasswell and Daniel Lerner. Cambridge: Massachusetts Institute of Technology Press.

O'Brien, Kevin J. and Lianjiang Li. 2000. "Accomodating 'Democracy' in a One-Party State: Introducing Village Elections in China." *China Quarterly* 162:465–89.

Oi, Jean C. and Scott Rozelle. 2000. "Elections and Power: The Locus of Decision-Making in Chinese Villages. *China Quarterly* 162:513–39.

O'Leary, Greg. 1998. "The Making of the Chinese Working Class." Pp. 48–74 in *Adjusting to Capitalism: Chinese Workers and the State,* edited by Greg O'Leary. Armonk, New York: M. E. Sharpe.

Parpart, Jane L. 1993. "Who Is the 'Other'?: A Postmodern Feminist Critique of Women and Development Theory and Practice." *Development and Change* 24: 439–64.

Parsons, Talcott. 1951. The Social System. New York: Free Press.

———. 1954. *Essays in Sociological Theory*. New York: Free Press.

———. 1968. "Professions." Pp. 536–47 in *International Encyclopedia of Social Sciences*, Vol. 12, edited by David L. Sills. New York: Free Press.

———. 1969."'The Intellectual': A Social Role Category." Pp. 3–24 in *On Intellectuals: Theoretical Studies/Case Studies*, edited by Philip Rieff. New York: Doubleday.

Pastor, Robert A. and Qingshan Tan. 2000. "The Meaning of China's Village Elections." *China Quarterly* 162:490–512.

Pearson, Margaret M. 1997. *China's New Business Elite: The Political Consequences of Economic Reform*. Berkeley: University of California Press.

Pei Minxin. 2000. "Rights and Resistance: the Changing Contexts of the Dissident Movement." Pp. 20–40 in *Chinese Society: Change, Conflict and Resistance,* edited by Elizabeth J. Perry and Mark Selden. London: Routledge.

Peng Jianpu 彭建甫. 1998. "Liangzhong Gaige Guan de Jiaofeng." 两种改革观的交锋 (Confrontation between two views on the current reform). *Dangdai Sichao* 当代思潮 (Contemporary thoughts) 5:51–8.

———. 1999. "Zuozhe Peng Jianpu Gei Du Ping de Xin." 作者彭建甫给杜平的信 (A letter from the author Peng Jianpu to Du Ping). *Dangdai Sichao* 当代思潮 (Contemporary thoughts) 1:59–62.

People's Republic of China Yearbook 1998.

Perry, Elizabeth. 1993. *Shanghai on Strike: The Politics of Chinese Labor*. Stanford: Stanford University Press.

———. 1997. "Shanghai's Strike Wave of 1957." Pp. 234–61 in *New Perspectives on State Socialism in China*, edited by Timothy Cheek and Tony Saich. Armonk, New York: M. E. Sharpe.

Perry, Elizabeth J. and Ellen V. Fuller. 1991. "China's Long March to Democracy." *World Policy Journal* 8(4)663–85.

Perry, Elizabeth J. and Mark Selden. 2000. "Introduction: Reform and Resistance in Contemporary China." Pp. 1–19 in *Chinese Society: Change, Conflict and Resistance,* edited by Elizabeth J. Perry and Mark Selden. London: Routledge.

Pickowicz, Paul G. 1995. "Velvet Prisons and the Political Economy of Chinese Filmmaking." Pp. 193–220 in *Urban Spaces in Contemporary China: The Potential for Autonomy and Community in Post-Mao China,* edited by Deborah S. Davis, Richard Kraus, Barry Naughton, and Elizabeth J. Perry. Washington D.C.: Woodrow Wilson Center Press.

Pollard, David E. 1976. "Chou Tso-jen: A Scholar Who Withdrew." Pp. 33–58 in *The Limits of Change: Essays on Conservative Alternatives in Republican China,* edited by Charlotte Furth. Cambridge: Harvard University Press.

Polumbaum, Judy. 1994a. "China's Press—Forget the Stereotype." Pp. 201–14 in *China at the Crossroads*, edited by Donal Altschiller. New York: H. W. Wilson Company.

———. 1994b. "To Protect or Restrict? Points of Contention in China's Draft Press Law." Pp. 247–69 in *Domestic Law Reforms in Post-Mao China*, edited by Pitman B. Potter. Armonk, New York: M. E. Sharpe.

Postiglione, Gerard A. 2000. "Internationalization and Professional Autonomy: The Academy in Hong Kong, Shanghai and Beijing." Paper delivered at the annual meeting of the Association for Asian Studies, San Diego, California, March 9–12.

Potter, Pitman. 1994a. "Riding the Tiger: Legitimacy and Legal Culture in Post-Mao China." *China Quarterly* 138:325–58.

———. 1994b. "The Administrative Litigation Law of the PRC: Judicial Review and Bureaucratic Reform." Pp. 270–304 in *Domestic Law Reforms in Post-Mao China*, edited by Pitman B. Potter. Armonk, New York: M. E. Sharpe.

———. 1998. "Economic and Legal Reform in China: Whither Civil Society and Democratization." Pp. 159–85 in *Market Economics and Political Change: Comparing China and Mexico*, edited by Juan D. Lindau and Timothy Cheek. New York: Rowman & Littlefield Publishers.

Pye, Lucian W. 1968. *The Spirit of Chinese Politics: A Psychocultural Study of the Authority Crisis in Political Development*. Cambridge: Massachusetts Institute of Technology Press.

———. 1981. *The Dynamics of Chinese Politics*. Cambridge: Oelgeschlager, Gunn & Hain, Publishers.

Qian Mu 钱穆. [1987] 1991. *Kongzi Zhuan* 孔子传 (A biography of Confucius). Taibei: Dongda Tushu Gufen Youxian Gongsi 台北东大图书股份有限公司.

———. [1981] 1999. "Zhongguo Zhishi Fenzi" 中国知识分子 (China's intellectuals). Pp. 53–86 in *Zhishi Fenzi Yinggai Gan Shenme* 知识分子应该干什么 (What intellectuals should do), edited by Zhu Yong 祝勇. Beijing: Shishi Chubanshe 北京时事出版社 (Current affairs press).

Qin Ling 秦岭. 1994. "Shichang Jinji yu Dangdai Zhongguo Zhishi Fenzi de Lishi Shiming" 市场经济与当代中国知识分子的历史使命 (Market economy and the historical mission of contemporary Chinese intellectuals), in *Shehui Kexue Ji Kan* 社会科学辑刊 (Magazine of social sciences) 2:39–41.

Qin Yan. 1999. *Zhongguo Zhongchan Jieji: Weilai Shehui Jiegou de Zhuliu* . 中国中产阶级: 未来社会结构的主流 (China's middle class: the future mainstream of the social structure). Beijing: Zhongguo Jihua Press 北京中国计划出版社.

Ragvald, Lars. 1978. *Yao Wenyuan as a Literary Critic and Theorist: The Emergence of Chinese Zhdanovism*. Ph.D. Department of Oriental Languages, University of Stockholm.

Rankin, Mary Backus. 1971. *Early Chinese Revolutionaries: Radical Intellectuals in Shanghai and Chekiang, 1902–1911*. Cambridge: Harvard University Press.

———. 1993. "Some Observations on a Chinese Public Sphere." *Modern China* 19(2)158–82.

Ren Jiantao 任剑涛. 1994. *Shan E de Bi An: Daxuesheng Daode de Shidai Zhuangkuang* 善恶的彼岸: 大学生道德的时代状况 (Between good and bad: the morals of college students in the contemporary times). Guangzhou: Zhongshan Daxue Chubanshe 广州中山大学出版社 (Zhongshan university press).

———. 2000. "Jiedu 'Xin Zuopai'" 解读 "新左派" (Understanding the "new left"). Pp. 191–214 in *Zhishi Fenzi Lichang: Ziyou Zhuyi zhi Zheng yu Zhongguo Sixiang*

Jie de Fenhua 知识分子立场: 自由主义之争与中国思想界的分化 (The intellectual stance: the debate on liberalism and the division of Chinese thought), edited by Li Shitao 李世涛. Changchun, Jilin: Shidai Wenyi Chubanshe 长春时代文艺出版社 (Art and literature of the time press).

Research Group of the Chinese Academy of Social Sciences. 1996a. "1995–1996 Nian Zhongguo Shehui Xingshi Fenxi yu Yuce Zong Baogao" 1995–1996 年中国社会形势分析与预测总报告 (General report on the analysis and forecast of Chinese social conditions from 1995–1996). Pp. 3–15 in *1995–1996 Nian Zhongguo Shehui Xingshi Fenxi yu Yuce* 1995–1996 年中国社会形势分析与预测 (An analysis of current Chinese society and forecast of its future: 1995–1996), edited by Jiang Liu 江流, Lu Xueyin 陆学艺, and Shan Tianlu 单天伦. Beijing: Zhongguo Shehui Kexue Chubanshe 北京中国社会科学出版社 (Chinese social science press).

———. 1996b. "1995–1996 Nian Shehui Xingshi: Zhuanjia Wenjuan Diaocha Zonghe Fenxi" 1995–1996 年社会形势: 专家问卷调查综合分析 (Social conditions in 1995–1996: a comprehensive analysis of surveys among experts). Pp. 35–45 in *1995–1996 Nian Zhongguo Shehui Xingshi Fenxi yu Yuce* 1995–1996 年中国社会形势分析与预测 (An analysis of current Chinese society and forecast of its future: 1995–1996), edited by Jiang Liu 江流, Lu Xueyin, 陆学艺, and Shan Tianlu 单天伦. Beijing: Zhongguo Shehui Kexue Chubanshe 北京中国社会科学出版社 (Chinese social science press).

Research Group on Private Enterprises in China. 1996. "1995 Chinese Private Enterprise Research: Data and Analysis" in *The Year Book of Chinese Private Economy 1996* 1996 年中国私营企业年鉴, edited by Zhang Xuwu 张绪武, Li Ding 李定, and Xie Mingwu 谢明午. Beijing: Zhonghua Gong Shang Lianhe Chubanshe 北京中华工商联合出版社 (Chinese industry and commerce united press) .

Rosen, Stanley. 2000. "Chinese Youth in the Year 2000: Internationalization, Nationalism, and Pragmatism." Paper prepared for the annual meeting of the Association for Asian Studies, San Diego, California, March 9–12.

Ross, Andrew. 1988. Introduction. Pp. 7–18 in *Universal Abandon?: The Politics of Postmodernism*, edited by Andrew Ross. Minneapolis: University of Minnesota Press.

Rowe, Willam T. 1993. "The Problem of 'Civil Society' in Late Imperial China." *Modern China* (19)2:139–57.

Rubin, Kyna. 1987. "Keeper of the Flame: Wang Ruowang as Moral Critic of the State." Pp. 233–250 in *China's Intellectuals and the State: In Search of a New Relationship,* edited by Merle Goldman with Timothy Cheek and Carol Lee Hamrin. Cambridge: Harvard University Press.

Saich, Tony. 1990. "Preface." Pp. vii–ix in *The Chinese People's Movement: Perspectives on Spring 1989,* edited by Tony Saich. Armonk, New York: M. E. Sharpe.

Saich, Tony and Hans J. van de Ven (eds.). 1995. *New Perspectives on the Chinese Revolution.* Armonk, New York: M. E. Sharpe.

Said, Edward. W. 1994. *Representations of the Intellectual.* New York: Pantheon.

Salisbury, Harrison E. 1992. *The New Emperors: China in the Era of Mao and Deng.* Boston: Little, Brown.

Scalapino, Robert A. (ed.). 1972. *Elites in the People's Republic of China.* Seattle: University of Washington Press.

Scalapino, Robert A. and George T. Yu. 1985. *Modern China and Its Revolutionary Process: Recurrent Challenges to the Traditional Order 1850–1920.* Berkeley: University of California Press.

Schein, Edgar H. with Inge Schneier and Curtis H. Barker. 1961. *Coercive Persuasion.* New York: Norton.

Schneider, Laurence A. 1976. "National Essence and the New Intelligentsia." Pp. 57–89 in *The Limits of Change: Essays on Conservative Alternatives in Republican China,* edited by Charlotte Furth. Cambridge: Harvard University Press.

Schoenhals, Michael. 1992. *Doing Things with Words in Chinese Politics: Five Studies.* Berkeley: Center for Chinese Studies.

Schram, Stuart R. (ed.). 1967. *Quotations from Chairman Mao Tse-tung.* New York: Bantam.

Schumpeter, A. Joseph. 1976. *Capitalism, Socialism and Democracy.* London: George Allen and Unwin.

Schurmann, Franz. 1968. *Ideology and Organization in Communist China.* Berkeley: University of California Press.

Schwarcz, Vera. 1986a. *The Chinese Enlightenment? Intellectuals and the Legacy of the May Fourth Movement of 1919.* Berkeley: University of California Press.

———. 1986b. Afterword. Pp. 247–56 in *China's Establishment Intellectuals*, edited by Carol Lee Hamrin and Timothy Cheek. Armonk, New York: M. E. Sharpe.

Schwartz, Benjamin I. 1976. "Notes on Conservatism in General and in China in Particular." Pp. 3–21 in *The Limits of Change: Essays on Conservative Alternatives in Republican China,* edited by Charlotte Furth. Cambridge: Harvard University Press.

Scruton, Roger. 1982. *A Dictionary of Political Thought.* New York: Hill and Wang.

Seymour, James D. 1968. *The Policies of the Chinese Communists toward China's Intellectuals and Professionals*. Ann Arbor, Michigan: University Microfilms International.

———. 1992. "A Half Century Later." Pp. 289–311 in *Roads Not Taken:The Struggle of Opposition Parties in Twentieth-Century China*, edited by Roger B. Jeans. Boulder, Colorado: Westview Press.

Shaw Yuming (ed.). 1986. *Mainland China: Politics, Economics, and Reform.* Boulder/London: Westview Press.

Shen Jiru 沈骥如. 1998. *Zhongguo Budang "Bu Xiansheng": Dangdai Zhongguo de Guoji Zhanlue Wenti* 中国不当 "不先生": 当代中国的国际战略问题 (China doesn't want to be Mr. No: the problems of contemporary Chinese international strategy). Jinri Zhongguo Chubanshe 今日中国出版社 (Today's China press).

Shen Lizhi 沈励志. 2001. "Minyun Shiren Liao Yiwu yu *Nanfang Zhoumo* Da Dizhen" 民运诗人廖亦武与《南方周末》大地震 (Democracy movement poet Liao Yiwu and the earthquake with the *South China Weekend*). *Qian Shao Yuekan* 前哨月刊 (Frontline monthly), October, pp. 64–9.

Shen Weiwei 沈卫威. 2000. *Qing Seng Kuxing: Wu Mi Zhuang* 情僧苦行: 吴宓传 (A sentimental monk's bitter journey: the biography of Wu Mi). Beijing: Dongfang Chubanshe 北京东方出版社 (East press).

———. 2001. "Wu Mi de Zhiye Lixiang yu Rensheng Beiju: Qian Qi Riji Jiedu" 吴宓的志业理想与人生悲剧: 前期日记解读 (Wu Mi's vocational ideal and his tragic life: an interpretation of his earlier diaries). Pp. 556–99 in *Jiexi Wu Mi* (An interpretation of Wu Mi), edited by Li Jikai 李继凯 and Liu Ruichun 刘瑞春. Beijing: Shehui Kexue Wenxian Chubanshe 北京社会科学文献出版社 (Social science literature press).

Sheng Hong 盛洪. 1995. "Shemo Shi Wenming" 什么是文明 (What civilization is). *Strategy and Management* 战略与管理 5:88–9.

Shi Jian 时间 (ed.). 1996. *Jingshen de Tianyuan: "Dongfang zhi Zi" Xueren Fangtan Lu* 精神的田园: "东方之子" 学人访谈录 (The field of spirit and vigor: the interviews of scholars in *"Sons and Daughters of the East.")* Beijing: Huaxia Chubanshe 华夏出版社 (China press).

Shijie 视界 (Horizons). 2001."'Qie Gevala' Dangan" (Archive of the play "Che Guevara"). *Shi Jie* 视界 (Horizons) 2:165–92.

Shils, Edward. 1969. "The Intellectuals and the Powers: Some Perspectives for Comparative Analysis." Pp. 25–48 in *On Intellectuals: Theoretical Studies/Case Studies*, edited by Philip Rieff. New York: Doubleday.

Shui Binghe 水秉和. 1989. "Zhishi fenzi de renwen qingxiang" 知识分子的人文倾向 (The humanistic tendency of intellectuals). Pp. 14–19 in *Xiandai Shehui yu Zhishi Fenzi* 现代社会与知识分子 *(*Modern society and intellectuals*)*, edited by Liang Congjie 梁从戒. Shenyang: Liaoning People's Press 辽宁人民出版社.

Sidel, Mark. 1995. "Dissident and Liberal Legal Scholars and Organizations in Beijing and the Chinese State in the 1980s." Pp. 326–46 in *Urban Spaces in Contemporary China: The Potential for Autonomy and Community in Post-Mao China,* edited by Deborah S. Davis, Richard Kraus, Barry Naughton, and Elizabeth J. Perry. Washington D.C.: Woodrow Wilson Center Press.

Siegrist, Hannes. 1990. "Professionalization as a Process." Pp. 177–202 in *Professions in Theory and History*, edited by Michael Burrage and Rolf Torstendhl. London: Sage Publications.

Simmel, Georg. 1950. *The Sociology of Georg Simmel,* edited by Kurt Wolff. New York: Free Press.

Simon, Denis Fred. 1987. "China's Scientists and Technologists in the Post-Mao Era: A Retrospective and Prospective Glimpse." Pp. 129–158 in *China's Intellectuals and the State: In Search of a New Relationship,* edited by Merle Goldman with Timothy Cheek and Carol Lee Hamrin. Cambridge: Harvard University Press.

Sing Lee and Arthur Kleinman. 2000. "Suicide as Resistance in Chinese Society." Pp. 221–40 in *Chinese Society: Change, Conflict and Resistance,* edited by Elizabeth J. Perry and Mark Selden. London: Routledge.

Siu, Helen F. 1993. "Cultural Identity and the Politics of Difference in South China," *Daedalus* 122(2)19–43.

Skocpol, Theda. 1994. *Social Revolutions in the Modern World.* New York: Cambridge University Press.

Smil, Vaclav. 1993. *China's Environmental Crisis: An Inquiry into the Limits of National Development*. Armonk, New York: M. E. Sharpe.

So, Alvin Y. 1992. "Democracy as an Antisystemic Movement in Taiwan, Hong Kong, and China." Sociological Perspectives 35(2)385–404.

———. 2000a. "Hong Kong's Problematic Democratic Transition: Power Dependency or Business Hegemony?" *Journal of Asian Studies* 59(2)359–81.

———. 2000b. "The Changing Patterns of Classes and Class Conflict in China." Paper presented to the annual meeting of the American Sociological Association, Washington, D.C., August 12–16.

Solinger, Dorothy. 1993. *China's Transition from Socialism: Statist Legacies and Market Reforms, 1980–1990*. Armonk, New York: M. E. Sharpe.

———. 1995. "The Floating Population in the Cities: Chances for Assimilation?" Pp. 113–39 *in Urban Spaces in Contemporary China: The Potential for Autonomy and Community in Post-Mao China*, edited by Deborah S. Davis, Richard Kraus, Barry Naughton, and Elizabeth J. Perry. Washington D.C.: Woodrow Wilson Center Press.

———. 1998. "Job Categories and Employment Channels Among the 'Floating Population.'" Pp. 3–47 in *Adjusting to Capitalism: Chinese Workers and the State*, edited by Greg O'Leary. Armonk, New York: M. E. Sharpe.

Solomon, Andrew. 1993. "Their Irony, Humor (and Art) Can Save China." *New York Times,* December 19, 1993.

Song Baoan 宋宝安 and Wang Yushan 王玉山. 1999. "Changchun Shi Xiagang Zhigong Zhuangkuang de Wenjuan Diaocha" 长春市下岗职工状况的问卷调查 (A survey on the situation of the laid-off workers in the city of Changchun). Pp. 255–70 in *1999 Nian Zhongguo Shehui Xingshi Fenxi yu Yuce* 1999 年中国社会形势分析与预测 (1999 analysis and prediction of social conditions in China), edited by Ru Xin 汝信, Lu Xueyi 陆学艺, and Shan Tianlun 单天伦, et al. Beijing: Shehui Kexue Wenxian Chubanshe 北京社会科学文献出版社 (Social science literature press).

Song Jingming 宋镜明. 1997. *Li Da* 李达. Shijiazhuang: Hebei Remin Chubanshe 石家庄河北人民出版社 (Hebei people's press).

Song Qiang 宋强, Zhang Zangzang 张藏藏, Qiao Bian 乔边, et al. 1996. *Zhongguo Keyi Shuo Bu* 中国可以说不 (China can say no). Hong Kong: Ming Bao Press 香港明报出版社.

———. 1996. *Zhongguo Haishi Neng Shuo Bu* 中国还是能说不 (China can still say no). Zhongguo Wenlian Chubanshe 中国文联出版社 (Chinese art and literature association press) .

Starr, John Bryan. 1973. *Ideology and Culture: An Introduction to the Dialectic of Contemporary Chinese Politics*. New York: Harper.

———. 1996. "China in 1995: Mounting Problems, Waning Capacity." *Asian Survey* 1:13–24.

State Statistical Bureau, People's Republic of China 中华人民共和国统计局 (ed.). 1994. *1994 Statistical Yearbook of China* 1994 年中国统计年鉴. Beijing: China Statistical Publishing House 中国统计出版社.

Su Wei and Wendy Larson. 1995. "The Disintegration of the Poetic 'Berlin Wall'" Pp. 279–93 in *Urban Spaces in Contemporary China: The Potential for Autonomy and Community in Post-Mao China,* edited by Deborah S. Davis, Richard Kraus, Barry Naughton, and Elizabeth J. Perry. Washington D.C.: Woodrow Wilson Center Press.

Su Xiaokang 苏晓康. 1990. "Guanyu Liyong Chuantong Ziyuan" 关于利用传统资源 (On how to use our traditional resources). *Democratic China* 民主中国 June.

———. 1991. "Dang Dai Zhongguo de Wenhua Jinzhang" 当代中国的文化紧

张 (The cultural tension in contemporary China). *Democratic China* 民主中国. February.

Su Xiaokang 苏晓康 and Wang Luxiang 王鲁湘. *He Shang* 河殇 (River Elegy). Beijing: Xiandai Chubanshe 北京现代出版社 (Modern press).

Sullivan, Michael J. 1995. "Development and Political Repression: China's Human Rights Policy Since 1989." *Bulletin of Concerned Asian Scholars*. October-December 4:24–39.

Sun Changjiang 孙长江. [1998] 1999."'Shijian Shi Jianyan Zhenli de Wei Yi Biaozhun' Fabiao Qianhou de Neimu" '实践是检验真理的唯一标准' 发表前后的内幕 (Before and after the publication of the article "practice is the sole criterion of truth"). Pp. 98–105 in *Yanlun Zhongguo: Guandian Jiaofeng 20 Nian* 言论中国: 观点交锋 20 年 (Discourse China: debating ideas over the past twenty years), edited by Jing Wu. Beijing: Zhongguo Jiancha Press 中国监察出版社.

Sun Yu 孙郁. 1999. "Wei Xueshu er Xueshu?" 为学术而学术? (Scholarship for scholarship's sake?) Pp. 421–8 in *Zhishi Fenzi Yinggai Gan Shenme* 知识分子应该干什么 (What intellectuals should do,) edited by Zhu Yong 祝勇. Beijing: Shishi Chubanshe 北京时事出版社 (Current affairs press).

Szelenyi, Ivan. 1991. "The Intellectuals in Power?" Pp. 269–73 in *After the Fall,* edited by Robin Blackburn. New York: Verso.

Szelenyi, Ivan and Eric Kostello. 1996. "The Market Transition Debate: Toward a Synthesis?" *American Journal of Sociology* 101(4)1082–96.

Szelenyi, Ivan and Bill Martin. 1991. "The Three Waves of New Class Theories and a Postscript." Pp. 19–30 in *Intellectuals and Politics: Social Theory in a Changing World,* edited by Charles C. Lemert. Newbury Park: Sage Publications.

Tam, Chen Hee. 1999. "Appendices: The Phenomenon of Falun Gong." Pp. 20–27 in *The Mystery of China Falun Gong: Its Rise and Its Sociological Implications,* by John Wong and William T. Liu. Singapore: World Scientific and Singapore University Press.

Tang Bo 唐勃. 1988. *Zhong gong yu zhishi fenzi* 中共与知识分子 (The Chinese Communist Party and intellectuals). Taibei: You Shi Cultural Enterprise Company 台北: 幼狮文化事业公司.

Tang Haoming 唐浩明. 1994. "Wo Xie *Zeng Guofan*" 我写 '曾国藩' (I Write *Zeng Guofan*). *Strategy and Management* 战略与管理 3:52–5.

Tang Jun 唐钧. 1999. "Zhongguo de Pinkun yu Fan Pinkun Xingshi Fenxi 中国的贫困与反贫困形势分析 (Analysis of China's situation of poverty and its efforts to fight it). Pp. 400–10 in *1999 Nian Zhongguo Shehui Xingshi Fenxi yu Yuce* 1999 年中国社会形势分析与预测 (1999 analysis and prediction of social conditions in China), edited by Ru Xin 汝信, Lu Xueyi 陆学艺, and Shan Tianlun 单天伦, et al. Beijing: Shehui Kexue Wenxian Chubanshe 北京社会科学文献出版社 (Social science literature press).

Tang Qinmei 唐青梅. 1997. "Wo Ban 'Duan he Duan'" 我办 "段和段" (I operate "Duan and Duan"). *People's Daily* (overseas edition) 人民日报海外版. October 31.

Tang Yongde 唐永德 (ed.). 1982. "Yu Shan Ju Yuan Jue Jiao Shu" 与山巨源绝交书 (A letter to sever relationship with Shan Ju Yuan). Pp. 75–7 in *Yuyan Wenxue Zixiu Daxue Jiangzuo* 语言文学自修大学讲座 (Lectures in language and literature by the self-study correspondence university). No. 8. Beijing: Dizhi Chubanshe 北京地质出版社 (Geology press).

Tang Yuyuan 唐宇元 (ed.). 1984. *Zhonghua Minzu Jiechu Renwu Zhuan (Di San Ji)* 中华民族杰出人物传 (第三集)(Outstanding personages in China. Vol. 3). Beijing: Zhongguo Qingnian Chubanshe 北京中国青年出版社 (China youth press).

Tao Baichun 陶百川. 1989. "Zhishi Fenzi Neng Wei Guojia Zuo Xie Shemo" 知识分子能为国家做些什么 (What intellectuals can do for the country). P. 108 in *Zhishi fenzi yu Taiwan fazhan* 知识分子与台湾发展 (Intellectuals and the development of Taiwan), edited by Zhongguo Luntan Bianwei Hui 中国论坛编委会 (China Forum Editorial Committee). Taibei: Zhongguo Luntan Zazhi 台北中国论坛杂志 (China forum magazine).

Tao Dongfeng 陶东风. 1994. "Zhongxin yu Bianyuan de Weiyi" 中心与边缘的位移 (The change of position between the center and the periphery). *Dongfang* 东方 (Orient) 4:18–22.

———. 2000. "Xiandai Xing Fansi de Fansi" 现代性反思的反思 (Reflecting on modern reflections). Pp. 431–48 in *Zhishi Fenzi Lichang: Ziyou Zhuyi zhi Zheng yu Zhongguo Sixiang Jie de Fenhua* 知识分子立场: 自由主义之争与中国思想界的分化 (The intellectual stance: the debate on liberalism and the division of Chinese thought), edited by Li Shitao 李世涛.Changchun, Jilin: Shidai Wenyi Chubanshe 长春时代文艺出版社 (Art and literature of the time press).

Teiwes, Frederick C. 1979. *Politics & Purges in China: Rectification and the Decline of Party Norms 1950–1965*. Armonk, New York: M. E. Sharpe.

Tempest, Rone. 1998. "China's New Premier Zhu Lays out Economic Plans." *Los Angeles Times,* March 19.

Tian Yuchuan 田玉川. 1999. *Zhongguo Shehui Bing yu Xin Qiannian* 中国社会病与新千年 (China's social ills and the new millennium). Beijing : Zhongguo Wenlian Chubanshe 北京中国文联出版社 (Chinese art and literature association press).

Torpey, John C. 1995. *Intellectuals, Socialism, and Dissent*. Minneapolis: University of Minnesota Press.

Trager, Frank N. and William Henderson (eds.). 1970. *Communist China, 1949–1969: A Twenty-Year Appraisal.* New York: New York University Press.

Tsou, Tang 邹傥. 1986. The Cultural Revolution and Post-Mao Reforms: A Historical Perspective. Chicago: University of Chicago Press.

———. 1994. *Ershi Shiji Zhongguo Zhengzhi: Cong Hongguan Lishi he Weiguan Xingdong de Jiaodu Kan* 二十世纪中国政治:从宏观历史和微观行动的角度看 (Twentieth-century Chinese politics: from the perspectives of macrohistory and micromechanism analysis.) Hong Kong: Oxford University Press.

Tu Wei-ming. 1976. "Hsiung Shih-li's Quest for Authentic Existence." Pp. 242–75 in *The Limits of Change: Essays on Conservative Alternatives in Republican China*, edited by Charlotte Furth. Cambridge: Harvard University Press.

———. 1991a. "Cultural China: The Periphery as the Center." *Daedalus* 120(2) (Spring).

———. 1991b. "A Meeting of East and West: Bill Moyers's Conversation with Dr. Tu Weiming," PBS Series: A World of Ideas. (Summer). Transcript.

———. 1993a. "Introduction: Cultural Perspectives." *Daedalus* 122 (2) (Spring).

———. 1993b, 2000. *Way, Learning, and Politics: Essays on the Confucian Intellec-*

tual. Albany: State University of New York Press. A Chinese translation of the book, *Dao, Xue, Zheng: Lun Rujia Zhishi Fenzi* 道, 学, 政: 论儒家知识分子 was published by Shanghai People's Press 上海人民出版社 (2000).

Tyler, Patrick. 1994a. "Discontent Mounts in China, Shaking the Leaders." *New York Times*, April 10.

———. 1994b. "Top Chinese Judge Warns of Serious Crime Problem in Rural Areas." *New York Times*, May 23.

———. 1994c. "A Tide of Pollution Threatens China's Prosperity." *New York Times*, September 25.

Van de Ven, Hans J. 1991. *From Friend to Comrade: The Founding of the Chinese Communist Party, 1920–1927*. Berkeley: University of California Press.

Wagner, Rudolf G. 1987. "The Chinese Writer in His Own Mirror: Writer, State, and Society—The Literary Evidence." Pp. 183–232 in *China's Intellectuals and the State: In Search of a New Relationship,* edited by Merle Goldman with Timothy Cheek and Carol Lee Hamrin. Cambridge: Harvard University Press.

Wakeman, Frederic Jr. 1975. *The Fall of Imperial China.* New York: Free Press.

———. 1980. "Duli Zizhu de Daijia—Zhishi Fenzi yu Ming Qing Zhengzhi" 独立自主的代价——知识分子与明清政治 (The cost of independence and autonomy—intellectuals and the politics of Ming and Qing dynasties). Pp. 271–314 in *Zhishi Fenzi yu Zhongguo* 知识分子与中国 (Intellectuals and China), edited by Zhou Yangshan 周阳山. Translation by Liu Tangfen 刘唐芬. Taibei: Shidai Chuban Gongsi 台北时代出版公司 (Times press company).

———. 1993. "The Civil Society and Public Sphere Debate." *Modern China* 19(2) 108–38.

Walder, Andrew George. 1978. *Chang Ch'un-ch'iao and Shanghai's January Revolution*. Ann Arbor: Center for Chinese Studies, University of Michigan.

———. 1991. "Workers, Managers and the State: The Reform Era and the Political Crisis of 1989." *China Quarterly* 129(467–92).

Wallerstein, Immanuel. 1996. "Social Science and Contemporary Society: The Vanishing Guarantees of Rationality." *International Sociology* 11(1)7–25.

Wang Binbin 王彬彬. 1999. "Juti er Shizai de Renwen Jingshen" 具体而实在的人文精神 (The concrete and solid humanist spirit). Pp. 339–41 in *Zhishi Fenzi Yinggai Gan Shenme* 知识分子应该干什么 (What intellectuals shoulddo), edited by Zhu Yong 祝勇. Beijing: Shishi Chubanshe 北京时事出版社 (Current affairs press).

Wang, Chen-main. 1999. *The Life and Career of Hung Ch'eng-ch'ou (1593–1665): Public Service in a Time of Dynastic Change*. Association for Asian Studies. Monograph and Occasional Paper Series. No. 59.

Wang Dan 王丹. 1998. Talk at USC-UCLA Joint Center for East Asian Studies at UCLA. May 22. (Personal notes).

———. 2000. Talk at a symposium in Montery Park, California. April 9. (Personal notes).

Wang Dingding 汪丁丁. 2000. "Ziyou: Yiduan Jiao Ta Shidi de Xushuo" 自由: 一段脚踏实地的叙说 (Freedom: a down-to-earth narration). Pp. 362–7 in *Zhishi Fenzi Lichang: Ziyou Zhuyi zhi Zheng yu Zhongguo Sixiang Jie de Fenhua* 知识分子立场: 自由主义之争与中国思想界的分化 (The intellectual stance: the debate on liberalism and the division of Chinese thought), edited by Li Shitao 李世涛.

Changchun, Jilin: Shidai Wenyi Chubanshe 长春时代文艺出版社 (Art and literature of the time press).

Wang, Edward. (Wang Qingjia.) 2001. *Inventing China Through History: The May Fourth Approach to Historiography.* Albany: State University of New York Press.

Wang, Fei-ling. 1997. "Ignorance, Arrogance, and Radical Nationalism: A Review of China Can Say No." *Journal of Contemporary China* 6(14)161–5.

Wang Gungwu. 1993. "To Reform a Revolution: Under the Righteous Mandate." *Daedalus* 122(2)71–93 (Spring).

Wang Hui 汪晖. [1997] 2000. "Dangdai Zhongguo de Sixiang Zhuangkuang he Xiandai Xing Wenti" 当代中国的思想状况和现代性问题 (Contemporary Chinese thought and the problem of modernity). Pp. 83–123 in *Zhishi Fenzi Lichang: Ziyou Zhuyi zhi Zheng yu Zhongguo Sixiang Jie de Fenhua* 知识分子立场: 自由主义之争与中国思想界的分化 (The intellectual stance: the debate on liberalism and the division of Chinese thought), edited by Li Shitao 李世涛. Changchun, Jilin: Shidai Wenyi Chubanshe 长春时代文艺出版社 (Art and literature of the time press).

Wang Hui 汪晖 and Zhang Tianwei 张天蔚. 1994. "Wenhua Pipan Lilun yu Dangdai Zhongguo Minzu Zhuyi Wenti" 文化批判理论与当代中国民族主义问题 (Theories of cultural criticism and contemporary China's nationalism). *Strategy and Management* 战略与管理 4:17–20.

Wang, Jing. 1996. *High Culture Fever: Politics, Aesthetics, and Ideology in Deng's China*. Berkeley: Univeristy of California Press.

Wang Jinshan 王金山. 1995. "Nuli Zuohao Xin Shiqi de Ganbu Jiandu Gongzuo" 努力做好新时期的干部监督工作 (To do well with cadre supervision in the new era). *Qiu Shi* 求是 12:28–31.

Wang Jinyuan 王金元. 1994."'Xinwen Toushi' de Toushi" '新闻透视' 的透视 (Penetrating "news penetration"). *Xinmin Evening News* 新民晚报. July 24, 1994.

Wang Meng 王蒙. 1994. "Renwen Jingshen Wenti Ougan" 人文精神问题偶感 (Some random thoughts on the humanist spirit). *Dongfang* 东方 (Orient) 5:46–50.

———. 1998. "Guanyu Jiushi Niandai Xiaoshuo" 关于九十年代小说 (On the novels of the 1990s). *Xinhua Wenzhai* 新华文摘 (Xinhua selection of essays). February.

Wang Ning. 1997. "The Mapping of Chinese Postmodernity." *boundary 2*. 23(3)19–40.

Wang Shicheng 王世城. 2000. "Mishi de Zhidu Wutuobang" 迷失的制度乌托帮 (The lost utopia). Pp. 407–12 in *Zhishi Fenzi Lichang: Ziyou Zhuyi zhi Zheng yu Zhongguo Sixiang Jie de Fenhua* 知识分子立场: 自由主义之争与中国思想界的分化 (The intellectual stance: the debate on liberalism and the division of Chinese thought), edited by Li Shitao 李世涛. Changchun, Jilin: Shidai Wenyi Chubanshe 长春时代文艺出版社 (Art and literature of the time press).

Wang Shubai 汪澍白 1990. *Mao Zedong Sixiang de Zhongguo Jiyin* 毛泽东思想的中国基因 (The Chinese genetics of Mao Zedong thought). Hong Kong: Shangwu Press 商务印书馆.

Wang Sirui 王思睿. 2000. "Jinri Zhongguo de Xin Baoshou Zhuyi" 今日中国的新保守主义 (Neoconservatism in today's China). Pp. 406–21 in *Zhishi Fenzi Lichang: Jijin yu Baoshou zhijian de Dongdang* 知识分子立场: 激进与保守之间的动荡 (The intellectual stance: between radicalism and conservatism), edited by Li Shitao 李世涛. Changchun, Jilin: Shidai Wenyi Chubanshe 长春时代文艺出版社 (Art and literature of the time press).

Wang Xiaodong 王小东. 2000a. "Minzu Zhuyi he Minzhu Zhuyi" 民族主义和民主主义 (Nationalism and democracy). Pp. 86–101 in *Zhishi Fenzi Lichang: Minzu Zhuyi yu Zhuanxing Qi Zhongguo de Mingyun* 知识分子立场: 民族主义与转型期中国的命运 (The intellectual's stance: nationalism and China's fate in the time of transition), edited by Li Shitao 李世涛. Changchun, Jilin: Shidai Wenyi Chubanshe 长春时代文艺出版社 (Art and literature of the time press).

———. 2000b. "Dangdai Zhongguo minzu zhuyi lun" 当代中国民族主义主论 (On nationalism in contemporary China). *Zhanlue yu Guanli* 战略与管理 (Strategy and management) 5:69–82.

Wang Xiaohui 王晓辉. 1997. "Zhongguo Zhuoli Zhuoba Kua Shiji Zhengzhi Yingcai" 中国著力擢拔跨世纪政治英才 (China works hard to promote political talents for the twenty-first century). *Overseas Chinese Daily.* August 26.

Wang Xiaoming 王晓明. 1995. "Women Nengfu Zouchu Shiyu de Kunjing" 我们能否走出失语的困境 (Can we emerge from the embarrassment of losing our discourse?). *Dongfang* 东方 (Orient) 3:72–8.

———. [1998] 1999. "Zai Didiao yu Gaodiao Zhijian" 在低调与高调之间 (Between the low tune and the high tune). Pp. 135–49 in *Zhishi Fenzi Yinggai Gan Shenme* 知识分子应该干什么(What intellectuals should do), edited by Zhu Yong 祝勇. Beijing: Shishi Press 时事出版社.

Wang Xingfu 汪幸福. 2000. *Yin Haiguan yu Jiang Jieshi* 殷海光与蒋介石 (Yin Haiguang and Chiang Kai-shek). Wuhan: Hubei Renmin Chubanshe 湖北人民出版社 (Hubei people's press).

Wang Xizhe 王希哲. 1997. "Fandui Jiang Zemin Fubi Tongdian" 反对江泽民复辟通电 (Open telegraph against the restoration of Jiang Zemin). *Beijing Spring* 北京之春 2:14. It was signed by over thirty democracy activists including Hu Ping 胡平, Xue Wei 薛伟, and Xin Ku 辛苦.

Wang, Y. C. 1966. *Chinese Intellectuals and the West: 1872–1949.* Chapel Hill: University of North Carolina Press.

Wang Ying 王颖, Zhe Xiaoye 折晓叶, and Sun Bingyao 孙秉耀. 1993. *Shehui Zhongjian Cen* 社会中间层 (The middle stratum of society). Beijing: Zhongguo Fazhan Press 中国发展出版社.

Wang Yuanhua 王元化. 1990. *Chuantong yu Fan Chuantong* 传统与反传统 (Tradition and antitradition). Shanghai: Shanghai Wenyi Press 上海文艺出版社.

———. 1993. Qing Yuan Ye Du 清园夜读. Shenzhen: Haitian Press 中国深圳海天出版社.

———. 1994a. "Xueshu Liangxin" 学术良心 (Academic conscience). *Wenhui Daily* 文汇日报. June 3.

———. 1994b. "Sibian Suibi Xu" 思辨随笔序 (Preface to random dialectical reflections). *Wenhui Reading Weekly*, July 23.

———. 1995. "Jinnian de Fansi" 近年的反思 (Reflections over the past few years). *Dongfang* 东方 (Orient) 1:72–6.

———. 2000. *Jiushi Niandai Fansi Lu* 九十年代反思录 (Reflections from the 1990s). Shanghai: Shanghai Guji Chubanshe 上海古籍出版社 (Shanghai ancient books press).

———. 2001. *Jiushi Niandai Riji* 九十年代日记 (Diaries from the 1990s). Hangzhou: Zhejiang Remin Chubanshe 杭州浙江人民出版社 (Zhejiang people's press).

Wang Zheng. 2000. "Gender, Employment and Women's Resistance." Pp. 62–82 in *Chinese Society: Change, Conflict and Resistance,* edited by Elizabeth J. Perry and Mark Selden. London: Routledge.

Wasserstrom, Jeffrey N. and Liu Xinyong. "Student Associations and Mass Movements." Pp. 362–93 in *Urban Spaces in Contemporary China: The Potential for Autonomy and Community in Post-Mao China,* edited by Deborah S. Davis, Richard Kraus, Barry Naughton, and Elizabeth J. Perry. Washington D.C.: Woodrow Wilson Center Press.

Weber, Max. 1946. *From Max Weber: Essays in Sociology,* edited by H. H. Gerth and C. Wright Mills. New York: Oxford University Press.

Webster, Andrew. 1990. *Introduction to the Sociology of Development,* 2nd ed. London: MacMillan Press.

Wei Jianxing 尉健行. 1996. "Jinyibu Jiada Fan Fubai Douzheng de Lidu" 进一步加大反腐败斗争的力度 (Further strengthening the anticorruption struggle). *Qiu Shi* 求是 4:2–6.

Wei Xiaodong 魏小东. 1996. "Zhishi Fenzi zai Shehui Zhuyi Geming he Jianshe Zhongde Zuoyong" 知识分子在社会主义革命和建设中的作用 (The function of intellectuals within the socialist revolution and construction). Pp. 122–49 in *Zhishi Fenzi yu Zhongguo Shehui Biange* 知识分子与中国社会变革 (Intellectuals and reform in Chinese society), edited by Jia Chun Zeng 贾春增. Beijing: Hua Wen Chubanshe 北京华文出版社 (Chinese language press).

Wen Chongyi 文崇一. 1989. "Zhongguo zhishi fenzi de leixing yu xingge" 中国知识分子的类型与性格 (The typology and character of Chinese intellectuals). Pp. 69–108 in *Zhishi Fenzi yu Taiwan Fazhan* 知识分子与台湾发展 (Intellectuals and the development of Taiwan), edited by Zhonghuo Luntan Bianwei Hui 中国论坛编委会 (China Forum Editorial Committee). Taibei: Zhongguo Luntan Zazhi 台北中国论坛杂志 (China forum magazine).

Wen Jize. [1942] 1994. "Diary of a Struggle," in *Wang Shiwei and "Wild Lilies:" Rectification and Purges in the Chinese Communist Party, 1942–44,* by Dai Qing. Armonk, New York: M. E. Sharpe.

Wen Shengtang 文盛堂. 1999. "1998 Nian: Zhongguo Fan Fubai Li Cha Da Yao An he Zhengsu Jun Jing yu Zhi Fa Duiwu" 1998 年: 中国反腐败力查大要案和整肃军警与执法队伍 (1998: China's anti-corruption effort focuses on key cases and the rectification of the army, police, and law enforcement agencies). Pp. 165–78 in *1999 Nian Zhongguo Shehui Xingshi Fenxi yu Yuce* 1999 年中国社会形势分析与预测 (1999 analysis and prediction of social conditions in China), edited by Ru Xin 汝信, Lu Xueyi 陆学艺, and Shan Tianlun 单天伦, et al. Beijing: Shehui Kexue Wenxian Chubanshe 北京社会科学文献出版社 (Social science literature press).

Wen Si 文思. 1994. "Daode Duoluo Shi Wenti zhi Suozai ma?" 道德堕落是问题之所在吗? (Is moral deterioration the problem?) *Dongfang* 东方 (Orient) 3:28–9.

White III, Lynn T. 1986. "Chinese Intellectuals and Party Policy." Pp. 205–55 in *Mainland China: Politics, Economics, and Reform,* edited by Shaw Yuming. Boulder, Colorado/London: Westview Press.

White, Tyrene. 2000. "Domination, Resistance and Accommodation in China's One-Child Campaign." Pp. 102–119 in *Chinese Society: Change, Conflict and Resistance,* edited by Elizabeth J. Perry and Mark Selden. London: Routledge.

Wilensky, Harold L. 1956. *Intellectuals in Labor Unions: Organizational Pressures on Professional Roles*. Glencoe, Illinois: Free Press.

Williams, James Harley. 1990. "Fang Lizhi's Expanding Universe." *China Quarterly* 123:459–84.

———. 1994. *Fang Lizhi's Big Bang: Science and Politics in Mao's China*. Ph.D. dissertation. University of California, Berkeley.

Wong, John. 1999. "The Mystery of *Falun Gong:* Its Rise and Fall in China." Pp. 1–19 in *The Mystery of China's Falun Gong: Its Rise and Its Sociological Implications,* by John Wong and William T. Liu. Singapore: World Scientific and Singapore University Press.

Wright, Erik Olin. 1985. *Classes*. London/New York: Verso.

Wu Jianguo 吴建国, Chen Xiankui 陈先奎, Liu Xiao 刘晓, and Yang Fengcheng 杨风城. 1993. *Dangdai Zhongguo Yishi Xingtai Fengyun Lu* 当代中国意识形态风云录 (Ideological battles in contemporary China). Beijing: Jingcha Jiaoyu Chubanshe 北京警察教育出版社 (Police education press).

Wu Mi 吴宓. [1927] 1998. *Wu Mi Riji 1925–27* 吴宓日记 (Wu Mi diary 1925–27). Beijing: Sanlian Press 北京三联出版社.

Wu Shuqin 武淑琴. 2000. "Qunian Renjun Shouru Zengfu Da" 去年人均收入增幅大 (Per capita income last year largely increased). *Overseas Chinese Daily* 侨报. February 18.

Wu Weihua 吴炜华. 1982. "Nan Bei Chao Shi Wen" 南北朝诗文 (Poetry and essays in Southern and Northern dynasties). Pp. 39–48 in *Yuyan Wenxue Zixiu Daxue Jiangzuo* 语言文学自修大学讲座 (Lectures in language and literature by the self-study correspondence university). No. 10. Beijing: Dizhi Chubanshe 北京地质出版社 (Geology Press).

Wu Xuan 吴炫, Wang Gan 王干, Fei Zhenzhong 费振中, and Wang Binbin 王彬彬. 1994. "Women Xuyao Zenyang de Renwen Jingshen?" 我们需要怎样的人文精神? (What kind of humanism do we want?) *Dushu* 读书 6:66–74.

WuDunn, Sheryl. 1993a. "Chinese Suffer From Rising Pollution as Byproduct of Industrial Boom." *New York Times*, February 28.

———. 1993b. "Layoffs in China: A Dirty Word, But All Too Real." *New York Times*, May 11.

Wylie, Raymond F. 1980. *The Emergence of Maoism: Mao Tse-tung, Ch'en Po-ta, and the Search for Chinese Theory, 1935–1945*. Stanford: Stanford University Press.

Xia Xinruo 夏信若. 2001. "Waizi Ru Gu Binggou Chuanmei Chongji Dang Tianxia" 外资入股并购传媒冲击党天下 (Foreign capital buys shares in the mass media and shakes the Party's dictatorship). *Qian Shao Yukan* 前哨月刊 (Frontline monthly), October, pp. 50–54.

Xia Yan 夏衍. 1994."'Wu Xun Zhuan' Shijian de Shimo" '武训传' 事件始末 (What happened before and after the movie "The Story of Wu Xun"). *Wenhui Daily* 文汇日报. July 21; also in *Strategy and Management* 战略与管理 1995 2:17–21.

Xiao Gongqin 萧功秦. 1994a. "Zhongguo Gaige Mianlin de Qianzai Weiji" 中国改革面临的潜在危机 (The potential crisis facing Chinese reform). *Strategy and Management* 战略与管理 1:8–11.

———. 1994b. "Zhishi Fenzi Fenhua he Lilun Jiaofeng" 知识分子分化和理论交锋 The division of intellectuals and their battles over theory). *Asia Weekly* 亚洲周刊, June 5.

———. 1994c. "Minzu Zhuyi yu Zhongguo Zhuanxing Shiqi de Yishi Xingtai" 民族主义与中国转型时期的意识形态 (Nationalism and ideology during China's transformative period). *Strategy and Management* 战略与管理 4:21–5.

———. 1999. "Wei Shemo Wo Fandui Jijin Minzu Zhuyi." 为什么我反对激进民族主义 (Why I am opposed to radical nationalism). *Ershi Yi Shiji* 二十一世纪 (Twenty-first century). August, 54:134–7.

———. 2000a. "Xin Zuopai yu Wenhua Langman Zhuyi." 新左派与文化浪漫主义 (The new left and cultural romanticism). <http://server12.hypermart.net.tursi/z/>, February 3.

———. 2000b. "Jijin de Minzu Zhuyi yu Shiji Zhijiao de Sixiang Fenhua" 激进的民族主义与世纪之交的思想分化 (Radical nationalism and diverse thought at the turn of the century). Pp. 508–13 in *Zhishi Fenzi Lichang: Minzu Zhuyi yu Zhuanxing Qi Zhongguo de Mingyun* 知识分子立场: 民族主义与转型期中国的命运 (The intellectual's stance: nationalism and China's fate in the time of transition), edited by Li Shitao 李世涛. Changchun, Jilin: Shidai Wenyi Chubanshe 长春时代文艺出版社 (Art and literature of the time press).

Xiao Ke 萧克, Li Rui 李锐, Gong Yuzhi 龚育之, et al. 1998. *Wo Qinli guo de Zhengzhi Yundong* 我亲历过的政治运动 (The political movements I have been through). Beijing: Zhongyang Bianyi Chubanshe 北京中央编译出版社 (Central compilation and translations press).

Xiao Shu 笑蜀 (ed.) 1999. *Lishi de Xiansheng: Bange Shiji Qian de Zhuangyan Chengnuo* 历史的先声: 半个世纪前的庄严承诺 (Voices in the past: a solemn promise from half a century ago). Shantou, Guangdong: Shantou Daxue Chubanshe 广东汕头大学出版社(Shantou university press).

Xiao Tongqing 肖同庆. 1995. "Xunqiu Jiazhi Mubiao yu Lishi Jincheng de Qihe" 寻求价值目标与历史进程的契合 (Seeking agreement between value goals and historical process). *Dongfang* 东方 (Orient) 1:19–20.

Xie Xiaoqing 谢小庆. 1995. "Pingjie Shemo Jianshou Jiazhi Tixi" 凭借什么坚守价值体系 (Relying on what to protect the value system). *Dongfang* 东方 (Orient) 3: 14–7.

Xie Yong 谢泳. 1999a. *Shiqu de Niandai: Zhongguo Ziyou Zhishifenzi de Mingyun* 逝去的年代: 中国自由知识分子的命运 (The bygone years: Chinese liberal intellectuals' destiny). Beijing: Wenhua Yishu Chubanshe 北京文化艺术出版社 (Art and literature press).

———. 1999b. *Jiaoyu zai Qinghua* 教育在清华 (Education at Qinghua). Tianjin: Baihua Wenyi Chubanshe 天津百花文艺出版社 (Hundred flower literature press).

———. 2000. "1949 Nian–1976 Nian jian Zhongguo Zhishi Fenzi Zisha Zhuangkuang de Chubu Kaocha" 1949 年–1976 年间中国知识分子自杀状况的初步考察 (A preliminary investigation of Chinese intellectual suicides between 1949 and 1976). http://www.netsh.com.cn/bbs/4145/messages/26/html.

Xu Feng and Wu Yiyi. 2000. "Laid-off Miner Riot Quelled in Liaoning." *Chinese News Digest, <www.cnd.org>*.

Xu Fuguan 徐复观. 1980. "Zai feichang bianju xia Zhongguo zhishi fenzi de beiju mingyun" 在非常变局下中国知识分子的悲剧命运 (The tragic fate of Chinese intellectuals in extraordinary times). Pp. 70–88 in *Zhishi Fenzi yu Zhongguo* 知识分子与中国 (Intellectuals and China), edited by Zhou Yangshan 周阳山. Taibei: Times Press Company 台北时代出版公司.

Xu, Jian. 1999. "Body, Discourse, and the Cultural Politics of Contemporary Chinese Qigong." *Journal of Asian Studies* 38(4)961–91.

Xu Jilin 许纪霖. 1991. Zhizhe de Zunyan: Zhishifenzi yu Jindai Wenhua. 智者的尊严: 知识分子与近代文化 (The dignity of the wise: intellectuals and modern culture). Shanghai: Xuelin Press 上海学林出版社.

———. 1992. Jingshen de Lianyu. 精神的炼狱 (The mental hell). Hong Kong: Joint Publishing Co. 三联书店(香港)有限公司.

———. 1997a. "Zouchu Gelou yihou." 走出阁楼以后 (After walking away from the ivory tower). Dushu 读书 (Reading) 9:15–24.

———. 1997b. Xunqiu Yiyi 寻求意义 (Searching for meaning). Shanghai: Sanlian Bookstore 上海三联书店.

Xu Jilin 许纪霖, Chen Sihe 陈思和, Cai Xiang 蔡翔, and Gao Yuanbao 郜元宝. 1999. "Daotong, Xuetong, yu Zhengtong" 道统, 学统与政统 (Dao, scholarship, and politics). Pp. 342–54 in *Zhishi Fenzi Yinggai Gan Shenme* 知识分子应该干什么 (What intellectuals should do), edited by Zhu Yong祝勇. Beijing: Shishi Chubanshe 北京时事出版社(Current affairs press).

Xu Jilin 许纪霖, Liu Qing 刘擎, Luo Gang 罗岗, and Xue Yi 薛毅. 2000. "Xunqiu di Santiao Daolu" 寻求第三条道路 (Looking for a third way). Pp. 309–33 in *Zhishi Fenzi Lichang: Ziyou Zhuyi zhi Zheng yu Zhongguo Sixiang Jie de Fenhua* 知识分子立场: 自由主义之争与中国思想界的分化 (The intellectual stance: the debate on liberalism and the division of Chinese thought), edited by Li Shitao 李世涛. Changchun, Jilin: Shidai Wenyi Chubanshe 长春时代文艺出版社 (Art and literature of the time press).

Xu Lie 徐列 (ed.) 2000. *Kandao Jiu Shuo: Nanfang Zhoumo Tegao* 看到就说: 南方周末特稿 (Say it as soon as you see it: special reports of South China Weekend). Beijing: Zhonghua Gongshang Lianhe Chubanshe 北京中华工商联合出版社 (China industrial and commercial united press).

Xu Linzheng 徐林正. 2001. *Wenhua Zuilian: Choulou de Zhongguo Wenyi Jie* 文化嘴脸: 丑陋的中国文艺界 (Cultural features: the ugly Chinese world of literature and art). Beijing: Taihai Chubanshe 北京台海出版社 (Taiwan straits press).

Xu Ming 许明. 1998. *Zhubian de Hua* 主编的话 (Words from the chief editor), in Ma Licheng and Ling Zhijun 马立成, 凌志军, *Jiaofeng:Dangdai Zhongguo Sanci Sixiang Jiefang Shilu* 交锋: 当代中国三次思想解放实录 (Confrontations: a truthful report on the three thought liberation campaigns in contemporary China). Beijing: Jinri Zhongguo Chubanshe 北京今日中国出版社 (Today's China press).

Xu Wenze 徐文泽. 1995. "Lun 'Bu Wei Shang, Bu Wei Shu, Zhi Wei Shi'" 论 '不唯上, 不唯书, 只唯实' (On "not relying solely on authorities and books but relying on reality). *Qiu Shi* 求是 14:8–12.

Xu Xiao 徐晓, Ding Dong 丁东, and Xu Youyu 徐友渔 (eds.). 1999. *Yu Luoke: Yizuo yu Huiyi* 遇罗克遗作与回忆 (You Luoke: works and recollections). Beijing: Zhongguo Wenlian Chubanshe 北京中国文联出版社 (Chinese literature and art association press).

Xu Xinxin 许欣欣. 1999. "1998–1999 Nian: Zhongguo Shimin de Guanzhu Jiaodian yu Weilai Yuqi" 1998–1999 年: 中国市民的关注焦点与未来预期 (1998–99: city people's concerns now and in the future). Pp. 84–100 in *1999 Nian Zhongguo Shehui Xingshi Fenxi yu Yuce* 1999 年中国社会形势分析与预测 (1999 analysis and prediction of social conditions in China), edited by Ru Xin 汝信, Lu Xueyi 陆学艺, and Shan Tianlun 单天伦, et al. Beijing: Shehui Kexue Wenxian Chubanshe 北京社会科学文献出版社 (Social science literature press).

Xu Xinxin 许欣欣 and Li Peilin 李培林. 1999. "1998–1999 Nian: Zhongguo Jiuye, Shouru he Xinxi Chanye de Fenxi yu Yuce" 1998–1999 年: 中国就业, 收入和信息产业的分析与预测 (1998–1999: analysis and prediction of employment, income, and the information industry in China). Pp. 18–42 in *1999 Nian Zhongguo Shehui Xingshi Fenxi yu Yuce* 1999 年中国社会形势分析与预测 (1999 analysis and prediction of social conditions in China), edited by Ru Xin 汝信, Lu Xueyi 陆学艺, and Shan Tianlun 单天伦, et al. Beijing: Shehui Kexue Wenxian Chubanshe 北京社会科学文献出版社 (Social science literature press).

Xu Youyu 徐友渔. 1999 [1996a]. "Xu" 序 (Preface) in *Yu Luoke Yizuo yu Huiyi* 遇罗克遗作与回忆 (Yu Luoke's works and recollections), edited by Xu Xiao 徐晓, Ding Dong 丁东, and Xu Youyu 徐友渔. Beijing: Zhongguo Wenlian Chubanshe 北京中国文联出版社 (Chinese literature and art association press).

———. 2000. "Ziyou Zhuyi yu Dangdai Zhongguo" 自由主义与当代中国 (Liberalism and contemporary China). Pp. 413–30 in *Zhishi Fenzi Lichang: Ziyou Zhuyi zhi Zheng yu Zhongguo Sixiang Jie de Fenhua* 知识分子立场: 自由主义之争与中国思想界的分化 (The intellectual stance: the debate on liberalism and the division of Chinese thought), edited by Li Shitao 李世涛. Changchun, Jilin: Shidai Wenyi Chubanshe 长春时代文艺出版社 (Art and literature of the time press).

Xu Zhijie 许志杰. 1994. "Xi You Can Ban Hua San Zi" 喜犹参半话三资 (Half happiness and half worries: talking about "three-capital" enterprises). *Democracy and Law* 民主与法律. July 15.

Ya Yi 亚衣. 1993. "Gongren Yundong yu Ziyou Gonghui Yundong" 工人运动与自由工会运动 (The workers' movement and the free union movement). *China Spring* 中国之春 5:69–75.

———. 1997a. "Duozhan Minjian Shehui Huodong Kongjian" 拓展民间社会活动空间 (Developing space for public social activities). *Beijing Spring* 北京之春 3: 69–77.

———. 1997b. "Buqu de Pingmin Fanpan Zhe" 不屈的平民反叛者 (An undaunted rebel out of a common man). *Beijing Spring* 北京之春 4:61–68.

———. 1997c. "Rang Shijie Jishi Liaojie Zhongguo" 让世界及时了解中国 (Let the world understand China in time). *Beijing Spring* 北京之春 6:69–76.

———. 1997d. "Zheli Yeyou Jiqing yu Shiyi" 这里也有激情与诗意 (Here there's also enthusiasm and poetry). *Beijing Spring* 北京之春 7:78–82.

———. 1997e. "Wo Xinzhong Yongyuan Guanzhu Zhongguo" 我心中永远关注中国 (China is forever the concern of my heart). *Beijing Spring* 北京之春 8:68–76..

Yan Buke 阎步克. 1989. "Shi dafu yu guanliao zhi" 士大夫与官僚制 (The literati and bureaucracy). Pp. 24–9 in *Xiandai Shehui yu Zhishi Fenzi* 现代社会与知识分子(Modern society and intellectuals), edited by Liang Congjie 梁从戒. Shenyang: Liaoning People's Press. 沈阳辽宁人民出版社.

———. 1996. *Shidafu Zhengzhi Yansheng Shigao* 士大夫政治演生史稿 (A history of the development of the scholar-official). Beijing: Beijing Daxue Chubanshe 北京大学出版社 (Beijing university press).

Yan Qingshi 颜清史. 1980. "Dong Han mo nian de zhishi fenzi yu zhengzhi" 东汉

末年的知识分子与政治 (Intellectuals and politics in the late Eastern Han). Pp. 247–254 in *Zhishi Fenzi yu Zhongguo* 知识分子与中国 (Intellectuals and China), edited by Zhou Yangshan 周阳山. Taibei: Shidai Chuban Gongsi 台北时代出版公司 (Times press company).

Yan Shi 严实. [1995] 1999. "Zunxun Jiben Silu, Ruiyi Gaige Chuangxin" 遵循基本思路, 锐意改革创新 (Follow the basic ways of thinking and be steadfast in reform and creative work). Pp. 270–8 in *Jujiao Jiaodian Fangtan* 聚焦焦点访谈 (A focus on "focused interviews"), edited by Yuan Zhengming 袁正明 and Liang Jianzeng 梁建增. Beijing: Zhongguo Da Baike Quan Shu Chubanshe) 中国大百科全书出版社 (China encyclopedia press).

Yan Tao and Lin Sheng. 1992. *Zhongguo Gudai de "Shi"* 中国古代的 "士" (The literati in ancient China). Zhengzhou: Henan Renmin Chubanshe 郑州河南人民出版社 (Henan people's press).

Yan Yaojun 阎耀军, Wang Jie 汪洁, Yang Wei 杨维 and Li Jiming 里继明. 1999. "Tianjin Shi Xiagang Zhigong Zhuangkuang de Wenjuan Diaocha" 天津市下岗职工状况的问卷调查 (A survey on the situation of the laid-off workers in Tianjin). Pp. 255–70 in *1999 Nian Zhongguo Shehui Xingshi Fenxi yu Yuce* 1999 年中国社会形势分析与预测 (1999 analysis and prediction of social conditions in China), edited by Ru Xin 汝信, Lu Xueyi 陆学艺, and Shan Tianlun 单天伦, et al. Beijing: Shehui Kexue Wenxian Chubanshe 北京社会科学文献出版社 (Social science literature press).

Yang, Benjamin. 1990. *From Revolution to Politics: Chinese Communist on the Long March.* Boulder, Colorado: Westview Press.

Yang Dongping 杨东平. 1994a. "Zhongguo Gaodeng Jiaoyu de Sulian Moshi" 中国高等教育的苏联模式 (The Soviet model of Chinese higher education). *Dongfang* 东方 (Orient) 3:35–9.

———. 1994b. Chengshi Jifeng: Beijing he Shanghai de Wenhua Jingshen 城市季风: 北京和上海的文化精神 (The trade winds of cities: the cultural spirits of Beijing and Shanghai). Beijing: Dongfang Chubanshe 北京东方出版社 (East press).

———. 1999. "1998 Nian: Zhongguo de Jiaoyu Fazhan" 1998 年: 中国的教育发展 (1998: China's development in education). Pp. 377–90 in *1999 Nian Zhongguo Shehui Xingshi Fenxi yu Yuce* 1999 年中国社会形势分析与预测 (1999 analysis and prediction of social conditions in China), edited by Ru Xin 汝信, Lu Xueyi 陆学艺, and Shan Tianlun 单天伦, et al. Beijing: Shehui Kexue Wenxian Chubanshe 北京社会科学文献出版社 (Social science literature press).

Yang Fan 杨帆. 1995. "Liyi Jiegou de Bianhua yu Shehui Zhenghe" 利益结构的变化与社会整合 (The change in interest structure and the normalization of society). *Dongfang* 东方 3:35–8.

Yang Jianye 杨建业. 1997. *Ma Yinchu* 马寅初. Shijiazhuang: Huashan Wenyi Chubanshe 石家庄花山文艺出版社 (Huashan literature and art press).

Yang Shoujian 杨守建. 2001. *Zhongguo Xueshu Fubai Pipan* 中国学术腐败批判 (A criticism of academic corruption in China). Tianjin: Tianjin Renmin Chubanshe 天津人民出版社 (Tianjin people's press).

Yang Weizhen 杨维桢. 1989. "Zhishi fenzi yu jishu guanliao" 知识分子与技术官僚 (Intellectuals and technocrats). Pp. 317–44 in *Zhishi Fenzi yu Taiwan Fazhan* 知识分子与台湾发展 (Intellectuals and the development of Taiwan), edited by Zhongguo Luntan Bianwei Hui 中国论坛编委会 (China Forum Editorial Committee). Taibei: Zhongguo Luntan Zazhi 台北: 中国 论坛杂志 (China forum magazine).

Ye Yonglie 叶永烈. 1988. Chenzhong de Yi Jiu Wu Qi 沉重的一九五七 (The heavy 1957). Hong Kong: Ming Xing Chubanshe 明星出版社 (Star press).

———. 1994. Hu Qiaomu 胡乔木. Beijing: Zhongyang Dang Xiao Chubanshe 北京中央党校出版社 (Central party school press).

———. 1997. *Lishi de Cangsang* 历史的沧桑 (The vicissitudes of history). Beijing: Zhongyang Dang Xiao Chubanshe 北京中央党校出版社 (Central party school press).

———. 1999. *Chen Boda Zhuan* 陈伯达传 (A biography of Chen Boda). Vols. 1–2. Beijing: Renmin Ribao Chubanshe 北京人民日报出版社(People's daily press).

Yi Cheng. 一程. 1999 [1998]. "Shuo Buzhun de Siying Qiye Zhu de Shehui Shuxing" 说不准的私营企业主的社会属性 (The unclear class position of private entrepreneurs). Pp. 290–2 in *Yanlun Zhongguo: Guandian Jiaofeng 20 Nian* 言论中国: 观点交锋 20 (Discourse China: debating ideas over the past twenty years), edited by Jing Wu. Beijing: Zhongguo Jiancha Press 北京中国监察出版社.

Yin Haiguang 殷海光. 1980. "Zhishi Fenzi de Zeren" 知识分子的责任 (The responsibility of intellectuals). Pp. 121–60 in *Zhishi Fenzi yu Zhongguo* 知识分子与中国 (Intellectuals and China), edited by Zhou Yangshan 周阳山. Taibei: Shidai Chuban Gongsi 台北时代出版公司 (Times press company).

———. 1982. "Daode de Chongjian"道德的重建 (The reconstruction of morality). Pp. 73–116 in *Wenhua chuantong de chongjian: Zhongguo wenhua de weiji yu zhanwang* 文化传统的重建: 中国文化的危机与展望 (Reconstructing traditional culture: the crisis of Chinese culture and its prospects), edited by Zhou Yangshan 周阳山 Taibei: Shidai Chuban Gongsi 台北时代出版公司 (Times press company).

Yin Li 尹力. 2001. *Jinri Shuofa: Zhongguo Ren de Falu Wucan* 今日说法: 中国人的法律午餐 (Law today: Chinese people's law for lunch). Vols. 1–4. Beijing: Zhongguo Renmin Gongan Daxue Chubanshe 北京中国人民公安大学出版社 (China people's public security university press).

Yu, Frederick T. C. 1964. *Mass Persuasion in Communist China*. New York: Frederick A. Praeger.

Yu Jie 余杰. 1999. *Wenming de Chuangtong* 文明的创痛 (The traumas of civilization). Tianjin: Baihua Wenyi Chubanshe 天津百花文艺出版社 (Hundred flower literature and art press).

Yu Luoke 遇罗克. [1966] 1999a. "He Jixie Weiwu Lun Jinxing Douzheng de Shihou Daole" 和机械唯物论进行斗争的时候到了(It is time to fight mechanical materialism). Pp. 108–11 in *Yu Luoke Yizuo yu Huiyi* 遇罗克遗作与回忆 (Yu Luoke's works and recollections), edited by Xu Xiao 徐晓, Ding Dong 丁东, and Xu Youyu 徐友渔. Beijing: Zhongguo Wenlian Chubanshe 北京中国文联出版社 (Chinese literature and art association press).

———. [1996] 1999b. "Riji" 日记 (Diaries). Pp. 112–22 in *Yu Luoke Yizuo yu Huiyi* 遇罗克遗作与回忆 (Yu Luoke's works and recollections), edited by Xu Xiao 徐晓, Ding Dong 丁东, and Xu Youyu 徐友渔. Beijing: Zhongguo Wenlian Chubanshe 北京中国文联出版社 (Chinese literature and art association press).

Yu Ying-shih 余英时. 1988. *Wenhua Pinglun yu Zhongguo Qinghuai* 文化评论与中

国情怀 (Cultural criticism and the feeling of being Chinese) Taipei: Yunchen Wenhua Shiye Corporation 台北允晨文化实业股份有限公司.

———. 1989. "Tian Di Bian Hua Cao Mu Fan" 天地变化草木蕃 (The world is changing and the grass and trees are flourishing). Pp. 481–2 in *Tiananmen* 天安门 *1989*, edited by Lian He Daily 联合日报. Taibei: Lianhe Press 联合出版社.

———. 1993. "The Radicalization of China in the Twentieth Century." *Daedalus* 122(2)125–50.

———. 1997a. "Minzu Zhuyi yu Zhongguo Qiantu Xu" 民族主义与中国前途序 (Preface to Nationalism and China's Future). *Beijing Spring* 北京之春 6:83–4.

———. 1997b. *Zhongguo Zhishi Fenzi Lun* 中国知识分子论 (On China's Intellectuals). Zhengzhou: Henan Renmin Chubanshe 郑州河南人民出版社 (Henan people's press).

———. [1987] 1999. "Zhongguo Zhishi Fenzi de Gudai Chuantong" 中国知识分子的古代传统 (The ancient tradition of Chinese intellectuals). Pp. 15–32 in *Zhishi Fenzi Yinggai Gan Shenme* 知识分子应该干什么 (What intellectuals should do), edited by Zhu Yong 祝勇. Beijing: Shishi Chubanshe 北京时事出版社 (Current affairs press).

Yu Zheng 余征 (ed.). 2000. *Zhenli de Zhuiqiu: Shi Nian Wencui 1990.7–2000.7* 真理的追求: 十年文萃 (The pursuit of truth: ten years of articles, July 1990–July 2000). Vols. 1–2. Beijing: Jincheng Press 北京金城出版社.

Yu Zuyao 虞祖尧. 1996. "Lishi shangde Zhongguo Zhishi Fenzi Jieceng" 历史上的中国知识分子阶层 (The historical class structure of Chinese intellectuals). Pp. 1–25 in *Zhishi Fenzi yu Zhongguo Shehui Biange* 知识分子与中国社会变革 (Intellectuals and reform in Chinese society), edited by Jia Chun Zeng 贾春增. Beijing: Hua Wen Chubanshe 北京华文出版社 (Chinese language press) .

Yuan Zhengming 袁正明 and Liang Jianzeng 梁建增. 1999. *Jujiao Jiaodian Fangtan* 聚集焦点访谈 (Focus on "focused interviews"). Beijing: Zhongguo Da Baike Quanshu Chubanshe 中国大百科全书出版社 (China encyclopedia press).

Yuan Zhiming 远志明. 1990. "Tansuo Weilai de Daolu" 探索未来的道路 (Searching for the road ahead: an interview). *Minzhu Zhongguo* 民主中国. June.

Yuan Ying 袁鹰. 1986. "Yu Sui." 玉碎 (Broken jade). Pp. 115–30 in *Lishi zai Zheli Chensi: 1966–1976 Nian Jishi* 历史在这里沉思: 1966–1976 年纪实 (History contemplates here: recollections from 1966–1976), Vol. 3, edited by Zhou Ming 周明. Beijing: Huaxia Chubanshe 北京华夏出版社 (China press).

Zhang Boli 张柏笠. 1997. "Yongyuan de Zhanshi" 永远的战士 (A fighter forever). *Beijing Spring* 北京之春 3:41–8.

Zhang Dainian 张岱年, Tang Yijie 汤一介, et al. 1997. *Wenhua de Chongtu yu Ronghe: Zhang Shenfu Xiansheng, Tang Yongtong Xiansheng, Liang Shuming Xiansheng Bainian Danchen Jinian Wenji* 文化的冲突与融合: 张申府先生, 梁漱溟先生, 汤用彤先生百年诞辰纪念文集 (Conflict and integration of culture: a collection of articles commemorating the hundreth anniversary of Profs. Zhang Shenfu, Tang Yongtong, and Liang Shuming. Beijing: Beijing Daxue Chubanshe (Beijing University press).

Zhang Dake 张大可. 1996."'Fanyou' he 'Wenge' Qijian de Zhongguo Zhishi Fenzi" "反右"和"文革"期间的中国知识分子(Chinese intellectuals during the periods of the Anti-Rightist Movement and the Cultural Revolution). Pp. 150–177 in *Zhishi*

Fenzi yu Zhongguo Shehui Biange 知识分子与中国社会变革 (Intellectuals and reform in Chinese society), edited by Jia Chun Zeng 贾春增. Beijing: Hua Wen Chubanshe 北京华文出版社 (Chinese language press) .

Zhang Guangnian 张光年 and Li Hui 李辉. 1995. "Tan Zhou Yang" 谈周扬 (On Zhou Yang). *Dongfang* 东方 (Orient) 6:50–2.

Zhang Hengshou 张恒寿. 1984. "Zhuang Zhou" 庄周 (Zhuang Zi). Pp. 97–119 in *Zhonghua Minzu Jiechu Renwu Xun* (Di San Ji) 中华民族杰出人物传 (第三集) (Outstanding personages in China), Vol. 3, edited by Tang Yuyuan 唐宇元. Beijing: Zhongguo Qingnian Chubanshe 北京中国青年出版社 (China youth press).

Zhang Heping 张何平 and Zhong Peiji 种培基. 1997. "He Kexue Kaiduo Zhe Wang Ganchang" 核科学隍开拓者王淦昌 (The atomic path-breaker Wang Ganchang). *People's Daily* (overseas edition) 人民日报海外版. November 11.

Zhang Houyi 张厚义. 1999. "1998–1999 Nian: Zhongguo Siying Qiyezhu Jieceng Zhuangkuang" 1998–1999 年: 中国私营企业主阶层状况 (1998–1999: The state of China's private entrepreneurial stratum). Pp. 482–91 in *1999 Nian Zhongguo Shehui Xingshi Fenxi yu Yuce* 1999 年中国社会形势分析与预测 (1999 analysis and prediction of social conditions in China), edited by Ru Xin 汝信, Lu Xueyi 陆学艺, and Shan Tianlun 单天伦, et al. Beijing: Shehui Kexue Wenxian Chubanshe 北京社会科学文献出版社 (Social science literature press).

Zhang Jian 张健. 2000. "Hefa Xing yu Zhongguo Zhengzhi" 合法性与中国政治 (Legitimacy and Chinese politics). *Zhanlue yu Guanli* 战略与管理 (Strategy and management) 5:1–15.

Zhang Longxi. 1992. "Western Theory and Chinese Reality." *Critical Inquiry* 19:105–32 (Autumn).

Zhang Maogui 张茂桂. 1989. "Ping 'Zhishi Fenzi yu Shehui Yundong'" 评 "知识分子与社会运动" (A critique of "Intellectuals and social movements"). Pp. 310–6 in *Zhishi Fenzi yu Taiwan Fazhan* 知识分子与台湾发展 (Intellectuals and the development of Taiwan), edited by Zhonghuo Luntan Bianwei Hui 中国论坛编委会 (China forum editorial committee). Taibei: Zhongguo Luntan Zazhi 台北中国论坛杂志 (China forum magazine).

Zhang Ming 张鸣. 2001. "Renao zhong de Leng Xiang" 热闹中的冷想 (Some cool thoughts amid the heat). *Dushu* 读书(Reading) 3:12–7.

Zhang Pengyuan 张鹏元. 1989. "Ping 'Zhongguo Zhishi Fenzi de Leixing yu Xingge' 评 "中国知识分子的类型与性格" (A critique of "The typology and character of Chinese intellectuals"). Pp. 109–14 in *Zhishi Fenzi yu Taiwan Fazhan* 知识分子与台湾发展(Intellectuals and the development of Taiwan), edited by Zhonghuo Luntan Bianwei Hui 中国论坛编委会 (China Forum Editorial Committee). Taibei: Zhongguo Luntan Zazhi 台北 中国论坛杂志 (China forum magazine).

Zhang Quanjing 张全景. 2001. "Jianding Gongchan Zhuyi de Lixiang Xinnian" 坚定共产主义的理想信念 (Consolidating Communist ideals and beliefs). *Zhenli de Zhuiqiu* 真理的追求 (The pursuit of truth). 7:1–14.

Zhang Qunli 张群力. 1993. "Daoyan Chen Jialin Tan Tang Ming Huang" 导演陈家林谈唐明皇 (Director Chen Jialin talks about his movie *Emperor Tang Ming Huang*). *Chinese TV News* 中国电视新闻. June 22.

Zhang Rulun 张汝伦. 2000. "Di Santiao Daolu" 第三条道路 (The third way). Pp. 334–43 in *Zhishi Fenzi Lichang: Ziyou Zhuyi zhi Zheng yu Zhongguo Sixiang Jie de*

Fenhua 知识分子立场: 自由主义之争与中国思想界的分化 (The intellectual stance: the debate on liberalism and the division of Chinese thought), edited by Li Shitao 李世涛. Changchun, Jilin: Shidai Wenyi Chubanshe 长春时代文艺出版社 (Art and literature of the time press).

Zhang Rulun 张汝伦, Ji Guibao 季桂保, Gao Yuanbao 郜元宝, and Chen Yinchi 陈引驰. 1994. "Wenhua Shijie: Jiegou haishi Jiangou" 文化世界: 解构还是建构 (The cultural world: deconstruction or reconstruction). *Dushu* 读书 (Reading) 7: 49–56.

Zhang Songru 张松如. 1987. *Lao Zi Shuojie* 老子说解 (An interpretation of Lao Zi). Jinan, Shandong: Qilu Shushe 齐鲁书社 (Qilu press).

Zhang Xianliang 张贤亮. 1996. "Zhang Xianliang." Pp. 230–4 in *Jingshen de Tianyuan: "Dongfang zhi Zi" Xueren Fangtan Lu* 精神的田园: "东方之子" 学人访谈录 (The field of spirit and vigor: the interviews of scholars on "Sons and Daughters of the East," edited by Shi Jian 时间. Beijing: Huaxia Chubanshe 北京华夏出版社 (China press).

Zhang Xiaochun 张晓春. 1989. "Zhishi fenzi yu shehui yundong" 知识分子与社会运动 (Intellectuals and social movements). Pp. 289–309 in *Zhishi Fenzi yu Taiwan Fazhan* 知识分子与台湾发展 (Intellectuals and the development of Taiwan), edited by Zhonghuo Luntan Bianwei Hui 中国论坛编委会(China Forum Editorial Committee). Taibei: Zhongguo Luntan Zazhi 台北: 中国论坛杂志 (China Forum Magazine).

Zhang Xiaoxia 张晓霞. 2000, 2001. *Zhongguo Gaoceng Zhinang* 中国高层智囊 (China's high-level advisors). Vols. 1–8 as a book series, *Yingxiang Dangjin Zhongguo Fazhan Jincheng de Ren* 影响当今中国发展进程的人 (People who have influenced the development of contemporary China). Beijing: Jinghua Chubanshe 北京京华出版社, Vols. 1,2; Beijing: Zhigong Chubanshe 北京致公出版社, Vol. 3; Xi'an: Shannxi Shifan Daxue Chubanse 西安陕西师范大学出版社 (Shaanxi Teachers' University press), Vols. 4–8.

Zhang, Xudong. 1997. *Chinese Modernism in the Era of Reforms: Cultural Fever, Avant-Garde Fiction, and The New Chinese Cinema*. Durham, North Carolina: Duke University Press.

———. 1998. "Nationalism, Mass Culture, and Intellectual Strategies in Post-Tiananmen China. Pp. 109–40 in Intellectual Politics in Post-Tiananmen China, a special issue of Social Text, edited by Xudong Zhang. Durham, North Caolina: Duke University Press.

Zhang Yi 张翼. 2000. "Zhongguo yi Kuaru Laoling Shehui" 中国已跨入老龄社会 (China is already an aging society). Pp. 282–96 in 2000 *Nian Zhongguo Shehui Xingshi Fenxi yu Yuce* 2000 年中国社会形势分析与预测 (2000 analysis and prediction of social conditions in China), edited by Ru Xin 汝信, Lu Xueyi 陆学艺, and Shan Tianlun 单天伦, et al. Beijing: Shehui Kexue Wenxian Chubanshe 北京社会科学文献出版社 (Social science literature press).

Zhang Ying 张鹰. 1999. "Cong Shanghai de Dadan Changshi Kan Gaoxiao Houqin Shehuihua" 从上海的大胆尝试看高校后勤社会化 (Viewing the contracting out of service departments in higher education from the perspective of Shanghai's courageous experiment). *Zhongguo Gaodeng Jiaoyu* 中国高等教育(China's higher education.) 4:10–15.

Zhang Yiwu 张颐武. 1994a. "Houxin Shiqi Wenhua: Tiaozhan yu Jiyu" 后新时期文化: 挑战与机遇 (Culture after the new era: challenges and opportunities). *Zhanlue yu Guanli* 战略与管理 1:112–4.

———. 1994b."'Xiandai Xing' de Zhongjie: Yige Wufa Huibi de Keti" "现代性"的终结: 一个无法回避的课题 (The end of modernity: an unavoidable subject). *Strategy and Management* 战略与管理 3:104–9.

Zhang Zhongdong 张中栋. 1989. "Wei ziyou Zhongguo zheng yanlun ziyou de Hu Shih" 为自由中国争言论自由的胡适 (Hu Shih: Struggling for freedom of speech to create a free China). Pp. 351–387 in *Zhishi Fenzi yu Taiwan Fazhan* 知识分子与台湾发展 (Intellectuals and the development of Taiwan), edited by Zhonghuo Luntan Bianwei Hui 中国论坛编委会 (China Forum Editorial Committee). Taibei: Zhongguo Luntan Zazhi 台北: 中国论坛杂志 (China forum magazine).

Zhao, Henry Y. H. (also Zhao Yiheng 赵毅衡). 1997. "Post-Isms and Chinese New Conservatism." *New Literary History* 28:31–44.

———. 2000. "Ruhe Miandui Dangjin Zhongguo Wenhua Xianzhuang" 如何面对当今中国文化现状 (How to understand the contemporary Chinese culture). Pp. 357–67 in *Zhishi Fenzi Lichang: Jijin yu Baoshou zhijian de Dongtang* 知识分子立场: 激进与保守之间的动荡 (The intellectual stance: between radicalism and conservatism), edited by Li Shitao 李世涛. Changchun, Jilin: Shidai Wenyi Chubanshe 长春时代文艺出版社 (Art and literature of the time press).

Zhao Huaquan 赵华荃. 2001. "Woguo Gongyou Zhi Jingji Suo Zhan Bizhong Hai Neng Zai Xiajiang ma?" 我国公有制经济所占比重还能在下降吗? (Can the rate of our country's public economic ownership continue to decline?) *Zhenli de Zhuiqiu* 真理的追求(The pursuit of truth) 7:19–26.

Zhao Jialing 赵佳苓. 1989. "Zhishi Fenzi Zhengzhi Juese de Fenhua" 知识分子政治角色的分化 (The proliferation of intellectuals' political roles). Pp. 5–9 in *Xiandai Shehui yu Zhishi Fenzi* 现代社会与知识分子 (Modern society and intellectuals), edited by Liang Congjie 梁从戒. Shenyang: Liaoning Renmin Chubanshe 沈阳辽宁人民出版社 (Liaoning people's press).

Zhao, Minghua and Theo Nichols. 1998. "Management Control of Labor in State-owned Enterprises: Cases from the Textile Industry." Pp. 75–100 in *Adjusting to Capitalism: Chinese Workers and the State*, edited by Greg O'Leary. Armonk, New York: M. E. Sharpe.

Zhao, Suisheng. 1997. "Chinese Intellectuals' Quest for National Greatness and Nationalistic Writing in the 1990s." *China Quarterly* 152:725–49.

Zhao, Yuezhi. 1998. *Meida, Market and Democracy in China: Between the Party Line and the Bottom Line*. Urbana/Chicago: University of Illinois Press.

Zheng Xian 郑宪. 1996. "Xinminzhu Zhuyi Geming yu Zhongguo Zhishi Fenzi" 新民主主义与中国知识分子 (New democracy and Chinese intellectuals). Pp. 93–121 in *Zhishi Fenzi yu Zhongguo Shehui Biange* 知识分子与中国社会变革 (Intellectuals and reform in Chinese society), edited by Jia Chun Zeng 贾春增. Beijing: Hua Wen Chubanshe 北京华文出版社 (Chinese language press).

Zheng Yefu 郑也夫. 1995. *Zou Chu Qiutu Kunjing* 走出囚徒困境 (Emerging from the prisoner's dilemma). Beijing: *Guangming* Ribao Chubanshe 北京光明日报出版社 (*Guangming* daily press).

Zheng Yi 郑义. 2001. "Sixiang Duli Jingshen Ziyou de Linghun Gongchengshi Men"

思想独立精神自由的灵魂工程师们 (Independent thinking, free spirited engineers of the soul). *Qian Shao Yuekan* 前哨月刊 (Frontline monthly), October, pp. 122–3.

Zhong Huai 钟怀. [1998] 1999. "Zhongguo You ge Jiao Qingtian" 中国有个焦青天 (China has an upright official named Jiao). Pp. 254–5 in *Jujiao Jiaodian Fangtan* 聚焦焦点访谈 (A focus on "focused interviews"), edited by Yuan Zhengming and Liang Jianzeng 袁正明, 梁建增. Beijing: China Encyclopedia Press 中国大百科全书出版社.

Zhongguo Gaodeng Jiaoyu 中国高等教育 (Chinese Higher Education). 1999. "Bange Shiji de Tansuo yu Huihuang: Gongheguo Gaodeng Jiaoyu Fazhan Licheng Huimu" 半个世纪的探索与辉煌: 共和国高等教育发展历程回眸 (Half a century's exploration and glory: looking back on developments in higher education in the People's Republic of China). 18:2–9.

Zhongguo Jingji Shibao 中国经济时报 (China economic news). [1996] 1999. "Gongren You Gonghui, Funu You Fulian, Siying Laoban You Gexie, Shui Ti Nongmin Shuo Hua" 工人有工会，妇女有妇联，私营老板有个协，谁替农民说话 (Workers have unions, women have women's associations, entrepreneurs have private associations; who speaks for peasants?). Pp. 317–8 in *Yanlun Zhongguo: Guandian Jiaofeng 20 Nian.* 言论中国: 观点交锋 20 年 (Discourse China: debating ideas over the past twenty years), edited by Jing Wu. Beijing: Zhongguo Jiancha Press 北京中国监察出版社.

Zhongguo Tongji Nianjian 1998 中国统计年鉴 1998 (China statistical yearbook 1998). Beijing: Zhongguo Tongji Chubanshe 中国统计出版社 (China statistical publishing house).

Zhongguo Tongji Zhaiyao 1998. 中国统计摘要 1998. (A statistical survey of China, 1998). Beijing: Zhongguo Tongji Chubanshe 中国统计出版社 (China statistical publishing house).

Zhonghua Renmin Gongheguo Nianjian 1998. 中华人民共和国年鉴 1998 (People's Republic of China yearbook, 1998). Beijing: People's Republic of China Yearbook Press 北京中华人民共和国年鉴出版社.

Zhou Yi 周易. 1996. "*Zhongguo Keyi Shuo Bu* zhi Qian Hou" 中国可以说不之前后 (What happened before and after *China Can Say No). Beijing Spring* 北京之春 10: 92–3.

Zhu Guanglei 朱光磊. 1994. *Da Fenhua Xin Zuhe: Dangdai Zhongguo Shehui Ge Jieceng Fenxi* 大分化新组合: 当代中国社会各阶层分析 (Great division breeds new organization: an analysis of social stratification in contemporary China). Tianjin: Tianjin Renmin Chubanshe 天津人民出版社 (Tianjin people's press).

———. 1998. "Shiji zhi Jiao Zhongguo shehui Jieceng Fenhua de Shi Da Qushi" 世纪之交中国社会阶层分化的十大趋势 (Ten tendencies of social stratification in Chinese society at the turn of the century). Nankai Scholarly Journal 南开学报 1: 1–9.

Zhu Qingfang 朱庆芳. 1999. "1998–1999 Nian: Zhongguo de Renmin Shenghuo Zhuangkuang" 1998–1999 年: 中国的人民生活状况 (Chinese living conditions: 1998–99). Pp. 353–67 in *1999 Nian Zhongguo Shehui Xingshi Fenxi yu Yuce* 1999 年中国社会形势分析与预测 (1999 analysis and prediction of social conditions in China), edited by Ru Xin 汝信, Lu Xueyi 陆学艺, and Shan Tianlun 单天

伦, et al. Beijing: Shehui Kexue Wenxian Chubanshe 北京社会科学文献出版社 (Social science literature press).

Zhu Ruikai 祝瑞开. 2000. *Ruxue yu Ershi Yi Shiji Zhongguo: Goujian, Fazhan "Dangdai Xin Ruxue"* 儒学与 21 世纪中国: 构建, 发展 "当代新儒学" (Confucianism and twenty-first century China: constructing and developing "contemporary neo-Confucianism"). Shanghai: Xuelin Chubanshe.

Zhu Yong 朱雍. 1999. "1998–1999 Nian: Zhongguo Guoyou Qiye Gaige de Xianzhuang yu Qianjing" 1998–1999:年中国国有企业改革的现状与前景 (1998–1999: Reforming China's state owned enterprises now and in the future). Pp. 123–46 in *1999 Nian Zhongguo Shehui Xingshi Fenxi yu Yuce* 1999 年中国社会形势分析与预测 (1999 analysis and prediction of social conditions in China), edited by Ru Xin 汝信, Lu Xueyi 陆学艺, and Shan Tianlun 单天伦, et al. Beijing: Shehui Kexue Wenxian Chubanshe 北京社会科学文献出版社 (Social science literature press).

Zhu Yunpeng 朱云鹏. 1989. "Ping 'zhishi fenzi yu jishu guanliao'" 评 '知识分子与技术官僚' (A critique of "intellectuals and technocrats"). Pp. 345–350 in *Zhishi Fenzi yu Taiwan Fazhan* 知识分子与台湾发展 (Intellectuals and the development of Taiwan), edited by Zhonghuo Luntan Bianwei Hui 中国论坛编委会 (China Forum Editorial Committee). Taibei: Zhongguo Luntan Zazhi 台北中国论坛杂志 (China Forum Magazine).

Zong Han 宗寒. 1994. "Gongyou Zhi de Zhuti Diwei Bunen Dongyao" 公有制的主体地位不能动摇 (The dominant position of state-ownership cannot be shaken). *Qiu Shi* 求是 10:13–8.

Zweig, David. 2000. "The 'Externalities of Development:' Can New Political Institutions Manage Rural Conflict?" Pp. 120–142 in *Chinese Society: Change, Conflict and Resistance,* edited by Elizabeth J. Perry and Mark Selden. London: Routledge.

Index of Chinese Names and Phrases

Note: Subjects and other important names are in the Subject and Name Index. The names here include those of most Chinese authors and intellectuals mentionded in the text.

Subject and Name Index

Note: For most Chinese names and phrases, see the Index of Chinese Names and Phrases.